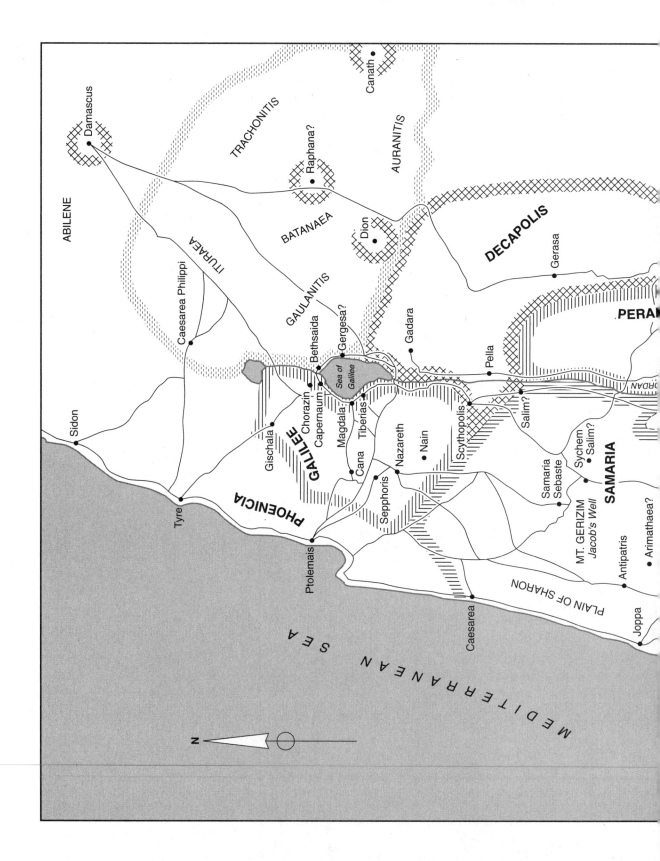

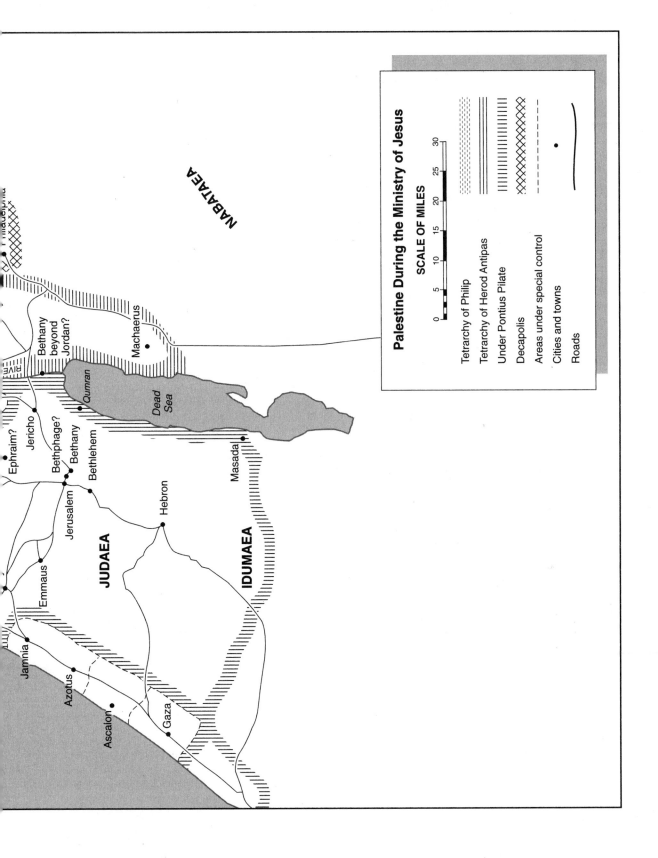

Palestine During the Ministry of Jesus

SCALE OF MILES

0 5 10 15 20 25 30

Tetrarchy of Philip
Tetrarchy of Herod Antipas
Under Pontius Pilate
Decapolis
Areas under special control
Cities and towns
Roads

NABATAEA

Machaerus

Bethany beyond Jordan?

Qumran

Dead Sea

Ephraim?
Jericho
Bethphage?
Bethany
Bethlehem

Jerusalem

Emmaus

JUDAEA

Hebron

Masada

IDUMAEA

Jamnia
Azotus
Ascalon
Gaza

www.wadsworth.com

wadsworth.com is the World Wide Web site for Wadsworth Publishing Company and is your direct source to dozens of online resources.

At *wadsworth.com* you can find out about supplements, demonstration software, and student resources. You can also send e-mail to many of our authors and preview new publications and exciting new technologies.

wadsworth.com
Changing the way the world learns®

THE NEW TESTAMENT

THE NEW TESTAMENT
A Critical Introduction

Third Edition

Edwin D. Freed
Professor Emeritus, Gettysburg College

 **Wadsworth**
Thomson Learning™

Australia • Canada • Denmark • Japan • Mexico • New Zealand • Philippines
Puerto Rico • Singapore • Spain • United Kingdom • United States

Religion Editor: Peter Adams
Assistant Editor: Kerri Abdinoor
Editorial Assistant: Mindy Newfarmer/Mark Andrews
Marketing Manager: Dave Garrison
Print Buyer: April Reynolds
Permissions Editor: Joohee Lee
Production Service: The Book Company

Text Designer: Devenish Design
Copy Editor: Pat Brewer
Cover Designer: Yvo Riezebos
Cover Printer: Von Hoffmann Press, Inc./Custom
Compositor: R&S Book Composition
Printer/Binder: Von Hoffmann Press, Inc./Custom

For more information, contact
Wadsworth/Thomson Learning
10 Davis Drive
Belmont, CA 94002-3098
USA
www.wadsworth.com

International Headquarters
Thomson Learning
290 Harbor Drive, 2nd Floor
Stamford, CT 06902-7477
USA

UK/Europe/Middle East
Thomson Learning
Berkshire House
168-173 High Holborn
London WC1V 7AA
United Kingdom

Asia
Thomson Learning
60 Albert Street #15-01
Albert Complex
Singapore 189969

Canada
Nelson/Thomson Learning
1120 Birchmount Road
Scarborough, Ontario M1K 5G4
Canada

Library of Congress Cataloging-in-Publication Data
Freed, Edwin D.
   The New Testament: a critical introduction/
Edwin D. Freed—3rd ed.
      p.   cm.
   Includes bibliographical references and index.
   ISBN 0-534-52139-8
   1. Bible. N.T.—Introductions.   I. Title.
   BS2330.2 .F73   2000
                                99-056609

To Ann

Contents

Part I: *Jesus and the First Three Gospels*   53

Chapter 1 *The First Three Gospels: Origins and Relationships*   54

Chapter 2 *The Gospel Writers as Authors and Some Techniques Used to Study Their Writings*   74

Preface

Only gradually is certain literature produced by a religious society accepted as sacred, that is, used in worship and recognized as authoritative for personal and communal faith. No writing in the New Testament (NT) was thought to be holy or sacred until long after it was written. The important thing, therefore, for those who read any writing produced by early Christians was not sacredness but content. There was no conviction that early Christian writings were especially "inspired" by God or the Holy Spirit.

Eventually a collection of writings composed and assembled by Christians was regarded as sacred, and it was designated the New Covenant. It was given that name because Christians believed that Jesus had initiated a new covenant with his followers (see Luke 22:20; 1 Cor 11:25; 2 Cor 3:6) as the Hebrew prophet Jeremiah had predicted (Jer 31:31–34; Rom 11:26–27). Christians believed that their covenant replaced that made by God with Abraham (Gen 17:1–21) and later with Moses (Exod 6:2–9; 34:10–28; Acts 7:8).

The Latin equivalent of the Greek word *diathēkē,* translated "covenant," is *testamentum,* from which we get the English word "testament." Therefore the English title of the collection of writings we are about to study is the NT. The Hebrew scriptures, the sacred writings of the Jews, were regarded as holy or sacred by the Christians as well as by the Jews. But after Christianity had become distinct from Judaism, Christians, not without bias, referred to the Jewish scriptures as the Old Testament (OT).

The writers of the NT did not write to replace the Jewish scriptures, or even to supplement them. Rather, NT writers in general used the Hebrew scriptures as proof for their convictions about Jesus' birth, life, death, and resurrection, as explanations for special events in early Christian history, and as support for theological views and moral exhortation.

Jewish writers during the NT period (200 BCE–200 CE) sometimes referred to their scriptures as the "holy" or "sacred books" (for example, I Macc 12:9; Josephus, *Life* 418; *Ant.* 20:12:1). Here the Greek word translated as "books" is the plural of either *biblion* or *biblos,* from which we get our English word Bible. Because Christians also accepted the Jewish holy books as sacred, by about 400 CE the Christian Bible included two parts, usually known as the OT and the NT. The Bible has influenced the thought, literature, institutions, values, and mores of Western culture for almost two thousand years.

The purpose of this introductory text is to help students learn about and participate in a critical study of the NT. Although it is not intended to be a "popular" treatment—the kind of book that usually oversimplifies material and presents it so rapidly that it rarely challenges thoughtful readers—this text avoids the technical language used in more advanced works. However, to satisfy the intellectual appetites of the very curious readers, some sections are rather detailed. For those who are less enthusiastic, a cursory reading of those sections will provide insight into the complex issues involved in the critical study of the NT. Through use of the most recent information available and through modern techniques of biblical study, this book provides a critical—in the sense of making judgments as objectively as possible—introduction to NT study.

The aim of the book has been to inform, not to convert, and to educate, not to indoctrinate. Evidence supporting diverse interpretations of the NT writings is presented to inform and enlighten readers on subjects about which certainty is too often assumed. This presentation should help students realize that the NT writings did not just drop from heaven, immune from open-minded discussion, and should encourage them to go beyond denominational and romantic approaches. The presentation of different opinions on controversial subjects provides enlightenment for students to make critical and objective judgments and to draw their own personal conclusions.

Several reviewers of earlier editions suggested that I should give my own conclusions more often on issues discussed. But rarely, if ever, is the evidence firm enough to warrant a totally conclusive opinion. Many times the critical investigator must be satisfied with presenting a consensus among scholars, and sometimes one cannot even speak of a consensus. Nevertheless, I now do sometimes give my own views, especially concerning some aspects of Jesus and Pauline studies. However, I do this as much to encourage students to participate in discussions with their instructors as to present my own opinions. Discussions often do more to enlighten students than the mere reading of opinions, no matter whose they are.

To help students achieve the aim of this book, the text is carefully organized and written in a clear-cut manner. For easy and frequent reference, the chronological table has been expanded to help students learn at a glance the time in which the various writings of the NT appeared. A more detailed table of contents makes it easy to find major and minor topics of discussion. And the widely acknowledged maps assist students in learning the locales of Jesus' work and the travels of the apostle Paul.

Scholars generally agree that it is increasingly more important for all who study the NT to understand it in light of the settings out of which it originated. I have, therefore, somewhat expanded the Introduction to include more on political developments, peoples and languages, schools and education, social and economic conditions, religion of the Greeks, Romans, and Jews, and Diaspora Judaism. I have added a section on early Hebrew religion so that students can learn that the basic theological views and the moral convictions of most NT writers stem from that religion. At the suggestion of several reviewers, I have divided the Introduction into parts A and B, because some instructors may prefer to have students read the second part later as an introduction to Paul and his letters.

The following are other important changes in this edition. All quotations from scripture have been changed from the *Revised Standard Version* (*RSV*) to the *New Revised Standard Version* (*NRSV*). All dates have been changed from B.C. and A.D. to BCE ("before the common era") and CE ("the common era"). The latter are more neutral designations, especially when referring to biblical events. This helps students realize and avoid the anti-Jewish bias that gave rise to the former terms.

To help clarify the specific situation or problems addressed by each NT writer, this book also contains introductions to each NT writing, including authorship, date and place of writing, special theological views, and literary style of most writers. Discussion of these topics helps broaden students' insights into the nature and content of the NT writers' works. It also helps them to develop their own critical thinking.

Outlines of and brief comments on each writing give structure to students' reading. A summary concludes each chapter and the book itself. All of these things help students stay focused on the most important subject matter of the many and diverse writings they are studying.

The main parts of this edition remain the same: Part I—Jesus and the First Three Gospels; Part II—Acts and Paul and His Letters; and Part III—Writings from Times of Oppression and Controversy. These divisions have been retained in spite of the fact that Paul's letters are the earliest writings in the NT. It is easier for students to begin their study with the gospels because the NT begins with them. Moreover, chronologically Jesus of Nazareth preceded Paul, and the memory of Jesus' life, teachings, and death, and the belief in his resurrection from the dead became the inspiration not only for the letters of Paul but also for the rest of the NT writings. By beginning with the gospels students more quickly become aware of these important truths.

Within the three main parts of the text there are important changes. At the suggestion of several reviewers, Chapter 7 has become Chapter 3, because it is more appropriate there as an aid for students in their critical study of Jesus and the gospels. There are new sections on Jesus studies and on feminist perspectives, so that students can become aware of the latest works on the former and the increasing significance of the latter. In Part I there is also new material on methods and approaches to NT study. In Part II sections have been added on the new quest for the "historical Paul," including some of the latest studies on that apostle, along with some of my own views on Pauline issues. These additions give students insights into some of the cutting-edge issues of NT study.

This book should be used with a modern translation of the NT. Readers will find it helpful to use a text of the first three gospels printed in parallel columns. A good one is *Gospel Parallels* (Nashville: Nelson, 1992). Unless indicated otherwise, translations from classical and Jewish writers are my own. However, I have used several different translations by other scholars, to whom I acknowledge my debt in this general way.

Since the last edition of this text, there has been an incomprehensible proliferation of works on almost all aspects of our study. For that reason the bibliography has been increased, sometimes with a descriptive word or phrase in the text, helpful to students and instructors alike who may be interested in a particular method or other aspect of critical study. Although the primary source for the critical study of the NT is the NT itself, students should be aware of the most important books on the subject as the basic tools for such study.

Because this textbook is written primarily for those who are beginning NT study, the references to scholarly works have been kept to a minimum. Those given are intended both to encourage interested students to do further study and to acknowledge the contributions of other scholars. However, I am indebted to many more scholars, both from this country and abroad, than are cited. I hereby express my appreciation to all whose work may be reflected in this book.

I want to thank members of the editorial staff of Wadsworth Publishing Company for help in various ways with this edition. I am grateful to Peter Adams, Editor, for his sympathetic concern and patience with me while working during the time of my serious illness. I appreciate the work of Kerri Abdinoor, Assistant Editor, in helping to get this edition started. I am especially grateful to Dusty Friedman of The Book Company of Ashland, Oregon, for her always friendly and efficient help in many ways in preparing this edition for the printer. And special thanks go to Pat Brewer, who copyedited my text; her helpful suggestions and meticulous editing have made this work much better in numerous ways.

Sincere gratitude is extended to the professors who reviewed the last edition in preparation for this one and made helpful suggestions, most of which have been followed: William E. Abshire, Bridgewater College; Larry Dunlop, Marymount College; J. Kenneth Kuntz, The University of Iowa; Christopher S. Langton, Principia College; and Thomas R. W. Longstaff, Colby College.

Very special and warm thanks go to my wife, Ann, for the photographs in this book—which are reproduced from her color slides—for many thoughtful suggestions, for always being around to give loving assurance and assistance, and especially for her help with the indexing. To her this edition is very affectionately dedicated.

Finally, for friendly encouragement and help in numerous ways during the writing of the first edition I am still very grateful to our daughter, Jane Freed Roberts.

Abbreviations

ABPR	Association of Baptist Professors of Religion
Alleg. Inter.	*Allegorical Interpretation of Genesis* by Philo
Ant.	*Jewish Antiquities* by Josephus
ApocJa	*Apocryphon of James*
BA	*Biblical Archaeologist*
BAR	*Biblical Archaeology Review*
BR	*Biblical Research*
BTB	*Biblical Theology Bulletin*
c.	*circa*, about
CBAA	Catholic Biblical Association of America
CBQ	*Catholic Biblical Quarterly*
CD	*Damascus Document*
CRBS	*Currents in Biblical Research: Biblical Studies*
DialSav	*Dialogue of the Savior*
Did.	*Didache*
Dis.	*Discourses* of Epictetus
ed.	editor, edited by, or edition
11QMelch	*Melchizedek* text from Qumran
esp.	especially
et al.	and others
4QpPs 37	*Commentary on Psalm 37* from Qumran
GEbi	*Gospel of the Ebionites*
GHeb	*Gospel of the Hebrews*
GNaz	*Gospel of the Nazoreans*
GPet	*Gospel of Peter*
GThom	*Gospel of Thomas*
Her.	*Against Heresies* by Irenaeus
Hist.	*Church History* by Eusebius
HR	*History of Religions*
HTR	*Harvard Theological Review*
IB	*Interpreter's Bible*
IDB	*Interpreter's Dictionary of the Bible*
InThom	*Infancy Gospel of Thomas*
JAAR	*Journal of the American Academy of Religion*
JBC	*Jerome Biblical Commentary*
JBL	*Journal of Biblical Literature*
JRH	*Journal of Religious History*
JSNT	*Journal for the Study of the New Testament*
Mor. Ep.	*Moral Epistles* by Seneca
NovT	*Novum Testamentum*
NRSV	*New Revised Standard Version*
NT	New Testament
NTS	*New Testament Studies*
OT	Old Testament
1 Macc	1 Maccabees
1QapGen	*Genesis Apocryphon* from Qumran
1QH	*Thanksgiving Hymns* from Qumran
1QM	*War Scroll* from Qumran
1QpHab	*Pesher [Commentary] on Habakkuk* from Qumran
1QS	*Manual of Discipline* from Qumran
1QSa	*Rule of the Congregation* from Qumran
par.	parallels
Perk Journ	*Perkins Journal*
POxy	*Oxyrhynchus Papyrus*
Pss. Sol.	*Psalms of Solomon*
Rev.	Revised by or revision
RSR	*Religious Studies Review*
SBLSP	*Society of Biblical Literature Seminar Papers*
Sir	Wisdom of Jesus the Son of Sirach
SNTSMS	*Society for New Testament Studies Monograph Series*
T. Benj.	*Testament of Benjamin*
T. Dan	*Testament of Dan*
T. Judah	*Testament of Judah*
T. Levi	*Testament of Levi*
T. Moses	*Testament of Moses*
T. Naph.	*Testament of Naphtali*
T. Sim.	*Testament of Simeon*
Tob	Tobit
Trans.	Translated by or translation
TS	*Theological Studies*
2 Bar	2 Baruch
2 Clem.	2 Clement
2 Esdr	2 Esdras
2 Macc	2 Maccabees
War	*The Jewish War* by Josephus
Wis	Wisdom of Solomon
W/K	Westminster/Knox

Chronological Table

Key Dates	Important Events in Hebrew/Jewish and Christian History (dates for NT writings are rather arbitrary)
900–400 BCE	Hebrew prophets of OT times
586	Babylonians destroy Jerusalem and temple
581	Babylonians take last group of captives to Babylon
550–530	Persian rule
538	First exiles return to Judea
520–515	Rebuilding of the temple
458–428	Ezra the scribe
332–331	Alexander the Great conquers Palestine
300–198	Ptolemies of Egypt rule Palestine
198–142	Seleucids of Syria rule Palestine
187	Death of Antiochus III (the Great)
175–164	Antiochus IV (Epiphanes)
168	Antiochus desecrates the temple
165	Judas Maccabee wins religious freedom; Hanukkah
161–143	Jonathan Maccabee
143–142	Jonathan and Simon Maccabee win political freedom
142–134	Simon
130 BCE–135 CE	Manuscripts left in Judean caves, including Qumran
142–63 BCE	Hasmoneans (Maccabees) rule Palestine
134–104	John Hyrcanus I
103–76	Alexander Jannaeus
76–67	Salome Alexandra; Hyrcanus II high priest
67–63	Aristobulus II king and high priest
63	Jerusalem and temple destroyed by Pompey of Rome
37–4	Herod the Great (Matt 2:1–22; Luke 1:5) begins rebuilding of temple; Jesus born c. 6–4 BCE; revolts after Herod's death
27 BCE–14 CE	Augustus emperor (Luke 2:1); divides Herod's kingdom among his three sons; Roman peace (*pax Romana*)
4 BCE–6 CE	Archelaus (Matt 2:22) rules Judea, Idumea, and Samaria
6 CE	Archelaus deposed by Augustus and his territory made a Roman province ruled by Roman prefect; Quirinius (Luke 2:2) becomes governor of Syria; Judas the Galilean (Acts 5:37) leads revolt because of census by Quirinius
4 BCE–34 CE	Philip (Mark 6:17; Matt 14:3; Luke 3:1) rules territory east and northeast of Sea of Galilee as tetrarch
4 BCE–39 CE	Antipas (Herod in Mark 6:14–22; 8:15; Matt 14:1–6; Luke 3:1, 19; 9:7, 9; 13:31–32; 23:7–15; Acts 4:27) rules Galilee and Perea as tetrarch; has John the Baptist beheaded (Mark 6:17–29; Matt 14:3–12)
14–37 CE	Tiberius emperor (Luke 3:1); Jesus goes public

26–36	Pontius Pilate procurator of Judea (Luke 3:1); Jesus crucified c. 30–33; conversion of Saul (Acts 9:1–22)
37–41	Gaius (Caligula) emperor; Paul escapes from Damascus and goes to Jerusalem, then to Tarsus; Caligula orders his statue placed in the temple but assassinated before accomplished
41–44	Agrippa I king of territory once held by Herod the Great; has James, brother of John, killed, Peter imprisoned but escapes (Acts 12:1–11)
41–54	Claudius emperor; expelled Jews from Rome (Acts 18:1–2); famine (Acts 11:27–28); Paul and Barnabas make first journey c. 46–49 (Acts 12:25–14:28); Paul's second journey (Acts 15:36–16:5) c. 50–52; 1 Thessalonians c. 51; Herod Agrippa II given rule of land NE of Sea of Galilee in 53; Galatians c. 48–54
44–46	Procurator Fadus executes rebel Theudas (Acts 5:36); Felix (52–60) and Festus (60–62) procurators of Judea; hostile revolts in Palestine; Paul apprehended in Jerusalem, before Sanhedrin, prosecuted by Ananias, hustled off to Caesarea by friends, makes defense before Felix; Festus takes Paul before Herod Agrippa II; upon his appeal as a Roman citizen, Paul is sent to Rome (Acts 21:27–27:2; 28:16); 1 and 2 Corinthians c. 53–56
54–68	Nero emperor; charges Christians for fire in Rome and persecutes them; third journey of Paul c. 54–58 (Acts 18:23–21:17); Romans c. 55; Philippians c. 55–58
50–100	Agrippa II (Acts 25:13–26:32) loyal to Rome throughout Jewish war against Rome (66–70); Philemon c. 56–64; Colossians c. 54–64; Ephesians c. 58–64; 2 Thessalonians c. 51–70; Hebrews c. 60–110
68–69	Galba, Otho, Vitellius emperors of Rome; Vespasian and then Titus defend Rome against Jews; severe revolution in Galilee and Judea
69–79	Vespasian emperor; Titus destroys Jerusalem and temple in 70; Romans rule Palestine; end of temple worship, Sadducean party, and Sanhedrin; Gospel of Mark c. 70
79–81	Titus emperor; Pharisees and rabbis outside of Jerusalem become teachers in Judaism
81–96	Domitian emperor; Revelation c. 68–96; perhaps some local persecution of Christians; Gospel of Matthew c. 85–110; Gospel of Luke and Acts c. 90–110; Gospel of John c. 90–120; 1, 2, and 3 John all after gospel; Letter of James c. 62–110
98–117	Trajan emperor; Jews revolt in regions outside Palestine (115–119); 1 Peter c. 70–115
117–138	Hadrian emperor; Jewish revolt under Bar Cochba (132–135); Jews driven from Jerusalem; Jerusalem becomes a thoroughly pagan city rebuilt as Aelia Capitolina; temple of Jupiter built on site of Jewish temple; letters of Jude and 2 Peter c. 100–125; 1 Timothy, 2 Timothy, and Titus c. 100–180

INTRODUCTION

The Settings of the New Testament

THE NEW TESTAMENT (NT) IS A COLLECTION of diverse religious literary works. It begins with the gospels, a distinctive literary form. They are followed by Acts, which is a history of the early church, and the letters of Paul. Then come other letters, written by a number of early Christians, and Revelation, representing a literary form known as *apocalypse* that is peculiar to Jews and Christians.

All the writings of the NT are the results of individuals or groups committed to their Christian faith when confronted with particular historical, social, and political situations. Therefore different emphases appear in different writings because each was addressed to a specific situation. And the particular social and cultural background of each writer, as well as the situation he was addressing, surely affected his response. These individual differences and approaches account for the diversity in faith and practice we find in the NT writings as Christianity was trying to establish its own identity in separating from its parent Judaism and to accommodate itself to a pagan environment in the Roman Empire.

It is important to understand that without exception NT writings were written for people of the writers' times whose language, education, society, history, politics, symbols, and customs were very different from those of today. So the more we learn about the writers' times, the better we can understand their writings.

Study of the history, religion, and literature of the NT is important for several reasons. Most important, perhaps, it helps us understand the Christian religion. Historically, the NT provides knowledge about the life and teachings of Jesus, that famous teacher whose followers came to regard him as both human and divine. Furthermore, the NT informs us about the way the early Christians, or followers of Jesus, lived and thought. It also provides insights into the life and work of Paul, whose writings inspired the religious reformation of the sixteenth century, a movement that gave birth to Protestantism as a separate entity from the Catholic church.

Since the Reformation, the NT has remained sacred scripture for Catholicism, Eastern Orthodoxy, and Protestantism, the main divisions of the Christian religion. Spiritually, the NT has inspired worship, study, and personal meditation for Christians throughout the world, and it has remained basic to Christian faith and practice. Beyond historical and spiritual significance, the NT, with the Old Testament (OT) of the modern Bible, has also had a major influence in shaping the systems of justice, governments, social institutions, and art of Western culture.

Jesus of Nazareth, a Jew from Galilee in ancient Palestine, was the inspiration for the whole NT. Jesus' first followers were all Jews, but gradually non-Jews, whom the Jews called Gentiles, also became his followers. All of these followers came to be called Christians, who formed religious communities known as churches, and the churches collectively formed an institution called the church. Members of the church wrote, collected, and published the diversified writings of the NT because they thought them useful for instruction in Christian faith and life. They did so during specific times in response to particular situations.

Although the NT writings provide historical insight into the life and work of Jesus and the Christian movement of its first century, the NT is not just a collection of historical writings. With the possible exception of the writer of the book of Revelation, no NT writer thought that what he was saying was so sacred that nothing should be added to or removed from it. However, Christian churches soon came to regard NT literature as scripture, that is, writings authoritative for faith, worship, and life. This is precisely why NT writings were preserved and other Christian writings were not.

In spite of the significance of the NT writings as scripture for Christians, the critical study of the NT for Christians and non-Christians alike must begin with open minds and a willingness to study these writings as products of the first century. This means analyzing NT writings just as we would any other writings. The aim is to understand the nature of the texts and why they came to be recognized as more than historical documents.

Having an open mind may mean admitting surprise, or even dismay, at learning something new or different and being willing to change one's mind in light of evidence. Sometimes evidence may not lead to conclusive opinions. Then, of course, one must ask more questions and seek new evidence, if possible, to arrive at new or different conclusions. If we keep our aim in mind, the study of the NT can be as interesting, exciting, and challenging as the study of any other subject.

In this Introduction we will study the settings out of which the NT writings developed during the first century of the Christian era to better understand how they originated and why they were written. This, in turn, can help provide insights into plausible interpretations of NT scriptures.

The first four books of the NT, the gospels, deal with the life and teachings of Jesus, and therefore are set in ancient Palestine, which was a part of the Roman Empire east of the Mediterranean. In Part A of this Introduction, we will focus on:

- Palestine's history and government as it was controlled by the Greeks, looking specifically at the influence of the complex phenomenon known as Hellenism—Greek culture as spread beyond Greece

- Palestine's history and government under Roman rule

- Peoples and languages

- Schools and education

- Social and economic conditions

- Graeco-Roman religions and the Jewish religion in ancient Palestine to understand the religious context in which Christianity developed

Because Jesus and most of his first followers were Jews, the early Christian church began as a sect within Judaism. As that sect separated from its parent, its followers were mostly non-Jews, or Gentiles. Therefore, it is important to study not only Judaism in first-century Palestine, but also other religions and influences of that land.

In Part B we will shift our attention from Palestine to the Hellenistic culture of the Roman

Empire north of the Mediterranean, where the early Christian church grew and developed. We focus on:

- Rome and her provinces under the emperors from Augustus to Trajan, because key cities in this area became centers of early Christianity
- Roman law
- Society and culture (peoples and languages, schools and education, social and economic conditions)
- Christians and the cities
- Roman religion and philosophy, because it is impossible to appreciate the thought of the NT without some knowledge of this religious competition for early Christianity

The literature from the time of the NT helps us better understand the NT's historical and cultural setting. Among Jewish sources, the OT is very important religious background for the NT. Two collections of Jewish writings from c. (*circa*, or about) 200 BCE–100 CE, the Apocrypha and Pseudepigrapha of the OT, are important for both the history and religion of the Jews, as are the works of the Jewish historian Josephus (c. 38–100 CE) and of the Jewish philosopher Philo of Alexandria (c. 20 BCE–50 CE) and the writings of the Sect of Qumran.

The Apocrypha are available in many editions, including one in the *New Revised Standard Version* (New York: Oxford, 1989). The most complete edition of the Pseudepigrapha is edited by J. H. Charlesworth 1983, 1985. Of innumerable works on the Qumran Scrolls, the following are excellent: F. M. Cross 1961; A. Dupont-Sommer 1962; H. Ringgren 1963; and G. Vermes 1994. For Josephus, see H. S. Thackeray 1967 and T. Rajak 1984. There are two excellent introductions to Philo, one by E. R. Goodenough 1986, the other by S. Sandmel 1979; see also H. A. Wolfson 1947. The writings of Philo and Josephus are available in English translation along with the Greek texts in the Loeb Classical Library, a collection of ancient Latin and Greek authors published by Harvard University Press.

Among Greek and Roman sources, the following are useful: the historical works of Livy (59 BCE–17 CE), Tacitus (c. 55 BCE–118 CE), Diodorus (c. 60–21 BCE), Dio Cassius (second century CE), and Pliny the Elder (c. 23–79 CE); *Description of Greece* by Pausanias (second century CE), *Geography* of Strabo (c. 64 BCE–21 CE), *Letters* of Pliny the Younger (61–112 CE), *Lives of the Caesars* by Suetonius (c. 69–140 CE), *Life of Apollonius of Tyana* by Philostratus (second–third centuries CE), *Moral Essays and Moral Epistles* of Seneca (c. 4 BCE–65 CE), *Morals* of Plutarch (c. 46–122 CE), *Discourses of Epictetus* (c. 55–135 CE) by Arrian (c. 90–175 CE), and the satires of Horace (65–8 BCE) and Juvenal (c. 50–130 CE). All of these works are in lucid English translations in the Loeb Classical Library.

For texts see C. K. Barrett 1987; D. G. Rice 1979; J. Shelton 1988; G. H. R. Horsley 1981–1987; M. W. Meyer 1987; M. E. Boring 1995 for Jewish and other texts relevant to the NT; D. R. Cartlidge 1994 for gospels; C. R. Holladay 1983–1996 for Hellenistic Jewish authors.

Remember that the conditions described in this chapter composed the setting for Christianity when it emerged as a small Jewish sect devoted to Jesus. Read this chapter, then, to gain insights into the environment in which Jesus lived and taught and in which the early Christians wrote the NT as the church grew into a religion of worldwide significance.

PART A
EAST OF THE MEDITERRANEAN: PALESTINE AND SYRIA

The gospels are set east of the Mediterranean, in lands that included Palestine and Syria. Although Jesus of Nazareth came from a northern region of ancient Palestine known as Galilee, when Palestine came under Greek rule in the fourth century BCE most Jews lived in Judea, a southern region about forty-five miles square, comprising Jerusalem and the surrounding country and villages.

(See the map of Palestine during the ministry of Jesus on front endsheet.)

HISTORY AND GOVERNMENT UNDER THE GREEKS (334–63 BCE)

From Alexander the Great to the Maccabean Rebellion (334–168 BCE)

From the time of Alexander the Great of Macedonia (a kingdom north of Greece) to the conquests by Rome, the period of Greek rule over lands of the East is known as the Hellenistic Age. Outside the Greek mainland, Greek culture—including political, socioeconomic, and religious aspects—is known as Hellenism; its military peak was reached with Alexander's conquests. (See Figure I.1.) Those living under Greek rule who adopted Greek culture (Hellenists) often contributed to the erection of theaters, gymnasia, and other buildings; many used Greek as their only language, and even wore distinctive Greek clothes. The majority of native peoples, however, continued to follow their own customs and lifestyles.

The process whereby Greek culture penetrated a region, especially its cities, is called Hellenization. To what degree Hellenization was effective in general is debatable, but it was very effective in creating an international language of commerce and communication. This is important to NT study because some groups living in foreign lands (for example, Jews in Alexandria, Egypt) gave up their native languages and used only Greek—requiring their scriptures, then, to be translated from Hebrew into Greek. That translation, known as the Septuagint and abbreviated LXX (from the Latin "seventy," because of the Jewish legend that seventy men independently had made the same translation), was the Jewish scriptures used by Christians.

The Jews of Palestine came under Greek rule with the conquests of Alexander the Great and his Greek successors c. 332 BCE. Governmental affairs were in the hands of a high priest, the supreme political and religious leader, who was assisted by a body of aristocratic priests and older

FIGURE I.1   *Sculptured head of Alexander the Great as a youth, in the museum in Pella, Greece, his birthplace.*

men known as the Gerousia. After Alexander's death in 323 BCE, his generals fought for control of his empire, which was divided into three parts, two of which are important in Jewish history: Seleucia and Egypt. Seleucia, comprising Syria, Phoenicia, and the surrounding regions north of Judea, was ruled by Greek enthusiasts from Antioch called Seleucids and Antiochids, and Egypt was ruled by Ptolemies, also Greek enthusiasts, from Alexandria. Until 198 BCE, Judea, the land of the Jews, was overrun by the forces of Seleucia and Egypt, who fought against each other to control it. Most of the time it was ruled by Ptolemies, who let the Jews live in comparative peace with their high priest in charge of local affairs.

In 198 BCE Antiochus III (the Great) of Seleucia gained control of Judea. Kind to the Jews, he settled many in new cities, allowed them to live by their laws, and eased tax burdens. From this point on, party politics among Jews themselves was as much responsible for the events that followed as any external conflict between Hellenism and Judaism. The pro-Seleucid party in Jerusalem was Hellenistic. But these Hellenists were regarded as unfaithful Jews by conservative Jews, who united under the name *Hasidim* (pious) and opposed all efforts of Hellenization.

Because Antiochus IV, successor to Antiochus III, offered the position of high priest to the highest financial bidder, the high priesthood changed quickly several times, and a clash developed in Jerusalem between the priestly aristocracy and those who wanted to preserve the legitimacy and sanctity of the priestly office. Antiochus IV, realizing that the strength of Jewish nationalism lay in its religion, and sensing the rebellious attitude of many Jews, determined to eliminate the Hasidim. He forbade circumcision, sabbath observance, and reading of scripture. He built an altar to Zeus in the temple and sacrificed a pig, an unclean animal according to Jewish law. Subsequently, devout Jews from the family Hasmon (later called Maccabees) rose in revolt (1 and 2 Maccabees; Josephus, *Ant.* 12–14; *War* 1).

The Maccabean Interruption (168–63 BCE)

Reaction of the Jews to the Hellenism of Antiochus IV was threefold. Some forsook their own religion and obeyed him (1 Macc 1:41–44, 52). The Hasidim, secretly following the law of Moses, passively resisted and preferred to die rather than submit. In the village of Modein, some rural Jews under the Maccabees actively rebelled when an aged Jewish priest, Mattathias, killed a Syrian officer and a Jew because they were about to sacrifice to Zeus. Mattathias and his five sons, including Judas, Jonathan, and Simon—all intensely devoted to Judaism—fled to the hills, where a group of nationalists joined them. Although greatly outnumbered and sometimes severely defeated, they ultimately gained complete freedom for the Jews by resorting to guerrilla warfare and clever diplomacy.

In 165 BCE Judas won religious freedom for the Jews. He and his followers cleansed the temple in Jerusalem, restored regular Jewish worship, and instituted the first Hanukkah, a festival

commemorating the dedication of the temple. By saving Jewish religious freedom, Judas aroused a new sense of Jewish nationalism founded on the law given by God.

Jonathan (161–143 BCE) and Simon (143–135 BCE) carried on the struggle and won political independence for the Jews in 142 BCE. Then, during the time of Hyrcanus (135–104 BCE), son of Simon, three major Jewish parties appeared: Pharisees, Sadducees, and Essenes (discussed below). Aristobulus (104–103 BCE) and Jannaeus (103–76 BCE), sons of Hyrcanus, expanded the territory of the Jews and secured its borders. Intrigue and murder in the ruling family, however, helped to erode that security, and a struggle between the Pharisees and Sadducees erupted into civil war. Alexandra (76–67 BCE), widow of Jannaeus, became a partisan of the Pharisees and for the first time appointed some of them to the Gerousia. Her apparently peaceful, powerful, and prosperous reign was marred by her murder of many Sadducees.

Upon the death of Alexandra, her sons Hyrcanus, a Pharisee, and Aristobulus, a Sadducee, waged civil war against each other. After a period of conniving and fighting (with foreign supporters on each side), envoys from both sides appealed to the most powerful person in the region, the Roman general Pompey in Damascus. A third delegation of Jews, wanting neither brother as ruler, preferred a return to pre-Maccabean government with a high priest and Gerousia. Pompey, who could not take over Jerusalem peacefully because Aristobulus's soldiers refused to surrender, then captured Jerusalem for Rome in 63 BCE.

HISTORY AND GOVERNMENT UNDER THE ROMANS (63 BCE TO BEYOND NT TIMES)

During early Roman rule (63–37 BCE), which began with Pompey's capture of Jerusalem, Pompey, Julius Caesar, Cassius, and Antony controlled Palestine. The lot of the Jews under Roman rule depended upon the nature of the individual ruler. Pompey broke into the Holy of

Holies, the most sacred part of the temple, where only the high priest was permitted to enter. Awed by the beauty of the place, he ordered that services be continued and left the temple treasury untouched. However, thousands of Jews were massacred, and all cities captured by the Maccabees were taken away from the Jewish state, including a harbor on the Mediterranean. Judea was placed under Hyrcanus II, without a royal title, and made subject to the Roman Scaurus, governor of the Roman province of Syria. Jewish independence was ended, and the high priest was a vassal of Rome. The Jewish spirit was crushed. Aristobulus and his family graced Pompey's triumphal procession in Rome in 61 BCE.

Julius Caesar made Hyrcanus hereditary high priest and ethnarch with all rights and privileges belonging to him as a Jew. He was also given permission to rebuild the walls of Jerusalem. Concessions granted to the Jews by Caesar included the return of Joppa, with its seaport, along with other lost territory. Jews in Alexandria were made Roman citizens, and those in Asia Minor were permitted full freedom of their religion.

When Cassius became master of Syria, he forced Judea to pay a large tribute, which was collected by Antipater and Herod. Towns too poor to pay were sold into slavery. Antony appointed Herod and Phasael, his brother, tetrarchs of Judea, so the authority of Hyrcanus came to an end. Because the Jews sided with the Parthians (an Iranian people who were Rome's greatest enemy in the East) for the overthrow of Rome while Antony was visiting Cleopatra, Hyrcanus was exiled to Babylonia, after his ears were bitten off. When the Parthians defeated the Romans in Palestine, Phasael committed suicide, and Herod secured his family in his fortress at Masada. From there he went to Rome to appeal to Antony. Antigonus, last ruler of the Hasmonean family, was made king and high priest by the Parthians in return for a large tribute and five hundred Jewish women. A somewhat better day was to dawn for the Jews with the rule of Herod (see Josephus, *Ant.* 14:5–13; *War* 1:8–13).

A born leader of untiring energy and crafty ambition, Herod vowed allegiance to Rome under all circumstances. In 40 BCE he fled from his Arab enemies in Nabataea (see map on front endsheet) to Rome where, in return for his ability and loyalty, the Roman Senate appointed him king of the Jews. With the aid of Roman troops, Herod returned to Jerusalem, capturing it and all of Palestine from the Parthians. This action and other deeds gained him the title Herod the Great.

Herod the Great (37–4 BCE), His Sons, and the Prefects of Judea (4 BCE–41 CE)

In the eyes of Rome, Herod was a faithful and able king with a strong interest in Hellenism. He built many splendid cities, including Caesarea and Samaria, the fortresses of Machaerus and Masada, theaters, amphitheaters, temples, aqueducts, baths, fountains, and public parks. (See Figure I.2.) Though a devotee of Hellenism, Herod at first was not hostile to Judaism, but his jealous and suspicious nature was responsible for the deaths of thousands of Jews, including many family members, such as the Jewess Mariamme, his favorite wife. Offended by his zeal for Hellenism, which they considered paganism, the Jews regarded Herod as a bloodthirsty tyrant, a self-seeking half-breed, and a murderer (*Ant.* 15–17; *War* 1:18–33).

Ironically, however, Herod brought an era of peace to the Jews that lasted longer than any they had known for years. The political hostility between the Pharisees and Sadducees ended, their controversy becoming one of ideas instead of weapons. Consequently, the rabbis Abtalion and Shemaiah and the Pharisaic teachers Hillel and Shammai, all of whom Herod befriended, were able to devote full time to religious study. Herod began rebuilding the Jewish temple, which was not completed until long after his death.

After Herod's death, the emperor Augustus ratified Herod's will, under which three sons inherited his kingdom. Archelaus (4 BCE–6 CE) received Judea, Idumea, and Samaria; Antipas (4 BCE–39 CE) received Galilee and Perea; and Philip (4 BCE–34 CE) received the territory northeast of the Sea of Galilee. Archelaus, violent and tyrannical, was deposed and exiled by Au-

FIGURE I.2
Roman aqueduct in Caesarea built by Herod the Great.

gustus in 6 CE and his territory made a Roman province known as Judea, which was to be ruled by a Roman prefect who served under the emperor. Because the welfare of the Jews depended upon their relations with the prefects, we must consider events during their times.

From 6 to 41 CE there were seven prefects, the most important being Pontius Pilate (26–36) because of his connection with Jesus (*Ant.* 18:2–4; *War* 2:9:2–4; Philo, *Embassy to Gaius* 38; gospels; also see Figure I.3). Appointed by the emperor, the prefect lived in Caesarea, the capital of the province, and served as commander in chief of the armies. Besides controlling the finances and assisting in collecting taxes he was a judicial authority and had the power to pass a death sentence (although Roman citizens could appeal to the emperor). Prefects also had the power to appoint and depose Jewish high priests.

Under the prefects, Jews had considerable freedom to govern themselves. Legal affairs were in the charge of the great Sanhedrin in Jerusalem and smaller sanhedrins in various cities. The supreme court of the Jews, the Sanhedrin was composed of seventy-one members, including Pharisees, Sadducees, and respected older men, over all of whom the high, or chief, priest presided. The Sanhedrin tried all civil, criminal,

and religious cases according to Mosaic (OT) law, but although it could pass and carry out laws (except over Roman citizens), the prefect may have had to confirm death sentences and always had the right to intervene. Nonetheless, the Jews were granted the power to kill any Gentile, even a Roman citizen, who ventured into the temple beyond the court of the Gentiles.

Philip (*Ant.* 18:2:1; 18:4:6; 18:6:10; *War* 2:9:1, 6) was the most respected of Herod's sons, and his rule was just, peaceful, and benevolent. The population of his territory was composed mainly of Greeks and Syrians, with only a few Jews. Philip rebuilt the ancient city of Panias, which came to be known as Caesarea Philippi (Mark 8:27; Matt 16:13), and Bethsaida, which he named Julias in honor of Augustus's daughter. After he died, his territory was given to Agrippa I, grandson of Herod the Great.

Antipas (*Ant.* 18; *War* 2:9:1, 6; *Life* 9, 12, 54), referred to as Herod in the gospels (see, for example, Mark 6:14–28; Matt 14:1–12; Luke 3:19–20), was as sly and ambitious as his father, though not as able. He built the towns of Sepphoris and Tiberias, among others, the former for the protection of Galilee, the latter as his capital. It was Antipas, according to both Josephus and the gospels, who executed the Jewish

FIGURE I.3   *Inscription of Pontius Pilate on a stone from a temple in Caesarea. Herod the Great built the temple in honor of Augustus.*

preacher John the Baptist. When the emperor Gaius (37–41) learned that Antipas had a large collection of arms that could be used to revolt against Rome, he deposed him and gave his territory to Agrippa I.

Agrippa I and Procurators of Palestine (41–66)

Agrippa I (41–44) ruled all of Palestine as a professed Jew and, for political reasons, defended Judaism at home and abroad, but he was a Hellenist at heart. At his own expense, he built a theater, amphitheater, and baths at Berytus, a Roman colony. Although differing in detail, Josephus and Acts agree that Agrippa I, dressed in a royal robe, died very suddenly in Caesarea while accepting the shouts of the crowd that he was a god. From his death in 44 to 66 all of Palestine became a Roman province with procurators under the supervision of the governor of Syria (sources: *Ant.* 18:6; 19:5–9; 20:1, 5–11; *War* 2:9–14; Philo, *Embassy to Gaius* and *Against Flaccus*; Acts 12:23–26; Tacitus, *Annals* 15:44 and *History* 5:9–10; Suetonius, *Lives of the Caesars*).

None of the procurators was a good ruler, and all lacked appreciation for Judaism, failed to reconcile the Jews to Roman rule, and severely suppressed any signs of Jewish unrest. Josephus says that the first two, Fadus and Alexander (44–48), "did not disturb the customs of the country and guarded the nation in peace" (*War* 2:11:6). Cumanus (48–52) was succeeded by Felix (52–60), whose rule marks the beginning of a constant hostility that culminated in the war of the Jews against Rome (66–73). During his time the Sicarii, Jews who got their name from carrying the Roman *sicae* (daggers) under their cloaks, intensified the hostility between Jews and Romans by committing violent acts. Such acts made the Roman and anti-Roman parties stronger so that "there were many daily murders" and "all Judea was filled with their madness" (*War* 2:13:3, 6).

Felix, with his wife Drusilla, heard the apostle Paul make his defense as a prisoner in Caesarea (Acts 23:23–24:27). When riots broke out in Caesarea between Jews and Syrians, Felix permitted soldiers to plunder their houses and sent the leaders of both groups to Rome. Although Felix was then recalled by the emperor Nero, Jewish hatred of Rome intensified.

Felix was succeeded by Festus (60–62), Albinus (62–64), and Florus (64–66). Albinus's one aim was to get rich by any means, so he stole public and private funds and sought bribes. When he learned that he was to be removed from his position by Nero, Albinus executed some prisoners and freed others, thus leaving the prisons empty of inmates and the land full of brigands. But Florus "was so bad and violent in exercising his authority . . . that the Jews praised Albinus as a benefactor" (*Ant.* 20:11:1). The stage was set for a tragic war against Rome that doomed the Jews to utter defeat (sources: *War* 2:14–7:11; *Life* 4–74; Tacitus, *History* 2:1–4,

79–83; 4:81; 5:1, 10, 12–26; Dio Cassius, *Roman History* 66:1, 4–7, 15; Suetonius, *Vespasian* 5–6 and *Titus* 4–5).

War of the Jews against Rome (66–73)

In 66 CE bitter fighting broke out between pro-Roman and anti-Roman Jewish forces. However, a victory over Cestius Gallus, the governor of Syria who attacked Jerusalem, united all Jews. An assembly of Jews in the temple made Josephus, the future historian, governor of Galilee despite the opposition of John of Gischala, a bitter foe of Rome, who felt Josephus was too friendly to Rome.

Nero placed Vespasian and his son Titus in charge of crushing the Jewish revolt, and when the Roman army arrived, Josephus and his disheartened troops fled (*War* 3:6–4:2:5). The Jews never had a chance against the skilled Roman troops, and by the end of 67 northern Palestine was again subject to Rome. John of Gischala and his radical anti-Roman followers, known as Zealots, fled to Jerusalem, where they engaged in a bloody civil war with less zealous Jewish forces under the leadership of Gorion. Other Jewish forces entered the civil war while Titus, whose father had gone to Rome to become emperor, prepared to attack Jerusalem. In August of 70 his army burned the temple along with the city, killing all they met.

Between 70 and 73 the last strongholds of the Jews were destroyed. The strongest opposition was given by Eleazar and his Sicarii forces, who had fortified themselves at Masada, a natural hill fortress on the southwest shore of the Dead Sea. When Eleazar saw there was no more hope of resistance against the forces of the Roman Silva, he persuaded his rebels to kill first their own families and then themselves rather than submit to Roman rule. When the Romans entered the fortress and saw the many dead Jews, "they rejoiced not as over enemies, but marveled at their noble purpose and the contempt of death carried out by so many without hesitation" (*War* 7:9:2).

The destruction of the Jerusalem temple brought an end to the Sanhedrin, all sacrificial worship, the Sadducean party, the priesthood, and all prospects for Jewish political independence. Judaism faced a severe religious crisis, but leading Pharisees who escaped from Jerusalem enabled Judaism not only to survive but to flourish as well. Under the leadership of the Pharisees and succeeding generations of rabbis, Jamnia, a town in western Judea, became the center of Jewish literary and religious activity. Jewish nationalism became identified with study and observance of the written and oral law. Christians had escaped to Pella, a town east of the Jordan (see map on front endsheet), and the fall of Jerusalem was a crucial event in the separation of Christianity from Judaism. For Jewish events after 70 CE see the Chronological Table.

PEOPLES AND LANGUAGES

Throughout its history, including the periods of Greek and Roman rule, Palestine was a land of many peoples. More Jews lived in Jerusalem and Judea than anywhere else, although there were some in Galilee. Greeks and Romans were present almost everywhere, and many cities, such as Caesarea and Tiberias, were predominantly Gentile.

Among the diverse people in Palestine were those known as Samaritans, who lived in the region of Samaria. The Jews regarded the Samaritans as neither fully Jews nor fully Gentiles, believing they were half-breed descendants of foreigners imported into Samaria by Assyrian kings and Israelites not deported by Assyria in the decades following 722 BCE. The Samaritans themselves, however, claimed to be descendants of Joseph's sons, Ephraim and Manasseh, and therefore authentic Jews. The Samaritans followed a version of the Pentateuch (first five books of the OT; also known as the Torah) that differed in several places from that of the Jews, and they worshiped in their own temple on Mt. Gerizim, not in the temple in Jerusalem.

In first-century Palestine four languages were spoken and written. Hebrew, the language of most of the OT, was the oldest. Many texts from the Jewish community at Qumran were written in Hebrew, confirming the literary use of that language. However, except for scrolls from Qumran, there is little evidence that Hebrew was widely used in first-century Palestine. Although it was probably used in parts of religious services and in Jewish schools, Hebrew was no longer universally understood among Jews.

Aramaic, the language of Aram (the OT word for Syria), was the most widely used language in Palestine in the first century CE and the one most commonly spoken by Jews. *Aramaic* is now a general term referring to a number of Semitic dialects closely related to each other and to Hebrew. Evidence from Qumran indicates that many texts in that community were also written in Aramaic.

After the conquests of Alexander the Great, Greek became the universal language throughout the Mediterranean world. The OT translated from Hebrew into Greek for Jews who lived outside Palestine was later used by some Jews within Palestine. Although all manuscripts of the NT are in Greek, it is possible that some were originally written in Hebrew or Aramaic and later translated into Greek. Such translations would have been made by Christians living in Hellenistic communities in Syria-Palestine or elsewhere.

In first-century Palestine Greek was very widely used not only by Jews in Graeco-Roman towns, but also by farmers and artisans, for whom Greek was surely a second language. Several kinds of documents written in Greek by Jews, including letters, business transactions, marriage contracts, and literary texts, have been discovered in Palestine. It is even conceivable that some Jews spoke and wrote only in Greek. At any rate, the Greek roots of the names of two distinctive Jewish institutions, the Sanhedrin and synagogue, illustrate the influence of Greek upon the Jews.

The newest language in Palestine was Latin, the language of Roman soldiers and some Roman officials. Evidence that Latin was used in first-century Palestine has been found in inscriptions dedicating public buildings and aqueducts, tombstones of Romans who died in Palestine, and signposts along Roman roads.

With four languages being spoken and written in first-century Palestine, scholars have speculated about the language Jesus used. If Jesus' visit to the synagogue in Nazareth is a historical fact, and if he read from the prophet Isaiah (Luke 4:16–22), then he could at least read Hebrew, since most of the OT was written in Hebrew. The consensus is that Jesus, like most other Jews, spoke Aramaic, not Hebrew, although some scholars believe he may also have spoken Greek. Because of the lack of substantial evidence, such views can only be speculation.

SCHOOLS AND EDUCATION

The words *school* and *education* do not occur in the NT in connection with Palestine. In Luke 2:46 we learn that as a boy Jesus was "in the temple, sitting among the teachers, listening to them and asking them questions"; this implies the existence of Jewish schools. Besides that passage there are no contemporary references to schools and education in first-century Palestine. However, in later literature of the rabbis (Jewish teachers) we learn about the Pharisaic schools of Hillel and Shammai. Rabbis frequently quoted opinions from "the school of Hillel," which was liberal, and less often from "the school of Shammai," which was more conservative. As an example of their differences, Shammai taught that a husband could divorce his wife only because of unchastity, the sole ground for divorce in Jewish law. Hillel, on the other hand, said a man could divorce his wife if she merely burned his food.

If we think of a school as an institution with a teacher, individuals who are being taught, and evidence of teaching, then there probably was such a school in Qumran, a community of Jews near the Dead Sea in Palestine. Among the excavations at Qumran were several stone tables, benches, and inkwells, and many believe that the area in which they were found was a scriptorium, a place for writing or copying scrolls. An *ostracon* (piece of pottery) was found on which Hebrew letters like those used in the scrolls were written. Some of the letters had been rewritten, indicating that someone was being taught to write and copy scrolls. The scrolls themselves, especially the *Man-*

ual of Discipline, now usually called *Rule of the Community,* are ample evidence for the teachings of the community. The *Rule* is addressed to "the instructor" of the new members of the community and gives instructions for living according to the *Rule* (see 1QS 1:1–11; 3:13–21).

The teacher at Qumran was known as the "Teacher of Righteousness" or "Righteous Teacher" and was regarded as one to whom God gave a special revelation and in whom his followers had faith (1QpHab 7:1–8:2). He may have founded the community (4QpPs 37) and written some of its scrolls. Although he was probably killed before the Christian era began, his influence lasted until the destruction of Qumran in c. 68 CE, and his followers wrote down many of his teachings.

There are reasons for thinking that Jesus and his disciples were a school. Jesus was addressed as "teacher," in both Hebrew (*rabbi*) and Greek (*didaskale*) forms of the word, more often than in any other way (see, for example, Mark 9:5; 10:17; 12:19; Matt 8:19; 17:24; Luke 18:18). When Jesus returned to his hometown, the people who remembered him as a carpenter or carpenter's son were amazed at his wisdom (Mark 6:2; Matt 13:54). He taught in the synagogue (Mark 1:21; 6:2) and the temple (Luke 19:47), where teaching usually took place, and discussed scholarly matters with other teachers (Mark 7:1–23; 12:28–34; Matt 15:1–20; 22:34–40; Luke 10:25–28). And Matthew reports that Jesus commissioned his disciples to "make disciples of all nations, . . . teaching them to obey everything that I have commanded you" (28:19–20). This coincides with the rabbinic saying "Raise up many disciples." Finally, Jesus' teachings were transmitted orally by his followers and later written into the gospels.

Although we do not know how many people in first-century Palestine were educated, the scriptures comprised the basis of education for both Jews and Christians. We do know that education of children began with the father's instructions in the commandments of God (Deut 6:2). Jews believed that by obeying, children would have insight as well as wisdom, so as not to be swayed by evil (Prov 1:8–16). Josephus says, "We are especially enthusiastic for the instruction of our children" and "The law commands that children be taught to read and learn the laws of their forefathers" (*Apion* 1:12; 2:25). The frequency of OT quotations and allusions in the NT shows that Christians were thoroughly familiar with scripture. Because scripture was the basis of religion for both Jews and Christians, it was imperative that they be familiar with scripture to develop a strong faith and to learn how to live properly.

SOCIAL AND ECONOMIC CONDITIONS

The biggest social division in Palestine was between Jews and non-Jews. Jews called non-Jews "the nations" or "Gentiles" (words that both translate the Greek word *ethnoi*). Jews thought of themselves as a race apart from others, a race based on the sacred covenant of circumcision (Gen 17:1–14). Besides circumcision, strict dietary and purity laws, sabbath observance, and an intense hatred of idolatry set Jews apart from Gentiles.

Within Jewish society itself there was also a cleavage between the wealthy Sadducean temple priests, on the one hand, and the Pharisaic synagogue officials and the rest of the people, on the other. The priests were proud of their hereditary office, which they believed was ordained by God (Exodus 28–29; Leviticus 8–9; Numbers 16–18). Many priests became very rich because they received most of the tithes and offerings that the Jews were required by law to take to the temple. For these reasons they looked down upon other Jews. Perhaps Jesus' reference to the temple as a "den of robbers" (Mark 11:17; Matt 21:13; Luke 19:46) reflects the feelings of many Jews of his time. Because the Pharisaic officials of the synagogues, especially the scribes, were well educated in the law, many of them also felt superior to the masses. Their attitude is expressed in John 7:49: "This crowd, which does not know the law . . . are accursed."

Ever since OT times, common Jews, the majority, were known as "the people of the land" (*ha 'am ha arez*). As the name implies, they farmed the land, and many of them owned the land they tilled. This means that they were not all poor, nor were they all ignorant of the Torah, as the rabbis later came to believe.

Josephus says that in the time of Herod the Great the land around Jericho was the most fertile, and the main crops were dates and balsam. From the dates, the best in the world (Pliny, *Natural History* 13:9:44), came honey not much inferior to that of bees (Josephus, *War* 1:1:6; 1:6:6; 4:8:3; *Ant.* 4:6:1; 14:4:1; 15:4:2). Josephus describes the Plain of Gennesaret in Galilee as a productive area for all kinds of plants, because the air is conducive to growing different varieties. Olives, fruits, grains, and vegetables were grown year-round in Galilee, and even the walnut, which prefers a cool climate, grows there. Grapes and figs ripen during most months of the year (*War* 3:10:8). And the soil is so rich and pasture so abundant that even the laziest persons are tempted to engage in agriculture (*War* 3:3:2).

There were also goats and, according to *Aristeas* (113), "many cattle of various sorts."

Presumably, men did the work in the fields, which were close to small villages, and the women did the housework. Men's work included tilling and harvesting, shearing sheep, and carding the wool. Women ground grain, baked bread, washed clothes, and kept the beds. (See Figure I.4.) They also prepared meals and did spinning and weaving to clothe the family.

Contrary to popular belief, Jewish men in Palestine did not wear Bedouin clothes and have long beards. Clothes were those of the Hellenistic world: men and women wore tunics and mantles. The tunic, a long piece of clothing wrapped around the body, came to the knees or slightly above. A mantle was worn over the tunic. Women covered their heads with a net or cloth that reached about to the shoulders. Men kept their hair short and were shaven or had closely trimmed beards. (For these items and for the use of utensils, glass, pottery, and stoneware, baking materials, and leather and cloth goods see Y. Yadin 1963 and E. P. Sanders 1992:119–126.)

FIGURE I.4
Peasant women sifting grain in Cappadocia, modern Turkey or ancient Asia Minor.

Among the three main groups of Jews—Pharisees, Sadducees, and Essenes—the Essenes were an economically classless community. Josephus writes: "They frown upon wealth, and their community is amazing; you will find that no one possesses more of anything than another. They have a law whereby those entering the sect must confiscate their property . . . so that there is neither excessive poverty nor wealth among them" (*War* 2:8:3). The Sect of Qumran was probably Essenes, and though it had a complicated hierarchy of authority, those entering the community were required to bring along all their possessions (1QS 1:11–13; 9:8–9).

The social cleavage between Jews and non-Jews and the economic differences within Jewish society itself were similar to the social and economic contrasts among Romans in Palestine. The greatest economic gap among Romans was between the officials and their soldiers and slaves. Apparently some military personnel were well-off. According to Acts, the Roman centurion Cornelius, who became the first Gentile convert to Christianity, "gave alms generously to the people" and "called two of his slaves and a devout soldier from the ranks of those who served him" (10:2, 7). Although not a high-ranking officer, he was rich enough to support a retinue.

Not many people like Cornelius became followers of Jesus. One rich young man approached Jesus but "went away grieving, for he had many possessions" (Mark 10:22; Matt 19:22). On the other hand, Zacchaeus, who "was a chief tax collector and was rich," was told by Jesus that "salvation" had come to his house (Luke 19:2, 9). Jesus was usually more successful among the "unimportant persons" and "poor classes" than among the "respectable men" about whom Josephus speaks (*Life* 9, 12). The parable of the rich man and Lazarus, although perhaps an exaggerated example, illustrates the extremes of luxury and pauperism within first-century Palestinian society: "There was a rich man who was dressed in purple and fine linen and who feasted sumptuously every day. And at his gate lay a poor man named Lazarus, covered with sores, who longed to satisfy his hunger with what fell from the rich man's table; even the dogs would come and lick his sores" (Luke 16:19–21).

Social and economic contrasts in ancient Palestine were also evident in its monarchial system. Luke begins the body of his gospel by describing the monarchial structure of Jesus' time: "In the fifteenth year of the reign of Emperor Tiberius, when Pontius Pilate was governor of Judea, and Herod was ruler of Galilee, and his brother Philip ruler of the region of Ituraea . . . during the high priesthood of Annas and Caiaphas" (3:1–2). It is clear that wealth is associated with the monarchy: "Look, those who put on fine clothing and live in luxury are in royal palaces" (Luke 7:25; compare Matt 11:8).

Although the mainstay of the ancient world's economy was agriculture, the wealthy class of the monarchial government in Palestine was supported by a variety of taxes and tolls. Censuses were taken to determine the number of people in the empire to be taxed, and money from imperial taxes went into the treasury in Rome. It may have been about such taxes that the Pharisees asked Jesus, "Is it lawful to pay taxes to the emperor, or not?" (Mark 12:14).

Taxes were often excessive, as in the time of Pompey, for example (*Ant.* 14:4:5), but Julius Caesar remitted some of them. Herod the Great's lifestyle and tremendous building programs required a lot of money. He received some revenues from the produce of the land (*Ant.* 15: 9:1) and others from relentlessly demanded taxes on purchases and sales (*Ant.* 17:8:4). The inhabitants of Jerusalem sometimes had to pay a tax on their houses, perhaps to pay for building the city walls. Jews twenty years of age and older (Exod 13:11–16) throughout the world had to pay a half-shekel annually to the temple (*Ant.* 18:9:1), and each year collectors traveled throughout Palestine to collect that tax. Both the collectors and the tax are mentioned in Matt 17:24, where "the collectors of the temple tax" asked Peter if his teacher (Jesus) paid the tax. After the fall of Jerusalem in 70 CE, Emperor Vespasian imposed a special tax payable to Rome that replaced the one formerly paid to the temple (*War* 7:6:6).

A tax collector's job was to collect taxes or tolls on all property—even slaves—transported from one place to another. For the job, a collector paid a certain amount that he agreed upon each year with the procurator, and then he tried to make a profit by hiring subordinates to do the collecting. The subordinates, in turn, could keep any excess money they collected. In the gospels such a subordinate is called *telōnēs* (tax collector). Tax collectors were never popular. Rabbinic writers called them robbers because of their corrupt practices, and in the gospels they are frequently linked with sinners (see, for example, Mark 2:15; Matt 11:19; Luke 15:1). In Luke 19:2, 7, for example, Zacchaeus is called "a chief tax collector," "rich," and "a sinner." Apparently he had gotten rich by hiring others to collect tolls near Jericho in Judea. But Sabinus, the father of the emperor Vespasian, was unlike most tax collectors. Suetonius writes that in the cities of Asia statues were erected in his honor and dedicated "to an honest tax collector" (*Vespasian* 1).

GRAECO-ROMAN RELIGIONS

From the beginning of Palestine's history, peoples who came there brought their religions. The Jewish religion was never the only one in Palestine, even in NT times. Remnants of old Canaanite, Syrian, Philistine, and other Near Eastern religions persisted but were gradually being absorbed into Graeco-Roman cults. The chief feature of these Graeco-Roman religious cults, therefore, was syncretism. *Syncretism* means a uniting or fusing of several different elements; thus religious syncretism is a fusing of elements from several religions. The syncretistic cults required participation in specific ceremonies or cultic acts, the aim of which was to get the gods to cooperate so the worshipers could be at peace with themselves. Performance of such acts, rather than adherence to ethical codes, constituted the piety of the worshiper.

Information about cults in first-century Palestine is limited and comes mostly from later sources. Although cults flourished in the Graeco-

Roman cities, such as Caesarea, they were evident everywhere, even in Jerusalem. Archaeological ruins near the pool of Bethesda may be those of a shrine to Asclepius, Greek god of healing. An inscription from Caesarea written in Latin mentions a public building, probably a temple, built by Pilate and dedicated to Augustus. Moreover, Herod had "filled his own region with temples" (*War* 1:21:4). In several cities Greek games were held regularly in honor of Graeco-Roman deities. Among the deities worshiped in Palestine by the end of the first century may have been Demeter, goddess of produce, especially corn, and Dionysus (Bacchus), primarily the god of wine.

Graeco-Roman religious ceremonies included sacrificial offerings through which worshipers believed they communed with the gods. A sacrifice involved the ritual killing of an animal or the offering of food, liquids, and incense. Animal sacrifices were thought more effective than grain or other offerings, and vital organs such as the heart, liver, and kidneys were considered the best sacrifices. The purpose of a sacrifice was to obtain a god's favor, to fulfill a vow, or to make amends for offenses. The most common sacrifices were pigs for Demeter, goats for Hermes (Mercury), and bulls for many gods, but poor people might be able to offer only a chicken or a cupful of grain.

The sacrifices were in the charge of several classes of priests. One class, the *augurēs*, was responsible for observing omens or signs (*omina*) to determine the action of the gods. This was a religious act as important as sacrifices and was accomplished by observing birds in flight, the eating habits of the sacred chicken, and thunder and lightning.

Emperor worship (see Figure I.5) was not demanded in Palestine before the reign of Emperor Gaius (37–41). Until then it had been sufficient for the Jews to offer "sacrifice twice a day in behalf of Caesar and the Roman people" (*War* 2:10:4). Gaius, however, displayed "his madness" for worship as a god everywhere in the Roman Empire (*Ant.* 19:1:1; Tacitus, *Annals* 11:3), but he died before he could have a statue

FIGURE I.5   *Headless statue at Caesarea, probably moved from a temple. The sculptured head of the reigning emperor (right) could be placed on the statue.*

of himself erected in Jerusalem as a reminder of his deity. Emperor Domitian (81–96) strictly enforced the collection of the former Jewish temple tax for the temple of Jupiter Capitolinus in Rome and severely punished anyone converting to Judaism.

RELIGION OF THE JEWS

Early Hebrew Religion

The basic tenets of the Hebrew religion, including worship and personal life, all originated before the time of Alexander the Great (334 BCE). The temple in Jerusalem, with its complex sacrificial cultus (see below), was the center of worship for centuries. Misunderstanding and misuse of temple worship was condemned by the great moral and social reformers, the prophets of Israel and Judah, who functioned as the consciences of the kings. The prophets believed that sacrificial worship apart from moral life was unacceptable to God. Amos preaches that a righteous God cannot accept sacrifices and offerings from sinful

people, "but let justice roll down like waters, and righteousness like an everflowing stream" (Amos 5:21–24; see also Amos 4:4–5; Isa 1:1–23; Jer 6:20–21; 14:10–12; Hos 8:13–14; 9:4). The righteousness of God and humans is a key concept in Paul's letters and in the gospel of Matthew, as also elsewhere in the NT.

Hosea says that God desires "steadfast love and not sacrifice, the knowledge of God rather than burnt offerings" (Hos 6:6). The prophets' viewpoint is reflected in the story of Jesus cleansing the temple (Mark 11:11; Matt 21:10–17; Luke 19:45–46; John 2:13–17). Micah asks if worshipers should come before the Lord with burnt offerings of calves and rams and thousands of rivers of oil. And then: "Shall I give my first-born for my transgression, the fruit of my body for the sin of my soul? . . . What does the Lord require of you but to do justice, and to love kindness, and to walk humbly with your God?" (Mic 6:6–8; see Matt 23:23; Luke 11:42).

The first question of Micah refers to child sacrifice, a form of worship practiced by the Canaanites and adopted by some Israelites. Another immoral form of worship widely practiced in the ancient world was so-called sacred prostitution. Under the influence of the prophets, both practices were forbidden by law during the time of the religious reformation under King Josiah about 626 BCE (see Deuteronomy 12–26, 28). Divination, augury, sorcery, necromancy, and other pagan practices were also forbidden by law (Deut 18:10–14; 23:17–18; see 1 Cor 6:15–16; Gal 5:15–20; Rev 9:21; 18:23; 21:8; 22:15). More positively, the reformers under Josiah sought to elevate religion from ritual to ethics both in worship and life (see Mark 7:1–23; Matt 15:1–20).

The prophets' conception of the Day of the Lord as a time of darkness, suffering, and gloom instead of one of light and levity was the beginning of later apocalyptic-eschatological thought developed extensively in the classic apocalypses (see below) of Daniel in the OT, later Jewish apocalypses, and the NT book of Revelation (see Amos 5:18–20; Isa 13:6–22; Jer 46:10–12; Joel 1:15–2:11, 30–32; Zeph 1:7–17; Mal 4:1–5; see also 1 Thess 5:1–11; 2 Thess 2:1–12; 1 Cor 5:3–5; 2 Cor 1:13–14; 2 Pet 3:1–13; Mark 13:5–37; Matt 24:4–36; Luke 21:8–36).

Jeremiah (c. 626–580 BCE) is important in the study of the NT for several reasons. His idea of a new covenantal relationship between God and his people as one by which the law is within human hearts (Jer 11:1–17; 31:31–34) is evident in some NT writers, especially in Paul's concept of "the Israel of God" (Gal 6:16; see also 1 Cor 11:25–26; 2 Cor 3:4–6; Rom 11:27; Mark 14:24; Matt 26:27–28; Luke 22:20).

Along with the idea of a new covenant, Jeremiah changed the concept of responsibility for sins. A popular proverb said: "Parents have eaten sour grapes, and the children's teeth are set on edge," an idea in the Torah (Exod 20:5; 34:7; Num 14:18; Deut 5:9). Jeremiah says that in the future "all shall die for their own sins; the teeth of everyone who eats sour grapes shall be set on edge" (Jer 31:29–30). Ezekiel applied the saying to his own generation: "It is only the person who sins that shall die," and the righteous shall be rewarded (Ezek 18:4; see all of Ezekiel 18). That the individual sinner is to be punished for sins

committed and the righteous rewarded is the presupposition of NT writers (e.g., see 2 Cor 5:10; Rom 2:5–11; 14:10–12; Jesus' parable of the last judgment in Matt 25:31–46; and many other passages).

All prophets, of course, emphasized morality, and Jeremiah's teachings on the subject appear especially in his parables (Jer 13:1–14; 18:1–17; 19:1–13; 24:1–10). In the same way, we shall see, morality is the point in some of Jesus' parables. Ezekiel's apocalyptic vision (1:1–3:15) portrays the supreme majesty and transcendence of God, who is everywhere and sees everything, a portrayal also shared by the writer of Revelation throughout. The final triumph of the righteous was emphasized by Malachi, who was confronted with confused moral standards among his own people and antagonism from non-Jews (Mal 3:13–4:6). With Malachi came the belief that before the coming of "the great and terrible day of the Lord" (Mal 4:5) the prophet Elijah would return, a view reflected in the gospels (Mark 8:27–29; 9:11–13; 15:35–36; Matt 17:10–12; 11:13; 27:47–49; John 1:19–22).

The designation "Jew" as a member of the land of Judah appears first in Neh 1:2; Jer 32:12; 40:11 and as a person distinct from Gentiles in Esth 9:15–19; Dan 3:8; Zech 8:23 (see Acts 14:1–2; John 4:9). "Jews" is also a designation for persons who worship the God Yahweh in Jerusalem after the Exile (Esth 3:4–6; Dan 3:8). The term *Judaism* does not occur in the OT; but, insofar as I know, it appears for the first time in the Jewish books of 2 and 4 Maccabees (2 Macc 2:21; 14:38; 4 Macc 4:26; see also Gal 1:13–14; Acts 13:43). It is important to know that for Jews Judaism does not mean a system of beliefs or dogma but refers to the totality of life as lived by Jews everywhere as regulated by the Torah (law) and revealed to them by their God Yahweh.

Idolatry was to be avoided under all circumstances (Exod 20:1–6; Deut 5:6–9). The prophets were the first to condemn idol worship, but in spite of their tirades against idols, idolatry continued to flourish among Israelites (Hos 4:17–19; 8:4–6; 11:2; Amos 5:25–27). You will find the following tirades against idolatry interesting: Isa 2:8–20; 41:21–29; 44:9–20; Jer 2:8–20.

Gentiles who were used to idolatry and became followers of Jesus caused Paul, a devoted monotheist, some anxiety, especially at Corinth (1 Cor 8:1–10; 10:14, 19; 12:2; 2 Cor 6:16; see also 1 Thess 1:9; Rom 1:23; 2:22; 1 John 5:21; Rev 2:14, 20; 9:20). However, after the Jewish exile in Babylonia (587–538 BCE) and the return of some Jews to Palestine, idolatry declined among Jews.

During the Exile or shortly thereafter the Jews became purely monotheistic. Although some scholars believe that Jewish monotheism dates from the time of Moses, others believe henotheism ("one god for one people") best describes early Hebrew belief. As henotheists Jews would have believed that their God Yahweh was only their God, without denying the existence of other gods for other peoples. At any rate, by the time of Second Isaiah (the name given to the writer of some or all of Isaiah 40–66) the belief in Yahweh as the only God in existence and, therefore, the God of all people was well established among Jewish religious thinkers. Listen to Second Isaiah: "I am the first and I am the last; besides me there is no god. . . . Is there any god besides me? . . . I know not one" (Isa 44:6, 8) and "I am the Lord, and there is no other; besides me there is no god" (Isa 45:5).

Thus, there is no other god in existence but the God of the Jews, so he is universally God, not just the God of Israel. Hence, it was thought that idols did not exist, because only God was living. Paul says of the Thessalonian converts: "how you turned to God from idols, to serve a living and true God" (1 Thess 1:9). This universal monotheism is the assumption behind all NT writers. Paul states the view clearly and succinctly for the Corinthians who lived in an especially pagan polytheistic city: "We know that 'no idol in the world really exists,' and that 'there is no God but one'" (1 Cor 8:4).

The Second Isaiah is important also for his concept of the coming of a special person he calls the Servant of the Lord, with his mission (Isa 42:1–4), destiny (49:1–6), discipline (50:4–9),

and suffering (52:13–53:12). The author of Acts refers to Jesus as God's servant (Acts 3:13) and his resurrection from the dead (3:26; see also Acts 4:27, 30). Although some scholars think several NT writers understood Jesus as the fulfillment of Isaiah's prophecies and that Jesus thought of himself as their fulfillment, the subject is a difficult one, with a wide difference of scholarly opinion about it. Second Isaiah also had visions of God's creation of a new Jerusalem (Isa 60:1–22; see also Jer 31:38–40) and of new heavens and a new earth (Isa 65:17–66:24). The writer of Revelation had similar visions (Rev 21:1–22:5).

With the rebuilding of the temple in Jerusalem (c. 520–516 BCE), the sacrificial cultus, under the leadership of the priests and Levites, was more firmly established in Jewish worship than ever before (see below). It was the place where several significant Jewish festivals (see below) were held annually in the time of Jesus and Paul (Mark 14:1–16; Matt 26:2–19; Luke 2:41; 22:1–15; John 2:13, 23; 7:2; 10:22; 11:15; Acts 2:1; 12:4; 20:16; 1 Cor 16:8). After Ezra the scribe returned from Exile (mid-fifth century BCE), scribalism became an institution, and it centered around the synagogue, which also probably developed during the Exile (see below). The first synagogue as an assembly may be recorded in Neh 8:1–8. Many scholars regard Ezra as the founder of Judaism. The gospels report that Jesus frequently taught and healed in the synagogues, which were located in every Jewish community (Mark 1:21, 39; 3:1; 6:1–2; Matt 12:9; 13:54; Luke 4:15–22; 13:10–17; John 6:59; 18:20). And early Christian missionaries proclaimed the gospel most frequently in synagogues (Acts 9:19–20; 13:4, 14–15, 43; 14:1; 17:1, 10, 17).

The scribes were the teachers of the Torah (see below), by which all personal, social, and religious life of the Jews was regulated. The synoptic gospels often refer to the scribes as a class (see also John 8:3; Acts 4:5; 6:12; 23:9) and sometimes to a scribe as an unnamed individual (Mark 12:28, 32; Matt 8:19). For law in Matthew see Chapter 5, and in Paul's letters see Chapter 11.

The scribes were succeeded by the great teachers of the Torah (rabbis) in the centuries following NT times. In Mark, Matthew, and John, Jesus is called rabbi (Mark 9:5; 11:21; 14:45; Matt 26:25, 49; John 1:38, 49; 3:2, 28; 4:31).

The religious developments among Jews just described and those that follow are extremely important as background for the study of the NT. During those developments the foundations for Judaism, the mother of Christianity, were laid.

Judaism flourished amidst the syncretistic Graeco-Roman religious cults evident everywhere. The Jews believed that God had revealed his will to Moses on Mt. Sinai as stated in the OT or Jewish scriptures. The distinctive Hebrew word for Jewish scriptures is *Torah*, which may be defined as teaching or instruction about the revealed will of God. *Torah* originally referred to the first five books of the OT, for which the Greek term is *Pentateuch*, but it was broadened to include all Hebrew scriptures. All Jewish life and religion was regulated by the Torah, and violations were tried in Jewish courts, the main one being the Sanhedrin in Jerusalem. Naturally, interpretations of the Torah varied as it was taught and transmitted from one generation to another, so there was a wide diversity of opinion within Judaism about belief and practice.

Holy Days

Jews observed several festivals or Holy Days. As with every other aspect of Jewish life, they were regulated by the Torah: "These are the appointed festivals of the Lord, the holy convocations, which you shall celebrate at the time appointed for them" (Lev 23:4). The Sabbath, observed from sundown Friday until sundown Saturday, was the most significant. At the third blast of a trumpet sounded from a synagogue roof, the sabbath lights were kindled, and the Holy Day was begun. It was primarily a day of rest from all work (Exod 20:8–11) except for the study of Torah, which was not considered a burden but a delight (Ps 1:2). Jews looked forward to the Sabbath for six days during which they collected delicacies to be eaten at the festive family meal, when they also drank wine blessed by a special prayer, the *kiddush*.

Pesach or Passover, described in detail in Exodus 12, is the oldest Jewish festival, and originally it celebrated the approach of spring. Later it became a historic holiday commemorating the deliverance of the Hebrews from Egypt. Its name derives from the belief that the angel of death passed over the doors of Hebrew households in Egypt, thus sparing them from death and helping to prepare them for their escape from bondage (Exod 11: 4–12:51).

As long as the temple in Jerusalem existed, the special feature of Passover was the slaughter of a sacrificial lamb or goat and eating the meat in a communal meal. After the destruction of the temple, the festival was celebrated at home and in the synagogue. Special features of the Passover meal were the prayer of blessing; unleavened bread, symbolizing the hasty departure from Egypt; bitter herbs, reminding the participants of the Israelites' suffering in slavery; and the recitation of some of Psalms 113–118, known as the *Hallel*.

Shavuoth, referred to as "the festival of weeks" in the OT (Exod 34:22; Deut 16:10), was held seven weeks after the sickle was first put to the standing grain (Deut 16:9). So the Greek term for it is *pentēkostē* ("fiftieth"), from which we get the English word *Pentecost* (2 Macc 12:32; Tob 2:1). It is the only Jewish festival that survived in the Christian religion (Acts 20:16; 1 Cor 16:8), where it celebrates the coming of the Holy Spirit and the birth of the church (Acts 2:1–43).

Originally an agricultural festival like Passover and Booths, which follows it, the festival of Weeks came to commemorate the giving of the Torah and the Covenant on Mt. Sinai. This transition, however, did not occur until after NT times. In Deut 16:9–12 Jews are exhorted to rejoice before God with all of their families and servants, sojourners, widows, and orphans among them. The kinds of offerings and sacrifices required by the Torah are given in detail in Num 28:26–31 and Lev 23:15–21.

After the middle of the third century CE, the Jewish New Year was called *Rosh Hashanah* (Hebrew, literally, "head of the year"). In the OT it is referred to as a day of blowing the trumpet (Num 29:1–6; Lev 23:23–24), apparently the distinctive feature of the festival. Another feature was the carrying of the *lulab* (palm) for seven days in the temple, but in the Diaspora for only one day. After the temple fell, Rabbi ben Zakkai (c. 1–80 CE) said it should be carried for seven days in the Diaspora in memory of the temple.

Yom Kippur (Day of Atonement) was the most sacred day of the Jewish year. It was a day of repentance for the forgiveness of sins: "On this day atonement shall be made for you, to cleanse you; from all your sins you shall be clean before the Lord" (Lev 16:30). The only historical sources for the observance of the Day of Atonement in NT times are Lev 16:29–34; 23:26–32; Num 29:7–11. The high priest performed the ritual for the purpose of cleansing the priesthood, the people of Israel, and the sanctuary of the temple. After 70 CE, services were held in the synagogue, of which the essence was prayer and confession, asking forgiveness for individuals and the community.

The Torah (Deut 16:16) required every male Jew to make three annual pilgrimages to the temple in Jerusalem. These were for the festivals of Passover, Weeks, and Booths. Booths (Hebrew, *sukkoth*) was a harvest festival held in the fall after the gathering of the grain and grapes (Deut 16:13). Apparently it was very popular in NT times, because Josephus calls it a festival thought by the Jews to be most sacred and important (*Ant.* 8:9:1). The historical occasion for the celebration of Sukkoth (trans. as either "booths" or "tabernacles") is stated in Lev 23:42–43: "You shall live in booths for seven days; all that are citizens in Israel shall live in booths, so that your generations may know that I made the people of Israel live in booths when I brought them out of the land of Egypt." Directions for the ritual observances in the temple are given in Lev 23:23–36; Num 29:12–38; Deut 16:13–15.

Sources for the elaborate ritual in the synagogue observance of Booths or Tabernacles are later than the NT era (but see Josephus, *Ant.*

3:10:4; 13:13:5). Perhaps the ritual included the carrying of palm branches and *ethrog* (citron) around the lectern and a water libation, probably a remnant of an old rain-making ceremony, because Booths came when autumnal rains were due. There probably was reading from the Torah and the Prophets, as well as the repetition of the refrain from Ps 118:25: "Save us, we beseech you, O Lord."

The rededication of the temple by Judas Maccabeus in 165 BCE was celebrated during the festival of *Hanukkah* (Hebrew, "dedication"). Accounts of its origin are given in 1 Macc 4:36–59 (see also 2 Macc 10:1–9). Josephus (*Ant.* 12:7:7) refers to it as the "festival of lights" because the right to worship was given to the Jews when they scarcely dared hope for it. Hanukkah originated after the OT, but we can observe from scant sources (1 Macc 4:52–58) that it was a festival of gladness lasting for eight days, with sacrifices, offerings, and music in the temple. There was also the carrying of ivy wreaths and palm branches and the singing of hymns of thanksgiving (2 Macc 10:5–7). Since Josephus refers to Hanukkah as a festival of lights, perhaps the lighting of the Hanukkah lights, so prominent in later observations, was already a part of the festival in his time.

Apocalyptic Eschatology, Messianic Expectation, and the Kingdom of God

Centuries of foreign oppression before the Christian era led to a renewed belief that the glorious earthly kingdom, long expected by the Jews, would not come until the end of time. Many Jews, therefore, wrote about the coming of the End, when God himself would intervene to end the present evil age and establish a glorious new age with a heavenly kingdom on a new earth. So within Jewish theology of NT times there was a renewed emphasis on a phenomenon known as *apocalyptic eschatology* or *apocalypticism*. These terms refer to both a system of thought and a religious movement. The word *eschatology* comes from the combination of two Greek words, *eschaton*, meaning "last" or "end," and *logos,* meaning "word." Thus eschatology is literally the word about the last things or what is to happen at the end of time. It refers to all events associated with the end of human life and the world, such as death, judgment, heaven and hell, and the resurrection of the dead. In Christian theology, belief in the Second Coming of Christ was also part of eschatology.

Eschatology is really part of a larger matrix of thought known as *apocalyptic* and is typical of a genre of Jewish literature called *apocalypse. Apocalyptic* and *apocalypse* are derived from the Greek *apocalyptō,* meaning "unveil" or "reveal." As a type of Jewish literature, apocalypse flourished from 200 BCE to 100 CE, but its origins go back into OT times. The matrix of apocalyptic thought includes such ideas as a distinction between this evil age and the future glorious age; a struggle between the forces of good and evil, with the eventual triumph of good; and a catastrophic cosmic upheaval that will usher in the new age with the last judgment and the resurrection of the dead. Among the literary characteristics of apocalypse are pseudonymity (with a false name), cryptic language, dreams and visions, angels, symbolism, ethical exhortation, and predictions or revelations concerning the destinies of people and nations.

Within Jewish apocalyptic eschatology of the two centuries BCE, there was a renewed hope for the coming of a Messiah. The term *messiah* means anointed one—in the ancient Hebrew concept of kingship, a priest or prophet of God anointed the king with oil in a religious ceremony. Thus the king was known as the Lord's anointed (messiah). Jewish messianism is a complex phenomenon, so what follows may be a simplification because Judaism was very diverse. There was no such thing as an absolute Judaism and no one idea or belief about a messiah to come, but various beliefs (see, e.g., J. Neusner 1987).

The idea of a future Messiah grew out of the hope for deliverance from the present age into a better one. To bring in a new age, a new and greater leader was necessary. Because Jewish writers looked back on the reign of David (c. 1000 BCE) as the golden age of Hebrew history, it was natural that they would want a descendant of David to bring about the new age and establish a kingdom of peace on earth. This Messiah from the line of David, a Messiah who from Jerusalem would rule over the tribes of Israel and over many Gentiles as well, was the most characteristic feature of Jewish messianism.

Messianism developed from a theological hope into a religious movement that was the strongest impetus behind rebellion against Hellenistic and Roman rule. To free the land of the Jews from foreign rule was an important part of messianism. At the same time, however, certain Jewish groups longed not for an earthly Messiah and an earthly kingdom, but awaited a Messiah sent from heaven by God, who himself would usher in the new age. This age would be preceded by a period of turmoil and suffering and a terrible judgment upon the godless, the Gentiles, and Satan and his forces. The Messiah would rule over faithful peoples of all times and all places, Gentiles as well as Jews. The messianic kingdom would be a universal kingdom in which all who survived would acknowledge the God of the Jews.

Some Jews came to believe in a general resurrection of the dead as part of the messianic hope. According to the older belief, only those living at the time would enjoy the new age, not those who had died before its arrival. Those who believed in a general resurrection of the dead, on the other hand, acknowledged that the faithful of previous generations would share in the new age. For various apocalyptic movements in the time of Jesus see R. A. Horsley 1984.

Now let us see how the preceding ideas are intermingled in several examples from Jewish apocalyptic literature of the NT period. But first, consider a few observations about the idea of the kingdom of God. The actual phrase "kingdom of God" does not occur in the OT, and it occurs only once (Wis 10:10) in Jewish literature of NT times. The phrase "his [God's] kingdom" does appear several times in that literature. Tobit, for example, prays: "Blessed is God who lives forever, and his kingdom" (Tob 13:1; see also Wis 6:4; *T. Moses* 10:1). This makes it extremely difficult to explain what the concept means. Some scholars say that the word *kingdom* is never appropriate to describe the concept and that "kingly rule" (of God) is the only accurate designation. Others suggest that the concept implies a special society wherein the will of God will be perfectly obeyed. As with most phenomena in Judaism, opinions concerning the kingdom of God are diverse with respect to its nature, coming, place, and duration.

From the beginning of their existence as a people, the Hebrews believed that God was directing their history. A natural outgrowth of their religious monotheism was their belief that God was not only directing their history but that of all peoples as well, that the outcome would be a better world, when God would be king of all the earth, and that God's will would be universally obeyed. A key passage in the OT is Zech 14:9: "The Lord will become king over all the earth; on that day the Lord will be one and his name one." Later the coming of the Messiah and his reign were included with the idea of God's universal and eternal rule. A good example of these ideas is *Psalms of Solomon* 17 and 18, where for the first time (c. 50 BCE) in an eschatological context the actual word *messiah* is used. The writer calls him "the Lord Messiah" (17:32; 18:7) or "the Messiah" (18:5).

In the *Psalms of Solomon* the Lord will be king forever and ever. God will raise up the Messiah, a descendant of David, who will rule over Israel, defeat his enemies, and reprove sinners. The Messiah will collect a holy people and lead them in righteousness. Heathen nations will serve under his rule during which there will be no unrighteousness, and the people will be holy. The Messiah will be free from sin, and God himself will be his king. The messianic figure is still a human (as in the OT, where only the concept, not the actual term *messiah*, appears), who will rule as a military leader over a kingdom on earth from Jerusalem as its center.

Different ideas appear in other Jewish literature. In *1 Enoch* 45:3–5, the "Elect One" will sit on a throne of glory, both heaven and earth will be transformed, and sinners and evildoers will be excluded from the kingdom (see Rev 21:1–22:5). In the *T. Moses* 10:1–10, the kingdom will appear throughout all creation, "the Heavenly One" will go forth from his royal throne, there will be an apocalyptic cataclysm of the earth, Israel will dwell firmly in heaven, and from there the Jews will look down upon their enemies on earth. Here there is only a heavenly kingdom, no earthly one.

In *1 Enoch* 90:20–104:13, there is a conglomeration of ideas associated with the kingdom of God. There will be an interim on earth before the heavenly age to come. Some of the wicked will then be destroyed, there will be a new Jerusalem and a resurrection of the righteous dead along with converted Gentiles, and the Messiah will come and establish the kingdom. There will be a judgment for the rest of the wicked, including Jews who were unfaithful. Ultimately the wicked will receive eternal punishment, and the righteous will be resurrected to everlasting bliss in heaven.

In *1 Enoch,* the duration of the interim is not stated. In 2 Esdr 7:26–61, however, after the apocalyptic woes, the Messiah will appear, and he and his company will reign with rejoicing for four hundred years. Then all the living, including the Messiah, will die. The messianic interim is a foretaste of the future glorious age. After a return of the earth to its primeval state for a week, there will be a resurrection for everyone and a final judgment. Those, few in number, who remain on earth will live in joy and bliss; those, the many, whose wicked deeds could not be concealed will receive torment and fire. Similar ideas occur in Rev 20:11–15, where the interim kingdom endures for one thousand years.

Apocalyptic eschatology was one of the most significant Jewish theological phenomena in the two pre-Christian centuries. In Chapter 3 we will examine its influence upon the development of early Christianity.

Wisdom

Wisdom (Greek, *sophia*) is a special subject in much of the Jewish literature from 200 BCE to 200 CE and, indeed, a genre of literature. Although there is a renewed emphasis on wisdom during that period, the phenomenon is much older in the ancient world and in Judaism goes back to about 1000 BCE. Wisdom books in the OT are Job, Proverbs, Ecclesiastes, and some of the Psalms (for example, 1, 49, 111). During the NT period, the Wisdom of Sirach and the Wisdom of Solomon are especially important wisdom writings, as well as sections of other works, including Tobit, *1 Enoch*, the *Testaments of the Twelve Patriarchs*, and the *Letter of Aristeas*.

The teachers of "wisdom" apparently were professional scribes, and much of the teaching, presumably, took place in the synagogues. The motto of the wisdom schools was "Fear of the Lord is the beginning of wisdom" (Ps 111:10; Prov 9:10; 15:33; Wis 7:7; Sir 1:1, 14, 20). And such fear included obedience to God's law, which sometimes was synonymous with wisdom (Ezra 7:25). The author of Sirach wrote so that those who love learning might "make even greater progress in living according to the law" (*Prologue*). Wisdom and the law were like two brooks that sometimes flowed separately, sometimes as one.

In general, wisdom writings were significant for several reasons. They taught a personal religion apart from any great concern for the national state. Wisdom could and should regulate the whole life of the common person as well as that of the wise person or sage. The religious life was emphasized apart from any duty of worship in the temple. And moral conduct was the chief goal of human life.

The good life included prayer, fasting, giving to charity, obedience to parents, sobriety, moderation, chastity, love for God and humanity, forgiveness, acting toward others as they were expected to act, and faith in the only God. Life was focused on keeping the law because the law said so. But there was also the strong belief that good deeds led to future reward (Tob 4:9; Sir 3:3–8, 14–15; 29:11–13).

With respect to the Wisdom of Sirach, the best example of wisdom writing in the NT period, the following observations are significant. Religion is for the individual, but a strong nationalism sometimes appears: "Israel is the Lord's own portion" (17:18; see also 36:1–17). The temple is the seat of the national religion,

and the author occasionally shows a special interest in the temple service and the priests (7:29–31; 24:10, 15; 36:13–14; 45:23–24; 50:1–21). But moral conduct is far more significant than temple ritual. Ritual and sacrifice are secondary, and they exist only because the law demands them (35:4–5). The sacrifice of an unrighteous person is in vain (7:8–9; 35:1–29); fasting without repentance is useless (34:26); God accepts only the offerings of the righteous (35:6–7). As in Judaism after the fall of the temple, keeping the law, doing good deeds, giving to charity, and abstaining from evil serve as offerings and sacrifices (3:3, 14–15, 30; 17:22; 35:1–3). As in Tobit, the Psalms, and elsewhere, personal piety finds its deepest expression in prayers or psalms (23:1–6; 36:1–17; 51:1–12). Many times the author says that prayers of various persons are effective (21:5; 35:13–17; 38:9, 13–14; 39:5).

Rewards for obedience to the law expressed in personal piety come in this life, as do punishments for doing evil (1:11–13; 2:7–11; 10:12–17; 11:14–19; 16:11–23). The author shows no knowledge of a philosophical belief in the immortality of the soul or of the Pharisaic idea of a resurrection of the body. The human is not immortal, but all persons are dust and ashes (17:30, 32; see also 41:2–4). The end of human life is vividly described in 10:11: "For when one is dead he inherits maggots and vermin and worms."

The writer's conception of God proceeds from his personal religion, not from philosophical speculation. He is a strict monotheist (36:1–5), although his work lacks any tirade against idolatry, which sometimes appears in similar writings (see 30:19; 46:11). God is mighty in power, sees everything, and knows every human act (15:18–19).

God created the earth and all things on it (16:24–30; 42:15–43:33) by his word (39:17–18; 42:15), and "all the works of the Lord are very good" (39:16). God created human beings in his own image from the earth, for a limited time, and gave them authority over all things on earth (17:1–4). God gave humans not only a tongue, eyes, and ears but also a mind for thinking (17:6; 38:6). Humans are responsible for their own wrongdoing and should not blame God for it (15:11–20). On the other hand, in 33:11–13 the lot of humans is in God's hands. The author remarks that those who serve wisdom serve the Holy One, "The Lord loves those who love her" (4:14). Sirach realizes, however, that those who serve God may have to endure affliction and testing and encourages them to continue their trust, for their reward will not be lost (2:1–9). (For this summary I am indebted almost entirely to R. H. Pfeiffer 1949:352–408.)

Readers who are curious about the Jewish concept of wisdom and want to learn about it first-hand will find the following subjects in the Wisdom of Sirach interesting and pertinent: the source of wisdom (1:1–30); honoring parents (3:1–16); courtesy toward and concern for the poor (4:1–11; 12:1–7); winning friends and friendship (6:5–17; 9:10; 12:8–13:23; 22:19–26; 27:16–21; 37:1–6); seeking wisdom (6:18–37); avoiding rash opinions about others (11:2–9); on virtues, including kindness (18:15–18), prudence (18:19–29), self-control (18:30–19:17), wisdom and folly (19:20–30), silence (20:5–8), restraint in speaking (20:18–27); evils of sex (23:16–27); on wisdom (24:1–29); father and son (30:1–13); health and wealth (30:14–17); table etiquette (31:12–24); sobriety (31:25–31); conduct at banquets (31:31–32:13); overeating (37:27–31); respect for physicians (38:1–15); death (41:1–13); and daughter and father (42:9–11).

From this list of subjects, we can see that the wisdom of Sirach the scribe was practical, dealing with virtues and vices of everyday life and exhorting proper conduct in sickness or in health, in poverty or in wealth, and in the affairs of family or community. According to Sirach, all who work at the job of acquiring such wisdom will "in God's time" receive their reward (51:30).

Religious Groups

In the gospels and Acts, there are references to two prominent groups of Jewish religious leaders—Pharisees and Sadducees. Josephus (*War* 1–5; *Ant.* 13, 15, 18; *Life* 2, 38), who is our only other source of information on these groups, also describes two other groups—Essenes and Zealots. (Besides Josephus, see Philo, *Every Good Man Is Free* 12–13; Pliny, *Natural History* 5:17:4; and the Qumran Scrolls.) Because both Josephus's account and the gospels are influenced by the writers' interests and circumstances, it is difficult to obtain accurate information about the groups. It is important to remember that since the groups were Jewish, what they had in common was far greater than what distinguished them from each other. Yet there were significant differences.

The origin of each group is obscure. The usual view is that the Pharisees developed from the pious party, or Hasidim, and the Sadducees from the Hellenists during the Maccabean struggles. *Pharisee* means "separatist," and perhaps the Pharisees got that name because they separated tithes and offerings required for the temple or because they set themselves apart from other Jews, especially the uneducated. The name *Sadducee* is probably derived from *Zadok,* the name of a priest who lived in the time of David and Solomon. The Essenes may have originated in Maccabean times, perhaps from the Hasidim. Although there is no consensus about the derivation of *Essene,* the name could have come from either of two Greek words, *hosios* or *isos,* meaning respectively "holy" and "equal," or from the Hebrew word *hasid,* "pious." Finally, the Zealots appeared during 67–68 CE as a party of Jews zealous for the overthrow of Rome.

Pharisees. According to Josephus, the Pharisees excelled other Jews in religious observances and in explaining the law. In addition to the written Torah (Hebrew OT), they developed a body of oral Torah or oral law referred to in the gospels (Mark 7:3–13; Matt 15:2–6; compare Gal 1:14) as "tradition" (*Ant.* 13:10:6). The oral Torah was a collection of additions, comments, interpretations, and anecdotes based on the written law, and the Pharisees observed it just as carefully as the written Torah. In the first five centuries of the Christian era the rabbis collected the oral Torah and produced an encyclopedic work known as the Talmud.

On the subject of fate (God's will) and free will (human will), the Pharisees took a middle position, believing that some things were the work of fate and others the result of human doing. They believed that bodies rose after death and that there were rewards for the righteous and punishments for the wicked.

The writers of Mark and Matthew present the Pharisees negatively, for the most part, perhaps because few Pharisees became converts to the new sect that came to be known as Christianity. They were Jesus' main adversaries, criticizing him for eating with tax collectors and sinners, for breaking the sabbath, for not fasting, and for eating with unwashed hands; and they plotted to kill him. Perhaps because he thought the Pharisees stressed ceremonial laws and neglected more important matters of the Torah, Jesus called them hypocrites, a generation of vipers, and "whitewashed tombs, which on the outside look beautiful, but inside they are full of the bones of the dead" (Matt 23:27).

More positively, we learn from the gospels that the Pharisees were concerned with sabbath observance, that they subscribed to an oral Torah, "the tradition of the elders" (Mark 7:3, 5), that they observed laws of ceremonial purity, especially when eating, and that they did not associate with people not observing such laws. All of this coincides with what we learn about the Pharisees in the Talmud and therefore may be accurate.

Luke, the author of Luke and Acts, is not always as harsh toward the Pharisees as Mark and Matthew are. He associates them with teachers of the law and says that Jesus ate in the house of a Pharisee three times (7:36; 11:37; 14:1). The saying about tombs is also milder in Luke 11:44: "You are like unmarked graves, and people walk over them without realizing it." The Pharisees warned Jesus to get out of Galilee because Herod wanted to kill him (13:31), and they called him teacher (19:39). From Acts we learn that the Pharisees believed in the resurrection of the body and the existence of angels and spirits (23:8). However, when reading what Luke says about the Pharisees, we must consider that one of Luke's motives, especially in writing Acts, was to reconcile Jewish and Gentile Christians.

Sadducees. Because Josephus was a Pharisee, he tends to disparage the Sadducees and place them below the Pharisees (see, for example, *War* 2:8:14). He says that in contrast to the Pharisees, the Sadducees said "it is necessary to keep only the written laws, not those transmitted by the fathers" (*Ant.* 13:10:6). Rejecting fate entirely, the Sadducees said that "a person is free to choose between good and evil" (*War* 2:8:14) and that humans were responsible for the evils that afflicted them. They denied life after death because there was no evidence for it in the scriptures, and from the gospels and Acts we learn that the Sadducees believed neither in the resurrection of the body nor in angels and spirits. As the priestly party, the Sadducees had access to the wealth of the temple and therefore had political power, unlike the Pharisees. They were the party with the high priest and, like the Pharisees, were members of the Sanhedrin (Acts 5:17; 23:6).

Essenes. The Essenes are not mentioned in the NT, but Josephus writes about them at length. They were an ascetic sect; that is, they renounced the privileges of society and lived in seclusion. Shunning pleasures and riches, they possessed everything in common, followed the same routine every day, including ritual purification baths, did not take oaths, were especially interested in the books of the ancients, honored Moses next to God, admitted members to the group only after three years of preparation, punished offenders severely, and observed the sabbath more strictly than other Jews. They observed the written Torah and may have developed some oral traditions of their own. The Essenes believed that "they should leave everything up to God," that there was life after death, and that all should strive for the rewards of the righteous.

Philo stresses that the Essenes were radically opposed to slavery and denounced slave owners, because slavery was contrary to their view that Nature created and nurtured all persons alike. In practice, however, not all persons were thought of as equals. Essenes generally disdained marriage but adopted children while they were young and could be reared according to Essene principles. According to Josephus, the reason for Essene celibacy was misogynist: women were wanton and could not be trusted to keep their marriage vows to one man (*War* 2:8:2). But Josephus also says that one order of Essenes did marry, because not to do so would mean the whole race would soon disappear. Josephus says, though, that married Essenes did not have sexual intercourse with their wives during pregnancy in order to show that the reason for marriage was to have children, not self-gratification (*War* 2:8:13).

It is generally believed that the largest community of Essenes was located in Qumran. The Sect of Qumran was an eschatological group of Jews who believed that they were to prepare themselves for the eschatological age when all evil would be abolished. A primary aim of the sect's members, therefore, was to transform their sinful human existence into a kind of superhuman way of life by trying to eliminate all evil in their bodies and suppressing natural desires that might lead to sin.

Although the Sect of Qumran is not mentioned in Josephus or the NT, it is presented here because its members are usually assumed to be Essenes. The Qumran settlement was discovered on the northwest shore of the Dead Sea in 1947. (See Figure I.6.) Among the discoveries were hundreds of manuscripts—usually referred to as the Qumran Scrolls—including whole or partial copies of all books of the OT except Esther, commentaries on books of the OT, copies of some books of the Apocrypha and Pseudepigrapha, a manual of discipline, a book of psalms, a war scroll, and many other writings in several languages, including Hebrew, Aramaic, and Greek. According to these writings, almost everything we learned about the Essenes in general is also true for the Qumran Sect, including the beliefs that God determined their destiny, that there would be a resurrection of the body, and that they should strive for future rewards.

The Sect of Qumran called itself the Covenant, the Community, or the Many. It is not

FIGURE I.6   *Water courses at Qumran.*

easy to determine the precise organization of the Community, but officially it comprised three classes: priests, Levites, and lay Essenes who were divided into thousands, hundreds, fifties, and tens, as in the time of Moses (Exod 18:21, 25; Deut 1:15). Within the Community, there was a judiciary Council composed of laymen and priests (1QS 8:1). These men were to be perfect in everything revealed in the Torah, to practice truth and righteousness, justice and loving kindness, to live humbly with each other, and to guard faithfulness in the land with a steadfast purpose and contrite spirit. The Council, under the leadership of the priests, sometimes assisted by the Levites (1QSa 1:22–2:3), governed the Community.

There was also an Overseer responsible for managing the financial affairs of the Community, for instructing the Many in the acts of God, for examining prospective members and assigning them their respective ranks in the Community, and for pitying members as a father pities his children (1QS 6:14–16; CD 13:7–19).

Presumably, any person wanting to join the larger Community had to spend three years in strict preparation, as for entrance into any Essene group. Any man wanting to join the Council of the Community had to be questioned by the Overseer of the Many concerning his understanding and deeds. If he passed subsequent instruction, the Overseer took him before the Council, where he was further questioned. The process went on for two years, during which time the candidate could not share in the privileges of the Council. After the first year, if it was decided under God that he was worthy according to the judgment of the priests and the majority of the members of the Covenant, his property and wages were submitted to the financial Overseer. He could not participate fully with the Many in the sacred meal until after the second year. Then after a final examination, if it was decided under God to accept him, he was assigned his rank among the members in accordance with the law, justice, purification rites, and the sharing of his property. And then he could give his opinion to the Community (1QS 6:14–23).

The two guiding principles of the ascetic Qumran Sect were ritual purity and apocalypticism. Their purity was maintained through routine daily water purifications. However, the sect was emphatic in saying that the water itself does not purify. "By a spirit of uprightness and humility his sins shall be atoned" and by walking perfectly in all God's ways (1QS 3:8–10). The sect's ascetic apocalypticism was perpetuated through the belief that their desert life was symbolic of the Israelites' wanderings under Moses. And that life was lived in preparation for the new age when they would experience perfect unity in brotherhood and love.

The nature of mankind and the problem of evil are explained by the doctrine of the two spirits, the spirits of truth and falsehood or of light and darkness. Members are instructed in these two ways in order "to enlighten the heart of man and to make clear before him the ways of true righteousness and to put fear in his heart about the judgments of God" (1QS 4:2–3). Those who live by the spirit of truth will experience healing, peace, long life, and everlasting blessings. Those who walk by the spirit of falsehood will experience greed, pride, lying, deceit, impiety, and jealousy, among other evils. Finally the Evil Spirit will be destroyed, and the Good Spirit will triumph at the last judgment.

As in the *Testaments of the Twelve Patriarchs* (*T. Sim.* 7:1–2; *T. Judah* 24:1–3), the sect believed in the coming of two Messiahs, the Messiah of Aaron (the priestly Messiah) and the Messiah of Israel (the royal or Davidic Messiah). Of these the priestly Messiah was to have the greater rank. The sect also expected the coming of the prophet predicted in Deut 18:18, a prophet like Moses (1QS 9:11; 1QSa 2:11–22).

The Community celebrated a daily sacred communal meal (1QS 6:4–5; 1QSa 2:17–22) at which the priest first blessed the bread and the wine. Like the ritual water purifications, the meal was intended for the purification of the Many, that is, those fully qualified as members of the Community. Novitiates could not fully participate in the meal until after two years. It may be that those meals were eaten in anticipation of the Messianic banquet in the new age, but scholars do not agree on this point.

The Qumran document known as the *Manual of Discipline* or the *Rule of the Community* (1QS) provides interesting insights into the life of the sect. The Manual begins by stating the purpose and ideals of the Community. Every member is to seek God with his whole being, to do what is good and right before God, to abstain from every form of evil, and to practice truth and righteousness. Those who enter the Community pledge to act according to all God's commands, to confess their past sins, and not to forsake God because of fear or any affliction if tempted by the power of Belial (Satan, also called the Angel of Darkness and the Evil Spirit).

A kind of high court was responsible for trying persons who violated the rules of the Community. Among specific rules mentioned in 1QS 5:1–9:26 are these: members of the Community must separate themselves from evil persons, swear to obey all the Mosaic law, reprove each other in humility and love, not speak in anger, sit each in proper rank with the priests first, not interrupt anyone speaking, and speak only in turn after getting permission to speak from the leaders of the Council or the Many.

For various offenses to the rules, the punishments were severe. If a member knowingly lied about his property, he was excluded from the Purification of the Many (perhaps the sacred communal meal) for one year, and one-fourth of his food was withheld. Whoever answered another disrespectfully or spoke to another impatiently was punished for a year. Death was the penalty for speaking evilly against God. The following were punishable for six months: speaking arrogantly or deceptively, bearing malice or taking revenge, and going naked without being seriously ill. For negligence to the extent of harming another or uttering a foolish word, the penalty was three months. Other offenses and punishments included interrupting another in speech, ten days; sleeping during the assembly of the Many or spitting in their midst, thirty days; laughing stupidly and loudly, thirty days; gesturing with the left hand (the significance of the "left" hand is unknown), ten days. For maligning one's fellow the penalty was separation from the Purification of the Many for a year, but for maligning the Many as a group the penalty was permanent dismissal.

Several sources other than Josephus mention that the community at Qumran included women. Some scrolls speak of married members and children. An *Appendix* to the *Manual of Discipline* speaks of all members gathering together, "including the children and the women," and says that a youth should not have sex with a woman before he is twenty years old and the woman knows good from evil (1QSa 1:4, 9–11).

The *Damascus Document* states that if a man gets a wife and has children he should do so in obedience to the law (CD 7:7–8; see Num 30:17; CD 16:10–12). The presence of women and children at Qumran has been confirmed by the bones of women and children found in a cemetery excavated there. On the other hand, the *Manual* itself says nothing about women and even warns men about "lustful eyes" (1QS 1:6). And thus far there has been no evidence of women in the main cemetery at Qumran. All the evidence together seems to indicate the presence of two orders of Essenes at Qumran, one that married and reared children and one that did not.

Because some crucial ideas previously thought to have originated with NT writers are expressed in the Qumran Scrolls, these scrolls provide a very important background for NT study. For example, the idea of a Holy Spirit occurs rarely in the OT but often in the scrolls. The following are some similarities between the Sect of Qumran and early Christians.

Members of the Qumran community thought of themselves as a congregation and a new covenant (1QS 3:11; CD 8:21; compare Mark 14:24; Matt 26:28). The Qumran Sect and the early Christians both thought of themselves as "the elect" or "chosen" (1QS 8:6; 1QH 2:13; Matt 24:22; Rom 8:33; 11:5; Gal 1:15; 2 Tim 1:9; 2:10). Both claimed special illumination and used the term *children of light* (1QS 1:9; Luke 16:8; John 12:36; 1 Thess 5:5). Both groups applied OT scripture to themselves, and both celebrated a sacred meal that included a blessing of bread and wine. Finally, one of the most important shared concepts is that of God's forgiveness or justification of sinners because of his own righteousness as we find it, for example, in 1QS 11:2–15 and Rom 3:20–26.

More detailed parallels between Qumran and the NT are given in J. A. Fitzmyer 1976, 1997. The titles "Son of God" and "Son of the Most High" occur in the same combination as in Luke 1:32, 35. In Matthew's infancy narrative, Joseph's uncertainty about the situation is paralleled with the doubt of Lamech in 1QapGen 2:1–27. The prohibition of divorce in the words of Jesus (Mark 10:11–12) is expressed also in a text from Qumran.

Besides the Qumran Scrolls, for Essenes see Josephus, *Ant.* 18:1, 2, 5; *War* 2:8; Philo, *Every Good Man Is Free* 12–13; Pliny, *Natural History* 5:17:4. In subsequent years after the discovery of

Qumran and the scrolls there, other manuscripts were discovered in more Judean caves. Along with the Qumran Scrolls, they are known as the Dead Sea Scrolls. These manuscripts together constitute the most important discovery relative to the OT, Judaism, and the origins of Christianity. However, there is still much debate about the relationship between the Qumran and other Dead Sea Scrolls. And some scholars believe that although the Qumran Sect has affinities with the Pharisees and Essenes, the sect has a distinctive identity and must remain as an unknown Jewish sect (see, e.g., L. H. Schiffman 1975).

Zealots. The Zealots were a fanatical war party of Jews who, along with the Sicarii, were largely responsible for the Roman defeat of the Jews in 66–73 CE. The Zealots fought not only against the Romans but against Jews who were unwilling to fight the Romans. Josephus says that since they believed "God was their only leader and master," they "had a passion for liberty hard to conquer." Their fanaticism was also grounded in the belief that they lived in a land that God had given to the Jews, a land that must continue to be under Jewish control. Otherwise, they agreed with all of the opinions of the Pharisees (*Ant.* 18:1:6).

Other Jewish Men and Women. The majority of Jews in Palestine did not belong to any of the four main groups described by Josephus. For common Jews, as for all other Jews, though to a lesser formal extent, the first five books of the Hebrew scriptures (the Torah or Pentateuch) regulated all aspects of their personal, family, social, civil, and religious life. They believed God gave the Torah to Moses and that it was, therefore, sacred and meant to be observed. So also for the rest of their scriptures. Life under the Law, especially the commands to be holy as God is holy and to love one's neighbor and the stranger (Lev 19:2, 34), set Jews apart from the rest of the world.

In Jerusalem there were many activities besides those in the temple and synagogue. We assume that most Jews, within a reasonable distance of the city, went there mainly for worship,

including the required sacrifices and offerings. At Passover times there were thousands of people, if not a million or two, in the city. Josephus estimates that at one Passover, when Nero was emperor of Rome, there were at least ten to twenty persons feasting on one paschal lamb. There were 255,600 lambs, so there were about 2,700,000 persons at the festival (*War* 6:9:3). Allowing for the usual exaggeration of Josephus, there were still a huge number of people there.

While at Passover, those who could afford it might buy "spices, precious stones, and gold . . . brought into the region by the Arabs," or other things in "the city . . . rich in crafts" (*Aristeas* 114).

(For a description of the temple see E. P. Sanders 1992:54–72, to whom I am indebted for some of the material in this section.) We turn now to the temple in Jerusalem.

Institutions for Worship

The Temple. The Sadducees and the Pharisees were closely associated with the two Jewish institutions for worship, the temple and the synagogue, respectively. As with the groups themselves, these two institutions differed significantly.

The first temple, built by King Solomon (962–922 BCE), was destroyed by the Babylonians in 586 BCE and rebuilt by Zerubbabel c. 516 BCE. This second temple, rebuilt by Herod c. 19 BCE, was known for its beauty and artistry. Herod hired "most skilled workmen" and trained others so that "it was thought no one else had so adorned the temple" (*Ant.* 15:12:3). Located in Jerusalem, it was the only temple for Jews all over the world, and several passages in the NT indicate that the temple was important in the religious life of Jesus and the first Christians. Jesus walked in the temple and taught there (Mark 11:27; 12:35; Luke 19:47; John 7:28; 8:20; Acts 2:46–47; 3:1–10). But some passages, such as those concerning the cleansing of the temple, show that there was opposition to some of its practices (Mark 11:15–19; Matt 21:12–13; Luke 19:45–48; John 2:13–17).

The chief officials of the temple, the priests, usually belonged to the Sadducean party and were presided over by the chief priest. There were many divisions of priests, who served in shifts for a week at a time. The priests performed all sacrifices, held daily morning and evening services (compare Heb 10:11), and conducted special rituals on the sabbath and on Jewish festivals, especially Passover, Pentecost, and Tabernacles.

Besides the high (or chief) priest and the priests, there were subordinate cultic officials known as Levites. They performed the more menial tasks around the temple, such as assisting the priests, maintaining the courts of the temple, cleaning the sacred utensils, and preparing the cereal offerings. The Levites also served in weekly shifts and went to the temple only at their designated times. Perhaps they also were responsible for the music in the temple; Josephus refers to them as hymn singers (*Ant.* 20:9:6).

We know almost nothing about temple worship in NT times. Everything was done according to the Torah, and the key word was *sacrifice*. Many services included various offerings (compare Mark 12:32–34; Luke 2:22–24), the slaughter of sacrificial victims such as sheep, goats, and pigeons, and the burning of flesh on a large stone altar. Animal sacrifices were a part of most ancient religions, including that of the Hebrews, as we know from the OT laws regulating sacrifices. Sacrifices were performed primarily to establish a favorable relationship between the sacrificer and the god(s) worshiped. For the Hebrews, this favorable relationship was accomplished through the forgiveness of sins, which was made possible by a proper sacrifice that was pleasing to God. Sacrifice was probably not the only aspect of temple worship. There also may have been singing—perhaps of some OT psalms—prayer, and scripture readings.

The Sect of Qumran did not participate in the temple worship in Jerusalem because it thought the temple priests were illegitimate and thus had defiled the temple. It considered praise of God and perfect conduct as the proper sacrifices (1QS 9:4–5), an idea that may have been shared even by Jews who participated in temple worship

(compare Hos 6:6, quoted by Jesus in Matt 9:13; 12:7).

The Synagogue. In contrast to the temple's origin, the origin of the synagogue is obscure, but the usual view is that the synagogue developed during the Jews' exile in Babylonia in the sixth and fifth centuries BCE. The Greek word *synagōgē* means "congregation" or "assembly," and translates a Hebrew word or two with the same meaning. Originally the synagogue was a meeting for worship and study, not a building. We do not know when or where the first synagogue was erected; but if some ruins at Masada are those of a synagogue, they are the oldest known. (See Figure I.7.)

The synagogue was a unique institution in the ancient world with a unique purpose, namely, to train all its adherents to become servants of God and good Jews personally and citizens of the Jewish nation. In contrast to the one temple, which was permitted only in Jerusalem, even before NT times there were many synagogues in Palestine and throughout the world, wherever there were communities of Jews. There was no sacrifice in the synagogue; instead, the key word there was *Torah*. The emphasis was on reading, study, and instruction in the Torah, so the synagogue was two institutions in one—a place of sabbath worship (Mark 6:2; Luke 4:16) and the Jewish school. The scribes were the teachers, and they usually belonged to the Pharisaic party. Philo (*Life of Moses* 2:39) calls Jewish places of prayer schools, and the gospels usually mention the synagogue with reference to Jesus teaching there (see, for example, Mark 1:21; Matt 13:54; Luke 6:6; John 6:59). In Acts, most apostolic preaching and the first conversions to Christianity took place in the synagogue.

We can be certain that reading of the Torah was a part of synagogue services in NT times (Luke 4:16–22; Acts 13:14–15). Eventually other parts were added, including the *Shema* (a statement of faith named from the first Hebrew word in Deut 6:4), a sermon, and prayers. The words of Jesus reported in Mark 11:25 (compare Matt 6:5; Luke 18:11)—"whenever you stand

FIGURE I.7
*Ruins of a synagogue
(?) at Masada.*

praying"—may show that worshipers stood for prayer. The words "best seats in the synagogues" (Mark 12:39; Matt 23:6; Luke 11:43; 20:46) indicate that worshipers sat according to rank of some kind, perhaps in order of age or authority, as in the Qumran community (1QS 6:8–9).

Several officers of the synagogue are mentioned in the gospels and Acts. The chief officer was an *archisynagōgos* ("leader of the synagogue"—Mark 5:22; Luke 8:49; 13:14; Acts 3:15; 18:8, 17). According to Luke 4:20, another officer was the *hypēretēs*, "attendant" or "minister." One of his duties was to bring out the scroll for reading and then replace it. Some officials were responsible for disciplining those who broke the law. (For the origin of the synagogue and its transformation from an assembly to an architectural structure in which assemblies for worship were held, see H. C. Kee 1990.)

The synagogue and the temple of the Jews flourished in the midst of Palestine as it was ruled first by the Greeks and then by the Romans. In addition to the Graeco-Roman religions and the other aspects of Palestinian society in the first century CE, the synagogue and the temple influenced Christianity as it began as a sect within Judaism in ancient Palestine.

Women as Models of Reverence for God

It is still generally thought that men, not women, were in complete control of the cults of the temple and the synagogue. These cults were crucial for Jewish understanding of the Torah and what its demands were for the worshipers. Women were on the periphery of things in both institutions. They could not serve as priests, nor could they participate in the leadership of the temple or synagogue. In fact, in the temple they were confined to the Court of the Women, well beyond the sphere of action. And in the synagogue they were restricted to a specific area, sometimes to a secluded balcony.

However, these views have been challenged by several women, notably B. J. Brooten 1982. Her study is based on evidence from Greek and

Latin inscriptions from the first century BCE to the sixth century CE. In some inscriptions women were given the titles "head of the synagogue," "leader," "mother of the synagogue," "elder," and "priest," titles that were not just honorary. According to the older view, such titles were only honorary and reflected fathers' and husbands' prestige in their communities. According to Brooten, no evidence exists for honorary titles for synagogue personnel or for wives assuming titles of their husbands. On the contrary, some women, especially in Diaspora Judaism in Africa, Asia Minor, Crete, Egypt, Greece, Italy, and even in Palestine, did occupy positions of leadership in synagogues.

Brooten argues that there is no literary or archaeological evidence for the segregation of women from men by having them sit in galleries during synagogue worship. Where galleries were a part of synagogue structures, there is no evidence that women sat there during worship. Moreover, some inscriptions show that women contributed money to synagogues, sometimes even donating one. Money was sometimes donated on behalf of women. And because money was traditionally associated with power, such donations suggest that women held positions of leadership in ancient Jewish communities.

How much of Brooten's evidence is helpful for NT times, especially in Palestine, is questioned by some scholars. Only one of nineteen inscriptions comes from Palestine, none of which is in Hebrew. There is no evidence that women were leaders of synagogues in Palestine, but six inscriptions about women contributing money to synagogues do come from there. Yet they are all from the fifth and sixth centuries CE.

In Orthodox synagogues today women are seated in galleries apart from men. Is this one of those practices that must not be read back into ancient times, as Brooten cautions? Or does it indicate that the tradition of separation of the sexes during Jewish worship has been very strong since ancient times? Recall that in the temple in Jerusalem women were confined to the Court of the Women. Nevertheless, Brooten's work must not be overlooked in future studies on women in all aspects of Judaism and early Christianity.

No matter about the role of women in ancient Palestinian synagogues, it is a fact that in certain Jewish literature, albeit apocryphal, a woman, not a man, is chosen to be the paragon of reverence toward God and of obedience to his law or as God's chief spokesperson. Four examples follow.

In the book of Judith a woman by that name is the heroine. The reader whose conscience is pricked by the conviction that the end never justifies the means may not even want to give the ancient author a fair hearing. Granted, Judith uses deceit and sexual allurement and even beheads a general (9:10–13; 10:3–5; 12:14–20; 13:3–10). Yet if one remembers that Judith was probably written when the Jews were fighting for their survival, perhaps during the Maccabean struggle, one can understand, if not accept, the author's attitudes and values. As with the author of Esther, the author of Judith chose a woman to deliver the Jews from their enemies. Judith (the name itself means "Jewess") is portrayed as his ideal and her noble deed as though God himself had acted through her for the deliverance of his people: "God . . . has not withdrawn his mercy from the house of Israel, but has destroyed our enemies by my hand this very night!" (13:14). Judged by the standards of the author's time, Judith was a pious and religious woman: "No one spoke ill of her, for she feared God with great devotion" (8:8).

The story ends with a hymn of praise sung by Judith and all the people: "The Lord Almighty has foiled them [the enemy] by the hand of a woman. For their mighty one did not fall by the hands of the young men. . . . but Judith daughter of Merari with the beauty of her countenance undid him" (16:5–7). Was the author unconcerned that because Judith became a sex object she overcame her enemies?

In two Jewish sections of a work dating from about 150 BCE to 80 CE and known as the *Sibylline Oracles,* the sibyl, a woman, has a dominant role in communicating God's will. Indeed, the name "sibyl," which refers to a female prophet, probably means "the counsel of God." Twice she is called "a prophetess of the Mighty God" (3:818; 4:4–6).

In one of the apocryphal additions to the OT book of Daniel called Susanna, the young man Daniel, because of his clever detective work, appears to be the hero of the story. But in reality he is only a foil for defending the virtue of Susanna, the heroine, and her faithfulness to God and the law. And in the earlier text (LXX) Daniel is not nearly so "dominant a figure" as in the later text of Theodotion (C. A. Moore 1977:115–116).

Susanna had been taught the law of Moses by her parents (3). Two elders, who were also judges among the people, plotted to assault her sexually one day as she was bathing (8–16, 19–21). Confronted by the men, who were recognized in the community as authorities on the law, Susanna decided to be falsely accused "rather than sin in the sight of the Lord" (23), that is, commit adultery, even though under duress. When Susanna was tried before a public assembly, the elders said that they had caught her having sex with a young man who fled when he saw them (37–40). Then comes the satire, the point of the whole story: "Because they were elders of the people and judges, the assembly believed them and condemned her to death" (41). But after Daniel exposed their boldfaced lies, the elders were convicted of false witness and put to death "in accordance with the law of Moses" (34–62).

Thus Daniel is often, though wrongly, thought to be the hero of this story. Rather, the story is one of contrasts between the elders, who as judges were the respected authorities on the law, and Susanna, a woman faithful to God and obedient to his law. When planning their action, the elders "suppressed their consciences and turned away their eyes from looking to Heaven or remembering their duty to administer justice" (9). In contrast, Susanna, falsely accused, "looked up toward Heaven, for her heart trusted in the Lord" (35). Need more be said about the noble example of Susanna's reverence for God and obedience to his law in the mind of the author of this story? But,

again, the patriarchal and sexist attitude of the day (if not of the author) is reflected in the fact that had it not been for the testimony of a male, Daniel, Susanna would have been killed because the people, including the good judges, did not let her testify in her own behalf.

The fourth example is from a writing known as Fourth Maccabees. It is a Hellenistic Jewish narrative strongly influenced by the philosophy of Plato and the Stoics. Its frequently reiterated philosophical theme is whether God-reverencing reason is sovereign over the emotions (for example, 1:1, 9, 13–14; 2:6–7, 10; 6:31).

Much of 4 Maccabees centers around the Jew Eleazar and seven Jewish brothers and their mother who all chose to die rather than break the Torah. When urged to share in the Greek way of life by eating food forbidden by the Torah, each in turn chose to suffer severe torment and death as a reward for virtue rather than yield. Thus God-reverencing reason (*eusebēs logismos*) ruled over the emotions.

After the account of the brothers (8:1–12:19), the author turns his attention to the mother (14:11–17:7). She is the greatest example of God-reverencing reason over the emotions, because she "bore the tortures of each of her children. Behold, how manyfold is the mother's love and affection toward her children. . . . But sympathy for the children did not move the mother of the youths. . . . When the mother had two choices, reverence toward God and the momentary salvation of her seven sons, . . . she loved reverence for God more which, according to God, saves for eternal life. . . . O, mother, who now experienced labors greater than in their birth pains! O, woman, who alone brought perfect reverence for God to birth. . . . If, thus, a woman—even an old woman—and the mother of seven sons, endured seeing her children tortured to death, it must be confessed that God-reverencing reason is the master over the emotions" (14:12–13, 20; 15:1–3, 16–17; 16:1; my trans.). Here again an author has chosen to write about a woman as the supreme example of Jewish reverence for God and obedience to his law.

PART B
NORTH OF THE MEDITERRANEAN: ASIA MINOR, GREECE, AND ROME

Although Christianity was born within Judaism east of the Mediterranean, it grew up amidst Hellenistic culture north of the Mediterranean. Asia Minor is the name given to much of the land east of the Aegean Sea and composed of several Roman provinces. It is not to be confused with the Roman province Asia. Study the map "The Journeys of Paul" (on back endsheet) to become familiar with the northern Mediterranean world of NT times. Later, in the chapters on Acts and Paul's letters, we will study the spread of Christianity from Jerusalem to Rome. Now we will examine Hellenistic culture as it affected NT writings from the northern Mediterranean world.

Roman emperors developed the government established by Julius Caesar. Augustus and Tiberius and several able successors consolidated the empire in the Mediterranean world. Under the rule of Roman emperors, Christianity grew and flourished in the cities of the Roman provinces in Asia Minor and Greece, and in Rome herself. This was possible because Greek was the universal language, good roads made missionary travel easy, Rome was tolerant, and there was peace.

ROMAN EMPERORS AND ROMAN PROVINCES

Augustus (27 BCE–14 CE), whose name means "consecrated," was the first emperor of the Roman Empire. He retained the name Caesar and, like Julius Caesar, had the title *imperātor,* "commander" (of the armies). Known as "Commander Augustus Son of Divine Caesar," he accepted divine honors in the eastern provinces but refused such recognition in Italy.

For an administrative career in Rome, one had to advance through a complicated system of ranks and promotions. The imperial guard (see Phil 1:13), one of the highest ranks in this complex system, was composed of an elite military group under Augustus. They were chief advisers and ministers to the emperors, and during the second century CE, they became a chief court of appeal in the Roman government.

From the time of Augustus to the end of the first century CE, many tasks of government and much of the record keeping was performed by personal slaves of the emperors. Those slaves and freedmen executed such tasks as minting the coinage required for the various armies and managing many of the fiscal affairs. These persons came to be known as "the emperor's household" (see Phil 4:22).

Augustus divided the provinces into two groups, the senatorial and the imperial. The former were governed by *proconsuls* who had no Roman troops but had the aid of *quaestors* who collected the taxes and paid them to the senate treasury. The latter were frontier provinces where an army was needed, so they were under the power of Augustus as *imperātor.* They were administered either by a *lēgātus* (legate) or a *praefectus* (governor) responsible to Augustus. Augustus controlled these administrators, and if they misgoverned, he deposed them.

Augustus tried to revive the state religion—that is, the public religion of Rome before influence from Hellenistic and oriental cults—by repairing temples and restoring ceremonies. As *pontifex maximus,* or high priest, Augustus had charge of the state religion. He encouraged morality and family life by discouraging divorce. In the provinces, Augustus also supported trade and commerce and built a system of roads. Because he wanted "to show that he was a prince who desired the public welfare rather than popularity" (Suetonius, *Augustus*), he established peace and security in the Roman provinces by freeing land and sea of robbers and pirates. The age of Augustus was called the *pax Romana,* or peace of Rome. Luke places Jesus' birth in the time of Caesar Augustus and John the Baptist's preaching in the time of his successor, Tiberius.

Tiberius (14–37), the second emperor, was succeeded by Gaius (37–41), who was the first to think of himself as a god, the incarnation of Jupiter. He ordered that his statue be placed in temples, and he appeared in public dressed as one of the gods. Claudius (41–54) was an excellent administrator who initiated reforms in Rome and the provinces. The statement in Acts that "Claudius had ordered all Jews to leave Rome" (18:2) is confirmed by Suetonius (*Claudius* 35:3).

Nero's reign (54–68) had grave consequences for both Jews and Christians. Through the influence of Nero's wife, Poppea, Florus was appointed procurator of Judea; this set the stage for the most tragic war in Jewish history, the war against Rome in 66–73. Nero was the first to persecute Christians, but the persecution was confined to Rome. When much of Rome burned in 64 and people began to blame Nero, he made the Christians the scapegoats. Some were clothed in animal skins and mangled by dogs, some were covered with pitch and became living torches in the emperor's gardens, and others were crucified.

Vespasian (69–79) was succeeded by Titus (79–81; see Figure I.8) and Domitian (81–96). Domitian expelled philosophers, mostly Stoics, and astrologers from Rome. He permitted Jews to have their own synagogues, but he forced collection of back payments of the tax previously paid to the temple in Jerusalem. Domitian had his father, Vespasian, deified and himself acknowledged as "lord and god." The final years of his reign were filled with terror and ended with his assassination by friends. In spite of this, Domitian ran the empire well. Although he increased taxes to pay for extensive roads, public works, and games, the provinces were loyal, peaceful, and contented.

Nerva (96–98) was followed by Trajan (98–117), who corresponded with Pliny, governor of Bithynia in northern Asia Minor. This correspondence is important because it relates to the study of several NT writings. Christian intolerance of the emperor cult and refusal to acknowledge pagan gods led the Romans to accuse the Christians of atheism. Because of their exclusive-

FIGURE I.8   *Arch of Titus in the Roman forum. The arch depicts Titus's victory over the Jews in 70 CE.*

ness, on the one hand, and their zeal for their religion on the other, Christians were also accused by non-Christians of being social misfits and fanatics. Although Christians were rarely persecuted by the Romans in NT times, Christianity was regarded as a "detestable superstition" and as having "a hatred of the human race" (Tacitus, *Annals* 15:44), an accusation sometimes brought against Jews at this time. *Superstition* was the term used for a foreign religion that came to Rome. The Christians concerned Pliny because of his subjects' complaints about them, so he wrote to Trajan about this situation. The fact that he wrote for information indicates that no imperial edict had been issued against the Christians.

In his letter to Trajan, Pliny writes that he has never been present at any trials of Christians, so he is not sure how to examine or punish Christian offenders. His procedure has been to ask those denounced to him as Christians if they are Christians. If they confess to being Christians, he questions them further and executes them. However, if the confessed Christians are Roman citizens, he sends them off to Rome. He claims that an investigation of charges that Christians were antisocial and immoral revealed that the sum of their guilt was, "They were accustomed to meeting on a fixed day . . . and to singing in alternate verses a hymn to Christ as to a god, and bound themselves by a solemn oath not to do any wicked deeds, never to commit any fraud, theft, or adultery, never to falsify their word, nor break a promise, nor deny a trust when called upon to make it good." Then they would adjourn and meet again to eat a meal of ordinary food.

Trajan replies that Pliny's procedure is proper and that no general rule can be applied to all cases. Pliny is not to search out Christians, but if they are guilty they must be punished, except for the person who denies being a Christian and proves it "by praying to our gods." Finally, Trajan reminds Pliny that if charges against Christians are to be valid, they must contain the names of the accusers in accordance with Roman custom (Pliny, *Letters* 10:97).

ROMAN LAW

The Roman law one thinks of as the legacy of Rome to much of the modern world was not in effect in the eastern provinces until the third century CE. It concerned regulations of private property and contracts and the individual's civic status. It was operative among Roman citizens but not among foreigners.

In imperial times the legal status of women and slaves was much improved. For example, women could engage in trade and manufacture and join some clubs with men. Slaves could own property and use it to buy their freedom, and they were legally protected against abuse. Roman law was more concerned with justice and fairness than with the strict observance of specific laws. Penalties for private violations were meant to right the

wrong done; penalties for public violations were usually vengeful and severe—for example, crucifixion. The emperors, as supreme rulers of the state, could make legally binding decisions, such as decrees requiring emperor worship.

The concern for law, justice, and fairness followed Rome into her provinces. As the correspondence between Trajan and Pliny indicates, the Roman provinces were governed by Roman law, the aim of which was to protect the state, its citizens, and public and private property. Governors of provinces were most concerned with keeping public order, always a primary interest of Rome. Governors set the penalties, but in times of crises, orders from the government in Rome took precedence over local regulations and privileges.

Roman officials respected the laws of others; however, their own law took precedence, especially for Roman citizens, who could appeal to the emperors. For example, the apostle Paul, a Roman citizen living in different places and appearing before different officials, was always under Roman law (Acts 21:33–28:31). After being tried before the procurator Festus, Paul was sent to Rome because he appealed to Caesar. Elsewhere he also appealed to his Roman citizenship. The authorities in Philippi were frightened to learn that they had put Paul and his companions in prison as Roman citizens, "beaten" and "uncondemned" (Acts 16:37–39; compare 22:25–29). It was against the law to beat Roman citizens for any reason, and as the letters between Pliny and Trajan indicate, Rome was always concerned that charges be properly obtained. In the Roman Empire, then, where the NT had its setting, society was governed by men who were always under Roman law. This law was a unifying force among the diverse peoples who populated that empire.

PEOPLES AND LANGUAGES

In rural areas and small villages in the Roman Empire, there were native peoples of many races and backgrounds, including Orientals (Easterners) and Occidentals (Westerners). When Greek and Roman rulers founded cities, they brought in peoples from many places to populate them. In some cities the population was predominantly Greek, in others predominantly Roman, but it was always mixed.

Because of the mixed population of the empire, there were several languages and many dialects. In the western part of the empire—Italy, Sicily, and Gaul, for example—Latin was the main language, and most Roman soldiers everywhere spoke only Latin. But in the eastern part, including Greece and Asia Minor, Greek remained the language of government and of the educated, many people having a sufficient knowledge of Greek to understand it and to make themselves understood. In some Jewish synagogues the scriptures were read in Hebrew and then translated into Greek so the people could understand. And Greek prevailed in many synagogues where the Greek OT, or Septuagint, was the scripture used and studied.

Evidence for the predominance of Greek and the diversity of language appears in the NT in John 19:20, where the title on Jesus' cross "was written in Hebrew, in Latin, and in Greek." In Acts, after Paul was arrested in Jerusalem, the Roman tribune said to him, "Do you know Greek?" Paul replied, "I am a Jew, from Tarsus in Cilicia, a citizen of an important city" (21:37, 39).

Paul's reply means that he could speak Greek, but many persons who used Greek may not have been able to understand some of the words in his letters. In light of the revived interest in sociological factors in early Christianity, we should note here that A. D. Nock 1933b wrote that when we turn to the Septuagint and the NT, "We find at once a strange vocabulary." The words *dikaioō* ("justify," for example, Gal 2:16–17; Rom 3:24–30; 5:1) and *doxa* ("glory," for example, Rom 5:2; 8:21; 10:31) are used "in peculiar senses." *Exousiai* ("authorities," for example, Rom 13:1; Eph 3:10) would be "entirely without meaning to a Greek." No Greek could naturally use *anathema* ("accursed," for example, Gal 1:8–9; 1 Cor 12:3; 16:27; Rom 9:3) without trying to explain it. "Such usages are the product of an enclosed world living its own life, a ghetto culturally and linguistically if not geo-

graphically; they belong to a literature written entirely for the initiated. . . . Apart from the magical papyri . . . we have no writings by men of esoteric piety addressed only to their spiritual brethren." In other words, its own jargon helped to make early Christianity a unique society.

SCHOOLS AND EDUCATION

During the Hellenistic period, one of the main places for education was the gymnasium, a public building maintained by a city. Some of the rooms were reserved for education, and teachers were often hired and paid by the person in charge of the gymnasium. Apparently there were three kinds of education—military, physical education or hygiene, and educational subjects, as we might call them, including instruction in reading and writing. Students also listened to lectures and did lessons.

For persons accustomed to thinking that education took place in school buildings, it may be surprising to learn that education also occurred on the streets of every large city. Traveling artists, poets, and philosophers—universal features of Hellenistic times—delivered prepared lectures to audiences always eager for learning.

We can best appreciate the concept of education in Graeco-Roman society by learning the meanings of several Greek words. *Scholē*, the word for school, meant "leisure," as did the Latin word *schola*, which came from the Greek. Both words were used for the place where leisurely discussions took place; hence, the meaning "school." Only people who had leisure could go to school and become scholars, or people at leisure. The word *scholē* occurs in the NT only in Acts 19:9, where Paul "argued daily in the lecture hall [*scholē*] of Tyrannus." That hall probably was not a school, but a place for public lectures or a meeting place for a trade association. The Greek word for education, *paideia*, originally meant the rearing and training of a child; hence, "education." *Paideia* occurs in the NT only in the sense of religious instruction or discipline (Eph 6:4; 2 Tim 3:16; Heb 12:5–11).

In the Greek tradition, *paideia* meant a very close personal relationship between the young man being educated and the older man, his teacher. The older man was not only his teacher but also his role model for the Greek way of life. Although the context is not a school in the sense we normally think of it, and although the word *paideia* does not occur, several things in 1 Thessalonians reflect these aspects of Greek education. Paul writes that the Thessalonian Christians became "imitators" of Paul and his companions (1 Thess 1:6). There was a very intimate relationship between the Christians at Thessalonica and the missionaries. The latter were "like a father with his children" among the Thessalonians, exhorting them to "lead a life worthy of God" (1 Thess 2:11–12). The missionaries were "gentle" among the converts "like a nurse tenderly caring for her own children," sharing the gospel and also their own selves, because they became beloved to the missionaries (1 Thess 2:7–8).

The word *exhort* is indicative of instruction or training (1 Thess 2:12; see also 4:1). Finally, Paul writes that the Thessalonians received rules about how to live (1 Thess 4:1–2). Through the intimate personal relationship with the converts at Thessalonica, Paul was concerned, of course, with their instruction in the Christian, not the Greek, way of life. Yet in writing as he does, Paul reveals a familiarity with the method of Greek education.

A series of words referring to teaching—*didaskō*, "to teach," *didaskalos*, "teacher," *didaskalia*, "teaching," and *didachē*, "teaching"—occurs in the NT. The first is used mostly in the gospels with reference to Jesus teaching and in Acts with reference to people teaching in the temple; the second, mostly in the gospels with reference to Jesus; the third, mostly in the latest writings of the NT in the sense of doctrine, whether true or false; the fourth, widely distributed and used for the teaching of Jesus, Pharisees, apostles, and others. All are used in a religious sense and occur least in the letters of Paul, indicating that terms and concepts of education arose with Jesus and his first followers in the religious schools of the synagogue and temple, not in the Gentile churches of the Roman provinces. The NT, therefore, shows little direct influence from the Graeco-Roman concept of schools and education.

In Graeco-Roman society teachers and scholars were people of leisure and did not do physical labor, which was the task of slaves. But in Jewish society the rabbis, or teachers, practiced trades in addition to their work as teachers. For example, Jesus was a carpenter (Mark 6:3) and Paul a tentmaker (Acts 18:2–3) who worked regularly during his missionary activity (1 Cor 4:12; 9:16).

Many subjects were taught in the schools of the Roman provinces, but the emphasis was on rhetoric (thought and forms of expression), declamation (reading aloud), and poetry. Teachers were highly respected by the emperors and were granted certain favors, for example, exemption from municipal taxes; sometimes the state paid their salaries. Many families engaged a *paidagōgos* (boy leader) to accompany boys to and from school and to teach them manners, morals, and Greek conversation. Some families provided such education for their children at home through a private tutor, usually a slave or freedman of the family. This aspect of education is reflected in Paul's letters when he writes that the Corinthians have numerous "guardians [*paidagōgous*] in Christ" (1 Cor 4:15) and tells the Galatians that "the law was our disciplinarian [*paidagōgos*] until Christ came" (3:24). Thus we see something of the educational setting in which Paul's letters were written.

Closely related to the subject of schools and education is "the scholastic aspect of early Christian communities" as emphasized by E. A. Judge 1960–1961; A. J. Malherbe 1983:45–47; and others. This is especially true for the communities established by Paul. His Roman citizenship (if, indeed, he was a Roman citizen) put him in an elite social class. So among the persons with whom Paul associated, there would be opportunities for lively discussions of ideas and of human behavior.

SOCIAL AND ECONOMIC CONDITIONS

Roman social position was determined more by birth and legal status than by ethnic origin, education, or wealth. In Rome there were several social classes, including senators and their families, equestrians, and plebians. The senators lived in luxurious houses, had so many slaves they did not know all of them, spent thousands of dollars on their sons' educations, and indulged in sumptuous banquets. The equestrians, including many merchants and political officials, were a rung below the senators in the social ladder. They were the financial speculators and the creditors of the senators. By buying cheap property and converting it into large sums, many equestrians also became very rich.

In strong contrast to those classes, the plebian class, to which most Roman citizens belonged, lived in cheap tenement houses and often in severe poverty. To keep the plebians peaceful and to secure their votes, wealthy Roman politicians, including the emperors, spent large sums of money supplying them with free grain and entertaining them with athletic games and gladiatorial contests. Below the plebians were freed slaves, who intermingled with citizens but rarely became citizens. And finally there were the slaves, who, with the freed slaves, performed most of the labor.

The greatest change in status for slaves came when they obtained their freedom, but not all freed slaves were better off than slaves. In Roman society slaves were not always "bound in servitude to a person or household." Some slaves owned slaves, some had businesses of their own, and many were skilled professionals, especially medics. Some slaves were even wealthy enough to pay high prices for their freedom. The emperors used slaves in the administration of the provinces, where they might win their freedom and rise to important positions.

Mobility and stability among social classes were not certain. So changes in economic fortune or education did not automatically mean a change in social status. The emperor always had the upper hand. He could encourage, even promote, mobility of officials in the empire. But he could also, independently, by policy or on impulse end the career of even his closest friend.

Agriculture was the main source of income through large estates in the provinces. The land was farmed for the landowners by tenants who were known as *coloni.* The *coloni* could make a decent living, but most of the income went to the owners themselves. In both Jewish and Roman society, rich absentee landowners sometimes cheated the workers. Such a situation is described exactly in Jas 5:4: "The wages of the laborers who mowed your fields, which you kept back by fraud, cry out." (See G. Theissen 1978, 1982; R. MacMullen 1981; H. I. Marrou 1956; R. Scroggs 1980.)

The cities were the support system of the Roman Empire. A city included the surrounding land that provided the food supply and the income for the city's rich people. Usually a city was run by a council of a hundred aristocratic citizens who were responsible for the city's administration, law enforcement, and taxation. People of other classes, whether freed slaves, slaves, aliens, or even citizens, could not participate in city government (R. MacMullen 1974:88–120).

In every large city in the provinces, as well as in Rome itself, there were artisans who did not think of themselves as laborers. People of the same craft had their shops on the same street and organized guilds that brought them political and social advantages. The names of some guilds or associations were "Mates and Marble-Workers" and "The Comrade Smiths" (R. MacMullen 1974:77). The guilds or associations were known as *collegia,* and their real purpose was to provide their members with a social life. Members were interested in companionship and the possibility of social advancement rather than in economic gain. In the second century Christianity was referred to by both pagans and Christians as a *thiasos,* one of the terms used for the associations (A. J. Malherbe 1983:84–91).

The associations often had a patron deity, as did "Demetrius and the artisans with him," who were devoted to Artemis (Acts 19:38). The artisans manufactured wares of bronze, images of gold and silver, pottery, glassware, and cloths of various kinds. Trade in these and other goods, together with agriculture, was the backbone of the commercial activity within the Roman Empire.

We know least about the vast majority of people, the persons on the street, and what they thought about various aspects of life. Perhaps the best description is that of Artemidorus of Ephesus (second century CE) in *The Interpretation of Dreams* (R. J. White 1975:21):

> These, then, are common customs. To venerate and honor the gods. (For there is no nation without gods, just as there is none without rulers. For different people reverence different gods, but the worship of all is directed towards the same power.) To nurture children, to yield to women and to sexual intercourse with them, to be awake during the day, to sleep at night, to take food, to rest when tired, to live indoors and not in the open air.

Artemidorus also writes that marriage and death are thought to be critical points in human life because similar things appear at weddings and burials—a procession of male and female friends, wreaths, spices, unguents, and written records of the possessions of the one married or buried.

CHRISTIANS AND THE CITIES, SOCIAL CLASSES, AND CITIZENSHIP

According to Acts and Paul's letters, Christianity was established in cities north of the Mediterranean. By the beginning of the second century, it had also spread to rural areas, as we know from Pliny's letter to Trajan: "This contagious superstition is not limited to the cities but has spread to the towns and rural areas." It was probably spread by traders who were also missionary preachers. In contrast to the images of Jesus and the gospels, those of Paul are mostly of the city and city life; and in contrast to the gospels' reflection of monarchial and rural society east of the Mediterranean, Acts and Paul's letters reflect a republican (governed by constitutions) and urban society.

Luke, the writer of Acts, uses terms for city officials that are confirmed by other sources. The terms include, for example, magistrates at Philippi, officially "a Roman colony" (16:12–39); city authorities (*politarchs*) at Thessalonica (17:6, 8); and a town clerk and *asiarchs* at Ephesus (19:31, 35). In each of these places, the

people took part in the actions against Paul, and the marketplace into which Paul was dragged was the people's courthouse. In Corinth Paul was brought before the *bēma* (tribunal), a place for public trials (18:12, 16) that has been discovered among the ruins of the city.

Just as Acts and Paul's letters reflect the urban society in which Christianity was established, they also provide clues about the early Christians themselves. The NT was written for the common people who were Christians, even though ordinary Christians did not write it. A person named Celsus (c. 180 CE) was the first pagan to oppose Christianity. We know his work through Origen, a Christian writer who responded to him. Celsus charged that the church refused the intelligent and sought the ignorant and uneducated. He said that Christians could convert only the foolish and stupid, along with women and children, but Christianity was more representative of the society of which it was a part than has often been thought.

We can make some assumptions about the socioeconomic status of early Christians by studying the names of people associated with Paul. Achaicus, Fortunatus, and Lucius in Corinth (1 Cor 16:17; Rom 16:21) and Clement in Philippi (Phil 4:3) had Latin names in Roman colonies where Latin was the prevailing language. "This *may* indicate that their families belonged to the original stock of colonists, who tended to get ahead" (W. A. Meeks 1983:56, to whose work I am much indebted). Moreover, Gaius (1 Cor 1:14; Rom 16:23) not only had a Roman name but had a home large enough for him to serve as host to Paul and "the whole church" in Corinth (Rom 16:23). Similarly, Philemon owned at least one slave, and his house had a guest room and was large enough for the church to meet there (Phlm. 2:22). Acts reports that "not a few of the leading women" and "women and men of high standing" (17:4, 12) joined the church and that Lydia was "a dealer in purple cloth" (Acts 16:14). Presumably these women had high social and economic standing; or if, as some suggest, they were "the wives of leading men," then their husbands had attained such status. The Asiarchs,

Paul's friends at Ephesus, were wealthy, as was the city treasurer (Rom 16:23), the only official whom Paul mentions in his letters.

According to some of the later NT writings, the conversion of richer people to Christianity caused social problems within the church. The writer of James warns his readers against showing partiality toward the rich (Jas 1:9–11; 2:2–7; 5:1–6; 1 Tim 6:8–10, 17–19; Rev 3:17). And Jas 4:13 is a clear reference to merchants who boast because of their wealth: "Come now, you who say, 'Today or tomorrow we will go to such and such a town and spend a year there, doing business and making money.'"

Persons became Roman citizens by birth in communities where their parents lived as Roman citizens. Non-Roman residents in the empire were considered "foreigners" (*peregrini*), living according to foreign legal systems. After Augustus, Roman emperors became more liberal in granting Roman citizenship to individuals for various reasons and even to whole communities in the empire. Residents in such communities had a feeling of being "citizens of the empire."

It is uncertain how many Christians were Roman citizens before the time of Pliny, who says he was lenient to them. No one in the NT is called a citizen, except Paul (Acts 21:39). But, as we shall see in our study of Paul, we cannot always trust Paul's biographer, Luke. Paul never mentions his Roman citizenship in his letters. He does say he was thrice "beaten with rods" (2 Cor 11:25), which was the official beating by Roman officers (lictors) for some legal offenses.

Citizenship was a necessity for social acceptance in the Roman Empire, and in Graeco-Roman society Christians felt as "strangers and aliens" (Eph 2:19), as "aliens and exiles" (1 Pet 2:11). They consoled themselves by thinking they were "citizens with the saints and also members of the household of God" (Eph 2:19) and by looking forward to being a "commonwealth" (colony) in heaven (Phil 3:20). Yet there were some citizens among the Christians in Rome. Paul writes to the Romans: "Let every person be subject to the governing authorities. . . . Pay to all what is due them—taxes to whom taxes are due, revenue to whom revenue is due, respect to whom respect is due, honor to whom honor is due" (13:1, 7). Since only Roman citizens had to pay taxes, this indicates that at least some Christians held Roman citizenship.

ROMAN RELIGION AND PHILOSOPHY

Most people in the Roman world were polytheistic; that is, they believed in and worshiped many gods and goddesses. Polytheism sharply distinguished Graeco-Roman religion from Judaism and then Christianity. Josephus probably reflects a typical Jewish attitude toward pagan religion when he criticizes Greek poets and lawgivers because they represent the gods to be "as many as they desire, born from one another and in all kinds of ways, and to whom they assign different places and ways of living, like species of animals, some under the earth, others in the sea" (*Against Apion* 2:33).

Polytheism "was far more general and far more deserving of the title 'spirit of paganism' than any piety of the mysteries" (see below). However, by the end of the first century CE, there was an increasing tendency toward monotheism. Plutarch, biographer and philosopher (c. 50–120), writes about this concept: "There are not different gods in different nations, barbarians and Greeks, southerners and northerners. Just as sun and moon and sky and earth and sea are common to all, though named differently by different peoples, so the one Reason ordering this world, the one Providence governing it, and the subordinate powers set over all have different honours and titles among different peoples according to their customs" (A. D. Nock 1964:29, 9).

Some deities were worshiped all over the Roman world; others were attached to certain local shrines. The primary purpose of all places of worship was sacrifice. However, in contrast to the Jews, whose sacrifices were regulated by the Torah and performed regularly, pagans made sacrifices whenever they felt like it. Although the Romans regarded sacrifice as a pious act, they expected some benefit such as good health or fertility in return. To help win the favor of the god being worshiped, sacrificers placed gifts, usually food of some kind, on the altar. Artemidorus writes (R. J. White 1975:112–113):

> Men sacrifice to the gods when they have received benefits or when they have escaped some evil. . . . Some gods can be apprehended only by the intellect [for example, Dioscuri, Heracles, and Dionysus] while others can be perceived by the senses [for example, Hecate, Pan, and Asclepius]. The majority . . . can be grasped by the intellect, whereas only a few can be perceived by the senses.

Some Roman gods had much in common with certain Greek gods or acquired characteristics that made them comparable, although the Roman Jupiter never became quite equal to the Greek Zeus, the father of the gods. The Greek Artemis became the Roman Diana, chiefly a goddess of fertility and childbearing, according to the usual view. But some scholars have maintained that Artemis "was not a fertility goddess at all but the mistress of destiny" (J. E. Stambaugh 1986:150). Hermes became Mercury, god of traders; Demeter became Ceres, goddess of grain; and Aphrodite became Venus, goddess of lovemaking and luck at games of chance. Apollo, who was god of many things, including music, archery, and care of flocks and herds, was worshiped as Apollo on the Capitoline Hill in Rome.

In the Hellenistic period Eastern cults, especially those attached to female deities, began to move westward. Old cults also died out or were changed, and new religious movements began. The cults were spread by artisans and traders. Settling in a city, they would find people from their homeland and set up shrines to their native gods. Eventually the supporters of a cult would establish their cult in a Greek temple, and the cult would then be accepted as part of a city's religious institutions.

These cults were part of the setting for religious competition in NT times. The people of the Roman Empire were, in the words of Paul at Athens, "how extremely religious you are in every way" (Acts 17:22). A century earlier Cicero, the Roman orator and statesman, had said that the Romans were wise enough to realize that all things were subject to the will and rule of the gods. The welfare of each community in the provinces depended upon the favor of its deities; therefore, an unexpected visitor might by chance be a god, and was always welcome. Twice Paul had to disillusion people. For instance, after he had healed a cripple at Lystra, the crowds exclaimed: "'The gods have come down to us in human form!' Barnabas they called Zeus, and Paul . . . Hermes" (Acts 14:11–12; compare Acts 28:6). Also at Lystra, "The priest of Zeus, whose temple was just outside the city, brought oxen and garlands . . . and wanted to offer sacrifice" to Paul and Barnabas (Acts 14:13). Such priests were political officials, not religious men, and served an old Roman religion that was itself political in nature.

Augustus had given permission to the city of Pergamum to build a temple dedicated to himself and to Rome. Such temples honoring emperors were built in the provinces, and gradually there was a universal imperial cult. Actually, emperor worship began with the deification of Rome, in the name of the goddess Roma, not with the worship of the emperor. Roma was symbolic of the power of Rome, and as early as 195 BCE a temple to Roma was erected in Smyrna in Asia Minor. It was a simple step, then, to think of the spirit of Rome as incarnate in one man, the emperor.

The emperor cult, politically helpful in unifying the various peoples, was a sign of solidarity in the empire, and it was promoted more by local provincial rulers to show their allegiance than by the emperors. In each province religious associations were formed to carry out religious duties and to maintain the cult. The officials in charge of such associations, the *asiarchs*, were in charge of the worship of the emperor in power.

Closely related to the imperial cult, but independent of it, were several Greek hero cults. The heroes of these cults were greater than humans but less than gods. A hero was thought to have had at least one divine parent, to have lived on earth and performed some important humanitarian service, and then, after death, to have achieved the status of demigod. One of the best-known Greek heroes was Heracles who, according to Cicero, had "passed into the number of the gods" (*Tusculan Disputations* 1:32). The Romans believed that through dreams dead heroes could advise or command humans.

The most popular Greek hero-god was Asclepius, who, in the literature of Homer, was just the "blameless physician," not a god. The myth developed, however, that he was the son of Apollo and had been reared by Chiron, who had taught him the medical arts. As a man he not only healed the sick but raised the dead. Zeus, fearing that humans might try to escape death altogether, killed Asclepius with a thunderbolt; but at Apollo's request, Zeus placed him among the stars. Visits of Asclepius from heaven were known in every region of the empire.

It is almost impossible to reconstruct imperial Roman religion and to be sure of its important features. The greatest religious quest was for escape or salvation from the world with its various evils. Romans shared the view, common in the ancient world, that evils in human existence were beyond human control. Remedies, therefore, had to come from the gods above. From this basic belief developed the longing for a savior from heaven to deliver humans from their evil lot. This expectation is clearly expressed in the writings of Virgil and Horace, poets of the first century BCE.

People sought to ascend to the world of freedom beyond by communicating with the one true god of the world above. The main techniques for achieving contact with the divine were magic and *theurgy,* the arts of persuading a god to reveal himself and to give salvation, healing, or other gifts. These techniques were practiced in the temples and cult institutions dedicated to the worship of particular deities.

Romans believed that religion should serve the state and that observance of religious rites helped assure political success. Consequently, Romans credited their success to scrupulous religious observance and attributed political failures to their neglect of the sacred rites. But such religious practices did not satisfy the people's need for a personal religion that gave assurance of a better life in the present and eternal life in the future. Other religions, instead, met that need for people who could no longer believe the myths about the classical Graeco-Roman deities.

The quest for salvation in Roman religions was one of the reasons Christianity could spread throughout the empire. Moreover, Rome tolerated the religions of her subjects if these religions did not disturb the peace or become too barbarous. From the evidence in the NT, with the exception of Revelation, it appears that the NT writers were as tolerant of Roman religion as Rome was of Christianity, perhaps for the sake of winning Rome to their faith. The writer of 1 Tim 2:1–4 urges "that supplications, prayers, intercessions, and thanksgivings be made for everyone, for kings and all who are in high positions" because God "desires everyone to be saved and to come to the knowledge of the truth" (compare Titus 3:1). The author of 1 Peter, who was writing when some Christians were being persecuted (1 Pet 4:12–19), advised his readers: "accept the authority of every human institution, whether of the emperor as supreme, or of governors, as sent by him. . . . Honor everyone. . . . Honor the emperor" (2:13, 17).

Philosophy was not just an intellectual "love of wisdom" (Greek, *philos,* "love," plus *sophia,* "wisdom"). It was an inclusive activity whose aim was to teach persons about themselves, the world, and God. It also tried not only to teach persons the right way to live but also to motivate them to live rightly. If persons subscribed to a philosophical idea, they obligated themselves to live as moral persons in a way that is not similar to the academic discipline we call philosophy. Ancient philosophy was thus closely allied with religion. The modern distinction between philosophy and religion did not arise until centuries after the Christian era began.

By the first century CE, philosophers had begun to question the existence and behavior of the Graeco-Roman deities and to renew the contemplative quest for one God. All schools of philosophy had become basically religious and moral.

Cynicism and Stoicism

Cynicism was a leading philosophy of NT times. Cynicism, from which Stoicism developed, was founded by Antisthenes (c. 455–360 BCE), a pupil of Socrates. For the Cynics, the supreme goal of life was virtue. Many, therefore, ate little and even begged for food, scorned all forms and customs of society, including marriage and the state, and sneered at wealth, honor, and pleasure—except for the pleasure that came from moral and ethical life.

For an excellent, though somewhat idealized, discussion of the Cynics, read Epictetus, *Dis.* 3:22, from which the quotation below comes. To the person who asks how it is possible for someone who has nothing, is naked, and lives in filth to live successfully, the Cynic replies:

> Look at me, I am without house, city, possessions, slave; I sleep on the ground; I do not have a wife or children, no governor's residence, but only earth, sky, and one little cloak, and what do I lack? Am I not without pain, am I not without fear, and am I not free? When has anyone of you seen me fail to get what I desire or fall into what I would avoid? When have I blamed God or human? When have I accused anyone? Has anyone of you seen me sad-faced? . . . Who, when he sees me, does not think he is seeing his king and his master?

(For Cynics and Jesus see B. L. Mack 1988:67– 69, 73–74.)

The most influential philosophy of the NT period was Stoicism. The name Stoicism was derived from the *stoa,* the Greek term for "porch," where its founder, Zeno (c. 335–260 BCE), taught in Athens. The basic belief of Stoicism was that the *logos* (word, reason) permeated the universe and gave it unity, order, and purpose. Stoics also believed that a seed of the *logos* existed within humans and that by obeying the seed they could learn their purpose in life.

Stoicism was more religious in nature than any other philosophy and reached its zenith during NT times under the influence of Seneca, tutor to Nero, and Epictetus, the Phrygian slave. Seneca, a statesman and philosopher, was born in Spain c. 5 BCE and was taken to Rome as a child by an aunt who nursed him through a sickly childhood and youth. He studied rhetoric and philosophy and rose to a political career, but he became involved in the affairs of Claudius's family and was banished. Later he returned to Rome, became adviser to the young Nero, and amassed a fortune. But his wealth and keen mind aroused the envy of Nero, who, encouraged by Seneca's enemies, accepted Seneca's request to retire and sent him away. In 65 CE Nero ordered him to commit suicide. Embracing his wife and begging her not to grieve, Seneca died a noble Stoic. Among his works are two collections known as *Moral Essays* and *Moral Epistles.*

Epictetus was born a slave in Hierapolis in Phrygia sometime between 55 and 60 CE. His master permitted him to attend the lectures of a Stoic, Musonius Rufus, and later set him free. Though lame and unhealthy, he began to teach philosophy in Rome. In 89 CE Domitian banished philosophers from Rome, so Epictetus went to Nicopolis, where he spent the rest of his life teaching. His pupil Arrian collected his teachings in a work known as *Discourses of Epictetus.* Although Epictetus did speculate in the area of theology, he was more interested in morality than in speculative philosophy. If his statements on morality and ethics were mixed with those of the NT, many people would not notice the difference.

With respect to the idea of God, Stoic thought is inconsistent. Stoics can speak of God and the gods, and the term *perfect being* is applied to Zeus, the universe, and nature. The Stoics also speak of a "supreme power" as Zeus, force, cause, creator, law, truth, destiny, necessity, providence, and other things. For Epictetus, providence is revealed in the order and unity of the universe, which is the work of God. Because the universe operates in cycles, it will be destroyed periodically by a world conflagration and then created all over again exactly the way it had been.

In such a system there was no place for a doctrine like the Jewish-Christian belief in the resurrection of the body or the Greek concept of the immortality of the soul, because bodies and souls could exist only until the next conflagration.

Seneca speaks about death in *To Marcia on Consolation:* "If you grieve at the death of your son, the blame begins at the time he was born; for his death was announced at his birth; into this state he was begotten, this fate accompanied him firmly from the womb" (10:6). For Seneca, then, death is the same state of existence as before birth—not existing. "What will be after me is what was before me" (*Mor. Ep.* 54:4–5). Epictetus agrees: Dying is "the time for the stuff from which you were put together to be restored to that again" (*Dis.* 4:7:15).

Older Stoics did not believe in the concept of free will, that is, the power to make choices in one's life. Everything was destined and had to be accepted as God's will. Although Epictetus retains a concept of destiny, he also speaks freely of choice, freedom, and free choice (see, for example, *Dis.* 1:1:4; 1:4:1–4, 11–15). "The power to reason," according to Epictetus, makes choices possible (1:1:4). Reason distinguishes humans from other animals, manifesting itself in assent and dissent, in desire and aversion, and in choice and refusal. Those actions are based on *phantasia,* usually translated as "external impressions." In dealing with those "impressions" one determines one's own good or evil. Things outside the realm of one's moral purpose are neither good nor evil and are "indifferent," that is, not subject to human control.

The moral purpose of life is "full happiness" (*eudaimonia*), sometimes defined as harmony of the human will with the will of God or the will of nature. If one reconciles one's own will to the will of God, then one is not disturbed by what is beyond one's own choice. Stoics speak often about virtue (*aretē*) and about how full happiness and serenity can come only from virtue. "If virtue holds out the promise of giving full happiness, freedom from emotion, and serenity, then assuredly progress toward virtue is progress toward each of these things" (*Dis.* 1:4:3).

Duty, a key concept in Stoicism, is basically a response to right reason or intelligent acts in personal and social relations. To various duties, such as citizenship, marriage, reverence to God, and care of parents, "we must subdue pleasure . . . as a servant, as a minister, in order to elicit our enthusiasm and to restrain us in our actions in accordance with nature" (*Dis.* 3:7:24–28).

The philosophy of Stoicism, then, was far more than the "empty deceit" with which the writer of Col 2:8 identified it. The following two quotations summarize well its essence. "I am not yet wise . . . nor shall I be. Therefore, demand of me, not that I be equal to the best, but that I be better than the bad. It is enough for me to take away daily something from my faults and to reprove my errors" (Seneca, *On the Happy Life* 17:3). "But what is philosophy? Is it not being prepared for the things happening to us?" (Epictetus, *Dis.* 3:10:6). Stoicism may have greatly influenced some of the writers of the NT. In our study of Paul's letters we will see how close some of his ideas are to those of Stoics (see Chapter 9).

Epicureanism

At Athens, the center of philosophical inquiry, Paul was challenged by Epicurean as well as Stoic philosophers (Acts 17:18). Epicureanism is named for its founder, Epicurus (c. 342–270 BCE), who was born on the island of Samos but spent his life in Athens. The Roman poet Lucretius (c. 94–55 BCE) was the most famous Epicurean of NT times. He wrote a complicated work, *On the Nature of Things,* on the atomic nature of the universe.

Contrary to popular views, Epicureans did not advocate a life of sensual pleasure. To them, pleasure was freedom from bodily pain and from mental anxiety. Nor did Epicureans always deny the existence of the gods. They only wanted to free humans from certain notions about the gods. Since the gods did not become involved with humans in any way, it was silly to be afraid of them, to pray to them for help, or to offer sacrifices to them. According to Lucretius, a human being consists of body and soul, and both are mortal, so one need not fear death or punishment by the gods after death. Nature has given all that is necessary to satisfy human needs and to live in ease, satisfaction, and pleasure. The wise person can live contentedly on little. To live like this and to be free from pain and suffering brings tranquil pleasure. To attain this pleasure, humans must study philosophy in order to overcome the fear of death and of the gods.

When Paul says, "Let us eat and drink, for tomorrow we die" (1 Cor 15:32), he is quoting the Greek text of Isa 22:13. But he also reflects a well-known Epicurean theme. Epicureans and Stoics chided him when he spoke about Jesus and the resurrection (Acts 17:18).

Middle Platonism and Neopythagoreanism

These two schools of philosophy were very closely related, and their representatives from the end of the first century to the third century were a diverse group. Philo of Alexandria and Plutarch are good witnesses to Middle Platonism, although when compared to Philo, Plutarch is only an amateur philosopher.

Middle Platonists held that belief in a supreme Being is basic. That Being is the supreme Intelligence and is sometimes referred to as "the One" or "the Good." Between the transcendent supreme Deity and the world and humans there is also a hierarchy of subordinate deities. Some of those deities serve as intermediaries between God and humans; some are good and some bad. The former are go-betweens from God to humans, the latter are those that pagan cults attempt to appease to avert evil in the world. The Ideas of Plato's doctrine are put in the mind of the supreme Being. The Middle Platonists thought that the Ideas, the archetypal models behind everything that exists, were God's ideas. Evil in the world is the result of either an evil world soul, coexisting with God but independent of him, or matter, coexisting with God but not derived from him. Humans are spiritlike and dwell in earthly bodies, so the aim of humans is to make "flights from the body" in ascents to the eternal world of spirit. Middle Platonists demanded a stern morality that was greatly influenced by the Stoics.

Neopythagoreanism gets its name from Pythagoras, mathematician and philosopher, who established a religious order in Italy in the sixth century BCE. A complicated system of numbers and their symbolism was the chief concern of the Neopythagoreans in the NT period. For example, "the One" was used to mean the basis of all good, perfection, order, and everything unchangeable and eternal. "The Two" was the basis of everything imperfect, evil, changeable, disorderly. The numbers 3 and 4 were sacred, the 3, for example, because it had a beginning, middle, and end.

As with the Middle Platonists, the Neopythagoreans believed in a supreme Deity with subordinate gods. God was thought to be both within experience and beyond experience, and next in rank to God was Intelligence or Mind, and then the World-Soul. Because human souls have sunk from an original state of purity, they must endure a long time of purification in this life and in an intermediate state hereafter, but finally they will return to heaven and immortality.

The best representative of Neopythagoreanism in the first century CE is Apollonius of Tyana (born c. 4 BCE), miracle worker and philosopher, whose *Life* was written by Philostratus (born c. 172 CE), rhetorician, sophist, and biographer. Apollonius rejected marriage, abstained from wine, refused to own property, and ate only vegetables. Dressed in linen to avoid wearing anything made from the skins of animals, he traveled far and wide, giving advice to those who wanted it and to those who did not. He condemned animal sacrifices to the gods because they involved killing animals and provided meat for poor people who would not otherwise eat meat. He walked barefoot or wore shoes made of bark. He never shaved, cut his hair, or took a bath. It is reported that Apollonius healed multitudes of sick people, drove out demons, raised the dead, knew all languages, and could even understand the language of birds and animals.

These philosophies as a whole endured for centuries because they gave "intelligible explanations of phenomena" to the naturally inquisitive minds of the Greeks. They also "offered a life with a scheme," a way of life (A. D. Nock 1933a:167). This is why some teachings of Paul, and perhaps some of Jesus as well, are so close to those of the popular philosophers. For some similarities and differences between Jesus and Paul and the philosophers see A. J. Malherbe 1987, 1989; W. A. Meeks 1986, 1993; J. E. Stambaugh 1986; F. G. Downing 1992.

Mystery Religions, Gnosticism, and Magic

Mystery religions is the name given to a conglomeration of cults, neither Jewish nor Christian, that flourished around the Mediterranean for centuries. Three key words were associated with them: *mystēria* (secrets), *orgia* (rites; our word *orgies*), and *teletē* (initiation). Considering these words all at once, we can say that the cults practiced secret, sacred rites of initiation that were known and understood only by the initiates. Main features shared by most mysteries were common meals, dances, and ceremonies—especially initiation rites in which death and rebirth or resurrection were portrayed symbolically. Through such ceremonies, the mysteries assured their initiates of a happy life both in the present and in the future, and gave them a personal satisfaction that the Roman state religion could not.

The most important Greek mystery was the cult of Demeter (grain goddess; Roman goddess Ceres) at Eleusis, but little is known about the actual rites of the cult or of its beliefs. Many prominent Romans were initiated into the Eleusinian mysteries. After his initiation, Cicero, for example, wrote that he understood the reasons for life and that he could live with joy and die with greater hope (*On Laws* 2:38).

Another mystery was that of Cybele, the great mother of the gods, and her consort Attis; both gods were included among Roman deities. Cybele was the universal mother, especially over nature. Initiates into her cult were taught that they had a special union with the goddess and that they could be certain of an afterlife. In the mystery of Isis, mother goddess from Egypt, and of her husband Osiris, god of vegetation, the initiation was preceded by a period of preparation. During that time candidates abstained from meat, wine, and sex.

The cult of Mithras, Persian god of light and wisdom, became prominent in the empire after the second century. Mithras came to be regarded as the giver of life, life being symbolized by a sacred bull that Mithras caught and sacrificed. By dying, the bull gave birth to the heavenly bodies and to the earth with plants and animals. There were seven stages of initiation, each of which consisted of baptisms, sacred meals, and other ceremonies. The Mithraic cult was the only one whose membership was limited to men.

The cult of Dionysus (also called Bacchus), god of fertility and wine, was the most significant mystery religion in the Hellenistic age. Along with Asclepius, Dionysus was a very popular deity. However, because of its wild and orgiastic rites, the Dionysian cult was greatly curtailed by the Roman Senate in the second century BCE. It became more prominent again in the second century CE.

At the same time that the mystery religions flourished, Gnosticism was developing into a system comprising religious and philosophical elements. Gnostic beliefs are so diverse that it is scarcely possible to define them. However, the basic concept of Gnosticism is that of a dualism between matter and spirit, the former evil and the latter good. Since the world is matter and God is spirit, the two are separate and incompatible. The world was not created by God but by a demigod. Since human bodies became involved in creation, they too are matter and evil. But in each body there is a divine spark (soul or spirit) that can be liberated from its prison—the body—by knowledge or *gnōsis,* from which the name *Gnosticism* comes. This *gnōsis* is as much personal mystical feeling as intellectual learning. For the Gnostics such knowledge, not faith, is essential for salvation; therefore, the more knowledge one has, the closer one gets to salvation, a state of complete spiritual existence. Those who have this knowledge are Gnostics or "the knowing ones."

Scholars disagree about whether Gnosticism as such existed before the Christian era or not; no known Gnostic document can be positively dated before the time of the NT. Consequently, there is no universal agreement about the importance of the phenomenon for NT study.

In 1945, near the town of Nag Hammadi in Egypt, some fifty documents were discovered in a cave. These documents were written in a third or fourth century CE Coptic script but translated from earlier Greek texts. The majority of these documents may be described as Gnostic writings of Christian heretics.

Because most scholars agree that Gnosticism of the second Christian century was a Christian heresy, does that confirm the existence of a kind of incipient Gnosticism already in the first century, evidence for which may be found in the NT itself and which came to maturity later? If there was an incipient Gnosticism, were some writers of the NT already in competition with that Gnosticism? Scholars now generally agree that we must consider the whole milieu of the late Hellenistic age as background for Gnosticism whenever and wherever it developed.

One of the most intriguing aspects in the Gnostic library from Nag Hammadi is the references to women. For example, the *Gospel of Philip* 63:32–35 reports that Mary Magdalene was the companion of Jesus, that he loved her more than all the disciples, and that he used to kiss her often. We must use extreme caution, however, in using such references to draw conclusions about the role of women in Gnosticism and especially in the NT. For example, in several of the Gnostic gospels women were included among Jesus' disciples. Women may, indeed, have been included among the disciples of Jesus, but in the NT itself there is no evidence that they were. The *Gospel of Thomas,* a document that many scholars think is crucial for the study of Jesus and the gospels, ends with statements about women quite unlike any attributed to Jesus in the NT gospels. Peter asks Jesus to send Mary away because "women are not worthy of life." Jesus replies that he will "make her male, so that she too may become a living spirit. . . . For every woman who will make herself male will enter the kingdom of heaven" (J. M. Robinson 1988:138).

For contrasting discussions of women in Gnosticism, see E. H. Pagels 1979 and R. E. Brown's 1980 review of Pagels's controversial book; see also J. A. Fitzmyer 1980. For Gnosticism and the NT, see also P. Perkins 1980; R. M. Wilson 1968a; C. W. Hedrick 1986.

In addition to Gnosticism and the mystery religions, magic was widely known and practiced in the ancient world, as was natural in polytheistic societies. Because of their number, the gods were limited in power and could not provide humans all they needed or desired. Consequently, humans turned to magic.

The terms *magician* and *magic* did not have the same meanings for the ancients as for us. The Greek words *magos* (magician) and *mageia* (magic) come from Persia. The former denotes a respected priest like the Hebrew priest; the latter literally means the "theology of the magicians," or priests. One of the earliest meanings of the Greek word *magos* was "quack," and in Sophocles' play *Oedipus, King of Thebes,* Oedipus refers to the soothsayer as "a tricky quack." In NT times magicians were artificers who used their technical ability in dealing with forces of nature, birth, death, sickness, demons, and love affairs. *Mageia,* the ability or power of the magicians, was often used by the magicians to aid patrons against their enemies.

Philostratus, writing in *Apollonius of Tyana* (7:39), digresses on magic and magicians, saying that merchants besieged by magic attribute their gains to the magician but their losses to their own failure. Lovers especially are addicted to the art and go to these "experts." They accept something like a box of stones, which they are to wear, and the magicians take huge sums from them but do nothing. If the experiment succeeds, the lover praises the art as able to do anything; but if it fails, he blames himself for doing something improperly. Philostratus concludes that he would denounce this art to prevent young men from keeping company with magicians, lest they become accustomed to such things.

DIASPORA JUDAISM

Judaism flourished in the midst of the influences of the major philosophies and other philosophical-religious systems in NT times. Diaspora (dispersion, scattering) Judaism is the name for the Jewish religion as it was practiced in lands outside Palestine. After Alexander the Great,

Jews were settled all over the Mediterranean world. Josephus (*Ant.* 14:7:2), quoting Strabo, says that Jews "have gone into every city, and it is not easy to find a place in the inhabited world which has not received this race and not been influenced by it." Philo (*Gaius* 36:283) speaks of myriad Jews "in every region of the inhabited world, whether in Europe, Asia, Libya, or in the mainlands, or on the islands, or on the seacoast or inland."

Usually living in separate quarters in each city, Jews were united through the synagogue; but they were not isolated from Gentiles, with whom they practiced the same trades, crafts, and professions. Because of the tolerance of Rome, Jews were free to practice their religion and were exempt from certain obligations. They could, for example, express superficial allegiance to the emperor without compromising their monotheism.

Jews living in the Hellenistic world had to learn Greek in order to communicate with their neighbors. Such Jews living in Alexandria found it necessary also to have their Hebrew scriptures translated into Greek. Diaspora Jews took on Greek ways of thinking and sometimes described Jewish content under Greek categories. Josephus (*Ant.* 18:1:2), for example, describes the religious groups of Jews under the heading "philosophies." The author of the *Letter of Aristeas* (c. 130 BCE) describes a Jewish high priest as having the character of a noble and good man (*kalokagathia*), typical Greek phraseology, and refers to the translators of the Septuagint as having distinguished Greek instruction (*paideia*). And Philo wrote volumes in which he tried to show the similarities between Judaism and Greek philosophy.

Jews outside Palestine retained a strong bond with fellow Jews in Palestine through the payment of the annual half-shekel tax to the temple. In fact, Josephus (*Ant.* 14:7:1–2) says that Diaspora Jews and non-Jewish worshipers in Jewish synagogues for a long time had contributed large sums of money to the temple. And Jews everywhere, even after the loss of the temple, maintained solidarity by worshiping the same God, observing the same Torah, and sharing the hope for a future leader who would unite all Jews in an age of peace. As in Palestine, circumcision, dietary laws, sabbath observance, ceremonial cleansings, and hatred of idolatry most distinguished Jews from non-Jews. But through the Greek scriptures Gentiles who attended synagogue services where those scriptures were read gained a better understanding of Judaism.

In many Jewish synagogues there were non-Jews who found satisfaction and peace in Jewish worship. The door to conversion was always open, but since circumcision was required of all males for full membership in Judaism, many continued to worship and learn the Torah without converting. Such people were known as God-fearers (compare Acts 10:22; 13:16, 26). On the other hand, many women did convert to Judaism. Among such converts and God-fearers, the apostles won their first converts to Christianity as "they proclaimed the word of God in the synagogues of the Jews" (Acts 13:5) throughout the lands north of the Mediterranean.

Philo of Alexandria

No discussion of Diaspora Judaism would be adequate without giving some space to Philo, the great Jewish philosopher of Alexandria. The only event in his life known with certainty is his trip to Rome in 40 CE to protest against the persecutions of the Jews and to try to persuade the Emperor Gaius (37–41 CE) not to force Jews to honor him as a god.

Through his voluminous works Philo has become the most important representative of Hellenistic Judaism. The depth of his Hellenism is clear from the fact that he quotes more than fifty Greek authors, including poets and the Stoics and especially the philosophers Plato and Aristotle. But Philo's works have a thoroughly Jewish religious foundation, and they really present religious ideas. Thoroughly loyal to Judaism, Philo confronted the challenge of being faithful to his religion, with its peculiar customs, and the opposing forces of accommodation to an alien environment. He met the challenge by writing to enlighten the Greeks about their Hellenism and his Judaism, with a view to having the Greeks accept Judaism.

As with any well-educated Jew, Philo was chiefly concerned with God, the law, and his fellow human beings. For Philo the Mosaic law was the absolute authority and contained all truth. Almost all Philo's works, therefore, are in the form of interpretations of the law. Apparently his aim was to reveal what had not previously been known. Everything that is true and good in Greek philosophy had much earlier been known and taught by Moses. So what Philo had learned in Greek schools he could also find in the Torah. Logically, then, Greek thinkers must in some way have been indebted to Moses and the law. To prove these presuppositions, Philo uses the allegorical method of interpretation.

Philo's use of the allegorical method does not mean that there is no literal or "historical" meaning in the OT, although he was hostile toward "literalism." Usually, however, he treats characters and events as symbolic of virtues and vices in human life or as metaphysical concepts. For example, in commenting on the Septuagint text of Gen 2:1, Philo says that Moses (who Philo believed was the author of the Torah) "symbolically calls the mind heaven, since in heaven natures are perceived by the mind; but sense perception he calls earth, because sense perception contains a bodily and more earthy composition. World . . . is all the incorporeal things discerned by the mind" (*Alleg. Inter.* 1:1). As with the Pythagoreans, Philo has a special interest in numbers; later in the same passage he digresses to discuss the number 7.

Nature rejoices in the number 7, for example, the seven planets and seven stars in the bear constellation. Humans become reasoning beings in the first seven years of life; during the second seven years they reach full maturity because they are then able to reproduce life; and during the third seven years growth is completed. The unreasoning aspect of the soul has seven parts: five senses, the organ of voice, and the reproductive organ. There are seven internal organs: stomach, heart, spleen, liver, lungs, and two kidneys. Likewise, of equal number are the parts of the body: head, neck, breast, hands, belly, abdomen, and feet. And the face, the noblest part of the living being, has seven openings: two eyes and two ears, two nostrils, and the mouth. In grammar there are the seven vowels, and in music there is the lyre with seven strings, the best instrument.

Perhaps Philo's most extensive and interesting, as well as most difficult, discussions concern the nature of God and humans' relationships to him. These subjects are so complicated that we can consider only a few aspects here; students can read more from the works on Philo, one of history's most important and interesting figures, listed on page 3. (I am indebted to those works.)

For Philo, God is a Unity or One, the One that alone exists, an absolute Being, absolutely incomprehensible and unchangeable. On the latter point Philo finds it difficult to maintain his position in his work *On the Unchangeableness of God.* For example, God's words in Gen 6:5–7, that he will eliminate man whom he had made from the face of the earth, may indicate that God was sorry that he had created man and that God, therefore, is changeable. Then Philo asks: "What greater impiety could there be than to think that the Unchangeable changes?" The words that God was angry that he had made the creatures on earth (Gen 6:7) give Philo even greater difficulty (see *Unchangeableness* 15–18).

Because God is incomprehensible and unchangeable, Philo uses terms to describe God that cannot be used with reference to other beings: unborn, impartial, nameless, invisible, and incomparable. Yet Philo describes God in more positive terms, as in the OT, such as good, most high, great, and merciful. The two chief powers of God are his goodness, by which he created all things, and his sovereignty, by which he governs the created things.

Although God is transcendent, he can become close to humans through various intermediaries. The one Philo stresses most is Reason (*logos*), a term that Philo uses hundreds of times with various functions. The *Logos* is the highest man can go in his effort to reach to God. Powers or Potencies are also intermediaries, among which are Goodness, symbolized in the OT by the name God, and Sovereignty, symbolized by the name Lord.

Mankind is the crown of creation, created in the image of God in that, like God, humans possess a mind and the power of thinking. Unique to humans among living creatures, the power of the mind is twofold. By having a mind, humans are rational beings and are able to discourse. "Nature," says Philo, "created man gregarious and law abiding, the most civilized of animals, and called him for concord and fellowship and gave him reason, which brings together harmony and the blending of dispositions" (*Decalogue* 25). "There are two kinds of man; the one is a heavenly man, the other earthly. The heavenly man, made in the image of God, is entirely without part in corruptible and earthly substance; but the earthly man is made of scattered material that [Moses] called dust." Thus the heavenly man was not formed but was stamped according to God's image; the earthly man is a formed thing of the Artificer, though not an offspring. The man formed from earth is mind entering into but not penetrating the body. This earthly mind is corruptible, if God did not breathe into it a power of real life. When this takes place, it no longer is formed but is a soul, not idle and unshapen, but one having a mind and living; for Moses says, "'man became a living soul'" (*Alleg. Inter.* 1:12).

As there are two kinds of humans, so there are two kinds of death, "one that of the human in general, the other that of the soul in particular. The death of the human is the separation of the soul from the body; the death of the soul is the corruption of virtue and the taking up of evil" (*Alleg. Inter.* 1:33). Elsewhere Philo talks about two souls in humans, an irrational one, which is corruptible and mortal, and a rational soul or mind, which is incorruptible and immortal.

Philo says that the account of the creation means that "the world is in accord with the law and the law with the world. The man keeping the law is assuredly a world citizen, directing his actions by the purpose of nature according to which the whole world is managed" (*On the Creation* 1:3). Thus the law is a charter for an ideal state.

The law is also the basis for Philo's ethics because it is unique in being revealed by God, not the result of human impulse or reason. Ethics is the means "by which the character is improved and desires the acquisition and use of virtue" (*On the Change of Names* 10:75). "One man showing concern for good character and conduct" has sometimes influenced a city, region, or nation. This is especially true for the one whom God has favored, for the righteous man is the support for the human race. He contributes whatever he has to the common lot for the benefit of all. What he does not have, he requests from God, who alone is very rich, and he opens his heavenly treasury and sends his good things (*Migration of Abraham* 21:120–122). Philo writes that the ladder in Jacob's dream (Gen 27:10–17) symbolizes the soul on which the words of God move up and down, and then he says: "Be zealous, then, O soul, to become a house of God, a holy temple, a most beautiful dwelling place" (*On Dreams* 1:23; compare 1 Cor 3:16–17; 6:19).

From this limited discussion, we can see that Philo, the Jew from Alexandria who lived during the time of Jesus and Paul, has made a tremendous contribution in religion, philosophy, and ethics not only to ancient Judaism but also to all who have been concerned with those disciplines since his time.

Jewish Women and Men

From Philo we learn about the intellectual concerns of an educated Jewish man who lived in the Diaspora in Egypt during the beginning of the common era. Philo sometimes writes specifically about women. Here are two examples. In his description of an ascetic Jewish community near Alexandria known as the Therapeutae, Philo (*On the Contemplative Life* 3) writes about women at worship. Members worship in a common sanctuary divided into two parts, one for men, the other for women, by a wall five or six feet high. This wall serves two purposes: the modesty of the female nature is preserved, and the women can hear what is said. But Philo also says that "women too often make up part of the audience with the same zeal and resolution becoming them." Does this imply that sometimes women participated in worship in the same audience with men?

Philo (*The Special Laws* 3:31) says that, with respect to public affairs, women are best suited to life indoors. Cities are ruled by statesmen, but the management of households belongs to women, who should appear in public very little. The audacity of women who defend their husbands in angry verbal exchanges or, worse yet, come to blows with men in loving defense of their husbands is highly reprehensible. A woman should not "unsex herself by a boldness beyond what nature permits but limit herself to the ways in which a woman can help" (Loeb trans.).

For some insights into the everyday life of uneducated Jewish men and women living at the same time and place as Philo we must turn to papyri from Egypt that have been preserved through the centuries. Here are several examples (from V. Tcherikover 1957–1964).

A Jew whose pregnant wife had been beaten by Johanna, another Jewish woman, writes to a village scribe to protest the incident. He asks the scribe to come to observe the beaten woman who had to go to bed to avoid a miscarriage and death. He hopes that Johanna will not go unpunished.

In a deed of divorce filed by a Jewess named Apollonia and her husband, both parties agree to dissolve the marriage contract, that the dowry has been returned, that neither will make any claim against the other about any matter based on the marriage contract, that both are free to marry again, and that whoever breaks the contract of divorce will be liable to a set penalty. Contrary to Jewish law, this woman was free to seek a divorce from her husband, and her name stands first in the contract.

Marcus makes a contract with Theodote that she will serve as a wet nurse for Marcus's slave baby for eighteen months in her own house. She is to be paid in money and olive oil, and if the child should die, Theodote agrees to nurse another child (presumably another slave baby) for Marcus without pay. Among other agreements Theodote makes is one to take the child to Marcus each month for inspection.

A father notifies the proper official about the death of his son, who was too young to pay the poll tax required of Jews. The official requires that the father verify his report, so at the end of the document the father, a Jew, takes an oath in the name of the emperor: "I swear by the Emperor Caesar Nerva Trajan Augustus."

Eudaimonis writes to her daughter Aline sometime during the revolt of the Jews in Egypt (115–117 CE). She hopes that Aline will bear her child soon and that it will be a son. She complains about not being able to find enough slave girls to help with her weaving. She reports that "our people" have been marching throughout the city requesting higher wages and that a child has been born to Aline's sister. "The little girl sends her greetings, and is persevering with her lessons." Eudaimonis says she will not pay any attention to God until her son returns, perhaps from the Jewish riots. Apparently she was facing rough economic times, because she is fearful of "being naked when winter starts."

In an application for a lease two women want to lease land owned by another woman. The husband of one woman and the son of the other have been appointed guardians for the women because they are illiterate. In another document, a woman files an official complaint to the city official about the theft of corn from the threshing floor of her deceased husband. She asks him to demand that the chief of police make a proper investigation and keep the guilty in custody to face fitting punishment.

As these examples verify, Jewish women in the Egyptian Diaspora had more freedom and greater privileges than their counterparts in Palestine.

Because of Philo's works and Jewish papyri, we know more about Diaspora Judaism in Egypt than in any other place. Through Philo we learn about the intellectual pursuits of one Jew thoroughly trained in Judaism and educated in Greek schools, while the papyri tell us about concerns of uneducated Jewish women and men in Egypt.

SUMMARY

The setting of the NT is the areas east and north of the Mediterranean Sea. In this chapter we have focused on both the political situation and the socioeconomic and religious conditions in those lands. While those lands were unified by the Hellenistic culture and Roman government, social, economic, and religious conditions were complex and diverse; and the NT reflects both the unity and the diversity of the times in which it was written. Likewise, the first Christians represented a cross section of the society of which they were a part. In Palestinian society the greatest social cleavage was between Jews and non-Jews, but the greatest economic distinctions east and north of the Mediterranean were between the rich and the poor, with some intermediate classes in both lands.

Judaism, the parent religion of Christianity, emphasized the study of the sacred law, or Torah, which Jews believed God had revealed to Moses. It also emphasized worship in the temple and synagogues, conducted by Sadducean priests and Pharisaic teachers, and apocalypticism, with its messianic hope. The important features of Hellenism were syncretism, the proliferation of Eastern cults, and a growing demand for emperor worship.

Philo of Alexandria is the best-known representative of Hellenistic Diaspora Judaism. A highly educated Jew, Philo wrote as an allegorist and philosopher who tried to persuade Greeks to accept Judaism while he tried to be faithful to his religion in an alien environment. He wrote extensively, especially about the nature of God and humans' relationships to him. His devotion to the Jewish law was the basis of his ethics because it was revealed by God and not the result of human effort.

In contrast to Philo, ordinary Jews in the Diaspora in Egypt were without formal education but knew the rigors of life. Like people everywhere, they were concerned with daily needs, family matters, paying taxes, and the realities of life and death.

Religion occupied a larger place in philosophy than ever before, especially in Stoicism, with its emphasis on the virtuous life. It was in this religious context that Jesus of Nazareth lived and taught in Palestine and that early Christianity grew and developed in the lands of the Mediterranean.

In Chapter 1 we will begin our study of the NT with an introduction to the first three gospels, which are records of Jesus' life and work. The focus is on the origins and relationships of these gospels. In subsequent chapters the gospel writers are examined as authors, several techniques and clues used in the critical study of the gospels are presented, and the questions of who Jesus was and the nature of his teaching, as well as his death and resurrection, are discussed.

For further study of the various backgrounds of the NT see the following. For general background and the political world: E. Schuerer 1973, S. Zeitlin 1962, D. Rhoads 1976, S. Sandmel 1967 (Herod), A. R. C. Leaney 1984, A. F. Segal 1986, F. F. Bruce 1972, E. Ferguson 1993, M. E. Boring 1995, M. Hengel 1980b, 1981b, B. J. Malina 1993, H. M. Mattingly 1959, C. J. Roetzel 1985, E. M. Smallwood 1976, K. C. Hanson 1998, V. Tcherikover 1966, J. H. Hayes 1998.

For the social world: J. Neusner 1984, P. F. Esler 1994, R. MacMullen 1974, W. A. Meeks 1986, J. E. Stambaugh 1986, H. I. Marrou 1956, L. M. White 1995, J. Shelton 1988, H. M. Mattingly 1959.

For the Dead Sea Scrolls: A. Dupont-Sommer 1962, G. Vermes 1981, 1994, Y. Yadin 1957, 1971, R. Eisenman 1993, W. S. LaSor 1972.

For Jewish groups: M. Hengel 1981b, 1997b, G. Stemberger 1995, A. J. Saldarini 1988; for Philo: E. R. Goodenough 1986, S. Sandmel 1979, H. A. Wolfson 1947, C. D. Yonge 1993.

For the religious world: F. C. Grant 1953, 1957, A. A. Long 1986, A. J. Malherbe 1989, J. Neusner 1975, 1987, S. Sandmel 1969, J. J. Collins 1986, P. Veyne 1988, J. Finegan 1989, H. R. Rose 1959, M. P. Nilsson 1961, L. H. Martin 1987, R. MacMullen 1981, W. Burkert 1985, F. J. Murphy 1991, E. P. Sanders 1992; for cults: M. W. Meyer 1987, R. Turcan 1996, J. Godwin 1981, F. W. Walbank 1982; for Gnosticism: H. Jonas 1963, E. Yamauchi 1983, K. Rudolph 1983, A. H. B. Logan 1983, 1996, R. M. Wilson 1958, 1968a and b, R. M. Grant 1961, 1966, J. Dart 1988, C. A. Evans 1992, P. Perkins 1980, C. W. Hedrick 1986, C. M. Tuckett 1986, E. H. Pagels 1979; for magic: H. C. Kee 1986, F. Graf 1997, J. M. Hull 1974.

PART I

Jesus and the First Three Gospels

CHAPTER 1

The First Three Gospels: Origins and Relationships

IN THE BEGINNING OF THE INTRODUC-
tion I stated that the NT is a collection of diverse literary works. It also contains a diversity of beliefs. Aware of these diversities, scholars have tried to find a central message or unifying theme throughout the whole NT. Such scholars generally emphasize theological factors, such as the messiahship and/or deity of Jesus, faith in him, his resurrection, and other christological themes, as well as an experience of the Spirit (for different views see J. D. G. Dunn 1977; J. Reumann 1991). These are all important themes and appear regularly.

Some reviewers have suggested that I stress diversity too much and unity not enough and that I should give my own views more often. Now I shall do both. Although I cannot defend my view in this volume, I believe the single most unifying theme throughout the whole NT is the emphasis on moral life. No matter what is said about faith, moral probity is to be the end result. This is the unifying thread that is woven into the whole fabric of NT literature, even in the letters of Paul where there is so much said about faith (see discussion of Paul and his letters in Part II). In every writing of the NT readers are told to do something good or to refrain from doing something evil.

I challenge you, as you study the literature of the NT, beginning with the first three gospels, and read what scholars say about it, to prove me right or wrong on the basis of material in the writings of the NT themselves.

The New Testament begins with the gospels—Matthew, Mark, Luke, and John—which record the story of a historical person, Jesus of Nazareth, who lived and taught in Palestine. Before the writing of these gospels, after the death of Jesus c. 30 CE, several Christian communities were established in Palestine, Syria, and in the Roman provinces north of the Mediterranean through the missionary activities of Jesus' followers, who were known as disciples and apostles. The historical and theological developments of this earliest period in the growth of Christianity—the apostolic age of the church—are recorded in the NT book of Acts and the letters of Paul. Paul's letters are the earliest writings in the NT and date from between c. 50 and 65 CE. During the time between Jesus' death and the first gospel, information about Jesus' life and teachings was transmitted orally. Some of this information was later recorded in the gospels of Matthew, Mark, and Luke, written between c. 70 and 110 CE. For convenience we use the names of the gospels also as the names of their authors.

Matthew, Mark, and Luke portray the life of Jesus, including his teachings and works, in essentially the same way. Because the gospel of John is unique in its presentation of Jesus and the content of his teachings, we will deal with it separately. Only the gospels of Matthew and Luke tell of Jesus' birth, but Matthew, Mark, and Luke all tell of Jesus' baptism by John the Baptist; his temptation; a period of teaching and performing miracles in Galilee and the surrounding regions; a journey to Jerusalem toward the end of his life; a final period of teaching in Judea, especially in and around Jerusalem; his encounter with Jewish and Roman authorities; and his arrest, trial, crucifixion, and resurrection.

In this chapter we will examine what a gospel is, why the gospels were written, and plausible reasons for the placement of the gospels in the NT. We will also consider noncanonical gospels. The chapter focus will then shift to a discussion of why and how Matthew, Mark, and Luke are closely related to one another in content and in the presentation of that content. The chapter includes analyses of gospel passages to illustrate how critical study of the likenesses and differences among the gospels can provide clues about the possible historical contexts in which the gospels were written and about the origin and literary relationships of the gospels.

WHAT IS A GOSPEL?

The English word *gospel* is the modern form of the Anglo-Saxon word *godspell*, meaning "a story about a god." When it was used to translate the Greek word *euangelion*, *gospel* acquired the popular meaning of "good news" or "glad tidings."

The Greek noun *euangelion* has its root in the verb *euangelizō*, which means to "bring good news" or "preach glad tidings." Both in the Old Testament (OT) and in Roman secular usage the verb *euangelizō* had acquired a religious significance. Isaiah used it to proclaim "good tidings" of deliverance for his people returning from captivity in Babylon (Isa 40:9; 52:7; 61:1). Both Isaiah and a psalmist use the word with reference to the proclamation of the good news of God's imminent salvation. The Greek text of Ps 95:2 reads in part, "Sing to the Lord, bless his name; preach good news of his salvation from day to day" (see also Isa 60:6).

The noun *euangelion* occurs only three times in the Greek OT (2 Sam 4:10; 18:22, 25), where it is used in the sense of "tidings" or "news," perhaps "good news." From a Greek inscription dated c. 9 BCE, we learn that the word *euangelion* in the plural was used in the Roman emperor cult in the pre-Christian era. On the inscription the reference is to the birthday of Augustus: "But the birthday of the god was for the world the beginning of tidings of joy on his account" (A. Deissmann 1927:345, 347, 366).

In its singular form, the word *euangelion* means "good news" or "glad tidings." Whether the word "gospel" in Mark 1:1 refers to the whole work Mark produced or only to the message of John the Baptist that follows or to the proclamation of and about Christ is a debatable question. Some scholars (for example, W. Marxsen 1968:117, 149–150 and H. Koester 1989) argue that Mark did not intend the word *gospel* as a designation for the literary work he wrote. Matthew begins his story, "*Biblos* (an account) of the genealogy of Jesus the Messiah . . ." (see also John 20:30). Luke refers to his work as *a kathexēs*, "an orderly account." In the preface to his second volume (Acts), Luke refers to his first volume as a *logos*, which literally means "word"; in Greek literature *logos* was used customarily to refer to a work of more than one volume. So Mark's word "gospel" is a special one. Whether he meant it to refer to his written work or to the proclamation of good news that he believed Jesus had brought, it is filled with religious meaning. The word *gospel,* in expressions like *preaching the gospel,* remains today symbolic of the Christian message.

Mark's first verse is "The beginning of the good news (gospel) of Jesus Christ, the Son of God." Besides the distinctive religious connotations of the word "gospel," other things indicate it is more expressive of faith than history. Mark takes the word "Christ" as part of Jesus' name, but it is actually an honorific title that translates the Hebrew term *messiah,* meaning "anointed one." The use of the title "Son of God," which Jesus did not claim for himself, makes Mark's work even more suspect as history. In the process of writing his account, Mark created a distinctive Christian literary type—gospel—a narrative in which preaching and teaching are combined with myth and history.

Although the gospels record the story of Jesus as a historical person, they are not historical records, since they are not narratives of events as they actually happened. The gospel writers, like other NT authors, did not think they were narrating mere human events, but rather what happened between God and human beings. The gospel writers thought that God, not human beings, was the master of human events, and for them God's sending Jesus was the greatest event in history. Because the gospels are not purely historical records of what actually happened, they do not belong to the literary genre or type known as history, nor are they biographies. Most things we associate with biography, in fact, are absent from the gospels. They are silent about Jesus' education, early life, and friends. There is no physical description of Jesus and nothing about his habits, his life at home, or whether he ever married. And there is no clue about how long he was active in public life.

C. H. Talbert 1977 has defended the view that the gospels are similar to Graeco-Roman biographies. But D. E. Aune 1981 disagrees with him and defends the view that the gospels are unique. P. L. Shuler 1982 maintains that the gospels, especially Matthew, fall within the category of the laudatory biography (*encomium*) genre of classical literature. For a more recent discussion of the subject of gospel genre, see C. H. Talbert 1988 and the response by D. P. Moessner 1988.

Some scholars refer to ancient biographies (Philostratus, *Life of Apollonius of Tyana,* for example) as *aretalogies* (literally, "accounts of virtuous persons"; Greek, *aretē,* "virtue"). Because there is no convincing evidence such a literary genre, with the concept of "divine man" (*theios anēr*) sometimes associated with it, ever existed, other scholars avoid that terminology when discussing Jesus and the gospels. However, P. Cox 1983 thinks that the aim of such ancient biographies was to evoke character rather than to convey historical truth. And, according to Cox, one can sense the biographer's own feelings in the narrative he composed and that he wanted to win followers. In those ways the gospels are biographies.

The gospels, then, are a rather distinctive kind of literature that arose to preserve traditional material about Jesus. Some of that material was undoubtedly historical, but as it was transmitted it was modified. Moreover, when it was recorded in a gospel, it was further altered by the convictions, interests, concerns, even biases of each author, who adapted the material to make it relevant to the problems and needs of a particular Christian community. So the gospels are theological, not historical, writings: their authors were more concerned with beliefs about God and Jesus and their relationships with human beings than with history. The gospel writers, therefore, frequently present information about Jesus that may be interpreted in different ways. As theological works, the gospels reveal how each author thought of Jesus and presented him to a particular Christian community. Each writer included deeds and sayings of Jesus that he thought would prove useful in the community to which he was writing. But through the use of modern techniques, like those discussed and illustrated in succeeding chapters, we can learn something about the activity and teachings of Jesus, the historical person from Nazareth. We can also learn some things about the community for which each gospel was written.

WHY GOSPELS WERE WRITTEN

After Jesus' death, when the first generation of his followers was dying and memories of him were fading, people began to record information about Jesus that had been transmitted orally. Judging from the way the gospels are written and from their content, we can hypothesize why gospels in general were written. As is true for every type of NT literature, the gospels were certainly meant to encourage people who were already Christians to become better ones and to remain faithful under difficult circumstances. They were written also to serve as propaganda, that is, as a means of propagating the religion of and about Jesus as the Christ. Moreover, as Jesus' first followers began to die, there developed the very practical need for some written records to meet the demands of growing Christian communities. Such communities would want some tangible reminder of what they had learned about the person and work of Jesus.

Since Jesus' first followers were all Jews, there was no need for early Christians to establish their independence from Judaism for several decades. But as Christianity became more and more separated from Judaism, Christians had to work out their own religious practices apart from such Jewish practices as circumcision and dietary laws. The gospels helped to establish such practices. Another reason for recording something about Jesus' life and teachings has to do with the conflict with Jewish and Roman authorities that resulted in persecution of one sort or another. Christians faced with persecution could find comfort from reading about Jesus' similar conflicts with authorities and his own suffering and death. On this important matter, as on all others, Christians would seek guidance in what was written about the man from Nazareth, who had now become for them more than just a man.

THE PLACE OF THE GOSPELS IN THE NEW TESTAMENT

In the arrangement of the books of the NT Canon, there may have been religious reasons for placing the gospels first. *Canon,* the designation for the sacred literature of a religious community, had its origins in the Hebrew word *qaneh,* which meant "reed." The Greek noun *kanōn* was used for a carpenter's rule, and the word acquired the meaning of "norm" or "standard." The NT Canon, then, is the list of books accepted by the church as official scripture, that is, books believed to be divinely inspired.

In that list the gospels may have been put first because they were thought to represent a new law and therefore to be comparable in importance to the Torah, the first division of the OT Canon, which is composed of Genesis, Exodus, Leviticus, Numbers, and Deuteronomy (see Canonical Criticism in next chapter). The word *torah,* as we learned, really means "teaching" or "instruction," but it is usually used in the sense of "law." As scripture, the Torah was the revelation of God's will to his people Israel. As the revelation of God's will, the Torah was meant to be obeyed and practiced in the lives and the cult of those who worshiped God. For Christians, then, the gospels contained a new revelation of God's will in the life and works of Jesus, and as in the Torah of the OT, God's will was to be practiced in life and cult.

The second division of the Hebrew Canon is the Prophets, and includes Joshua, Judges, Samuel, Kings, Isaiah, Jeremiah, Ezekiel, and the twelve so-called Minor Prophets (Hosea to Zechariah), as Christians sometimes refer to them. The Torah and the Prophets are the two basic divisions of Hebrew scriptures, and selections from both are read in the synagogue every sabbath today as in ancient times. The gospels have several features in common with the prophetic books of the OT, which may also help to explain why they were placed first in the NT.

As in the prophetical books, the basic literary unit of the gospels is the spoken word or oracle. Like the prophets, Jesus delivered his message in direct confrontation with his hearers. Then later his spoken words, like those of the prophets, were collected, sorted, edited, and written down by those who remembered them as best they could. Although several prophets may originally have written down some of their own oracles, their works were edited in the process of transmission. Those who edited the prophetical books were little concerned with biographical details of the prophets whose messages they were recording. Usually, however, there was a superscription to each book that gave the prophet's family connections and the kings during the time he prophesied. In the same way, the gospel writers give little biographical information about Jesus, except for his family connections and the rulers at the time of his birth (Matthew 1–2; Luke 1–2) and at the time of his forerunner, John the Baptist (Luke 3:1–6).

NONCANONICAL GOSPELS

Many gospels or fragments of gospels written by early Christians have been discovered, none of which is included in the NT. They are, therefore, usually referred to as *noncanonical gospels* (see R. Cameron 1982). NT scholars continue to debate the importance of these documents for the study of Jesus and his teachings. A main problem in trying to assess the documents' significance is that many of them cannot be specifically dated within several decades or even a century or more, from the middle of the first century CE to the end of the second century and later.

Scholars who think that some of these noncanonical gospel texts represent sayings of Jesus from a tradition independent of the canonical gospels tend to date the texts in question as early as the first century and think they are very important for the study of Jesus. Other scholars argue that the noncanonical texts cannot be dated so early and, therefore, think that they have little value for the study of Jesus because, in all probability, they depended on the canonical gospels. Still other scholars maintain that there is no verifiable new information about Jesus in the noncanonical gospels and that only a few different sayings may possibly come from the historical Jesus.

Despite these vast differences of opinion about the significance of the noncanonical gospels for the study of Jesus, these gospels do show that traditions of Jesus and his teachings were still being selected, collected, and revised for some time after the canonical gospels were composed. And the noncanonical gospels also show the diversity among Christian communities as they used—according to the view of modern scholars—"authentic" and "inauthentic" material about Jesus in mission activity, instruction, and meditation in the decades or centuries following the composition of the canonical gospels.

One scholar who thinks that at least four of the noncanonical gospels are extremely significant for the study of gospel traditions is J. D. Crossan 1985. He argues that the *Gospel of Thomas* "is a completely separate and parallel stream of the Jesus tradition. It is not dependent on the inner four and they are in no way dependent on it. They are parallel traditions." There is a direct relationship between *Egerton Papyrus 2* and both John and Mark, and "Mark is dependent on it directly." Besides being very early, this papyrus "shows a stage before the distinction of Johannine and Synoptic traditions was operative."

Canonical John and Mark "know" the *Secret Gospel of Mark* (see our discussion of this text in Chapter 4); John knows it indirectly and Mark knows it directly. Both canonical Mark and the *Secret Gospel of Mark* "must come from the same school or even author, but canonical Mark has dismembered its units and redistributed them beyond recovery across his own text." *Secret Mark* and *Egerton 2* were narrative, not discourse, gospels and are concerned with both the words and deeds of Jesus.

The *Gospel of Peter* is "both independent of" and "dependent on" the four canonical gospels, according to Crossan. The "Passion-Resurrection Source" of the *Gospel of Peter* "is earlier than and independent of the intracanonical gospels. Indeed, all four of them know and use this source." In its final form, *Peter* "attempts to preserve that independent tradition by uniting it with units from the intracanonical gospels and placing the new complex under the pseudepigraphical authority of Peter."

Crossan concludes that scholarly discussion on the four canonical gospels "needs some rather radical revision." Crossan 1986 sets out some five hundred sayings of Jesus in both canonical and noncanonical forms in four genres: parables, aphorisms, dialogues, and stories. Only continuing scholarly research, discussion, and criticism will show whether Crossan is right. For a series of recent essays on the historical Jesus and the noncanonical gospels, see C. W. Hedrick 1988, and for a response to Crossan see R. E. Brown 1987.

On the following pages, whenever texts from the first three gospels are printed, references to parallel passages from the noncanonical gospels are listed at the bottom of the printed passages. Students who want to can then check out the parallels and study all the passages together. To begin, see R. W. Funk 1985.

RELATIONSHIPS AMONG THE FIRST THREE GOSPELS

A distinctive literary type, the gospels evolved to meet needs in the worship and lives of early Christians. Because Matthew, Mark, and Luke are so closely related in content, they are called *synoptic gospels* or *synoptics,* and their authors are often referred to as *synoptists.* The designation *synoptic* is derived from the Greek word *synoptikos,* which really means "seeing with," that is, "seeing the whole together." In other words, the first three gospels present the whole of Jesus' life, teaching, and work in a similar way.

When the first three gospels are studied together, it becomes clear that they are related not only in content but also in literary characteristics. Although these gospels agree on the main points in Jesus' life and activity, they often differ in the details about Jesus and his teachings. Studying some of these similarities and differences carefully and critically will provide a more enlightened understanding of the synoptic gospels.

In order to analyze some of the likenesses and differences, turn to Mark 1:1–6, in which the writer tells about the appearance of John the Baptist, and compare it with the accounts of Matt 3:1–6 and Luke 3:1–6 (Example 1.1). For reasons given below, we assume that Mark, not Matthew, was the first gospel written and that in writing their gospels Matthew and Luke each used Mark. So read Mark first and then compare Matthew and Luke.

Several differences are readily noticeable. Because Mark's account of John the Baptist is in the beginning of his gospel, he starts with an immediate reference to Jesus, who is his main concern. In contrast to Mark, Matthew and Luke have already introduced their readers to Jesus with the narratives of his birth. Matthew begins immediately with the coming of John the Baptist, but Luke first places John's coming in historical context. This is consistent with Luke's special historical interest. Luke also expands the quotation from Isaiah to include the words in v 6, "and all flesh shall see the salvation of God," because he believes Jesus came to bring salvation to all people, Gentiles as well as Jews.

Although the differences in this account may be more obvious than the likenesses, Matthew and Luke do agree with Mark on several points. They follow Mark in reporting that John the Baptist comes preaching before Jesus appears in public, that John preaches repentance, that John's preaching takes place near the Jordan River, and that John appears in the wilderness. Furthermore, Matthew and Luke follow Mark in quoting from Isaiah.

Some similarities and differences of a more literary nature are also apparent. Notice that Luke agrees with Mark in the precise wording of "proclaiming a baptism of repentance for the forgiveness of sins" (Mark 1:4; Luke 3:3). Matthew, on the other hand, has "proclaiming, 'Repent, for the kingdom of heaven has come near'" (3:1, 2). Notice also that Mark introduces John as "the baptizer" (literally, "the one baptizing"), but that Matthew says "the Baptist" (a noun in Greek, rather than a participle as in Mark). Luke does not refer to John as the baptizer or baptist, apparently to avoid the view that Jesus was actually baptized by John. Instead, Luke introduces John with the biographical phrase "son of Zechariah" (see Luke 1:5–25, 57–80). After that Luke refers to him simply as John (3:15, 16, 20; so Mark 1:6, 9; Matt 3:4, 13, 14). Matthew retains Mark's description of John as a person wearing camel's

EXAMPLE 1.1   *The Appearance of John the Baptist*

Matt 3:1–6	Mark 1:1–6	Luke 3:1–6
In those days John the Baptist appeared in the wilderness of Judea, proclaiming, ²"Repent, for the kingdom of heaven has come near." ³This is the one of whom the prophet Isaiah spoke when he said, "The voice of one crying out in the wilderness: 'Prepare the way of the Lord, make his paths straight.'" ⁴Now John wore clothing of camel's hair with a leather belt around his waist, and his food was locusts and wild honey. ⁵Then the people of Jerusalem and all Judea were going out to him, and all the region along the Jordan, ⁶and they were baptized by him in the river Jordan, confessing their sins.	The beginning of the good news of Jesus Christ, the Son of God. ²As it is written in the prophet Isaiah, "See, I am sending my messenger ahead of you, who will prepare your way; ³the voice of one crying out in the wilderness: 'Prepare the way of the Lord, make his paths straight.'" ⁴John the baptizer appeared in the wilderness, proclaiming a baptism of repentance for the forgiveness of sins. ⁵And people from the whole Judean countryside and all the people of Jerusalem were going out to him, and were baptized by him in the river Jordan, confessing their sins. ⁶Now John was clothed with camel's hair, with a leather belt around his waist, and he ate locusts and wild honey.	In the fifteenth year of the reign of Emperor Tiberius, when Pontius Pilate was governor of Judea, and Herod was ruler of Galilee, and his brother Philip ruler of the region of Ituraea and Trachonitis, and Lysanias ruler of Abilene, ²during the high priesthood of Annas and Caiaphas, the word of God came to John son of Zechariah in the wilderness. ³He went into all the region around the Jordan, proclaiming a baptism of repentance for the forgiveness of sins, ⁴as it is written in the book of the words of the prophet Isaiah, "The voice of one crying out in the wilderness: 'Prepare the way of the Lord, make his paths straight. ⁵Every valley shall be filled, and every mountain and hill shall be made low, and the crooked shall be made straight, and the rough ways made smooth; ⁶and all flesh shall see the salvation of God.'"

Cf. *GEbi* 2–3.

hair and a leather girdle and eating locusts and wild honey, but he apparently puts Mark's description in his own words. Luke omits that description of John.

Finally, Mark, Matthew, and Luke each quote a prophecy from Isaiah (40:3) as being fulfilled in John's coming; but Mark makes a mistake when he also attributes to Isaiah the words "See, I am sending my messenger ahead of you, who will prepare your way." Those words are not from Isaiah but from Malachi (3:1). Perhaps Mark made

this error because he was quoting from memory and simply confused his OT prophets. The important thing to note is that both Matthew and Luke appear to correct Mark's passage by omitting the words from Malachi.

After examining just this one section of the synoptic gospels, it is clear that they are closely related in content. Likewise, we can readily discern a literary relationship among them. Trying to determine and explain this literary relationship on the basis of the gospels' similarities and differences—for example, in content and literary style—is referred to as the synoptic problem.

THE SYNOPTIC PROBLEM

There is obviously a relationship of literary dependence among the synoptic gospels. They are strikingly similar in some places, yet noticeably different in others. The similarities suggest the existence of a primary source from which the others copied. Part of the synoptic problem, therefore, is to explain how the similarity came about. Who copied from whom? It seems clear that Mark was the basic text and that Matthew and Luke each copied Mark. However, while the likenesses indicate that Mark was a common source used by Matthew and Luke, the differences show that Matthew and Luke were not simply copying Mark. These differences help to confirm a literary relationship among the synoptic gospels, and the differences are also a part of the synoptic problem.

Trying to solve the synoptic problem is important, because the more nearly we can determine the primary text, the more accurately we can learn about the life and sayings of Jesus. We can also gain clearer insight into the way the gospels were composed. We can learn the peculiar literary traits, special interests, and theological beliefs of each gospel writer. In seeking solutions to the synoptic problem we must work with three groups of data: material common to all the gospels, material common to Matthew and Luke but not in Mark, and material peculiar to each gospel.

The Priority of Mark

The most widely accepted theory suggested to help solve the synoptic problem is known as "the priority of Mark." The essence of this theory is that Mark, not Matthew, was the first gospel written and that, in writing their gospels, Matthew and Luke each used Mark as a primary source. In the section of the gospels we just examined, Mark seems to be the basic text because it appears that Matthew and Luke used Mark, sometimes exactly and sometimes each in his own way by altering, adding, and omitting at will. In this short section a definite pattern emerges: Matthew can differ from Mark and Luke, and Luke can differ from Matthew and Mark, but Matthew and Luke together usually do not differ from Mark, at least not on larger points. With few exceptions, this pattern recurs throughout the synoptic gospels.

Matthew reproduces 90 percent of the content of Mark, or about 606 of 661 verses, and uses most of the same words. Luke, however, reproduces only slightly more than half of Mark, or about 350 of Mark's verses. Luke supplements the Markan material with a considerable number of items that come from a tradition or source peculiar to Luke (see below). In an average pericope—that is, a unit of material that occurs in the three gospels—Matthew and Luke, either together or individually, repeat the same words of Mark. Similarly, Matthew and Luke generally follow the order of incidents in Mark, and if one abandons Mark's order, the other usually follows it.

Mark's writing style and grammar are not very refined. He also sometimes uses words from the Aramaic language, the language probably spoken by Jesus and by most Jews during the NT period. Words and phrases in Mark that might cause offense or misunderstanding are sometimes toned down, changed, or omitted by Matthew and/or Luke. This is clearly illustrated in the following two passages. The first passage (Example 1.2) narrates healings of Jesus.

According to Mark, *all* who were sick were brought to Jesus, who cured *many.* Although the writer of Mark may have believed that Jesus could heal all sick people brought to him, Matthew and Luke wanted to make certain that there was no misunderstanding on that point. So Matthew changed Mark's "he cured many" to "cured all," and Luke changed Mark to "each of them and cured them." Notice also that Matthew adopted Mark's opening phrase, "that evening," but that Luke composed his own introductory clause. Characteristically, Matthew adds that Jesus' action fulfilled an OT prophecy.

EXAMPLE 1.2   *Healings by Jesus*

Matt 8:16–17	Mark 1:32–34	Luke 4:40–41
[16]That evening they brought to him many who were possessed with demons; and he cast out the spirits with a word, and cured all who were sick. [17]This was to fulfill what had been spoken through the prophet Isaiah, "He took our infirmities and bore our diseases."	[32]That evening, at sundown, they brought to him all who were sick or possessed with demons. [33]And the whole city was gathered around the door. [34]And he cured many who were sick with various diseases, and cast out many demons; and he would not permit the demons to speak, because they knew him.	[40]As the the sun was setting, all those who had any who were sick with various kinds of diseases brought them to him; and he laid his hands on each of them and cured them. [41]Demons also came out of many, shouting, "You are the Son of God!" But he rebuked them and would not allow them to speak, because they knew that he was the Messiah.

The second passage (Example 1.3) is taken from the story of Jesus' rejection by the people of his hometown of Nazareth (Mark 6: 1–6; Matt 13:54–58; Luke 4:16–30). It contains some interesting and important differences among the three gospels.

First of all, notice how the people of Nazareth characterize Jesus. Each of the gospels gives the impression that the people are astonished at Jesus' teaching because they recognize him as a member of a family they know. In Mark the people refer to Jesus as "the carpenter, the son of Mary." It was customary for Jews to refer to a man not as the son of his mother but as the son of his father, whether or not the father was still living. The best example of an exception to the rule in the OT is Judg 11:1: "Now Jephthah . . . the son of a prostitute, was a mighty warrior." The Markan expression "the son of Mary," like the one used with reference to Jephthah, could be taken as insulting or even as implying illegitimacy. (For differing views on this subject, compare E. Stauffer 1960:15–18 and H. K. McArthur 1973). As a Jew, Matthew might have realized that his readers would understand the people's question about Jesus as insinuating his illegitimate birth. To avoid that possibility Matthew changed Mark's reading to "Is not this the carpenter's son?" Luke's characterization of Jesus as "Joseph's son," the most definite of the three, is in har-

mony with his understanding of the paternity of Jesus in 2:16 and in several other places in his narratives of Jesus' birth (see also John 1:45 and 6:42, where Jesus is also referred to as "the son of Joseph"). Recall Luke's reference to John the Baptist as "son of Zechariah" (Luke 3:2).

The second point to notice in the passage about Jesus' rejection at Nazareth is that, in spite of Mark's reported exclamation of the people, "What deeds of power are being done by his hands!" (6:2) and Mark's remarks that Jesus did lay his hands upon a few sick people and heal them, Matthew and Luke apparently were not happy with Mark's words. Matthew's change is significant. There is a vast difference in meaning between Mark's comments that Jesus "*could do no deed of power* there" and that "he was amazed at their unbelief" and Matthew's shortened statement, "And he *did not do* many deeds of power there, because of their unbelief" (emphasis mine). Luke may have used another source here besides Mark. At any rate, Mark's remarks are omitted in Luke's version, so any possibility of misunderstanding is avoided.

These two passages, then, support and illustrate one argument for the priority of Mark— that Matthew and Luke sometimes tone down or omit words in Mark that might lead to misunderstanding or cause offense. Another argument that supports the priority of Mark is stated by

---

EXAMPLE 1.3   *Jesus' Rejection at Nazareth*

Matt 13:54–58	Mark 6:1–6	Luke 4:16, 22–24
[54]He came to his hometown and began to teach the people in their synagogue, so that they were astounded and said, "Where did this man get this wisdom and these deeds of power? [55]Is not this the carpenter's son? Is not his mother called Mary? And are not his brothers James and Joseph and Simon and Judas? [56]And are not all his sisters with us? Where then did this man get all this?" [57]And they took offense at him. But Jesus said to them, "Prophets are not without honor except in their own country and in their own house." [58]And he did not do many deeds of power there, because of their unbelief.	He left that place and came to his hometown, and his disciples followed him. [2]On the sabbath he began to teach in the synagogue, and many who heard him were astounded. They said, "Where did this man get all this? What is this wisdom that has been given to him? What deeds of power are being done by his hands! [3]Is not this the carpenter, the son of Mary[b] and brother of James and Joses and Judas and Simon, and are not his sisters here with us?" And they took offense at him. [4]Then Jesus said to them, "Prophets are not without honor, except in their hometown, and among their own kin, and in their own house." [5]And he could do no deed of power there, except that he laid his hands on a few sick people and cured them. [6]And he was amazed at their unbelief.	[16]When he came to Nazareth, where he had been brought up, he went to the synagogue on the sabbath day, as was his custom. He stood up to read, [22]All spoke well of him and were amazed at the gracious words that came from his mouth. They said, "Is not this Joseph's son?" [23]He said to them, "Doubtless you will quote to me this proverb, 'Doctor, cure yourself!' And you will say, 'Do here also in your hometown the things that we have heard you did at Capernaum.'" [24]And he said, "Truly I tell you, no prophet is accepted in the prophet's hometown."

Cf. *POxy* 1:6; *GThom* 31.

B. H. Streeter, who developed that theory: "The way in which Marcan and non-Marcan material is distributed in Matthew and Luke respectively looks as if each had before him the Marcan material *in a single document,* and was faced with the problem of combining this with material from other sources." (Except for the passages to illustrate the theory, I am primarily indebted to B. H. Streeter 1951 for what I say about the priority of Mark.)

The Two-Source Theory

Keeping in mind what we have learned thus far about the relationships among the gospels, we can now illustrate the first step in a diagram that shows the sequence of composition of the synoptic gospels as well as their literary relationships.

This diagram demonstrates that Mark was the first gospel written and Matthew and Luke each used Mark as a main source when composing their gospels. However, Mark was not the only source for Matthew and Luke, as Example 1.4 illustrates.

Notice that Matthew and Luke have a paragraph essentially the same, except for a different introductory sentence. In fact, in the Greek text

---

EXAMPLE 1.4   *Preaching of John the Baptist (Q)*

Matt 3:7–10	Mark	Luke 3:7–9
[7]But when he saw many Pharisees and Sadducees coming for baptism, he said to them, "You brood of vipers! Who warned you to flee from the wrath to come? [8]Bear fruit worthy of repentance. [9]Do not presume to say to yourselves, 'We have Abraham as our ancestor'; for I tell you, God is able from these stones to raise up children to Abraham. [10]Even now the ax is lying at the root of the trees; every tree therefore that does not bear good fruit is cut down and thrown into the fire."		[7]John said to the crowds that came out to be baptized by him, "You brood of vipers! Who warned you to flee from the wrath to come? [8]Bear fruits worthy of repentance. Do not begin to say to yourselves, 'We have Abraham as our ancestor'; for I tell you, God is able from these stones to raise up children to Abraham. [9]Even now the ax is lying at the root of the trees; every tree therefore that does not bear good fruit is cut down and thrown into the fire."

Cf. *ApocJa* 9:24–10:6.

---

the paragraphs themselves are exactly alike in all but three words. Since not a word of that material is in Mark, Matthew and Luke must have each used another common source besides Mark. German scholars who discussed this source were probably the first to give it the name *Quelle,* meaning "source," and it is commonly referred to as Q. Q, therefore, is the symbol used loosely to indicate the material that Matthew and Luke have in common but that is not in Mark. Q does not exist in the form of a document like Mark, and it is not known whether the Q material was in oral or written form when used by Matthew and Luke. We can theorize about its contents only by studying the synoptic gospels, especially those verses in Matthew and Luke that are not in Mark. However, it is often difficult to tell whether to designate a certain passage as belonging to Q or to another source.

The diagram of synoptic relationships can now be expanded.

This diagram indicates that, in the composition of their gospels, Matthew and Luke each used two sources in common, Mark and a source called Q. This view is known as the two-source theory or the two-document hypothesis. The two-source theory was first proposed at the end of the eighteenth century and is accepted today by the majority of NT scholars.

The assumption of a common source (Q) besides Mark for Matthew and Luke helps to explain three phenomena: the agreements in wording in material that Matthew and Luke have in common but that is not in Mark; the existence of doublets, that is, the same sayings that occur in one form in Mark and in another form in Q (see, for example, Mark 10:11 = Matt 19:9; Matt 5:32 = Luke 16:18; one saying is Markan, the other Q); and the order of incidents common to Matthew and Luke.

Nature, Content, and Origin of Q. There is no universal agreement among scholars regarding the nature, content, or origin of Q. Q consists mostly of short sayings of Jesus and longer accounts of his teachings; therefore, it contains little narrative material. Some scholars include in Q only the narrative of the healing of the centurion's slave (Matt 8:5–13; Luke 7:1–10). Others also include John the Baptist's preaching of repentance (Matt 3:7–10; Luke 3:7–9; see above), parts of the temptation story (Matt 4:1–11; Luke 4:1–13; see also Mark 1:12, 13), some narratives about and sayings of John the Baptist (Matt 11:2–19; Luke 7:18–28; 7:31–35; 16:16), and other verses here and there. Conspicuous by their absence in Q are any narratives concerning Jesus' passion—that is, his trial, suffering, and crucifixion.

Most of Jesus' references to matters of everyday life and the world of nature are contained in Q: vipers, stones, grass and trees, wheat and the granary, chaff and the threshing floor, salt, lamps, bushel measure, birds, flowers, beam of timber, loaf of bread, fish, scorpions, gifts for children, fruit of trees, and bramble bushes. Whether Jesus actually used such illustrations or whether they were put into his mouth by early Christians responsible for the gospel material, they helped to make the teaching effective for those who heard or read it. To get a general idea of the nature, content, and extent of Q, skim the material in the *Gospel Parallels* in the columns of both Matthew and Luke but not in Mark.

Although it is impossible to determine the original sequence of Q material, Luke may have preserved the arrangement more accurately than Matthew, since Luke seems to present the material in simple units. On the other hand, Matthew tends to combine material from Q with Mark and with some of his own material; and he distributes it, as he does the Markan material, so that it fits into his own arrangement of the gospel into alternate sections of narrative and discourse.

The usual view has been that the content and purpose of Q are didactic (intended to teach something). According to this view, the purpose of Q was to instruct recent converts to early Christianity in personal and social morality and ethics. To this type of material certainly belong the sayings about serving two masters (Matt 6:24; Luke 16:13), the eye as the lamp of the body and the light within (Matt 6:22, 23; Luke 11:34–36), and the sayings on the forgiveness of sins (Matt 18:15, 21, 22; Luke 17:3, 4). Many

scholars believe that as much as 90 percent of the Q sayings is religious and moral instruction, analogous to that in the prophetic and wisdom books of the OT and in other Jewish writings. Many of these sayings concern the kingdom of God and its coming, something that is emphasized in Jesus' teaching.

Some scholars have presented evidence for the view that the predominant element in Q is eschatology (doctrine of last things), especially as it pertains to Jesus' future return as Son of Man and the coming of God's kingdom. Others maintain that a prominent element in Q is prophecy. R. A. Edwards 1976a has suggested that in Q there is an interaction of three emphases—eschatology, prophecy, and wisdom (see also M. E. Boring 1976; W. Schmeichel 1976; J. R. Michaels 1976; R. A. Edwards 1976b; J. S. Kloppenborg 1987, 1992; I. Havener 1987).

Members of the community in which the Q source originated viewed their role as similar to that of Israelite prophets. They proclaimed the will of God by repeating sayings of Jesus, the Son of Man. Like the prophets, Jesus had been persecuted, so members of the community in which Q originated thought they would be mistreated until the End. But prophecy is only one element in a larger complex of thought, including wisdom sayings. Such sayings usually teach that proper conduct results from knowledge of God, the creation, and human life. Wisdom sayings in Q imply that the last days have given Christians new insights into the relationship between humans and the creation.

As with the gospels themselves, it is impossible to determine the date and place of origin for Q. Like each of the gospels, it has a theology of its own, and it grew out of particular situations in an early Christian community. The Q sayings were preserved by a community that shared the same interests and theological concerns. Since Q contains no passion narrative, it may have originated earlier than Mark. On the other hand, the compilers of Q may not have been aware of, or perhaps were not interested in, Jesus' passion.

Those who maintain that the predominant element of Q is eschatology think that Q originated

Matt	Mark	Luke 3:10–14
		[10]And the crowds asked him, "What then should we do?" [11]In reply he said to them, "Whoever has two coats must share with anyone who has none; and whoever has food must do likewise." [12]Even tax collectors came to be baptized, and they asked him, "Teacher, what should we do?" [13]He said to them, "Collect no more than the amount prescribed for you." [14]Soldiers also asked him, "And we, what should we do?" He said to them, "Do not extort money from anyone by threats or false accusation, and be satisfied with your wages."

EXAMPLE 1.5   *John the Baptist's Preaching (L)*

within Palestinian Christianity, perhaps in Jerusalem, where Christians and Jews were in lively discussion with each other. People who find the hortatory element strongest suggest Antioch as the place of origin. There, a document like Q would have been useful for teaching people who were in the process of becoming Christians, especially Gentiles. Indeed, Q would have been useful in any Gentile missionary community.

Challenges to Q. A notable challenge to the hypothesis of Q has been made by the Oxford scholar A. M. Farrer 1955. He argues that Matthew is "an amplified version" of Mark for which no source is presupposed except Mark. Luke, in turn, used only Mark and Matthew as sources. Obviously, Farrer's argument makes it unnecessary to postulate a hypothetical source such as Q to explain the material common to Matthew and Luke that is lacking in Mark. Today few scholars defend this view, though M. D. Goulder 1989:1:27–71 has argued for the "identity of Q and Matthew" because they "share the same decade and the same knowledge of Jesus' ministry" and have a common vocabulary and theology. But Goulder leaves open the question of whether Matthew is its author or its editor.

The Four-Source Theory

Notice that the material in Example 1.5 occurs only in Luke. In addition to Mark and Q, there-

fore, Luke must have used a source not known, or at least not employed, by Mark and Matthew. Scholars have used the letter *L* as a symbol for the material peculiar to Luke. Our diagram illustrating the literary relationships among the gospels can now be further expanded.

In any given verse or verses appearing only in Luke, it is sometimes difficult to determine whether Luke is editing Mark or Q or inserting material from his peculiar source. Examples of peculiar Lukan material occur in the narratives of Jesus' birth (chaps. 1–2), John the Baptist (3:1, 2, 10–14), and Jesus' passion and resurrection (22:35–38; 23:6–16, 26–49; 24:13–53).

Much of Luke's special material is inserted into the center of the gospel, usually referred to as Luke's special section or his travel narrative (9:51–18:14). Some of that material, however, is editorial interpretation and expansion of material from Mark, and more material from Q. But much of the material in this section is clearly from Luke's special source and contains many of Jesus' best-known parables, including the good Samaritan (10:29–37), the rich fool (12:13–21), the prodigal son (15:11–32), the rich man and Lazarus (16:19–31), and the Pharisee and the tax collector (18:9–14). This section also con-

---

EXAMPLE 1.6 *Teaching of Jesus (M)*

Matt 5:33–37	Mark	Luke
[33] "Again, you have heard that it was said to those of ancient times, 'You shall not swear falsely, but carry out the vows you have made to the Lord.' [34] But I say to you, Do not swear at all, either by heaven, for it is the throne of God, [35] or by the earth, for it is his footstool, or by Jerusalem, for it is the city of the great King. [36] And do not swear by your head, for you cannot make one hair white or black. [37] Let your word be 'Yes, Yes' or 'No, No'; anything more than this comes from the evil one.		

---

tains some familiar miracle stories, such as the one about the woman who was ill for eighteen years (13:10–17) and the healing of the ten lepers (17:11–19). The raising of the widow's son at Nain is also only in L (7:11–17).

The passage in Example 1.6 shows that some material appears only in Matthew, so Matthew, like Luke, must have used a separate source.

The letter *M* is used to designate material found only in the gospel of Matthew. Our diagram now looks like this:

This diagram indicates that, in the composition of their gospels, Matthew and Luke together used four sources: Mark, Q, M, and L. This view is known as the four-source theory or four-document hypothesis. Most scholars have considered this theory the best partial solution to the synoptic problem, a problem that may never be completely solved.

As in the case of L, peculiar Matthean material occurs in the narratives of Jesus' birth (chaps. 1–2), John the Baptist (3:14, 15), and Jesus' passion and resurrection. Among the latter narratives are the death of Judas (27:3–10), Pilate's wife's dream (27:19), Pilate washing his hands (27:24), and the saints coming from the tombs (27:52, 53). The story of the coin in the mouth of the fish (17:24–27) is also only in M. Perhaps a few

verses dealing with Jesus' miracles are also in M: two blind men (9:27–31; see also 20:30) and a dumb demoniac (9:32–34; see also 12:22).

Nature, Content, and Origin of M and L. Doubtless both Luke and Matthew colored some of the material from their special sources, as they did that from Mark, with their own special interests and theological concerns. For example, the material peculiar to Luke presents Jesus as showing concern for outcasts and sinners (7:36–50; 14:13; 19:1–10). There is such a special concern for the poor, in fact, that it becomes at the same time a bias against the rich (6:20–26; 12:13–21; 16:19–31). An interest in women unlike that anywhere else in the gospels is also very apparent (7:11–17; 8:1–3; 10:38–42; 11:27, 28). Jesus message is intended for non-Jews as well as Jews, but especially for Samaritans (9:51–55; 10:29–37; 17:11–19). Contrast the attitude of M in Matt 10:5, 6. For L see also the citations on the previous page.

Although some characteristics of L indicate that it may have originated in Palestine, L does not contain as much material on the Jewish law as M. Because L is concerned with the reception of non-Jews into Christianity, some scholars think it originated among Galilean Christians. It might have gotten into the hands of Samaritan Christians (see Acts 8), from whom it would then have been passed on to the writer of Luke at Caesarea, Antioch, or elsewhere.

A special characteristic of peculiar Matthean material (M) is the use of quotations from the

OT. There are three of these in the birth narratives, the first of which is from Isa 7:14 in Matt 1:23: "Look, the virgin shall conceive and bear a son, and they shall name him Emmanuel" (see also 2:6, 18). Similar quotations occur regularly throughout the gospel (4:14–16; 8:17; 9:13; 12:7, 17–21; 13:14, 15, 35; 21:4, 5, 16; 27:9).

The teaching material of Jesus is the most important and characteristic feature of M. Most of Jesus' teachings occur in the form of short sayings and parables in his five main discourses. Among the sayings are several beatitudes in the Sermon on the Mount (5:4, 5, 7–10) and other short sayings of several kinds (see, for example, 5:14, 16; 10:5b, 6, 41). Among the parables are those of the weeds (13:24–30), the hidden treasure and the pearl (13:14–16), the net (13:47–50), the householder (13:51, 52), the unmerciful servant (18:23–35), the laborers in the vineyard (20:1–16), the two sons (21:28–32), the ten maidens (25:1–13), and the last judgment (25:31–46).

Other types of material in M are hard to classify, such as Jesus' words on the law (5:17, 19, 20), murder (5:21–23), and adultery (5:27, 28), and the sayings on swearing (5:33–37), almsgiving, prayer, and fasting (6:1–8, 16–18). Some of this material may go back to Jesus, but some could be rules developed for the Christian community where M originated, or the material could have been written by the author of the gospel himself. M also contains material anti-Pharisaic in nature, some of which is in the form of woes (see, for example, 23:2, 3, 5, 7–10, 15–22, 32, 33). Again, it is difficult to decide how many, if any, of these sayings actually go back to Jesus, or whether, and to what extent, they reflect the antagonisms that developed later between Jews and Christians (see Acts 6:8–13; 14:1–7; 15; 17:1–15).

How much of the peculiar material in Matthew belongs to authentic teaching of Jesus is debatable. Many scholars have recently argued that the Matthean beatitudes (5:4, 5, 7–10) and most or all of the antitheses ("You have heard that it was said . . . but I say to you") in the Sermon on the Mount are authentic. Since some of the material is legalistic in nature (5:19, 20) and seems to be opposed to accepting Gentiles

(10:5b, 6; 15:24) into the Christian community, it could have originated in a Jewish environment in Palestine, perhaps even in Jerusalem. Its date of origin would, of course, have to be earlier than that of the gospel of Matthew.

The material peculiar to Matthew may sometimes be taken from Q material omitted by Luke, or it may sometimes be editorial expansion by the writer of Matthew. In many passages referred to above (except the parables) it seems that the writer took Q material and combined M material with it as he wished. At any rate, the material peculiar to Matthew is very similar in form and content to that of Q.

Markan Material Omitted by Matthew and Luke. In trying to understand the synoptic problem it is important to examine not only the passages in Mark that are included by Matthew and Luke but also the material they exclude. By considering omissions as well as inclusions, we gain further insight into the way Matthew and Luke use their source Mark.

Actually, Matthew omits only about fifty of Mark's verses, among which are the following stories: healing of the demoniac in the synagogue at Capernaum (1:23–28 = Luke 4:33–37); the deaf mute (7:33–37; also omitted by Luke); the blind man of Bethsaida (8:22–26; also omitted by Luke); the parable of the seed growing secretly (4:26–29; also omitted by Luke); the strange exorcist (9:38–41; shorter version in Luke 9:49, 50); and the widow's gift (12:41–44; shorter version in Luke 21:1–4).

Luke omits much more of the Markan material than Matthew, and except for the so-called great omission (Mark 6:44–8:26), the omissions occur throughout the gospel. Some of Luke's omissions are Jesus' walking on the water (6:45–52 = Matt 14:22–27, 32, 33), what defiles a man (7:1–23 = Matt 15:1–20), the Syrophoenician woman (7:24–30 = Matt 15:21–28), feeding of the four thousand (8:1–10 = Matt 15:32–39), Pharisees seeking a sign (8:11–13; see also Matt 16:1–3; 12:38, 39; Luke 11:29; 11:16; 12:54–56), and the blind man of Bethsaida (8:22–26; also omitted by Matthew). Several reasons for these omissions have been suggested. Luke may have used an (earlier?) edition of Mark that did not contain the material missing in Luke, or perhaps the scroll of Luke's gospel would have become too unwieldy. Luke may have had personal reasons for omitting some or all of the stories.

Lukan omissions are of two kinds: those for which there are no replacements and those for which Luke substitutes similar traditions from another source. The following are examples of material omitted and not replaced, with likely reasons for the omissions: introduction of John the Baptist, his food, and clothing (1:4–6 = Matt 3:4–6), because Luke plays down the Baptist; Jesus beside himself (3:20, 21; also omitted by Matthew), because it would give offense; the seed growing secretly (also omitted by Matthew), perhaps because it did not fit his theology of the kingdom; the death of the Baptist (6:17–29 = Matt 14:3–12), because it may not have coincided historically with another account Luke may have known; the Syrophoenician woman (7:24–30 = Matt 15:21–28), because it would have offended Luke's Gentile readers; the feeding of the four thousand (8:1–10 = Matt 15:32–39), because Luke considered it a variant version of the feeding of the five thousand; and what defiles a man (7:1–23 = Matt 15:1–20), because it was not important for, or would not have been understood by, Luke's Gentile readers.

The following are examples of Markan material that is omitted by Luke but replaced by material from another source: the call of first disciples (1:16–20 = Matt 4:18–22), replaced by the miraculous catch of fish and inserted a little later (Luke 5:1–11); casting out of demons by Beelzebul (3:22–30), replaced by a similar story (perhaps from Q; see also Matt 12:22–30); and Jesus' rejection at Nazareth (6:1–6 = Matt 13:54–58), replaced by a longer and rather different version and used as an introduction to Jesus' public ministry (Luke 4:16–30). Similarly, Luke omits the scribes' question (12:28–34 = Matt 22:34–40) in chap. 20, probably because

he had already used a question by a lawyer (so Matt 22:35) as a preface to the parable of the good Samaritan (10:25–28). And he omits the anointing at Bethany (Mark 14:3–9 = Matt 26:6–13) in chap. 22, probably because he had already used a similar story in 7:36–50.

Luke also omits parts of Mark's passion narrative, which he uses very freely. He transposes a dozen passages, omits some passages (for example, the mocking by the soldiers—Mark 15:16–20 = Matt 27:27–31), and inserts material apparently from other traditions (for example, Jesus' trial before Herod—23:6–16; see also 23:27–32, 39–43).

These examples help to explain and illustrate further the theory of the priority of Mark and the literary dependence of Matthew and Luke upon Mark. Such dependence can be observed not only in the way each writer reproduces material from Mark, but also in the way each, especially Luke, omits and supplements Markan material at will.

Beyond the Four-Source Theory

In addition to Mark, Q, M, and L, other sources and traditions undoubtedly were used in the composition of the synoptic gospels. Traditions, such as those of Jesus' birth, for example, contributed to the writing of Matthew and Luke. Similarly, earlier editions of some present gospels may have been sources themselves for the NT gospels. In this section we will examine only the theories of a proto-Luke and a proto-Matthew, although a proto-Mark has also been frequently suggested.

Only chapters 1–2 of Matthew and Luke contain narratives about Jesus' birth. These narratives cannot be printed in parallel columns because there are too many differences between them. So Matthew and Luke must have had separate traditions for those narratives. Taking into account the stories of Jesus' birth recorded in Matthew and Luke, we can expand the diagram of the four-source theory (bottom of page).

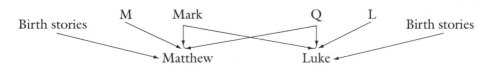

But what about Mark? Why are there no birth stories in his gospel? Several answers are possible. Perhaps the stories originated too late to be incorporated into his gospel. But the gospel of John is the latest of all the gospels, and it also lacks birth narratives. Mark could have been aware of birth narratives but for some reason did not use them. Theologically for Mark, Jesus became Son of God at his baptism (1:11), so perhaps Jesus' baptism was more important than his birth.

A Proto-Luke Hypothesis. We have now examined and illustrated the prevailing view of the priority of Mark and the two- and four-source theories as attempts to solve the synoptic problem. An aspect of those theories advocated by some scholars since Streeter (who was quoted above in connection with the priority of Mark) is that of a proto-Luke, that is, an earlier edition of Luke. According to this view, Luke used Q not in its original form but as part of a combination of Q and L. Q and Mark stand apart from this combination. Although Mark was important for Luke, the document Q + L was his main source. This document of Q + L may be called "Proto-Luke." It was a first edition of Luke's gospel written by Luke himself, who later enlarged the earlier work by prefixing the birth narratives and a preface, by inserting material from Mark, and by adding an account of Jesus' passion and resurrection. The result is the present gospel of Luke. Taking into consideration the theory of a proto-Luke, we can illustrate the synoptic relationships thus:

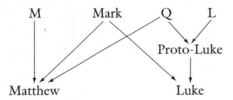

Passages that may have been part of Proto-Luke are the stories of John the Baptist (3:1–20); the baptism, genealogy, and temptation of Jesus (4:1–13; 3:21–38); the rejection at Nazareth (4:16–30); the miraculous catch of fish (5:1–11); the sermon on the plain (6:20–49); the centurion's servant (7:1–10); the widow's son at Nain (7:11–17); John's question to Jesus and Jesus' reply (7:18–35); the woman with the ointment and the ministering women (7:36–8:3); the material in Luke's special section (9:51–18:14), including much Q material and miracles and parables found only in Luke; and much of the material in Luke 19 and 22:14–24:53, without material inserted from Mark.

Obviously, we cannot be certain that specific passages belong to Proto-Luke, but those listed above show that either Luke deviates significantly from the outline of Mark or that the relationship to Mark is uncertain and difficult to determine. This indicates that Luke may not be directly dependent upon Mark. Indeed, according to Streeter, Luke seems to have preferred his Proto-Luke over Mark. Streeter believed that Proto-Luke was sometimes superior to Mark and represented a source for the life of Jesus as early as Mark and not dependent upon Mark.

The Proto-Luke hypothesis was developed, among other reasons, to account for the differences in wording between Q as it appears in Matthew and Luke, and the deviations of Luke from Mark when the two are parallel. A main difficulty with the theory is the big gaps between 8:3–9:51 and 19:48–22:14. For these and other reasons the theory of a proto-Luke has not won the general acceptance of scholars.

The Griesbach Hypothesis. With regard to the priority of Mark and the use of Mark by Matthew and Luke, the hypothesis of the eighteenth century critic J. J. Griesbach has been revived and defended by several scholars. (See especially W. R. Farmer 1964 and H. Stoldt 1980, who discuss both the history of the problems and the arguments involved. For a response to Farmer, see C. H. Talbert 1972. For contrasting points of view, see also C. M. Tuckett 1984; A. J. McNicol 1987; G. N. Stanton 1989; B. J. Malina 1992; W. O. Walker 1978.)

According to the Griesbach hypothesis, Matthew is the first gospel written, Luke the second, and Mark an abbreviated combination of both. The agreements between Matthew and Luke, then, are the result of Luke's use of Matthew.

EXAMPLE 1.7 *Agreement of Matthew and Luke against Mark*		
Matt 26:67–68	**Mark 14:65**	**Luke 22:64**
[67]Then they spat in his face and struck him; and some slapped him, [68]saying, "Prophesy to us, you Messiah! Who is it that struck you?"	[65]Some began to spit on him, to blindfold him, and to strike him, saying to him, "Prophesy!" The guards also took him over and beat him.	[64]they also blindfolded him and kept asking him, "Prophesy! Who is it that struck you?"

Cf. *GPet* 3:9.

The agreements in order and content between Mark and Matthew are due to Mark following the common order of Matthew and Luke; when they deviate from each other, Mark usually follows the order of one or the other. In short, Mark composed a gospel to meet the needs of his readers by reformulating the material in Matthew and Luke as he wished. He abbreviated, omitted, or expanded the material he was using to suit his purpose.

According to the Griesbach hypothesis, the synoptic relationships should be:

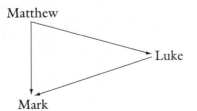

Griesbach believed that his theory best explained three special characteristics of Mark: the order, the content, and the way Mark sometimes conforms to Matthew, sometimes to Luke. Almost all of Mark's content is parallel to that of Matthew and Luke. Since Mark (because of his relationship to Peter, one of Jesus' disciples) knew the story of Jesus so well, he chose the material deliberately from Matthew and Luke. And because Mark sometimes agrees with Matthew, sometimes with Luke, he must have used both at the same time.

Now turn back to the story of Jesus' rejection at Nazareth (Example 1.3: Mark 6:1–6; Matt 13:53–58; Luke 4:16, 22–24) and observe how

Professor Farmer 1964, an ardent defender of the Griesbach hypothesis, explains the parallels. Instead of Matthew and Luke being dependent upon and changing Mark, Mark takes up Matthew's order, according to Farmer, because Luke had recorded the story much earlier. But Mark follows Luke in reporting that the incident happened on the sabbath, so he must have remembered or turned to the parallel in Luke. Mark's wording follows that of Matthew very closely. The Matthean and Lukan stories are vastly different, but Mark deliberately copied the story from Matthew, not Luke, whose order is so different. Here "the close agreement between Mark and Matthew . . . is to be compared with Mark's close agreement with the text of Luke in the preceding passages, where in following Luke's order he had to deal with Matthean parallels which were in quite a different order." This illustrates Mark's pattern of sometimes following the order of one source, sometimes that of the other.

Current defenders of the Griesbach hypothesis find their strongest point in the many "minor agreements of Matthew and Luke against Mark," which make it more plausible that Mark had Matthew and Luke before him when he wrote than that Matthew and Luke copied independently from Mark. The arguments in support of this point are too complicated for us to deal with, but Example 1.7 shows some of the evidence. Another good example is in the Greek text of Matt 9:7 and Luke 5:25, where the words "went to his home" agree against Mark 2:12, "went out before all of them."

The problem of the minor agreements of Matthew and Luke is one not easily solved. In the most meticulous examination of them, F. Neirynck 1974 concludes that they correspond to the way Matthew or Luke generally redacts Mark. However, this problem, as others, in synoptic studies will continue to be debated (see M. D. Goulder 1989:1:6–10; 47–51; A. J. Bellinzoni 1987).

In important contributions to synoptic studies, P. Parker 1953, 1981 has combined much from the work of Griesbach and Streeter. This is Parker's central thesis: "*Our* Matthew did not derive from *our* Mark. Instead, both canonical Gospels came from a common *Grundschrift* [basic document], which for convenience I labelled 'K.'" *K* stands for *koinos progonos,* "common ancestor." Parker's view is based on a two-source theory—a first edition of Matthew and a first edition of Luke. Parker's diagram below illustrates his view of the synoptic relationships. This view eliminates Q by explaining the "Q" or "double tradition" in Matthew as derived from Proto-Luke. And of course Luke's "Q" material, which is often more primitive than that of Matthew, comes from his first edition, Proto-Luke.

Another Challenge to the Four-Source Theory. M. D. Goulder 1989 strongly challenges all the hypotheses of the four-source theory except the priority of Mark. According to Goulder, "parts of Mark go back to the events and words of Jesus' lifetime," but it is "doubtful that there are reliable traditions in the non-Marcan sections of the other Gospels. The Marcan traditions were collected . . . by the Jerusalem community under Peter, James and John, which amplified and eroded them. They were written down by Mark about 70, with further amplifications and erosions of his own. There was no lost sayings–source common to Luke and Matthew. Q is a total error."

Matthew is an "expansion of Mark," and "the Q and M matter" in Matthew "is almost entirely his elaboration of Mark." Luke combined Mark and Matthew, "re-wrote Matthew's birth narratives with the aid of the Old Testament, and he added new material of his own creation, largely parables, where his genius lay." Goulder says that new material in Luke "can almost always be understood as a Lucan development of matter in Matthew. There was hardly any L." John "drew on all three Synoptists, but especially Matthew, and developed them freely." The gospel of Thomas should not be given serious attention because it is "a gnosticizing version of the Gospels, especially Luke" (1:22–23).

Goulder's drastic "erosions" of the four-source theory will have to be reckoned with. Personally, I have long ago argued that John knew and used the synoptic gospels (E. D. Freed 1965), and I have come to believe that much of the material designated L, according to the four-source theory, is the creation of Luke (see E. D. Freed 1987). The works of Goulder and those of others mentioned here who have challenged the prevailing source theories of the composition of the gospels must be continually considered and evaluated.

Remember that the views presented here are only theories, and they should be understood as theories. Some scholars still accept the traditional order of the gospels—Matthew, Mark, Luke—as the authentic order. Such scholars see no problems with the gospels and their relationships to each other, because they simply regard the likenesses and differences as developing naturally from the fact that different writers were report-

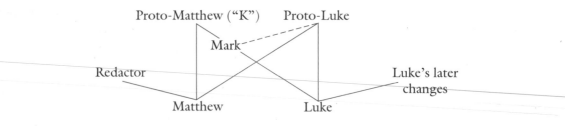

ing the same incidents or sayings of Jesus in the same or different ways. Just as naturally, also, the different writers would not always choose to report or not to report the same sayings or incidents from Jesus' life.

SUMMARY

That there are close relationships in content and in literary characteristics among the first three gospels is a fact. Most NT scholars believe that these relationships among the synoptic gospels can best be explained by the theory of the priority of Mark and by the four-source hypothesis. According to the prevailing view, Mark was the first gospel written, and in the composition of their gospels the writers of Matthew and Luke each used Mark and another common source called Q. In addition, the writers of Matthew and Luke each used a source of his own, namely, M and L, respectively. Each perhaps used other sources and traditions as well, such as the birth stories. However, an increasing number of scholars believe that Matthew was the first gospel

written, Luke the second, and that Mark is a synopsis of the others.

In our study of Jesus and the first three gospels we will accept the four-source theory of gospel relationships. However, in considering the sections of the gospels presented thus far, it may have become evident that Matthew and Luke—and presumably Mark also—were not simply copying sources but were including some of their own ideas.

There is a vast difference of opinion about the value of noncanonical gospels for the study of Jesus and the canonical gospels. However, the noncanonical gospels show that diversity of thought and practice continued in Christian communities after the NT period. In those communities, traditions of Jesus and his teachings were still being selected, collected, and revised.

In the next chapter we will use the techniques discussed in this chapter. In doing so we will learn that each gospel writer was not only using sources but, as an author, was also editing or redacting sources to convey special interests and to suit particular evangelistic purposes.

CHAPTER 2

The Gospel Writers as Authors and Some Techniques Used to Study Their Writings

DESPITE THE DIFFERENT THEORIES ON the origins and relationships of the synoptic gospels, there is general agreement that their close literary relationship confirms the use of sources in their composition. It is also widely accepted that before the gospels were written, the message of "good news" was transmitted orally.

In this chapter we will learn about historical criticism, or the historical-critical method, including the techniques of literary, form, and redaction criticism within that broad method. These techniques are used to study the gospels critically in order to identify factors—including oral traditions and written sources—that influenced the writing of the gospels. Particular attention is given to form and redaction criticism because of their value in studying the gospel writers as authors. While form criticism is used to study the pregospel oral material, redaction criticism is used to provide insight into the gospel writers as authors who redacted—that is, edited—their sources. That Matthew, Mark, and Luke were not simply copying sources but were influenced by their special interests, the needs of the community being addressed, and their individual Christian faith is clear from the differences among them. In spite of their common sources, the gospel writers, as creative authors, used those sources to suit their own purposes and concerns and to make their unique contributions to the gospel narratives.

Then we will analyze some gospel passages to illustrate the historical-critical method, especially the techniques of form and redaction criticism. These analyses demonstrate how techniques of critical study can be used to illustrate the individual contributions of the gospel writers as authors and, in turn, to provide clues about authentic words and deeds of Jesus. Finally, we will briefly consider some other approaches to the study of the NT.

THE ORAL GOSPEL

Before any gospel was written, there was an orally transmitted "gospel." In the oral period the word "gospel" was always used by NT writers to refer to God's good news as it was preached, not written. Between the time of Jesus' death and the time of our first gospel, Mark, the unwritten gospel was communicated by the apostles. This oral gospel contained sayings of Jesus and narratives about him, such as those about his miracles and his baptism by John the Baptist.

We learn about the oral gospel from the apostle Paul's letters, which were all written (c. 50–65 CE) before Mark. Paul refers to this gospel about fifty-six times, and does so in every letter; in each instance the word "gospel" means something oral, not something written. Paul writes that he is "not ashamed of the gospel" (Rom 1:16), that he has "fully proclaimed the gospel of Christ" (Rom 15:19), and that the gospel he preached was not of human origin (Gal 1:11). According to Acts, when the apostles and elders were assembled in a conference at Jerusalem to consider whether Gentile Christians should be circumcised and should obey the law of Moses, Peter told the group that by his mouth "the Gentiles would hear the message of the gospel and become believers" (15:7). In these passages "gospel" refers to the oral message about Jesus.

To distinguish it from the written gospels, the material from and about Jesus that was spread orally from one generation to another is usually designated by the general term *oral tradition*. Taking this oral tradition into consideration, we can now expand our diagram of the sequence of the writing of the gospels and the relationships among them. (See diagram below.)

A number of methods used in critical study reveal how both the oral traditions and written sources influenced the gospels as we know them today. One of these methods is historical criticism.

HISTORICAL CRITICISM OR THE HISTORICAL-CRITICAL METHOD

The word *criticism* often has the negative connotation of finding fault or disapproving, but when used in NT study, it has a positive meaning. The word *criticism* is derived from the Greek verb *krinō*, "to separate," "distinguish," "choose," "decide," or "judge." The historical-critical method in itself is neutral. It seeks to prove nothing but is primarily concerned with acquiring information. Therefore, people who use the historical-critical method act as historians and judges and try to determine the truth of the matter under consideration.

When applied to biblical studies, historical criticism involves determining the oldest text, its literary nature, the circumstances that gave rise to it, and its original meaning. When used in the study of Jesus and the gospels, historical criticism involves trying to separate legend and myth from fact; to learn why gospel writers often report a saying of Jesus differently in different contexts; and, insofar as possible, to determine original sayings of Jesus. Those who use the historical-critical method must make judgments and state conclusions in light of available evidence. Within this broad method are other methods sometimes called tools or techniques, including textual, literary, form, and redaction criticism.

Textual Criticism

None of the original manuscripts of NT writings has been preserved. However, a multiplicity of handwritten manuscripts, with many textual traditions from the second to the fourteenth centuries, has survived. Textual critics, first of all, try

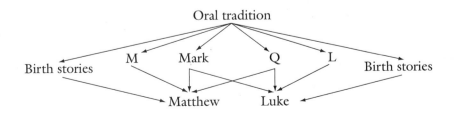

to determine the most likely words of the earliest text as accurately as possible, but always without any sure results. Why? Because such a text is actually nonexistent. Next, textual critics compare the many different manuscripts of a biblical writing in order to fix a text that is thought to be best. That text is known as a "critical text," for which variant readings called the *apparatus criticus* ("critical apparatus") are listed below the page of text. Most modern translations of the Bible are made from such established critical texts.

Textual criticism is a very technical aspect of the critical study of the Bible that requires not only a thorough knowledge of biblical languages but also special skill in reading styles of handwriting over several centuries. Those of you who know some Greek and are interested in learning more about textual criticism should consult these very helpful works for an introduction to the subject: B. M. Metzger 1994; J. K. Elliott 1995; J. H. Greenlee 1995; C. M. Tuckett 1987:21–40.

Clues for Understanding a New Testament Text

Here are some suggestions for how to gain as much insight as you can into a NT writing. We will use them throughout our study:

1. If the literary form of a writing or of a particular passage, such as gospel, letter, parable, miracle story, or some other form, is not obvious, try to determine what form it is by using the techniques of literary criticism (see below).

2. Use any references to historical persons or events to help fix the approximate time the work was written. For the time of Jesus see Herod (Matt 2:3, 7; Luke 1:5), Caesar Augustus, Quirinius, Tiberius, and Pontius Pilate (Luke 2:1–2; 3:1; 13:1; Mark 15:1; Matt 27:2; John 18:29). For early Christianity see Gamaliel (Acts 5:33–34), Theudas and Judas the Galilean and the events associated with them (Acts 5:36–37), and Herod the king (Acts 12:1). For Paul see Sergius Paulus (Acts 13:7), the Roman governors Felix and Festus (Acts 23:26; 24:2–27; 25:13), and Agrippa the king (Acts 25–26).

3. Once you establish some chronology, look for other written evidence, such as inscriptions or Jewish and Graeco-Roman literature that seems to show parallels in language and thought to the passage under consideration.

4. Learn as much as you can about the political, socioeconomic, and religious milieu of the time of the author and his work. Think of some questions. Does the setting of the writing throw any light on what the author says, and how do some things the author says seem to relate to that setting? Do the language and thought of the author seem similar to that of any other writing in the NT? Does one of the writings help to explain something in the other? Compare, for example, the gospel of John and the letter 1 John and the gospel of Luke and the book of Acts.

5. Within a writing study each particular section in light of its immediate context and in light of the whole writing. Do not take words, phrases, or sentences out of context, because words and phrases may have different meanings in different contexts. At the same time, though, the way the same author uses some words in various contexts may help to determine the meaning in another context.

6. Finally, ask yourself if there may be more than one possible interpretation of the passage you are considering. If so—and sometimes there may be—what is the evidence for each interpretation?

Literary Criticism

As the term implies, literary criticism deals with literary or written works. Originally, literary criticism involved studying literature as an expression of art forms, including words and phrases, rhythm, sentence and paragraph structure, and the form of the parts in their relationship to the whole structure of a literary work. Sometimes literary criticism is confined to the study of sources and is then properly called source criticism.

When used in studying the gospels, literary criticism tries to establish the literary relationships among the gospels in an effort to determine the sources behind them. It also seeks to identify differences and peculiarities in language and style, as well as variations in theological viewpoints. Some literary critics have combined literary criticism, in the classical sense of the term, with biblical criticism to provide new perspectives on the literary forms of the NT. Thus we have gained new insights into religious and theological impressions conveyed by those forms.

Literary criticism has become extremely complicated and requires special skills for the use and understanding of language, especially with respect to the role of imagination and symbol. (For example, see R. M. Frye 1970; basic works in America are A. N. Wilder 1978, 1982; for a summary see W. A. Beardslee 1989.) Especially helpful is C. M. Tuckett 1987:174–183.

Form Criticism

There is little doubt that before the accounts of Jesus' words and deeds were written in the gospels, they were shaped by factors that influenced oral tradition. The explanation of those factors is one of the aims of form criticism. "Form criticism" is the English translation of the German word *Formgeschichte,* which literally means "form-history" or "history of form" and which appeared for the first time in the title of a book by the German scholar M. Dibelius in (1919) 1935. As the result of the works of Dibelius and two other German scholars, K. L. Schmidt 1919 and R. Bultmann (1921) 1963, during the First World War, form criticism was established as a method for NT study.

When form criticism is applied to the study of Jesus and the gospels, two basic assumptions are that a period of preaching about Jesus by those who believed in him preceded the writing of gospels and that during this period material from

and about Jesus was circulated mostly as separate oral units that can be determined and classified by their forms. Our gospels, then, did not originate from the biographical, historical, or literary interests of the writers. Rather, the gospels are the result of the sorting and editing of the material that had come down to the writers in various fixed and characteristic forms. These assumptions are based on the realization that in Paul's letters and elsewhere in the NT there are fragments of hymns, creeds, and parts of liturgies, as well as lists of virtues and vices and duties for members of households, including slaves. Such fragments and lists were used in early Christian churches, the former in worship and the latter for moral and ethical instruction of church members. So materials in fixed literary forms were already being used by Christian communities before the gospels were written.

W. H. Kelber 1983:214 has suggested that the gospel was written as a radical alternative to, rather than as an evolution from, antecedent oral traditions. Those traditions were determined by social interests, and many such interests resulted in various traditions. But "the written gospel is ill accounted for, and in fact misunderstood, as the sum total of oral rules and drives." The gospel was written to restore confidence and assurance during the crisis following the events in 70 CE.

Proceeding under their assumptions, form critics try to determine the forms taken by the material from and about Jesus during the period of its oral transmission. They also try to determine the situation in the life (in German writings, *Sitz im Leben,* a term now used also by people writing in English) of the early church that gave rise to the various forms.

Dibelius defines the *Sitz im Leben* as "the historical and social stratum in which precisely these literary forms were developed." The situations included mission work, preaching, worship, and instruction. Scholars now consider the broader social and cultural settings in trying to determine the *Sitz im Leben* for all NT writings, not just the gospels.

The following categories of forms were articulated by Dibelius and Bultmann. Both scholars assume that an early *passion narrative* existed as a unit because preaching required such a text whether for use in mission work or in worship.

A *paradigm* (Dibelius) or *apothegm* (Bultmann) is a miracle story or other narrative about Jesus. Characteristics of this form are brevity and simplicity, edifying style, emphasis on words of Jesus, and a concluding thought useful in preaching. Examples of pure paradigms are the healing of the paralytic (Mark 2:1–12 = Matt 9:1–8 = Luke 5:17–26; the equals sign indicates that the passages are very similar because Mark is the basic text used by Matthew and Luke), Jesus' true relatives (Mark 3:31–35 = Matt 12:46–50 = Luke 8:19–21), and the question of tribute to Caesar (Mark 12:13–17 = Matt 22:15–22 = Luke 20:20–26).

Tales, types of miracle stories, are like paradigms in that they are "individual stories complete in themselves" (Dibelius). They contain more detail than paradigms; include a brief history of the illness, the technique used in performing the miracle, and the miraculous act; and end abruptly without any saying useful for preaching. The emphasis is on Jesus as miracle worker. Examples are the healing of the leper (Mark 1:40–45 = Matt 8:1–4 = Luke 5:12–16), the Gerasene demoniac (Mark 5:1–20 = Matt 8:28–34 = Luke 8:26–39), the feeding of the five thousand (Mark 6:30–44 = Matt 14:13–21 = Luke 9:10–17), and the blind man of Bethsaida (Mark 8:22–26).

Legends are "religious narratives of a saintly man in whose works and fate interest is taken" (Dibelius). They deal with the thought and life of a human being directed by God. The characteristics of legend are clear in the story of Jesus in the temple at twelve years of age (Luke 2:41–52). Legends are not meant to confirm history, but some legends do have historical content.

Sayings of Jesus are divided by Bultmann into three main groups: wise sayings or proverbs (for example, Matt 12:34b; Luke 5:39; Matt 10:16b), prophetic and apocalyptic sayings (for example, Matt 11:5–6 = Luke 7:22–23; Mark 8:35; Luke 14:15), and those dealing with legal matters and church regulations (for example, Matt 12:34;

Mark 3:4 = Matt 12:12 = Luke 6:9; Mark 11:25; Matt 6:14–15). Dibelius has a single category, exhortations (for example, Matt 5:44 = Luke 6:27; Matt 6:25 = Luke 12:22; Mark 9:43–47 = Matt 18:8–9).

Similitudes, parables, metaphors, and other forms are numerous. The meaning of most parables cannot be recovered because the parables do not go back to Jesus but are the formulations of the church.

Myths are defined by Dibelius as "stories which in some fashion tell of many-sided doings of the gods." According to Dibelius, the only mythological stories in the gospels are the baptism, temptation, and transfiguration of Jesus. Bultmann considers these stories legends and the narratives of Jesus' birth sometimes as legendary, sometimes as mythological.

Other Literary Forms. We have learned that gospel is a distinctive literary form. Within a gospel there are separate literary forms such as parables and miracle stories (see Chapter 7). The book of Acts is a rather unique form, but many scholars regard it as history (see Chapter 8). Revelation is a form peculiar to Judaism and Christianity known in Greek as apocalypse (see Chapter 15). The letters of Paul and other NT writers are, of course, well-known literary forms. Other literary forms are the sermon (Hebrews), speeches (those of Paul in Acts), religious essays or tracts (1 John, James, Jude), and poetry (Luke 1:46–55, 68–79; parts of John and 1 John).

A literary type, frequent in Paul's letters, is moral or ethical exhortation or *topos,* as it is now called. *Topos* is a Greek word that literally means "place" or "passage" in a book, but metaphorically it can also mean "topic." Words such as "exhort" (*parakaleō*), "exhortation" (*paraklēsis*), "beseech" (*erōtaō*), "charge" or "command" (*parangellō*), "order" or "precept" (*parangelia*), and "admonish" (*noutheteō*) are clues that moral exhortation or *topos* follows.

An important question about *topos* is whether the topics relate to general concerns of everyday life, such as friends, sexual relations, wine, food, relationships with others, or to specific situations, such as those in Paul's churches. According to T. Y. Mullins 1980, *topoi* have three essential elements: injunction (warning or command), reason for it, and discussion. A good example is Rom 13:8–10:

Injunction: "Owe no one anything, except to love one another;"

Reason: "for the one who loves another has fulfilled the law."

Discussion ("explanation" might be a better term): "The commandments," etc.

The following passages in Paul's letters contain examples of *topos*: 1 Thess 2:10–12:4; 4:1–12; 1 Corinthians 7; Romans 13 (see also Eph 4:17–6:20). For differences of opinion concerning *topos* as a literary type see D. G. Bradley 1953, T. Y. Mullins 1980, J. C. Brunt 1985. For many other literary forms in the NT see J. L. Bailey 1992.

Form criticism is important in NT study for several reasons. Basically, it shows that even Mark, the earliest written gospel, does not take us directly back to the earthly Jesus and his genuine teachings. Form criticism also teaches us to ask and answer questions about what shaped the oral tradition and the earliest written traditions into the units that appear in the gospels. To recover the probable original form of a saying or story, we must work backward from the gospels. First, we must determine what adaptations each gospel writer made; then we must try to discover the context in the life of the early church. Contexts included missionary preaching, a need for exhortation or warning (discipline in a community), or a need for strengthening the faith of Christians. Finally, we can surmise the original form of a saying or story and also the likely setting in the life of Jesus.

Most scholars today accept the basic validity of the results of form criticism and generally agree on the following points.

- The gospel as a literary form is not essentially history or biography. The main purpose of a gospel writer, even Mark, was theological.

- Before the gospels were written, the gospel circulated orally; so the written gospels are not personal reminiscences, and the original order of events and the original contexts of Jesus' teachings were almost certainly lost in the transmission of the material.

- Particular needs of a Christian community—such as preaching, teaching, worship, and apologetics (formal defense of the Christian faith)—and differences of opinion shaped the Christian gospel at every stage in its transmission.

- Certain forms of material, such as parables and miracle stories, were created before they were incorporated into the gospels.

Following are some reservations many scholars share concerning the results of form criticism. Form critics do not always agree on the specific forms of material or on the situation in the community that gave rise to the forms. It is difficult if not impossible to determine the situation in life for some of the material from and about Jesus that has survived in the written gospels. Except for the parables and perhaps some miracle stories, it is difficult to classify the material by forms. Each gospel writer shaped the material that he included in his gospel more than the form critics realize, because no gospel writer simply copied down material from his sources, whether oral or written.

Remember these cautions regarding form criticism when studying any unit of gospel material. Some of these cautions, especially the last, led to the development of another method for the study of the NT—particularly the synoptic gospels—called redaction criticism.

Redaction Criticism

The attempt to identify a gospel writer's sources and the oral traditions behind those sources may have tended to leave the impression that the authors' works were only compilations of sources and traditions. However, a gospel writer brought to his work his own writing style, a special vocabulary, his own opinions and interpretations shaped by personal theological convictions, his own emphases, and above all, his creative thought.

Aware that such factors entered into the composition of the gospels, W. Marxsen 1969 and other scholars have shown that form critics tended to bypass the writers themselves in their extreme concern for the tradition behind the gospels. To help students and scholars pay more attention to the gospel writers' unique contributions, Marxsen invented the word *Redaktionsgeschichte* and used it in his book on the gospel of Mark. Literally, *Redaktionsgeschichte* means "redaction-history," but it is translated into English as "redaction criticism." In the context of NT studies, redaction is editing or changing for publication. (For redaction critical studies in Matthew, see G. Bornkamm 1963; for Luke, see H. Conzelmann 1960. Their works were anticipated by those of W. Wrede 1901; R. H. Lightfoot 1934; N. Perrin 1969.)

Redaction criticism accepts the assumptions of the four-source theory and form criticism, but it goes beyond them by trying to determine how the gospel writers used the materials they had at hand. Redaction criticism also tries to understand why gospel writers wrote as they did and to learn what material they added to their compositions. Redaction critics are concerned with what a writer includes, excludes, and changes of the sources and traditions known to him, rather than with the forms, sources, and traditions themselves. They ask such questions as these: Why does Mark emphasize the passion of Jesus so much? Why is Luke's quotation from Isaiah longer than that in his source Mark (Mark 1:3; Luke 3:4–6) when Luke is reporting about John the Baptist? Why does Matthew report the appearance of the resurrected Jesus only in Galilee and Luke only in and near Jerusalem? In raising and answering questions like these, redaction critics have shown how the gospel writers altered their sources and shaped the traditions they were using, as well as how their special interests, theological viewpoints, and even biases influenced what and how they wrote. (For a critical discussion of the problems involved in form and redaction criticism, see E. Guettgemanns 1979.) The best way to understand the historical-critical method, especially the techniques of literary, form, and redaction criticism, is to analyze several passages as critical scholars do.

ANALYSES OF PASSAGES

Example 2.1 contains excerpts from Jesus' Sermon on the Mount, known in Luke's gospel as the Sermon on the Plain. Observe the following differences. The sermon takes place on a mountain only in Matthew and is recorded before the call of the twelve disciples (Matt 10:1–4). On the other hand, Luke says that Jesus "stood on a level place" (6:17) after he came down from the hills where he had chosen the twelve apostles. Luke (6:12–16) follows Mark (3:13–19) in saying that Jesus went into the hills where the twelve were selected and named, but Matthew does not. So both the setting of Jesus' teaching in this passage and its place in the gospel differ in Matthew and Luke. Matthew makes the "sermon" (5–7) the first of his five major discourses of Jesus, whereas Luke, who usually distributes teaching material and frequently adds some of it to a section from Mark, adds material to Mark.

Since the first passage occurs in both Matthew and Luke but not in Mark, it comes from the source Q. The form of the teaching is a beatitude, a rather common type of teaching in Jewish literature. By looking closely at the language of the first verse, we can see two important differences between the two versions, both of which are reported as words of Jesus. Matthew has "poor in spirit"; Luke has "you who are poor." But what does Matthew mean by "poor in spirit"? Humble? Downcast? Contrite? A spirit or an attitude that is not good? We cannot be certain what Matthew means. On the other hand, the meaning of Luke's "poor" is certain—without money or possessions, not wealthy. Notice also that Matthew's version is in the third person, Luke's in the second person. Form and redaction critics would try to figure out what the original words of the saying in Q were and what Jesus himself really said.

EXAMPLE 2.1	*Teachings in the Sermon on the Mount (Plain)*

Matt 5:3, 6	Mark	Luke 6:20–21
[3]"Blessed are the poor in spirit, for theirs is the kingdom of heaven." [6]"Blessed are those who hunger and thirst for righteousness, for they will be filled."		[20] "Blessed are you who are poor, for yours is the kingdom of God. [21] Blessed are you who are hungry now, for you will be filled."

Matt	Mark	Luke 6:24–26

		[24] "But woe to you who are rich,
		    for you have received your consolation.
		[25] Woe to you who are full now,
		    for you will be hungry.
		Woe to you who are laughing now,
		    for you will mourn and weep.
		[26]Woe to you when all speak well of you, for that is what their ancestors did to the false prophets."

Cf. *GThom* 54; 69b.

Although it is impossible to answer these questions fully, several answers may be suggested. Since Jewish beatitudes were usually formulated in the third person, Matthew's third person may be original. Luke's shifts to the second person in vv 20 and 21 would then be his own doing to make them conform to the second person (in v 22) where Matthew (v 11) also has the second person. This was probably the original form of the saying in Q. Yet Luke's regular style is to have Jesus address his hearers in the second person.

Many commentators think that Luke's "poor" is more original than Matthew's, and that Matthew sees the poor in the source not just as impoverished and humble, but also perhaps as oppressed. Therefore, Matthew, and perhaps Jesus himself, had in mind a class of people whom the psalmists of the OT refer to as *ani'im* or *anawim*. This word represents a plural form of the Hebrew word meaning "poor," "humble," or "afflicted"—see, for example, Pss 10:8–12; 34:2; 35:10; 140:12. However, evidence elsewhere in Luke's gospel indicates that the author has a special interest in the poor and the rich, perhaps even a bias in favor of the poor and against the rich. Notice that in the second passage of Example 2.1 (only Luke 6:24–26) Luke adds a series of woes that are in sharp contrast to the beatitudes. Luke is not content just to report Jesus' words as "Blessed are you who are poor"; he also reports Jesus as saying, "But woe to you who are rich." Luke's special interest in the poor and the rich is clear also from his much more frequent use of the words "poor" (ten times; Mark, five; Matt, five) and "rich" (eleven times; Mark, two; Matt, three), and only Luke uses the verb "to be rich" (twice).

In the preceding chapter we learned that the peculiar Lukan material (L) shows a special interest in the poor and the rich. Only there do we find the parable of the rich fool (12:13–21), the story of the rich man and Lazarus (16:19–31), and the rich tax collector named Zacchaeus (19:1–10; see also 4:18; 14:12, 13; 16:1). But Luke's special interest in the poor and the rich is evident not only in his special source, but also in the way Luke treats his sources Mark and Q.

Now look at Example 2.2, which presents excerpts from the story of the rich man who asked Jesus what he should do to inherit eternal life. The words in quotation marks are Jesus' reply to the man. Notice that Jesus' command to sell "what you own" in Mark and "your possessions" in Matthew—which is the same thing—is a command to sell "all that you own" in Luke. "All" makes Jesus' command more demanding; it is absolute (see Luke 5:11: "They left everything and followed him"). And Luke's "distribute" implies a greater dissemination of the riches than Mark's "give" (followed by Matthew). The description "he had many possessions" in Mark (also Matthew) becomes "he was very rich" in Luke.

In the verses following those in Example 2.2, Jesus addresses the rich man directly in Luke ("Jesus looked at him") when he says, "How hard it is for those who have wealth to enter the kingdom of God!" and "It is easier for a camel to go through the eye of a needle than for someone who is rich to enter the kingdom of God." This direct address is characteristic of Luke. In Mark (also Matthew) those sayings are addressed to the disciples, not to the rich man. Notice also that the word "perfect" in Matt 19:21 is probably Matthew's own touch added to Jesus' speech, because the thought expressed corresponds exactly to that in Matt 5:48: "Be per-

fect." The word "perfect" is a Matthean word and occurs nowhere in Mark or Luke.

Two passages from Q show Luke's work as an author. The first (Example 2.3) is from the parable of the marriage feast (Matt 22:1–10) or the great banquet (Luke 14:15–24). In Matthew the invitation to the meal is inclusive, "everyone you find," but in Luke it is limited to the handicapped, including the poor. In the second passage from Q (Example 2.4), which is Jesus' reply to John the Baptist's disciples, the poor are included in Matthew's version, "the poor have good news brought to them" (Matt 11:5 = Luke 7:22), as they are in Luke's version. So here Luke apparently did not need to alter his source Q.

While in the peculiar Lukan source (L) the special interest in the rich and the poor seems really to be a bias in favor of the poor and against the rich, Luke himself has revealed that special interest in the way he works with his sources Mark and Q. Therefore, we suspect that as an author Luke may have permitted his bias to influence what he wrote about the rich and poor when he was using and reporting material from his peculiar source L.

Now turn again to the beatitudes. With respect to the first beatitude, there is probably no difference in meaning between Matthew's "kingdom of heaven" and Luke's "kingdom of God," a concept never explicitly defined in any gospel. Luke always uses "kingdom of God," never "kingdom of heaven." Except for Matt 12:28;

EXAMPLE 2.2   *Excerpts from Story of the Rich Man*

Matt 19:21	Mark 10:21	Luke 18:22
[21]Jesus said to him, "If you wish to be perfect, go, sell your possessions, and give the money to the poor, and you will have treasure in heaven; then come, follow me."	[21]Jesus, looking at him, loved him and said, "You lack one thing; go, sell what you own, and give the money to the poor, and you will have treasure in heaven; then come, follow me."	[22]When Jesus heard this, he said to him, "There is still one thing lacking. Sell all that you own and distribute the money to the poor, and you will have treasure in heaven; then come, follow me."

Cf. *GNaz* 16.

EXAMPLE 2.3	*Excerpt from Parable of the Marriage Feast*	
Matt 22:9	**Mark**	**Luke 14:21**
9'Go therefore into the main streets, and invite everyone you find to the wedding banquet.'		21'Go out at once into the streets and lanes of the town and bring in the poor, the crippled, the blind, and the lame.'

Cf. *GThom* 64.

EXAMPLE 2.4	*Jesus' Reply to John the Baptist's Disciples*	
Matt 11:4–6	**Mark**	**Luke 7:22–23**
4Jesus answered them, "Go and tell John what you hear and see: 5the blind receive their sight, the lame walk, the lepers are cleansed, the deaf hear, the dead are raised, and the poor have good news brought to them. 6And blessed is anyone who takes no offense at me."		22And he answered them, "Go and tell John what you have seen and heard: the blind receive their sight, the lame walk, the lepers are cleansed, the deaf hear, the dead are raised, the poor have good news brought to them. 23And blessed is anyone who takes no offense at me."

19:24; and 21:31, 43, Matthew always uses the latter expression. Matthew's "heaven" is probably a substitute for God, in accordance with the Jewish practice of avoiding the utterance of the divine name. Luke, a Gentile, did not share that practice, so he would not hesitate to mention the word *God*. In this respect he may be following the style of Mark, who always uses "kingdom of God."

With respect to the second beatitude in Example 2.1 (Matt 5:6 and Luke 6:21), the meaning of Matthew's "hunger and thirst for righteousness" is again uncertain. Perhaps, as with "poor in spirit," the words are intended to imply a spiritual condition. On the other hand, it is quite clear that with Luke's words a physical condition of hunger is meant. The word "righteousness" is a Matthean touch—it does not occur in Mark and occurs only once in Luke (1:75). Matthew uses it five times in the Sermon on the Mount (5:6, 10, 20; 6:1, 33); its use is probably due to Matthew himself, or even to his source M and the tradition behind it, rather than to Jesus.

Matthew also inserts the word "righteousness" into his sources Mark and Q, as the texts presented in Examples 2.5 and 2.6 show.

Example 2.5 presents Jesus' words concerning cares about earthly things as reported in a Q passage. These two beatitudes, which apparently stemmed from Q, are reported as words of Jesus in the form of a beatitude but are stated in accordance with each writer's special interests. Although a traditional form (beatitude) of Jesus' saying has been preserved, in each case its original meaning has been lost, so it is impossible to determine what Jesus really said.

In the story of Jesus' baptism (Example 2.6), Mark is again the basic text. The word "immediately" (1:10; Greek text), a favorite of Mark's (forty-one times; Matt, five; Luke, one) here copied by Matthew ("suddenly" in *NRSV*), shows Mark's editorial hand. When the accounts of Matthew and Luke are compared with Mark there are agreements and differences. They agree with Mark on these points: Jesus was baptized, the heavens opened, the Spirit descended, and a

---

EXAMPLE 2.5   *Teaching of Jesus*

Matt 6:33	Mark	Luke 12:31
[33]"But strive first for the kingdom of God and his righteousness, and all these things will be given to you as well."		[31]"Instead, strive for his kingdom, and these things will be given to you as well."

EXAMPLE 2.6   *Story of Jesus' Baptism*

Matt 3:13–17	Mark 1:9–11	Luke 3:21–22
[13]Then Jesus came from Galilee to John at the Jordan, to be baptized by him. [14]John would have prevented him, saying, "I need to be baptized by you, and do you come to me?" [15]But Jesus answered him, "Let it be so now; for it is proper for us in this way to fulfill all righteousness." Then he consented. [16]And when Jesus had been baptized, just as he came up from the water, suddenly the heavens were opened to him and he saw the Spirit of God descending like a dove and alighting on him. [17]And a voice from heaven said, "This is my Son, the Beloved, with whom I am well pleased."	[9]In those days Jesus came from Nazareth of Galilee and was baptized by John in the Jordan. [10]And just as he was coming up out of the water, he saw the heavens torn apart and the Spirit descending like a dove on him. [11]And a voice came from heaven, "You are my Son, the Beloved; with you I am well pleased."	[21]Now when all the people were baptized, and when Jesus also had been baptized and was praying, the heaven was opened, [22]and the Holy Spirit descended upon him in bodily form like a dove. And a voice came from heaven, "You are my Son, the Beloved; with you I am well pleased."

Cf. *GNaz* 2; *GHeb* 2; *GEbi* 4.

---

voice spoke. But Matthew and Luke differ on every point. Matthew agrees with Mark in saying that Jesus came from Galilee, but he omits Nazareth, and Luke omits the geographical reference. Mark and Matthew locate the scene at "the Jordan." Although Matthew and Luke agree with Mark in saying that Jesus was baptized, they do not say "by John." For Mark's "the Spirit," Matthew has "the Spirit of God" and Luke has "the Holy Spirit," his characteristic expression for the phenomenon. To Mark's "like a dove," Matthew adds "and alighting on him" and Luke has "in bodily form." Among differences in the Greek text, not noticeable in English, is the word for "opened," which is the same in Matthew and Luke (*anoigō*) against Mark (*schizō*; lit., "to rend" or "tear"). Matthew has a different word for "came" (3:13) than Mark (1:9). Matthew has the word *hōsei* for "as" instead of Mark's *hōs*, which is retained by Luke in the phrase "like (as) a dove." And Luke retains Mark's "You are," whereas Matthew has "This is" ("this" is Matthew's favorite demonstrative pronoun).

One of Luke's special interests evident here is Jesus at prayer. Whereas Matthew agrees with Mark in saying that the Spirit came upon Jesus after he got out of the water, Luke says the Spirit came upon Jesus as he "was praying." In Mark all aspects of the religious experience are confined to Jesus himself. In this way Mark keeps Jesus' messianic identity a secret that only the readers know. Only Jesus sees the Spirit descending upon him like a dove, and only he hears the voice. Matthew follows Mark in the first instance, and Luke follows Mark in the second. Look carefully, and you will notice other differences in the texts. Now consider the theological implications of the passage, especially Matthew's addition in vv 14–15.

The story of Jesus' baptism has been regarded as legend, myth, and historical fact. Regardless of which is correct, the story was composed under the influence of the OT and contemporary Jewish ideas either by Mark or, perhaps to some extent, by the author of his source. In v 10 Mark's Greek is "he saw the heavens torn apart," which echoes the prayer of Isa 64:1: "O that you [God] would tear open [LXX, "open"; so Matthew and Luke] the heavens and come down." The Spirit descending reflects the idea of God putting his Spirit in the midst of the Israelites during the Exodus (Isa 63:11, 14). Usually in the OT the Spirit was given for someone to do a specific task; for example, "The spirit of the Lord came upon him [Othniel], and he judged Israel" (Judg 3:10; see also 6:34; 2 Kgs 2:9). Such texts no doubt helped shape the tradition of Jesus' baptism.

Mark reports exactly what was believed would happen to the Messiah. In Mark 1:2–3 he quotes passages from the OT to show that a forerunner would precede the Messiah; now he alludes to other ideas current in messianic thought. John the Baptist exits from the stage, and Jesus becomes the focus of attention. Messianic expectations are fulfilled in Jesus through the power of God manifested by his Spirit. According to *T. Levi* 18:1–6, when the Lord (God) raises up the new priest (Messiah), "all the words of the Lord shall be revealed to him. . . . The heavens shall be opened, and . . . sanctification shall come upon him with the Father's voice. . . ." "And the heavens shall be opened to him [Messiah] to pour out the Spirit as a blessing of the Holy Father" (*T. Judah* 24:1; see also Isa 42:1). According to Mark 1:4, John came "proclaiming a baptism of repentance for the forgiveness of sins." The readers of Mark might therefore assume that Jesus, like others, came to John to be baptized for forgiveness. But the Messiah was to be "pure from sins" (*Pss. Sol.* 17:41). Mark's report that Jesus submitted to John's baptism for the forgiveness of sins caused an embarrassing problem in the early church.

Now look at Matthew's account. Matthew may have composed vv 14–15 to meet the question concerning the sins or sinlessness of Jesus. The passage shows Matthew's editorial hand at work with one of his favorite words, "righteousness." Moreover, the word "prevented" occurs only here in the NT, and the word "proper" occurs nowhere else in the gospels. The words "saying," "answered," "now," "fulfill," "then," and "consented" are all characteristic of Matthew's linguistic style. According to Matt 3:13, Jesus came to John wanting to be baptized, as the expression "to be baptized" makes clear. Jesus' wanting to be baptized is in accord with the theological explanation Matthew put in Jesus' words in v 15. The meaning of the words "to fulfill all righteousness," although known to Matthew and perhaps to his readers, is unknown to us. But by that explanation, by Jesus wanting to be baptized, and by John consenting, Matthew presents Jesus as the best possible example to motivate and support baptism in the church of Matthew's time. John's hesitation before baptizing Jesus is an acknowledgment of Jesus' superiority to John, something John had previously admitted: "The one who is more powerful than I is coming after me" (Mark 1:7 = Matt 3:11 = Luke 3:16).

By not mentioning John's name and by barely referring to the act of Jesus' baptism, Luke emphasizes only Jesus. He focuses attention on Jesus' praying and on the coming of the Holy Spirit (see 1:34, 41; 2:25; 4:1; 10:21; 11:13; 12:12)—two Lukan special interests. In the OT and elsewhere the dove is a symbol of Israel (Hos 11:11; Pss 68:13; 74:19; 2 Esdr 5:26). Is it likely, as some have suggested, that the dove, especially for Luke, represents the Christian community as the new Israel? Luke's words "bodily form" would then stress the reality of the Spirit in the community in which Jesus is God's representative as Son of God.

This partial analysis shows that, in reporting what may have been a historical incident in Jesus' life, each gospel writer shaped the written narrative with his own literary style and theological concerns. Perhaps even before Mark the tradition had been shaped by the Jewish ideas alluded to in Mark.

We turn now to a more difficult passage in order to illustrate further how the gospel writers acted as authors. The excerpts in Example 2.7 give the reason for Jesus' speaking in parables. On the assumption that Mark believed Jesus taught in parables in order to help his hearers understand his message about the kingdom of God and be forgiven, this passage has caused difficulty for interpreters. Here Mark clearly reports that Jesus says he speaks in parables "in order that 'they may indeed look, but not perceive, and may indeed listen, but not understand; so that they may not turn again and be forgiven.'" For the very reason that Jesus' saying contradicts what Mark himself believed about Jesus, according to an older interpretation of the passage, it was regarded as an authentic saying of Jesus. In other words, even though Jesus' saying contradicted Mark's own view of Jesus, Mark nevertheless reported it because it was an authentic saying.

According to Mark, it is clear that Jesus speaks in parables to prevent those outside the inner circle from being forgiven. The Greek construction beginning with "in order that" is a purpose clause expressed by the Greek conjunction *hina* (a three-letter word in Greek) plus the subjunc-

---

EXAMPLE 2.7   *Reason for Jesus' Speaking in Parables*

Matt 13:10–14	Mark 4:10–12	Luke 8:9–10
[10]Then the disciples came and asked him, "Why do you speak to them in parables?" [11]He answered, "To you it has been given to know the secrets of the kingdom of heaven, but to them it has not been given. [12]For to those who have, more will be given, and they will have an abundance; but from those who have nothing, even what they have will be taken away. [13]The reason I speak to them in parables is that 'seeing they do not perceive, and hearing they do not listen, nor do they understand.' [14]With them indeed is fulfilled the prophecy of Isaiah that says:"	[10]When he was alone, those who were around him along with the twelve asked him about the parables. [11]And he said to them, "To you has been given the secret of the kingdom of God, but for those outside, everything comes in parables; [12]in order that 'they may indeed look, but not perceive, and may indeed listen, but not understand; so that they may not turn again and be forgiven.'"	[9]Then his disciples asked him what this parable meant. [10]He said, "To you it has been given to know the secrets of the kingdom of God; but to others I speak in parables, so that 'looking they may not perceive, and listening they may not understand.'"

Cf. *GThom* 41; *ApocJa* 7:1–10; 8:24–27.

tive mood. Matthew clearly did not want to convey Mark's view to his readers, so he changed Mark's purpose clause to one of cause by using a different three-letter word (*hoti*) with the indicative mood. In doing so, Matthew shifts the reason for the people not perceiving and being forgiven from Jesus to the people themselves—"is that 'seeing, *they* [emphasis mine] do not perceive,'" and so on. Moreover, by being that way the people are fulfilling a prophecy of Isaiah (6:9–10). Remember that the fulfillment of OT prophecy is one of Matthew's special interests.

Mark 4:12 is also an allusion to Isaiah 6:9–10, part of the record of Isaiah's vision in which he received God's call to become a prophet. The purpose and the result of Isaiah's work are blended into one present reality: Isaiah's hearers hear but do not understand; they see but do not perceive. Since purpose and result can be expressed grammatically in the same way in Hebrew, some commentators have explained Mark 4:12 by saying that Mark has stated the result of Jesus' teaching in parables as the purpose of the teaching.

Although some scholars accept the saying as authentic (for example, T. W. Manson 1945:76–80), perhaps most believe that the whole of Mark 4:10–12 is an editorial compilation for two main reasons. First, the question in v 10 concerns the parables in general, whereas the one in Mark 4:13 (not printed) presumes the parable of the sower just told. So the original question in Mark's source must have been similar to the one in Luke 8:9, and the original questioners in Mark's source probably were either "those who

were around him" or "the twelve." One or the other group of questioners and the clause "when he was alone" derive from Mark himself.

Second, vv 11–12 do not represent the thought of Jesus. Rather, they either represent the thought of the early church behind the source Mark used, or they convey the thought of Mark himself. E. Schweizer 1976:92–94 says that the quotation in v 12 is closer to the Aramaic than to the other versions and originated in "the Aramaic-speaking church," presumably in Palestine, where "those outside" referred to Gentiles or unbelievers. The saying became much harsher as it was translated into Greek. The concept "mystery" (another translation of the Greek word *mysterion,* translated as "secret" in our text), is prominent in Jewish apocalyptic writers, Qumran, and Paul, but not present elsewhere in Mark. According to this concept, only a small group of people, in contrast to those outside, are given insight into God's plan. That concept was typical of the church but not of Mark, who believed that Jesus' parables were intended for everyone (compare 4:1 with 2:13 and 6:34, and 3:23 with 4:3, 9; see also esp. 4:21–25, 33).

If you look at chap. 4 of Mark, you will see that it contains a group of parables and not one but two explanations for Jesus speaking in parables. The first explanation (4:10–12), which we have been discussing, separates the interpretation of the parable of the sower from the parable itself. The second (Example 2.8) concludes the chapter and is given in the writer's own words, not in Jesus' words, as the first one is.

EXAMPLE 2.8	*Writers Give Reasons Why Jesus Speaks in Parables*	
Matt 13:34–35	**Mark 4:33–34**	**Luke**
[34]Jesus told the crowds all these things in parables; without a parable he told them nothing. [35]This was to fulfill what had been spoken through the prophet: "I will open my mouth to speak in parables; I will proclaim what has been hidden from the foundation of the world."	[33]With many such parables he spoke the word to them, as they were able to hear it; [34]he did not speak to them except in parables, but he explained everything in private to his disciples.	

It is difficult to believe that the same author could, in the same chapter, propose two such different explanations for Jesus' use of parables. How, on the one hand, could he report that Jesus spoke in parables to keep those outside— that is, the masses of Jews or Gentiles—from hearing and understanding and, on the other hand, say that Jesus spoke to them "many such parables . . . as they were able to hear"? Which explanation came from the source Mark was using, and which did Mark simply retain, however inappropriately, in the text? And which represents Mark's own thought?

V. Taylor 1957:257 says that the first passage as it now stands in 4:11–12 "represents the beliefs of Mark." In contrast to Taylor, E. Trocme 1975:161 maintains that the passage in 4:33–34 is Mark's own and that he included 4:10–12, "the traditional explanation of the parable of the Sower," with v 13, as "the germ of a 'parables theory' which he spelled out" in vv 33–34. He gives as linguistic support for his view the fact that the words "when he was alone" and "the secret" occur only in Mark 4:10–12, which also contains "bizarre" Greek expressions such as "those about him with the twelve" and others. But vv 33–34 contain usual Markan expressions, such as "he spoke the word" (see also 2:2; 8:32) and "privately" (6:31–32; 7:33; 9:2, 28; 13:3). "Privately" is a characteristic feature of Mark's style and is his typical editorial device for having Jesus explain in private what he had said in public.

Now notice that in the second explanation, as in the first, Matthew sees the fulfillment of OT prophecy (Ps 78:2) in Jesus' use of parables. Having made that observation, we return to Matthew's treatment of Mark 4:10–12. Verse 12 is an insertion that is out of context and breaks the connection between vv 11 and 13. The first half of the saying apparently refers to disciples of Jesus and the second half to others, but those others who have not been given the secret of the kingdom cannot be forced to give up what they do not have. The same saying occurs in another context with another saying or two (Mark 4:21–25 = Luke 8:16–18), where apparently both halves of the saying in question refer to disciples. Also, observe that Matthew has added the verb "know" and uses the plural "secrets" instead of the singular of Mark. We cannot be certain whether the plural was added by Matthew, since it also occurs in Luke. The meaning of "the secret" in Mark cannot be determined with certainty, though many think it refers to the eschatological coming of the kingdom. But in Matthew, if not also in Luke, "the secrets" may be doctrines of the church, or perhaps the interpretations of the parables that follow. Or an eschatological meaning may be intended.

Luke has shortened and toned down the Markan saying by limiting the question to the single parable of the sower and by omitting (as does Matthew) the reference to Jesus being alone with the disciples. The disciples ask the question in the presence of the crowd that has heard the parable (8:4). Although the original form of the question in Mark's source may have been similar to that in Luke, Luke has formulated the question as an introduction to v 10, as we know from his characteristic use of the optative mood (a form of the verb used to express a wish, condition, or possibility) in Greek indirect questions. The statement about Jesus being alone with the disciples may have been omitted to avoid the impression of Jesus speaking only to a select few. Although Luke retains the idea that Jesus' parabolic teaching was to be understood only by those to whom it was "given," his words "to others" are not so emphatic as Mark's "for those outside." And Mark's severe conclusion from the prophecy of Isaiah, "so that they may not turn again and be forgiven," is omitted. Perhaps Luke's differences are due to his strong interest in Jesus' message reaching all people, "those outside" as well as those on "the inside."

Having considered one of the most difficult passages in the gospels, we turn now to several other sayings of Jesus (Example 2.9). Notice that there are apparent, if not real, contradictions in the sayings about peace. The word "peace" is one of Luke's favorites (thirteen times; Mark, one; Matt, four). In Mark 5:34 (= Luke 8:48) Jesus uses it in a common dismissal formula ("go in peace") that echoes OT usage (1 Sam 1:17; 20:42; also Luke 7:50). Matthew uses the word "peace" only in Jesus' discourse to his disciples as he sends them out, including the second passage quoted below (10:34) and the one in 10:13 (Example 2.10).

Luke has a peculiar account of the sending out of the seventy (10:1–16; not printed). The passages in Example 2.10 are from the sending out of the twelve, with Jesus' instructions to his disciples. In Matt 10:13 and Luke 10:5–6 "peace" seems to be a kind of objective, even personified, spiritual existence that can "come," "rest," and "return." In part, the use of "peace" here reflects the Hebrew *shalom*, which includes in its meaning not only the absence of war or

---

EXAMPLE 2.9   *Sayings of Jesus*

Matt 5:9	Mark	Luke
9"Blessed are the peacemakers, for they will be called children of God."		

Matt 10:34–36	Mark	Luke 12:51–53

34"Do not think that I have come to bring peace to the earth; I have not come to bring peace, but a sword.
 35   For I have come to set a man against his father,
        and a daughter against her mother,
        and a daughter-in-law against her mother-in-law;
 36   and one's foes will be members of one's own household."
	Mark	51"Do you think that I have come to bring peace to the earth? No, I tell you, but rather division! 52From now on five in one household will be divided, three against two and two against three; 53they will be divided:
		        father against son
		            and son against father,
		        mother against daughter
		            and daughter against mother,
		        mother-in-law against her daughter-in-law and daughter-in-law against mother-in-law."

Cf. *GThom* 16.

EXAMPLE 2.10   *Jesus Speaking to His Disciples*

Matt 10:11–13	Mark 6:10	Luke 9:4
11"Whatever town or village you enter, find out who in it is worthy, and stay there until you leave. 12As you enter the house, greet it. 13If the house is worthy, let your peace come upon it; but if it is not worthy, let your peace return to you."	10He said to them, "Wherever you enter a house, stay there until you leave the place."	4"Whatever house you enter, stay there, and leave from there."

other hostility, but also such blessings from God as harmony, good order, safety, and prosperity (see Isa 9:7; 32:17; 48:18; Jer 16:5; Pss 29:11; 37:11; Prov 3:2). Luke's "peace to this house" (10:5) is similar to the Hebrew greeting *shalom leka,* "Peace be to you," and his "son of peace" (10:6; Greek text) is a Semitic idiom.

Peace seems to be a special theme in Luke. In the song after the birth of John the Baptist, Zechariah includes a prophecy of peace: "to guide our feet into the way of peace" (1:79). At the birth of Jesus the angels sing, "Glory to God in the highest heaven, and on earth peace among those whom he favors" (2:14), and after Jesus' circumcision and presentation in the temple, Simeon says, "Master, now you are dismissing your servant in peace" (2:29). In the account of Jesus' entry into Jerusalem, only Luke adds, "Peace in heaven, and glory in the highest heaven!" (19:38). And in Luke 24:36 the risen Jesus greets the disciples with the words "Peace be with you." Three times in Luke (Greek text) the word "peace" means the absence of war (11:21; 14:32; 19:42). How can we account for Luke's special interest in peace in its various meanings? Perhaps he was influenced by the OT idea of *shalom,* or perhaps the pervasive *pax Romana* of the Augustan age had left an impressive image on his mind. Was the peace associated with the coming of Jesus meant to stand in contrast to the peace of the Augustan age?

In light of Luke's association of peace with Jesus, it is highly unlikely that Luke would have omitted the Matthean beatitude on the peacemakers if it had been in his source. So we must ask whether the beatitude goes back to Jesus or whether Matthew added it to the series of beatitudes in Q. At least the phrase "sons of God" (Greek text) may be a Matthean touch, since for Matthew Jesus is the Son of God and his disciples are sons of God (5:45, not in Q of Luke 6:27–28; 13:38). The word "peacemakers" occurs in the NT only in Matt 5:9 and is usually thought to mean those who settle quarrels. This is true especially in light of Matt 5:21–24 and 5:24–26 = Luke 12:57–59. So in Matthew the

word may reflect quarrels among family members about accepting or rejecting Jesus.

If the beatitude on peacemakers is an authentic saying of Jesus, the saying about peace and a sword in the Q passage (Matt 10:34 = Luke 12:49–53) is ironic, to say the least. In that saying "peace" and "sword" are not used with reference to war but to family quarrels or divisions. So again we must ask the usual question: Does this saying go back to Jesus? If so, then Jesus realized that his coming would not bring "peace" because each person would have to make a decision about whether to follow him or not. A decision to follow Jesus would cause division even in the same family, when some members chose not to follow him (see Matt 10:21). We can imagine, for example, that Zebedee, father of James and John, was a little angry when his sons decided to leave their father to follow Jesus. The peace in Zebedee's household was surely disrupted. If the saying about peace and a sword does not go back to Jesus, then it would have originated from the disquieting experiences of the early church.

The words "from now on" (12:52) are a Lukan expression, so the rest of the verse may be his own expansion of Q. Verse 35 in Matt (= v 53 in Luke) is based on Mic 7:6. Matthew agrees with Micah that the hostility is that of the younger generation toward the older, but in Luke the hostility between generations is mutual. Luke omits the part of the quotation retained in Matt 10:36. In Mic 7:6 the prophet is describing the corrupt social life of his time in an eschatological context. The church, seeing in its own experience of trial and division the fulfillment of Micah's prophecy, put Micah's prophecy on the lips of Jesus as a sign that the end of the world was soon to come. So according to some form critics, the sayings of Jesus in Matt 10:34–36 = Luke 12:51–53 did not originate with Jesus but developed out of the experience of the early church. Again, more than one understanding of the passage is possible.

Now turn to the passages in Example 2.11. Mark 14:46–47 and parallels are part of the nar-

EXAMPLE 2.11	*Excerpts from the Account of Jesus' Capture*

Matt 26:50–54	Mark 14:46–47	Luke 22:49–51
Then they came and laid hands on Jesus and arrested him. [51]Suddenly, one of those with Jesus put his hand on his sword, drew it, and struck the slave of the high priest, cutting off his ear. [52]Then Jesus said to him, "Put your sword back into its place; for all who take the sword will perish by the sword. [53]Do you think that I cannot appeal to my Father, and he will at once send me more than twelve legions of angels? [54]But how then would the scriptures be fulfilled, which say it must happen in this way?"	[46]Then they laid hands on him and arrested him. [47]But one of those who stood near drew his sword and struck the slave of the high priest, cutting off his ear.	[49]When those who were around him saw what was coming, they asked, "Lord, should we strike with the sword?" [50]Then one of them struck the slave of the high priest and cut off his right ear. [51]But Jesus said, "No more of this!" And he touched his ear and healed him.

rative of Jesus' capture recorded in Mark 14:43–52 = Matt 26:47–56 = Luke 22:47–53. It has been suggested that the narrative in Mark 14:43–52 originally followed Mark 14:26–31 and that the primitive framework on which Mark constructed his narrative of Jesus' passion is Mark 14:1–2, 10–11, 12–16, 17–21, 26–31, 43–52. As the tradition grew, that framework was embellished with legendary, apologetic, and liturgical material. We can see how such embellishment took place in the section quoted. The original narrative probably ended with Jesus' arrest in Mark 14:46, to which Mark added the verses that follow. He has loosely appended the incident of the bystanders who struck the slave of the high priest. The crowd from which the bystander comes is not described, and his act is committed impulsively to avenge Jesus' arrest. Mark also uses several words here not used elsewhere in the gospel, including those for "draw a sword," "to strike," "to cut off," and the particular word for "ear."

Matthew and Luke have changed and embellished Mark's account. The crowd is described as "those with Jesus" (Matthew), and as "those who were around him" (Luke). But in Luke the crowd senses in advance what is about to happen and volunteers communal action, with a question to Jesus addressed as Lord, a title for Jesus especially characteristic of Luke. In the legendary element of the ear being cut off, Luke specifies the "right ear" and adds that Jesus touched the ear of the man and healed him. In Matthew, as in Mark, Jesus is seized before the sword-wielding incident, but in Luke Jesus is not seized until he has finished speaking. In Matthew, Jesus' response to the incident is an embellishment, especially the proverb in v 52, which may have been made into a saying of Jesus (see Rev 13:10). It is out of place in the narrative because it makes the rejection of the sword a general rule, not a remark that arises naturally from the specific situation. And finally, according to Matthew, the scriptures concerning Jesus as the Son of God (implied from "my Father") cannot be fulfilled if resistance is offered (see also Mark 12:49 and Matt 26:56). Both Son of God and fulfillment of scripture are characteristic Matthean traits.

Our final passage to illustrate how an author's own understanding of Jesus and his teachings influenced what he wrote is a short one (Example 2.12). Each excerpt shows differences in emphasis and interpretation with respect to the main subject of Jesus' teaching—the kingdom of God. Mark frequently uses the expression "and he said to them" as a connecting link and as an indication that the saying that follows is separate and is not in its original context here. Among the three excerpts, there are no important differences before the words "taste death," an idiom for "die." The clause containing those words means, "who will not die until," and so on. But the words following that clause are different in each gospel, so we will focus on them.

In Mark the emphasis is on the kingdom of God and the manner of its coming, expressed in eschatological language. The words "with power" probably mean in its fullness and perhaps with cataclysmic signs to be observed (see Luke 17:20). The kingdom will break in upon the world from the outside. In Matthew the emphasis is on the Son of Man who is to come along with the kingdom, a kingdom that is his, not God's. The coming of the Son of Man is a major concern elsewhere in Matthew's gospel. The coming of the kingdom is still eschatological, but because of the omission of "with power," the violent aspect is not so emphatic in Matthew as in Mark. Presumably, for Matthew the Son of Man in his kingdom will also break in upon the world from the outside.

The most significant difference in this reported saying of Jesus occurs in its Lukan form. Although Luke omits the verb "come," the time is probably still the future. But by omitting that word and the words "with power," and by using "see," Luke shifts the emphasis from the eschatological coming of the kingdom to the people ("they") and to the experience ("see") of the kingdom. The Greek word translated "see" means "discern" or "perceive," so Luke's clause could be interpreted to mean that some people will still be living to perceive the kingdom of God when it comes upon the world, perhaps from the outside. But the word "see," in its broader sense, can also mean "experience." So Luke's language could also signify that before the people mentioned ("they") die, they themselves will experience the phenomenon of the kingdom of God. In other words, in this passage Luke may be saying that the kingdom of God will be a personal, subjective experience for some before they die. Luke perceives the kingdom of God in that way in the following passage, which appears only in Luke (Example 2.13). The Greek phrase translated "among you" may also mean "in the midst of you" or "within you." Since in this passage and in Luke 9:27 the concept of the kingdom of God differs radically from Mark's usual eschatological conception, which is taken over by Matthew, the words "within you" convey the theology of Luke, and therefore are probably not part of an authentic saying of Jesus. In this passage, as in the previous one, Luke "de-eschatologizes" the kingdom of God; that is, Luke leaves out the idea of its coming at the end of time and makes the kingdom of God a present personal experience. For Jesus and the kingdom of God see B. D. Chilton 1979, 1984, 1987, 1994.

EXAMPLE 2.12 *Jesus Teaching about the Kingdom of God*		
Matt 16:28	**Mark 9:1**	**Luke 9:27**
[28]"Truly I tell you, there are some standing here who will not taste death before they see the Son of Man coming in his kingdom."	"Truly I tell you, there are some standing here who will not taste death until they see that the kingdom of God has come with power."	[27]"But truly I tell you, there are some standing here who will not taste death before they see the kingdom of God."

EXAMPLE 2.13	*Jesus Teaching about the Kingdom of God*	

Matt	Mark	Luke 17:20–21
		[20]Once Jesus was asked by the Pharisees when the kingdom of God was coming, and he answered, "The kingdom of God is not coming with things that can be observed; [21]nor will they say, 'Look, here it is!' or 'There it is!' For, in fact, the kingdom of God is among you."

Cf. *POxy* 654, 3; *GThom* 3; 113.

METHODS USED IN ADVANCED STUDY

Some methods and approaches that have been used in other disciplines are now practiced in biblical studies as well. Most are too complicated for students at the introductory level. However, you ought to be aware of them in case you become interested in more advanced study.

Canonical Criticism

Before you read this section please review the first section in Chapter 1 about the *canon*.

J. A. Sanders 1972, an OT professor, was the first to use the phrase "canonical criticism" as a method of interpretation supplementary to form and redaction criticisms. He sought to discover the interpretation according to which parts of scripture were adapted to new situations in the development of the canon. Sometimes an effort is made to determine the form of a biblical writing "as originally given" (F. F. Bruce 1988). The process of canonical criticism spans the whole development of the canon, not only the final form of a writing as it appears in the Bible. Included in the process is the attempt to determine the theology of a biblical text, along with the significance of that theology and how it functioned in the religious community that kept the text in existence.

Although he refuses to accept canonical criticism as a method like form and redaction criticisms, the approach of B. Childs 1979 and 1984, another OT scholar, is similar to that of canonical critics. Childs shares some of the same aims of canonical criticism mentioned above, but his main goal is to fix a position whereby the Bible is to be read and studied "as sacred scripture" (1979:82).

It seems fair to say that Childs is chiefly concerned with determining the theological power of each canonical book in its relationship to the canon as a whole, not only for early generations of Christians but for generations of all time. Childs's canonical approach "concerns itself . . . with theological function" of NT works, not with "historical reconstruction" (1984:52, 23).

For a somewhat different approach and for further study of canonical criticism see H. Y. Gamble 1985, L. M. McDonald 1988, and J. A. Sanders 1984. Students will find C. M. Tuckett 1987:5–20, 168–174 and B. M. Metzger 1997 helpful.

Narrative Criticism

"A narrative" presents events that may be actual or fanciful and reported for some reason or other. Since the time of Aristotle, literary critics had thought of narratives as distinct literary forms, such as myths, legends, parables, novellas, sagas, etc. But modern narrative critics generally use the term "story" with respect to the literary work being studied. They think of the gospels, for example, as stories, not as gospels. And narrative critics are really often not concerned whether the events narrated in the stories actually occurred. Take, for example, the so-called Passion Narrative in the gospels (Mark 14–15; Matthew 26–27; Luke 22–23). How much of that story is actual event or fanciful report by Christian storytellers is really not a problem for modern narrative critics. They concentrate on what can be learned from the text itself, without concern for historical veracity within the text.

Narrative critics, it seems to me, need vivid imaginations, because they think in terms of what is "inferred" or "implied" in a story. They infer things about those who first heard or read what was spoken or written, the real audience of the author. That audience is to be distinguished from the persons the author had in mind when he wrote, the implied audience. The implied audience can only be imagined. In the same way, narrative critics infer from the narrative the one who is the implied author, and he is to be distinguished from the person who actually wrote the story, the real author.

An excellent work for interested novices to learn about narrative criticism and how it is used is D. Rhoads 1999. Good examples of narrative critics' works are N. R. Petersen 1978; M. A. Powell 1990; R. A. Culpepper 1983, for gospel of John; J. D. Kingsbury 1988, for Matthew.

Structuralism

As a method of interpretation, structuralism is very difficult to define for people just beginning NT study. Structuralism has been a part of many disciplines, including mathematics, sociology, physical sciences, and philosophy. It came into biblical criticism from the structural anthropology studies of C. Levi-Strauss and others. As the term implies, structuralism is concerned with the total structure or form of a literary work and with almost nothing else. There is little or no concern for history and other factors that might have had a bearing on the work being studied. However, structure is not an obvious outline of a work and the structures within a work are so hidden that one must be specially trained to uncover them. Indeed, the structures are often so deeply hidden that, as a person untrained in the skill, I cannot discern them.

Interested novices should see D. Patte 1976b; R. M. Polzin 1977:1–43; C. M. Tuckett 1987: 151–156. Others see, for example, J. Calloud 1976 and D. Patte 1987; for the letters of Paul see D. Patte 1983.

Social/Sociological Criticism

Although the application of social concepts as a method of biblical exegesis did not emerge until the 1970s, basic groundwork had been done a century before by German and American scholars.

As early as 1923 S. J. Case 1923 wrote that when Christianity spread to the Gentiles a Christian "could not afford to surrender the economic quest, and if he desired to exert a real influence in society he must maintain immediate contacts with the forces that were native to the social order in which he was living." Case and his colleagues at the University of Chicago (the "Chicago School") were concerned with the social teachings of Jesus and their application ("the social gospel") to American society. Today scholars investigate the socioeconomic, political, and religious factors in the milieu of the NT in order to understand NT texts. In doing this social criticism also tries to show how particular authors were influenced by social conditions and if and how their work shows responses to those conditions.

The Chicago School has been revived with the work of G. Theissen 1978, whose methodology and conclusions have been challenged by R. A. Horsley 1989b, who, nevertheless, acknowledges Theissen's work as substantive and groundbreaking. The thesis of Horsley's book is that Jesus was a social revolutionary, much like some OT prophets, who wanted to liberate all the people of Israel (Jews) from oppression by the wealthy class. Horsley 1989a has applied the same method in his study of the infancy narratives in Matthew and Luke. For my response see my forthcoming book, *The Stories of Jesus' Birth: A Critical Introduction.*

E. A. Judge 1960 has described "a range of social forms of the age to which Christians, as members of earthly society, would consider themselves obligated." On the other hand, some scholars have maintained that the norms of the NT were not conditioned by the environment.

J. H. Elliott 1993:7 defines social-scientific criticism as "that phase of the exegetical task which analyzes the social and cultural dimensions of the text and of its environmental context through the utilization of the perspectives, theory, models, and research of the social sciences." It is related to the other criticism we have been discussing and may, of course, be used in the study of any NT text.

For a discussion of both sides of the issue see B. Holmberg 1990:20–76. Novices see esp. C. M. Tuckett 1987:136–150. See also D. Tidball 1983:65–122; C. Osiek 1989; H. C. Kee 1980, 1989; J. Neusner 1988:109–232; J. G. Gager 1975; A. J. Malherbe 1983:29–59, 1987; G. Theissen 1978, 1982, 1992; J. E. Stambaugh 1986; J. H. Elliott 1986, 1993.

Rhetorical Criticism

The word "rhetoric" is derived from the Greek *rhētorikē* or the Latin *rhētorica,* meaning the "art of oratory or speaking." Basically, it deals with the principles of communication, either to inform or persuade others, so almost everyone who speaks uses it. Originally rhetoric involved the creation or composition of a spoken message, but it has come to be used in the interpretation or analysis of a message in literature. Thus, it is an aspect of literary criticism, which is the way it is used in biblical studies. In NT studies it is practiced especially in analyzing the letters of Paul.

Literary rhetorical analysis has three main parts: (1) A brief introduction (*exordium* or *prooemium*). (2) The central part, composed of two main sections, the *propositio* and *argumentatio*. The *propositio* may include a listing of points to be argued (*partitio*) and a recital (*narratio*) of issues relevant to the *propositio*. The *argumentatio,* of course, is giving evidence or

proofs and a refutation of (*refutatio*) the opposing arguments. (3) Conclusion (*peroratio* or *conclusio*), the purpose of which is to convince the judges or audience (or readers) that the arguments have been proven.

A notable rhetorical study of Paul's letter to the Galatians is that by H. D. Betz 1979, who organizes his commentary on Galatians on the following rhetorical scheme: Epistolary Prescript (1:1–5), *Exordium* (1:6–11), *Narratio* (1:12–2:14), *Propositio* (2:15–21), *Probatio* (3:1–4:31), *Exhortatio* (5:1–6:10), and Epistolary Postscript or *Conclusio* (6:11–18).

On the other hand, G. A. Kennedy 1984, a classical scholar, especially in the field of rhetoric, says that the theory of literary genres was not very developed in antiquity. He implies, therefore, that biblical scholars should be more concerned with rhetorical methods than with types of narratives. In particular, Kennedy maintains that Betz misunderstands the rhetorical aspects of Galatians, which is deliberative or persuasive, not apologetic or judicial (Betz). Moreover, according to Kennedy, Betz stresses the existence of narrative in Galatians at the expense of exhortation. That, it seems to me, is a common shortcoming in Pauline studies (see below).

For recent studies on rhetorical criticism see W. C. Booth 1983, W. Wuellner 1987, and S. E. Porter 1993.

Moral/Ethical Criticism

For more than four centuries the presupposition for many, if not most, NT studies has been the basic doctrine of the Protestant Reformation of the sixteenth century. That doctrine in essence is that individuals are justified or saved by the grace of God (alone) through faith in Jesus Christ. Texts from the letters of Paul, especially as interpreted by Martin Luther, have biased the approach, and subsequently the results as well, of too many NT studies, especially in Europe but also in America, even late into the twentieth century.

A favorite presuppositional text has been Gal 2:16: "We know that a person is justified (made righteous) not by the works of the law but through faith in Jesus Christ." This text, along with others (Rom 3:21–22, 26; Gal 2:20; 3:22; Phil 3:9), has been generally misinterpreted by most scholars in two main ways: justification has been taken to mean the same thing as salvation, and "faith" has been understood to be that of the believer. In the last several decades, however, some scholars have argued that Paul's Greek in Gal 2:16 (*dia pisteōs Iēsou Christou*) should be taken as "through the faith of Jesus Christ." This makes the faithfulness that of Jesus and not of the believer, a view with which I agree. However, most scholars still seem to think that for Paul justification and salvation are in essence the same thing, a view with which I do not agree. But enough of negative criticism. (For my views on the subject see E. D. Freed 1994.)

Positively, I suggest that we begin to study the NT, especially the letters of Paul, with some different texts as our presuppositions. In doing this, our method could be called "moral/ethical criticism."

> For you were called to freedom, brothers and sisters; only do not use your freedom as an opportunity for self-indulgence, but through love become slaves to one another. For the whole law is summed up in a single commandment, "You shall love your neighbor as yourself." [Gal 5:13–14]

> For he [God] will repay according to each one's deeds: to those who by patiently doing good seek for glory and honor and immortality, he will give eternal life; while for those who are self-seeking and who obey not the truth but wickedness, there will be wrath and fury. There will be anguish and distress for everyone who does evil . . . but glory and honor and peace for everyone who does good. [Rom 2:6–10]

Other texts support this change in our presuppositions, for example, 2 Cor 5:10: "For all of us must appear before the judgment seat of Christ, so that each may receive recompense for what has been done in the body, whether good or evil." See also 1 Cor 6:9–20; Rom 13:8–10; 14:7–12; Gal 5:16–26; and many others.

These passages show that, according to Paul, "eternal life" (= "salvation") lies in the future, whereas justification occurs in the present and is associated with conversion and baptism. The basic text here is 1 Cor 6:9–11. Please read that passage now.

The use of moral/ethical criticism might lead to a truer understanding of much of the NT, especially Paul's letters. We would, therefore, also understand Paul in his own century and not put him in the sixteenth or twenty-first century. As with other methods of NT study, if we are concerned with meaning, this approach would be valid and provide insight into moral/ethical teachings of the NT frequently overlooked.

For a summary of my views as the result of using such a method see *Paul as a "Christian" Thinker* in Chapter 9, and for details see E. D. Freed 1994 and bibliography there for different viewpoints.

SUMMARY

Our analyses of passages illustrated the use of the historical-critical method and the techniques of literary, form, and redaction criticism in studying the gospels. Because many sources—both pregospel oral traditions and written sources—were used in unique ways by the gospel writers as creative authors, the content of our gospels is not merely words of Jesus and historical narratives of actual facts and events. Methods of critical study help us understand the gospels as theological works influenced by the particular interests, concerns, theological convictions, and even biases of Mark, Matthew, and Luke. As creative authors, the gospel writers used the pregospel oral traditions and their sources in their own unique ways.

Through the use of the historical-critical method, those who study the NT act as historians and make judgments in trying to get to the truth behind what they are studying. Literary criticism is especially helpful in trying to determine the sources used by the gospel writers and the peculiar traits of the writers' vocabularies and styles. Form criticism is important because it teaches us that although Mark is the earliest gospel, we cannot be certain of Jesus' actual words and deeds as recorded even in that gospel. Form criticism also gives us insight into why and how early Christians shaped traditions about Jesus before they were written down. Redaction criticism is helpful in identifying how the gospels were shaped by the gospel writers as authors and in determining the authors' theological viewpoints.

Up to this point we have learned about the relationships among the first three gospels, the gospel writers as authors, and methods and approaches used in the critical study of the NT. In the next chapter we will learn about the critical study of Jesus in light of those gospels and what we have learned thus far.

CHAPTER 3

The Critical Study of Jesus and the Synoptic Gospels

THE HISTORICAL-CRITICAL METHOD, with the techniques of literary, form, and redaction criticism, provides insight into the gospel writers as creative authors through the critical study of the texts, sources, and literary relationships of the gospels. In this chapter we will try to gain insight into the life and teachings of Jesus as revealed in the first three gospels.

Because the gospels were influenced by oral traditions, written sources, and the unique contributions of the gospel writers as authors, they contain information about Jesus that frequently may be interpreted in different ways. To study Jesus' life and teachings critically, therefore, it is essential to learn about several clues used to understand the gospel material about Jesus: apocalyptic eschatology, the *kērygma,* myth, Christian prophecy, criteria for determining the authenticity of Jesus' sayings, phases of earliest Christianity, and Christianity as a millenarian movement. Several more recent approaches, such as special interests interpretations, including feminist studies and liberation theology, and the approaches of the Jesus Seminar and the most recent quest for the historical Jesus are also considered.

Unfortunately, critical study reveals more uncertainties than certainties; nevertheless, critical study does provide several clues about Jesus. So this chapter concludes with some general considerations about Jesus as teacher, preacher, and healer, with special attention to Jesus as teacher and to the nature of his teaching and to his death and resurrection.

APOCALYPTIC ESCHATOLOGY

One clue that many scholars have found useful in the study of Jesus and the gospels is eschatology. Remember that eschatology is essentially the doctrine of last things. Almost a hundred years ago, as part of the first quest for the historical Jesus, two German scholars, J. Weiss and A. Schweitzer, maintained that eschatology was the most prominent theme in Jesus' teaching and in the faith of NT writers. Considering passages like Mark 9:1—"Truly, I tell you, there are some standing here who will not taste death until they see that the kingdom of God has come with power"—Schweitzer 1945 maintained, in his classic book, that Jesus was a thoroughgoing eschatologist. Influenced by Jewish apocalyptic thought (see the Introduction), Jesus proclaimed the imminent end of the present age. All of Jesus' teachings are to be read in light of that proclamation, and therefore were not meant for Christians of a later time. They were only an interim ethic intended to sustain the disciples through the last days, the interim between Jesus' time and the imminent end of the world, and to prepare them for that end. According to Schweitzer, the kingdom of God preached by Jesus would come only in the future and at God's command; humans could do nothing to delay or hasten its coming. Schweitzer's view that Jesus was an apocalyptic eschatologist, although sometimes strongly challenged (C. H. Dodd 1961; W. G. Kuemmel 1961), has had far-reaching effects on most studies of Jesus and the first three gospels.

It is one thing, of course, to emphasize that Jesus expected the end of the world to come soon, but quite another to say that all of Jesus' teaching was oriented toward the future. The early church, in fact, found much of his teaching that applied to the present useful even after time had proven Jesus wrong about the nearness of the End.

THE *KĒRYGMA*

Another clue widely used in trying to understand Jesus, the gospels, and early Christianity is a phenomenon known as the *kērygma*. The term is used with reference to the process as well as to the content of Christian preaching. *Kērygma* is a Greek noun meaning "preaching" or "proclamation" and comes from the verb *keryssō*, "to preach," "herald," or "proclaim." So the kērygma is the message about what God did through Jesus, as preached by early Christians. We can get the best idea of the nature and con-

tent of the kērygma or missionary preaching by reading parts of Peter's sermon at Pentecost in Acts 2:16–36:

> [16]No, this is what was spoken through the prophet Joel:
> [17]   'In the last days it will be, God declares,
>   that I will pour out my Spirit upon all flesh,
>   and your sons and your daughters shall prophesy. . . .
> [22]"You that are Israelites, listen to what I have to say: Jesus of Nazareth, a man attested to you by God with deeds of power, wonders, and signs that God did through him among you, as you yourselves know— [23]this man, handed over to you according to the definite plan and foreknowledge of God, you crucified and killed by the hands of those outside the law. [24]But God raised him up, having freed him from death. . . . [32]This Jesus God raised up, and of that all of us are witnesses. [33]Being therefore exalted at the right hand of God. . . . God has made him both Lord and Messiah.

According to this passage, the kērygma included these points: OT prophecy was fulfilled in Jesus and his coming; miracles attested to the power of Jesus; Jesus was crucified and raised from the dead according to God's plan; Jesus was exalted at God's right hand; and God made Jesus both Lord and Messiah. From Paul's letters and elsewhere in Acts, we can add the beliefs that Jesus was descended from David and that he would come again as judge of humanity. (See Chapter 8 for speeches in Acts.)

Many scholars have maintained that the kērygma was the main concern of NT writers, and is therefore an important clue in the study of the NT, including the gospels. For example, the first verse of Mark's gospel—"The beginning of the gospel of Jesus Christ, the Son of God"—indicates that the author was recording a version of the kērygma. This verse shows immediately that the Christology of the kērygma, not a narrative of events, was the writer's main interest.

Christology, a term frequently used in the study of Jesus, comes from two Greek words, *christos,* "anointed one," and *logos,* "word." *Christ* is the English equivalent of *christos,* so Christology is literally the word about Christ, or more specifically the doctrine (something taught) about Christ. It includes all aspects of Christian thought regarding God's revelation in Jesus as the Christ. Thus, it is concerned with showing the relationship of Christ to God in metaphorical and mythological imagery and is an aspect of theology.

Those who have most strongly emphasized the kērygma as a clue have argued that the gospels are so permeated with faith in Jesus' resurrection and in Jesus as Lord and Christ that there can be no recovery of authentic incidents in Jesus' life or of his authentic sayings. They claim that the Christians responsible for the gospels and the other NT writings never wanted to, nor could, distinguish between their own christological conceptions of the resurrected or exalted Lord or Christ and the earthly or historical Jesus of Nazareth. Most scholars today, however, have abandoned this radical approach involving the kērygma. Readers interested in a more philosophical-theological approach to the study of Jesus should read the classical work by M. Kaehler 1964. For a more moderate approach, see the influential little book by C. H. Dodd 1936.

MYTH

Ever since D. F. Strauss published his work on the life of Jesus in 1835, the idea of myth has remained a controversial factor in the study of Jesus and the gospels. Strauss's work was a reaction against two prevalent nineteenth-century views of interpreting the Bible: the supernaturalistic and the rationalistic. Those who held the supernaturalistic view accepted everything in the Bible as literal fact, including angels, demons, and all miracles, while those who held the rationalistic view tried to explain everything by eliminating what could not be accepted on the basis of reason—for example, miracles and demons.

According to Strauss, myth is not a fiction invented by its author to deceive the reader, so it is essential to discover the idea that gave rise to the myth in the first place. With reference to the gospels, a myth is a religious conception that represents "the spirit of a people or a community." Therefore, the interpreter of myth, "in searching out the ideas which are embodied in the narrative, is controlled by regard to conformity with the spirit and modes of thought of the people and of the age."

Strauss identifies three kinds of myth: evangelical, pure, and historical. The first is "a narrative relating directly or indirectly to Jesus, which may be considered not as the expression of a fact, but as the product of an idea of his earliest followers." The story of the virgin birth of Jesus is such a myth. The second kind of myth—pure myth—has two sources: the messianic ideas in Judaism before Jesus and "that particular impression which was left by the personal character, actions, and fate of Jesus, and which served to modify the Messianic idea in the minds of his people." The transfiguration story (Mark 9:2–8) comes from the first source, and the story of the curtain of the temple being torn in two (Mark 15:38) comes from the second. Finally, historical myth "has for its groundwork a definite individual fact which has been seized upon by religious enthusiasm, and twined around with mythical conceptions culled from the idea of the Christ." For example, sayings of Jesus such as those about "fishing for people" and the barren fig tree may actually have been spoken by Jesus, but in the gospels they appear "transmuted into marvellous histories" (quotations from 1972:86–87).

According to Strauss, some aspects of myth are present in most gospel narratives, but the strongest mythological elements are in the narratives of Jesus' birth and childhood; the miracles, including the transfiguration story; the entry into Jerusalem; the predictions of the passion, and much of the passion narrative itself; and the resurrection and ascension of Jesus. Strauss accepts a core of historical truth: Jesus did live, became a follower of John the Baptist, called disciples, believed he was the Messiah, moved about Galilee and taught in discourses, many of which are authentic, and believed he would return as Son of Man; he was arrested, tried, found guilty, and executed.

Strauss's thought influenced another German scholar, R. Bultmann 1960, who has done more than anyone else to try to interpret Jesus and the NT from the standpoint of myth. Bultmann 1961 begins his discussion of the NT and mythology by saying that the biblical view of the world "as a three-storied structure," with heaven above, the underworld below, and the earth in the middle, is obsolete. Scientific advances have also made it impossible to believe in good or evil spirits, mythical eschatology (which is "untenable for the simple reason that the parousia [second coming] of Christ never took place as the New Testament expected"), the strange statements about the Spirit and the sacraments, death as punishment for sin, the doctrine of the atonement (the belief that Christ died to forgive human sin), and the resurrection of Jesus. Despite such drastic criticism of the NT mythology, Bultmann says that the NT proclamation can be preserved and can give meaning to human existence now, if stripped from its mythical framework—that is, if demythologized.

According to Bultmann, Jesus was a mythological figure to the extent that he was a preexistent being and Son of God. But as Jesus of Nazareth, whose father and mother were known by others and whose life ended on a cross, he was also a real historical figure. In this "unique combination of history and myth," a number of difficulties arise from within the NT itself—for example, the inconsistency between the virgin birth of Jesus in Matthew and the doctrine of his preexistence in Paul and John. Bultmann explains the mythological language used in describing the preexistence of Christ and the virgin birth as an attempt "to explain the meaning of the Person of Jesus for faith."

Bultmann demythologizes the cross and resurrection in such a way, he believes, that they retain their significance for salvation. The real meaning of Jesus' death and resurrection is to be found in Christian faith as it was preached (the *kērygma*) in the early church, not in the crucifixion and resurrection as historical events. It is

faith in the saving effect of Christ's death and resurrection, as "proclaimed through preaching," that makes Christian life authentic.

The views of both Strauss and Bultmann have influenced many studies of Jesus and the gospels, generally because of extreme reactions by other scholars to their views. On the one hand, some have used their views to deny the possibility of recovering any of Jesus' sayings and even to cast doubt on the historical reality of Jesus himself. On the other hand, some have reacted by arguing for the historical character of the gospels, including virtually all of Jesus' teachings. Used more moderately, their views have aroused an awareness of the difficulties involved in the critical study of Jesus and the gospels.

CHRISTIAN PROPHECY

Another clue for the study of Jesus and the gospels, though quite different from myth, is early Christian prophecy. (For definitions of Christian prophecy, see M. E. Boring 1973; G. F. Hawthorne 1975.) A number of passages (Matt 5:12; 7:15, 22–23; 10:19–20, 41; 13:17; Luke 10:24; Acts 13:1) indicate that some early Christians, perhaps living in small communities in different places, thought they possessed the gift of prophecy. This is also clear from the first chapters of Acts, which reflect early Jewish Christianity at Jerusalem, and from Paul's letters, which reflect Gentile Christianity in the Graeco-Roman world. These Christians believed they had received words of God through the living and resurrected Jesus. The writer of Revelation may have felt that he was such a prophet: "The revelation of Jesus Christ, which God gave him to show his servants what must soon take place. . . . Blessed is the one who reads aloud the words of the prophecy" (1:1, 3; see also 10:11; 11:6; 19:10; 22:9–10, 18–19).

As we know from the speech put into Peter's mouth at Pentecost (Acts 2:14–36), some early Jewish Christians in Jerusalem thought of themselves as fulfilling the prophecy of Joel quoted in that speech. They believed they were living in the last days before the end of the world. This is clear from the writer's changing of the word "afterward" in Joel to "in the last days" (Acts 2:17), thus making the prophecy apply to the eschatological community of Christians. That these Christians believed they had the gift of prophecy is clear because the words "and they shall prophesy" (Acts 2:18), which are not in the text of Joel, are added in Peter's speech.

In 1 Corinthians 11–14, Paul had to deal with speaking in tongues, that is, inspired but unintelligible utterances, and with revelation, knowledge, prophecy, teaching, healing, and other phenomena that were regarded as significant in Christian experience. According to Paul, prophets rated second to apostles: "And God has appointed in the church first apostles, second prophets, third teachers . . ." (1 Cor 12:28). Paul stresses the superiority of prophecy to other gifts, especially speaking in tongues, which the Corinthians thought was their special gift. He writes: "Strive for the spiritual gifts, and especially that you may prophesy. . . . Now I would like all of you to speak in tongues, but even more to prophesy. One who prophesies is greater than one who speaks in tongues, unless someone interprets, so that the church may be built up" (1 Cor 14:1–5; see also 11:4–5; 13:9; 12:28–29; 14:24–39).

In light of early Christian interest in prophecy, it is likely that certain sayings about prophets and prophecy attributed to Jesus, especially in Matthew, actually do not go back to Jesus. Instead, they may reflect controversy within Christian groups in Palestine. Take, for example, the saying of Jesus reported only in Matt 7:22–23: "On that day many will say to me, 'Lord, Lord, did we not prophesy in your name? . . .' Then I will declare to them, 'I never knew you; go away from me, you evildoers.'" Because the parallels in Luke 6:46 and 13:26–27 lack the words about prophesying, some scholars suggest that Matthew directs the saying—which originated in some Christian group and not with Jesus— against another Christian group that, like the one in Corinth, had the power of prophecy. By using the saying as he does, Matthew reveals his opposition to the group of Christians who

thought of themselves as prophets (see E. Kaesemann 1969a:82–107).

Soon after Jesus' crucifixion, some Christians began to ponder the question "Who then is this?" (Mark 4:41; Matt 8:27; Luke 8:25). As their theological insight developed, they came to apply several titles to Jesus, such as Son of God and Lord, in answer to that question. One title was that of prophet. Perhaps an awareness of a saying attributed to Jesus—"because it is impossible for a prophet to be killed outside of Jerusalem" (Luke 13:33)—made it easy for them to apply that title to Jesus. At any rate, the book of Acts (3:22–26; see also John 6:14; 7:40) gives some evidence that Christians at Jerusalem believed Jesus was the prophet whom Moses had predicted God would raise up among them and whom they were to obey (Deut 18:15–19).

If we consider early Christian prophecy as a clue in the study of Jesus, what can we learn about Jesus through it? Perhaps Jesus thought of himself as a prophet. If he did, early Christians may have regarded themselves as prophets in imitation of him. But if he did not, some early Christians may have thought of Jesus as a prophet only after they thought of themselves as endowed with the spirit of prophecy. If so, did they come to those decisions after Jesus' death, when prophets, teachers, and miracle workers were competing with each other in the developing church? We can't be certain.

CRITERIA FOR DETERMINING AUTHENTICITY OF SAYINGS OF JESUS

Some scholars find clues for the study of Jesus in certain criteria established to determine the authenticity of sayings of Jesus. For several reasons it is difficult to distinguish between a genuine saying of Jesus and one composed by early Christians and then attributed to Jesus. First, Jesus did not write a word, so we know him only by what others have reported. Second, there was an interval of about forty years between the time Jesus died (c. 30 CE) and the first gospel, Mark, was written (c. 70 CE). Third, our gospels are the culmination of a long process of oral transmission during which sayings of Jesus were fashioned to meet the interests, needs, faith, and even biases of early Christians, including the gospel writers.

Theological or religious interests, or even biases, may also influence a person's decision about the authenticity of a saying of Jesus. For example, a pacifist might regard Jesus' words that those "who take the sword will perish by the sword" (Matt 26:52) as authentic and his saying "I have not come to bring peace, but a sword" (Matt 10:34) as not authentic. A militarist, on the other hand, might take the opposite point of view. Even a proposed criterion for determining the authenticity or inauthenticity of Jesus' sayings could be the result of a special interest or bias.

There are extreme viewpoints regarding sayings of Jesus. Some scholars believe that "it is the inauthenticity, and not the authenticity, of the sayings of Jesus that must be demonstrated" (J. Jeremias 1971:37). Others maintain that the gospel tradition *"is such that the burden of proof will be upon the claim to authenticity"* (N. Perrin 1967:39). Between those extremes there is a variety of opinions based on several criteria for determining authenticity.

One criterion is that of "dissimilarity"; that is, "the earliest form of a saying we can reach may be regarded as authentic if it can be shown to be dissimilar to characteristic emphases both of ancient Judaism and of the early Church." (The terminology and definitions are those of N. Perrin 1967:39–47. I am also indebted to H. K. McArthur 1969:139–144.) This means that if a saying of Jesus coincides with something we know from Judaism or from primitive Christianity as reported in the book of Acts—particularly the first half—or in Paul's letters, which were written before our gospels, then the saying is to be regarded as suspect, if not rejected. For example, some scholars have argued that Jesus' use of the word *abba* (the Aramaic equivalent of our word "daddy") in addressing God (for example, in Mark 14:36) is original because it was not used in Jewish prayers. But as others have pointed out, since Paul uses the word in Rom 8:15 and Gal 4:6, Jesus' usage is not dissimilar to that of the early church; therefore, the saying is not genuine after all. Hence this criterion can be manipulated either to prove or disprove a saying of Jesus.

The criterion of dissimilarity must be used cautiously for several reasons. Jesus was a Jew, so naturally his teaching would reflect much of the Jewish religion of his time, but what is most original or creative in his teaching differs from Judaism. Yet just because some of the sayings attributed to Jesus concern distinctive features of Judaism, such as sabbath observance and the commandments, does not mean they are not authentic. We must not assume that Jesus taught in a vacuum and that he had no ties with Judaism, or that he did not influence those followers of his who were to become the early church. For criticism of the criterion of dissimilarity and especially of its misuse, see M. D. Hooker 1972.

A second criterion is that of "coherence"; that is, "material from the earliest strata of the tradition may be accepted as authentic if it can be shown to cohere with material established as authentic by means of the criterion of dissimilarity." This means that if a saying could not be judged authentic in itself by the criterion of dissimilarity, it may still be regarded as authentic if it can be found to cohere with or to echo a saying judged as genuine by the criterion of dissimilarity. It is logical that once a saying of Jesus has been judged authentic, then another saying reported to come from Jesus that is in accord with the idea of the authentic saying is more likely to be authentic than one not in accord with such an idea. On the other hand, there was nothing to prevent early Christians from composing sayings of Jesus that were in harmony with or in coherence with sayings of Jesus that were regarded as authentic. Again, this criterion is not absolute and must also be used with caution.

A third criterion is "multiple attestation." "This is a proposal to accept as authentic material which is attested in all, or most, of the sources which can be discerned behind the synoptic gospels." This criterion does not mean that just because a saying of Jesus occurs in three gospels it can therefore be accepted as authentic.

Such a situation might mean only that Matthew and Luke both took the saying from Mark, not that there are three separate attestations. This criterion is more useful for determining motifs in Jesus' teaching than for authenticating specific sayings. For example, the incident reported in Mark 2:15–17 about Jesus eating with tax collectors and sinners is not reported in any of the sources of the gospel writers, Q, M, or L. But Jesus' concern for such people is evident in all strands of material, so it is truly historical, that is, not invented by the early Christians when transmitting the material about Jesus. The criterion of multiple attestation is probably most useful when a saying of Jesus occurs in two or more forms, as in a parable and elsewhere.

These criteria for determining authentic sayings of Jesus must be used with caution. In general, they are more valid for establishing the general characteristics and motifs of Jesus' teaching than for determining the authenticity of individual sayings, and the subject of criteria and that of the quest for the historical Jesus discussed below is not greatly significant when trying to determine the particular views of the gospel writers as authors discussed in the last chapter.

For balanced assessments of the criteria for determining authenticity, see C. F. D. Moule 1967; M. D. Hooker 1967; R. H. Fuller 1966:69–103; H. Riesenfeld 1970; and R. S. Barbour 1972. For the criteria mentioned and for others that have been proposed, see R. H. Stein 1980. For a list of passages that "competent scholarly opinion would recognize as authentic" and reasons for their authenticity, see N. Perrin 1976:41.

For the view, severely criticized by many, that like Jewish rabbis, Jesus deliberately taught his disciples to memorize his sayings to ensure their accurate transmission, see B. Gerhardsson 1964a, 1964b, 1979; see also W. Kelber 1983.

PHASES OF EARLIEST CHRISTIANITY

Another clue for the study of the gospel material about Jesus is the development of Christianity among Palestinian Jews and then among Gentiles. Like Jesus, most of his first followers were Jews. After Jesus' death they formed communities in Jerusalem and elsewhere in Palestine (Acts 1–12) that represented Palestinian Jewish Christianity. They were the oldest and probably the most conservative groups of Christians with respect to requirements for conversion to the new religion and a mission to Gentiles. Palestinian Jewish Christians would have been likely to insist that the Jewish rite of circumcision and dietary laws should be observed by those who became Christians. They had their special interests and theological ideas, and they left their influence on the gospels. They even helped shape some of Jesus' sayings, such as those about prophets.

Some of Jesus' earliest followers may not have been Jews; the names of Andrew and Philip, for example, are Greek. Since Andrew and Philip are associated with the rest of Jesus' early disciples (Mark 3:16–19 = Matt 10:2–4 = Luke 6:13–16; Acts 1:13), whose names are Jewish, we think of them and people like them as early Palestinian Christians. Andrew and Philip may have been Greeks or Greek-speaking Jews (known as Hellenists), and they and others like them represented Hellenistic Jewish Christianity. In Jesus' time there were Greeks and Greek-speaking Jews in Palestine, and since there were elements of Hellenism in Christianity from the start, we should not make too sharp a distinction between what we call Jewish and Hellenistic phases in earliest Christianity.

Tensions in Jerusalem between Christians who were strictly Jewish and those who were Hellenistic Jewish are shown in the book of Acts (6:1–6). The Palestinian Jewish Christians, under the leadership of Peter, James, and others, remained in Jerusalem (Acts 8:1–2; 15:1–29; Gal 1:18–2:15). The Hellenistic Jewish Christians were probably the ones scattered abroad from Jerusalem because of persecution after Stephen's death (Acts 7:59–8:1). They were the moving force behind the spread of Christianity throughout the Graeco-Roman world. The NT volumes of Luke-Acts, with their theme of the spread of Christianity from Jerusalem to Rome, are the literary and theological products of this phase of Christianity.

The Hellenistic Jewish Christians also influenced the gospel material. Some scholars believe that this group's influence is especially strong in certain miracle stories such as the ones about the Gerasene demoniac (Mark 5:1–20 = Matt 8:28–34 = Luke 8:26–29) and the deaf mute (Mark 7:31–37; see also Matt 15:29–31). Theologically, Hellenistic Jewish Christians may have been responsible for the transition of the Jewish title *messiah,* meaning "anointed one," to its Greek equivalent, *christos* (Christ), but the original technical meaning of "anointed one" would scarcely be retained. For example, in an expression such as "Jesus who is called the Christ," which occurs only in Matthew (1:16; 27:22; see also 11:2; 23:10), the word "christ" for Jewish Christians would mean "the anointed one" (of God). But when "christ" is used in the name Jesus Christ, as in Mark 1:1, it would be taken as only part of a proper name like Julius Caesar. Hellenistic Jewish Christians would have been apt to discontinue the title "Son of Man" because it meant nothing in Greek. Instead of that title, which may have originated within the Palestinian Jewish group of Christians, Hellenistic Jewish Christians may have preferred the titles "Son of God," "Lord," and "Savior." Each of these three titles, as applied to Jesus, has affinities with its use in Judaism and Hellenism.

Christianity eventually separated from its parent, Judaism. Tensions arose between Jews who accepted Jesus as the long-expected Messiah and those who did not. Those who accepted Jesus as Messiah accused those who didn't of having a hand in his death. Recall Peter's words: "Jesus of Nazareth, a man attested to you by God . . . as you yourselves know—this man . . . you crucified and killed by the hands of those outside the law" (Acts 2:22–23; see also 4:23–28; 10:39). Besides difficulties of this kind, religious fervor resulting from their faith in the risen Jesus led Jewish Christians to seek converts among Gentiles. Hellenistic Jewish Christians became leaders in the Gentile mission, which was set into full swing by Stephen's death (Acts 7), an incident that was the culmination of differences among Jewish Christians in Jerusalem. As the result, "a severe persecution began against the church in

Jerusalem, and all except the apostles were scattered throughout the countryside of Judea and Samaria. . . . Now those who were scattered went from place to place, proclaiming the word . . . the Messiah to them" (Acts 8:1–5). Some of those Hellenistic Jewish Christians were the ones in the synagogues in Damascus whom Paul wanted to bring back "bound to Jerusalem" (Acts 9:1–2).

As Christianity confronted the polytheistic religions, especially the mystery cults, of the northern Mediterranean world, it increasingly emphasized its belief in the saving power of Christ. Christianity could not avoid creating a cult of its own hero, Jesus, with its recital of the kērygma, its initiation rite of baptism, and its sacred common meal. Almost all of the NT, including the gospels, was written as the result of the mission to the Gentiles. Paul's letters and Acts 6–28, supplemented with material from the gospels, are our chief sources of information for that mission.

Mark has a special interest in Gentiles, evident from such statements as "the gospel must first be proclaimed to all nations" (13:10; see also Matt 24:14), the elect are to be gathered "from the ends of the earth" (13:27; see also Matt 24:31), and "the gospel is proclaimed in the whole world" (14:9; see also Matt 26:13). The statement that the curtain of the temple was "torn in two, from top to bottom" (Mark 15:38; see also Matt 27:51) may be symbolic of the spread of Christianity from Jews to Gentiles. The climax of Mark's interest in Gentile Christianity comes with the confession of the centurion, a Gentile: "Truly this man was the Son of God!" (15:39). The title Son of God was widely used in the Graeco-Roman world.

Matthew's concern for Gentile Christianity is less obvious than Mark's. In Matthew some parables show a universal interest, in spite of a rather strong Jewish bias occasionally shown elsewhere (see, for example, Matt 10:5, 17). But in the parables of the two sons (21:28–32), the wicked tenants (21:33–46), and the wedding feast (22:1–14), Matthew presents the Jews, in contrast to others, as rejected because of their lack of faith. This intense anti-Jewish feeling is at the same time pro-Gentile, not only in the heightened woes against the scribes and Pharisees, but also in the emotion-filled statements about the innocence of Pilate (27:24) and the guilt of some Jews (27:25). Only Matthew (4:12–16) presents Jesus as going to live in Capernaum, in "Galilee of the Gentiles," to fulfill the prophecy of Isa 9:1–2 (see also LXX of Joel 4:4; 1 Macc 5:15). Finally, although the authenticity of Jesus' words at the end of the gospel is disputed, these words are the acme of universalistic expression for the writer: "Go therefore and make disciples of all nations" (28:19).

As is especially clear in Acts, the first history of the spread of Christianity into Gentile lands, the apostles are Jesus' "witnesses . . . to the ends of the earth" (1:8). This is the underlying theme of the gospel of Luke as well: "all flesh shall see the salvation of God" (Luke 3:6). Quite intentionally Luke places the story of Jesus' rejection at Nazareth, his hometown (4:16–30), early in the gospel as Jesus' first public appearance. There Jesus first appeared to Jews as their Messiah but was rejected, so Christianity must be preached to all people. That theme not only shaped the presentation of Jesus and his message in Luke's gospel, but also created the outline for Acts. Luke's first volume begins with the kērygma about Jesus as a "horn of salvation for us" (Jews) and as a bringer of "knowledge of salvation to his people" (1:69, 77). His second volume ends with Paul preaching to Jews in Rome, "Let it be known to you then that this salvation of God has been sent to the Gentiles; they will listen" (Acts 28:28).

Thus, because of the break with Judaism, the gospel writers, while retaining contact with Judaism but living as Christians among Gentiles, were forced to make their works vehicles of the Gentile mission.

CHRISTIANITY AS A MILLENARIAN MOVEMENT

On the basis of views expressed by sociologists, anthropologists, and psychologists, J. G. Gager 1975 argues that earliest Christianity meets five basic criteria common to all millenarian cults and therefore "deserves to be designated a millenarian movement." Gager uses the terms "millennial" and "millenarian" in the "sense of movements that expect a new order of reality in the near future," without any relationship to a rule of a thousand years to occur in the future.

The five criteria are (1) "the promise of heaven on earth—soon," (2) "the overthrow or reversal of the present social order," (3) "a terrific release of emotional energy," (4) "a brief life span of the movement itself," and (5) "the central role of a messianic, prophetic, or charismatic leader."

According to Gager, the figure of Jesus—not necessarily the historical Jesus—rather, *"images of Jesus,"* as we find them in early Christian literature, stood at the center of the movement. The gospels portray Jesus in the role of a millenarian prophet as "one who articulates aspirations in such a way that a visible movement will erupt from a bed of amorphous discontent." Jesus was the perfect image of a prophet who challenges traditional assumptions with respect to new standards of value and integrity that arise as part of the moral regeneration of millenarian movements. He centered his attention on the two redemptive media of his time, the temple and the interpretation of the law.

When compared with the third to the fifth centuries of Christian history, the relative absence of theology in the first generations but great emphasis on community and ethics shows that Christianity was a millenarian movement in the beginning but later was not. Christianity survived not as a millenarian movement but in a changed form.

Christianity survived in spite of its disappointment concerning the coming of the new world order and the return of Jesus. Psychologists call the experience of distress and doubt resulting from disappointment *cognitive dissonance*. In millenarian movements such dissonance gives rise to pressures to alleviate or eliminate it. One of the most common and effective ways of doing that is proselytism, which explains the terrific energy expended in the mission activity of early Christianity.

As with all important millenarian movements, Christianity was a movement of the disinherited. Early Christianity was disinherited politically because of the rebellious nature of the Galileans, with whom some associated the movement from the beginning. The fact that Rome controlled the money in the empire was also a contributing factor. The situation of earliest Christians was one of deprivation, so they developed a clearly formulated ethic of poverty. This does not mean that all Christians were very poor, but the ideology of poverty, although exaggerated and idealized, reflects the reality.

The failed millennial hope came to life in the experience of the Christian community through which Christianity, as with other new religions, "created a world so that certain ideas of God and salvation, and not others, seem peculiarly appropriate." Such community was the only alternative for continued existence within the confines of the social structure. Christians were so zealously concerned with the unity and stability of their congregations not only "to defend apostolic prerogatives" but even more "to preserve the only meaningful form of social existence for a liminal community (so regarded by Jews and pagans alike)."

Some essential features of the Christian community were the lessening, or even elimination, of status distinctions and the absence of fixed structure. In his letters Paul does not single out any specific leaders, and there is no evidence of definite structure in the Christian communities. Rather, the emphasis is on the local congregation as a whole.

During the mission activity of the church, certain earlier beliefs had to be disconfirmed. Among these was the death of Jesus, which constituted a problem for the church. There had been no preparation for the death of Jesus the Messiah. This problem was met by rationalizing Jesus' death to the degree that it was "both necessary and beneficial." If Jesus had predicted his own death, then his death confirmed the prediction, and it would, therefore, aid rather than hinder mission activity.

Both internal and external conflicts functioned positively in the survival and maturing of early Christianity. Fighting heretics on the inside more than pagans on the outside strengthened the church in trying to consolidate as an institution.

External factors that facilitated the ultimate triumph of Christianity included the Augustan empire and Hellenistic Judaism. "A single, overriding *internal* factor" was "the radical sense of Christian community—open to all, insistent on absolute and exclusive loyalty, and concerned for every aspect of the believer's life."

(Along with the work of J. G. Gager, several works of H. C. Kee 1977b, 1980,1986, 1989 are important for studying the social origins of the NT; see again discussion of the social/sociological method in Chapter 2.)

SPECIAL INTERESTS INTERPRETATIONS

Feminist Studies

I use the term "special interests interpretations" with respect to feminist studies because, it seems to me, such studies have the unique interest in determining and extolling the role of women in the early church. I shall say more about this later. Roman society in the first century of the common era did not encourage literary activity by women. Almost certainly no writing in the NT was produced by a woman. So all we know about women in early Christianity and about attitudes toward them we learn only from writings by men. That is why some women scholars (C. C. Kroeger 1995) have designed a study edition of the Bible using the *NRSV*. Their theory is that they have things to say about the NT that men cannot say or that they have not yet said. Recently L. Schottroff 1995 has used her own experience of patriarchal oppression in her interpretation of NT material.

As we have seen, Luke has a special interest in and concern for women in both of his works. But the historian must be cautious in assessing Luke's word on the subject because his account may, to some degree at least, represent his own bias rather than historical fact. Nevertheless, it seems certain that women did play influential roles in some Christian communities, yet we do not have their own accounts of their work or of their experiences as women.

More and more women today are challenging the ways men have treated, or failed to treat, women in the NT in studies on the NT thus far produced mostly by men. Most feminist NT scholars, in light of their own experiences as women, try to interpret NT texts and traditions completely and with sensitivity. C. Osiek 1985:93–105 suggests "five alternative responses to the question of feminist biblical hermeneutics" that "arise from five different sets of women's experiences and assumptions about the Bible . . . : rejectionist, loyalist, revisionist, sublimationist, and liberationist." We are concerned with them only as they relate to the study of Jesus and the NT.

The rejectionist method, as its name implies, regards the Bible as unauthoritative and useless; some who follow this method even reject the whole religious tradition represented in the Bible. Almost the opposite of this method is the loyalist one, according to which "the fundamental premise is the essential validity and goodness of the biblical tradition as Word of God, which cannot be dismissed under any circumstance." God's authority is ultimately found in scripture, and all humans must obey it. But as God's Word the scripture cannot be oppressive. If it seems to be so, the interpreter is at fault, not the message in the Bible, whose aim is to promote happiness and human freedom for all. Passages that appear to demand submission of females (for example, 1 Cor 14:34 and 11:5 and 1 Tim 2:12 and Titus 2:3) are by exegesis (critical interpretation) shown to prove that women are not at all given a lower status than men.

The middle ground between the first two alternatives is the revisionist hermeneutic, the basic premise of which is that the patriarchalism of the Judeo-Christian tradition is determined historically but not theologically. The male-dominated, androcentric, and discriminatory characteristics resulting from social and historical factors can be separated from the tradition and so are "not intrinsic to it." By using a positive approach in examining the sources, this method interprets the role of women in the NT and in the early church from the presentation of women in the gospels, letters of Paul, and other early Christian literature. The anti-feminist texts "are explained by a combination of exegetical method and interpretation of the influence of cultural context."

Sublimationism in biblical studies "takes the form of the search for and glorification of the eternal feminine in biblical symbolism." This method centers on the symbols of the church as the "bride of Christ and mother of the faithful" and "Mary as virgin-mother who symbolizes . . . the church, and the feminine mystique."

Liberation Theology

Beginning with the perspective of liberation theology, the liberationist interpretation of the NT "proclaims that the central message of the Bible is human liberation, that this is in fact the meaning of salvation." A chief advocate and developer of this hermeneutic alternative is E. S. Fiorenza 1983, to whose book *In Memory of Her* we now turn briefly.

The title of Fiorenza's book is taken from Jesus' words to the woman who anointed his head: "Wherever the gospel is proclaimed in the whole world, what she has done will be told in remembrance of her" (Mark 14:9). Contrary to Jesus' prediction, according to Fiorenza, Judas and Peter, rather than the woman, have been remembered by Christians. This typifies the forgetting of women in history.

In trying to understand early Christian communities, Fiorenza centers her attention on NT texts that rise above the patriarchal and androcentric. In doing so, she tries to reconstruct, if not rewrite, the history of early Christianity from "a feminist critical hermeneutics of liberation" (26).

Fiorenza presumes the priority of Mark and the source theory of the composition of the synoptic gospels. For example, Luke (7:36–50) redacts the story of the woman who anointed Jesus' head (Mark 14:3–9; Matt 26:6–13) to characterize her as a sinner, "that is, a prostitute." The formula "your faith has saved you" here and in the story of the woman with the flow of blood indicates that these stories were associated with the baptism tradition in the early church. And the stories "assert . . . that Jesus and his movement invited into their table community . . . sinners, prostitutes, beggars, tax collectors, the ritually polluted, the crippled, and the impoverished—in short, the scum of Palestinian society. . . . And many of these were women" (129–130).

By including everyone, the Jesus movement brought about a wholly different idea of God, "a God of graciousness and goodness who accepts everyone and brings about justice and well-being for everyone without exception" (130). In the earliest traditions about Jesus, this God is perceived in the form of a woman "as divine *Sophia* (wisdom)," even by Jesus, and that he thought of himself as the child and prophet of Sophia. Fiorenza believes that the "very old saying" of Jesus in Luke 7:35 may have had its setting in Jesus' table fellowship "with tax collectors, prostitutes, and sinners" (132). She also discusses other passages in the synoptic gospels, Paul's letters, Colossians, and the prologue of John where Jesus is interpreted as Wisdom. In the pre-Johannine prologue hymn, the feminine *Sophia* became the masculine *Logos,* probably under the influence of Philo, who was not a feminist (191).

In contrast to Fiorenza, from a socioeconomic and feminist viewpoint, W. Munro 1998 argues that Jesus was born of a slave woman, had the status of a slave, and lived as a freed man only conditionally.

Fiorenza stresses the significance of house churches and the family of Chloe (1 Cor 1:11) in the missionary activity of early Christianity. Phoebe (Rom 16:1–2) is "not a deaconess of the women, but a minister of the whole church" (170).

The statement in Gal 3:28 that there is neither Jew nor Greek, slave nor free, male nor female, for all are one in Christ Jesus is a pre-Pauline baptismal statement. Paul interprets and adapts it to the community at Corinth to "unequivocally affirm the equality and charismatic giftedness of women and men in the Christian community." By encouraging women to remain free from the marriage bond, Paul makes it possible for them to have "a new independent lifestyle," thus af-

firming Christian freedom and equality. At the same time, "he subordinates women's behavior in marriage and in the worship assembly . . . and restricts their rights not only as 'pneumatics' but also as 'women,'" because Paul does not give the same kind of restrictions about men's behavior "*qua* men" ("in the capacity or character of" men) in public worship (235–236).

W. Stegemann 1997 reviews Fiorenza's thesis that Jesus initiated a gender-equality movement and considers the role of women in the Jesus movement. Although, according to Stegemann, the textual evidence is limited and the interpretations of the gospel writers favor a patriarchal point of view, there is no doubt that women played an important part in early Christianity. It seems to me the fact that women played a more important role in the early Christian movement than heretofore recognized is the bottom line in feminist studies.

As is usually true when very different proposals are offered, many scholars do not agree with Fiorenza's "reconstruction of Christian origins." However, Fiorenza and other feminists raise many significant questions that must be considered in any attempt to recover the work and words of Jesus and to reconstruct Christianity in its early stages. Perhaps feminist scholars in general are most vulnerable in reading into biblical texts what is not there and in failing to acknowledge that ancient realities and modern causes, however noble, are often not the same.

For further study of women in the NT, see J. LaPorte 1982; R. Ruether 1979; B. McHaffie 1986; E. Stagg 1978; B. Witherington 1985, 1988; W. Munro 1982; B. B. Thurston 1989; G. Theissen 1998; E. M. Tetlow 1980; J. M. Arlandson 1997; E. S. Fiorenza 1994.

THE JESUS SEMINAR AND THE NEW JESUS QUEST

The Jesus Seminar is the name given to a group of NT scholars, sometimes as many as seventy, who met semiannually to evaluate the gospel accounts of what Jesus said and did. Founded in 1985 by R. W. Funk and J. D. Crossan as cochairs, the seminar has probably been the best advertised event in the history of biblical research. Why? Because from the start some members sought publicity through the news media, including leading newspapers, news journals, and television. As a result, the group have been accused of being ultraliberal and of creating a circus-like atmosphere whenever they appear. The seminar has now turned its attention to the letters of Paul.

At the meetings members read papers and discussed texts, varying in length from several words, phrases, and sentences to a whole unit of material from both canonical and noncanonical gospels. Sayings of Jesus were assigned various colors to indicate their relative authenticity. By using beads of different colors, members voted on the relative authenticity, or lack of it, of sayings of Jesus. I say "relative" because different colors signify different possibilities of authenticity in descending likelihood. Red means that Jesus said the words in question, or something close to them; pink means he probably said something like them; gray means Jesus did not say them, but the idea behind them may be his; and black means Jesus did not say them. This color scheme has appeared graphically in a publication by R. W. Funk 1993. The volume gives the full text of the canonical gospels, plus the *Gospel of Thomas,* which up to this time has generally been regarded as apocryphal (see Chapter 1).

Only about twenty percent of sayings attributed to Jesus are regarded as authentic by the seminar members. The reason for the low number is that they assume a saying was not uttered by Jesus unless proven otherwise. However, many scholars still hold to the principle that a saying attributed to Jesus is genuine unless determined to be unauthentic. Notice that I said "determined" instead of "proven." Scholars cannot "prove" a saying attributed to Jesus is authentic or unauthentic any more than classical scholars can do so for a saying attributed to Socrates by Plato.

The translation in Funk's work is not one of the standard versions but that of the seminar members called the *Scholars Version (SV).* For this and other reasons some critics of the seminar believe that its members assume persons who do not belong to the group or its sponsor, the Westar Institute in Sonoma, California, are not scholars. On the other hand, some scholars critical of the seminar members think some of them are not scholars.

I shall not enter that arena of personal debate. Those of you who become interested in the work of the seminar should read the lengthy introduction to the *SV* of the gospels and one or more of the books on Jesus mentioned below. For a conservative scholar's view of *The Five Gospels* (R. W. Funk 1993) see D. A. Carson 1994.

The most severe, if not vituperative, attack against the Jesus Seminar is that of L. T. Johnson 1995. He does not want people to think that the views of the seminar represent a "consensus" of most NT scholars. Johnson is not satisfied to criticize the writings of seminar scholars but also disputes their qualifications. He accuses the seminar members of limited historical knowledge and tries to demolish their assumptions and methodology. History, according to Johnson, cannot prove the truth about Jesus and the gospels. On that point Johnson also faults the "fundamentalist" and "conservative" scholars for going to other extremes.

For Johnson, Christian faith is based on the "real Jesus" as "both Lord and Christ" (Acts 2:36), not on events taken to be historical. The resurrection of Jesus may have happened as a historical event, but the historian cannot determine if it did. The historicity of the resurrection occurs in the effect it has on the believer. Indeed, according to Johnson, no reconstruction of Jesus as a historical person has relevance for Christian faith, worship, or theology.

Johnson's separation of faith from history is unacceptable to many scholars, conservative and liberal alike. Is Johnson's "real Jesus" any less tenuous than the Jesus of the scholars Johnson lambastes? Perhaps most scholars still think the real Jesus needs some grounding in history. Philosophers and theologians may perform their tasks apart from historical considerations, but can critical biblical scholars do so?

SOME CONTEMPORARY STUDIES ON JESUS

Some twenty years ago there began a revived interest in the study of Jesus that is still strong as we enter the twenty-first century. Some of the studies are written by persons in the Jesus Seminar, some are not, though perhaps occasioned by it. With few exceptions, the studies are concerned with and based on a knowledge of the socioeconomic, political, and religious conditions of the time of Jesus.

A number of scholars have claimed to write about Jesus with an interdisciplinary approach and without Christian presuppositions. The apocalyptic-eschatological views of J. Weiss and A. Schweitzer that for Jesus the end of the age was imminent has largely faded from view. I think it is fair to say that in general Jesus' Son of Man sayings are regarded as unauthentic, and those on the kingdom of God, which is often no longer regarded as the basis of Jesus' teaching, do not point to the end of the world. Rather, Jesus was a teacher of wisdom or a prophet and social reformer much like the great Israelite prophets or a sage as divine Wisdom personified in the flesh of Jesus (B. Witherington 1994). Jesus emerges as a model for socioeconomic, political, and religious reforms and often, it seems, in that order of importance. Contemporary studies are enhanced by feminist and other social/psychological criticism that presents Jesus as an advocate of a new, even radical, social vision that includes all people, regardless of gender or social status. (For a review of contemporary Jesus studies see M. J. Borg 1994a.)

M. J. Borg has written several volumes on Jesus. In the first (1984; new ed. 1998) he argues that interpretations of Jesus' teachings have been unduly influenced by the apocalyptic-eschatological views of J. Weiss and A. Schweitzer. Consequently many teachings of Jesus that cannot be fitted into that mold have been neglected. Much of that teaching deals with Jesus' conflict with authorities within the institutions of Judaism concerning the Jews and their destiny, but not without political consequences.

According to Borg, the teaching of Jesus can best be understood by considering the Jewish piety of NT times and understanding how the social conflict between the Jews and Rome shaped those times. The conflict between Jesus and Jewish authorities must be understood within that broader conflict. The chief issue, as the title of Borg's book implies, was the holiness of the Jews. The quest for holiness was the attempt to imitate the holiness of God by keeping apart from all impurity through devotion to the law and the temple service. That quest best explains the resistance to Rome. Jesus challenged that quest, which was pursued by the ruling elite. The works of Borg do show a concern for historical-critical research and for Christian faith and life (see also M. J. Borg 1987, 1994b).

For somewhat similar, yet contrasting, studies see those of J. P. Meier 1991, 1994. The first volume is a moderate and thorough investigation of all aspects of Jesus' life based on the canonical gospels. The gospel of John is given almost equal value with the synoptics, but Meier does not regard the *Gospel of Thomas* of like value. Meier's second volume deals with John the Baptist as Jesus' mentor and with the Baptist in his own right. Meier discusses the kingdom of God, present and future, along with its background. Then he discusses ancient and modern views of miracles and all kinds of miracles and healings attributed to Jesus. Meier concludes that Jesus as a prophet and miracle worker is the best way to think that his contemporaries understood him (see also J. P. Meier 1996).

The work of J. D. Crossan 1991 is one of the most radical of the new studies of Jesus when compared with most of those of previous generations. He attempts to reconstruct the real teachings of Jesus in the real world and events of the real person, Jesus of Nazareth. For Crossan, though, phenomena from Judaism, such as the law and prophecy, are not considered, because they do not help in getting to understand Jesus. There was no trial of Jesus before Jews because he was crucified by the Romans. For views that differ from those of Crossan about Jesus and

Judaism see E. P. Sanders 1985, and J. H. Charlesworth 1988.

Crossan bases his study on restructured versions of Q and on apocryphal gospels that he thinks date before 60 CE. However, many scholars still believe those gospels date from the second century (see R. E. Brown 1987). According to Crossan, Jesus was a Jewish Cynic and Galilean peasant who, in light of contemporary socioeconomic and political society, was on a social mission for an egalitarian community to replace the divisive culture of the times. In light of Satanism and devil cults in some of our current culture, especially among the youth, it is interesting to note that Crossan thinks demons were nonexistent for Jesus. Jesus did, however, free some people from oppression that they thought was demon possession.

With respect to the beginning and end of Jesus' life, the stories of Jesus' birth are fictitious, and the stories of his passion were motivated by passages from the OT. Jesus did not rise from the dead, and it is likely that dogs ate his unburied body. Although Jesus was a historical person, no reconstruction of the historical Jesus is relevant for Christian faith, worship, or theology (see also J. D. Crossan 1994). Perhaps the most vehement critic of Crossan's work and similar studies of Jesus is L. T. Johnson 1995 (see The Jesus Seminar above; see also J. D. Crossan 1994).

In several volumes N. T. Wright 1993, 1996a, 1996b labels some contemporary works on Jesus as caricatures whose authors find a couple of true aspects in their portrayals of Jesus but, in spite of that, wind up with fallacious conclusions. As for his own views, Wright believes Jesus was conscious of God as Father, believed he was the Messiah, and in his own salvific fulfillment of OT scriptures. According to Wright, Jesus did teach about the kingdom of God, its coming, and entrance into it. Jesus was crucified but believed he would ultimately return. For criticism of Wright see M. Casey 1998 ("Where Wright is Wrong"). In a recent volume Borg and Wright 1998, whose views, obviously, are opposed to each other, discuss their respective positions regarding the virgin birth of Jesus, his deity, resurrection, and his second coming.

In a book just off the press G. Luedemann 1999, using his own criteria for determining authentic sayings of Jesus, concludes that the traditional Christian faith cannot be confirmed by those criteria. Although Jesus was a deeply sympathetic person and remains as one of the great religious personalities of all time, Christians cannot honestly appeal to Jesus without participating in a "great deception" (see the title in the bibliography).

Luedemann's book is too recent for me to present any scholar's reaction to his view. However, please consider it carefully, along with the view of others presented here, as you study the stories of Jesus' life and work suggested in the following pages and especially as you read about Jesus in the first three gospels.

One thing in Jesus research that must be understood clearly is that in NT times persons who claimed to be or were thought to be the Messiah were not present everywhere, contrary to implications in some works on Jesus. Whether Jesus actually thought of himself as the Messiah is still a debatable question according to information in the synoptic gospels. However, in the gospel of John Jesus readily admits that he is (John 4:25–26; see Mark 14:61–62; see also John 1:41; 11:27).

Of course, we must remember that John's stated purpose for writing was to convince his readers to "believe that Jesus is the Messiah, the Son of God, and that through believing you may have life in his name" (John 20:31). If Jesus did claim to be the Messiah, he was the first known Jew to do so before Simon bar Cochba, who led the final Jewish revolt against Rome in 132–135 CE (see Chronological Table). The illustrious Rabbi Akiba supported his claim. For views that Jesus was the Messiah and/or was proclaimed to be the Messiah see B. Witherington 1995b (last chapter). For a variety of opinions on messianic ideas and persons in Judaism before Jesus see J. H. Charlesworth 1992.

For balanced studies on Jesus from different perspectives see R. A. Horsley 1987; B. D. Chilton 1994; B. Witherington 1995b; N. T. Wright 1992, 1996a and b; I. Wilson 1997. On Jesus as Messiah see M. de Jonge 1977, 1991.

So then, after learning about only several of the recent views about Jesus, what conclusions can we suggest about Jesus, the central figure behind the NT writings who continues to be the focus of a vast body of current literature? We consider that question in the pages that follow.

JESUS' LIFE AND WORK

The question "Who then is this?" (Mark 4:41) is put on the lips of Jesus' disciples after the stilling of the storm. Ever since the gospels were written, many thoughtful people have wondered "what sort of man" Jesus was (Matt 8:27). No matter what techniques or clues are used in an effort to arrive at the truth about Jesus and what he said and did, subjective judgments do enter into the process, and the results of such effort are always based on inconclusive evidence.

Consider, for example, the question of Jesus' physical appearance. How could a painter or a sculptor possibly portray Jesus authentically? In the gospels there is not a hint about Jesus' physical stature, deportment, appearance, complexion, color and length of his hair, or the color of his eyes. But close your eyes for a moment and let a picture of Jesus come into your mind. Whose painting of Jesus do you imagine—that by Leonardo da Vinci, Raphael, Sallman, or some other? Undoubtedly you have some image of Jesus. It is probably inevitable that one begins the study of Jesus with impressions that are not based on evidence in the gospels.

Jesus as Teacher, Preacher, and Healer

In the Introduction it was suggested that Jesus and his disciples constituted a school, and there is evidence in the gospels for Jesus as a teacher. The evidence is corroborated by early Christian writers after the NT period and by Jewish sources that are hostile toward Jesus (W. D. Davies 1964:418–419). Mark, as the oldest gospel, is the oldest tradition for Jesus as teacher. Q, the source besides Mark that Matthew and Luke have in common, is composed mostly of teachings of Jesus, and reporting Jesus' teachings is a common interest of Matthew and Luke. Jesus is portrayed primarily as a teacher, but it is also reported that he sometimes preached and healed sick people.

Although Mark reports considerably fewer of Jesus' teachings than either Matthew or Luke, his favorite title by which others address Jesus is teacher, both in the Greek (*didaskale*) and Hebrew (*rabbi*) forms of the word. (For possible reasons why Mark reports fewer teachings see M. E. Boring 1977; R. T. France 1980.) Jesus is so addressed not only by his disciples (Mark 4:38; 9:38; 10:35; 13:1), but also by others (Mark 5:35 = Luke 9:38; see also Matt 8:19; 9:11; 12:38; 17:24; Luke 7:40; 9:38; 10:25; 18:18), including those hostile to him, among whom are scribes, Pharisees, Herodians, and Sadducees (Mark 12:14, 19, 32 = Matt 22:16, 24, 36 = Luke 20:21, 28, 39). Mark also uses the verb "to teach" (*didaskō*) and the noun "teaching" (*didachē*) with reference to Jesus more often than either Matthew or Luke does.

It is not certain when the term *rabbi*, which literally means "my teacher," was first used as a title of respect or to indicate that a person with that title belonged to a professional group of Jewish teachers. It may not have been so used during Jesus' lifetime. However, on an ossuary (a container for the bones of the dead) discovered on the Mount of Olives and dated early in the first century, the Greek word *didaskalos* (teacher) is used as a title. So if *didaskalos* represents the Hebrew *rabbi*, "rabbi" could have been applied to Jesus during his lifetime. At any rate, by the time Mark wrote his gospel, the title "rabbi" was applied to Jesus by his disciples (9:5; 11:21; 14:45 = Matt 26:49; see also Matt 26:25). And when Matthew wrote his gospel (c. 80 CE), he understood the terms "rabbi" and "teacher" as synonymous honorific titles applied to leaders in the community. This is clear from one of Jesus' statements to his disciples: "But you are not to be called rabbi, for you have one teacher" (23:8). Luke avoids the use of the word "rabbi," as he does other non-Greek words.

It is significant also that many times Matthew and Luke change Mark's use of the titles "teacher" and "rabbi": "rabbi" in Mark 9:5 to "Lord" in Matt 17:4 and to "Master" (*epistata*) in Luke 9:33; "rabbi" in Mark 10:51 to "Lord" in both Matt 20:33 and Luke 18:41; and "rabbi" in Mark 11:21 omitted by Matthew in an incident that Luke does not contain. Matthew usually portrays the disciples as addressing Jesus with the reverential title "Lord" (8:25; 17:4) instead of the Markan "teacher" (4:38; 13:1) and "rabbi" (9:5), or he omits the title in Mark (see Mark 10:35 and Matt 20:20; Mark 13:1 and Matt 24:1; Mark 11:21 and Matt 21:20). Luke also uses "Lord" instead of Mark's "rabbi" in 18:41, and "Master" instead of "teacher" in 8:24 and 9:33, 49.

After studying about Jesus from the perspectives of modern education, J. T. Dillon 1995 concludes that, irrespective of his success or effectiveness, it can be shown that Jesus was a good teacher. According to B. L. Mack 1988:67–74, because of his "style of social criticism," and because "his themes and topics are much closer to Cynic idiom" than to those of public Jewish piety, Jesus can best be thought of as a Cynic teacher.

As the church developed a higher theology of Jesus as Lord, the more primitive and historical tradition of Jesus as teacher was suppressed. The designation of Jesus as teacher was superseded by titles that later more adequately expressed the faith of Christians in their Lord. Nevertheless, the fact that Jesus had been a teacher was never forgotten, and the efforts of some early Christians to collect, transmit, and interpret material about Jesus as teacher and about his teachings were largely responsible for the first three gospels as they now exist.

Among the offices of the early church, teachers ranked third after apostles and prophets (1 Cor 12:28–29) or after prophets and ministers (Rom 12:6–8; see also Eph 4:11). Since teachers ranked only third, there would hardly have been so much emphasis on Jesus as a teacher in the traditions underlying the gospels if he had not actually been regarded as a teacher.

G. Vermes 1973:69, 224–225 thinks that evidence in the gospels indicates that Jesus had supernatural abilities derived "from immediate contact with God," not from secret powers. Jesus was "a genuine charismatic" in a long line of prophetic religious figures, the *Hasidim* or Pious. Two such contemporary Jewish figures were Honi the Circle-Drawer and Hanina ben Dosa, whose background perhaps was Galilee, though this is purely conjectural.

In one way, more than any other, Jesus surpassed his contemporaries and prophetic predecessors who preached on behalf of the poor and defended widows and orphans oppressed by the rich and powerful. Jesus not only proclaimed the poor as blessed, "he actually took his stand among the pariahs of his world, those despised by the respectable." Vermes concludes that on the basis of the earliest gospel tradition, "considered against its natural background of first-century Galilean charismatic religion," Jesus was "the just man . . . Jesus the helper and healer, Jesus the teacher and leader, venerated by his intimates and less committed admirers alike as prophet, lord and *son of God*."

The concept of Jesus presented by Vermes has affinities with the image of the "divine man" (*theios anēr*), thought by some scholars to be represented in the portrayal of Jesus by the gospel writers. The term *theios anēr* originated within Hellenism and designated a man who was truly wise because his wisdom and life were thought to be in harmony with the Divine. Moses, Socrates, Apollonius of Tyana, and other historical persons were thought to be such figures. The designation came to be applied especially to persons believed to have the power to perform miracles. But a variety of other traits were ascribed to "divine men," including wisdom, prophecy, ecstatic speech, and rhetorical skill. "Divine men" were usually itinerants who wanted to win reverence for their persons and adherence to their teachings. Some scholars maintain that the "divine man" concept is inappropriately applied to Jesus because of lack of documentary evidence in the first century CE. For differences of opinion, see the works by M. Hadas 1965; D. L. Tiede 1972; T. J. Weeden 1971; C. R. Holladay 1977.

In contrast to the frequency with which Jesus is called "teacher" and referred to as one who teaches, he is never referred to as a preacher and only rarely as one who preaches. Mark refers to Jesus as preaching just four times (so also only in Matt 4:23; 9:35; 11:1; Luke 4:44; 8:1), and only in the first chapter after he has presented John the Baptist as one who came preaching (1:4, 7). Then Mark says, "After John was arrested, Jesus came into Galilee, proclaiming the gospel of God, and saying, 'The time is fulfilled, and the kingdom of God has come near; repent, and believe in the gospel'" (1:14, 15). These words are an apocalyptic-eschatological message, and John had preached the same message. It seems, therefore, that in these verses Mark's source or Mark himself was intentionally presenting Jesus as imitating both the manner and the content of John's message. Although Mark again refers to Jesus as preaching in 1:38, 39, for Mark, Jesus was a teacher whose teaching was the basis of his authority.

Immediately after the call of the first disciples, Mark says that Jesus "went to Capernaum . . . entered the synagogue and taught. They were astounded at his teaching, for he taught them as one having authority, and not as the scribes" (1:21–22). Now turn to Mark 1:21–28 in Example 3.1.

Notice that Mark has used vv 21–22 and vv 27–28, which present Jesus as teacher, to serve

---

EXAMPLE 3.1	*Jesus Teaching in the Synagogue in Capernaum*	
Matt 7:28–29	**Mark 1:21–28**	**Luke 4:31–37**
[28]Now when Jesus had finished saying these things, the crowds were astounded at his teaching, [29]for he taught them as one having authority, and not as their scribes.	[21]They went to Capernaum; and when the sabbath came, he entered the synagogue and taught. [22]They were astounded at his teaching, for he taught them as one having authority, and not as the scribes. [23]Just then there was in their synagogue a man with an unclean spirit, [24]and he cried out, "What have you to do with us, Jesus of Nazareth? Have you come to destroy us? I know who you are, the Holy One of God." [25]But Jesus rebuked him, saying, "Be silent, and come out of him!" [26]And the unclean spirit, convulsing him and crying with a loud voice, came out of him. [27]They were all amazed, and they kept on asking one another, "What is this? A new teaching—with authority! He commands even the unclean spirits, and they obey him." [28]At once his fame began to spread throughout the surrounding region of Galilee.	[31]He went down to Capernaum, a city in Galilee, and was teaching them on the sabbath. [32]They were astounded at his teaching, because he spoke with authority. [33]In the synagogue there was a man who had the spirit of an unclean demon, and he cried out with a loud voice, [34]"Let us alone! What have you to do with us, Jesus of Nazareth? Have you come to destroy us? I know who you are, the Holy One of God." [35]But Jesus rebuked him, saying, "Be silent, and come out of him!" When the demon had thrown him down before them, he came out of him without having done him any harm. [36]They were all amazed and kept saying to one another, "What kind of utterance is this? For with authority and power he commands the unclean spirits, and out they come!" [37]And a report about him began to reach every place in the region.

Cf. *InThom* 19:2.

as an introduction and conclusion, respectively, to the original miracle story (vv 23–26) that was in his source. In this way Mark associates Jesus' function as teacher with his function as healer in the first miracle story he reports (see also Mark 6:2). By enclosing the miracle story with references to Jesus' teaching, he makes the teaching superior to Jesus' working of miracles. Now look at the parallel in Luke 4:31–37, especially vv 36–37. Luke changes the crowd's response into a reaction to the miracle alone, not to the teaching of Jesus. This corresponds to Luke 4:16–27, Jesus' first public appearance in Luke. There Luke presents Jesus as a preacher (vv 21–22) and teacher (vv 22–24) who defends his activity as a miracle worker with a reference to the healings by Elijah and Elisha. Thus, Luke gives equal weight to Jesus as preacher, teacher, and healer in the first public incident in Jesus' career.

Several different conclusions can be drawn from what I have just said. If, as seems entirely likely, Mark did compose vv 21–22 and 27–28 to frame the paradigm—that is, the healing story (vv 23–26) that was in his source—we can conclude that Mark presented Jesus as a teacher because he wanted to stress teaching as Jesus' main role. On the other hand, we can conclude that because Mark actually knew Jesus was a teacher, he enclosed the miracle story in his source with references to Jesus as an authoritative teacher in order to acknowledge that Jesus was also a healer.

Belief in miracles and miracle workers was taken for granted everywhere in the Graeco-Roman world. Therefore, in order to present Jesus as a successful teacher in the world of Mark's time, Mark had to portray him also as a person who had the power to perform miracles, especially healings. But in spite of Mark's special interest in reporting miracles of Jesus, he never links Jesus' teaching, preaching, and healing as does Matthew (4:23; 9:35). Luke sometimes combines "preaching" and "bringing the good news" (8:1); the latter phrase, which is one word in Greek (*euangelizō*), is one of Luke's favorites. He uses it several times with reference to Jesus' preaching, where it is synonymous with "to preach" (see, for example, 16:16; 20:1). Mark

never uses the word *euangelizō*, which has more theological implications than the expression "to preach," and it occurs in Matthew only once, in a Q passage (Matt 11:5 = Luke 7:22).

All gospel writers, then, present Jesus as a teacher, preacher, and healer, with the least emphasis on Jesus as a preacher. In Mark the emphasis is clearly on Jesus as a teacher who also performs miracles, and in Matthew and Luke the emphasis is on actual teachings of Jesus.

Nature and Content of Jesus' Teaching

As a Jewish teacher, Jesus could assume a number of things about his hearers. He could assume that because of the diversity of opinion on every subject within Judaism during his time, he would be given a hearing. He could also assume that his hearers expected a Messiah, a day of judgment with rewards for the righteous and punishment for the wicked, and a resurrection of at least the righteous dead. Jesus could take for granted among his hearers the world view current among Jews, a belief in the existence of God, the conviction that God's will as revealed in the Torah invoked the responsibility for obedience, a moral and ethical awareness stemming from the commandments, and a feeling of guilt when disobedience was called to the attention of his hearers.

Much of Jesus' teaching is of a hortatory nature, such as that preserved in the Q source, in some of Matthew's special material in the so-called Sermon on the Mount, and sometimes elsewhere. This hortatory material was transmitted and used in the early church as the need for such material arose when Gentiles, many of whom were used to living lives much different from those of Jews and Christians, were being admitted into the church. For example, Paul specifically refers to commands of Jesus (1 Cor 7:10–11; 9:14), and sometimes Paul's language and thought are close to those of Jesus as recorded in the gospels. Here are some examples:

Bless those who persecute you. [Rom 12:14]

Pray for those who persecute you. [Matt 5:44]

Do not repay anyone evil for evil. [Rom 12:17]

Do not resist an evildoer. [Matt 5:39]

Be at peace among yourselves. [1 Thess 5:13]

Be at peace with one another. [Mark 9:50]

You shine like stars in the world. [Phil 2:15]

You are the light of the world. [Matt 5:14]

Paul occasionally reminds his readers of something they have learned. To the Roman believers recently converted from paganism Paul writes, "You, having once been slaves of sin, have become obedient from the heart to the form of teaching to which you were entrusted, and that you, having been set free from sin, have become slaves of righteousness" (6:17–18; see also 2:17–24; 16:17–19). And he writes to the Thessalonians, "We ask and urge you in the Lord Jesus that, as you learned from us how you ought to live and to please God . . . you should do so more and more" (1 Thess 4:1).

The evidence from Paul tends to support the synoptic gospel tradition of Jesus as a teacher and the hortatory nature of his teaching. On the other hand, the Pauline concept of *dikaiosynē*, translated either as "justification" or "righteousness," is absent from the synoptic gospels in the Pauline sense. The word "grace" (*charis*), which occurs only in Luke's gospel, is not used in the Pauline sense (but see 2:40). The same is probably true for "justification" (but see Matt 12:37; Luke 16:15; 18:14). The silence of the gospels on these and other doctrines of apostolic Christianity, such as that of the Holy Spirit, suggests that we can be in touch with some genuine sayings of Jesus in the gospels. Yet many teachings of Jesus reported by the gospel writers probably do not go back to him.

Because Jesus was a Jewish teacher, it seems reasonable to assume that he would have talked about things of interest and concern to Jews. Almost all the reported teachings of Jesus have parallels in the OT, the writings from Qumran, or other writings of the Judaism of his time. Judging from what we know of Judaism, there certainly is much of what we would call "old stuff" in the synoptic gospels. Does that mean, though,

that whatever has a parallel in Judaism is not from Jesus? It may indeed, as many believe. Yet wouldn't Jesus as a Jew be likely to speak about things Jewish? In fact, maybe precisely those parts of his teaching that correspond with Judaism originally come from him. It should be no surprise that Jesus repeated things that had been said before, since newness or originality or uniqueness in a teacher is not the same as that of an inventor. Jesus was concerned with what was most essential in religion (Mark 12:28–34).

In spite of Mark's report that, after the exorcism in the synagogue in Capernaum, some Jews asked among themselves, "What is this? A new teaching!" (1:27), novelty was never a charge raised by Jesus' opponents. In this respect Jesus' experience was different from that of Socrates, who was formally charged with introducing new and strange deities (Plato, *Apology* 11; 14; Xenophon, *Memorabilia* 1:1:1). The same motif is reflected in the account of Paul at Athens (Acts 17:18–20): "He seems to be a proclaimer of foreign divinities. . . . May we know what this new teaching is that you are presenting? It sounds rather strange to us, so we would like to know what it means." In strong contrast, the gospel writers do not present Jesus as the developer of a new religion but as the fulfiller of the prophecies of the old. Yet there must have been at least some new emphasis in Jesus' teaching, or how could we explain the Jews' opposition to him?

It was not the content of Jesus' teaching that was new, but the emphases he gave it. His demands seemed extreme, even in his own day, but that is all the more reason to suspect that they belong to the historical record. His words were uncompromising: "Do not resist an evildoer." "Love your enemies." "Pray for those who persecute you." Many Jewish leaders were willing to make concessions to retain their control, but they became hostile when faced with the uncommon and unconditional demands of Jesus.

Certainly one way Jesus differed from more professional teachers and leaders of his time was in eliciting responses from the unlearned people who met him. Mark's report that "the great crowd heard him gladly" (12:37; Greek) is probably not an idle one. Jesus didn't bring new concepts of love and forgiveness for sinners; he just gave the old ones concrete expression as he associated with people. When he did that, he was rejected by those who presumed that they were righteous and welcomed by sinners. Jesus' regular association with outcasts, even sinners, was a source of constant irritation to his critics.

Jesus' teaching is different not only in what it emphasizes, but also in what it doesn't stress. Conspicuously absent from Jesus' teaching, for example, is a message of faith. In fact, faith is scarcely mentioned in the reported sayings of Jesus, except in connection with healing miracles. Jesus only once asks his hearers to believe in him (Mark 9:42). Indeed, Jesus regularly directs attention toward God, not toward himself. Most of Jesus' sayings are intended to motivate people not toward faith of any kind, but toward action, including the proper behavior of humans toward God and toward one another. Jesus seems to have been trying to prepare people for the kingdom of God, either as it existed in his own time or as it would come in some form in the future. Any reference to faith as a requirement for entrance into the kingdom is conspicuously absent from Jesus' teaching.

Although Jesus did not direct faith toward himself and rarely ever mentioned faith, early Christians developed a profound faith in the person of Jesus. Although there is sufficient evidence in the gospels, especially Mark, that Jesus was regarded as a teacher, his first followers came to regard him as more than a teacher. Another phase in the development of faith in the person of Jesus was the conviction that he was the long-promised and expected Messiah. Andrew's words to his brother Peter reported in the gospel of John are the joyful expression of that conviction: "We have found the Messiah" (1:41).

Death and Resurrection of Jesus

When the first followers of Jesus began trying to convert others to their faith in Jesus as the Messiah and to their way of life, the death of Jesus was a major obstacle to the conversion not only of

Jews but of Gentiles as well. This is clear from Paul's statement in 1 Cor 1:23: "Christ crucified, a stumbling block to Jews and foolishness to Gentiles." No group of Jews was expecting a Messiah who would suffer, let alone die, especially on a Roman cross. (For Jewish messianic beliefs, see R. A. Horsley 1984, 1987, 1988; J. Neusner 1987.) Except for the first followers of Jesus who came to believe he was the Messiah, Jews simply were not prepared to accept the death of the person they had hoped was "the one to redeem Israel" (Luke 24:21). And long after the time of the first generation of Jewish Christians and Paul, certain pagans, although admiring the Christians' high moral standards, ridiculed the Christians because "they still reverence that man, the one who was fixed on a stake in Palestine" (the satirist Lucian, *Death of Peregrinus* 11; see also Origen, *Against Celsus* 2:39–44).

If, as Christians came to believe, Jesus had predicted his own suffering, death, and resurrection and then fulfilled his predictions, then the suffering and death of Jesus as the Messiah (Christ) would not remain a stumbling block but become an asset to mission preaching. However, many scholars believe that the predictions of Jesus' passion belong to the traditions of the early church and do not go back to the historical Jesus.

In the first prediction of Jesus' passion, we can detect the problem the church faced with the suffering and dying Messiah (Mark 8:27–33; Matt 16:13–23; Luke 9:18–22; see also Mark 9:12; Luke 17:25; 24:6–7). In response to Jesus' question about who he is, Peter replies, "You are the Messiah." Here Peter speaks for himself and for all who believe that Jesus was the Messiah. Then Jesus says that he must suffer many things, be rejected by Jewish leaders, be killed, and rise again. Peter then rebukes Jesus and in Matt 16:22 says: "God forbid it, Lord! This must never happen to you." Peter's rebuke and response indicate that he is unable to comprehend or accept the idea of a suffering Messiah (so also the disciples in Mark 9:32; Matt 17:23; Luke 9:45; 18:34). Jesus' response to Peter is a rebuke followed by "Get behind me, Satan! For you are setting your mind not on divine things but on human things." Thus Peter's faith in God is questioned, apparently because he does not understand that Jesus must suffer and die. Peter's incomprehension represents, as well, the view of those Jews for whom a crucified Messiah was unthinkable.

Very early, therefore, Christians developed apologias for the suffering and death of Jesus. These apologias have survived in several traditions that frequently include Jesus' resurrection, which came to be linked theologically with his passion.

Perhaps one of the earliest apologias was that by Jesus' suffering and death (as well as his resurrection) he actually fulfilled OT prophecies. This was a firm conviction of the early church, although there are no known precisely relevant OT passages to support the belief (but see Hos 6:1–2; Ps 16:8–11, quoted in Acts 2:25–28; Isa 33:10 [LXX]). This apologia appears in the kērygma of Acts: "God fulfilled what he had foretold through all the prophets, that his Messiah would suffer" (Acts 3:18). In the synagogue at Thessalonica, Paul argued from the scriptures before both Jews and Greeks "that it was necessary for the Messiah to suffer and to rise from the dead, and saying, 'This is the Messiah, Jesus, whom I am proclaiming to you'" (Acts 17:2–3; see also Acts 2:22–34; 8:32–35; 17:11; 18:28; 26:22–23; 1 Cor 15:3–4; 1 Pet 1:11).

According to one tradition, preserved only in Luke's gospel, the risen Jesus himself explained that his death was in accordance with the scriptures to some disappointed and doubting followers: "'Oh, how foolish you are, and how slow of heart to believe all that the prophets have declared! Was it not necessary that the Messiah should suffer these things and then enter into his glory?' Then beginning with Moses and all the prophets, he interpreted to them the things about himself in all the scriptures" (Luke 24:25–27; see also 24:32, 44–46).

The writer of the gospel of John believed that particular aspects of Jesus' passion were in accordance with OT scriptures: betrayal by Judas (13:18; see Ps 41:10; Mark 14:18, 21; Luke

22:22); Jesus hated without cause (15:25; see Pss 35:19; 69:5; 119:157, 161); dividing Jesus' clothes (19:24; see Ps 22:19; Mark 15:24; Matt 27:35; Luke 23:34); Jesus' thirst (19:28; see Pss 63:2; 69:22); and piercing Jesus' side (19:36–37; see Exod 12:10, 46; Num 9:12; Ps 34:21; Zech 12:10; Matt 24:30).

The author of John refers to Jews of his time (the end of first century CE) who continued to reject Jesus as the Messiah: "They agreed that if anyone should confess him as the Christ, he should be put out of the synagogue" (9:22; my trans.; see also 12:42). According to John, Jesus predicted that this would happen (16:2). One view of the author, therefore, is that Gentiles scattered abroad would come to believe in Jesus and join believing Jews as "children of God" (11:53; see also Mark 12:1–12; Matt 21:33–46; Luke 20:9–19).

As the Christian movement grew and spread among Jews and Gentiles, Christians developed theological explanations for Jesus' suffering, death, and resurrection. One of the earliest of these is Paul's view in 1 Thess 4:14–18 and 5:9–10 that assures the converts at Thessalonica of their own future bliss in the resurrection because of Jesus' death and resurrection (see also 1 Cor 15:12–57; Phil 3:10–11; 1 Pet 1:3–5). This early view, perhaps even pre-Pauline, included the idea also (see 1 Thess 5:9–10) that the death of Christ served to atone for past sins of converts: "Christ died for our sins in accordance with the scriptures" (1 Cor 15:3–4; see also Gal 1:4; 2:19–21; Rom 4:24–25; 5:6–11; 6:1–11; 8:34; Heb 2:9–10; 1 Pet 3:18; Isa 53:4–5 [LXX]).

Early Christian missionaries found it useful to present witnesses to Jesus' resurrection to reinforce theological views. "With great power the apostles gave their testimony to the resurrection of the Lord Jesus" (Acts 4:33; see also 1:22; 2:32; 3:15). According to Acts, Peter says that the risen Jesus did not appear to all the people "but to us who were chosen by God as witnesses, and who ate and drank with him after he rose from the dead" (10:40–41; see also 1 Cor 15:5).

As a comparison among the accounts of resurrection appearances reported in 1 Cor 15:5–8, in the four gospels, and in Acts indicates, the testimony was preserved in differing traditions. In the gospel of John the earthly Jesus sometimes speaks as his own witness to the resurrection and promises eternal life that already begins with belief in him (John 11:25–26).

In all of the gospels, as you will learn, women are portrayed in the role of proclaiming the news of Jesus' resurrection. On that evidence, C. Setzer 1997 maintains that in the rest of the gospels or even in the pregospel traditions the role of women was silenced and their witness discredited (see also P. Perkins 1984; D. C. Allison 1985).

The writer of Hebrews presents a unique view of the efficacy of Jesus' suffering and death as atonement for sins in portraying Jesus as a priest or high priest. Although Jesus "was a Son," presumably from his birth, "he learned obedience through what he suffered; and having been made perfect, he became the source of eternal salvation for all who obey him" (Heb 5:8–9; see also 2:9–10, 18; 9:13–14). According to another tradition shared by Paul and the writer of Acts, Jesus was "declared to be Son of God . . . by resurrection from the dead" (Rom 1:4; Acts 13:33; see also Acts 2:29–36).

An increasing number of scholars think that the evidence in the gospels is not decisive enough to confirm the physical resurrection of Jesus. G. Luedemann 1994, after carefully analyzing the earliest traditions about the resurrection of Jesus in Paul's letters and the gospels, says that they confirm the sudden belief expressed in such passages as Acts 13:30, "God raised him from the dead," and similar passages in Paul's letters. Two passages have historical value (Luke 24:34; John 21:15–17). The first is an auditory report, and the second shows that Peter had a profound experience of God's love and forgiveness in a visionary encounter with the risen Jesus. The resurrection appearances in Jerusalem are efforts to reconcile later stories of the empty tomb with earlier traditions of the resurrection. In sum, the resurrection experiences were a combination of visionary and auditory encounters as the reactions to Jesus' suffering and death.

Other scholars seek to explain the resurrection stories from even greater perspectives of psychology. J. J. Pilch 1998 says that the psychological idea of altered states of consciousness makes it plausible that those who had "seen" Jesus did experience his "real self." This would be the cultural equivalent of humans experiencing non-human beings such as angels, demons, or even God.

The books below give more traditional discussions of Jesus' passion and resurrection. For works on the development of the passion and resurrection narrative, see J. D. Crossan 1988 and P. Pokorny 1987:63–235; see also J. L. Houlden 1987; U. Wilckens 1978; T. L. Miethe 1987; C. F. D. Moule 1968; P. Perkins 1984; R. H. Fuller 1971; W. Marxsen 1970; and pages from Chapter 4 and later in this chapter.

As Christians began to experience abuse and persecution from various groups in the communities where they lived, they became convinced that Jesus had predicted their sufferings as well as his own. The gospels report that Jesus said his followers would be beaten in synagogues, persecuted, hated by all, brought before authorities, put in prison, and expelled from synagogues (Mark 13:9; Matt 10:17, 23; 23:34; Luke 12:11; 21:12; John 15:20; 16:2). Moreover, some Christians believed that Jesus had promised a state of blessedness for those who suffered such fates: "Blessed are those who are persecuted" (Matt 5:10). "Blessed are you when people hate you, and when they exclude you, revile you" (Luke 6:22; see also Matt 5:11).

Christians found comfort from such promises in their times of danger, suffering, and persecution and looked to the example of Jesus who had suffered for them to sustain them. At such times Christians apparently tried to imitate his conduct and even felt that when they suffered they "shared" in Christ's suffering. Paul writes to the Corinthians: "When reviled, we bless; when persecuted, we endure; when slandered, we speak kindly" (1 Cor 4:12–13; see also Rom 12:14–15). For the sake of Christ, Paul was content with insults and persecutions (2 Cor 12:10; see also Rom 8:35–39).

Christians felt that just as Christ's sufferings were abundant for them, so they would share abundantly in his consolation (2 Cor 1:5–8; see also Rom 8:17). Paul writes to the Philippians that it has been granted to them that for the sake of Christ they should not only believe in him but also suffer for his sake (Phil 1:29; see also 3:10–11; Heb 10:32–39). The writer of 2 Timothy urges his readers to "share in suffering like a good soldier of Christ Jesus" (2 Tim 2:3; see also 2:8–13; Heb 12:1–11).

The writer of 1 Peter believed that the true test of Christians' status as God's people was suffering and that through various trials they should remain faithful to God and never fail to do what was right (1 Pet 1:6–7; 2:11–12). 1 Pet 2:19–24 provides an excellent summary of the Christian belief that the suffering and death of Jesus were effective for the forgiveness of past sins and of the conviction that the best witness to such faith is moral living:

> If through a consciousness of God one endures pains of suffering unjustly, this is a sign of grace. For what credit is it if when you do wrong and get beaten you endure? But if when you do good and suffer and you endure, this is a sign of grace from God. For this purpose you have been called, because Christ also suffered for you, leaving you a model that you should follow in his footsteps. . . . When reviled, he did not revile in return; when suffering he did not threaten. . . . He himself bore our sins in his body on the tree, in order that having no part in sins we might live to righteousness. [my trans.; see also 1 Pet 3:13–18; 4:1–19; Heb 12:1–17]

Christians came to believe that the suffering, death, and resurrection of Christ were effective for the forgiveness of past sins. They also believed that in their own times of suffering, they should follow his example and felt themselves blessed to "share" in his sufferings. And from the beginning, Christians also believed that moral life went hand in hand with the theological doctrines of the passion of Jesus. Doubtless they also thought that Christ was their model for that moral life. In fact, doctrines of Christ's passion are almost always put in the context of moral exhortation, as in the passage from 1 Peter just quoted.

Taking Jesus' conduct as an example, Paul believed it was a part of his apostolic mission to make the model of Christian moral life perfectly clear. He felt that he was not only a preacher and teacher but also a model—one whose conduct readers should imitate (Phil 3:17; see also 2 Thess 3:7–9). Paul writes to the Corinthians to be imitators of him as he is of Christ (1 Cor 11:1; see also 1 Cor 4:16; Eph 5:1).

The reference to Christ as "paschal lamb" is put in the context of exhorting the Corinthian Christians to remove immoral persons from among them (1 Cor 5:1–13). And so it is in every letter of Paul: theological doctrine and exhortation to moral life are inseparably bound together. "Christ died for our sins. . . . Do not be deceived. Bad companionships corrupt good ways. Become properly sober in your minds and do not sin" (1 Cor 15:3, 33–34; my trans.). God "raised Jesus our Lord from the dead, who was handed over to death for our trespasses and was raised for our justification. . . . Do not let sin exercise dominion in your mortal bodies, to make you obey their passions" (Rom 4:24–25; 6:12).

Many scholars believe that the story of Jesus' passion and resurrection was the first written narrative about Jesus. But they hold different opinions about whether the narrative was pre-Markan or a creation of Mark and whether it first circulated as independent units, like much of the other gospel material, but was put in its final form by Mark.

As Christianity spread from the first Jewish followers of Jesus who acknowledged him as the Messiah to Hellenistic Jews and Gentiles, other titles such as "Son of God," "Lord," "Savior," and, rarely, "God" were applied to Jesus in an effort to promote faith in him. But the same combination of theological doctrine and moral exhortation that occurs in Paul's letters, the earliest NT writings, is just as clearly and strongly emphasized in the later NT literature.

SUMMARY

Several clues used in the critical study of Jesus and the first three gospels help to provide a better understanding of Jesus' words and deeds. Some scholars think the best clue is the apocalyptic eschatology (that is, the beliefs about the end of the world and the last judgment) of Jesus and the gospel writers. Others prefer to consider the kērygma—early Christian preaching about what God did through Jesus—as revealed especially in the speeches of Acts. Some scholars have stressed the study of myth, in the sense of a religious conception representing theological insights into Jesus' life and activity, as the best way to arrive at the truth about Jesus. Still other scholars believe that the truth about Jesus can best be approached through the study of early Christian prophecy and by means of several criteria for determining the authenticity of Jesus' sayings.

Some scholars have proposed that Christianity began as a millenarian movement, at the center of which stood Jesus in the image of a prophet who challenged traditional assumptions about values. Christianity failed as a millenarian movement because the new world order failed to appear. Christianity succeeded because of its radical sense of community without social distinctions and its concern for all aspects of believers' lives.

An increasing number of women are involved in NT studies, and from their perspectives women played a much more influential role among Jesus' followers and in the early church than male scholars have heretofore acknowledged. Sometimes passages that appear to be unfavorable toward women are explained by exegesis and interpretation of cultural context to show that women were not given a lower status than men. By including all kinds of persons, Christianity brought about a different idea of God, a God of goodness who accepts everyone without exception. It has even been argued that in the earliest traditions about Jesus, God was perceived in the female form as "divine *Sophia.*"

Because the gospels are theological works and not histories or biographies, it is difficult to determine exactly how Jesus was regarded by his first followers. This problem, like the others considered in this chapter, can be only partially solved through the use of certain clues and techniques in studying Jesus and the gospels. However, evidence indicates that the earliest followers

of Jesus thought of him as a teacher and as the Messiah. As a teacher, Jesus' uniqueness lay not in the content but in the emphases of his teaching. Perhaps the most striking feature of Jesus' teaching was his radical moral and ethical demands.

Jews were not prepared to accept a crucified Messiah, so Jesus' followers became convinced that he had predicted his own death and resurrection. As Christianity spread from Jews to Gentiles, Christians developed theological explanations for Jesus' death and resurrection, especially that Jesus' death served to atone for past sins of converts. Theological faith in Jesus also included the concepts of Jesus as Son of God and Lord, common designations for special individuals in the Hellenistic world. As Christians began to suffer persecution, they came to believe also that Jesus had predicted their sufferings as well as his own, and that faith sustained them.

Through some insights into several contemporary studies on Jesus we have learned that there is a renewed quest for "the historical Jesus." In general, it seems fair to say that compared with studies in former quests, many are more negative than positive, even with respect to the canonical gospel accounts. Sometimes one or more of the noncanonical gospels are given equal, or even greater, value in the consideration of Jesus than the canonical gospels. Positively, Jesus emerges as a Galilean peasant, a teacher of wisdom, and even as the personification of divine Wisdom. Perhaps Jesus is more often portrayed as a prophet and/or social reformer, even a radical one, and, therefore, as a model for socioeconomic, political, and religious reforms.

In the next three chapters we will consider the synoptic gospels individually, beginning with Mark, the earliest. We will discuss the questions of authorship, date and place of writing, and likely communities addressed. We will also discuss the literary style of each author and the structure of his work, along with an outline and brief commentary.

CHAPTER 4

The Gospel of Mark

THE GOSPELS ARE THE CULMINATION OF a long process involving oral traditions and written sources. Although the first three gospels are very similar in content and have close literary relationships, these synoptic gospels also have important differences. The differences are due to the gospel writers shaping their own narratives by the way they used their sources and by their own theological convictions, concerns, and interests. In this chapter we will focus on the gospel of Mark in order to understand the origin and purpose, the particular use of sources, and the structure of that work. We will also examine the literary style and special interests of Mark to become more familiar with Mark's distinctiveness as an author. As you read the gospel of Mark in your study of this chapter, observe Mark's theological emphasis on Jesus as the messianic Son of God and his use of miracle stories to strengthen his view of Jesus as a teacher.

ORIGIN, PURPOSE, AND DATE OF MARK

Most NT scholars agree that the gospels are anonymous and that the present titles probably were not added until sometime in the second century. Because the form of the title is the same for every gospel, a title was probably given to each only after the gospels had been collected as a group of four. Then the name of a well-known person was included in the superscription of each gospel. But the superscriptions read, "the gospel according to," not "the gospel by" Matthew or Mark or Luke, so the gospels as we now have them are anonymous.

There is no firsthand information about the authors of the synoptic gospels, and except for Luke, no author tells us why and to whom he was writing. However, several ancient traditions exist for the authorship of Matthew, Mark, and Luke, the oldest of which is that from Papias (c. 70–146), bishop of Hierapolis in Phrygia, Asia Minor, who wrote *The Interpretations of the Sayings of the Lord*. This work has not survived, but

Papias's statements about the writing of the gospels have been preserved in the *Church History* of Eusebius (c. 260–340), historian and bishop of Caesarea. Papias wrote:

> Mark, who became the interpreter of Peter, wrote accurately as much as he remembered, but not in order, of the things said and done by the Lord. . . . Peter used to do teaching as there was need, but did not make, as it were, an arrangement of the Lord's sayings, so that Mark did not go wrong in thus writing down single points as he remembered them. [*Hist.* 3:39:15; see also 6:14:6]

Thus Peter, one of Jesus' disciples, was thought to be the authority behind Mark's gospel.

Similarly, a tradition from Clement of Alexandria (c. 150–220), also preserved in Eusebius (6:14:6), associates Mark with Peter in Rome. Many scholars still believe that Mark was written in Rome shortly before or after the destruction of Jerusalem in 70 CE. The author was writing to those who were already Christians, and he may have wanted to encourage the first Christians in Rome who were persecuted during and after the time of Nero (54–68).

There are, of course, notable exceptions to the general opinion about the origin and purpose of Mark. W. Marxsen 1969:54–116, following earlier scholars, has proposed Galilee as the place of origin for Mark. And W. Kelber 1974 has presented a case for the writing of Mark in Galilee not long after 70 CE. According to Kelber, Mark wrote to sustain Christians displaced and without hope because of the fall of Jerusalem. H. C. Kee 1977a has presented evidence for concluding that Mark was written in southern Syria in the late 60s during the Jewish revolt against Rome (66–73), before the overthrow of Jerusalem. Mark wrote to a community of Christians who did not want to identify with any of the Jewish groups during that tumultuous period. Those Christians, who were under the suspicion of both Jews and Gentiles, were a "community whose members travelled as itinerant charismatics, carrying forward the tasks of preaching and healing inaugurated by Jesus, ready to follow

him to death, if God willed" (176). Included in the evidence for Kee's view is the linguistic character of Mark; though written in Greek, Mark shows Semitic influence and cultural features of the rural areas or villages of regions east of the Mediterranean.

The period of the Jewish revolt against Rome from 66 to 73 was a particularly difficult time for Christians because the Romans regarded them as Jews, but to the Jews they were outcasts. Apocalyptic-eschatological expectations of Christians who were living between the time of Jesus' death and his expected second coming were intensified. Christians living in Rome, Syria, or Galilee would have been affected by the tumultuous times. Mark wrote to instruct and encourage such Christians, especially by emphasizing Jesus' passion.

Because the gospel of Mark was used by Matthew and Luke, it must have been rapidly transmitted soon after it was written. Its author had a special interest in a mission to Gentiles, so the gospel probably originated in some church center of Gentile Christianity. Rome, Antioch in Syria, or even some Greek-speaking community in Palestine are possibilities.

MARK'S USE OF HIS SOURCES

Although Mark is the earliest gospel, it surely was not written "from scratch." Like other gospel writers, Mark used sources, but it is very difficult to determine what they were, and scholars differ widely concerning their nature and number. Some think Mark used only oral tradition or at most only a few written collections of material, while some think Mark is an abridgment of Matthew or another earlier gospel. The idea of an earlier or "primitive Mark" (*Urmarkus*) is often used to explain Luke's omission of Mark 6:45–8:26 and the agreements in wording between Matthew and Luke against Mark. Other scholars maintain that Mark used many sources, including a passion narrative (14–15), collections of parables (4:1–34) and miracle stories (5; 7), an apocalypse (13), instructions for disciples (10:2–45), and controversy stories (2:1–3:6). Although Mark may have used such collections of material, there is no evidence that they had been written as a continuous narrative about Jesus.

In Paul's letters, all written before Mark, we find that the passion and resurrection of Jesus play an important part in Paul's theology. 1 Cor 11:23–25 is the earliest extant account of the Last Supper (compare Mark 14:22–24), and in 1 Cor 15:4–7 Paul lists resurrection appearances of Jesus. So there were Christian traditions for these things before Mark, and he probably had access to them. However, if he did, he did not include any of the resurrection appearances of Jesus in his gospel because it ends with the story of the empty tomb.

Although we cannot determine the content of the passion narrative in Mark's source, we know that Mark himself is preoccupied with Jesus' passion. He had added his own touches, including the view that Jesus' death fulfilled OT scripture (see, for example, 14:27, 34, 62; 15:34) and thus was in accord with God's will, that Jesus fulfilled his own predictions of his suffering and death (compare 14:41 and 8:31), and that Jesus' death on the cross made him truly "a Son of God" (15:39). The oldest manuscripts of Mark contain no resurrection appearances of Jesus. There has thus far been no satisfactory explanation for this fact.

N. Perrin 1982 has observed that a "possible pre-Markan unit of tradition is a cycle of stories giving an account of (a) a feeding, (b) a crossing of the lake, (c) a controversy with Pharisees, and (d) teaching concerning bread." There are two such cycles of stories (compare 6:30–44 and 8:1–10; 6:45–56 and 8:10; 7:1–13 and 8:11–13; and 7:14–23 and 8:14–21). Finally, it is very likely that Mark used miracle stories from earlier Christian tradition. P. J. Achtemeier 1970 has proposed that Mark used two catenae ("chains"; from the Latin *catena,* "chain") of miracles that were in existence when he wrote. Mark incorporated a cycle of two catenae, each consisting of a sea miracle, three healings, and a feeding miracle, into the structure of his gospel (see Figure 4.1).

FIGURE 4.1 *Catenae of Miracles in Mark*
Stilling of the Storm (4:35–41)
The Gerasene Demoniac (5:1–20)
The Woman with a Hemorrhage (5:25–34)
Jairus' Daughter (5:21–23, 35–43)
Feeding of the 5,000 (6:34–44, 53)
Jesus Walks on the Sea (6:45–51)
The Blind Man of Bethsaida (8:22–26)
The Syrophoenician Woman (7:24b–30)
The Deaf-Mute (7:32–37)
Feeding of the 4,000 (8:1–10)

Studies dealing with Mark's use of his sources have generally proceeded from the assumption of the two-source theory as the best solution to the synoptic problem. However, D. B. Peabody 1987 has approached the subject of Mark as a composer in a way that "presupposes no particular solution to the Synoptic Problem and . . . employs minimal presuppositions about 'redactional passages' within the gospel." Peabody has two aims: "(1) the collection and systematic display of potentially redactional features of the text of Mark as a whole and (2) the isolation of those redactional features within this larger body of potentially redactional material that have the highest probability of coming from the hand of the author/composer of the gospel." The focus is on the recurrence of words or phrases as "habitual expressions" of Mark in order to determine his technique as a composer.

A very different approach to Mark's use of his sources is that of B. L. Mack 1988. The "pre-Markan materials of memory" are filled with hostility between the synagogue and followers of Jesus, but that material does not suggest "that any connection had been made in the minds of the followers of Jesus between that conflict and the crucifixion of Jesus in Jerusalem. This means that Mark's story is probably Mark's fiction."

In his fabrication, Mark "brought together two distinctively different types of written material representative of two major types of early sectarian formation." One was "that of movements in Palestine and southern Syria that cultivated the memory of Jesus as a founder-teacher," the other "that of congregations in northern Syria, Asia Minor and Greece wherein the death and resurrection of the Christ were regarded as the founding events." The apocalyptic picture of Christian origins is a myth fabricated by Mark, and it was the basis for the social formation of Christianity.

In 1958 Morton Smith 1973a discovered a manuscript of Mark's gospel that had been used by the church of Clement of Alexandria (c. 150–220). Known as the *Secret Gospel of Mark*, this gospel is similar to the Mark of the NT with some additions, particularly the raising of a young man, apparently a version of John 11. A few scholars (H. Koester 1983; J. D. Crossan 1985; 1988:283–286) have maintained that the *Secret Mark* is older than the Mark in the NT and that, indeed, the latter gospel was derived from it. For a response to Koester, see D. B. Peabody 1983. Scholars have generally rejected the view that *Secret Mark*, or any other apocryphal gospel was written before Mark of the NT.

R. E. Brown 1987 criticizes current challenges, including that of Crossan, to the canonical gospels in support of noncanonical writings. Brown criticizes the arguments, methods, and the relationships between the *Gospel of Peter* and the NT gospels proposed by canon critics. According to Brown, the *Gospel of Peter* "does not constitute or give the earliest Christian account or thoughts about the passion," as Crossan and others claim (see also A. Kirk 1994). However, the noncanonical gospel has worth in that it is "another window into popular Christianity of the 1st half of the 2nd century."

THE STYLE OF MARK

Many stylistic features of an author are more noticeable in the original language than in transla-tion. Translation from one language into another always causes problems of accuracy and nuance of meaning, and so leaves some uncertainty. Nevertheless, we can observe important aspects of style even in English translation. One of these aspects involves the phrase *kai elegen autois,* "and he said to them." It is Mark's way of introducing sayings of Jesus and is most frequently used that way (see, for example, 2:27; 4:2, 11, 21, 24; 7:9), although it also occurs in a narrative context (see, for example, 6:4, 10; 11:17). Another distinctive feature of Mark's style is his use of the Greek adverb *euthys,* "immediately." Skim through the first chapter of Mark, and notice how often the word "immediately" occurs. In vv 10–43 it occurs eleven times, although it is often omitted in the *NRSV.* It occurs forty-one times in Mark, compared with five times in Matthew, once in Luke, and four times in the rest of the NT.

Mark frequently depicts Jesus as taking his disciples aside to explain something or to give them instructions privately. In this connection Mark uses the word *proskaleomai,* which means "to call to oneself." The synonymous phrases *kat' idian,* meaning "privately," "in private," or "by oneself" (see, for example, 4:34; 6:31–32; 7:33; 13:3), and *kata monas,* meaning "by oneself" or "alone," are even more precise about the privacy intended. The last phrase is best illustrated in Mark 4:10: "When he was alone, those who were around him along with the twelve asked him about the parables." Jesus speaking in private to his followers is a peculiar trait of Mark's presentation of Jesus (with Mark 4:10 compare Matt 13:10 and Luke 8:9).

Another characteristic of Mark's style is his frequent use (twenty-six times) of *archomai,* meaning "to begin," as a helping verb. The passages in Example 4.1 illustrate Mark's unique style. The first is from the healing of the Gerasene demoniac, the second from the introduction to the sending out of the twelve, and the third from Jesus' third prediction of his passion (see also Mark 4:1; 6:34; 8:11; 10:28 and par.).

EXAMPLE 4.1   *Mark's Use of "Begin" as a Helping Verb*

Matt 8:34	Mark 5:17	Luke 8:37
they begged him to leave their neighborhood.	[17]Then they began to beg Jesus to leave their neighborhood.	[37]Then all the people of the surrounding country of the Gerasenes asked Jesus to leave them
Matt 10:1	**Mark 6:7**	**Luke 9:1–2**
[1]Then Jesus summoned his twelve disciples and gave them authority over unclean spirits, to cast them out, and to cure every disease and every sickness.	[7]He called the twelve and began to send them out two by two, and gave them authority over the unclean spirits.	[1]Then Jesus called the twelve together and gave them power and authority over all demons and to cure diseases, [2]and he sent them out to proclaim the kingdom of God and to heal.
Matt 20:17	**Mark 10:32**	**Luke 18:31**
he took the twelve disciples aside by themselves, and said to them	He took the twelve aside again and began to tell them what was to happen to him	[31]Then he took the twelve aside and said to them

SPECIAL INTERESTS OF MARK

A study of Mark reveals not only peculiar stylistic traits but also the writer's special interests or emphases. All gospel writers present Jesus as a person who is more than a mere man—that is, as in some sense divine (Christ, Son of God, and so on)—without stressing Jesus' own awareness of his uniqueness. Mark, however, seems to present Jesus as conscious of his uniqueness and to let others gradually become aware of it. In Mark's gospel, Jesus becomes conscious of his divine Sonship at his baptism, when the voice from heaven says, "You are my beloved Son" (1:11). Then in the synagogue at Capernaum the man with the unclean spirit addresses Jesus as "the Holy One of God," but Jesus rebukes him and commands him to be silent (1:24–25). Jesus "would not permit the demons to speak, because they knew him" (1:34), and he demands that people he has healed keep silent (1:43–44; 3:12; 5:43; 7:36; 8:29–30; 9:9).

The secret of Jesus' messiahship is only gradually revealed (Mark 8:27–33; 9:2–10). Then at his trial before the Sanhedrin, to the high priest's question "Are you the Christ, the Son of the Blessed One?" Jesus responds, "I am" (14:61–62). And finally, when the Gentile centurion sees that Jesus has "breathed his last," he confesses, "Truly this man was the Son of God!" (Mark 15:39). This statement is the climax to the gradual revelation of Jesus' uniqueness. The purpose of Mark is clear. He wants Jewish and Gentile Christians to understand that Jesus' uniqueness as Messiah and Son of God is to be comprehended not in his working of miracles, or even in his teaching, but in his suffering and death.

The passages dealing with Jesus' identity and its gradual unfolding, along with those dealing with his private instructions to disciples and his private interpretation of some parables, are usually referred to as Mark's "messianic secret," an idea first proposed by the German scholar W. Wrede 1971. Although challenged from time to time (see W. G. Kuemmel 1975:89–93), the theory of the messianic secret as a theological motif of Mark himself, not of Jesus, is generally accepted.

With respect to the messianic secret, the consensus has been that there is no sign of such a secret in Matthew. However, J. D. Kingsbury 1986 has argued that "the secret of Jesus' divine sonship is in fact a major motif in Matthew's story." Kingsbury demonstrates how the parable of the wicked tenants (Matt 21:33–46) "plays a critical role in the development of the motif." In that parable for the first time "the Jewish public, in the persons of the leaders, is confronted with the claim that Jesus is the Son of God."

Another significant emphasis in Mark is on the passion of Jesus. The German philosopher-theologian M. Kaehler (1835–1912) 1964 was the first to observe that "one could call the Gospels passion narratives with extended introductions." This is especially true for Mark. From the first prediction of the passion at Caesarea Philippi (8:27–33) on, Mark stresses the necessity of Jesus' suffering and death, and every main section of the gospel contains references to Jesus' coming death (see, for example, 3:6; 8:31; 10:45). Indeed, Mark worked no differently in composing his passion narrative in chaps. 14–16 than he did in composing chaps. 1–13. He edited, combined, and added new material to create a whole sequential narrative from chap. 1 to chap. 16 (W. Kelber 1976).

Mark is interested in the passion of Jesus not only as a means for conveying the significance of the person and work of Jesus, but also for conveying to his readers the meaning of true discipleship. Each passion prediction has the same structure: Jesus' prediction, the disciples' misunderstanding, and Jesus' sayings about what is required of those who follow him (chaps. 8–10; N. Perrin 1974:110–111). This pattern is hardly to be attributed to pre-Markan tradition. Rather, it appears to be conscious redaction by Mark, and it is intended to convince readers that true discipleship means following Jesus by living lives of service and by sharing in his suffering. For a discussion of various views of discipleship in Mark, see E. Best 1977, 1981.

Mark is more interested in reporting Jesus' miracles than his teachings, in spite of the fact that Mark emphasizes Jesus as teacher. Miracles are the prevailing interest in the first half of the gospel, and they include three basic types: healings (including exorcisms), nature miracles, and resuscitations. Jesus' adversaries accused him of casting out demons by Beelzebul, the prince of demons, and his friends thought he was "out of his mind" (3:21–22). But for Mark, Jesus was the Son of God who cast out demons because that was part of his mission (1:32–39). Mark took over the tradition of Jesus as a miracle worker and put it in the perspective of Jesus' passion. That is why the taunt of the priest and scribes is significant: "He saved others; he cannot save himself. Let the Christ, the King of Israel, come down from the cross now, so that we may see and believe" (15:31–32). Mark's readers were to believe not because Jesus had worked miracles or because he could save himself from the cross, but because of the miracle of God, who through the cross had made Jesus uniquely the Son of God (15:39).

Mark also presents Jesus as the Son of Man. As Son of Man Jesus has the authority to forgive sins (2:10) and is Lord even of the sabbath (2:28). The Son of Man must suffer, be rejected, killed, and rise again (8:31; 9:9–12, 31; 10:33). He came not to be served but to serve (10:45). But Mark also writes about the eschatological Son of Man coming on the clouds with power and glory (13:26).

The problems of the origin, meaning, and functions of Jesus as Son of Man as compared with Jesus as Son of God are still far from solved. This is confirmed by the works of two scholars, B. Lindars 1984 and S. Kim 1985, who wrote during the same year (1983) but on different continents. Lindars wrote from Great Britain and Kim from Korea, and their works were published in America in different years. Each author used different methods but much of the same evidence, and neither author knew the work of the other. They agree on several things, for example, that in Judaism Son of Man was not used as a title, but differ on most of the important problems. For example, Kim is certain that Jesus used the designation "the Son of Man" with reference to himself, but Lindars thinks that Jesus used the title only in a vague way to refer to himself, though not exclusively so. Lindars rejects the eschatological saying of Jesus in Mark 14:62 as inauthentic, whereas Kim accepts it as genuine.

THE STRUCTURE OF MARK

Papias clearly says that Mark did not write in chronological order what he remembered of the things Jesus said and did, so the order of incidents and the sequence of Jesus' sayings in Mark are those of the author himself. From an analysis of Mark, it appears that the author has structured the gospel according to both a geographical and a theological outline. Mark's geographical outline of Jesus' activity is as follows: Galilee (1:14–6:13), outside Galilee (6:14–8:26), journey from Caesarea Philippi to Jerusalem (8:27–10:52), and Jerusalem (11:1–16:8).

Theologically, the author of Mark has structured his gospel around the basic theme of Jesus as the Son of God. The confessional statements of the writer in his first verse—"The beginning of the gospel of Jesus Christ, the Son of God"— and of the centurion while Jesus was on the cross—"Truly this man was the Son of God!" (15:39)—are the theological framework within which Mark has structured his gospel. If the summarizing and transitional statements are taken into account, the theological structure is as follows:

I. *Introduction (1:1–13)*

II. *Transitional summary (1:14–15)*

III. *As Son of God, Jesus manifesting his authority in teaching, healing, and in conflicts with scribes and Pharisees (1:16–3:6)*

IV. *Transitional summary (3:7–12)*

V. *The Son of God rejected by his own people (3:13–6:6a)*

VI. *Transitional summary (6:6b)*

VII. *Jesus' own disciples not understanding him as Son of God (6:7–8:21)*

VIII. *Transitional story of the blind man of Bethsaida, marking the shift in geography from Galilee to Caesarea Philippi and to the emphasis on Jesus' passion and its importance for true discipleship (8:22–26)*

IX. *The passion of Jesus as Son of God, putting Christian discipleship in its proper perspective (8:27–10:45)*

X. *Transitional story of blind Bartimaeus, marking the shift in geography to Jerusalem and to the conflicts with Jewish authorities before Jesus' death (10:46–52)*

XI. *Jesus' confrontation with authorities in Jerusalem and Mark's introduction to Jesus' apocalyptic discourse (11:1–13:5a)*

XII. *Jesus' apocalyptic discourse to his disciples (13:5b–37)*

XIII. *The passion narrative (14:1–16:8)*

Transitional and summarizing passages like those in the outline above and others (see, for example, 1:21–22, 32–34, 39; 2:13; 4:1; 5:1; 6:12–13, 30, 53–56; 10:1), which are evident in the structure of Mark, are a characteristic of the writer's style. Mark has carefully placed them in order to call attention to the geographical regions of Jesus' activity and to what is included in that activity, especially exorcisms and healings.

So as an author, Mark has a characteristic literary style and special interests, especially an interest in Jesus as Son of God. Try to observe this and other special traits as you read the gospel of Mark. The outline and comments below are intended to assist you in analyzing and interpreting the gospel.

Outline and Comments

I. *Introduction (1:1–13)*

Unlike Matthew, which begins with the genealogy of Jesus (1:1–17), and Luke, which begins with a formal preface (1:1–4), Mark begins with a dynamic statement of faith (1:1). There is no record of Jesus' birth or childhood in Mark, so through John the Baptist's preaching Jesus is introduced as an adult whose baptism makes clear that Jesus is chosen by God. The summary account of the temptation could be intended to show that Jesus, like Moses (Exod 34:28), Elijah (1 Kgs 19:8), and the children of Israel (Num 14:33), who were also chosen by God, had to spend some time in the desert to be sure of God's will.

II. Transitional summary (1:14–15)

Jesus moves from private to public life with the beginning of his activity in Galilee.

III. As Son of God, Jesus manifesting his authority in teaching and healing, and in conflicts with scribes and Pharisees (1:16–3:6)

Jesus first calls four disciples (1:16–20); then his exorcism of the demon from the man in the synagogue at Capernaum (1:21–28; see Figure 4.2) makes him famous throughout Galilee. Healing and preaching in Galilee, where the demons recognize his uniqueness (1:34), Jesus asks the demons and others healed to be silent (1:43). This editorial device ("messianic secret")

serves two purposes: it prepares the readers not to hold Jesus responsible for the conflict with the authorities that is about to develop, and it explains how, after he had healed so many, Jesus' uniqueness was not recognized by everyone. Mark's motive is to show Jesus' increasing popularity (1:45), not the actual sequence of events.

In Mark 2:1–3:6 there is a series of controversy narratives in which the authority of Jesus is pitted against that of the scribes and Pharisees. As Jesus' popularity grows, opposition to him increases. The healing of the paralytic (2:1–12) presents Jesus as the earthly Son of Man who has authority to forgive sins. The responses "were all amazed" and "We have never seen anything like this!" (2:12) echo the writer's feelings. The call of Levi shows not only that one called by Jesus should immediately follow him, but also that Jesus can disregard custom by eating with sinners and tax collectors (2:13–17).

The result of the question about fasting (2:18–22), which shows Jesus' independence from Jewish law, is a prophetic statement anticipating the passion: "The days will come when the

F I G U R E   4 . 2   *Ruins of a synagogue at Capernaum in Galilee, from sometime between the second and fourth centuries CE.*

bridegroom is taken away from them, and then they will fast on that day" (2:20). The question itself sets Jesus apart not only from the Pharisees but also from John the Baptist's disciples. The difficult sayings about the garment and wineskins (2:21–22) became attached to the independent unit in 2:18–20. The original contexts of the sayings are lost, and we cannot say whether they were already attached to the story about fasting or whether Mark added them. Although they mean that something new must be attached to something new or put in new containers, we do not know what practical application was intended by Jesus—if the sayings go back to him. Mark may have wanted the sayings to show that as representatives of a new religious movement the disciples of Jesus were not to be bound by an old tradition such as fasting. At any rate, the sayings probably indicate conflict between Jews and Christians, but the circumstances of the conflict are unknown. In Christian tradition before Mark, what is new was contrasted with what was old (see, for example, Rom 7:6).

The stories about plucking grain (2:23–28) and healing the man with the withered hand (3:1–6) show Jesus as Son of Man not hesitating to violate the sanctity of sabbath law. The plot of the Pharisees and Herodians (those loyal to Herod Antipas, ruler of Galilee and Perea) to destroy Jesus again anticipates the passion.

IV. Transitional summary (3:7–12)

The vocabulary and style of these verses indicate that they were composed by Mark himself. The content is also typically Markan: Jesus' popularity because of his healings, the demons acknowledging Jesus' uniqueness—"You are the Son of God!"—and Jesus' charge not to make that uniqueness known.

V. The Son of God rejected by his own people (3:13–6:6a)

The disciples become more prominent and are associated with Jesus in his work of healing. People, including Jesus' friends and relatives, misunderstand and reject Jesus. Jesus appoints twelve to share his work (3:13–19); several dis-

tinctively Markan ideas are presented in connection with them. Jesus' friends think he is crazy (3:21), and the scribes think Jesus is possessed by Beelzebul, by whom "he casts out demons" (3:22). But Jesus retaliates with his statement about a house divided (3:23–26).

The sayings about the strong man (3:27) and blasphemy (3:28–29) may have been added from another collection of sayings, since they have also been preserved in Q. Mark may have added the first saying in this context to show that Satan, the strong man, has been overcome and his helpers, the demons, defeated by the works of Jesus. The second saying is used to defend Jesus against the Jewish charge that he casts out demons under Satanic influence. Jesus works under supernatural influence, but it is the influence of the Spirit. Those who deny the results of that influence commit the unforgiveable blasphemy (that is, "speaking evily against"). Mark 3:30 is an editorial explanatory comment.

The story about Jesus' true relatives (3:31–35) may reflect the historical fact that during his earthly career Jesus' own friends and relatives (see 3:21; 6:4) did not follow him. Mark certainly found the story useful for stressing to his readers that physical descent carries with it no special privilege in a Christian community: "Whoever does the will of God is my brother and sister and mother" (3:35).

Except for the stilling of the storm, chap. 4 deals with parables (see Chapter 7). Again the disciples are given a prominent place. They alone know "the secret of the kingdom of God" (4:11), and to them Jesus "explained everything in private" (4:34). And yet, the disciples completely fail to understand Jesus. Most scholars regard the interpretation of the parable of the sower (4:13–20), like other parable interpretations in the gospels, as stemming from the later church, not from Jesus. As it now stands, the parable of the sower (4:1–9) and its interpretation stress that all who hear Jesus' word are to respond by bearing fruit. Apparently Mark took several of Jesus' sayings from a source or collection he was using and inserted them, along with editorial comments, to help explain the purpose of Jesus' parables (4:21–25), something he also tried to do in 4:33–34.

The parable of the seed growing secretly (4:26–29) is the only parable found exclusively in Mark's gospel; like most of Jesus' parables, it deals with the kingdom of God. Although the original contexts of Jesus' parables are lost—and perhaps most of the original meanings also—as it now stands, the parable of the mustard seed illustrates the growth of the kingdom (4:30–32).

In 4:35–5:43 each of the three miracle stories appears to stress faith, but the nature or object of faith is not always clear. In the stilling of the storm, after he has calmed the sea Jesus asks the disciples: "Why are you afraid? Have you still no faith?" (4:40). But faith in whom or in what? Faith in God or faith that Jesus could control nature's hostile forces? With the words "Peace! Be still!" did Jesus calm the fears of the disciples and not the stormy sea? Or did Mark want to show that as Jesus was victorious over the forces of nature, so he would be triumphant over his human foes? At any rate, according to Mark, the disciples still do not understand: "Who then is this, that even the wind and the sea obey him?" (4:41).

Faith is not mentioned in connection with the healing of the Gerasene demoniac (5:1–20), who even from afar recognizes Jesus as "Son of the Most High God" and worships him. Here Jesus does not demand silence on the part of the one healed, but in language that is clearly Markan, he commands the man to go tell his friends what God has done for him (5:19). Does Mark include such a command because Jesus is outside Galilee, in non-Jewish territory, and because Mark wants the story to show how Christianity appeals to Gentiles? Jesus tells the woman with the hemorrhage that her faith has made her well, and he says to the people from Jairus's household, "Do not fear, only believe" (5:21–43). The raising of Jairus's daughter from the dead is the only resuscitation miracle in Mark.

Jesus is rejected in his hometown of Nazareth and can do no mighty work there because of the people's "unbelief" (6:1–6a). The word "unbelief" (*apistia*) had been used by Paul to designate the Jews' disbelief in Jesus (Rom 3:3; 11:30). Jesus has all but finished his activity in Galilee, where he has been dramatically and tragically rejected by his own people, the Jews. His rejection at Nazareth is a significant episode in the gospel of Mark, for it anticipates a new phase in Jesus' activity in which the disciples become more actively involved in the mission to Gentiles.

Recall the titles under which Mark has presented Jesus thus far. In the first verse of the gospel Mark introduces Jesus as the Son of God; then a voice from heaven confirms Jesus in that role. Twice as Son of Man Jesus asserts his authority, first with the power to forgive sins (2:10) and then in the disregard for sabbath law (2:28). And finally, Jesus is again twice acclaimed Son of God (3:11; 5:7). In this way Mark discloses his understanding of Jesus' uniqueness.

VI. Transitional summary (6:6b)

Although this is the shortest of the summaries, it is important. It reveals Mark's fondness for Jesus' activity in the more rural areas of Palestine (see 1:38; 5:14; 6:36, 56; 8:23, 26, 27; 11:2). After being rejected by his own people, Jesus devotes more time to his disciples, who are given a special mission in the next phase of Jesus' work.

VII. Jesus' own disciples not understanding him as Son of God (6:7–8:21)

Two cycles of stories deal with a feeding of a multitude, a crossing of the sea, a controversy with Pharisees, and teaching about bread. Vocabulary and style indicate that Mark himself composed the narrative of the sending out of the twelve (6:6b–13) as a parallel to 3:13–19 (see also 1:17–20). Jesus' sayings in 6:8–11 come from an earlier collection, probably used also by Matthew (10:9–14). The words "no bread" point forward to the miracles of feeding, when Jesus will give bread to all.

The narrative of the disciples' mission (6:7, 12) and their return (6:30) is interrupted with the records of Herod's opinion of Jesus (6:14–16) and the death of the Baptist (6:17–29). The feeding of the five thousand (6:30–44) and Jesus walking on the water (6:45–52) continue Mark's portrayal of Jesus as Son of God because of his miracles and the idea of the disciples' misunderstanding (6:51–52). Unlike Matthew (14:33), Mark does not actually use the title "Son of God" here. After using "Son of God" and "Son of Man" (1:1–5:7), he avoids the use of any title for Jesus until Peter's confession of Jesus as "the Christ" (8:29). Jesus' power of healing is so great that even the touching of his garment is effective (6:53–56; see also 5:28).

The section titled "What Defiles a Person" (7:1–23) contains two pronouncement stories (7:1–8; 7:9–13) and a parabolic saying (7:14–23). A pronouncement story is a brief narrative that ends with a pronouncement from Jesus dealing with some aspect of life or religious belief or behavior. All of these sayings show that Jesus is opposed to the oral law (referred to as "tradition" in Mark) that the Pharisees observed as conscientiously as the written Torah. The sayings further show Jesus' authority as Son of God in opposition to the Pharisees and scribes from Jerusalem, who stand in contrast to the crowds in Galilee that recognized Jesus and brought sick people to be healed (6:53–56).

The most difficult saying in this section is that about Corban (7:9–13). *Corban* is a Greek transliteration of the Aramaic word meaning "offering" or "gift given to God." Jesus gives a concrete example to show how adherence to the oral Torah contradicts what God commands in the written Torah (see Exod 20:12 = Deut 5:16; Exod 21:16–17; Lev 20:9). Thus, Jesus shows his belief that the written law is binding and that the Pharisees are using a legal loophole to permit people to retain money that, according to the written Torah, should be used to support their parents. In v 14 the author makes the transition from the Corban saying to the answer to the question asked of Jesus in v 5. The answer is addressed not only to the Pharisees but to all the people, and again the disciples ask Jesus about the parabolic saying because they "fail to understand" (7:17–18). It is difficult to say how much, if any, of the explanation that follows goes back to Jesus. The list of virtues and vices does not appear elsewhere in sayings attributed to Jesus, but similar lists were used by Paul (see, for example, Gal 5:19–26). These facts, along with the statement declaring all foods clean, may indicate early Christian teaching for Gentiles, for whom Jewish law and tradition meant nothing.

The healings of the Syrophoenician woman's daughter (7:24–30) and the deaf mute (7:31–37) are meant to show Jesus' attitude toward Gentiles. The first is performed at a distance and is not so important as the conversation between Jesus and the woman that precedes it. The deaf mute is healed by Jesus' touch and a special word, two common elements in Hellenistic miracle stories. With the words "They were astounded beyond measure" (7:37) Mark links these miracles with those in previous sections (see 1:27; 4:41).

The feeding of the four thousand (8:1–10) is generally regarded as a variant version of the feeding of the five thousand. It is only loosely attached to what precedes it. Because of the stories' different geographical settings, the feeding of the five thousand is associated with Jews and the feeding of the four thousand with Gentiles, and commentators suggest symbolic meanings in the different vocabularies of the two stories. The five loaves for the five thousand represent the five books of Jewish Torah; the seven loaves for the four thousand are reminiscent of the seven Gentile deacons of Acts 6:3–6 (see also the seven Gentile churches of Asia in Revelation 1–3). In the same way, the twelve baskets in the former miracle represent the twelve tribes of Israel, and the seven baskets in the latter again stand for Gentiles. The word for basket (*kophinos*) in the first story was regularly used by the poorer class of Jews in Rome, whereas the word for basket (*sphuris*) in the second story refers to a common kind of basket. Since Mark repeats the two words in 8:19–20, the distinction is hardly accidental. The fragments remaining in each case show that Jesus can meet the needs of all people, both Jews and Gentiles.

The dispute with the Pharisees who seek a sign (8:11–13) is followed with the discourse on leaven (8:14–21). Mark sees a meaning in Jesus' miracles as well as in his parables, and for those who can understand that meaning no further sign is necessary. Those to whom "has been given the secret of the kingdom of God" should understand. But the disciples do not yet perceive, so Mark brings another main section of his gospel to its climax with Jesus' question "Do you not yet understand?" (8:21; see also 6:52; 7:18).

VIII. *The transitional story of the blind man of Bethsaida, marking the shift in geography from Galilee to Caesarea Philippi and to the emphasis on Jesus' passion and its importance for true discipleship (8:22–26)*

This miracle story and the one about the deaf mute are the only ones recorded exclusively in Mark. They have the following points in common: each follows a geographical reference (see Figure 4.3); the man is brought to Jesus by others who beg Jesus to touch him; Jesus leads the man away from the people; emphasis is on the techniques Jesus uses; Jesus spits and touches the man; the man is completely healed; and the healing is not to be made known.

The main difference between the two stories is that the blind man is healed in two stages. Perhaps this is a reason why Matthew and Luke omit that story. It could be taken to imply that Jesus' first touch was not effective. Perhaps Mark thinks of the story as symbolic of the phases of the disciples' insight into the uniqueness of Jesus and its true meaning. Up to this point in the gospel the disciples have been repeatedly and emphatically blind to the uniqueness of Jesus as revealed in his miracles and parabolic teachings. In what follows there is another series of incidents by which Jesus attempts to open the eyes of the disciples, but without success.

IX. *The passion of Jesus as Son of God, putting Christian discipleship in its proper perspective (8:27–10:45)*

Commentators' opinions differ concerning the historical veracity of this material, especially the passion predictions. Many think it highly improbable that Jesus actually foresaw his passion, and they therefore regard the predictions of his sufferings as the interpretation of the church.

FIGURE 4.3   *Site of ancient Caesarea Philippi, including one of the sources of the Jordan River.*

Others think that Mark took the materials from tradition but arranged them with a view to the catechetical (teaching) needs of his community. And some regard the material, including the passion predictions, as actual reminiscences of Peter passed on to Mark; they therefore regard the details of every story and the words of every saying as accurate.

No matter how one regards the material with respect to its historicity, it is clear that this section is built around three predictions of the passion. Each prediction is introduced with a geographical reference and followed with misunderstanding on the part of the disciples, teaching of Jesus, and some inserted units of material. After each prediction the readers are brought closer to Jesus' actual passion by the christological content of Jesus' teaching and by the movement of Jesus geographically toward Jerusalem, the scene of the passion.

Jesus' first prediction follows Peter's response, "You are the Christ," to Jesus' question about who he is. Although we do not know all the implications of the term "messiah" among different groups of Jews at the time, for every group the Messiah was to be a person of exceptional or miraculous power who would bring in a new and glorious era of peace and prosperity like that of David. In such a view there was no room for the thought that the Christ "must undergo great suffering, and be rejected" by the authorities. Peter's response, therefore, was inaccurate because he had failed to perceive that it was God's will for Jesus as the Son of Man to suffer and be rejected. Any attempt to persuade Jesus to reject his fate was tantamount to Satan's temptation of Jesus in the wilderness (8:27–33).

Jesus' sayings on the conditions of discipleship (8:34–9:1) were inserted by Mark to teach the first lesson in true discipleship—the necessity for taking up the cross. Contemporaries of Mark who want to follow Jesus must be willing to suffer a similar fate of rejection and suffering. Only by doing so will they have life in the world to come.

Based on the account of Moses' theophany at Sinai (Exod 24:15–18; 34:29–30; see also 40:34–38) and the Jewish apocalyptic manifesta-

tions of the Son of Man (Daniel 7–8; 10; *Enoch* 14; 60; 71; see also 2 Esdr 10:25–33), the transfiguration of Jesus (9:2–8) lets privileged disciples recognize, if only for a passing moment, the uniqueness of Jesus. Jesus' prediction that he must suffer and be rejected as Son of God accords fully with God's will (9:7) and anticipates the resurrection of Jesus (9:9). Only after the crucifixion and resurrection of Jesus will the uniqueness of Jesus as Son of God, symbolically portrayed in the transfiguration, be fully comprehended. Here, as at the confession of Jesus' messiahship by Peter, the disciples are charged to tell no one (8:30; 9:9), quite in keeping with Mark's theme of the messianic secret.

Because Elijah is referred to in the transfiguration story, which anticipates Jesus' resurrection, Mark found this the opportune place to introduce the early Christian belief that John the Baptist was Elijah returned. According to Mal 4:5–6 (see also Sir 48:1–3), Elijah was expected to return before the day of the Lord and the general resurrection of the dead. The Jews believed that Elijah would come before the Messiah appeared; and for the early Christians, including Mark, Elijah had appeared as John the Baptist, the forerunner of Jesus the Messiah (9:9–13).

Because both Moses and Elijah appear with Jesus, some scholars think that Mark's emphasis on Jesus as Son of God marks the end of the time of the law and the prophets and the beginning of the era of the risen Christ until his return.

Unlike most miracles in Mark, which take place in private, the healing of the epileptic boy (9:14–29), like the healing of blind Bartimaeus (10:46–52), is performed before a crowd. It is a composite story of two or three scenes, each with narrative and dialogue, in which lessons on faith and prayer have become combined. The emphatic cry of the father, "I believe; help my unbelief!" (9:24), and Jesus' comments on prayer (9:29) echo the spiritual needs of the early church when confronted with opposing forces. Mark has placed the story in its present context for several reasons. God's revelation of Jesus as Son of God is confirmed by Jesus' victory over opposing demonic forces. At the same time, the disciples' failure to perceive the uniqueness of Jesus is reflected in their inability to exorcise the demon from the boy. Thus, they are placed in sharp contrast to the strange exorcist (9:38–41), who is not a disciple of Jesus, but who successfully casts out demons in Jesus' name. In this way Mark dramatically presents the motif of the disciples' misunderstanding and inadequate discipleship. The words in vv 26–27, "the boy was like a corpse," "he is dead," and "he arose" (Greek), anticipate Jesus' own death and resurrection.

The second prediction of the passion (9:30–32), again with a Markan comment about the disciples' failure to understand, is followed with a teaching about true discipleship (9:33–37). True disciples belong to the Christian religion not for what they can get out of it but for what they can give to it through service. The strange exorcist (9:38–41) shows that the early church (see also Acts 8:18–24; 19:13–17) had to face the problem of exorcism. In Mark 9:42–50 are several sayings that were used to teach that suffering is necessary for the kingdom of God. Such teaching was directed toward Mark's readers in Rome or elsewhere who were suffering because of their faith. The words "believe in me" occur only here in the synoptic gospels and indicate that the sayings come from the church, not from Jesus. "Faith in" Jesus developed only after his death.

Unless the Pharisees had heard about Jesus' teaching on the subject, their question about divorce (10:1–12) is strange. Jews were concerned only with proper grounds for divorce, not its prohibition. Jesus' view that marriage is to be permanent (vv 6–9) is not found in the OT, Qumran, or rabbinical literature. The expression "in the house" (7:24; 9:33; 14:3) and the disciples' questioning of Jesus are traits of Mark. The idea that a man who divorces his wife and marries another commits adultery is a departure from Jewish practice, and in Judaism, at least in Palestine, the woman rarely, if ever, had the right to divorce her husband. From all of these things we can draw several conclusions about the sayings of Jesus. Since they differ from Judaism, they may have originated with Jesus, or they may have originated in a non-Jewish community that thought Jesus had prohibited divorce. Since in Roman so-

ciety the woman did have the legal right to divorce her husband, v 12 originated in or was at least accommodated to Graeco-Roman society.

The blessing of the children (10:13–16) may reflect the custom of bringing Jewish children to scribes in the synagogue for a blessing on the eve of the Day of Atonement. The teaching is that the kingdom of God "belongs," is "received," and is to be "entered into." Such language concerning the kingdom is hard to explain, to say nothing of the meanings of the expressions "to such" and "as a child." What do you think those expressions mean?

With the story of the rich young man (10:17–31), Mark returns to the subject of requirements for discipleship. Jesus' reference to God and not to himself as good, and his radical demand for more than observance of the law—"Go, sell what you own, and give the money to the poor"—may have originated with Jesus. Notice that Matthew makes the reply of Jesus conditional—"If you wish to be perfect" ("perfect" is a Matthean word). Does Mark use this pronouncement story to illustrate the "to such as these that the kingdom of God belongs" of the preceding verses? And if so, what is Jesus' answer to the man's question? Is it "Go, sell what you own, and give the money to the poor," or is it "Come, follow me"? The words "you will have treasure in heaven" go with the first command, and because of those words the man's countenance falls. So perhaps the words "come, follow me" are added. Did Mark add them as a call to discipleship?

The sayings in vv 23–27 and 28–31 may be appended; at least 24a and 26a are editorial comments. The words about a camel and the eye of a needle may have been a proverb used for emphasis. There is no textual evidence for the suggestions that the Greek word *kamīlos*, meaning "rope," should be read for *kamēlos*, "camel," or that the needle's eye represented a city gate. The double amazement of the disciples seems odd because it implies that the disciples were rich. In some Jewish literature, especially wisdom writings (see, for example, Prov 10:2, 5, 27; 18:11), riches were a sign of God's favor, though they were not to be gained treacherously. But the moral and spiritual pitfalls of wealth were well known. Plato had said that it was hard for a person to be very rich and very good at the same time (*Laws* 5:3). The words "eternal life" in v 30 and v 17 are the only occurrences of that expression in the synoptics and are the framework within which Mark has set the story. As usual Mark has the promise of reward for discipleship, along with the possibility of "persecutions."

The third prediction of the passion (10:32–34) is followed by the disciples' misunderstanding of Jesus' mission and the role of discipleship. After Mark 10:32–34, the third prediction of the passion, the *Secret Gospel of Mark* inserts a story about Jesus raising a young man from the dead after a reverential request from his sister (for text, see J. D. Crossan 1985:111).

There are two answers to the two disciples' request (vv 38–40 and vv 41–45), but we cannot tell which is the more original. Actually, v 40 alone is a complete answer to the request. Verses 38b–39 allude to Jesus' death in metaphorical language which, in spite of their previous ignorance, the disciples now understand. In the OT and in Judaism, immersion in waters (baptism in vv 38–39) and the word "cup" represent trouble (see, for example, Pss 11:6; 42:7; Isa 30:27–28; 43:2; 51:17, 22; *Pss. Sol.* 8:14–15; 1QpHab 11:10–15). The pericope teaches that disciples are not to be concerned about sharing Jesus' glory (this is beyond their control) but with being willing to suffer and serve.

X. Transitional story of blind Bartimaeus, marking the shift in geography from Galilee to Jerusalem and to the conflicts with Jewish authorities before Jesus' death (10:46–52)

Along with 8:22–26 this story frames Mark's section on teaching and ends a main section of the gospel. Bartimaeus is a shining example of one who does understand Jesus (vv 47–48), sees, and follows him on the way to his passion (v 52).

XI. Jesus' confrontation with authorities in Jerusalem and Mark's introduction to Jesus' apocalyptic discourse (11:1–13:5a)

Up to this point the disciples and the crowds have been blind to the real Jesus, but now Jesus enters Jerusalem and is acclaimed as the Messiah (11:1–10). "The coming kingdom of our ancestor David" makes the story messianic. Matthew makes Jesus' entry the fulfillment of OT prophecy, and Mark may also have been influenced by Zech 9:9. The branches and the allusion to Psalm 118 probably show influence from the Jewish Feast of Dedication, at which that psalm was sung. This feast celebrated the purification of the temple after its desecration by Antiochus IV (2 Macc 10:5).

Was the entry into Jerusalem a historical incident? If so, what impression did Jesus really want to give? Did he believe he was the Davidic Messiah? Notice that Matthew shifts the attention from the kingdom to the "Son of David," and Luke shifts it to "the King."

Mark places the story of the cleansing of the temple (11:15–19) between the two halves of the fig tree story (11:12–14; 11:20–25). The story of the fig tree is difficult because it presents Jesus as demanding something unreasonable and contrary to nature. Several explanations have been suggested: the story illustrates the divine power of Jesus; it is an acted parable to teach a lesson on faith; it symbolizes the fruitless and faithless Jewish people (see also Jer 8:13; Hos 9:10; Joel 1:6–7). At any rate, vv 20–25 are used by Mark to shift the emphasis from the negative to the positive with the catchwords "faith" and "prayer." At the same time, by inserting the cleansing story as he does, Mark wants his readers to see a connection between it and the story of the fig tree. The Messiah has come to cleanse Jewish worship of its corrupt sacrificial cult, for which faith in God and prayer are substitutes. "All the nations" (11:17) can participate in such worship.

It is difficult to see how Jesus could settle down and teach the people (vv 17–18) after his forceful, if not violent, action (vv 15–16). It is important to notice that Mark again stresses Jesus as teacher and that opposition is to his teaching, not to his action. In the series of questions that follows, Jesus' authority is challenged by the authorities in the temple (11:27–33): Pharisees and Herodians (12:13–17), Sadducees (12:18–27), and a scribe (12:28–34). Jesus is portrayed as victorious in academic debate. "And after that no one dared to ask him any question" (12:34).

Jesus may have engaged in "scholastic dialogues" like those reported after the cleansing of the temple. But as these dialogues now exist, they were probably formulated by the church and reflect its later controversy with Judaism. Evidence for such controversy is especially clear in a passage like Mark 12:13: "They sent to him some Pharisees and some Herodians to trap him in what he said." The word "trap" reflects controversy, and its intensity comes out in the parable of the wicked tenants (Mark 12:1–12 = Matt 21:33–46 = Luke 20:9–19). In that parable the Jews' rejection of the OT prophets culminates in their murder of Jesus. This is a clue, of course, that the present form of the parable was written after Jesus' death.

Among the four controversy dialogues, the one in Mark 12:28–34 about the great commandment may be closer to an original account than any of the others. In the Markan form it lacks the idea of testing Jesus that is present in Matt 22:35 and Luke 10:25. The fact that the scribe compliments Jesus twice (12:28, 32) and that Jesus tells the scribe that he is "not far from the kingdom of God" indicates that the controversy reflected in some other dialogues is absent here.

In the discussion about David's son (12:35–37a), we cannot tell whether Jesus applies the psalm to himself as Lord or to the expected Messiah. The teaching of the scribes is criticized, and in the passages that follow—the woes against the Pharisees (12:37b–40) and the widow's gift (12:41–44)—their practices are attacked. The section closes with Jesus' prediction of the imminent destruction of the temple (13:1–2) and with the setting of the scene "privately" for the apocalyptic discourse (13:3–4). Jesus' prediction provides a clue to the date of Mark's gospel. If the prediction is taken literally, then the gospel was written shortly before the fall of Jerusalem in 70 CE. If, on the other hand, the prediction is taken as one made after the event and written into Jesus' words, then Mark was written soon after 70.

XII. Jesus' apocalyptic discourse to his disciples (13:5b–37)

This discourse is typical of the apocalypse genre and of Jewish apocalyptic thought. It is a composite composition based on apocalyptic thought of the OT (compare, for example, 13:12 and Mic 7:6; 13:19 and Dan 12:1; 13:24–25 and Isa 13:10 and 34:4), sayings reflecting the sufferings of early Christians (13:9–13) and their concern with being prepared for the End (13:28–37), signs of the End and exhortations (13:5–8, 14–23), and Son of Man sayings (13:24–27). It is impossible to tell how much, if any, of this material goes back to Jesus, how much Mark found in his source, and how much is Mark's editorial work. For Mark the purpose of the discourse was to encourage his readers in troubled circumstances. He wanted them to persevere in their hope for the glorious coming of the Son of Man and to endure in order to be saved (v 13).

XIII. The passion narrative (14:1–16:8)

Many scholars think the story of Jesus' passion was the first to be written as a continuous narrative. If this is true, then perhaps the traditions about Jesus "developed backward." According to this view, Mark prefixed "the passion narrative with the tradition of Jesus, and . . . that tradition with the tradition of the Baptist" (W. Marxsen 1969:31).

It is impossible to tell how much of an earlier narrative is preserved in Mark and how much he shaped the material he received. However, there is general agreement that Mark's version is the oldest preserved and that the plan of the other synoptists follows that of Mark. Many scholars think that the framework on which Mark constructed his narrative consisted of the conspiracy of the authorities against Jesus (14:1–2), Judas's agreement to betray Jesus (14:10–11), preparation for the Passover (14:12–16), the mention of the traitor (14:17–21), the prophecy of Peter's denial (14:26–31), and Jesus' being taken captive (14:43–52). Then, as the tradition grew, apologetic, liturgical, legendary, and even mythological material was added. Contrary to usual views about the passion narrative, originally Mark may have ended with the apocalyptic discourse (see E. Trocme 1975:224–240).

Several factors in the development of the church may account for some of the embellishment of the framework of the passion narrative. The story of Gethsemane (14:32–42) could have originated to explain Jesus' death—it was God's will. Peter's denial (14:54, 66–72) would have been good for teaching Christians never to deny their religion or fail to confess their faith.

Many questions arise in connection with the study of Jesus' trial, crucifixion, and resurrection that are too complicated for us to consider in detail. However, it is important for all who study the NT to consider several basic issues. With respect to the trial of Jesus, for example, consider these two points: the legitimacy of the trial before the Sanhedrin and the charge against Jesus. A trial on the day of a Jewish festival, on the eve of a festival, or on the eve of a sabbath (Mark 15:42; Matt 27:57; see also John 19:31) runs counter to Jewish law as recorded in the *Mishnah* (*Sanh.* 4:1). The *Mishnah* is a collection of Jewish law and lore edited after 200 CE, and the *Sanhedrin* is one of its tractates.

Blasphemy is suggested as a possible charge against Jesus (Mark 14:64; Matt 26:65). Although we do not know what constituted blasphemy in Jesus' time, according to Lev 24:16 (see also *Sanh.* 7:5), blasphemy was the speaking of evil against "the name of the Lord." But no evidence is presented against Jesus for speaking in such a manner. The penalty for blasphemy was death by stoning, and Jesus was not stoned by the Jews but crucified by the Romans. One of the crimes punishable by Roman crucifixion was sedition. Some scholars have suggested that Jesus had become involved with the Zealots who were advocating rebellion against Rome. Most scholars, however, think there is insufficient evidence for such a charge.

Archaeological evidence for crucifixion in Palestine during the first century CE makes even the method of Jesus' crucifixion problematic. The skeleton of a young man named John was discovered in a tomb within the bounds of Jerusalem. Among other details, evidence indicates that one nail had been driven through both heel bones. Also, a small seat had been fastened on the upright part of the cross to support the buttocks of the victim, perhaps to prolong the agony and prevent a quick death. This evidence does not support the usual view of Jesus' crucifixion—that his hands were nailed to the horizontal bar of the cross. Other evidence, however, seems to indicate that both hands and feet of the victim were nailed to the cross and that flogging was a usual part of the execution (see M. Hengel 1977:31–32).

With respect to the physical resurrection of Jesus, there are interesting and important points to be discussed. Most important, perhaps, is the biomedical proposition stated by D. F. Strauss (1972:736) more than a century ago: If a dead man came to life, could he have been "wholly dead," and if actually dead, could he "really become living"? The gospels are unanimous, however, in saying that Jesus did become living again, but the evidence concerning the nature of his resurrected body is inconclusive. Was it a physical or a spiritual body (see 1 Cor 15:44)? The statements that Jesus talked and ate (Matt 28:9; Luke 24:13–35) support the notion of a physical body. On the other hand, Jesus' appearance in a form not recognized by his followers and his unexpected presence (Luke 24:15, 36; John 21:4), and especially his entering a room with the doors closed (John 20:19), support the notion of a spiritual existence.

These are some of the most critical problems confronting those who study the trial, crucifixion, and resurrection of Jesus. Here are some questions for further study of the passion narrative. Why did the story of the anointing at Bethany (14:3–9), which interrupts the narrative of the conspiracy against Jesus, become a part of the passion narrative? How would Christians have learned about Judas's negotiations with Jewish authorities? Why is the name of Judas not mentioned in the story of the traitor (14:17–21)? Why would a known criminal like Barabbas be released instead of Jesus? Why does Mark—unlike Matthew, Luke, and John—not contain any narratives of Jesus' resurrection appearances?

Remember that Mark was not writing history or biography, and this is true no less for the passion narrative than for any other part of the gospel. The main motive behind the passion narrative (and all of the gospel) was religious. As the numerous allusions to OT texts show, the death of Jesus was thought to be God's will. The proclamation "He has been raised" (16:6) shows Jesus' triumph over all human authority, both Jewish and Roman. For Mark the passion narrative is the climax to his gospel (*euangelion*, "good news"), which ends as it began—with the confession that Jesus is "the Son of God."

SUMMARY

Because Mark is the earliest gospel, it is much more difficult to identify Mark's sources than those of Matthew and Luke. Mark probably had access to miracle stories of Jesus and to an account of Jesus' passion. Although Mark presents Jesus as a teacher, he is more concerned with reporting Jesus' miracles than his teachings because the miracles reinforce Jesus' authority as a teacher. References to Jesus' passion and the passion narrative occupy a disproportionate amount of space in Mark's gospel compared to that in Matthew and Luke. Perhaps the reason is that Mark wrote to encourage Christians during suffering.

A unique feature in Mark's presentation of Jesus is his emphasis on Jesus speaking privately to his disciples. This is one of the ways Mark encouraged true discipleship among his readers, one of his special interests. Mark also presents Jesus as conscious of his messiahship and of being the Son of God. Jesus becomes aware of his uniqueness at his baptism, but this uniqueness is disclosed only gradually in the gospel. This feature of Mark's story of Jesus is known as the messianic secret of Mark. Mark begins and ends his gospel with the theme of Jesus as the Son of God, and it is around this theme that he has developed the theological structure of his gospel.

For further study of Mark, see V. Taylor 1957; E. Schweizer 1976; E. J. Mally 1968; T. J. Weeden 1971; P. J. Achtemeier 1975; C. F. D. Moule 1965a; R. P. Martin 1976b; L. W. Hurtado 1983; C. M. Tuckett 1983a; J. D. Kingsbury 1983; V. K. Robbins 1984; D. B. Peabody 1987; B. L. Mack 1988; M. Hengel 1985; S. P. Kealy 1982; C. S. Mann 1986.

These books will be helpful in studying the trial and crucifixion of Jesus: P. Winter 1974; J. Blinzler 1959; E. Bammel 1970; W. R. Wilson 1970; J. A. Fitzmyer 1978; D. R. Catchpole 1976; W. Kelber 1976; S. Légasse 1997. The definitive work, and very readable, on the passion of Jesus is R. E. Brown 1994—for bibliography see 1:97–100. In addition to the works listed above see W. Telford 1985, various interpretations; H. C. Waetjen 1989, sociopolitical; M. A. Tolbert 1989, literary-historical; C. A. Bryan 1993; J. G. Cook 1996, linguistic; J. K. Elliott 1993, language and style; J. D. Kingsbury 1989, conflict in Mark; E. S. Malbon 1986, narrative, structuralism, myth; J. Painter 1997, conflict; N. R. Petersen 1980, perspectives; D. O. Via 1985, ethics; A. Y. Collins 1992; D. Rhoads 1999, story, narrative. For passion narrative see J. R. Donahue 1973; D. Senior 1984; D. Juel 1977.

In the next chapter we will consider Matthew's gospel.

CHAPTER 5

The Gospel of Matthew

FOR MATTHEW, AS FOR MARK, JESUS IS the messianic Son of God, but Matthew's special designation for Jesus is "Son of David." For Matthew Jesus is to be confessed as Lord, especially in the worshiping community of Matthew's readers. Whereas Mark has a special interest in reporting Jesus' miracles, Matthew is more concerned with stressing his teachings. Observe these major points as we consider why Matthew was placed first among the gospels, the origin, purpose, and structure of the gospel, and the writer's use of sources, his style, and his special interests.

The gospels may have been placed first in the NT because they were thought to represent an important new law comparable to the Torah, the first division of the OT. The Torah was considered the revelation of God's will through Moses, the gospels the revelation of God's will through Jesus. Like the commands of the Torah, the teachings of the gospels were meant to be practiced in religious life.

But why was Matthew placed first among the gospels? The second word of the gospel is *genesis* (the title of the first book of the LXX), and this immediately suggests a parallel with the Torah. Note, however, that the first word of Mark—*archē*—meaning "beginning," could have the same significance as *genesis*. But Matthew portrays Jesus as presenting a new law that requires greater obedience and righteousness than the Jewish law. Matthew had a special interest in the church, and the church also had a special interest in Matthew's gospel. It found in Matthew a guide for itself as a growing institution and for its organization. Matthew could help to regulate the life of church members and to remind them of the church's origins.

ORIGIN AND DATE OF THE GOSPEL

As with the other gospels, Matthew was an anonymous work. Its title probably came from a tradition originating in the story of the tax collector by that name in Matt 9:9–13. The name is also in the list of the twelve disciples in Matt 10:1–4. The earliest evidence for the authorship of Matthew, as for Mark, comes from Eusebius, who reports that Papias had written, "Matthew compiled the sayings [*ta logia*] in the Hebrew language [Aramaic], and each person interpreted them as he was able" (*Hist.* 3:39:16). But this statement is of no value in establishing authorship. The *logia* are not the same as a gospel; at most, they may refer to some source of sayings, such as Q or M, or to a collection of OT texts used by Christians. Because there is no evidence elsewhere that Matthew was written in Hebrew (Aramaic), there is universal agreement that it was originally written in Greek. The dependence of Matthew on the Greek text of Mark has been demonstrated even for the story of the call of Matthew, the tax collector. For these and other reasons most scholars regard Matthew as an anonymous gospel.

There is no tradition for the place of origin of Matthew, but certain clues suggest a strongly Jewish provenance. A number of passages in the letters of Ignatius, bishop of Antioch in Syria (110–115 CE), seem to allude to Matthew, so the gospel was probably known early in Syria and may therefore have originated in Antioch.

Internal evidence indicates that Matthew is a Jewish gospel, written by a Jew for Jews, but with an interest also in Gentiles (see 4:12–16; 12:15–21; 21:43, 45; 28:19–20). As a devout Jew, Matthew usually uses "the kingdom of heaven" instead of "the kingdom of God," substituting "heaven" to avoid the use of the divine name. Similarly, Matthew speaks of Jerusalem as "the holy city" (4:5; 27:53), a designation used only by Jews. He knows Jewish law (7:12; see also Luke 6:31) and assumes that his readers know what is meant by "the tradition of the elders" (15:2); therefore, he does not have to explain it, as Mark (7:1–5) does. Matthew is also familiar with Jewish belief and practice: almsgiving (6:1–4), prayer (6:5–8), and fasting (6:16–18), phylacteries and fringes worn by orthodox Jews (23:5), and tithes even of small things (23:23).

At the same time, Matthew is disgusted because his fellow Jews have not responded to Jesus and his teaching as Matthew would have liked them to respond. Therefore he writes very harshly against the Jews. Several times he adds, "Woe to you, scribes and Pharisees, hypocrites!" to his Q source (23:13, 15, 23, 29). In light of Jesus' teaching, Matthew's readers are to "beware . . . of the teaching of the Pharisees and Sadducees" (16:12). According to Matthew, "the kingdom of God will be taken away from you [priests and Pharisees] and given to a people that produces the fruits of the kingdom" (21:43). Passages like these may indicate that Matthew was a converted scribe. Converts from one religion to another are often angry about the religion they left. Such anger may be especially evident in Matthew's report of the Gentile Pilate's declaration of innocence concerning Jesus' death—"I am innocent of this man's blood"—and the terrible response of Jesus' Jewish accusers—"His blood be on us and on our children!" (27:24–25).

The supposition that Matthew may have been a converted Jew helps to explain two difficulties in the gospel. The first is inaccurate statements about Jewish leaders. Although there were distinctive differences between the Pharisees and Sadducees in belief and practice, Matthew sometimes refers to them as one group: "Pharisees and Sadducees" (3:7; 16:1, 6, 11–12). Similarly, he links other groups in unlikely combinations—for example, "the chief priests and scribes of the people" (2:4; see also 20:18) and "the elders and chief priests and scribes" (16:21). This reflects greater concern with total opposition of Jewish officials to Jesus than with historical accuracy.

The second difficulty is the glaring contradictions in the gospel with respect to Jesus' teaching and that of the Jews. Matthew reports Jesus as saying, "Whoever breaks one of the least of these commandments, and teaches others to do the same . . ." and "Unless your righteousness exceeds that of the scribes and Pharisees . . ." (5:19–20), sayings that support observance of the law. Yet he repeats from his Markan source (7:1–7) Jesus' charge that the Pharisees and scribes are hypocrites because they follow "the tradition of the elders" (15:1–9), a sign of Jewish piety. More important, perhaps, is Jesus' positive comment about the teaching of the scribes and Pharisees, reported only by Matthew: "Do whatever they teach you" (23:3). But this contradicts Matthew's explanatory comment about Jesus' teaching on leaven, a teaching meaning that the disciples are "to beware . . . of the teaching of the Pharisees and Sadducees" (16:12). These contradictions certainly could indicate that as a convert from Judaism to Christianity, Matthew found it difficult to reconcile the old teaching with the new.

In light of the mission command in Matt 28:19–20 to "make disciples of all nations," some scholars say that Matthew intended the Christian faith to be universal. His Jewish-Christian teachings, therefore, were to be used to promote a universal Christianity that was neither typically Jewish nor typically Gentile. But Matthew's background is thoroughly Jewish, despite his interest in Gentiles.

Antioch may be the place of origin for the gospel, because interest in and conflicts between Jewish and Gentile Christianity were keen there. Most scholars agree that Matthew was written somewhere in Syria-Palestine where Judaism was strong and Christianity was trying primarily to enlighten Jewish converts and to win others.

On the other hand, J. A. Overman 1990, using sociological categories to determine the setting of Matthew, concludes that Galilee, not Antioch in Syria, is the place of origin for the gospel. At any rate, from Matthew we learn about a specific early Christian community struggling to work out its own beliefs and practices of worship as it was separating from Judaism.

Several passages may provide clues for determining the date of Matthew. The statement in the parable of the marriage feast that "The king was enraged. He sent his troops . . . and burned their city" (22:7) probably refers to the destruction of Jerusalem in 70 CE. If it does, then the gospel was written sometime after 70. The sayings about woes to the scribes and Pharisees reflect a situation later than Jesus when Christianity was in conflict with Judaism. Matthew refers to "their synagogue(s)" (9:35; 10:17; 12:9; 13:54) as if Christians were not associated with the synagogue; this may reflect the fact that the Jews

forbade Christians to be members of the synagogue after c. 85 CE. These clues and the likelihood that Ignatius and his readers knew the gospel of Matthew make a date sometime between c. 85 and 110 plausible.

PURPOSES OF MATTHEW

Matthew, like Mark, never tells why he wrote his gospel, so again we must find clues in the gospel itself. Remember that Mark 1:1 gives a clue to his presentation of Jesus as the Christ, the Son of God. Similarly, the first verse of Matthew provides a clue to his portrayal of Jesus: "An account of the genealogy of Jesus Christ, the son of David." Although the most widely stressed aspect of messianic belief was that the Messiah would be a descendant of David, the title "Son of David" was not used with reference to the Messiah before the first century BCE. Then it was used of the political ruler who would restore the kingdom of Israel (*Pss. Sol.* 17:23). It is not used in the NT except in the synoptic gospels, where it is first applied to Jesus as a healer of blind Bartimaeus (Mark 10:47–48; Matt 20:30; Luke 18:38).

Apparently Matthew took over both the title "Son of David" and the idea of healing associated with it from Mark, using them to convince his Jewish opponents that Jesus' Davidic messiahship was expressed in healings. That this was disputed is clear from several passages. After the healing of two blind men and a dumb demoniac, the Pharisees accuse Jesus of casting out demons "by the ruler of the demons" (9:27–34; also 12:22–24). After the crowds proclaim Jesus as the Son of David during his entry into Jerusalem, he heals the blind and lame in the temple. "But when the chief priests and the scribes saw the amazing things that he did, and heard the children crying out . . . 'Hosanna to the Son of David,' they became angry" (21:9–15). By contrast, the Gentile Canaanite woman (15:21–28), who addresses Jesus as Lord and as Son of David, is healed because of her great faith. No sign of dissension is present in that story.

One of Matthew's purposes, then, was to promote faith in Jesus as the messianic Son of David, as evidenced in his healings. Matthew's efforts, which represented an aspect of early Christology, were resisted by his Jewish opponents, especially the Pharisees and scribes. This clearly reflects the controversy between the church and synagogue of Matthew's time. Another of Matthew's purposes was to present Jesus as the Messiah who fulfilled OT prophecy. Throughout the gospel, Matthew reports incidents in Jesus' life as happening in accordance with a quotation from the OT that is usually introduced with a formula like "this took place to fulfill what had been spoken by." Examine these passages: Jesus' virgin birth (1:22–23; Isa 7:14), his birth at Bethlehem (2:5–6; Mic 5:2), Jesus' return from Egypt (2:15; Hos 11:1), Herod's killing of male children (2:16–18; Jer 31:15), Jesus' living in Nazareth (2:23; Heb. of Isa 11:1?), Jesus' living and teaching in Galilee (4:12–16; Isa 9:1–2), the reason for speaking in parables (from Mark, but reinterpreted in light of Isa 6:9–10; also in 13:35; Ps 78:2), entry into Jerusalem as King (21:4–5; Isa 62:11; Zech 9:9), and the price of Jesus' life (27:9–10; Jer 32:6–15; 18:2–3; Zech 11:12–13).

Matthew's use of so many quotations with a standardized formula raises two important questions. The first is too difficult for us to deal with: Did Matthew use the Hebrew or Greek (LXX) text of the OT, or did he find his quotations in a special collection of OT prophecies called *testimonia* ("witnesses") that was used in the early church to confirm the messiahship of Jesus? The second question is a historical one: Did Matthew report actual events in Jesus' life and then show that they fulfilled OT prophecy? Or, being familiar with OT texts, did he create incidents in the life of Jesus to match the texts? Sometimes, of course, he found an incident in Mark and then interpreted or supplemented it with a quotation, as, for example, in the story of the entry into Jerusalem. Similarly, since Luke also refers to the virgin birth of Jesus, we know that it was in the tradition and that Matthew did not invent it. But how about the stories of Herod's killing male children and the flight to Egypt and the return? And did Jesus really go to live in Capernaum, or did Matthew use the OT passage "Galilee of the Gentiles" to support the Gentile mission of the church?

One of Matthew's purposes was to write a gospel for the church, as is clear again from several clues within the gospel itself. Matthew is the only gospel in which the word "church" is used. According to Matthew, the church was established by Jesus himself with Peter as the main charter member and chief authority (16:17–19). Built upon a rock, like the house in the parable at the end of chap. 7, it will endure as a power even over death (as Jesus did). It is to serve as an arbiter in disputes among its members (18:15–17) and assures God's presence even "where two or three are gathered" for Christian worship (18:20). The church gives advice and encouragement in time of persecution (5:10–12, 44; 10:17–39). Through the example (3:13–15) and authority of Jesus (28:18–20), it has the authority to baptize, and it gives instructions for proper almsgiving, prayer, and fasting (6:1–18). The Sermon on the Mount (5–7) and other passages (for example, those dealing with children and "little ones"—Matthew's favorite word for Christians) tell what kind of behavior is expected of church members. The passages in Example 5.1 show that for Matthew the church is sometimes the kingdom of heaven.

Observe that in the Markan passage, used to teach the nature of true discipleship, the dispute about greatness occurs among the disciples themselves. Now notice that in vv 1 and 4 Matthew changes the discussion to a question about who is greatest in the kingdom (= the church). Notice also that the tense in v 3 is future—"will enter"—which is Mark's form. But in v 4, which is Matthew's addition, the tense is present, as in v 1. Here Matthew's editorial hand helps him convey his conception of the church. At the same time, the passage reflects a struggle for prestige within the church.

Example 5.2 is from the institution of the Lord's Supper. Notice three changes in Matthew. Mark's command "Take" becomes "Take, eat," and the simple narrative "all of them drank from it" becomes a command, "Drink from it, all of you." Matthew's account reflects a liturgical service in the church. Notice also Matthew's addition, "for the forgiveness of sins," the very phrase Matthew (3:2–4) left out of Mark's ac-

---

EXAMPLE 5.1   *Kingdom of God as the Church in Matthew*

Matt 18:1–4	Mark 9:33–36; 10:15	Luke 9:46–48; 18:17
At that time the disciples came to Jesus and asked, "Who is the greatest in the kingdom of heaven?" [2]He called a child, whom he put among them, [3]and said, "Truly I tell you, unless you change and become like children, you will never enter the kingdom of heaven. [4]Whoever becomes humble like this child is the greatest in the kingdom of heaven."	[33]Then they came to Capernaum; and when he was in the house he asked them, "What were you arguing about on the way?" [34]But they were silent, for on the way they had argued with one another who was the greatest. [35]He sat down, called the twelve, and said to them, "Whoever wants to be first must be last of all and servant of all." [36]Then he took a little child and put it among them; and taking it in his arms, he said to them, [15]Truly I tell you, whoever does not receive the kingdom of God as a little child will never enter it."	[46]An argument arose among them as to which one of them was the greatest. [47]But Jesus, aware of their inner thoughts, took a little child and put it by his side, [48]and said to them, [17]Truly I tell you, whoever does not receive the kingdom of God as a little child will never enter it."

Cf. *GThom* 12; 22; *Acts of Philip* 34.

EXAMPLE 5.2   *Changes in Matthew's Account of the Last Supper*

Matt 26:26–28	Mark 14:22–24	Luke 22:19–20
[26]While they were eating, Jesus took a loaf of bread, and after blessing it he broke it, gave it to the disciples, and said, "Take, eat; this is my body." [27]Then he took a cup, and after giving thanks he gave it to them, saying, "Drink from it, all of you; [28]for this is my blood of the covenant, which is poured out for many for the forgiveness of sins."	[22]While they were eating, he took a loaf of bread, and after blessing it he broke it, gave it to them, and said, "Take; this is my body." [23]Then he took a cup, and after giving thanks he gave it to them, and all of them drank from it. [24]He said to them, "This is my blood of the covenant, which is poured out for many."	[19]Then he took a loaf of bread, and when he had given thanks, he broke it and gave it to them, saying, "This is my body, which is given for you. Do this in remembrance of me." [20]And he did the same with the cup after supper, saying, "This cup that is poured out for you is the new covenant in my blood."

Cf. *GEbi* 7; *Did.* 9:15.

---

count (1:4) of John's preaching. Thus, Matthew makes sure forgiveness is to come not from John's baptism ceremonies, but from Jesus' sacrificial death, which is symbolized in the Lord's Supper. This coincides with the command to Peter, the exemplary cornerstone of the church, to forgive a fellow Christian "seventy times seven" (18:21–22).

Apparently Mark's gospel no longer served the requirements of Matthew's community, so Matthew modified and expanded Mark to fill the community's needs. Matthew was a document easy to refer to for matters of faith, conduct, and worship. The fact that Matthew calls his work a "book" (Greek, *biblos*)—assuming that the word refers to the whole gospel and not just to the first two chapters—indicates that it was meant to serve a practical purpose.

In light of what we have learned about Matthew and the law, one of the practical purposes of Matthew may have been to counter a group in his community who were opposing the law (antinomians) and/or were disobeying the law. That Matthew has a special interest in the law (*nomos*, "law," especially God's law) and lawlessness (*anomia* [four times; not in Mark or Luke], especially disobedience to God's law), tends to support such a view. Some passages thought to support the view that Matthew is opposing antinomians are 5:17-20, 48; 7:12-27; 13:41; 22:34-40; 24:10-12; 23:28.

G. Barth 1963:94, 159 was the first person to defend in detail the view that Matthew was polemicizing against antinomians. "Against the antinomians he defends the abiding validity of the whole Old Testament law. . . . They dispute that the law and the prophets still hold for the Church." Among those who support Barth's thesis is C. Carlston 1968, among those disagreeing are W. D. Davies 1964, J. Rohde 1968, and J. E. Davison 1985.

MATTHEW'S USE OF HIS SOURCES, ESPECIALLY MARK

On the hypothesis that Matthew used both Mark and Q, it is easier to separate redaction from tradition in his gospel than in Mark, for which we have no certain source. By studying the way Matthew uses his sources, we can discover important features of his style and his special interests.

At the beginning of his gospel, Matthew expands Mark's outline by supplementing the story of the Baptist with a genealogy of Jesus (1:1-17) and narratives of Jesus' birth (1:18-2:23), and at the end by adding resurrection appearances (28:9-20) to Mark's story of the empty tomb. He arranges Jesus' sayings in Q (see also Luke 6:20-49), adds others from elsewhere in Q, and combines all of them with material of his own (5-7). Similarly, he collects other sayings and inserts them in blocks into Mark's outline (10-11; 13; 18; 23; 24-25). He also adds quotations from the OT to individual pericopes, as in the sections on Jesus' living in Capernaum (Mark 1:14-15; Matt 4:12-17; Luke 4:14-15) and on the reason for speaking in parables (Mark 4:10-12; Matt 13:10-15; Luke 8:9-10). Matt 3:14-15 and 28:16-20 are good examples of material Matthew probably wrote himself. The curious thing about many of Matthew's additions to Mark is that they seem to be legends either created by Matthew or taken over from an earlier tradition: some of the birth narratives (2:1-23), Peter's walking on the water (14:28-31), the shekel (coin) in the fish's mouth (17:24-27), the dream of Pilate's wife (27:19), Pilate washing his hands (27:24-25), the opening of the tombs and the rising of the saints (27:51b-53), and the guard at the tomb (27:62-66).

Matthew combines and rearranges material from Mark. He neatly combines the miracles in Mark 2:1-3:6 and 4:35-5:43 into one section (8-9). In chap. 13 he takes the parables of the sower and the mustard seed from Mark and inserts between them the parable of the weeds (from M or from his own reworking of Mark's parable of the seed), instead of using Mark's parable of the seed growing secretly. Then he takes the parable of the leaven from Q and adds the parables of the treasure and the pearl, the net, and the householder.

In Matt 13:53-28:8 the author follows Mark's order rather carefully, but from 3:1 to 13:52 there are frequent changes in order. If you have *Gospel Parallels,* leaf through it now, beginning with page 11, and observe Matthew's arrangement of Markan with Q and M material. Notice that Matthew sometimes condenses Mark's narrative, mostly in the miracle stories, apparently to save space for more of Jesus' teaching. Look at the story of Peter's mother-in-law (p. 21), and you will see that Matthew's version is shorter than Mark's. The same thing is true for the stories of the Gerasene demoniac, Jairus's daughter, and a woman's faith (pp. 81–85).

Matthew sometimes tones down or omits things in Mark that might cause offense or misunderstanding. Remember that Matthew changes Mark's "could do no deed of power" to "he did not do many deeds of power." Matthew omits Jesus' emotions and his need to ask questions. Here are some examples of what Matthew omits that is in Mark: "moved with pity" (1:41); "he looked around at them with anger; he was grieved at their hardness of heart" (3:5); "he sighed deeply in his spirit" (8:12); "he was indignant" (10:14); "What is your name?" (5:9); "Who touched my clothes?" (5:30). The self-seeking of James and John in asking Jesus to do for them whatever they ask (10:35) is attributed by Matthew to their mother (20:20). Matthew, unlike Mark, does not want to put the disciples in a bad light. In the same way, Matthew usually does not share Mark's idea of Jesus speaking and acting in secret, so he omits the significant words "He did not want anyone to know it" (9:30).

Matthew sometimes omits details or adds touches to Mark's miracle stories in order to intensify the miraculous. For example, he omits the vivid details in the story of the epileptic boy in order to emphasize the healing by Jesus' word: "Jesus rebuked the demon, and it came out of him, and the boy was cured instantly" (17:18). Matthew stresses the suddenness of a healing by adding a statement such as "And instantly (lit., "from that hour") the woman was made well" (9:22; see also 15:28; 17:18).

In sum, Matthew redacts his sources by adding, omitting, interpreting, rearranging, rewriting, and condensing, and at other times by being careful to follow Mark's precise wording.

THE STRUCTURE OF MATTHEW

Although Matthew reproduces most of the narrative material in Mark and in general follows Mark's framework, about half of the gospel is composed of teachings of Jesus that do not come from Mark, including shorter sayings and parables. These teachings are arranged in five main sections, each of which ends with a similar formula, "and when Jesus had finished. . . ." Not all of these teachings, usually referred to as discourses, go back to Jesus or even to only one earlier source. Some do go back to Jesus, some come from various traditions in the church, and some may have been composed by Matthew himself. Matthew collected them, arranged them, and fitted them into the Markan framework. That they have been arranged by Matthew is clear because a number of the sayings Matthew has grouped together are separated in Luke. You can see this by looking at the following parallels: Matt 5:13–16 = Luke 14:34–35 and 11:33; Matt 7:1–5 = Luke 6:37–38, 41–42; Matt 7:12–14 = Luke 6:31 and 13:23–24.

Between each main discourse (roughly chaps. 5–7; 10; 13; 18; 23–25) Matthew has inserted narrative material and added introductory and concluding narratives. With this in mind we can outline the general structure of the gospel as shown in Figure 5.1.

Notice that Matthew not only closes each discourse with a similar formula, but also introduces each with a statement about Jesus as "teaching" or "saying." In the same way, most narrative sections begin and end with references to crowds or with words that imply a large following. Thus crowds are associated with what Jesus says and does. The only exceptions are the beginnings of the narratives before the first and third discourses; they begin with statements about John the Baptist. These statements keep the readers aware that the one who is teaching and healing, not John, is the Messiah. The disciples and the crowds, the two groups constantly intermingled, represent Christian missionaries and the converts they are teaching.

Most scholars still think Matthew structured his gospel around the five main discourses (first proposed by B. W. Bacon 1930 but questioned by W. D. Davies 1964 and J. P. Meier 1979, 1983). But this view has been challenged. For

FIGURE 5.1   *General Structure of Matthew*

Prologue:	birth narratives (1:1–2:23).
Introductory narratives:	(3:1–5:1).
Opening formula:	"In those days John the Baptist appeared in the wilderness of Judea" (3:1).
Closing formula:	"And great crowds followed him. . . . When Jesus saw the crowds . . ." (4:25–5:1).
First discourse:	the new law for Christians (5:2–7:29).
Opening formula:	"Then he began to speak, and taught them, saying . . ." (5:2).
Closing formula:	"When Jesus had finished saying these things, the crowds were astounded at his teaching, for he taught them as one having authority, and not as their scribes" (7:28–29).
Narratives:	mostly miracles (8:1–9:36).
Opening formula:	"When Jesus had come down from the mountain, great crowds followed him" (8:1).
Closing formula:	"When he saw the crowds, he had compassion for them" (9:36).
Second discourse:	teaching for Christian missionaries (9:37–11:1).
Opening formula:	"Then he said to his disciples . . ." (9:37).
Closing formula:	"When Jesus had finished instructing his twelve disciples, he went on from there to teach and proclaim his message in their cities" (11:1).
Narratives:	mostly controversy material (11:2–13:2).
Opening formula:	"When John heard in prison what the Messiah was doing . . ." (11:2).
Closing formula:	"Great crowds gathered around him that he got into a boat and sat there" (13:2).
Third discourse:	parables about what "the kingdom of heaven is like" (13:3–53).
Opening formula:	"And he told them many things in parables, saying . . ." (13:3a).
Closing formula:	"When Jesus had finished these parables, he left that place" (13:53).
Narratives:	miracles, controversies, and the church (13:54–7:22a).
Opening formula:	"He came to his hometown and began to teach them in their synagogue, so that they were astounded" (13:54).
Closing formula:	"As they were gathering in Galilee . . ." (17:22a).
Fourth discourse:	the church and behavior in it (17:22b–19:1a).
Opening formula:	"Jesus said to them . . ." (17:22b).
Closing formula:	"When Jesus had finished saying these things . . ." (19:1a).
Narratives:	mostly controversy material (19:1b–22:46).
Opening formula:	"He left Galilee and went to the region of Judea . . . Large crowds followed him" (19:1b–2).
Closing formula:	"No one was able to give him an answer, nor from that day did any one dare to ask him any more questions" (22:46).

(continued)

FIGURE 5.1 *Continued*

Fifth discourse:	woes, apocalyptic, and need for watchfulness (23:1–26:2).
Opening formula:	"Then Jesus said to the crowds and to his disciples . . ." (23:1).
Closing formula:	"When Jesus had finished saying all these things, he said to his disciples, 'You know that after two days the Passover is coming, and the Son of Man will be handed over to be crucified'" (26:1–2).
Concluding narratives:	the conspiracy against Jesus to the resurrection (26:3–28:20).
Opening formula:	"Then the chief priests and the elders of the people gathered in the palace of the high priest . . . and they conspired to arrest Jesus" (26:3).
Closing commission:	"Go therefore and make disciples of all nations . . ." (28:19–20).

---

example, J. D. Kingsbury 1975:1–39 points out the peculiar Matthean formula in 4:17 and 16:21: "From that time Jesus began. . . ." With that formula as a starting point, Kingsbury divides the gospel into three main parts: "The Person of Jesus Messiah (1:1–4:16)," "The Proclamation of Jesus Messiah (4:17–16:20)," and "The Suffering, Death, and Resurrection of Jesus Messiah (16:21–28:20)." See also D. R. Bauer 1988. Because of the diversity of the material, it is impossible to work out a completely satisfactory structural outline of the gospel. Most scholars agree, however, that Matthew adapted and supplemented the outline of Mark and that in doing so he reveals his own style and special interests.

THE STYLE OF MATTHEW

Matthew frequently repeats the same or similar phrases, such as "and when Jesus had finished," weeping and gnashing of teeth (8:12; 13:42, 50; 22:13; 24:51; 25:30), and going to hell (5:22, 29, 30; 10:28; 18:9; 23:33). This is evident also in the way he begins the parables. Six begin with "the kingdom of heaven is like" (13:31, 33, 44, 45, 47; 20:1), and three begin with "the kingdom of heaven may be compared to" (13:24; 18:23; 22:2; see also 25:1). In three parables,

these formulas are preceded with "another parable" and followed by "he put before them another parable" (13:24, 31), or "he told them" (13:33; see also 21:33). Another favorite repetition is "You have heard that it was said . . . but I say to you" (see, for example, 5:21–22, 27–28, 38–39).

Matthew has a way of balancing out statements in his sources. To Mark's "forty days" (1:13; also Luke 4:2) Matthew adds "and forty nights" (4:2). The passages in italics in Example 5.3 are just a few examples of this stylistic feature in Matthew's use of his sources Mark and Q.

The word "righteousness" is a favorite of Matthew's, and he inserts it into his sources Mark and Q. (For the meaning of the term in Matthew, see J. D. Kingsbury 1977:86–90.) Figure 5.2 displays other favorite words and phrases, with numbers pertaining to their usage by the three synoptists. Notice the words and phrases as you work through Matthew's gospel.

Matthew likes to put things in threes: three incidents after Jesus' birth (2:1–23); teaching, preaching, and healing (4:23; see also Mark 1:39; Luke 4:44); three signs of righteousness—almsgiving, prayer, and fasting (6:1–18); three negative commands (6:19–7:6); three positive commands (7:7–20); three parables of sowing (13:1–32); and three hopes (6:9–10) and three petitions (6:11–13) in the Lord's Prayer (6:9–13).

EXAMPLE 5.3   *Balanced Statements Showing Matthew's Style*

Matt 4:18–22	Mark 1:16–20	Luke
[18]As he walked by the Sea of Galilee, he saw *two brothers,* Simon, who is called Peter, and *Andrew his brother,* casting a net into the sea—for they were fishermen. [19]And he said to them, "Follow me, and I will make you fish for people." [20]Immediately they left their nets and followed him. [21]As he went from there, he saw *two other brothers,* James son of Zebedee and *his brother John,* in the boat with their father Zebedee, mending their nets, and he called them. [22]Immediately they left the boat and their father, and followed him.	[16]As Jesus passed along the Sea of Galilee, he saw Simon and his brother Andrew casting a net into the sea—for they were fishermen. [17]And Jesus said to them, "Follow me and I will make you fish for people." [18]And immediately they left their nets and followed him. [19]As he went a little farther, he saw James son of Zebedee and his brother John, who were in their boat mending the nets. [20]Immediately he called them; and they left their father Zebedee in the boat with the hired men, and followed him.	

Cf. *GEbi* 1.

Matt 16:14–15	Mark 11:25	Luke
[14]*"For if you forgive others their trespasses, your heavenly Father will also forgive you;* [15]but *if you do not forgive others, neither will your Father forgive your trespasses."*	[25]"Whenever you stand praying, forgive, if you have anything against anyone; so that your Father in heaven may also forgive you your trespasses."	

Matt 6:22–23	Mark	Luke 11:34
[22]"The eye is the lamp of the body. So, *if your eye is healthy, your whole body will be full of light;* [23]but *if your eye is unhealthy, your whole body will be full of darkness.* If then the light in you is darkness, how great is the darkness!"		[34]"Your eye is the lamp of your body. If your eye is healthy, your whole body is full of light; but if it is not healthy, your body is full of darkness."

Matt 18:8	Mark 9:43, 45	Luke
[8]"*If your hand or your foot* causes you to stumble, cut it off and throw it away; it is better for you to enter life maimed or lame than to have *two hands or two feet* and to be thrown into the eternal fire."	[43]"If your hand causes you to stumble, cut it off; it is better for you to enter life maimed than to have two hands and to go to hell, to the unquenchable fire. [45]And if your foot causes you to stumble, cut it off; it is better for you to enter life lame than to have two feet and to be thrown into hell."	

Cf. *GThom* 24; *DialSav* 125:18–126:2.

FIGURE 5.2   *Favorite Matthean Words and Phrases*

The numbers on the left, from left to right, indicate times inserted in parallel material, times in peculiar Matthean material, and times shared with one or both of Mark and Luke. Numbers on the right indicate times in Matthew, Mark, and Luke (statistics from R. H. Gundry 1982:641–649).

(15,8,8)	truly I say to you	(31,13,6)
(25,7,0)	kingdom of heaven	(32,0,0)
(34,9,19)	behold	(62,7,57)
(10,2,2)	called, with names	(14,2,2)
(7,0,0)	now (*arti*)	(7,0,0)
(10,2,1)	Father in heaven	(13,1,1)
(38,6,8)	come to (*proserchomai*)	(52,5,10)
(66,17,7)	then (*tote*)	(90,6,14)
(4,0,1)	little faith	(5,0,1)
(8,3,2)	hypocrite	(13,1,3)

SPECIAL INTERESTS OF MATTHEW

Recall that Matthew has a special interest in reporting Jesus' teachings, that he inserts five main discourses into the general framework of Mark, and that he frames each discourse with a reference to Jesus teaching or speaking. Although some scholars have challenged the prevailing view that Matthew intended the five discourses to parallel the five books of Moses, the beginning and end of the Sermon on the Mount show that Matthew was comparing Jesus with Moses as lawgiver. In contrast to Luke, who prefixes his account of the sermon with "He . . . stood on a level place" (6:17), Matthew says, "He went up the mountain" (5:1). Compare Matthew's words with those about Moses: "The Lord summoned Moses to the top of the mountain, and Moses went up" (Exod 19:20; see also 19:3). And compare Matthew's statement "When Jesus had come down from the mountain, great crowds followed him" (8:1) with that about Moses: "Moses went down from the mountain to the people" (Exod 19:14; see also 19:21). Surely the similarity is not just a coincidence.

Jews of Matthew's time regarded Moses as the supreme lawgiver and the scribes as the chief teachers of the law. Matthew does not seek to do away with the Jewish law or scribalism, as certain passages make clear: Jesus did not come "to abolish the law or the prophets" (5:17); all will be "accomplished" (5:18); every Christian "scribe who has been trained for the kingdom of heaven" can bring "out of his treasure what is new [Jesus' teachings] and what is old" (the law and the prophets; 13:52).

That Matthew has retained an interest in Jewish law is clear from the way he uses the terms "law" and "the law and the prophets." Since Mark never uses either of those terms, Matthew did not find them in Mark. The term "law" occurs in peculiar Matthean material in 5:18 and 12:5, and is inserted into Q in 23:23 and into Markan material in 22:36. Except for the Q passage Luke 16:16 = Matt 11:13, from which Matthew may have taken it, the combination "the law and the prophets" occurs only in Matthew (see Luke 24:44). It occurs in Matthean material (5:17), is inserted into Q in Matt 7:12 (= Luke 6:31), and is added to Markan material in 22:40.

Matthew, however, is interested in convincing his readers that Jesus brought a new law, radical in its demands for obedience. For those who want to enter the kingdom of heaven (the church), Christian righteousness must exceed that of the scribes and Pharisees (5:20). This is the point of the antitheses in the Sermon on the Mount. The conclusion to the antitheses is "Be perfect [*teleios*], therefore, as your heavenly Father is perfect" (5:48). But the old law had required just as much: "You shall be perfect [Hebrew; LXX, *teleios,* "perfect"] with the Lord your God" (Deut 18:13). For the view that Matthew intentionally constructed his narrative about Jesus as a Moses typology on the basis of traditions and his own theological interests see D. C. Allison 1993.

EXAMPLE 5.4   *Matthew's Use of the Word "Coming" for the Parousia*

Matt 24:3	Mark 13:4	Luke 21:7
and what will be the sign of your coming and of the end of the age?"	and what will be the sign that all these things are about to be accomplished?"	and what will be the sign that this is about to take place?"
Matt 24:37	**Mark**	**Luke 17:26**
37"As the days of Noah were, so will be the coming of the Son of Man."		26"As it was in the days of Noah, so too it will be in the days of the Son of Man."

Some of the ideas discussed under Matthew's purposes for writing—Jesus as Son of David, his use of the OT, and the church with Peter as its most prominent member—are also special interests. Christologically, for Matthew Jesus as Son of David is a royal Messiah. Herod plots to kill the Christ, king of the Jews (2:2, 4), who is to govern Israel (2:6). Jesus rides into Jerusalem as the humble king predicted by the prophet (21:5). And the charge against Jesus in Mark, "The King of the Jews" (15:26), becomes a confession of the Romans who put Jesus on the cross: "This is Jesus, the King of the Jews" (27:37; also in Matt 27:42 from Mark 15:32).

As Messiah, Jesus is also Son of God. As a baby, Jesus is called out of Egypt as God's Son in fulfillment of OT prophecy. Then, in contrast to the secret messianic Sonship of Jesus in Mark, Jesus' Sonship is announced publicly at his baptism: "*This* [not "You," of Mark] is my beloved Son" (3:17; emphasis mine). For Matthew, the taunts of the Jews while Jesus is on the cross, "If you are the Son of God, come down from the cross" and "for he said, 'I am God's Son'" (27:40, 43; both absent in Mark), become the confession of the church. After Peter exemplifies the doubting disciple (14:30–31), the worshiping community, represented by all the disciples, confesses: "Truly you are the Son of God" (14:33). Finally, to Peter's confession in Mark, "You are the Christ" (8:29), Matthew adds, "the Son of the living God" (16:16). Recall here that in our discussion of the messianic secret in Mark

we learned that J. D. Kingsbury 1986 says that it is also a prominent motif in Matthew.

Matthew also has a special interest in Jesus as eschatological Son of Man who, as a glorious heavenly figure, will come again (especially in M, for example, 19:28; 25:31; see also 16:28; 24:30–31; 26:64). Several key words provide clues to the writer's thought. *Palingenesia* (lit., "rebirth") was a technical term used by Stoics and other philosophers for the new world that would appear after the destruction of the old. Matthew is the only writer in the NT who uses it in that sense: "At the renewal of all things, when the Son of Man is seated on the throne of his glory . . ." (19:28; see also Mark 10:29; Luke 22:28–30). In the early church the word *parousia* (lit., "presence," "arrival," "coming") had become a technical term for the second coming of Christ (see, for example, 1 Cor 15:23; 1 Thess 2:19; 3:13; 4:15). Of the gospel writers, only Matthew uses it in that way (24:3, 27, 37, 39). The passages in Example 5.4 show how he inserts it into his sources.

Other things in Matthew also indicate his interest in eschatology. Among the circumstances to accompany the end of the age is "weeping and gnashing of teeth"; this expression is repeated several times in Matthew, but otherwise is used in the NT only in Luke 13:28. The parables of the ten maidens (25:1–13), the talents (25:14–30), and the last judgment (25:31–46), all of which appear only in Matthew, stress the need for watchfulness and proper conduct in preparation for the imminent End.

Finally, Matthew has a special interest in conveying his christological concept of Jesus as Lord. Mark has a special interest in portraying Jesus as a teacher, and his portrayal may be accurate. In Mark Jesus is addressed as "rabbi" or "teacher"—terms of respect—by disciples and others who believe in him as well as by strangers and opponents. But in Matthew, disciples and others who believe in Jesus address him as "Lord" (see, for example, 8:8, 25; 14:28; 17:4). On the other hand, a scribe (8:19), scribes and Pharisees (12:38), someone unknown to Jesus (19:16), Pharisees and Herodians (22:16), Judas the traitor (26:25, 49), and others who are unfaithful, unknown, or unfriendly, address Jesus as "teacher." This shows that in the church of Matthew's community, Jesus had become an exalted, authoritative figure not comprehended in the same way by outsiders. Peter is made the example of the church member who is doubting and faithful at the same time. As a "man of little faith" (14:31), his doubt is to be rejected; but as a model disciple, his confession, "Lord, save me!" (14:30), is to be imitated in the church.

Although Peter is the most prominent disciple in each of the synoptics, Matthew exceeds all others in giving him prominence. Besides the things already noted, observe these. Only Matthew puts "first" before the name of Simon (Peter) in the list of the twelve (10:2), and only Peter is called "blessed" by Jesus (16:17). Peter asks Jesus to explain his words about what defiles a person (13:15), and he asks the question about how often to forgive his brother (18:21). Matthew, indeed, has a special interest in the exemplary disciple in the church.

Observe this interest and the other special interests and traits mentioned as you study Matthew with the help of the outline and comments below.

Outline and Comments

I. Prologue: birth narratives (1:1–2:23)

The birth narratives are early Christian legend, not history, and reveal the creative imagination and theological insights of Matthew. Typically, in the genealogy (1:1–17) the writer presents the ancestors of Jesus in three sets to prove that, as the Son of Abraham, Jesus fulfills God's promise that in Abraham "all the families of the earth shall be blessed" (Gen 12:3). As the Son of David, the Messiah Jesus "will save his people from their sins" (1:21). So the purpose of Jesus' coming as Messiah is theological, not political; and the significance of Jesus' coming lies not in the manner of his birth, but in the meaning of his name Emmanuel, "God is with us." Thus, the gospel begins and ends with the assurance of the divine presence: "I am with you always, to the end of the age" (28:20).

One of Matthew's purposes for writing, as we have learned, was to present Jesus as the fulfiller of OT prophecy, especially his conception by a virgin (Matt 1:23 and Isa 7:14). Although Matthew was primarily concerned with portraying Jesus as the one who would "save his people from their sins" and be God's presence among them (1:21–23), he also wrote that Jesus was conceived by a virgin in order that Isaiah's prophecy might be fulfilled.

Much has been written about the circumstances of Jesus' birth, and I think it is fair to say that an increasing number of scholars reject the literal view of Jesus' virgin birth. J. Schaberg 1987 writes that the conception of Jesus was not virginal but biologically normal, although illegitimate. For feminist interpretations of Matthew's infancy narrative see J. Schaberg 1997. G. Luedemann 1999 says that a blending of piety, faith, and fantasy has shrouded the person of Mary to make her more believable and human and that Jesus was born from a premarital union. R. A. Horsley 1989b, typically, takes a sociopolitical approach to the infancy narratives, but he also discusses different viewpoints. M. D. Goulder 1989:1:205–291 views the narratives as the creation of a creative writer. And M. Coleridge 1993 considers Luke's birth narrative from a detailed literary critical analysis. He argues throughout that the important thing is not what actually happened but why Luke narrated it.

The definitive work, and very readable, on all aspects of the birth narratives is R. E. Brown 1943. For a very broad approach, which is also very lucid and thorough, see J. A. Fitzmyer

FIGURE 5.3
*Olive press at
Capernaum.*

1981:303–448. Perhaps you also want to see my forthcoming book, *The Stories of Jesus' Birth: A Critical Introduction,* written from the perspectives of the authors' literary styles and theologies.

Two statements in the story of the Magi (2:1–13) provide clues for our understanding of Matthew's thought. Jesus as "king of the Jews" has been rejected by his own people, Israel, symbolized by Herod. The Magi, who "knelt down and paid him homage," represent the Gentiles who accepted Jesus. This theme of Jewish rejection and Gentile acceptance is a major one throughout the gospel.

The narrative of the flight to and from Egypt (2:12–23) is full of symbolism. Like Moses, who went to Egypt and returned because God told him to do so, Jesus goes to Egypt and returns. The boy Moses was saved from death at the hands of Pharaoh in Egypt (Exod 1:15–2:10), and the boy Jesus is saved from death at the hands of Herod by going to Egypt. In the Exodus story Pharaoh is the enemy of Moses and Is-

rael; in Matthew, Archelaus is the enemy of Jesus and the church. Notice the close similarity between the angel's words to Joseph and those of God to Moses: "Go to the land of Israel, for those who were seeking the child's life are dead" (2:20), and "Go back to Egypt; for all those who were seeking your life are dead" (Exod 4:19). Jesus goes to live in Nazareth to fulfill OT prophecy. Nazareth, which like Capernaum is a town in "Galilee of the Gentiles" (see Figure 5.3), ties the birth narratives in nicely with the body of the gospel and with the beginning of Jesus' public life in Galilee.

II. Introductory narratives (3:1–5:1)

    *A. John the Baptist and Jesus' baptism
    (3:1–17)*

    B. The temptation (4:1–11)

In the first verses both Matthew and Luke appear to follow Mark. They agree that the Spirit motivated Jesus to go to the wilderness, where for forty days he was tempted and hungry. But after that Matthew and Luke agree only in the quotations from the Septuagint. The order of the final two temptations is reversed, and the phraseology is so different that if Matthew and Luke used the same source, one writer freely reworked it.

At his baptism Jesus is proclaimed Son of God, so the clause "If you are the Son of God" is significant. Those words, along with the reference to the Spirit, indicate that in mythological terms the writer is objectifying theological concepts. Perhaps one idea for Matthew is that as Son of God Jesus is under God's power, and therefore not in Satan's league, as was later charged by Jesus' Jewish opponents.

The OT passages quoted by Jesus are all from Deuteronomy and refer to God's testing of the Israelites to see if they deserve the land he has promised them. Compare Matt 4:1–2 with Deut 8:2: "Remember the long way that the Lord your God has led you these forty years in the wilderness . . . testing you to know . . . whether or not you would keep his commandments." Like Israel (Hos 11:1; Jer 31:9), Jesus is God's Son; but unlike Israel, Jesus has passed the test.

Another important OT passage for our interpretation of Matthew is the brief account (Exod 34:28) of Moses writing the ten commandments: "He was there with the Lord forty days and forty nights; he neither ate bread nor drank water. And he wrote on the tables [of stone] the words of the covenant, the ten commandments." Thus, as Moses fasted before he gave the old law, so Jesus fasted before he gave the new law.

C. Calling of disciples, preaching, and healing in Galilee (4:12–5:1)

III. First discourse: the new law for Christians (5:2–7:29)

The repeated reference to disciples and crowds provides an insight into Matthew's purpose. The disciples represent Christian teachers, the crowds the anticipated recipients of the new teaching, the Sermon on the Mount. The new teaching is required for entrance into the kingdom of heaven (= the church). At the same time, the discourse reflects Matthew's controversy with his Jewish opponents.

A. Beatitudes, two parables, and words on the law (5:2–20)

B. The antitheses (5:21–48)

In each instance, the new teaching of Jesus is more radical in its demands than the old law of Moses. The antitheses explain what is meant by the Christian righteousness that is to exceed "that of the scribes and Pharisees" (5:20).

C. Almsgiving, prayer, and fasting (6:1–18)

These three basic acts of Jewish piety are to be continued by Christians but practiced privately, not publicly. In each case, an antithesis is stated between the proper and the improper act of piety. The repetition of certain phrases, especially "truly, I tell you," reveals that the passages are written in Matthew's style. Notice also the repetition of such phrases as "whenever you give alms," "pray," "fast," and "your Father who sees in secret." Moreover, the words translated as "heap up empty phrases" and "many words" (6:7) are used nowhere else in the NT. Matthew seems to be critical of Jewish almsgiving and fasting, but the words "do not heap up empty phrases [lit., "chattering"] as the Gentiles do" allude to pagan practices.

Luke's version of the Lord's Prayer may be closer than Matthew's to the original because Matthew's additions are characteristic of his style and are probably liturgical expansions.

D. Sayings on material possessions (6:19–34)

Matthew has collected some sayings from Q, which occur in various contexts in Luke, and put them together. The theme seems to be "Do not store up for yourselves treasures on earth" (6:19). In that context, the sayings about the healthy eye can be taken in two ways. "Healthy" (*haplous*) literally means "single," that is, "directed toward one object." In light of the preceding verses, the meaning seems to be "Keep your heart set on things in life that bring 'treasures in heaven.'" The sayings that follow seem to confirm this meaning, but in both Judaism and the NT (see, for example, Prov 11:25, LXX; 1 Chr 29:17;

Rom 12:8; 2 Cor 8:2) *haplous* and its cognates (related words) often signify generosity. So the healthy eye could refer to a person who is generous. The word translated "unhealthy," *ponēros*, means "evil" or "malicious," so the saying also has moral implications—generous vs. stingy or good vs. evil.

E. Detached sayings (7:1–29)

Except for the most difficult saying, the one on profaning the holy, these sayings also come from Q. "Dogs" and "swine" were derogatory terms for Gentiles as enemies of the Jews. If "what is holy" and "pearls" refer to the Christian religion, then the saying is representative of the anti-Gentile tone of much of the material designated M. This would then be one of the most anti-Gentile passages and would limit church membership to Jews.

Notice a typical Matthean threefold formula in the section on prayer (7:7–11): ask—be given, search—find, and knock—be opened. God is more generous than human fathers who, though they may be evil, will provide food for their children.

The golden rule (7:12), like the sayings on judging (7:1–5) and the gate (7:13), gives advice for true disciples. Matthew's addition to the rule—"this is the law and the prophets"—concludes the section on the radical demands of the new law, which began with Jesus' statement that he did not come "to abolish the law or the prophets" (5:17).

Finally, Christians have a choice between two courses of action: the one that leads to life or the one that leads to death (7:13–14). The choice between two ways is a common Jewish idea. God, through Moses, gave the Israelites the same choice: "I have set before you today life and prosperity, death and adversity. If you obey the commandments . . . then you shall live. . . . But if your heart turns away . . . you shall perish" (Deut 30:15–18; see also Jer 31:8; 1QS 3:18–4:26).

The rest of the sayings graphically illustrate the destinies of those who choose the way of life and those who choose the way of destruction. The passages dealing with "prophets" indicate dissensions within the church.

IV. Narratives: mostly miracles (8:1–9:36)

All of the miracle stories except the one about the centurion's servant, which comes from Q, are taken from Mark. They are characteristically condensed in Matthew, and there are other Matthean touches, such as a heightening of the miraculous (8:13) and the use of favorite words and phrases (8:12, 25).

Matthew has presented the teaching of the authoritative teacher: "For he taught them as one having authority, and not as their scribes" (7:29). Now Matthew presents Jesus as the authoritative healer and concludes each series of three miracles with a statement showing Jesus' authority. For example, when the crowds see the healing of the paralytic, Matthew reports, "They glorified God, who had given such authority to human beings" (9:8; see also 8:17–18; 9:33).

A. First series: leper, centurion's servant, and Peter's mother-in-law (8:1–15)

To emphasize the miraculous power of Jesus, Matthew omits stages in healing as well as unnecessary gestures, such as spitting (Mark 7:33–34; 8:22–26). Jesus heals by a simple touch or command, usually after the person concerned has acknowledged him as Lord or Son of God.

The law was specific and detailed about how lepers should behave, what offerings should be made for their cleansing after they were pronounced free of the disease by the priest, and the priest's duties in their cleansing (Leviticus 13–14). However, the law could legislate but not cure. After the leper's confession of faith, Jesus heals him and tells him to do what the law requires: "Show yourself to the priest, and offer the gift that Moses commanded" (8:4). By placing this miracle first, Matthew stresses the truth of Jesus' statement that he did not come to abolish the law but to fulfill it (5:17).

The healing of the centurion's servant stresses the faith of a Gentile and reveals Matthew's controversy with the Jews because of their unwillingness to believe. After the healing of Peter's mother-in-law with a touch, Matthew ends the first series of three miracles by inserting the Markan story about Jesus healing many sick people (Mark 1:32–34). But Matthew adds, "This was to

EXAMPLE 5.5		*Differences in Versions of the Nature of Discipleship*
Matt 8:18–22	**Mark**	**Luke 9:57–60**
[18]Now when Jesus saw great crowds around him, he gave orders to go over to the other side. [19]A scribe then approached and said, "Teacher, I will follow you wherever you go." [20]And Jesus said to him, "Foxes have holes, and birds of the air have nests; but the Son of Man has nowhere to lay his head." [21]Another of his disciples said to him, "Lord, first let me go and bury my father." [22]But Jesus said to him, "Follow me, and let the dead bury their own dead."		[57]As they were going along the road, someone said to him, "I will follow you wherever you go." [58]And Jesus said to him, "Foxes have holes, and birds of the air have nests; but the Son of Man has nowhere to lay his head." [59]To another he said, "Follow me." But he said, "Lord, first let me go and bury my father." [60]But Jesus said to him, "Let the dead bury their own dead; but as for you, go and proclaim the kingdom of God."

Cf. *GThom* 86.

fulfil what had been spoken through the prophet Isaiah, 'He took our infirmities and bore our diseases'" (8:17). Thus, Matthew casts Jesus in the role of the servant of Yahweh, about whom Isaiah had written. Jesus is the authoritative healer.

B. The nature of discipleship (8:18–22)

In Example 5.5, Matthew's transition verse (18) may be a version of Mark 4:35. Matthew uses it to set the scene for the miracle at sea (8:23–27) and the one at Gadara, across the Jordan (8:28–34). The word translated "he gave orders" (*keleuō*) is a favorite of Matthew's and emphasizes the authority of Jesus, whose followers do as he says. Luke places these sayings from Q at the beginning of Jesus' journey through Samaria, on the way to Jerusalem, and adds a third saying (9:61–62). The original context of the sayings is lost, but they are linked by the word "follow." Matthew uses that word to link the sayings with the next section (v 23).

Notice that the sequence "someone" and "another" in Luke is natural and that the sequence "a scribe" and "another of his disciples" in Matthew is not so natural, unless, of course, the scribe is a disciple. The scribe addresses Jesus as "teacher," a title of respect, and the disciple addresses Jesus as "Lord," a confession of faith. For Matthew, then, if the scribe is a disciple, he has not yet achieved the ultimate understanding of Jesus urged in Matthew's community.

Jesus' response to the scribe means that a disciple must be willing to be a wandering follower of Jesus who, like Jesus, would be without a home and an income. Jesus' answer to the disciple is difficult to interpret. Several interpretations have been suggested with respect to the "dead": they are the spiritually dead, those not willing to follow Jesus; forget the past, and follow the present call; Judaism is dead, compared with Christianity; let the burier of the dead do the burying; and let the matter take care of itself. Since Jews stressed the obligation of children to bury their parents, the point may be that discipleship demands giving up even the most pressing family duties (see 10:37).

C. Second series of miracles: calming of the storm, the Gadarene demoniacs, and the paralytic (8:23–9:8)

D. Call of Matthew and question about fasting (9:9–17)

The section on fasting is difficult to understand. Matthew's editorial hand is at work immediately with the use of two favorite words, "then" and "come to" (v 14). In Mark "people" ask the question, but Matthew puts the question on the lips of John's disciples and the Pharisees. For Matthew, then, those groups represent Judaism, and Jesus' disciples represent Christianity. This helps to explain the parables that follow (vv 16–17). But what does Jesus' reply in v 15a mean? Matthew changes Mark's "fast" to "mourn," so does the reply mean that the new age of the kingdom of God is a time for joy, not sorrow? The early church took the saying as an allegory (also in Mark): the bridegroom is Jesus and the guests are the disciples. The saying in v 15b (= Mark 2:20 = Luke 5:35) is from the church because it alludes to Jesus' death and the practice of fasting among early Christians.

The parables of the cloth and wineskin are not a continuation of the previous saying, and their original meaning is lost. In the early church "old" and "new" were used to contrast Judaism and Christianity (see, for example, Rom 7:6). The sayings reflect Matthew's concern about the law and Christian teaching (see 5:17–20; 23:1–3). It may be difficult, though not impossible (as for Mark), to mix the two. The words "so both are preserved," added by Matthew, show that he thought Christianity and Judaism could mix.

E. Third series of miracles: Jairus's daughter, a hemorrhaging woman, and the blind and dumb (9:18–36)

Perhaps these stories are meant to illustrate the power of Christianity (= the church or the kingdom) over Judaism: health instead of sickness, life instead of death, and sight instead of blindness. The woman's faith has made her well (= "saved"), and the blind men are healed after their confession of Jesus as Lord. The climax comes in 9:33: "Never has anything like this been seen in Israel."

V. Second discourse: teaching for Christian missionaries (9:37–11:1)

The discourse is composed of diverse material from Q and the expansion of Mark. Matt 10:5–10 reflects the Christian mission to the Jews, who are "harassed and helpless, like sheep without a shepherd" (9:36; see also 1 Kgs 22:17;

Zech 10:2). The disciples, like John the Baptist (3:2) and Jesus (4:17), are to preach to the Jews that "the kingdom of heaven has come near" (10:7), and like Jesus they are to heal the sick.

Since Matt 10:9–16 contains instructions similar to those in Luke 10:3–12, these instructions may have been intended for the Hellenistic Jewish mission. The sayings that follow (10:17–42) are appropriate for missionaries and disciples among both Jews and Gentiles (10:17–18). They reflect persecutions from without and difficulties within the church, even in families within the church.

VI. Narratives: mostly controversy material (11:2–13:2)

Jesus' healings confirm his messiahship (11:2–6). John was Elijah, who was expected to appear before the Messiah (11:7–15). Verses 12–19 are very difficult, and we cannot be sure what they mean. Not used in Mark or Luke, the word *harpazō*, translated "take it by force," is used in 12:29 and 13:19 and indicates violent action. Were some people trying to force their way into the kingdom or the church? Was John "the prototype of persecuted Christians"? Or is the meaning that the Zealots were trying to force the coming of God's kingdom?

In general, the point of vv 16–19 is that the same people criticized both John and Jesus even though each practiced a different lifestyle. "This generation" (see 12:39, 41, 45; 23:36) is used in anti-Jewish contexts and refers to those Jews who have not repented and followed Jesus. They are like children who refuse to join other children in playing games. But "wisdom is vindicated by her deeds." This may be an adaptation of a proverb that can here be interpreted in different ways. Wisdom may refer to God; if so, then God is vindicated because some "children" did respond to the work of John and Jesus. This interpretation is more fitting for Luke, who actually uses "children" (= Gentiles ?). "Deeds" in Matthew may refer to "the deeds of the Christ" (11:2; Greek). His deeds are justification enough! This meaning seems clear from the following verse, in which Jesus rebukes the cities where "most of his deeds of power had been done, because they did not repent" (11:20–24). Those who have repented are the unlearned and lowly (11:25–26), who can bear Jesus' yoke (a rabbinic metaphor for obedience to the law), which is light (11:28–30) compared to the burdens of the scribes and Pharisees (23:4).

The sabbath controversies that follow (12:1–14) are taken over from Mark. Was Matthew not aware that in reporting Jesus' breaking of the sabbath he was contradicting his statements about Jesus and the law (5:17–20)? Or, by redaction, was Matthew careful to show that Jesus and his disciples do not actually break the law? Notice that the disciples pluck grain because they "were hungry" (not in Mark) and are, therefore, like David, "guiltless" (12:7; not in Mark). Notice also that Jesus' question in Mark 3:4 becomes a declaration in Matt 12:12: "It is lawful to do good on the sabbath."

In Matt 12:15 there is a third summary of Jesus' healings (see also 4:23–25; 8:16–17). Aware of the Jews' plot to kill him, Jesus "departed." This may be symbolic of Jesus' leaving the synagogue, and his action anticipates that of the church going to the Gentiles. Jesus' command not to make him known (the messianic secret in Mark) introduces the quotation from Isaiah. As in 8:17, Jesus fulfills the role of God's servant, but here especially as a hope for Gentiles.

Another series of controversy narratives (12:22–45) concludes this section. In general, the material is close to that of Mark and Q. The story of Jesus' true relatives (12:46–50) serves as a transition to the next section. Jesus' rejection by the Jews means that his true family is those who do the will of God, those who respond to the message of Jesus. Some of the parables that follow illustrate that point.

VII. Third discourse: parables about what "the kingdom of heaven is like" (13:3–53)

Matthew adds to Mark's group of parables and uses them to suit his purpose. Probably at least a nucleus of each parable goes back to Jesus, but the interpretations of the parables may be those of the church, not Jesus. The parables of the sower, weeds, mustard seed, and leaven are told to the crowds, representing those who reject Jesus and his message. Matthew closes the first section of the chapter with a comment that Jesus speaks in parables to fulfill prophecy (13:35). The comment also makes the transition from the crowds to the disciples, to whom Jesus tells the parables of the weeds, the treasure and the pearl, the net, and the householder. The disciples represent those who respond to Jesus' message.

These parables, generally, illustrate the theme of response and rejection, especially the parables of the sower, the weeds, and the net. Those who respond, "the righteous" (13:43, 49), will be rewarded; those who do not respond, "evildoers," will be punished (13:41–42, 50). This may also be the theme of the other parables. Perhaps the parables of the mustard seed and leaven illustrate the growth of the kingdom. The parable of the treasure and the pearl teaches that those who renounce all for the kingdom find joy as a reward. The parable of the householder teaches that in the kingdom there is room for both the old law and the new Christian teaching.

VIII. Narratives: miracles, controversies, and the church (13:54–17:22a)

This material follows that of Mark closely, and in previous chapters we have already dealt with much of it. The passage about Peter and the church in 16:17–19 is one of the most difficult in the NT. There are two main issues: what was the origin of the saying, and what does it mean? On its origin, two commentators on Matthew have different opinions. F. W. Beare 1981:354–355 says that the tone of these verses is Semitic and that Matthew used an Aramaic source. The saying arose "out of some controversy in the Palestinian church, and is intended to justify the exaltation of Peter in the face of attempts to give an equal or even a higher status to some other Christian leader." In contrast, R. H. Gundry 1982:330–333 argues that the stylistic features of Matthew, such as parallelism and vocabulary, theological ideas, OT influence, and echoes of other passages from Matthew, indicate that Matthew composed the verses himself. Many, however, think that all or most of the saying goes back to Jesus.

With respect to the meaning of the saying, the crucial passage is "You are Peter [*petros,* masc.], and on this rock [*petra,* fem.] I will build my church" (16:18). Technically, because the second "rock" is feminine, it cannot refer to Peter, for whom the word "rock" is masculine. Of course, if Jesus spoke Aramaic and we had the Aramaic text, there would be no problem, because in Aramaic the same word for "rock" (*kepha;* see John 1:42; 1 Cor 1:12; 15:5) would be used both times. But we have only Matthew's Greek text, so what does the second "rock" stand for?

In spite of Matthew's imperfect grammar, the context seems to make his point clear. Therefore, an increasing number of scholars (since the work of O. Cullmann 1962) think Matthew meant to say that Peter was, in some sense, the foundation on which the church was built. However, some scholars still think that the "rock" refers to Christ himself or to Peter's confession that Christ is the Son of God. It has been suggested (R. H. Gundry 1982:334) that the "rock" is the same as that in 7:24, where it is "these words" of Jesus. Therefore, the church is built on the words of Christ. But the meaning of the word "church," which occurs only here and in 18:17 in the gospels, is uncertain. Most agree that it probably does not go back to Jesus, after whose time the word became the designation for a (or the) Christian community. On the other hand, the word translated "church" (*ekklēsia*) is used regularly in the LXX for Israel as the community of God, and the metaphor of building a community on a foundation or rock occurs in the Qumran Scrolls (1QS 8:4–8; 1QH 6:25–28; see also Isa 28:16). So perhaps Jesus did use some metaphor of a community on a rock, and Matthew adapted it to the church.

Since the expression "the keys of the kingdom of heaven" occurs only here, it is impossible to say exactly what it means. The kingdom may be the equivalent of the church, since the binding and loosing by Peter takes place on earth. This conception agrees with 23:13, where Jesus accuses the scribes and Pharisees of not allowing those who want to enter the kingdom to do so. If this view is correct, then "heaven" in v 19b is a substitute for "God" and means that God would approve Peter's actions. The usage of Matthew goes back to Isa 22:22, where the prophet says God speaks about Eliakim as one to whom authority will be given: "I will place on his shoulder the key of the house [that is, the palace] of David; he shall open . . . he shall shut." The key was the symbol of the steward's authority to lock and unlock the palace and to admit or reject visitors. In the same way, apparently Matthew thought of Peter as the steward of the church.

There is no biblical background for the phrase "binding and loosing," so we cannot determine exactly what it means. The same phrase occurs in 18:18, where Jesus uses it with reference to the disciples as a group. There it refers to actions taken toward members in the church. The phrase signifies some kind of authority, but what kind of authority and how it was to be used are not stated.

IX. Fourth discourse: the church and behavior in it (17:22b–19:1a)

The story of the coin in the fish's mouth is typically Matthean legendary material. The tax, remember, was the one formerly paid to the temple, but in Matthew's time it was paid to Rome. The story immediately puts Peter in the spotlight as an authority for the group. The subsequent discussion of Jesus and Peter probably means that the disciples as Christians are children of God. As "children" and as Christians, therefore, they would not, like other Jews, have to pay the tax. But they do pay in order not to put a stumbling block (= "give offense") in the way of other Jews who might want to become Christians but still feel obligated by law (Exod 30:11–16) to pay the tax.

The rest of the section (18:1–19:1a) deals with relationships among Christians. It reflects struggles within the church for positions of authority (18:1–5) and over moral problems (18:6–9, 15–35). Church members are to care for other members (18:10–14).

X. Narratives: mostly controversy material concerned with Jesus' time in Judea and Jerusalem (19:1b–22:46)

With the exception of several sayings about the kingdom and the way to get into it (19:10–12; 20:1–16; 21:28–32; 22:1–14), the material is taken from Mark. Matthew makes Jesus' teaching on divorce conform to the strictest Jewish teaching and introduces the consideration of celibacy (19:3–12). Matthew inserts the parable of the laborers in the vineyard (20:1–16) to illustrate the teaching of the preceding verses (19:27–30) about benefits in the kingdom.

XI. Fifth discourse: woes, apocalyptic, and need for watchfulness (23:1–26:2)

Matthew has taken over Jesus' apocalyptic discourse (24:4–36) from Mark. Before it he adds his own material on the woes against the scribes and Pharisees (23:1–36), and after it he adds more apocalyptic teaching from Q (24:37–51) and another series of parables (25:1–46). The parables are an emphatic conclusion to Jesus' teaching as Matthew understands it. The parables of the ten maidens (25:1–13) and the talents (25:14–30) illustrate the Q sayings (24:37–51) and emphasize the need for watchful, wise behavior in light of the coming of the Son of Man and his judgment.

The parables also contrast the deeds of Christians, "the righteous" (25:37), to the deeds of the Jewish leaders who "teach, but do not practice" (lit., "do"; 23:3–4) what counts. The parable of the last judgment (25:31–46) is the climax to Jesus' teaching: the new law requires obedience that is evident in kind deeds.

XII. Concluding narratives: the conspiracy against Jesus to the resurrection (26:3–28:20)

Except for minor editorial changes, the addition of fulfillment quotations, and several legendary narratives, Matthew follows Mark very closely. But Matthew frames this last section with sayings of Jesus: "You know that after two days . . . the Son of Man will be handed over to be crucified" (26:2) and "Go therefore and make disciples of all nations . . . teaching them to obey everything that I have commanded you" (28:19–20). Up to this point, according to Matthew, Jesus has charged his disciples only to preach and heal (10:7–8). Now, at the end, Matthew reports Jesus' command to his disciples to continue his teaching. The disciples intended are the readers of the gospel.

Matthew's conclusion is most effective in a gospel written to be used for teaching in the church. Jesus' last words, "Remember, I am with you always, to the end of the age" (28:20), are a vivid expression of the meaning of Emmanuel, "God is with us" (1:23), with which the gospel began.

For further study see J. L. McKenzie 1968; O. L. Cope 1976; A. W. Argyle 1963; A. H. McNeile 1952; J. C. Fenton 1963; J. P. Meier 1983; G. N. Stanton 1983. Additional bibliography is at end of chapter.

SUMMARY

Matthew presents Jesus as the messianic Son of David whose healings confirm his messiahship and whose life and work fulfill OT prophecy. For Matthew Jesus is also the eschatological Son of Man who will eventually return for a final judgment, but above all else, Jesus is to be confessed in the church as Lord. The fact that the word "church" occurs in the gospels only in Matthew is a clue that Matthew wrote his gospel for the church, which could turn to Matthew's book (1:1) for guidance on matters of faith and religious life.

Matthew combines and rearranges material from Mark by concentrating miracles in one section and parables in another. He also arranges Jesus' teachings in five main blocks known as discourses and structures his gospel around them.

Between each discourse Matthew inserts narrative material. He frames each discourse with references to Jesus teaching, and each narrative with references to crowds following Jesus. All of this is intended to encourage Christian missionaries in their work among potential converts. Jesus' teachings represent God's will delivered by Jesus, just as the Torah represents God's will delivered by Moses. Jesus' teachings demand an even higher righteousness than the Torah, but like the Torah they are to be practiced in everyday life.

Additional bibliography, mostly for advanced study: E. Schweizer 1975; D. Senior 1977, 1983, 1985, passion; G. N. Stanton 1983, 1992; J. D. Kingsbury 1975, 1988, story; C. S. Keener 1997a; R. T. France 1998, Matthew as first gospel and Jesus as teacher; D. Patte 1996, structural analysis; R. A. Edwards 1985, literary criticism. For passion of Jesus see especially R. E. Brown 1994, bibliography 1:100–101. For Sermon on Mount: W. D. Davies 1964; R. A. Guelich 1982; H. D. Betz 1985a, 1995; G. Strecker 1988; W. Carter 1994.

In the next chapter, after introductory matters, we will study redaction in Luke and L and the similarities between Luke and the gospel of John. Finally, we will examine Luke's literary style and his many special concerns, including his unique interest in Jesus' prayers, around which he structures his gospel.

CHAPTER 6

The Gospel of Luke

THE GOSPEL OF LUKE IS THE FIRST PART of a two-volume work known as Luke-Acts, which comprises more than a fourth of the NT. Not only are both volumes addressed to the same man—Theophilus (Luke 1:3; Acts 1:1)—but on the basis of literary style, emphases, and special interests, all scholars agree that the volumes were indeed written by the same author, who is traditionally referred to as Luke (see H. J. Cadbury 1920, 1958 and C. H. Talbert 1974). Luke and Acts, then, were written to be read together. But when the gospels were collected and put into their present order, Luke became separated from Acts and was given the title "gospel," and Acts was called "acts of apostles."

Recently, although not disputing the view that Luke wrote both volumes, M. C. Parsons 1993 presents reasons for saying that it would be more accurate to use the designation "Luke and Acts" instead of "Luke-Acts."

In this chapter we will consider the authorship, origin, and date of the gospel of Luke. We will then study the author's purposes for writing, use of sources, literary style, and special interests. Finally, in examining the structure and content of the gospel through the outline and comments, we will pay particular attention to Luke's birth narratives because of their unique function in Luke's special story of Jesus.

As you read this chapter, it will become clear that Luke, like Matthew and Mark, was more of a theologian than a historian. However, Luke places the ministry of Jesus in historical context and thinks of his gospel as the third stage in the tradition about Jesus, after eyewitnesses and servants of the word (Luke 1:2). As a gospel, Luke is distinctive because it is the first volume of two written by the same author and because the central section deals with Jesus on the way to Jerusalem. Specific interests and concerns also clearly distinguish the two-volume work of Luke-Acts from the synoptic gospels. Perhaps most noticeable is Luke's emphasis on non-Jews. Just as Mark stressed Jesus as the messianic Son of God and Matthew stressed Jesus as the messianic Son of David, Luke's peculiar christological title for

Jesus is "Savior," and as Savior Jesus brings a message of salvation for all people, especially women, Samaritans, and social outcasts. All who hear Jesus' message belong to the church and are true people of God. Watch for all of these things as you study Luke and this chapter.

AUTHORSHIP, ORIGIN, AND DATE OF LUKE

The earliest tradition for the writing of Luke-Acts comes from a collection of NT writings known as the Muratorian Canon, which probably originated in Rome c. 180–200 CE. According to its author, Luke the physician wrote after Paul had taken him along on his travels. This tradition stems from Paul's statements that Luke was one of his "fellow workers" (Phlm 24; see also 2 Tim 4:11) and that he was "the beloved physician" (Col 4:14). In this way Paul, a great leader in the church, was recognized as the authority behind Luke, as Peter was for Mark.

The tradition of Luke's association with Paul became embellished so that Eusebius (3:4:6), for example, writes that Luke was a native of Antioch, a physician, and a long-time companion of Paul's, and that he spoke carefully with other apostles and left us two volumes of medicine for souls. But there is no clue in either the gospel or in Acts that a person named Luke is the author, so Luke, like the other gospels, was originally anonymous.

The traditional view that Luke was a physician and that his works contain a special medical vocabulary (see W. K. Hobart 1957; A. Harnack 1907) has been abandoned. Nevertheless, because in Col 4:14 Luke is referred to as "the beloved physician," many lay people today still think of him as an ancient doctor. However, H. J. Cadbury 1920 has shown that the positions of Hobart and Harnack are no longer tenable. According to Cadbury, the so-called medical language of Luke-Acts can be found in the Septuagint and in Hellenistic writers such as Josephus and Plutarch, for example, who definitely were not doctors. On the other hand, "the absence of marked medical traits does not prove that a doctor did not write Luke and Acts." The work of Xenophon, a soldier and historian, contains as much medical language as that of his contemporary Ctesias, a physician. Thus, we cannot use the alleged medical language of Luke to argue for or against his authorship of Luke-Acts.

The tradition that the author of Luke-Acts was a companion of Paul's is still frequently discussed. Support for this tradition comes primarily from the "we passages" in Acts (which imply that the writer sometimes traveled with Paul), the statements in Phlm 24 and Col 4:14, and the similarities between the ideas attributed to Paul in his speeches in Acts and those in his letters. On the other hand, scholars have argued that Luke was not familiar with any of Paul's letters, that Paul as a prisoner would hardly refer to a fellow worker, and that Colossians may not be a genuine letter of Paul. (M. D. Goulder 1989: 1:25, 129–146 maintains that Luke was influenced by some of Paul's letters, especially 1 Corinthians and 1 Thessalonians.)

Opinions also vary about whether Luke-Acts was written by a person named Luke. Some scholars think that before the second century Luke-Acts circulated anonymously, while others agree with J. M. Creed 1942:xiii: "If the Gospel and Acts did not already ["in the apostolic age"] pass under his name there is no obvious reason why tradition should have associated them with him."

There is also no universal agreement about whether Luke was a Gentile or Jewish Christian. The main argument in support of Luke as a Christian convert from Judaism is his use of LXX and Hebrew expressions, such as "it came to pass that." Arguments in favor of Luke as a Gentile who was converted to Christianity from a pagan background are the excellence of his Greek, his avoidance of Semitic expressions, and his omission of Jesus' controversies with Jewish authorities over legal observances. J. A. Fitzmyer 1981:42 has argued that on the basis of Luke's name and the tradition connecting him with Antioch, Luke was "a non-Jewish Semite, a native of Antioch, where he was well educated in a Hellenistic atmosphere and culture."

The place of composition for Luke-Acts is uncertain, but most agree that it was written outside Palestine. The traditional sites of Achaia, Rome, Caesarea, the Decapolis (a region in Palestine east of the Jordan River), and some place in Asia Minor have been suggested. If we accept the four-source theory of the composition of the gospels and date Mark at c. 70, then Luke is later than Mark (see Luke 19:39–44; 21:20, 24). Consequently, most scholars agree that Luke was written c. 70–90.

PURPOSES OF LUKE

Luke is the only gospel writer to state his purpose in a formal, literary Greek preface (1:1–4):

> [1]Since many have undertaken to set down an orderly account of the events that have been fulfilled among us, [2]just as they were handed on to us by those who from the beginning were eyewitnesses and servants of the word, [3]I too decided, after investigating everything carefully from the very first, to write an orderly account for you, most excellent Theophilus, [4]so that you may know the truth concerning the things about which you have been instructed.

> [1]In the first book, Theophilus . . . (Acts 1:1).

The word "account," often used in historical writings, indicates that Luke intended to write a historical work in the ancient sense of the term; and he wanted to write accurately (*akribōs*, trans. "closely"), "orderly," and truthfully. To see that Luke's preface is like those of ancient historical writers, compare it with the one by Josephus in *Against Apion* (1:1–3; 2:1:1).

> I assume that in the history of the *Antiquities,* most excellent Epaphroditus, I have made clear to those who come upon it the nature of the Jewish race. . . . But since I see that many influenced by the malicious slanders of certain persons, do not believe what I wrote concerning our antiquity . . . I thought I ought to write briefly about all these things, to convict those who insult us . . . to correct the ignorance of some, and to teach all who want to know the truth about our antiquity.

> In the first book, my most esteemed Epaphroditus. . . .

In the prefaces of Luke and Josephus, the Greek is carefully written, the work is addressed to a respected person, the writing of others is implied to be unsatisfactory, and the writer states his purpose. (For the pitfalls of trying to determine an author's purpose on the basis of the preface, see S. Brown 1978.) Luke, like Josephus, intended the preface to his first volume to serve also for the second; and Luke's preface, like that of Josephus, indicates a historical purpose. This is clear because immediately after the preface Luke places the Baptist's birth in historical context: "In the days of King Herod of Judea, there was a priest named Zechariah" (1:5). Similarly, he places the birth of Jesus (2:1–7) and the public appearance of the Baptist (3:1–3) in historical contexts. Luke, in fact, is the only NT writer who mentions Roman emperors by name—Augustus (Luke 2:1), Tiberius (Luke 3:1), and Claudius (Acts 11:28; 18:2). But Luke's references to the census of Quirinius (Luke 2:1–2), the priesthood of Annas and Caiaphas (Luke 3:2), and the uprisings of Theudas and Judas the Galilean (Acts 5:36–37; see also Josephus, *Ant.* 20:5:1–2) cause real problems for the interpreter because of discrepancies with information elsewhere. They therefore raise doubts about Luke's accuracy as a historian. However, his purpose was not to write history for history's sake. Indeed, Luke is primarily a theologian, not a historian, as certain words in the preface already demonstrate. But, as A. Harnack 1909:301 observed, if the heroes Peter and Paul "had found no historian, it is highly probable that in spite of Marcion we should have had no New Testament."

The words translated as "have been fulfilled," "handed on," and "the truth" all have theological implications. The first word may be interpreted in several ways, but it is probably a synonym for others that Luke uses to refer to the fulfillment of scripture (see, for example, 4:21; 22:37). Luke, then, is saying that events took place in order to fulfill scripture. The words "handed on" were regularly used in the early church with reference to Christian teaching or tradition passed on to others (see, for example, Rom 6:17; 1 Cor 11–2; 15:3; Acts 16:4). "The truth" is literally "firmness" or "certainty." The certainty Luke hopes to give Theophilus and the readers is that through Jesus salvation can come to everyone. This is Luke's primary theological purpose for writing. For the intertwining of prophecy and history in Luke-Acts, see D. L. Tiede 1980; for Luke as a theologian, see J. A. Fitzmyer 1989. For all aspects of Luke's prologue see J. A. Fitzmyer 1981:287–302.

Of the synoptists, only Luke uses the words "Savior" and "salvation" with reference to Jesus. Jesus was born "a Savior, who is the Messiah, the Lord" (2:11; see also 1:69; Acts 3:13–15). Salvation is not to be confined to the Jews—"all flesh shall see the salvation of God" (3:6). Moreover, Acts is a record of the spread of salvation from Jerusalem, the center of the Jewish world, to Rome, the center of the Gentile world (see Acts 1:8).

Luke wrote primarily for Gentile readers, whom Theophilus represents, and his interest in Gentiles is more noticeable in Acts than in the gospel. The apostles usually preach first to Jews in the synagogues, but the emphasis is on God opening the way of salvation to the Gentiles (see, for example, Acts 9:15; 10:45; 11:18; 13:45–47). Although Luke's communication with Gentile readers is more subtle in the gospel than in Acts, he obviously omits things of special interest only to Jews, such as the ritualistic traditions of the Pharisees in Mark 7:1–23. Not so obvious, however, are his substitutions of good Greek words for Hebrew or Aramaic terms. For example, Luke (5:24) uses *klinidion,* a correct word for the couch of a sick person, instead of Mark's colloquial *krabattos,* "mat" (2:11); he substitutes *epistatēs,* "teacher" (9:33), for the Hebrew *rabbi* (Mark 9:5) and *kurie,* "Lord" (18:41), for the Aramaic *rabbouni* (Mark 10:51); and he omits the Aramaic *abba,* "Father" (22:42) in Mark 14:36. Yet despite all of this, Luke seems to be especially familiar with the scripture reading, organization, and discussion within Jewish synagogues (Luke 4:16–30; Acts 13:14–43; 15:21). For challenges to the usual view that Luke-Acts is directed primarily to Gentile readers, and for the role of Jews in bringing the message of salvation to Gentiles, see J. Jervell 1972; J. Drury 1977; R. L. Brawley 1987; J. B. Tyson 1988, 1992; D. L. Tiede 1988.

In sum, Luke seems to have a historical purpose for writing, at least to the extent of setting the story of Jesus and of salvation for all people in a historical context. Nevertheless, Luke is not primarily a historian but is instead the greatest synoptic theologian (but see I. H. Marshall 1971); he wrote his story in two volumes for readers who were mostly Gentiles.

LUKE'S USE OF HIS SOURCES

In writing his gospel, Luke, like Matthew, uses the framework of Mark. He follows Mark's sequence of incidents closely but uses Mark more creatively than Matthew does and reproduces less of it. Matthew expands the framework of Mark by adding sayings of Jesus from Q and M. Luke also expands Mark's outline, but he alternates between blocks of Markan and non-Markan material. Moreover, he occasionally changes incidents in Mark in such a way that he seems to be adding new information or substituting another narrative. He may have a source other than Mark for John the Baptist's preaching (Mark 1:7–8; Matt 3:11–12; Luke 3:15–18) and for the temptation story (Mark 1:12–13; Matt 4:1–11; Luke 4:1–13), or perhaps he uses Mark and Q in his own way. Luke presents his stories of Jesus' rejection at Nazareth (Mark 6:1–6; Matt 13:54–58; Luke 4:16–30), the call of the fishermen disciples (Mark 1:16–20; Matt 4:18–22; Luke 5:1–11), Jesus being anointed by a woman (Mark 14:3–9; Matt 26:6–13; Luke 7:36–50), and the Beelzebul controversy (Mark 3:22–27; Matt 12:22–26; Luke 11:14–23) quite independently of Mark's order and content.

If you use the *Gospel Parallels,* you can observe the following to learn how Luke actually uses his sources. Luke 3:1–4:15 is the first block of material based on Mark (1:1–15), and Luke alternates among Markan, Q, and L material. He departs from Mark's order in 3:19–20 by recording John's imprisonment early, apparently to have him out of the picture before Jesus' public life begins. John's role is diminished, then, even in Jesus' baptism. The sources for the rejection at Nazareth are uncertain but are probably a combination of Mark and Q. Luke places this story first in his gospel to stress Jesus' fulfillment of scripture and to symbolize the rejection of Jesus by his own people and his acceptance by Gentiles.

Luke 4:31–6:19 constitutes the second block of Markan material (1:21–3:19). Luke replaces the call of first disciples in Mark 1:16–20 with the miraculous catch of fish by Simon and his partners (5:1–11). Thus, it is more logical that they would follow Jesus after hearing about his teaching and healing. Then Luke switches the call of the twelve (6:12–16) and the healing of the multitudes (6:17–19) to assure Jesus an audience for the sermon on the plain (6:20–49).

Luke 6:20–8:3 represents the smaller of two insertions into Markan material. Here Luke alternates between Q and L material. Then in the third block of material from Mark (4:1–9:40), Luke (8:4–9:50) is entirely dependent upon Mark, but he excludes a large section (6:45–8:26). In 8:4–9:50 Luke also omits the coming of Elijah (Mark 9:9–13), perhaps because it would not interest Gentile readers or because he had already said enough about the Baptist (7:24–35). He also shifts the incident about Jesus' true relatives (Mark 3:31–35) from before to after the parable of the sower and its interpretation (8:19–21). In this way Jesus' words "My mother and my brothers are those who hear the word of God and do it" (8:21) illustrate the teaching of the parable: true followers of Jesus not only hear the word of God, but also "bear fruit with patient endurance" (8:15).

Luke 9:51–18:14, composed of alternate L and Q material, is a large insertion into the Markan framework and has been called "Luke's special section" or "travel section." (For travel in Acts see Chapter 8.) Although the first description is accurate, the second is not, especially if a structured itinerary is implied. That Jesus is on a journey is clear (9:51–56; 10:1, 38; 13:22, 33; 17:11–12; 18:31; 19:1), but what he does is rarely connected with specific places. Moreover, Jerusalem is the real goal of Jesus' journey—"He set his face to go to Jerusalem" (9:51); in fact, the journey motif is not primarily geographical, but theological—"Because it is impossible for a

prophet to be killed outside of Jerusalem" (13:33). Beginning at 9:50, Luke omits all of Mark 9:41–10:12 (but see also Luke 17:2 and Mark 9:42; 14:34 and 9:50), perhaps to prevent the readers' misunderstanding (Mark 9:42–48) and disinterest (Mark 10:1–12) or to save space for his own view of Jesus.

In 18:15 Luke picks up the Markan material (10:13–13:32) again for another section (18:15–21:33), follows Mark's order, and only rarely inserts material from Q and L. He omits the request of James and John (Mark 10:35–40), perhaps because it puts the disciples in a bad light. Luke also omits the cursing of the fig tree and its explanation (Mark 11:12–14, 20–25), perhaps because he does not want to attribute such action to Jesus and because of his earlier parable of the fig tree (Luke 13:6–9). And he omits the question about the great commandment (Mark 12:28–34) because he has already used a similar story (10:25–28).

The last block of Markan material (14:1–16:8) occurs in Luke 22:1–24:11. Luke shifts the prediction of the traitor (Mark 14:18–21) from before to after the Last Supper (22:21–23) and attaches other sayings (22:24–38). In order to have Jesus appear only once before the Sanhedrin and to put the material about Peter in one place, Luke inverts the questioning before the Sanhedrin. In Mark the high priest questions Jesus (14:55–64), Jesus is mistreated (14:64–65), and then he is denied by Peter (14:66–72); in Luke Jesus is denied by Peter (22:54–62), mistreated (22:63–65), and then questioned (22:66–71). Luke incorporates the mocking of Jesus into his own accounts of the trial before Herod (22:11–12; see also Mark 15:16–20) and the men who arrested Jesus (22:63–65). Luke omits the anointing at Bethany (Mark 14:3–9), perhaps because he has used similar material earlier (7:36–50).

So although Luke follows Mark's outline of incidents, he sometimes omits Markan material, inserts Q and L material in Mark's framework, and alternates among Markan, Q, and L material. Sometimes he redacts or edits most of the material he uses. Although Matthew avoids Markan expressions of anger, love, and other of Jesus' emotions, Luke eliminates some that apparently

FIGURE 6.1   *Similarities Between Luke and John*

Luke	Incident	John
3:2	Annas, a high priest	18:13, 24
3:15–16	Question about John as the Christ	1:19–22, 27
5:4–9	Miraculous catch of fish	21:5–11
6:16	Two disciples named Judas	14:23
7:36–50	Jesus anointing a woman	12:1–8
9:10–17	Only one feeding story	6:1–13
10:38–42	Mary and Martha, Jesus' friends	11:1–44
16:19–31	Lazarus alive after death	11:38–44
19:37–38	Jesus entering Jerusalem as King	12:12–17
22:3	Satan entering into Judas	13:2, 27
22:54–71	Only a daytime trial of Jesus	18:12–24
22:21–38	Jesus' final discourse with disciples	14–17
22:50	Right ear of high priest's slave cut off	18:10
23:4, 14, 22	Pilate three times saying that Jesus is innocent	18:38; 19:4, 6
23:53	Jesus buried in an unused tomb	19:41
24:4–5	Two angels speaking at Jesus' tomb	20:12–13
24:13–53	Resurrection appearances in Judea	20–21

did not upset Matthew—for example, Jesus' sorrow in Gethsemane (Mark 14:34; Matt 26:38; see also Luke 22:40–41) and his cry on the cross (Mark 15:34; Matt 27:46; see also Luke 23:44–46). Similar omissions include Jesus' being actually "asleep" during the storm at sea (4:38), Jesus' rebuke of Peter (Mark 8:33), and the details of Jesus' forceful action in the temple (11:15–16). Luke even omits Jesus' physical contact in healings. Compare, for example, Luke 4:39 with Mark 1:31 and Matt 8:15, and Luke 9:42 with Mark 9:27.

Luke redacts Mark so as not to disparage the disciples. For example, although the disciples sometimes do not understand Jesus, Luke likes to give a reason for it—"what he said was hidden from them" (18:34; see also 24:16). Although they fall asleep in Gethsemane, they are "sleeping because of grief" (22:45); and although they

do not believe Jesus has risen from the dead, they disbelieve "in their joy" (24:41). Luke also redacts Mark's trial narrative to show that Jesus was not condemned as a criminal like the "two others" (23:32), but as the Christ. In the trial before the Sanhedrin, others bring no testimony against Jesus, no charge of blasphemy, and no condemnation, as in Mark 14:55–64. Rather, the account is condensed and centers on the statement "If you are the Christ, tell us" (22:67), and the question "Are you then the Son of God?" (22:70). Only in Luke does Pilate say, "I find no basis for an accusation against this man" (23:4).

In studying Luke's use of his sources, we discover some curious and interesting similarities between Luke's special source (L) and certain passages in John's gospel. Figure 6.1 displays some of these similarities. Although it is unlikely that Luke used John's gospel, these similarities raise the questions of whether John used Luke's gospel or whether both used a common written or oral source. The consensus is that both Luke and John used an independent tradition, perhaps written but probably oral. On this point, see J. A. Bailey 1963; R. E. Brown 1966:xlvi–xlvii; F. L. Cribbs 1971, 1978; J. A. Fitzmyer 1981; G. B. Caird 1963.

In contrast to what I have said about Luke and his sources, we should note the view of C. H. Talbert 1982, who shares with some other scholars the loss of confidence in the two-source theory. Therefore, he tries not to assume any source theory but considers Luke as a whole literary unit in its own right. Talbert acknowledges likenesses and differences and makes comparisons among Luke and the other synoptic gospels. However, he does so without presuppositions of dependency of Luke on any other gospel. In this way he finds literary patterns and theological themes often overlooked by scholars who regard Luke as dependent on either Mark or Matthew.

THE STYLE OF LUKE

Although the Greek used by NT writers varies, Luke's is close to that of classical authors. At the same time, it shows influence from Semitic usage, especially in chaps. 1–2. Even though Luke sometimes substitutes good Greek words for Hebrew or Aramaic ones, his Greek vocabulary shows influence from Hebrew in such expressions as "angel" (1:11), "order" of priests (1:5), "measure" (*batos,* from Heb. *bat; NRSV,* "jugs"; 16:6), and "mammon" (Greek; from Q; *NRSV,* "wealth"; 16:13).

Luke's Greek vocabulary is especially rich. Compared with Mark (77) and Matthew (102), Luke uses 284 words in his gospel that are not used elsewhere in the NT, and compared with Mark (41) and Matthew (95), Luke uses 151 words or phrases that are characteristic of his gospel. The following occur more than twenty times in Luke (numbers in parentheses are occurrences in Luke, Mark, and Matthew; Greek): "man" (27,4,8), "and also" (25,2,3), "it hap-pened that" (38,3,6), "but he said" (59,0,0), "Jerusalem" (*Hierousalēm;* 27,0,2), "people" (*laos;* 36,2,14), "to" (*pros*) with verb of saying (99,5,0), "with" (*syn;* 23,6,4), and "a certain" (38,2,1).

Only Luke introduces parables of Jesus with "And he told a parable," both in his peculiar material and when using his other sources (see, for example, 5:36; 6:39; 12:16; 13:6; 19:11; 20:9). Luke likes to omit or tone down emphatic words, such as "great," "many," and "much," when used in Mark. Compare "a windstorm" (8:23) with "a great windstorm" (Mark 4:37; Matt 8:24), "the mountain" (9:28) with "a high mountain" (Mark 9:2; Matt 17:1), and "the crowd" (8:40) with "a great crowd" (Mark 5:21). On the other hand, Luke sometimes emphasizes what Mark does not—for example, "a high fever" (4:38) for "a fever" (Mark 1:30), "many crowds" (5:15) for "people" (Mark 1:45), and "all the people" (3:21), which is not in Mark. With the exception of Matthew (14:21), Luke is the only NT writer who uses "about" with numbers (compare, for example, 9:14 with Mark 6:40, 44 and 23:44 with Mark 15:33 and Matt 27:45).

Luke prefers to use a participle instead of a finite verb and does so in several ways. In the following I transliterate the Greek words and then translate them literally to show the difference both in the Greek and English. *Iēsous ebaptisthē,* "Jesus was baptized" (Mark 1:9) and *Iēsou baptisthentos,* "Jesus having been baptized" (Luke 3:21); *kai lyousin,* "and they untie" (Mark 11:4) and *lyontōn de autōn,* "and as they were untying" (Luke 19:33). Luke sometimes substitutes a participle for the first of two verbs joined by "and" (*kai*): *aron kai hypage,* "take and go" (Mark 2:11) and *aras poreuou,* "having taken up, go" (Luke 5:24). In the following, Luke substitutes a participle for the second of two verbs joined by "and": *autou hēpsato kai legei,* "he touched him and says" (Mark 1:41) and *hēpsato autou legōn,* "he touched him, saying" (Luke 5:13).

Luke usually avoids the historic present tense, that is, a present tense used to narrate past events as though happening in the present. Mark uses 151 historic presents, and Luke changes all but one of them to a past tense or substitutes a participle. Here are good examples (from the Greek): "And when they draw near to Jerusalem . . . he sends two of his disciples . . . and says to them" (Mark 11:1–2) and "As they drew near to Bethany . . . he sent two of his disciples . . . saying" (Luke 19:29–30). This passage is from Q: "The devil takes him to a very high mountain and shows him" (Matt 4:8) and "having taken him up, the devil showed him" (Luke 4:5)

In spite of Luke's good Greek elsewhere, Greek that literally translates Hebrew expressions (Septuagint Greek) occurs frequently. Here are some examples in literal translation: "laid them up in their hearts" (1:66), "they feared with a great fear" (2:9), "before the face of all peoples" (2:31), "and Simon answered and said" (5:5), "the one who did mercy with him" (10:37), "he added to send another servant" (20:11), and "sons of this age" (20:34).

P. L. Dickerson 1997 has shown an interesting aspect of Luke's style. Whenever Luke introduces a new character, he uses variations of a typical phrase. After an introduction and character description, he tells the story. Such "new character narrative" occurs thirty-one times in Luke and twenty-five times in Acts without a sign of it in either Mark or Matthew.

Such things give a distinctiveness to the style of Luke, who also has distinctive interests.

SPECIAL INTERESTS OF LUKE

Within the broad purpose of showing that Jesus' teaching was intended for all people, Luke has a special interest in minorities, including the poor and the outcast, women, and Samaritans. A special interest in women appears already in the birth narratives. In contrast to Matthew's account, where Joseph is the focus of attention, Mary is much more prominent in Luke. Only Luke has the story of Elizabeth, mother of John the Baptist, and Anna, the prophetess (2:36–38). In the body of the gospel, only Luke

records the raising of the widow's son (7:11–17), the names of women healed (8:2–3), the story of Mary and Martha (10:38–42), the exclamation of blessedness expressed toward Jesus by a woman (11:27–28), the healing of the woman with an infirmity (13:10–17), and the parable of the widow and the judge (18:1–8).

In Acts, women play a prominent part in the church. The disciples devoted "themselves to prayer, together with certain women, including Mary the mother of Jesus" (1:14). "Devout women of high standing," as well as "the leading men," are mentioned (13:50; see also 17:4). Sapphira, along with her husband, was a member of an early Christian commune and shared rights and responsibilities (5:1–11). Other women specifically mentioned include Tabitha (Dorcas), "devoted to good works and acts of charity" (9:36–41); Mary, mother of John Mark, in whose house people worshiped (12:12); Lydia, "a worshiper of God," who became a Christian (16:14–15, 40); and Priscilla who, with her husband, became a leader in the church at Ephesus (18:1–3, 18–21, 26). Luke also includes women in his summaries of the growth of the church (5:14; 8:3, 12; 9:2; 17:12, 34; 22:4).

Scholars differ in assessing Luke's treatment of women. Some (E. S. Fiorenza, for example) think that Luke does not rise above patriarchalism and relegates women to menial chores. On the other hand, R. Ryan 1985 says that women played a role in and always were a part of Jesus' ministry. They also shared with the twelve disciples in announcing the coming of the kingdom of God. B.E. Reid 1996 takes the middle ground. Although there are positives in the Lukan stories, negatives also emerge.

After studying research on some Lukan passages, R. J. Karris 1994 concludes that Luke used his own literary style "to narrate a more positive view of women than we had previously thought" (19). J. Dewey 1997 studied the portrayal of women in the synoptic gospels and concludes that their authors are androcentric. The writers give more details for men, men speak more to Jesus, and are spoken to more by him. Sometimes men discuss the behavior of a woman if she does act. Hence, the description "seen but not heard" may aptly be used of Luke's women.

As you study the gospel of Luke and the book of Acts, pay special attention to Luke's portrayal of women. Do you think he should or should not be thought of as the first Christian feminist?

In order to draw attention away from the Palestinian setting in his gospel and to stress the universal significance of Jesus' teaching, Luke sometimes omits references to specific locations. For example, his not mentioning Caesarea Philippi (9:18; see also Mark 8:27; Mark 16:13) as the place of Peter's confession—"The Christ of God"—implies that the confession of Jesus as the Christ can take place anywhere. On the other hand, Samaria, not mentioned in Mark or Matthew, is mentioned in Acts, where it is referred to in connection with the growth of the church (8:1–17; 15:3), as well as in Luke 17:11–19. Although Mark does not mention Samaritans and Matthew does so only to say that their cities are to be avoided in the disciples' mission (10:5), Luke has a special interest in Samaritans. Jesus and his disciples go through Samaria on their way to Jerusalem. When some Samaritans will not receive Jesus, James and John want to "command fire to come down from heaven and consume them," but Jesus turns and rebukes them (9:51–55). And only Luke has the parable of the good Samaritan (10:29–37) and the healing of a Samaritan leper (17:11–19).

Luke also has a special interest in the (Holy) Spirit. Although Mark uses the word "spirit" (nineteen times; Matthew, fourteen) as often as Luke, Luke uses "Holy Spirit" (fourteen times) more than Mark (four) and Matthew (five) together. From the beginning of Luke to the end of Acts, the Spirit is the motivating force behind the main characters. In Luke, Zechariah (1:67), the Baptist (1:15), Elizabeth (1:41), Mary (1:35), and Simeon (2:25–27) are portrayed as motivated by the Spirit. After his baptism, Jesus is "full of the Holy Spirit" (4:1), is "led by the Spirit" into the wilderness (4:1), and returns "with the power of the Spirit" into Galilee (4:14). Luke prefaces Jesus' gratitude to the Father in Q (Matt 11:25–27) with the words "re-

joiced in the Holy Spirit" (10:21–22). Also in Q, the statement of Matt 7:11 that God will "give good things to those who ask him" in Luke is "give the Holy Spirit to those who ask him" (11:13). In Acts, the church begins with the outpouring of the Spirit as prophesied by Joel so that Christians who are assembled are all "filled with the Holy Spirit" (2:4–21). The Spirit is the motivating power behind the apostolic mission and is responsible for the church's growth (9:31). Acts closes with a reminder from Paul that "the Holy Spirit was right in saying . . . through the prophet Isaiah" that the Jews would reject the "salvation of God," which "has been sent to the Gentiles" (28:25–29).

Luke also has a special interest in Jesus as a man of prayer and in Christians praying. Only Luke records Jesus at prayer at important times in his life: at his baptism (3:21), before his first controversy with Pharisees and Jewish teachers (5:16), before he chooses the twelve (6:12), before he asks the disciples who he is (9:18), before his transfiguration (9:39), before the Lord's Prayer (11:1), and before he dies on the cross (23:46). Only Luke has the parables of the friend at midnight (11:5–13) and the unjust judge (18:1–8), which teach persistence in prayer. The parable of the Pharisee and the tax collector (18:9–14), also only in Luke, teaches humility in prayer. Only Luke says that Jesus instructed his disciples to "pray that you may not come into temptation" (22:40), and in the birth narratives Zechariah's prayer for a son is heard (1:13).

Likewise, there is a reference to prayer in most chapters of Acts. Like Jesus in the gospel of Luke, the Christians in Acts pray at critical moments. After Jesus' ascension the disciples and the women "were constantly devoting themselves to prayer" (1:14). They pray before the selection of the person to take the place of Judas (1:24–26), before receiving the Holy Spirit (8:15), before sending out apostolic missionaries (13:1–4; see also 14:23), and before receiving visions from heaven (10:1–16; 11:5). Even the sailors taking Paul to Rome "prayed for day to come" when they feared they "might run on the rocks" (27:29).

Finally, Luke seems to have a special interest in portraying Jesus as a prophet like the Elijah/Elisha figure in the OT. Only in Luke does Jesus appeal to the examples of Elijah/Elisha to defend himself when rejected at Nazareth (4:25–28). Throughout the gospel there are some striking parallels between Luke's story of Jesus and the stories of Elijah/Elisha. In examining 1 Kings 17–19 and 2 Kings 1–6 and the gospel of Luke, we find that the following incidents are associated with both Elijah/Elisha and Jesus: raising a widow's son, multiplying food, motivation by the Spirit, spending time in the wilderness, fasting for forty days, fire coming from heaven to consume others, ascension into heaven, healing of a leper who returns to give thanks, and ministering in Samaria. Obviously, the Elijah/Elisha figure is a prototype for the Lukan Jesus.

Although opinions about Luke's theological interests differ considerably, most scholars agree that Luke emphasizes eschatology in Jesus' teaching less than Matthew and Mark do. Jesus' saying in Mark 9:1—"There are some standing here who will not taste death until they see that the kingdom of God has come with power"—in Luke is, "There are some standing here who will not taste death before they see the kingdom of God" (9:27). For Luke "the kingdom of God is not coming with things that can be observed" because "the kingdom of God is among you" (17:20–21). Moreover, Luke omits Mark's opening proclamation of Jesus: "The time is fulfilled, and the kingdom of God has come near; repent, and believe in the gospel" (1:15). Instead, Luke substitutes Jesus' preaching in the synagogue at Nazareth on the text of Isaiah (4:16–21). Jesus' comment "Today this scripture has been fulfilled in your hearing" (4:21) implies that the kingdom is already present for those who accept it.

Other texts, however, contradict this view. For example, the statement that "the kingdom of God has come near" (Luke 10:9) is repeated in 10:11 (see also Matt 10:7, 14–15). Luke retains the idea of Q that one should be prepared for the unexpected End (12:45–46; Matt 24:48–51). Even Luke 17:20, "the kingdom of God is not coming with things that can be observed," is contradicted by 21:31: "when you see these things taking place, you know that the kingdom of God is near."

Perhaps most scholars still agree with H. Conzelmann 1960 that Luke wrote at a time when the Christian expectation of the end of the world was subsiding. Christians had to face up to the present world, so Luke wrote to help the church meet that challenge. He presents Jesus' ministry as coming in the middle period of God's plan (see also Acts 2:22–24) for the history of salvation. The first period consisted of Israel's history from creation to John the Baptist; the work of the church, beginning with Pentecost and extending to the end of the world, constituted the third period.

Some scholars, however, challenge Conzelmann's view that Luke eliminated references to the approaching end of the world in order to deal with the delay of Jesus' second coming. For example, E. Franklin 1975:6–47 believes that Luke reinterpreted rather than reduced the traditional emphasis. Though Luke fully included the End in his thinking, it was "no longer thought of as the event which guaranteed the claims made on behalf of Jesus. This for him was rather provided by the ascension." Luke wrote "to gain a response to the message that the ascension proclaimed—that Jesus really is Lord and that the eschatological action of God was effective through him."

According to C. H. Talbert 1970, Luke wrote to combat "over-realized eschatology," that is, the idea that the kingdom of God had already come with Jesus' last days in Jerusalem. The disciples had mistakenly believed that Jesus' going to Jerusalem and his ascension were to be identified with the coming of the kingdom of God, the Parousia: "he was near Jerusalem, and . . . they supposed that the kingdom of God was to appear immediately" (19:11; see also 9:51). According to Talbert 1974:89–110, Luke wrote to correct the view that Jesus' ascension was identical with the Parousia.

Luke, then, in both his gospel and in Acts, clearly shows special interests in women, the poor, Samaritans, the Holy Spirit, prayer, and—in the gospel—an Elijah/Elisha motif. Because of contradictory passages, Luke's precise views on eschatology are less certain than those interests. For critical study of Luke's interest in prayer see S. F. Plymale 1991, a theological approach with respect to salvation history; D. M. Crump 1992, christological approach through redaction criticism.

THE STRUCTURE OF LUKE

Because Luke contains detached, unrelated, and even contradictory statements and episodes, it is impossible to develop a logical outline of Luke. Most scholars agree on this general chronological scheme: preface (1:1–4); preparation for Jesus' ministry (3:1–4:13), Jesus' Galilean ministry (4: 14–9:50), Jesus' journey to Jerusalem (9:51–19:27), Jesus' ministry in Jerusalem (19:28–21:38), the passion narrative (22:1–23:56), and the resurrection narrative (24:1–53). Except for the first two chapters, the structure of Luke in general follows that of Mark.

Any effort to develop a nonchronological outline of the gospel is clearly subjective and therefore open to criticism. Nevertheless, assuming that Luke wrote to inform and instruct his readers and that he had a reason for inserting seven references to Jesus praying at crucial moments in his life, we can divide the religious and theological content of the gospel as follows by using the seven references as dividing points.

I. *Preface (1:1–4)*

II. *Prologue: narratives of the births of John and Jesus (1:5–2:52)*

III. *Introduction: John the Baptist preaching, baptizing, and imprisoned (3:1–20)*

IV. *Jesus teaching and healing under the guidance of the Spirit (3:21–5:15)*

V. *Jesus confronting Jewish authorities (5:16–6:11)*

VI. *Jesus teaching his disciples and healing (6:12–9:17)*

VII. *Jesus, as Christ, Son of God, and God's Chosen One, teaching all who listen to him (9:18–10:42)*

VIII. *"Your kingdom come": proper prayer, doing God's will, resisting evil, and facing opposition and death (11:1–23:46a)*

IX. *Conclusion: Jesus' burial, resurrection from the dead, and ascension to heaven (23:46b–24:53)*

This framework is the basis for the outline and comments below.

Outline and Comments

I. *Preface (1:1–4)*

The use of a formal, literary preface does not necessarily mean that Luke was a historian by profession. Nor does "an orderly account" mean that he had done careful research, like a modern scholar. In fact, whatever history Luke's work contains cannot be separated from his Christian theological proclamation and ministry. He wrote so that his readers might "know the truth" as he believed it. To assure a wide reading, Luke used the kind of preface familiar to readers living in the Hellenistic environment in which he wrote.

II. *Prologue: narratives of the births of John and Jesus (1:5–2:52)*

Because Luke's birth narratives are among the most popular literature in the Bible, and because they are not always studied critically, we will consider them in some detail. First of all, notice the similarities and differences between the Matthean and Lukan accounts in Figure 6.2.

Notice that, in spite of some differences in details, there is basic agreement on fifteen points (2–4, 7–13, 15, 21–22, 27–28). But differences in style, approach, and content show that the two accounts were written independently. All of this suggests that there was a traditional core of material about Jesus' birth that each writer used and to which he added materials from other sources, including some of his own creation. For example, Bethlehem as the place of Jesus' birth was already fixed in Christian tradition because both Matthew and Luke use the story. Matthew explains the tradition as the fulfillment

FIGURE 6.2   *Similarities and Differences in Birth Narratives*

Matthew 1–2	Luke 1–2
1. Gospel begins with genealogy of Jesus (1:1–17)	Gospel begins with formal preface (1:1–4); genealogy is in chap. 3
2. Jesus is a descendant of David (1:1)	Jesus is a descendant of David (1:32)
3. Mary engaged to Joseph (1:18)	Mary engaged to Joseph (1:26; 2:5)
4. Joseph and Mary had not had sexual intercourse (1:18, 25)	Joseph and Mary had not had sexual intercourse (1:27, 34)
5. Joseph, husband of Mary (1:19)	Mary has no husband (1:34)
6. Mary, wife of Joseph (1:20)	Joseph, father of Jesus (2:48)
7. Joseph in lineage of David (1:20)	Joseph in lineage of David (1:27; 2:4)
8. Mary with child of Holy Spirit (1:20)	Mary with child of Holy Spirit (1:35)
9. Joseph told of coming birth by an unnamed angel (1:20)	Mary told of coming birth by angel Gabriel (1:26–35)
10. Joseph told by angel, "You are to name him Jesus" (1:21)	Mary told by Gabriel, "You will name him Jesus" (1:31)
11. Jesus "will save his people from their sins" (1:21)	Jesus is "a Savior, who is the Christ, the Lord" (2:11)
12. Joseph and Mary live together before birth of Jesus (1:24–25)	Joseph and Mary live together before birth of Jesus (2:4–7)
13. Prophecy implies Mary is a virgin (1:22–23)	Mary called a virgin (1:27)
14. Joseph and Mary live in Bethlehem (2:1, 11)	Joseph and Mary go to Bethlehem from Nazareth for taxation (2:1–5)
15. Jesus born in house in Bethlehem (2:1, 11)	Jesus born in stable in Bethlehem (2:7, 12)
16. Birth in Bethlehem fulfills OT prophecy (2:5–6)	Birth in Bethlehem coincidental with stay there for census (2:1–6)
17.	Birth of Baptist promised by Gabriel to the father, Zechariah (1:5–24)
18.	Mary visits kinswoman Elizabeth, mother of Baptist (1:39–56)
19.	Birth of Baptist (1:57–80)
20.	Poetic sections based on passages from OT (1:14–17, 32–33, 46–55, 67–79; 2:29–32, 34–35)
21. Visit of wise men (2:1–12)	Visit of shepherds (2:8–20)
22. Visitors had been informed of Jesus' birth in supernatural manner (2:1–2, 7–10); visitors return from whence they came	Visitors had been informed of Jesus' birth in supernatural manner (2:8–18); visitors return from whence they came
23. Flight to Egypt and Herod's massacre of male children fulfill OT prophecies (2:13–18)	Simeon predicts rejection and persecution by some (2:34–35)

(continued)

FIGURE 6.2 *Continued*

Matthew 1–2	Luke 1–2
24.	Circumcision and presentation of Jesus in temple, and Mary's purification (2:21–39)
25.	Joseph and Mary referred to as parents of Jesus and as father and mother of Jesus (2:27, 33, 41, 43, 48, 51)
26.	Mary herself refers to Joseph as father of Jesus (2:48)
27. Joseph and family return from Egypt to Judea and then go to Nazareth to live—both to fulfill OT prophecies (2:19–23)	Joseph and family return from Bethlehem to Nazareth, "their own town," to live (2:39)
28. Herod, king of Judea (2:1, 3, 7, 12–16, 19, 22); Archelaus succeeds his father, Herod (2:22)	Herod, king of Judea (1:5)
29.	Augustus, emperor of Rome (2:1)
30.	Quirinius, governor of Syria (2:2)
31.	Jesus in temple at twelve years of age (2:41–52)

---

of prophecy (2:1–6); Luke explains it through the census by Augustus (2:1–7). The tradition of Jesus' origin in Nazareth had also been established, and again, Matthew explains it as fulfillment (2:19–23); but for Luke it was logical that Jesus' parents would take him back to Nazareth, "their own town" (2:39).

So was Jesus actually born in Bethlehem? If so, did Matthew (or his source?) interpret Mic 5:2 and other OT texts as supporting Jesus' messiahship in light of his birth there? Or did early Christians regard Mic 5:2 as a prediction of the Messiah's birth at Bethlehem and then invent the story of Jesus' birth there to fulfill the OT prophecy? By the same reasoning, are Luke's statements that there was no room in the inn, that Jesus was laid in a manger to be accepted as historical because there is no OT prophecy about them? Think about these questions as we turn to Luke's narratives of Jesus' birth.

Luke's Birth Narratives

Luke's birth narratives, including the material peculiar to Luke, differ from the rest of the gospel in two main ways. The Greek is less classical and more Semitized, like that of the Septuagint, and the narratives show strong influence from the OT. There are many verbal parallels—such as "your wife Elizabeth will bear you a son" and "the child grew," for example—between the stories of Abraham and his wife Sarah (Genesis 17–18) and Zechariah and Elizabeth (Luke 1:5–25). (For OT influence on other sections of Luke's narrative, see R. E. Brown 1977:235–495 and J. A. Fitzmyer 1981:303–448.)

It is impossible to say how much of the material in the Baptist narratives Luke took from tradition and how much he invented on the basis of the OT. He probably took bits of information from tradition—for example, "John son of Zechariah" (3:2)—and wrote his account to serve his own literary and theological purposes. Because of common literary features in the birth narratives and elsewhere in Luke-Acts, this seems to be the view of most scholars today. One of these features is two series of comparisons between John and Jesus (1:5–38 and 1:57–2:52), separated by the episode of Mary's visit to Elizabeth (1:39–56). Notice these parallels between the stories of John and Jesus: the parents, who do not expect a child, are presented; after an angel has appeared to each, Zechariah and Mary are both troubled but told not to fear; a hymn describes the character and work of the son, who "will be great"; both Zechariah and Mary question the angel's message; all are surprised at the news of the birth; and "the child grew and became strong."

Such parallels represent the kinds of repetition and variation typical of Luke's literary style in the rest of chaps. 1 and 2 and elsewhere in the gospel and Acts. But why did Luke use narratives of John's birth, along with those about Jesus, in the introduction to his gospel? By reading the narratives carefully, you will notice that there is a strong Christological motive behind them in that Luke presents John and Jesus as agents in God's plan of salvation. But Jesus' side of the story always is superior, something that is true for Jesus' parents as well as for Jesus himself. Both conceptions are miraculous, but John's comes about naturally through sexual relations. Jesus' conception, however, comes about without sexual intercourse, through the Holy Spirit coming upon Mary. John "will be called the prophet of the Most High" (1:76), but Jesus "will be called the Son of the Most High" (1:32) and "holy . . . Son of God" (1:35), and Jesus is born "a Savior, who is the Christ, the Lord" (2:11). John "will turn many of the people of Israel to the Lord their God . . . to give knowledge of salvation to his people," that is, Jews (1:16, 77), but Jesus comes not only for the glory of Israel (2:30–32) but to bring salvation for all peoples, "a light for revelation to the Gentiles."

A subtle subordination of John to Jesus was present in Luke's sources, Mark and Q. John says that "one who is more powerful than I is coming" (3:16; Mark 1:7; Matt 3:11), and John is "more than a prophet . . . yet the least in the kingdom of God is greater than he" (7:26, 28; Matt 11:9, 11). The same ideas occur in Acts (see 13:23–25). Acts 18:24–19:7 reflects differences, if not controversy, between followers of John and of Jesus. Luke retains the Q passage in which Jesus defends John, as well as himself,

against his critics: "John the Baptist has come eating no bread and drinking no wine, and you say, 'He has a demon'" (7:33; Matt 11:18). This statement provides Luke a tie-in with the infancy narrative in the angel's words to Zechariah: "He must never drink wine or strong drink" (1:15). Luke's own statement, "All were questioning in their hearts concerning John, whether he might be the Christ" (3:15), implies that some people thought John was the Messiah.

According to Luke, the history of Israel began as the first era in God's plan for the salvation of humankind with the birth of Isaac to Abraham and Sarah. The birth of John—the account of which is modeled on that of Isaac—signaled the end of that era, and the birth of Jesus marked the beginning of the next one. "The law and the prophets were in effect until John came; since then the good news of the kingdom of God is proclaimed" (Luke 16:16; see also Matt 11:12–13). Luke's theological convictions that Jesus, not John the Baptist, was the Christ and that he brought in a new era in God's plan for human salvation influenced what he wrote in the birth narratives and elsewhere in the gospel. At the same time, what he said was a subtle polemic or defense against those followers of John who had not joined the Christian movement.

Luke 1:35. Although it is not practical to comment on each section in the birth narratives, I will do so for three passages. First, Luke 1:35: "The Holy Spirit will come upon you, and the power of the Most High will overshadow you." "Most High," a synonym for God used often in the OT, occurs most frequently in Luke. Besides in the birth narratives (1:32, 35, 76), Luke uses it in 6:35 and Acts 7:48 and 16:17, whereas Matthew does not use the expression and Mark uses it only once (5:7 = Luke 8:28).

Luke is the only gospel writer to use the word "come upon" (*eperchomai*); in Acts 1:8 he uses it of the Holy Spirit coming upon the disciples. And the expression "filled with the Holy Spirit" is peculiar to Luke in the NT (Luke 1:15, 41, 67; Acts 2:4; 4:8, 31; 9:17; 13:9). These expressions indicate Luke's special hand at work in using, if not composing, 1:35. There is no parallel in the OT to the idea of the Holy Spirit coming upon the person who is to give birth to the messianic ruler.

Since in Luke 1:35 the two sentences are in parallel, some scholars have said that God himself could be regarded as participating in the act of physical union. Consequently, they have seen here a mythological notion derived from pagan sources. (For references, see J. Machen 1932: 317–379 and T. Boslooper 1962:135–186.) Indeed, two passages from Plutarch, biographer and philosopher at the end of the first century CE, contain ideas like those in Luke 1:35. Below are literal translations of two passages, one from Plutarch's *Lives* and the other from his *Morals:*

> And yet the Egyptians make a distinction which they think is not incredible, namely, that it is possible for a spirit of God to come near a woman and to create certain beginnings of generation, but there is not sexual intercourse. [*Numa* 4]

> And I do not think it terrible if God, not coming near in the manner of a man, but by some other touches or through other contacts, alters the mortal nature and makes it pregnant with a more divine offspring. (*Symposiacs* 8:1:3]

Look back to the discussion of the virgin birth in Outline and Comments in Chapter 5.

The Birth of Jesus (2:1–20). That Jesus was born in the time of Augustus is hardly debatable, but an incident scarcely defensible historically is that of the shepherds with the angelic messengers. Many proposals have been offered as to why Luke incorporated this story into his account of Jesus' birth (R. E. Brown 1977:392–434). As you read that story, notice that 2:8–20 is not a necessary part of the account of Jesus' birth. Verse 21 follows naturally after v 7 and serves as a conclusion to vv 1–7. At the same time, v 20 forms a fitting conclusion to a unit that begins with v 8. It seems, therefore, that Luke composed the story of the shepherds and inserted it into that of Jesus' birth between vv 7 and 21. Verse 21, then, serves as a conclusion to the whole unit (2:1–21). Verses 15 and 16 tie the shepherd story in with what precedes it, and v 17, "When they saw this, they made known what had been told them about this child," provides a tie-in with 4:14: "and a report about him spread through all the surrounding country."

Unlike a number of other words in the infancy narratives, "shepherd" is not Lukan and occurs in Luke only in 2:8–20. In fact, in Mark 6:34 and 14:27, passages that both Luke and Matthew reproduce, Luke omits the word (Luke 9:11; 22:39–40). Matthew omits the word in the first passage (14:14), but he uses it in 9:36: "like sheep without a shepherd," the same expression as in Mark 6:34. In the second passage, Matthew (26:31) retains the Markan saying, and he uses the word "shepherd" also in an M passage (25:32).

The average person today thinks of shepherds as relatively gentle, unaggressive, even affectionate people because of images from well-known biblical passages such as "the Lord is my shepherd" (Ps 23:1) and Jesus as the good shepherd (John 10:7–16). But when Luke wrote, shepherds did not have a good reputation and were often considered dishonest and lawless because they pastured their sheep on the lands of others. Perhaps Luke avoided the term "shepherd" elsewhere because he was aware of its objectionable connotations; and perhaps, therefore, he did not originally compose the shepherd story in the birth narratives, but only used it to suit his purposes.

However, the shepherd story has many Lukan touches. For example, in the same line where Luke first mentions shepherds, the expression translated as "keeping watch over their flock by night" is literally "watching the watches of the night over their flock." Luke's fondness for using cognate expressions, such as "watching the watches" (*phylassontes phylakas*), is a characteristic of his literary style. He uses a similar expression again in the next verse. "They were terrified" is literally "they feared a great fear" (see also 7:29; 11:46; 22:15).

Why did Luke include the story of the shepherds? Some have suggested they are symbolic of the sinners whom Jesus was sent to save (see, for example, 4:43; 5:32; 15:1–7). In support of this view is the angel's statement to the shepherds: "to you is born this day in the city of David a Savior" (2:11). Or perhaps Luke was influenced by Hellenistic culture, since in the mythology of the mystery religions, shepherds came worshipfully to present the infant Mithra the first fruits of their harvests and flocks (F. Cumont 1956:132).

Although we do not know why Luke used the story of the shepherds, the following observations may be helpful. Within the story of the shepherds are three phenomena associated with Augustus: joy at his birth, "savior," and peace. An inscription with reference to Augustus reads, "But the birthday of the god was for the world the beginning of tidings of joy on his account." Since Augustus was hailed as savior of the world, Luke could well have presented Augustus as giving a decree that was to affect the whole world. As the founder of the Roman Empire, Augustus had brought peace to the world by putting an end to the brutal wars after the murder of Julius Caesar. The *pax Romana* (see Introduction) meant not only cessation of war but also order within the empire. So for thousands of Romans Augustus marked the fulfillment of the "glorious age" that Virgil (*Eclogue* 4:11) had predicted.

In his own subtle way, Luke was offering Christian propaganda to Jews and non-Jews alike—that the birth of Jesus, not that of Augustus, was the real occasion of "good news of great joy for all the people" (2:10). The peace that Jesus came to bring was proclaimed not by humans but by "a multitude of the heavenly host" and was to be experienced by all mortals with whom God was pleased. Augustus had begun a new age in Roman history, but Jesus began a new era in the history of the world. For Luke, Jesus was not only Savior; he was also Christ the Lord (2:11). The combination "Christ the Lord" occurs in the same way nowhere else in the NT (see 2:26). For Luke, God made Jesus "both Lord and Christ" (Acts 2:36), a figure superior to the great Augustus. Thus Luke may have used the story of the shepherds as a foil for showing the superiority of Jesus to the emperor Augustus. At the same time, he made his account a gentle rebuff of Au-

gustus in the hope of winning Gentile readers to Christianity.

Neither Matthew nor Luke mentions the actual date Jesus was born, nor is a date for that event mentioned anywhere else in the NT. So how do we know when he was born? We really do not know for sure, but to determine it as accurately as we can, we must try to fix the event at a time that coincides with contemporary events or persons whose dates are reasonably certain.

Christians did not become concerned about developing a calendar of their own until several centuries after the birth of Jesus, when they tried to fix dates for events in his life. First, they tried to establish a date for the last Passover of Jesus with his disciples (Mark 14:12–25; Matt 26:17–29; Luke 22:7–23). They did this, of course, because they wanted to determine the date of Easter (the celebration of Jesus' resurrection), which became the most important Christian festival.

As time went on, Christians also became interested in fixing the time of Jesus' birth. And to do that they tried to establish the date of Herod's death, since he died soon after Jesus was born. However, that was not an easy task for several reasons. First, Jews reckoned dates from the time of the creation of the world, which corresponds with our date of 3761 BCE. But Christians wanted to date their festivals from the time of Jesus' birth. Second, Christians did not have easy access to published and official calendars like those today. And third, Romans dated events from the time of the founding of the city of Rome (*ab urbe condita* [*a.u.c.*], "from the founding of the city").

By the sixth century CE Christians began fixing dates for Jesus' birth and his resurrection. Perhaps it was the Roman monk Dionysius Exiguus (called "Dennis the Little") who thought Herod the Great died in 754 *a.u.c.* Because there is no date 0 BCE or CE, Herod's death would have occurred in the last year before Jesus was born, or 1 BCE, as now designated. However, later someone else fixed the date of Herod's death at 750 *a.u.c.*, which corresponds with 4 BCE. So, if we allow two years for Herod's decree for the death of children (Matt 2:16) to be effective, we have the time of 6–4 BCE as the most likely date of Jesus' birth.

Circumcision of Jesus, Presentation in the Temple, and Jesus at Twelve Years (2:21–52). The last two sections of Luke's birth narratives seem to be independent units of material, each with separate beginnings (2:22 and 2:41) and endings (2:39–40 and 2:51–52). Perhaps they come from a time and source before the virginal conception was known, since Joseph and Mary are referred to as the parents of Jesus (2:27, 41, 43), and especially since Joseph is called Jesus' father (2:33, 48). Scholars have disagreed about their origin and content, but whether or not Luke composed them, he at least Lukanized them. Or if Luke wrote them himself, he did so before he learned about the special conception of Jesus.

"Parents" (*goneis*) is a Lukan word, which Luke inserts twice (8:56; 18:29) where it does not occur in Mark and retains the one time when it is used in Mark (Luke 21:16; Mark 13:12 = Matt 10:21). In the NT only Luke (3:23; 4:22) and John (1:46; 6:42) refer to Jesus as the son of Joseph. Other Lukan touches in the two sections are the Holy Spirit guiding Simeon, Jerusalem as a place of special interest, and the summaries in 2:40 and 2:52. Distinctive Lukan words include the verb translated "went" (2:41) and the words translated "as usual" (2:42) and "in great anxiety" (2:48). The use of these words and others ties these sections in with Lukan style and content elsewhere.

There is probably no better tie-in between the birth narratives and the rest of the gospel than the temple/Jerusalem motif. It may be reflected in the temptation story, where Luke reverses the final two temptations and places the temptation of Jesus to throw himself from the pinnacle of the temple last. In doing so Luke makes the temple scene the climax of the temptations. In the central part of the gospel (9:31, 51), Jerusalem becomes Jesus' destination, "because it is impossible for a prophet to be killed outside of Jerusalem" (13:33; see also 13:22; 17:11; 19:11). Jesus

spent much of the time during his final week teaching in the temple (19:47; 21:37–38). In Mark and Matthew Jesus' resurrection appearances take place in Galilee, but in Luke they occur in and near Jerusalem (24:13–49). Jesus' final words to his disciples, recorded only in Luke, are that "repentance and forgiveness of sins is to be proclaimed . . . to all nations, beginning from Jerusalem" (24:47). Then Jesus tells them to "stay here in the city, until . . . clothed with power [the coming of the Holy Spirit] from on high" (24:49). Acts opens where the gospel of Luke ends—in Jerusalem with Jesus' followers who receive the Holy Spirit as promised.

Having examined Luke's birth narratives in detail because they are so interesting and perplexing, we will now consider the rest of the gospel, though in less detail.

III. Introduction: John the Baptist preaching, baptizing, and imprisoned (3:1–20)

Verses 3:1–6 seem like the beginning of a book and support the view that chaps. 1 and 2 are from a separate source. John's preaching (3:7–14) is a combination of eschatology and ethics in which the message is "Bear good fruit," that is, "Live right or else!" John gives examples of what is expected of the readers. The meaning of 3:16–18 is that Jesus the Messiah is "more powerful than" John and that Jesus will baptize in a more dramatic and effective way.

IV. Jesus teaching and healing under the guidance of the Spirit (3:21–5:15)
A. Baptism of Jesus (3:21–22)

Theologically, these verses mark the transition from the introduction to the body of the gospel. For Luke, the Holy Spirit came to Jesus as the answer to his prayer, not as the result of his baptism. Under the influence of the Spirit, Jesus faces his temptations and then begins his work in Galilee.

B. Genealogy of Jesus (3:23–38)

Although this section and Matt 1:1–17 are referred to as genealogies, neither Luke nor Matthew uses the Greek term *genealogia*, which occurs in the NT only in 1 Tim 1:4 and Titus 3:9. In 1 Tim 1:4 the writer urges the readers not "to occupy themselves with myths and endless genealogies"; in Titus 3:9 the writer includes genealogies with "stupid controversies" to be avoided. These passages reflect a negative attitude toward genealogies, the first passage placing them in the same literary category as myths.

The two genealogies were probably written independently of each other by people who did not write the other material, including the birth narratives, in the respective gospels. This becomes obvious after a few observations. Matthew and Luke proceed in reverse order. Matthew begins with Abraham and comes through David to Joseph, father of Jesus. Luke, on the other hand, starts with Jesus, the son of Joseph, and works backward through David to Adam, whom he calls "son of God." Both lists agree in names between Abraham and David, but from David to Joseph Matthew lists twenty-five names and Luke gives forty, and they agree on only two, Zerubbabel and Shealtiel. Moreover, Jesus had two paternal grandfathers, Jacob (Matthew) and Heli (Luke).

Whoever composed the genealogies thought Jesus had a father through whom Jesus' lineage could be traced, so the genealogies were probably completed after Jesus' death but before belief in his unique birth was widespread. One difference between the Lukan and Matthean genealogies is significant for understanding both writers' points of view. By tracing Jesus' ancestry back only to Abraham, the progenitor of Jews alone, Matthew limits Jesus' ancestry to Jews. However, by tracing Jesus' descent back to Adam, the progenitor of all peoples and races, Luke includes Gentiles in the extended family of Jesus. Perhaps that is why Luke places the genealogy close to the story of Jesus' rejection by the Jews at Nazareth.

Jewish Christians who believed Jesus was the Messiah soon claimed that he was in the line of David. Paul had already asserted that Jesus "was descended from David according to the flesh" (Rom 1:3). The genealogies were written, then, to show that, as a descendant of David, Jesus was the legitimate Messiah. We have no record, though, that Jesus himself ever claimed such descent.

C. Jesus tempted in the desert, returns to Galilee, and teaches and heals (4:1–44)

In 4:15 Luke omits Jesus' eschatological preaching in Mark 1:15, but he closes the section (4:43–44) with an addition to Mark in Jesus' words: "I must proclaim the good news of the kingdom of God . . . for I was sent for this purpose." "Proclaim the good news" translates *euangelizō*, one of Luke's favorite words. It ties the preceding stories in nicely with Jesus' reading and applying of the passage from Isaiah to himself in the synagogue at Nazareth (4:18–21). The same word also ties in the narratives in this section (4:14–44) with the "good news" of the births of John (1:19) and Jesus (2:10). Only in Luke is Jesus already recognized as "the Holy One of God" (4:34 = Mark 1:24), "the Son of God," and "the Christ" (4:41). Thus the promises of the angel (1:32, 35) are fulfilled, and theologically, Luke has tied the birth narratives in with the first narratives about Jesus' preaching and healing.

D. The miraculous catch of fish and the healing of a leper (5:1–15)

Luke composes the first story from Markan and L material and follows Mark closely for the second. By transposing and redacting the Markan call of disciples, Luke shows that Jesus becomes well known—after his rejection at Nazareth—through his healing of the demoniac (4:31–37), Peter's mother-in-law (4:38–39), and others (4:40–41). Presumably Gentiles as well as Jews are present at the healings. The miraculous catch evokes from Peter an attitude of worship, a confession of sins, and an acknowledgment of Jesus as Lord (5:8). In contrast to Jesus' statement about fishing for people, which is addressed to the group in Mark (1:17 = Matt 4:19), Jesus speaks only to Peter in Luke 5:10: "You will be catching people." This looks forward to Peter's role as leader of the twelve.

V. Jesus confronting Jewish authorities (5:16–6:11)

The statement in 5:16 about Jesus praying marks the transition to the next section of the gospel. The prayer prepares Jesus to face his opponents for the first time. The fact that Luke earlier omitted Mark's reference to Jesus praying (1:35) and inserts such a reference here supports the view that Luke thinks another phase of Jesus' career is beginning.

Luke follows Mark closely for the controversy narratives of the healing of the paralytic (5:17–26), the call of Levi (5:27–32), the question about fasting (5:33–35), plucking grain on the sabbath (6:1–5), and the healing of the man with the withered hand (6:6–11). At the end of the sayings about the garment and the wineskins, Luke adds a difficult verse that may be understood in several ways. As in Mark, the two sayings illustrate the impossibility of mixing the new (Christianity) with the old (Judaism). Then Luke adds a proverbial saying: "No one after drinking old wine desires new wine, but says, 'The old is good'" (5:39). This seems to contradict the preceding sayings and thus to support the Jewish rejection of Jesus' teaching, but it can be taken ironically to mean just the opposite. Or it may be a statement that represents those who are satisfied with the old (Judaism) and are therefore not likely to join the new (Christianity).

VI. *Jesus teaching his disciples and healing (6:12–9:17)*
A. *The call of the twelve and the healing of multitudes (6:12–19)*

In the transitional verse (6:12), Jesus prays before the selection of the twelve and the healings and teachings that follow. By transposing the call of the twelve and the story of the multitudes, Luke assures Jesus of "a great crowd of his disciples and a great multitude of people" (6:17) for what follows. The transposition places the crowd of disciples who now follow Jesus in contrast to the Pharisees and scribes who had opposed him in the preceding episodes.

B. *Sermon on the plain (6:20–49)*

Luke gives no indication that Jesus withdrew from the crowds mentioned in 6:17–19, so "disciples" in 6:20 is to be taken in the sense of followers in general, rather than the twelve in particular. Jesus' words "I say to you that listen" (6:27) and "someone is like who comes to me, hears my words, and acts on them" (6:47) show that Luke wanted the sermon to influence the behavior of his readers. The sermon contains three forms of teaching: beatitudes, with corresponding woes (6:20–26), exhortations (6:27–38), and parables (6:39–49). The omission of the antitheses in Matthew's version may make Jesus' demands seem less radical than they do in Matthew, but the exhortations to "Love your enemies" and "Do good to those who hate you" (6:27) must have seemed radical enough to all who heard and read.

C. *A series of incidents showing that Jesus is well received (7:1–8:3)*

Material from Q and L reflects Luke's special interests and concerns and provides concrete evidence that Jesus practiced what he had just preached (6:20–49). Luke shows careful literary skill in conveying his theological convictions, especially in the words of the people: "'A great prophet has risen among us!' and 'God has looked favorably on his people!'" (7:16).

1. *The centurion's slave and the widow's son at Nain (7:1–17)*

These miracles set the stage for Jesus' discourse with John's disciples that follows in 7:18–23—"The disciples of John reported all these things to him" (7:18). The story of the centurion's slave is essentially the same as in Matthew, and for both writers the centurion represents believing Gentiles. Verses 3–6 are added by Luke; they show Luke's sociological and theological concerns and the close connection of the gospel with Acts. The centurion does not approach Jesus directly but sends two delegations, "some Jewish elders" and "friends." This centurion must have been rich because he built a synagogue for the Jews. So Luke not only brings Jews and Gentiles together before Jesus, but he also presents several social classes together before him: a wealthy Roman military man, a slave, Jewish leaders, and possibly a fourth class represented by the centurion's friends. Here is a superb example of the fulfillment of the passage quoted only by Luke in the introduction to his gospel: "All flesh shall see the salvation of God" (3:6). One of the main themes of Luke-Acts is the harmonization of Jewish and Gentile Christians. The words Luke adds in 7:3–6 express this theme, and the scene foreshadows a similar one in Acts.

Now turn to Acts 10 and compare the words about the centurion in Luke 7:4–5 with those about the centurion Cornelius in Acts 10:2: "a devout man who feared God . . . gave alms generously to the people and prayed constantly to God." Cornelius represents Gentile and Peter Jewish Christians. Since Luke-Acts is one work, Luke 7:3–6 is meant to indicate Jesus' approval of the kind of missionary activity among Gentiles that is described in Acts.

Luke, with a special interest in widows, uses the word "widow" nine times in the gospel and three times in Acts. Matthew does not use the word, and Mark uses it only in the story of the widow's gift (12:41–44), which Luke rewrites to emphasize her gift. The miracle of the widow's son and the parable of the widow and the judge (18:1–8) especially convey Luke's concern (see 4:25–26; 20:47; Acts 6:1; 9:39, 41). The miracle of the widow's son presents Jesus as a prophet like Elijah/Elisha, and the words "God has looked favorably on his people" provide an excellent tie-in with the birth narratives: "for he has looked favorably on his people and redeemed them" (1:68). Although spoken with reference to John's birth, the words foreshadowed the mission of Jesus, which Luke sees as being fulfilled in the stories before us.

2. Jesus' words about John (7:18–35)

The raising of the widow's son and the works of Jesus mentioned in 7:21 (not in Matthew), all done in the presence of John's disciples, add concrete evidence to the Q statement "Go and tell John what you have seen and heard" (7:22 = Matt 11:4). This passage echoes the synagogue scene at Nazareth and shows that Jesus' healing of lepers and raising of the dead surpass what had been prophesied.

3. The woman with the ointment and the ministering women (7:36–8:3)

These stories are proof of Luke's special interest in women. The former, like that of the tax collector Zacchaeus later (19:1–10), provides grounds for the charge in 7:34 that Jesus is "a friend of tax collectors and sinners." The same stories also show that "the Pharisees . . . rejected God's purpose for themselves" (7:30), but most importantly they portray Jesus as a bringer of salvation. The account of the ministering women shows Jesus' willingness to help and be helped in his work of "bringing the good news of the kingdom of God" (8:1).

D. A series of parables and miracles (8:4–9:17)

1. Teaching on hearing and responding to the word of God (8:4–21)

As in the sermon on the plain (6:27, 47), the emphasis in the parable of the sower (8:4–15) is on hearing and responding to God's word as preached by Jesus. (See Figure 6.3.) True followers of Jesus are "those who hear the word of God and do it" (8:21).

FIGURE 6.3 *Peasant with primitive plow in field north of Jerusalem.*

2. *A series of miracles (8:22–56)*

Luke follows Mark in presenting four stories illustrating the four types of Jesus' miracles: power over nature, casting out of demons, healing of the sick, and raising of the dead. This arrangement conveys the progressive revelation of Jesus' powerful word.

3. *The sending out of the twelve, Herod's reaction, and the feeding of the five thousand (9:1–17)*

Since Luke used Mark 6:1–6a earlier, the sending story comes after the account of Jesus' miracles just presented. This makes good sense because, like Jesus, the disciples are sent out with "power and authority over all demons and to cure diseases" (9:1). Notice that only Luke includes a command to "proclaim the kingdom of God" (9:2).

VII. *Jesus, as Christ, Son of God, and God's Chosen One, teaching all who listen to him (9:18–10:42)*

A. *Peter's confession and what it means (9:18–27)*

Omitting Mark 6:45–8:26, Luke returns to Mark's order with Peter's confession. As the reference in 9:18 to Jesus praying shows, Luke is beginning another section in his theological portrayal of Jesus. By omitting everything about Peter (see also Mark 8:32–33; Matt 16:17–23) except his answer to Jesus' question, Luke focuses on Jesus as "the Christ of God" (9:20). Peter's confession is the counterpart to the author's statement in the birth narratives that Simeon would not die "before he had seen the Lord's [that is, God's] Christ" (2:26). As the earthly Christ, Jesus must suffer, be rejected, and be killed, but he will rise again (9:22). Through Jesus' resurrection, according to Luke, "God has made him both Lord and Christ" (Acts 2:36) in the fullest sense. Recall that in the birth narratives the angel announced that on the day of his birth Jesus was "a Savior, who is the Messiah, the Lord" (2:11).

Luke closely links the sayings on discipleship (9:23–27) to what precedes them with the words "He said to them all," which hark back to "Who do the crowds say that I am?" (9:18). Those who follow Jesus as the Christ in Luke's time must be willing to go the whole way—even to death.

B. *Transfiguration of Jesus, and episodes that follow (9:28–10:42)*

1. *Transfiguration (9:28–36)*

The reference to Jesus at prayer again marks an important incident in his life and in the Lukan theological scheme. But since the reference does not interrupt the sequence of episodes, as do the other references to Jesus praying, it does not introduce a major division of the gospel.

When Jesus was praying after his baptism, he received the Holy Spirit, and a voice announced Jesus' Sonship. That experience prepared Jesus for his Galilean mission. Similarly, in this story Jesus has a spiritual experience while praying, and a voice proclaims his Sonship. Jesus is now prepared for his mission outside Galilee, which is about to begin. For Luke, however, the primary significance of the transfiguration is theological, not geographical, as Luke's addition in 9:31–33a makes clear. Recall that in the birth narratives Jesus' parents "brought him up to Jerusalem to present him to the Lord" (2:22), and that as the Christ (9:20) and Son of God, his greatest accomplishment is to take place at Jerusalem (9:31). This reference to Jerusalem, not the one in 9:51, is the crucial one in the theological journey motif in Luke. Before this, people from Judea and Jerusalem have come to see and hear Jesus (5:17; 6:17) where he was. But at Jerusalem, through his departure (9:31) to the Father—"Father, into your hands I commend my spirit" (23:46)—he will become a heavenly figure like Moses and Elijah (9:30). The disciples on the mountain with Jesus have a glimpse of "his glory," as do the two disciples on the road to Emmaus (24:13–35). In the Emmaus story, Jesus' question provides Luke's own commentary on the transfiguration incident: "Was it not necessary that the Christ should suffer these things and then enter into his glory?" (24:26). Compare Luke's comments with respect to

Stephen in Acts 7:55: "But filled with the Holy Spirit, he gazed into heaven and saw the glory of God and Jesus standing at the right hand of God."

2. A healing and teachings (9:37–50)

Because Luke omits the story of Elijah's coming (Mark 9:9–13), the healing of the epileptic boy (9:37–43a) follows immediately after the transfiguration and provides a fitting sequel to it. Luke's only interest in presenting the story is to provide a setting for his own comment: "All were astonished at the greatness of God" (9:43).

3. Entry into Samaria and teaching (9:51–10:42)

"When the days drew near for him to be taken up, he set his face to go to Jerusalem" (9:51) ties in with the statement about Jerusalem in 9:30–31. From 9:51 to 18:14 (Luke's "special section"), where Luke again picks up Mark's account, there are many disconnected episodes from Q and L. In that material, as in the material from 18:15–19:27, the motif of the journey to Jerusalem is prominent (see 13:22; 17:11; 18:31; 19:11).

Jesus' entry into Samaria (9:52–56) prefigures the Samaritan mission of Acts 8, and the sending out of the seventy (10:1–16) represents a mission to Gentiles. This view is supported by the Jewish belief that there were seventy Gentile nations and by Luke's inclusion of the Q saying about the repentance of Tyre and Sidon, both Gentile cities, with the sending story. The sending story in Luke 10:1–16 corresponds with Paul's missions to the Gentiles in Acts (13:1–21:17; C. H. Talbert 1974:15–23). Notice that in 9:51–10:42 Luke inserts three references to the kingdom (9:60, 62; 10:9), thus anticipating a main theme of the gospel's next major section.

VIII. "Your kingdom come": proper prayer, doing God's will, resisting evil, and facing opposition and death (11:1–23:46a)

Theologically, Luke frames this large section in two ways. It begins with Jesus at prayer and with the Lord's Prayer, and ends with Jesus'

prayer on the cross (23:46a). The beginning of the Lord's Prayer includes the petition "your kingdom come" (11:2). At the end of the section only Luke reports the criminal's words, "Jesus, remember me when you come into your kingdom" (23:42). The kingdom of God, mentioned before rather incidentally without any description of it, is the main theme in this section. Luke shifts the kingdom parables of the mustard seed in Mark and the leaven in Q and the house divided in Mark to this section from earlier points in Mark and Matthew. He also places all the parabolic sayings that can be taken to refer to the kingdom or to the judgment in this section: salt and light, a lamp, on anxiety, the narrow gate, fearless confession, divisions in households, and seeking signs. On the way to Jerusalem, Jesus presents the way of the kingdom in various figures. Theologically, the journey motif actually began with Jesus praying at the transfiguration.

Many episodes in this section are disconnected, and it is difficult to determine their purposes in the gospel. If you follow the passages in the *Gospel Parallels,* the meaning will be clear from the outline.

> A. First half of the journey, with teachings on the kingdom (11:1–13:30)
>
> 1. The Lord's Prayer and persistence in prayer (11:1–13)
>
> 2. The kingdom already present in Jesus' casting out of demons (11:14–28)
>
> 3. Miraculous signs not needed to confirm Jesus' messiahship for those who observe the light of his teaching (11:29–36)
>
> 4. Pharisees at fault for neglecting justice and the love of God, and for being hypocritical in their observances (11:37–54)
>
> 5. Teaching to disciples (12:1–53)

Learning from the Pharisees, disciples of Jesus must acknowledge and never hypocritically deny him (12:1–12). Followers of Jesus must not amass possessions or be anxious about bodily needs, but seek the kingdom that God gives (12:13–34). Christians of Luke's time must be prepared for the Parousia (13:35–40), and in the meantime church leaders must not become abusive or corrupt, or they will be punished (12:41–48). Jesus' coming will divide households (12:49–53).

6. Teaching to the multitudes (12:54–13:30)

Jesus' hearers (and Luke's readers) must learn to interpret the signs of the times and settle their accounts, or pay the penalty (12:54–59). They must repent or perish, bear fruit or be cut down (13:1–9). In the work of the kingdom in overcoming Satanic powers, healing takes precedence over the sabbath (13:10–17), and from such small beginnings the kingdom grows (13:18–21). Strive to enter the difficult path to the kingdom before it is too late; on the way, Gentiles have a better chance than Jews (13:22–30).

B. Second half of the journey, with more teachings on the kingdom (13:31–19:27)

1. Transition in the journey motif (13:31–35)

This is the second of two major transitions in the journey motif, the first of which was 9:51–56. There are minor transitions at 13:22; 17:11; 18:31; and 19:11. Such geographical transitions do not affect the theological aspect of the motif, an aspect that began with Jesus praying at the transfiguration (9:29–32). Verses 34–35 reiterate that aspect of the motif.

2. A healing and a parable on humility (14:1–24)

Humility and the invitation of the poor to dinner are requirements for entrance into the kingdom (14:1–14). Another parable teaches that the poor will replace Jews who do not accept the invitation to the kingdom, and Gentile outcasts will replace self-satisfied Christians (14:15–24).

3. Reckoning the cost and paying the price of discipleship (14:25–35)

4. The repentance of sinners (15:1–32)

5. *Prudence and faith—marks of Christian stewardship (16:1–15)*

6. *Detached sayings (16:16–18)*

7. *Fate of the rich and the poor in the kingdom (16:19–31)*

8. *Teachings on temptation, forgiveness, faith, and lack of reward for doing what is expected (17:1–10)*

9. *Ten lepers healed (17:11–19)*

10. *The kingdom of God already present (17:20–21)*

11. *The coming of the Son of Man (17:22–37)*

12. *Parables teaching persistence and humility in prayer (18:1–14)*

13. *The kingdom and "children" (18:15–17)*

After his special section, which began at 9:51, Luke now returns to Mark's narrative, probably because of its teachings on the kingdom.

14. *Selling possessions and distributing to the poor (18:18–30)*

15. *On the way to Jerusalem—the third prediction of the passion (18:31–34)*

16. *Healing of Bartimaeus (18:35–43)*

17. *"Salvation" for Zacchaeus (19:1–10)*

After he agrees to right his wrongs, Zacchaeus becomes "a son of Abraham," that is, one who shares in God's promise of salvation.

18. *A conflated parable teaching that discipleship means proper activity, and that those who have rejected the Messiah will be punished (19:11–27)*

C. Jesus in Jerusalem (19:28–23:46a)

From this point on Luke follows Mark and inserts some material of his own. In studying the last chapters of Luke, remember that Acts is his second volume. If you read Acts 21–27, you will discover many parallels between Paul's last visit to Jerusalem and that of Jesus (C. H. Talbert 1974:17–18).

1. Jesus as Christ the King (19:28–44)

Jesus brings peace (only in Luke) and inspires praise to God, as at the time of his birth (19:28–38; see also 2:13–14, 20), but the Pharisees reject him.

2. Cleansing the temple and teaching there (19:45–21:38)

Luke frames this section with two references to Jesus teaching daily in the temple (19:47; 21:37). Except for occasional touches, he follows Mark closely. Jesus' farewell speech (20:45–21:36) reflects the time of Luke. Jesus is questioned about his authority (20:1–8) and tells the parable of the wicked tenants (20:9–19). He is questioned also about tribute to the emperor and about the resurrection (20:20–40), and comments about David's son (20:41–44). Jesus speaks woes against the Pharisees (20:45–47) and observes the widow giving her gift (21:1–4). He predicts the destruction of the temple (21:5–7) and delivers the apocalyptic discourse (21:8–36), with an indication that "the kingdom of God is near" (21:31). Luke adds a special ending to this discourse, in which he urges the readers to be morally prepared, to watch, and to pray for strength for what is to "come upon all who live on the face of the whole earth" (21:34–36). Then Luke summarizes Jesus' days in Jerusalem (21:37–38).

3. Narratives of Jesus' passion, from the conspiracy against Jesus to his death (22:1–23:46a)

Although the general outline of Luke's account probably comes from Mark, Luke used other sources and redacted Mark. The kingdom continues to be a Lukan theme. Luke has two references to the kingdom in the narrative of the institution of the Lord's Supper (22:16, 18), while Mark and Matthew have only one reference to the kingdom (Mark 14:25; Matt 26:29) in this section of the gospels (but see Mark 15:43 = Luke 23:51). In a passage from Q, Jesus promises that those who continue with him in his trials will eat and drink in the kingdom and share in the judgment (22:28–30; see also 23:42).

In a passage akin to Mark 10:42–45 (= Matt 20:25–28), which, like the one in Mark, reflects dissension in the church, the words "to give his life a ransom for many" are omitted by Luke. This indicates that Luke did not think Jesus died for the sins of humankind. For this reason the same idea is not a part of Luke's account of the institution of the Lord's Supper (compare Luke 22:15–20 with Mark 14:22–25 and Matt 26:26–29).

Luke believed that Jewish authorities alone were responsible for Jesus' death (22:66; 23:1–2, 10, 13, 18; Acts 2:23; 3:14; 5:27, 30; 7:52; but see also 4:27–28). Neither the Roman Pilate nor Herod finds Jesus guilty of any of the charges against Jesus (23:4, 13–16), and the Roman centurion remarks at Jesus' death, "Certainly this man was innocent" (23:47). These passages are only in Luke (see Matt 27:19, 24).

With respect to these statements and those that follow, we should note the view of R. J. Karris 1986. He argues that the word translated as "innocent" (*dikaios*) should be translated as "righteous." The Jesus of Luke was not a martyr. As "the righteous one" Jesus' "way of righteousness is opposed to that of the religious leaders who plot his death. . . . God has not abandoned his suffering righteous son" but "graciously vindicates that Jesus and creates salvific trust in those who trust in his justice."

Another passage only in Luke (22:35–38) is very difficult and is to be explained in light of the writer's theology. The quotation "And he was counted among the lawless" (Luke 22:37; see also 23:33) indicates that Luke believed Jesus fulfilled the role of God's suffering servant prophesied by Isaiah (53:12; compare Luke 2:30, 32 and Isa 52:10; 42:6; 49:6; and Acts 8:32–33 and Isa 53:7–8). The quotation foreshadows and explains Jesus' crucifixion with criminals, but Luke omits any reference to the servant's sacrificial death. For Luke, Jesus died an innocent death, as the last of a long line of martyrs, and his martyrdom is a model for his followers (C. H. Talbert 1982:212–213). In contrast to the time when the disciples were sent out without purse or bag or sword, they must now be prepared to share in

Jesus' rejection and suffering for days to come. The mere sight of swords is enough to indicate that the prophecy is fulfilled. This is a part of God's plan (Acts 2:23).

The final references to the kingdom (23:42) and to Jesus' last prayer, by which he commits his spirit to God (23:46a), mark the end of the final section and the body of the gospel. The gospel began with the descent of the Holy Spirit upon Jesus and ends with Jesus' committing his spirit to God. This is the geographical end of the journey to Jerusalem motif.

IX. Conclusion: Jesus' burial, resurrection from the dead, and ascension to heaven (23:46b–24:53)

Theologically, the Jerusalem motif continues as Jesus is buried in a new tomb, appears alive in and near Jerusalem, and ascends to heaven. It ends with the ascension, when Jesus "withdrew from them" (24:51). Thus, the motif ends as it began in 9:31—with a reference to Jesus' departure. In the second volume of Luke's story, the Jerusalem motif continues. The church begins in Jerusalem with the descent of the Holy Spirit upon Jesus' followers. Historically, Jerusalem remained the center of Jewish Christianity until the Romans destroyed it in 70 CE.

For further study of Luke, see W. Manson 1930; E. J. Tinsley 1965; C. Stuhlmueller 1968; F. W. Danker 1976, 1988; E. E. Ellis 1981; I. H. Marshall 1978b; E. Schweizer 1984; D. L. Tiede 1988; H. Moxnes 1988; and especially M. D. Goulder 1989. For Luke and Acts see C. H. Talbert 1970, redaction criticism for theology; 1974, 1978, 1984, literary-theological; 1982, literary-theological commentary on Luke; J. D. G. Dunn 1975, Jesus and Spirit; R. P. Menzies 1991, Spirit in Luke-Acts; H. E. Toedt 1965, Son of Man; A. J. B. Higgins 1980, Son of Man; R. C. Tannehill 1986, unity of Luke-Acts; J. Knight 1998, Luke as narrative; J. B. Green 1997, commentary; J. D. Kingsbury 1997, narrative and social criticism; R. E. Brown 1994, passion narrative, bibliography 1:102–104.

SUMMARY

Luke's work is distinctive in that his story of Jesus in the gospel is followed by a second volume—Acts—on the history of the church. Although perhaps a historian in the ancient sense of the term, Luke, like Mark and Matthew, was primarily a theologian. He wrote the gospel to present Jesus as a bringer of salvation to all peoples as part of God's plan. Theologically, he wrote also to counteract the view that Jesus' going to Jerusalem and his ascension meant that the kingdom of God had already fully come. Within his broad purpose, Luke shows a special interest in minorities, including the poor, outcasts, and women. Other special interests are the influence of the Holy Spirit, Jesus as a type of Elijah/Elisha prophetic figure, and the prayers of Jesus. Jesus' prayers at important times in his life provide a clue to the theological structure of the gospel.

With this chapter we conclude our study of the individual synoptic gospels. In the next chapter, we will consider some of Jesus' parables and miracles as reported in those gospels.

CHAPTER 7

Parables and Miracles of Jesus and Kingdom of God

THE GOSPEL WRITERS PRESENT WHAT Jesus said in two basic ways: short, terse sayings and longer stories, usually called parables. Among the longer narratives in the gospels are the stories of Jesus' miracles. Both the parables and miracles were used by the early church to promote faith and to instruct converts. In this chapter, our main purpose will be to examine certain reported parables and miracles of Jesus to see how the gospel writers used them in their compositions, as well as the kingdom of God as associated with both.

PARABLES

The Greek word usually translated "parable" is *parabolē*. It comes from the verb *paraballō*, "to place beside" or "compare," so a parable is a placing beside or a comparison. In the Septuagint *parabolē* translates the Hebrew word *mashal*, which stems from the verb meaning "to be like." The ideas of comparison, being like, and parable are combined in Mark 4:30 and Luke 13:18. Mark 4:30 reads, "With what can we compare the kingdom of God, or what parable will we use for it?" In Luke 13:18 the words "like" and "compare" are from the same root: "What is the kingdom of God like? And to what should I compare it?" The teller of a parable, then, takes an illustration from everyday life and puts it alongside something less familiar in order to explain the latter.

The Hebrew *mashal* can refer to a variety of verbal figures, including proverbs (1 Sam 24:13; Ezek 18:2–3), riddles (Ps 78:2; Ezek 17:2–3), taunts (Isa 14:4; Ezek 16:44), wisdom sayings (Prov 10:1, 26), allegories (Ezek 17:2–3), and oracles (Num 23:7; 24:3). In the gospels, *parabolē* is also applied to different figures of speech or is given different meanings. In Luke 4:23, for example, the word translated "proverb" in the NRSV is really "parable" (*parabolē*). And in Mark 13:28 (= Matt 24:32; see also Luke 21:29), "from the fig tree learn its lesson," the word "lesson" is literally "parable." Jesus taught about "many things in parables" (Mark 4:2; Matt 13:3; see also Luke 5:36; 6:39; 14:7).

The parable is closely related to three other figures of speech that involve comparison—metaphor, simile, and allegory. Although none of these terms occurs in the gospels, Jesus used the first two figures and probably the third. In all three, similarities are assumed between the things compared, although in reality the things are very different.

Metaphor comes from the Greek *metapherō*, "to carry over" or "transfer," so a metaphor is literally a transference. In a metaphor certain characteristics, qualities, descriptions, or functions are transferred from one of the things being compared to the other. "You are the salt of the earth" (Matt 5:13) is a metaphor meant to teach that Jesus' disciples are to function in some way like salt—provide taste, healing, or cleansing (?) in their communities. They are to serve some useful purpose, although what that purpose is remains unclear. In the metaphoric expression "Beware of the yeast of the Pharisees" (Mark 8:15), the meaning is even more unclear.

Simile comes from the Latin word *similis,* "similar." In a simile the comparison is indicated by the use of *as* or *like*. Sometimes the qualities compared are clear, as in "Be wise as serpents and innocent as doves" (Matt 10:16), sometimes not clear, as in "Whoever does not receive the kingdom of God as a little child will never enter it" (Mark 10:15 = Luke 18:17). What childlike qualities are intended (see Matt 18:3–4)?

Allegory comes from the Greek *allēgoreō,* "to say something other." In an allegory the comparison is made by substituting other images for those in the story itself. In the gospels the parable of the weeds (Matt 13:24–30) is taken as an allegory (Matt 13:37–39): "The one who sows the good seed is the Son of Man; the field is the world, and the good seed are the children of the kingdom; the weeds are the children of the evil one, and the enemy who sowed them is the devil; the harvest is the end of the age, and the reapers are angels." Something is substituted for everything in the story; every detail must be decoded, so to speak. This is exactly what those who tell or write allegories want the hearers or readers to do.

SKETCH OF PARABLE INTERPRETATION

Until the twentieth century the parables of Jesus were usually interpreted allegorically. Then a German scholar, A. Juelicher 1910, first outlined a method for interpreting the parables as parables, not allegories. His work became the foundation on which most parable research has been built. He wrote that the parable is a comparison in which two ideas are placed in parallel, so that the hearer or reader can make a comparison between them. Just one point of comparison between the two places one idea in relationship to the other. For Juelicher, Jesus' parables were vivid, clear pictures from everyday life that could easily be understood. They were instructional in nature and illustrated moral truth.

C. H. Dodd 1961 brought the parables into the discussion of the kingdom of God in Jesus' teaching. In contrast to the form critics, Dodd argued that sometimes we must take a parable from its setting in the church and try to discover its original setting in Jesus' time. He focused on the historical context of the parables as sayings of Jesus and on their eschatological context as proclamations of the kingdom of God. He emphasized Juelicher's point that the parables are vivid pictures from the life of Jesus' time. "At its simplest the parable is a metaphor or simile drawn from nature or common life, arresting the hearer by its vividness or strangeness, and leaving the mind in sufficient doubt about its precise application to tease it into active thought."

J. Jeremias 1963, building on the work of Juelicher and Dodd, rejects the notion of the parables as allegories. Like Dodd, he emphasizes the eschatological context of the parables. But reacting to Dodd's "realized eschatology"—the idea that the kingdom came in its fullness with Jesus' work—Jeremias thinks that the eschatology was still being realized in Jesus' time. From the parables' place in the gospels, Jeremias retraces the stages in the transmission of the parables back to the words of Jesus. Jeremias's main aim, however, is not to interpret the parables themselves, but to recover the genuine words (*ipsissima verba*) of Jesus.

N. Perrin 1976 writes not only that the kingdom of God and the parables are closely related, but also that "the Kingdom of God is the ultimate referent of the parables of Jesus" and that "the whole message of Jesus focuses upon the Kingdom of God, while the parables are today the major source for our knowledge of that message." However, E. Breech 1978 maintains that the approach of Perrin and others is mistaken because it rests "on the assumption that Jesus did proclaim the kingdom." According to Breech, this assumption is not supported by an investigation of Jesus' kingdom sayings.

One approach to the parables has centered on the "language event" because "something decisive happens here through what is said" (E. Linnemann 1966:30–33. Her existential ("what it means to me") approach is that of others also, for example, J. D. Crossan 1973). The interpreter's task is to make that event intelligible and meaningful to those who study the parables. Discussion of the parables, especially in America, has centered on their literary features (A. N. Wilder 1978, 1982; R. W. Funk 1966, 1982; D. O. Via 1967, 1976; N. Perrin 1976). Another approach to the parables is through a method known as structural analysis. It is concerned only with analysis of the linguistic structure of the parables, not with their authenticity as teachings of Jesus, their historical contexts, or their function in the gospels. (For an introduction to structural analysis, see D. Patte 1976a; for the use of this method in the study of parables, see R. W. Funk 1974 and J. D. Crossan 1974.) Some interpreters of the parables have taken a psychological approach. For example, the parable of the unjust judge (Luke 18:1–8) is taken "as a representation of a problem in male psychology" and as "a metaphor of the unrealized self" (D. O. Via

1976:1–32; for responses to Via see articles in the same volume; for a history of parable research, see W. S. Kissinger 1979).

J. R. Donahue 1988 joins study of the parables to the results of redaction criticism. He examines major parables "as texts in context" and tries "to show how the parables simultaneously influence and reflect the major theological motifs of the individual Gospels" (194).

After determining the meaning of parables and their use in the OT and in other Jewish literature that the first Christian writers inherited from Jewish tradition, J. Drury 1989 wants to understand the parables in the contexts of the gospels in which they occur. In contrast to most parable research, Drury revives "the historical interest: not, this time, to search for the historical Jesus, but rather for the structures and specifications to which parables were made in the first century and in the neighborhood of Christianity" (1, 3). In doing so, Drury does not "resort to the hypothesis of Q" but assumes that Luke used Matthew.

TRANSMISSION OF THE PARABLES

Jesus told parables directly to his hearers, who were living in essentially the same setting in Palestine as he was. As some of Jesus' first hearers died, others retold the parables to people living in new and varied settings. Like other forms of Jesus' sayings, the parables were used by early Christians to teach converts. Thus, the parables were subjected to powerful exegetical forces as they were repeated in different situations. As a parable was adapted to an immediate practical and teaching context, even the wording would be altered. Thus, for most parables both the original wording and the context are lost. It is difficult, therefore, if not impossible, to determine the original meanings of such parables. The last stage in the transmission of the parables, of course, was their incorporation into the gospels. Then sometimes the same parables were given different contexts in different gospels, and all were fit into the context of each gospel as a whole.

Now leaf through the *Gospel Parallels* if you have it. Observe that Mark, who includes the fewest parables, concentrates several in chap. 4. Matthew, who includes many more than Mark, does the same thing in chap. 13. Luke, however, distributes the parables as he does other sayings of Jesus. Consider also how each gospel writer uses parables. For example, Matthew uses the parable of the unmerciful servant (M) to illustrate Jesus' teaching on forgiveness that precedes it. It is difficult to tell whether Luke uses the parable of the good Samaritan (L) to illustrate Jesus' response to the lawyer or whether he uses the scene of the lawyer and Jesus as an introduction to the parable. The story of the friend at midnight (L) is placed between the Lord's Prayer (Q) and Jesus' teaching on prayer (Q) in order to teach the effectiveness of persistence in prayer. The parable of the rich fool (L) serves as a setting for Jesus' teaching about earthly things (Q), and Jesus' dinner with a Pharisee is the setting for two parables on invitations to dinner, one from L and the other from Q.

Luke places the parable of the mustard seed (Mark) and the parable of the leaven (Q) in a different context than the ones they have in Mark and Matthew. Luke inserts the parable of the rich man and Lazarus (16:19–31) between Jesus' teachings on divorce (16:16–18) and on temptations to sin (17:1–2). Matthew uses the parable of the lost sheep (18:12–14) after the teachings on temptations to sin (18:6–11), which reflect conditions in his own community (18:15–24). Luke uses the parable of the lost sheep in Jesus' defense after the Pharisees and scribes have accused him of receiving and eating with sinners (15:1–10). Luke uses the parable, then, to show that Jesus, like God, seeks to save sinners.

The gospel writers thus use Jesus' parables in a variety of ways and in various contexts. Notice also that the parables seem to reflect each writer's special interests. Mark adapts his few parables to his theme of the secret of the kingdom of God and the disciples' failure to understand that secret. The parables are to help them understand. Matthew centers the parables around the theme of a coming judgment and around instructions for Christians of his day. The parables in Luke reflect Luke's special interests in the rich and the poor, and four of them (the Samaritan, the rich fool, the rich man and Lazarus, and the Pharisee and the publican) provide examples to be imitated.

As a gospel writer adapted a parable to a particular context, he would naturally alter the wording, which had already been changed in the tradition. In his own vocabulary and style, the writer would give new meaning to the parable in order to suit his own practical and theological needs. So in speaking about "a parable of Jesus," we must remember that the vocabulary, context, and message are, to some degree at least, those of the gospel writer. This is true especially for the interpretations of the parables.

BACKGROUND OF JESUS' PARABLES

The background of Jesus' parables is thoroughly Jewish. The prophets told parables and sometimes acted them out. Isaiah wrote the parable of the vineyard (5:1–6) with its interpretation (5:7). He walked the streets of Jerusalem naked for three years to dramatize parabolically the fates of Egypt and Ethiopia at the hand of Assyria (20:1–6; see also Jer 13:1–14; 18:1–11; 19:1–13). Jotham told a parable (Judg 9:7–15) with an interpretation (9:16–21) unfavorable to the people of Shechem. Perhaps the OT parable most familiar to Jesus' hearers was the one the prophet Nathan told to David, who had arranged the death of Uriah so he could marry his wife (2 Sam 12:1–7):

> [1]And the LORD sent Nathan to David. He came to him, and said to him, "There were two men in a certain city, the one rich and the other poor. [2]The rich man had very many flocks and herds; [3]but the poor man had nothing but one little

ewe lamb, which he had bought. He brought it up, and it grew up with him and with his children; it used to eat of his meager fare, and drink from his cup, and lie in his bosom, and it was like a daughter to him. [4]Now there came a traveler to the rich man, and he was loath to take one of his own flock or herd to prepare for the wayfarer who had come to him, but he took the poor man's lamb, and prepared that for the guest who had come to him." [5]Then David's anger was greatly kindled against the man. He said to Nathan, "As the LORD lives, the man who has done this deserves to die; [6] he shall restore the lamb fourfold, because he did this thing, and because he had no pity."

[7]Nathan said to David, "You are the man!"

David had acted wrongly and the parable is told to reprove David's action. It is a parable of action—a traveler comes, and the rich man steals a lamb and makes a dinner. The images are taken from everyday life. The hearer of the parable—David—responds in anger and realizes that the wrong action should be atoned for. Nathan bluntly interprets the parable for David—"You are the man."

In general Jesus' parables conform to the one by Nathan and are essentially action stories composed of images from everyday life. Jesus directed his parables to those whose attitudes and actions differed from his. Consequently, he told them in response to specific situations and aimed to change the hearers' attitudes and actions. Both Jesus and the gospel writers used the parables to persuade their hearers and readers to see things their way.

The immediate response desired to a controversy parable like Nathan's is self-perception— "He is talking about us." Matthew's comment after the parable of the wicked tenants (21:45; see also Mark 12:12; Luke 12:41; 20:19) expresses this point clearly: "When the chief priests and the Pharisees heard his parables, they realized that he was speaking about them." But unlike David, the hearer in Nathan's parable who repented, the ultimate reaction of Jesus' hearers is rarely stated. When reactions are given, they are failure to understand on the part of the disciples or rejection on the part of Jesus' critics.

These reactions may reflect Jesus' time, but they may also reflect the times of the gospel writers, when the Christian message was not always accepted.

Like Nathan's parable, other OT parables have the narrator's interpretations. This gives us a reason for suspecting that Jesus may sometimes have interpreted his parables. Finally, like Jotham's parable and those of Jeremiah, some of Jesus' parables originated during times of controversy.

The use of parables was especially characteristic of contemporary Judaism, so Jesus' parables are a sign of his Jewishness. B. H. Young 1989 argues that parables were a unique kind of teaching preserved only in the gospels and Rabbinic literature. Jesus used parables to inspire his hearers and convey his message.

By their nature, parables many times are more obscure than clear. In the OT and in contemporary Jewish literature they were equated with riddles (see, for example, Sir 47:15). Only the person devoted to "the study of the law of the Most High" (God) would be able to penetrate "the subtleties" and be "at home with the obscurities of parables" (Sir 39:2–3). "The discerning of parables requires hard work of the mind" (Sir 13:26; from the Greek). We will now look at several of Jesus' parables and try to determine how much of the parable may go back to Jesus, what verses were added in its transmission and why, the original point of the parable, and the meaning in its present context.

ANALYSIS OF PARABLES

The Mustard Seed

The parable of the mustard seed (see Example 7.1; from Greek text) represents one of the main themes of Jesus' parables—biological growth. In Mark and Matthew it is the third of three seed parables, although the second one is different in the two gospels. Mark frames the three with his comments in 4:2—"He began to teach them many things in parables"—and 4:33—"With many such parables he spoke the word to them." Other parables of growth are those of the sower

---

EXAMPLE 7.1   *Parable of the Mustard Seed*

Matt 13:31–32	Mark 4:30–32	Luke 13:18–19
[31]Another *parable* he put before them, saying, "*The kingdom* of heaven is like a grain of mustard which a man took and sowed in his field; [32]it is the *smallest of all the seeds*, but *when* it has *grown* it is the *greatest of the shrubs* and becomes a *tree*, so that *the birds of the air* come and *dwell in its branches*."	[30]And he said, "How may we *compare the kingdom of God*, or what *parable* may we use for *it*? [31]It is like a *grain of mustard, which*, when *sown* upon the ground, is the *smallest of all* the seeds on earth; [32]yet *whenever* it is sown it grows up and *becomes the greatest of all the shrubs*, and puts forth large *branches*, so that *the birds of the air* can *dwell under its* shade."	[18]He said therefore, "What is *the kingdom of God like?* And to what shall I *compare it*? [19]It *is like a grain of mustard which a man took* and threw in his garden; and it *grew and became* for a *tree*, and *the birds of the air dwelt in its branches*."

Cf. *GThom* 20.

(Mark 4:1–9; Matt 13:1–9; Luke 8:4–8), the seed growing secretly (Mark 4:26–29), the weeds (Matt 13:24–30), the leaven (Matt 13:33; Luke 13:20–21), the abundant harvest of the rich fool (Luke 12:13–21), the fig tree (Luke 13:6–9), and three vineyard parables (Mark 12:1–12 = Matt 21:33–46 = Luke 20:9–19; Matt 20:1–16; 21:28–32).

In both Mark and Matthew, the parable of the mustard seed is one of a series, but in Luke it follows the story of Jesus healing the woman with the infirmity. By placing the parable in that position, Luke may have wanted to indicate that from such small beginnings as Jesus' healings the kingdom grows.

The italicized words indicate a maximum of similarities in the Greek text, but there are also many differences, many of which are not evident in translation. Notice that Luke typically puts the present-tense verbs into past tenses. "Compare" is in a different person in Mark and Luke—"we compare" and "I compare." "Sow" is the same verb in Mark and Matthew but is in a different form. Luke literally reads "threw," not "sowed," and has "for a tree" instead of "a tree," as in Matthew. Notice also the differences among "ground" (Mark), "field" (Matthew), and "gar-

den" (Luke). And as usual, there are differences among the introductory statements. The questions and vocabulary make Mark and Luke closer to each other than either is to Matthew.

The similarities between Matthew and Luke, such as "a tree" and "in its branches," may indicate that the parable was preserved in both Mark and Q. It is generally agreed that, because of its unity and brevity, Luke reproduces Q. Matthew's use of the Q words for "grow," "tree," and "in its branches," and of Mark's words for "smallest of all the seeds," "greatest of all the shrubs," and "sow" shows that Matthew conflates Mark and Q. The vast differences among the three accounts indicate how far we are from Jesus' actual words.

Now look at Mark's text. "It is like" is not to be taken literally, because the kingdom is not like a seed but is to be compared with it in the sense that what happens to the mustard seed is what is happening to the kingdom. Mark inserts phrases into his source and then repeats the preceding phrase. The underlined words are probably Mark's insertions. The remaining text is close to that of Q as represented by Luke. There is still a problem with "and becomes," which is also in Q. If Mark inserted the phrases mentioned, then the main point of the parable for him is the contrast between the meager beginnings of the kingdom and the magnitude of its growth. But Mark is also concerned with the stages of growth: "sown upon the ground," "grows," "becomes," and "puts forth large branches."

The words "so that the birds of the air can dwell under its shade" (Mark) are an allusion to one or more OT passages. The last part of Mark 4:32 reads literally, "so that under its shade the birds of the heaven can dwell." The words of Ps 103:12 (LXX) are closest: "By them the birds of the heaven shall dwell." This psalm praises God as Creator, and the "them" is the waters God provides for his creatures. If Jesus (or Mark) was alluding to the psalm, was he saying that when the kingdom grows to its greatest, God will provide for all of his creatures? Such an interpretation fits well with Jesus' teaching on anxiety (Matt 6:25–34) or earthly things (Luke 12:22–31). That teaching ends with the words "Strive for his kingdom, and these things will be given to you as well" (Luke 12:31; see also Matt 6:34). Harmony among all of God's creatures was anticipated for the messianic age (see, for example, Isa 11:1–10).

In Mark's version of this parable there is nothing about the eschatological kingdom of the future. For Mark the seed is the Christian community represented by the kingdom. "Grows up" and "becomes" are verbs indicating present and continuing action, but how the kingdom grows Mark does not say.

Now turn to Matthew to notice some significant differences from Mark. Fortunately, the parable of the weeds, which precedes, and its interpretation, which follows, help us to understand Matthew's version of the parable of the mustard seed. The words "before them" are important. They immediately tie the parable in with the one before it (13:24) and remind us that the setting is the "great crowds" of 13:2—mostly Jews, of course (see also "to them" in 13:10–11, 13). Thus, Matthew begins the parable with his mind on the Jews, and he ends it by thinking of Gentiles.

The words "a man took and sowed in his field" provide a link with a similar expression in 13:24.

From the interpretation of the parable of the weeds, we know that "a man" is Jesus as "the Son of Man" (13:37) and that "the field is the world" (13:38). Matthew's verbs in the past tense, "took and sowed," mean that for Matthew, Jesus has already established the kingdom and that the kingdom is the church. Even though "the ground" and "upon the ground" (Mark 4:31) are favorite expressions of Matthew's (forty-three; Mark, nineteen; Luke, twenty-five), which he often inserts into his sources, he uses "field." This word emphasizes the magnitude of the kingdom and requires the use of the symbolic "tree" from Q. Scholars have different opinions about whether "tree" accurately describes a grown mustard herb. Nevertheless, the point is the parabolic contrast between the proverbial smallness of the mustard seed in Judaism and the seed's ultimate growth.

Now notice that after "sowed" the verbs are in present tense. Jesus brought the kingdom (church) to the world; however, it did not come in a cataclysmic way, as expected by the Jews. Rather, it came through Jesus and had a meager beginning. For Matthew the kingdom was already great—"the greatest of the shrubs"—and it was in the process of becoming greater. It was becoming a tree.

The last lines of Matthew's version are also an allusion to the OT, and the passages usually suggested are Ezek 17:22–23; 31:6; and Dan 4:10–12. There are some parallels between each of these passages and Matt 13:32, but the closest is Ezek 31:6 (LXX). There the prophet is describing Egypt mythologically as a cedar before her fall to Babylonia. Egypt is a great tree above all the trees of the forest: "All the birds of the heaven made nests in its branches . . . and in its shade dwelt all great nations." The Greek word translated "nations" is also the word for Gentiles. Like the mighty empire of ancient Egypt, the kingdom of God (church) is established, and Gentiles as well as Jews belong to it. Moreover, in the eastern Mediterranean world, birds and trees were cosmological symbols (A. J. Wensinck 1921:25–35). So Matthew ends the parable as it began (field = world)—with the worldwide significance of the kingdom of God.

Luke places this kingdom parable with that of the yeast and with all other kingdom sayings after the prayer for the kingdom to come (11:1–2). From elsewhere in the gospel we may get a clue to what the parable of the mustard seed meant for Luke. He especially associates the kingdom of God with Jesus' healings. Only Luke reports that Jesus spoke to the crowds "about the kingdom of God, and healed those who needed to be cured" (9:11; see also 10:9). After the Lord's Prayer, Luke uses the story of Jesus casting out a demon (11:14) and the Q saying "If it is by the finger of God that I cast out the demons, then the kingdom of God has come to you" (11:20). Then, immediately before this parable, Jesus heals the woman thought to be under the power of Satan (13:16). So the parable of the mustard seed, Luke's first on the kingdom, illustrates the coming of the kingdom. This coming is demonstrated in Jesus' healing and in his powers over Satan. Luke does not stress either the growth or the contrast so clear in Mark and Matthew. There is no sowing or growth. A man throws the seed in his garden, and it grows, becomes a tree, and the birds make their nests in its branches. The Jews usually sowed mustard seed around a field, so Luke's "garden" is an adaptation to an urban environment. The whole process seems to have happened all at once. Thus, in Luke this parable illustrates Jesus' saying "It is your Father's good pleasure to give you the kingdom" (12:32). Through Jesus' work, God gave the kingdom, and people of all nations have already entered it.

In the *Gospel of Thomas* (20), the parable of the mustard seed is much condensed. The disciples ask Jesus to tell them "what the kingdom of heaven is like." Jesus replies: "It is like a mustard seed. It is the smallest of all seeds. But when it falls on tilled soil, it produces a great plant and becomes a shelter for birds of the sky" (J. M. Robinson 1988:128). All versions emphasize the smallness of the seed. The main difference is the "tilled soil" in *Thomas*. It may mean that only genuine Gnostics are prepared to receive the seed for growth.

Having examined one parable in detail, we will examine several others of different kinds in less detail.

The Unmerciful Slave

The parable in Example 7.2 (from the Greek) is the conclusion to the fourth major discourse of Jesus in Matthew (17:22b–19:1a) and deals with the church and behavior in it. If you turn back to the beginning of chapter 18, you will see that the main theme is sin. Repentance ("change" is the Greek equivalent of the Hebrew word for "repent") and humility are required for entrance into and prestige in the kingdom (church; 18:1–5). "Little ones" (Matthew's favorite expression for Christians) should overcome temptations to sin in order to avoid hell (18:6–9). That God does not want one of those little ones to perish is illustrated in the parable of the lost sheep (18:10–14). Sins against fellow Christians that cannot be reconciled among the Christians themselves should be reconciled by the church (18:15–20). Then comes Peter's question to Jesus about how often Peter should forgive a brother, with Jesus' reply, "seventy times seven" (18:21–22). All of this provides the context of the parable of the unmerciful slave, as well as clues for understanding it. Although the "therefore," a Matthean expression, connects the parable only loosely with what precedes, this is to be expected, since the original context is lost. However, "brother" in v 35 is a clear tie-in with "brother" in v 21. It seems, then, that Matthew is using the parable to illustrate Jesus' answer to Peter's question, even though the parable does not mention repeated forgiveness.

Most scholars agree that "the kingdom of heaven may be compared to" is a Matthean formula that is not to be taken literally. The same formula is used in two other parables in which Matthew stresses the consequences of a final judgment. Because of their style and because of Matthew's emphasis on a final judgment, vv 34–35 are probably his addition to the version of the parable in his source. (R. H. Gundry 1982: 371–375 makes a strong case for Matthew's

---

EXAMPLE 7.2 *Parable of the Unmerciful Slave*

Matt 18:23–35	Mark	Luke
23"Therefore the kingdom of heaven may be compared to a king who wished to settle accounts with his slaves. 24When he began the reckoning, one was brought to him who owed ten thousand talents; 25and, as he could not pay, his master ordered him to be sold, with his wife and children and all that he had, and to pay. 26So the slave fell on his knees, imploring him, 'Have patience with me, and I will pay you everything.' 27And out of pity for him the master of that slave released him and forgave him the debt. 28But that same slave, as he went out, came upon one of his fellow slaves who owed him a hundred denarii; and seizing him, choked him and said, 'Pay what you owe.' 29So his fellow slave fell down and begged him, 'Have patience with me, and I will pay you.' 30But he refused and went and threw him in prison till he should pay the debt. 31When his fellow slaves saw what had taken place, they were greatly distressed, and they went and told their master all that had taken place. 32Then his master summoned him and said to him, 'You wicked slave! I forgave you all that debt because you begged me; 33and should not you have had mercy on your fellow slave, as I had mercy on you?' 34And in anger his master handed him over to the torturers, till he should pay all that he owed. 35So also my heavenly Father will do to every one of you, if you do not forgive your brother from your heart."		

---

composition of the whole parable.) Without the introductory formula and vv 34–35, the parable is probably close to Jesus' original.

There is no agreement about whether the parable originated in a Jewish or Gentile environment. Of course, if the parable goes back to Jesus, then it would have a Palestinian origin. But some scholars say that only the slave of some king outside Palestine would have been rich enough to owe ten thousand talents (ten million dollars). Others say, however, that in parabolic speech such figures are not meant to be taken literally but to emphasize contrast. There is no evidence in Judaism that a wife as well as her husband and children could be sold to pay a debt (see 2 Kgs 4:1, the only relevant text). Seizing by the neck or choking reflects Roman law (Livy, *Hist. of Rome* 4:53), but there is a reference in the *Mishna* to a creditor seizing a debtor "by the throat" (*Baba Bathra* 10:8). Except, perhaps, in the time of Herod the Great,

Jews in Palestine would not have been turned over to "torturers" for failure to pay a debt. And the central imagery of the parable—debt for sin—would have originated among and have been understood only by Jews. Compare "Forgive us our debts" (Matt 6:12) and "Forgive us our sins" (Luke 11:4).

But what is the teaching of the parable? Let me make some comments and raise some questions for you to think about. No matter what the parable's original teaching and how much of it may go back to Jesus, the word "brother" indicates that Matthew intended the whole parable as instruction for his readers. If the parable originally ended with v 33, then, as is usually stated, the point is that as people have been forgiven, they must forgive. But there is more than that. The words "because you begged me" (v 32) are important. The slave is forgiven because he asks for forgiveness. This echoes other reported teachings of Jesus, for example, "Ask, and it will

EXAMPLE 7.3	*Parable of the Good Samaritan*	
Matt	**Mark**	**Luke 10:29–37**
		[29]But he, wanting to justify himself, said to Jesus, "And who is my neighbor?" [30]Jesus replied, "A certain man was going down from Jerusalem to Jericho, and he fell among robbers, who stripped him, beat him, and went away, leaving him half dead. [31]Now by chance a certain priest was going down that road; and when he saw him he passed by on the other side. [32]So likewise a Levite, when he came to the place and saw him, passed by on the other side. [33]But a certain Samaritan, as he journeyed, came to where he was: and when he saw him, he was filled with pity, [34]and went to him and bound up his wounds, pouring on oil and wine; then he set him on his own beast and brought him to an inn, and took care of him. [35]And the next day he took out two denarii and gave them to the innkeeper, saying, 'Take care of him; and whatever more you spend, I will repay you when I come back.' [36]Who of these three, do you think, was a neighbor to the man who fell among the robbers?" [37]He said, "The one who showed mercy on him." And Jesus said to him, "Go and do likewise."

be given you" (Matt 7:7; Luke 11:9, Q). But here there is more than asking. The word translated as "fell down" could mean "worshiping." The "master" in the slave's words could then refer to Jesus as Lord. The slave's change in attitude and his promise to pay everything change the attitude of the lord (= master) from one of anger to pity (see Zacchaeus's change of attitude and promise to make amends, and Jesus' reply, in Luke 19:8–9).

Do these things indicate that Matthew was telling his readers that in the kingdom of God (church) those who worship Jesus as Lord and ask forgiveness receive forgiveness, and that the experience of such forgiveness brings the obligation to forgive others? Whether Matthew meant the parable to be taken in this way, the point in v 33 remains: those who have been forgiven (by God or others) must forgive. This idea could go back to Jesus, even though Matthew may have composed much of the parable and used it for his own purposes.

If vv 34–35 belong to the parable, then we must deal with an additional theme: that of the slave—forgiven, yet refusing to forgive—being punished for his improper attitude and action to-

ward his fellow servant. Verse 34 is then necessary to complete the point of the whole parable in v 33. The slave's failure to forgive a small debt brings out the sensitivity of his fellow slaves, and their report changes the master's attitude from pity to anger. The person who has received forgiveness must then forgive others or suffer severe, if not eternal, punishment. Does this reflect the Hebrew-Christian conception of God? Does such teaching go back to Jesus or only to Matthew (see 5:22, 29–30; 18:9; 23:15)? Did Jesus share his view of hell with some Jews? Would Jesus' parable have been more or less impressive to his hearers if it had ended with the question in v 33?

The Good Samaritan

Because of what precedes the passage displayed in Example 7.3 (from Greek text), Jesus (according to Luke) is telling the parable to a fellow Jew. In Luke 10:25 Jesus is addressed as teacher, an equal, and not as Lord, a superior, as he is in places where influence from the church is clear. On the other hand, "test" usually signifies controversy between Christians and Jews after

Jesus' time. The parable illustrates Jesus' positive attitude toward a part of Jewish law by showing his radical understanding of what the command to love one's neighbor as oneself really means. Luke uses the parable to answer the question "Who is my neighbor?" The parable illustrates how a true neighbor really acts and provides an example for Christians to imitate. But at the same time it shows Luke's universal interest in Jesus' teaching, and especially his concern for justifying a Christian mission to Samaritans.

In the original context in which the parable was told, the words "but a certain Samaritan" would have shocked any Jew; but because Luke has a special interest in Samaritans, the Samaritan is the one who showed mercy. This is obviously the point of comparison in the parable. It may be that for Jesus, however, the contrast between the Jewish priest and Levite and the Samaritan had two more subtle points. Could the hearers of the parable have failed to observe that the priest and the Levite, representatives of the temple cultus, had not met the challenge to love a fellow human being in a neighborly way? And wouldn't Jews hearing the parable have felt a truer sense of love for their neighbor in realizing that a fellow Jew had accepted the mercy of a Samaritan, with whom Jews had no dealings?

The Unrighteous Manager

The parable in Example 7.4 (from Greek text) of the unrighteous manager is not only the most difficult of Jesus' parables, but also one of the most difficult passages in the NT. There is no final solution to the problems of its unity or its interpretation. Opinions vary widely about where the text of the parable ends. At one extreme, some scholars limit it to vv 1–7; at the other extreme, some include vv 1–13. If we limit it to vv 1–7, the parable lacks a conclusion and a point of comparison. If v 13 is the end of the parable, there are problems of unity and interpretation.

This parable is the second of three in Luke's special section, or journey narrative, dealing with a rich man. The others are the parables of the rich fool (12:13–21) and the rich man and Lazarus (16:19–31). In each instance the rich man is the loser. Now look at the first eight verses of the parable of the unjust or unrighteous manager. The rich man in v 1 becomes the master in vv 5 and 8. But in v 8 is the master still the master of the parable, as some think, or is he Jesus, as others believe? According to one popular interpretation of the parable, the manager is confronted with a crisis brought on by Jesus' preaching of the eschatological coming of the kingdom, and he has to make an immediate decision. The parable, therefore, was not addressed to the disciples (v 1) but to those in the crowds who were not followers of Jesus (J. Jeremias 1963:46–48, followed by N. Perrin 1967:114–115 and D. O. Via 1967:155–162).

The point of the parable is in v 8, but is the emphasis on the master or on the manager? Would Jesus commend an unrighteous person even in a time of crisis? If so, this goes against every teaching of Jesus and of the early church. In Thessalonica some Christians thought the end of the world was coming soon and were living it up, but Paul reminded them that the nearness of the End was no excuse for misconduct (1 Thess 2:10–12; 4:3–12; 5:1–22). Ananias and Sapphira were killed on the spot because they lied about withholding some of the money from the sale of property (Acts 4:32–5:11). And really, would any rich man congratulate a manager who had just swindled him out of so much?

Now look at vv 8b–13. Although it is uncertain what v 8b really means, "the children of light" (see also John 12:36; 1 Thess 5:5; Eph 5:8) probably represent those in or destined for the kingdom of God as opposed to those who are not, "the children of this age." But whatever the meaning, v 8b does not fit with what precedes or follows. In v 9 is "I" the master in the parable or Jesus? Here, as elsewhere, "I tell you" is Luke's favorite way of introducing Jesus' explanation of a parable (see also 11:8; 15:7; 18:14). The words "may welcome you into the eternal dwelling places" (v 9b) may be a tie-in with "may receive me into their houses" (v 4). The point seems to be security in the future as the result of action in the present, but vv 9a and 11

EXAMPLE 7.4		*Parable of the Unrighteous Manager*

Matt	**Mark**	**Luke 16:1–13**
		[1]Jesus said to the disciples, "There was a certain rich man who had a domestic manager, and a complaint was made to him that this man was squandering his possessions. [2]And he called him and said to him, 'What is this that I hear about you? Turn in the account of your management, for you can no longer be manager.' [3]And the manager said to himself, 'What shall I do, since my master is taking the management job away from me? I am not strong enough to dig, and I am ashamed to beg. [4]I have decided what to do, so that people may receive me into their houses when I am put out of the management job. [5]So, summoning his master's debtors one by one, he said to the first, 'How much do you owe my master?' [6]He said, 'A hundred containers of olive oil.' And he said to him, 'Take your bill, sit down quickly, and write fifty.' [7]Then he said to another, 'How much do you owe?' He said, 'A hundred containers of wheat.' He said to him, 'Take your bill, and write eighty.' [8]The master praised the unrighteous manager because he had acted wisely; for the children of this age are wiser in dealing with their own generation than the children of light. [9]And I tell you, make friends for yourselves by means of wealth gotten unjustly, so when it fails they may welcome you into the eternal dwelling places. [10]"The one who is faithful in a very little is faithful also in much; and the one who is unrighteous in a very little is unrighteous also in much. [11]If then you have not been faithful with the wealth gotten unrighteously, who will entrust to you the true riches? [12]And if you have not been faithful in that which is another's, who will give you that which is your own? [13]No household slave can serve two masters; for either he will hate the one and love the other, or he will be devoted to the one and despise the other. You cannot serve God and wealth."
Cf. GThom 47; 2 Clem. 8:5.		

contradict v 13, a saying of Jesus from Q (see Matt 6:24). It has been suggested that everything from 8b on is Luke's attempt—a poor one at that—to explain Jesus' parable in vv 1–8a. Verses 8b–13 may be separate sayings of Jesus from other contexts, used here by Luke for that purpose. Luke used those sayings, which he thought were related to the parable, to exhort his readers and to encourage faith.

Finally, Luke often presents parables of Jesus that use a disreputable character to make a point, but such characters are always placed in contrast to a reputable person. This is true in the parables of the rich man and the poor Lazarus, the unjust judge and the poor widow, and the Pharisee and the publican. Even in the parable of the prodigal son, which immediately precedes that of the unrighteous manager, the two rich boys are contrasted in order to bring out the point of the story. The parable of the unrighteous manager is about two people, both probably disreputable in Luke's mind, but the usual contrast is lacking.

This may indicate that something is missing from the parable. Verses 8–13 may represent the efforts of the tradition and of Luke to supply the missing part.

The gospel writers, then, used parables in different ways—ways that reflect not only the writers' special interests, but also their literary styles, their theological concerns, and the immediate needs of the communities to which they were writing. Parables that may have originated with Jesus, therefore, are ultimately reported in different contexts and with different interpretations in different gospels. This is also true of miracle stories.

Besides works already cited, for further study of the parables, see B. T. D. Smith 1937; J. D. Kingsbury 1969; C. W. F. Smith 1975; C. E. Carlston 1975; M. Boucher 1977; M. A. Tolbert 1979; R. H. Stein 1981; P. Perkins 1981; J. Lambrecht 1981; B. B. Scott 1989; D. Wenham 1989; C. L. Blomberg 1990; R. W. Funk 1974, 1982; C. Westermann 1990.

MIRACLES OF JESUS

In Chapter 2 we learned that the main subject of Jesus' teaching as a whole is the kingdom of God/heaven. It is, therefore, the main subject of Jesus' parables as well. We also learned that, in contrast to Matthew and Luke, Mark is concerned with portraying Jesus as teacher but that he is more interested in reporting miracles of Jesus than teachings. Although Mark reports many fewer parables of Jesus than Matthew and Luke, as with them, he does associate the kingdom of God with Jesus' parables (Mark 4:11, 26, 30; 7:14–21; 12:1–12). Elsewhere in Mark the kingdom of God is associated with teaching of Jesus apart from parables or miracles. It is curious, though, that Mark does not associate the kingdom of God with a miracle of Jesus. This is in marked contrast to Matthew and Luke who do link together the kingdom of God and mighty deeds of Jesus (Matt 8:11–13; 10:7–8; 12:28; [see also Matt 4:23; 9:35]; Luke 8:1–3; 9:1–6, 11; 11:20).

I have just spoken about miracles or mighty deeds of Jesus. But what do we mean by "miracle"? Our word "miracle" comes from the late Latin form *miraculum,* from the verb *miror,* which means to "wonder," "be astonished." So a *miraculum* is "a wonderful thing," "prodigy" or, as we might say, "miracle."

Because modern conceptions of natural phenomena, medicine and healing, death and dying, and psychology differ from related concepts in the ancient world, I shall not attempt to give a definition of miracle. Moreover, the concept of miracle depends upon the presuppositions with which one considers the phenomenon. For example, if one believes or does not believe that things happen that seem to or do (?) run counter to natural occurrences, the results of one's study of miracles may differ accordingly. There might be as many definitions of miracles as there are students in a class. At any rate, no one word in the NT is used for our word "miracle"—no matter how it is conceived—which comes from language later than NT times.

NT writers had essentially five Greek words to use for what we call miracles, each with a unique aspect included in its meaning. The word *thauma,* "marvel," or "wonder," with a concrete meaning, is used several times by Philostratus (see below). It occurs in the NT only two times, both in the abstract sense of the term: "And no wonder!" (2 Cor 11:14) and "I wondered . . . with a great wonder" (Rev 17:6; my trans.). The word *ergon,* "work" or "deed," is the actual deed performed. *Dynamis* includes the "power" or "might" behind the deed. *Teras,* "startling portent" or "extraordinary occurrence," includes the reaction of awe or fright. And *sēmeion,* "sign" or "visible indication" of an unusual happening, includes something that lies beyond or behind the sign itself (for signs see Chapter 14). As with most scholars, I continue to use the word "miracle" in the broadest sense to include all the kinds of phenomena covered by the terms just described.

So, with that said, we turn to some miracle stories in the first three gospels.

Remember that Mark incorporates miracle stories from the tradition into patterns in his gospel, and that Matthew abbreviates the miracle stories from Mark to save space for more teachings of Jesus. Recall also how the gospel writers use miracle stories to illustrate or serve as settings for Jesus' teaching. Although we are not concerned with whether Jesus actually performed miracles or with how to explain them, we will consider how the gospel writers used them to elicit faith in Jesus as Christianity spread from Jews to Gentiles.

The gospel writers and the writer of Acts (see, for example, 2:22) believed that Jesus performed miracles. The gospel writers report three basic types of miracles:

- Healings, including the exorcism of demons—for example, the healing of Peter's mother-in-law (Mark 1:29–31 = Matt 8:14–15 = Luke 4:38–39) and the Gerasene demoniac (Mark 5:1–20 = Matt 8:28–34 = Luke 8:26–39)

- Demonstrations of powers over nature, such as the stilling of the storm (Mark 4:35–41 = Matt 8:23–27 = Luke 8:22–25) and the feeding of the five thousand (Mark 6:30–44 = Matt 14:13–21 = Luke 9:10–17)

- Raising of the dead (resuscitations)—for example, Jairus's daughter (Mark 5:22–24, 35–43 = Matt 9:18–19, 23–26 = Luke 8:41–42, 49–56) and the widow's son at Nain (Luke 7:11–17).

However, the sources of the gospels may not be unanimous in attributing miracles to Jesus. If, as some believe, the story of the centurion's slave is not a part of Q, then Q contains no miracle story. No miracle occurs in both Mark and Q, and M may not contain any miracles, since many scholars regard Matt 9:27–34 and 12:22 as Matthean compositions (so also 14:14; 19:2; 21:14–17).

Because of conflicting evidence, it is impossible to tell how Jesus felt about miracles. Although Q contains no actual miracle stories, Jesus implies that he has done "deeds of power" (Luke 10:13; Matt 11:21), and also in Q Jesus tells the Baptist about his healings, and his raising of the dead (Luke 7:22; Matt 11:4–5). In L

Jesus tells the Pharisees to tell Herod that he casts out demons and performs cures (13:32), and it is reported that Jesus believed his exorcism of demons to be a sign that the kingdom of God was present (see, for example, Mark 3:22–26; Luke 11:19–20; Matt 12:27–28). But in other places Jesus is reported to be indifferent or negative as far as miracles are concerned. When told that, because of his healings, "*Everyone* is searching for you," Jesus replies, "Let us go on to the neighboring towns, so that I may proclaim the message there also; for that is what I came out to do" (Mark 1:37–38; see also Luke 4:42–43). Jesus refuses to perform a miracle when the Pharisees ask for a sign to convince them of his uniqueness (Mark 8:11–12; Matt 12:38–39; 16:1–4). He says that people would not be persuaded to change their ways "if someone rises from the dead" (Luke 16:31).

Although the background and the setting for Jesus' parables are Jewish, most scholars believe that the miracle stories were shaped more by a Hellenistic than by a Jewish milieu. The gospels were written in a world filled with tales of the miracle worker. Josephus writes that exorcism of those possessed by demons was a "very great power among us" and that he saw a fellow countryman free those possessed by demons (*Ant.* 8:2:5). Suetonius (*Vespasian* 7) reports that Vespasian restored sight to a blind man with spit and healed a lame man with a touch (see also Tacitus, *Hist.* 4:81). Between pagan stories of healings and exorcisms and those of the gospels there are three general similarities: the staging of the cure, including a consideration of the nature of the problem; the cure itself, including the technique, such as a special command, gesture, or touch; and a proof that a cure has occurred, including some visible sign or a reaction by witnesses.

Now compare Philostratus's account of Apollonius raising the girl from the dead with Mark's account of Jesus healing Jarius's daughter (Example 7.5; trans. F. C. Conybeare 1912:1:457, 459, 391, 393). The two stories have these common features: a girl, the daughter of a public official; presence of a crowd; weeping and lamentation led by people hired for that purpose (see

---

EXAMPLE 7.5   *Raising of Jairus's Daughter*

Mark 5:35–43	*Life of Apollonius 4:45*
[35]While he was still speaking, some people came from the leader's house to say, "Your daughter is dead. Why trouble the teacher any further?" [36]But overhearing what they said, Jesus said to the leader of the synagogue, "Do not fear, only believe." [37]He allowed no one to follow him except Peter, James, and John, the brother of James. [38]When they came to the house of the leader of the synagogue, he saw a commotion, people weeping and wailing loudly. [39]When he had entered, he said to them, "Why do you make a commotion and weep? The child is not dead but sleeping." [40]And they laughed at him. Then he put them all outside, and took the child's father and mother and those who were with him, and went in where the child was. [41]He took her by the hand and said to her, "Talitha cum," which means, "Little girl, get up!" [42]And immediately the girl got up and began to walk about (she was twelve years of age). At this they were overcome with amazement. [43]He strictly ordered them that no one should know this, and told them to give her something to eat.	A girl had died just in the hour of her marriage, and the bridegroom was following her bier lamenting as was natural his marriage left unfulfilled, and the whole of Rome was mourning with him, for the maiden belonged to a consular family. Apollonius then witnessing their grief, said: "Put down the bier, for I will stay the tears that you are shedding for this maiden." And withal he asked what was her name. The crowd accordingly thought that he was about to deliver such an oration as is commonly delivered as much to grace the funeral as to stir up lamentation; but he did nothing of the kind, but merely touching her and whispering in secret some spell over her, at once woke up the maiden from her seeming death; and the girl spoke out loud, and returned to her father's house, just as Alcestis did when she was brought back to life by Hercules. And the relations of the maiden wanted to present him with the sum of 150,000 sesterces, but he said that he would freely present the money to the young lady by way of a dowry.

"flute players" in Matt 9:23; Josephus, *War* 3:9:5); miracle worker speaks to the crowd; crowd does not understand what is about to happen; miracle worker turns to girl, touches her, and speaks to her; girl gets up and walks away as a sign of her being raised; crowd reacts favorably; miracle worker responds to crowd's reaction; and uncertainty about whether the girl was actually dead. Thus, the stories are remarkably similar. Two obvious differences, however, are Jesus' words about believing and the girl's relatives offering money to Apollonius. Now compare those stories with the ones of Elijah/Elisha raising the dead boy (1 Kgs 17:17–24; 2 Kgs 4:18–37) and of Jesus raising the son of the widow at Nain (Luke 7:11–17).

Below is the story of Apollonius (4:20) casting a demon out of a man. Compare it with the story of the Gerasene (see Figure 7.1) demoniac (Mark 5:1–20; Matt 8:28–34; Luke 8:26–39).

Then Apollonius looked up at him and said: "It is not yourself that perpetrates this insult, but the demon, who drives you on without your knowing it." And in fact the youth was, without knowing it, possessed by a devil; for he would laugh at things that no one else laughed at, and then he would fall to weeping for no reason at all, and he would talk and sing to himself. Now most people thought that it was the boisterous humour of youth which led him into such excesses; but he was really the mouthpiece of a devil, though it only seemed a drunken frolic in which on that occasion he was indulging. Now when Apollonius gazed on him, the ghost in him began to utter cries of fear and rage, such as one hears from people who are being branded or racked; and the ghost swore that he

FIGURE 7.1   *Unusual circular Roman forum in ancient Jerash, perhaps ancient Gerasa.*

would leave the young man alone and never take possession of any man again. But Apollonius addressed him with anger, as a master might a shifty, rascally, and shameless slave and so on, and he ordered him to quit the young man and show by a visible sign that he had done so. "I will throw down yonder statue," said the devil, and pointed to one of the images which were in the king's portico, for there it was that the scene took place. But when the statue began by moving gently, and then fell down, it would defy anyone to describe the hubbub which arose thereat and the way they clapped their hands with wonder. But the young man rubbed his eyes as if he had just woke up, and he looked towards the rays of the sun, and won the consideration of all who now had turned their attention to him; for he no longer showed himself licentious, nor did he stare madly about, but he had returned to his own self, as thoroughly as if he had been treated with drugs; and he gave up his dainty dress and summery garments and the rest of his sybaritic way of life, and he fell in love with the austerity of philosophers, and donned their cloak, and stripping off his old self modelled his life in future upon that of Apollonius.

Notice these common features. Both accounts describe in forceful detail the abnormal behavior of the demoniac. Also in both, people other than the exorcist and the demoniac are present and are aware of the demoniac's situation. The demoniac recognizes the exorcist, and the exorcist talks with the demon at two different times. Both exorcists command the demon to come out of the man. In the Apollonius story, the demon agrees to give a sign that he has left the man. In Mark, Jesus agrees to let the demons go into the pigs, and the drowned pigs are the sign that the man is cured. In both stories, the people acknowledge the man's cure and return to normal life, and each man becomes a devotee of the exorcist. Again, in spite of some differences, the similarities are striking.

FUNCTION OF MIRACLE STORIES IN THE SYNOPTIC GOSPELS

It seems clear that in the oral period stories of Jesus' miracles were adapted to a Hellenistic environment from a Palestinian setting. In Palestine, stories of Jesus' miracles would be concrete evidence for Jews that Jesus was the Messiah. There is no evidence, however, that Jews would deny that people other than the Messiah had miraculous powers. Yet they would hardly regard a person as the Messiah, or even as a prophet (see Mark 6:14–15; Luke 7:15–16; John 7:31), if he did not perform miracles. In the northern part of the Mediterranean world miracle tales would always attract attention, so the miracle story became a main medium for prompting faith in Jesus as the church spread from Jews to Gentiles.

In the synoptic gospels, the words "believe" and "faith" almost always occur in connection with a miracle story. This usage is always true in Mark, and, with the exception of the "woe saying" in Matt 23:23, the same is true for Matthew. In the miracle stories, there are three expressions that originate in Mark or his source: "When he [Jesus] saw their faith" (Mark 2:5), "Your sins are forgiven" (Mark 2:5, 9), and "Your faith has made you well" (Mark 5:34; 10:52). Luke uses the last expression not only in passages based on Mark (8:48; 18:42), but also in material peculiar to him. To the Samaritan leper, the only one of ten healed who returns to thank Jesus, Jesus says (17:19), "Your faith has made you well" (or "saved you," since the same Greek word, *sōzō*, means either "save" or "heal").

Faith, however, is not always associated with the person healed but is sometimes attributed to someone else. In the story of the paralytic, we read that "when Jesus saw *their* faith," he said to the paralytic, "*Your* sins are forgiven" (Mark 2:5 = Matt 9:2 = Luke 5:20; emphasis mine). The conversation between Jesus and the Jews in this story reflects the Jewish view that sickness was the result of sin, so the gift of healing meant also the power to forgive sins. In fact, the healing of the man's paralysis and the forgiveness of his sins were regarded as the same phenomenon. That is why in miracle stories where it occurs, the Greek word *sōzō* may be translated either "heal" or "save." Therefore, Jesus' words to blind Bartimaeus (Mark 10:52) or to the blind man (Luke 18:42) may be rendered either as "Your faith has healed you" or "Your faith has saved you" (lacking in Matt 20:34; see Mark 5:34 = Matt 9:22; Luke 8:48; 17:19).

We will consider just one passage to illustrate the important connection between miracle and faith in the redaction of the gospel tradition. It is the story of the Syrophoenician (Canaanite) woman (Mark 7:24–30; Matt 15:21–28; see Example 7.6). As a whole, this story is of interest because it relates Jesus' dealings with a non-Jewish woman and especially because it shows the change in Jesus' attitude as the dialogue progresses. Each account reveals characteristic features of its author's vocabulary and style. Both compositions also reflect the controversy among early Jewish Christians concerning a mission to Gentiles. This is true even for Mark, but more so for Matthew because of added details. Matthew adds that the disciples begged Jesus to send the woman away and that Jesus refused to respond to her initial plea, as well as the repeated insistence of the woman. These details and the Matthean expression "to the lost sheep of the house of Israel" (see Matt 10:6) reflect a hostile attitude toward a Gentile mission.

Notice that the narrative in Matthew is more advanced theologically than the one in Mark. In addition to Mark's she "bowed down" (see Mark 3:11; 5:22), a sign of utmost respect and sorrow, Matthew has the woman address Jesus as "Lord" three times. Notice also that whereas in Mark Jesus changes his mind toward the woman because of her clever response ("for saying that"), in Matthew Jesus does so because of the woman's great faith.

Mark and Matthew believed they were reporting an actual healing miracle by Jesus. However, both are also concerned with reporting the conversation between Jesus and the woman. Jesus' response is made to serve as instruction concerning a prominent and difficult question in the early church—should there be a mission to the Gentiles? Hence, this miracle story is not transmitted among the more usual reports of miracles (for example, Mark 4:35–5:43 and parallels and Matthew 8–9), but in the context of a controversy between Jesus and the Jews concerning Jewish legal matters (Mark 7:1–23 = Matt 15:1–20).

EXAMPLE 7.6 *Story of the Syrophoenician (Canaanite) Woman*

Matt 15:21–28	Mark 7:24–30	Luke
[21]Jesus left that place and went away to the district of Tyre and Sidon. [22]Just then a Canaanite woman from that region came out and started shouting, "Have mercy on me, Lord, Son of David; my daughter is tormented by a demon." [23]But he did not answer her at all. And his disciples came and urged him, saying, "Send her away, for she keeps shouting after us." [24]He answered, "I was sent only to the lost sheep of the house of Israel." [25]But she came and knelt before him, saying, "Lord, help me." [26]He answered, "It is not fair to take the children's food and throw it to the dogs." [27]She said, "Yes, Lord, yet even the dogs eat the crumbs that fall from their masters' table." [28]Then Jesus answered her, "Woman, great is your faith! Let it be done for you as you wish." And her daughter was healed instantly.	[24]From there he set out and went away to the region of Tyre. He entered a house and did not want anyone to know he was there. Yet he could not escape notice, [25]but a woman whose little daughter had an unclean spirit immediately heard about him, and she came and bowed down at his feet. [26]Now the woman was a Gentile, of Syrophoenician origin. She begged him to cast the demon out of her daughter. [27]He said to her, "Let the children be fed first, for it is not fair to take the children's food and throw it to the dogs." [28]But she answered him, "Sir, even the dogs under the table eat the children's crumbs." [29]Then he said to her, "For saying that, you may go—the demon has left your daughter." [30]So she went home, found the child lying on the bed, and the demon gone.	

Although Mark's narrative reflects the controversy concerning a Gentile mission, Mark is primarily concerned with the healing itself. This is clear from the details in his final verse. On the other hand, Matthew's final verse is abrupt and formal. In Matthew, the whole narrative moves toward the climax in v 28. In both accounts there is a healing, but in Matthew the healing has taken place instantly by the efficacy of the woman's faith.

It appears that in reporting the story about Jesus and the non-Jewish woman, both Mark and Matthew have the question of a Christian mission to Gentiles in mind. Mark wants to show prospective Gentile converts that Jews have priority over them (see "first" in v 27; some scholars see influence here from Paul's thought in Rom 1:16: "to the Jew first and also to the Greek"), but for Matthew Jesus represents a stricter Jewish-Christian viewpoint. For Matthew, Jesus' response to the woman's faith is meant to teach that Gentiles enter the Christian church through faith in Jesus as Lord (see the Q passage in Matt 8:10; Luke 7:9).

SUMMARY

Again, the synoptic writers were not just reporting Jesus' words and deeds in recording parables and miracles. Instead, they were adapting their accounts to meet practical and theological needs as the church grew and spread from Jews to Gentiles. In the synoptic gospels, parables and miracle stories are the most prevalent types of longer narratives. Although we can seek clues to the historical Jesus in both parables and miracle stories, these narratives are more important for studying the special attributes of the gospel writers as authors and for understanding the contexts of the synoptic gospels themselves.

The following articles are very readable and useful for further study, in addition to works already cited: J. D. Kingsbury 1978; J. P. Heil 1979. See also P. J. Achtemeier 1978; H. J. Held 1963. Older books that are still useful include C. J. Wright 1930; A. Richardson 1941; R. H. Fuller 1963; C. F. D. Moule 1965b; H. V. D. Loos 1968; E. Keller 1969; A. Fridrichsen 1972; D. L. Tiede 1972. For more recent works see H. Hendrickx 1987; C. Brown 1984; for differences between pagan magicians and Jesus see J. P. Meier 1994:507–1038; for miracles in the pagan world and the NT see H. C. Kee 1983.

Thus far we have considered the origins and relationships of the first three gospels, the gospel writers as authors, methods and approaches used in the critical study of the NT, the first three gospels individually, and some parables and miracles in the synoptic gospels. Next we turn to Part II of our study—Acts and Paul and his Letters—beginning with the book of Acts in the next chapter.

PART II

Acts and Paul
and His Letters

CHAPTER 8

Acts of the Apostles

IN THE NT, ACTS STANDS BETWEEN THE gospels and the letters of Paul, an early Christian who was very influential in the Christian mission to Gentiles. Acts, then, provides a natural transition from the first three gospels, which deal with Jesus and his teachings, to Paul's letters, which along with Acts, provide information about the development of early Christianity after Jesus' death.

Because Acts is the second of Luke's two volumes on the origin and spread of early Christianity, it might be helpful for you to review the discussion in Chapter 6 about Luke's purposes, his special interests, and date and place of writing. In this chapter we will examine Luke's purposes for writing Acts, as well as the sources and structure of that work. Next we will study Luke's extensive use of speeches and dialogues and the nature of his relationship with Paul. Then we will consider the origin and meaning of the term "Christian," which appears for the first time in the NT in Acts.

The oldest title of Luke's second volume, though not affixed by the author himself, is "acts of apostles." However, Luke is concerned with only two apostles, Peter and James, although he lists eleven (Acts 1:13) and records the selection of a twelfth to take Judas's place (1:15–26). Peter is the center of attention during the first twelve chapters of Acts and is sometimes accompanied by John, who never speaks. Luke reports the death of James but says nothing about the reasons for, or the manner of, that death. After chap. 12 Paul, who was not one of the twelve disciples or apostles, becomes the main character in the narrative of the spread of Christianity to the Gentiles.

Acts is important in NT study for a number of reasons. Significantly, Acts provides the first history of the Christian church. Let me say, though, that if we think of "history" as "a record of events as they actually happened," then Acts is not history, nor is any other NT writing. Acts also introduces the life and work of Paul. But how much Luke really knew about Paul and his thought and the controversy over Gentile Christians is continually debated (see J. A. Fitzmyer 1981:27–29, 47–51).

Set east of the Mediterranean Sea, the first twelve chapters are primarily concerned with the activities of Peter and of early Jewish Christianity as it centers around the temple in Jerusalem. Then, for chaps. 13–28, the setting shifts to lands north of the Mediterranean, including Asia Minor, Greece, and Rome. This final part of Acts conveys Luke's main theme: the spread of Christianity from Jerusalem to Rome and from Jews to Gentiles through the apostles, who are under the guidance of the Holy Spirit. This final part of Acts also presents Paul as the super apostle of Gentile Christianity, which was centered in Antioch, Syria. From there Christianity spread, largely through activities of Jewish synagogues, to key cities on the way to Rome.

PURPOSES OF ACTS

In his gospel, Luke was writing with a historical purpose—"an orderly account of the events that have been fulfilled among us" (1:1). According to the preface of Acts, he believed he had fulfilled that purpose—"In the first book . . . I wrote about all that Jesus did and taught" (1:1). Luke thought the action recorded in Acts had been commissioned by Jesus himself: "You will receive power when the Holy Spirit has come upon you; and you will be my witnesses in Jerusalem, in all Judea and Samaria, and to the ends of the earth" (Acts 1:8). In recording the fulfillment of that commission—and in trying, of course, to enlighten and strengthen his readers' faith—Luke wrote about the Christian church. Beginning with a token group of disciples in Jerusalem, Acts records the Christian movement westward through key cities in the Roman Empire to Rome itself—"the ends of the earth." Although Acts is not a history in the fullest sense of the term, it has expanded our knowledge of early Christianity and the church after Jesus' death.

The commission of Jesus stated in 1:8 becomes the theme of the book: the spread of Christianity from Jerusalem to Rome and from Jews to Gentiles through the apostles, Paul, and others who are under the guidance of the Holy Spirit. As in the gospel, in Acts the writer stresses the influence of the Spirit. In the gospel Jesus begins his public career with a proclamation that "the Spirit of the Lord" is upon him (4:18), and in Acts the history of the church begins with the descent of the Spirit upon Jesus' followers in Jerusalem (2:1–21). Peter (4:8), Stephen (6:5), and others (8:17, 29; 9:17; 10:47; 13:52) are filled with the Spirit. Ananias and Sapphira lie not only to Peter but also to the Holy Spirit (5:3, 9). Filled with the Holy Spirit, Paul strikes Elymas, the magician, blind (13:6–11). The same Spirit forbids Paul to speak the word in Asia (16:6) and does not allow him to go to Bithynia (16:7). The Holy Spirit is responsible for the growth of the church (9:31), and "the Holy Spirit was right in saying" to the Jewish fathers that since they would not respond to the Christian mission, "this salvation of God has been sent to the Gentiles" (28:25–29).

Luke's purposes, therefore, are religious as well as historical. I. H. Marshall 1971 and 1978b has argued that "Luke was primarily an Evangelist or preacher, concerned to lead men to Christian belief on the basis of a reliable record of the historical facts" (1971:9). Acts does reflect local color accurately (H. J. Cadbury 1955), but that does not mean that the history presented is also accurate. Indeed, at least three passages cast doubt about the trustworthiness of Luke as a historian: the date of the census (Luke 2:1–5), the time and number of Paul's visits to Jerusalem compared with Gal 1:15–2:10, and the inverted sequence of the incidents caused by Theudas and Judas the Galilean (Acts 5:36–37).

G. Luedemann 1988, 1989 maintains that "*only for the traditions* that have been reworked in Acts" is Acts "an important source for the history of early Christianity" that goes beyond that in Paul's letters.

In fact, Luke writing more as a preacher and storyteller than as a historian was customary of "historians" of his day, so every detail of Acts is not to be taken literally any more than in the gospels. For example, in Luke 24:50–51 Luke tells a story of Jesus' ascension, and he does so also in Acts 1:9–11. However, in Luke the ascension occurs soon after Jesus' resurrection, but in Acts Jesus appeared among the disciples (apostles) for forty days after his resurrection. If you read the two stories, you will notice other differences. These differences indicate that Luke's purpose was not to convey historical details. Rather, for him the gospel story signifies the end of Jesus' earthly life and work, while the story in Acts marks the beginning of the disciples' ministry about Jesus "to the ends of the earth" (1:8).

The basic scheme of Acts is, nevertheless, corroborated by Paul's letters. Christianity began with a nucleus of Jews in Jerusalem under the leadership of Peter. They continued in close touch with Jews who worshiped in the temple, but they called themselves a "church." From the beginning that group included some Greek-speaking Jews known as Hellenists, who were more liberal in their attitude toward the Jewish law and were eventually persecuted and dispersed. As a result, Christianity spread to Greek-speaking Jews and Gentiles in Antioch and other cities outside Palestine; Paul and others assumed leadership in the churches of these cities.

One of Luke's purposes was to secure for Christianity, as it spread in the Roman Empire, the same status as Judaism. Perhaps that was *collegia licita*, whereby Christians, like Jews, could organize into *collegia* and meet together for the observance of their religion (see Philo, *Embassy to Gaius* 23; Josephus, *Ant.* 14:10:8–12; *War* 6:6:2; H. Conzelmann 1960:137–149). One way he does this is to show that Christianity originated within, and is a continuation of, Judaism, as the following examples indicate. Jesus was a Jew, circumcised according to the law (Luke 2:21), as were Paul and Timothy, leaders in the church. Furthermore, Luke uses many OT passages to show that Jesus' work and the incidents that followed it had been predicted in Jewish scriptures and were being fulfilled. "The God of Abraham, the God of Isaac, and the God of Jacob, the God of our ancestors has glorified his

servant Jesus" (3:13) and raised him from the dead (3:15). In his travels, Paul regularly went into the synagogue first to talk with Jews. He even faced death to reach Jerusalem in time for Pentecost (20:16; 21:7–15), and while there he observed a strict Jewish vow in order to prove the falseness of the charges that he had taught Jews living among Gentiles not to circumcise their children or to observe Jewish customs (21:17–26). And Gamaliel, the famous Jewish teacher, advised his fellow Jews to stop attacking the Christians (5:33–39).

To further his purpose of winning Rome's recognition of Christianity as an approved religion, Luke stresses the Jews' responsibility for Jesus' death and the innocence of the Roman Pilate (Luke 23:4, 22; Acts 3:13–15; 13:26–28). Luke also is unique in that he portrays Herod Antipas as innocent of responsibility for Jesus' death by sending Jesus back to Pilate (Luke 23:6–17). Pilate also escapes responsibility for Jesus' death by handing him over to the Jews as they wished (Acts 23:18–25). Similarly, when Jews were responsible for Paul's arrest, Roman officials regularly released him: the magistrates at Philippi (16:19–39), Gallio at Corinth (18:12–17), and Felix and Festus in Jerusalem (23:26). Before Festus, Paul confesses complete innocence: "I have in no way committed an offense against the law of the Jews, or against the temple, or against the emperor" (25:8). Agrippa and Festus agree that Paul "could have been set free if he had not appealed to the emperor" (26:30–32).

Finally, Luke shows that not only did Roman officials favor Paul, but Roman officials and people of social standing became members of the new sect. Cornelius, the centurion at Caesarea, was the first Gentile convert. At Cyprus "the proconsul, Sergius Paulus, an intelligent man . . . believed . . . for he was astonished at the teaching about the Lord" (13:7–12). At Beroea "not a few Greek women and men of high standing" believed (17:12). At Athens Dionysius the Areopagite, probably a wealthy person, joined Paul and believed (17:34).

Another purpose for writing becomes clear in Acts. From several of Paul's letters, particularly

Galatians (all written before Luke-Acts), we learn that there was dissension between the leaders of Jewish Christianity at Jerusalem and Paul and other leaders of Gentile Christianity at Antioch and elsewhere. Some of the conservative leaders of the church in Jerusalem, including Peter and James, believed that Gentiles who wanted to become Christians should first become Jews by being circumcised and obeying some Mosaic law. Paul wrote Galatians specifically to refute that position, and in his refutation he reveals considerable hostility between himself and those in Jerusalem. According to Paul, people become Christians by faith in Christ, not by circumcision and works of the law. Luke wrote to mitigate or reconcile the two factions, the Jewish faction in Jerusalem and the Gentile faction represented by Paul and his companions.

The question about Gentiles becoming Christians arises several times in Acts, especially in chaps. 11, 15, and 21. Each time the problem is settled without harsh feelings. Luke portrays the spread of Christianity from Jews to Gentiles as harmonious and free of the controversy that, according to some of Paul's letters, was a part of that development. To report such a harmonious development, then, was one of Luke's purposes.

SOURCES OF ACTS

The first two verses of the preface to Luke indicate that the writer used sources: "Many have undertaken to set down an orderly account." We have identified some of the sources Luke used for his gospel and how he used them. It would have been natural for him also to use sources in writing Acts, but we cannot be certain which sources he used or how he used them. (On the question of sources, see R. H. Fuller 1966:123–126; C. S. C. Williams 1957:7–13; W. Neil 1981:22–25; E. Haenchen 1971:81–90; C. H. H. Scobie 1979; H. Conzelmann 1987: xxxvi–xl.) However, since Luke gives so much space to Paul's travel from city to city, we may assume that he had a source for those travels. With that assumption in mind, turn to Acts 14:1–20.

Paul and Barnabas had to flee Iconium because Gentiles and Jews wanted to stone them. They "fled to Lystra and Derbe . . . and to the surrounding country; and there they continued proclaiming the good news" (vv 6–7). Then comes the interesting story of Paul and Barnabas at Lystra (vv 8–19). They do not actually get to Derbe until after Paul has been stoned at Lystra (v 20). Thus, it looks as though Luke supplemented the travel source dealing with Lystra and Derbe with the story of Lystra, which he inserts between vv 7 and 20 of the travel source.

If you follow Paul's journeys in Acts and on the map (see back endsheet), you will see that Paul usually visits a city several times. But typically, as in the case of Lystra, Luke reports stories about Paul in a city only once, usually during his first visit. It is possible, of course, that the events took place during these first visits as reported in Acts, but it is unlikely that stories connected with only one of Paul's visits to a city would have survived. Thus it seems that, in addition to a travel source, Luke had access to anecdotes about Paul and his travels, and that he consistently inserted these anecdotes into the travel source in connection with Paul's first visit to a city (see M. Dibelius 1956:5–25).

Within the travel source there are peculiar passages known as "we sections" because in them the author suddenly shifts from "they," "he," or "them" to "we" and "us" (16:10–18; 20:5–16; 21:1–18; 27:1–28:16). Look at 16:9–10, for example: "During the night *Paul* had a vision. . . . When *he* had seen the vision, *we* immediately tried to cross over to Macedonia, being convinced that God had called *us* to proclaim the good news to them" (emphasis mine). It is generally agreed that these sections come from the diary of one of Paul's companions, but there is no agreement about whose diary it was. Four main explanations have been given: (1) the "we sections" came from Luke himself, who traveled with Paul—this is the traditional view; (2) Luke got them from the diary of one of Paul's companions; (3) Luke invented them to give credibility to his work; and (4) they have nothing to do with any source of Luke but are due to a literary technique often found in the ancient Mediterranean world (V. K. Robbins 1975, 1978; J. A. Fitzmyer 1989:16–22, however, finds the evidence of Robbins from ancient literature unconvincing). The third explanation is least popular.

Beyond what we have said about sources of Acts, the matter gets very complicated. Some scholars suggest a Jerusalem or Palestinian source for passages like 1:6–2:40; 3:1–4:31; 5:17–42; and 12:1–23. Others suggest an Antiochene source for 6:1–6; 6:8–8:4; 11:19–30; and 15:3–33. Still others think that, except for the "we sections," 9:1–30; 13:3–14:28; and 15:35–28:31 came from Paul. There is no consensus, however, about what sources Luke used for Acts or whether he used sources at all. Most scholars seem to agree that if he did use sources, he imposed upon them his own vocabulary and style. One feature of Luke's style in Acts is his frequent use of speeches.

In Chapter 3 we learned about the *kērygma* as a clue to understanding Jesus, the gospels, and early Christianity with a quotation from Acts 2:14–36. Review what is said there in order to help you understand the speeches in Acts.

THE SPEECHES IN ACTS

It was customary for ancient historical writers to embellish their works with speeches of the characters involved. Although one writer might follow another's work rather closely, he always reworked it into his own style and composed the speeches himself. Thus we sometimes find different speeches on the lips of the same character in two different writers who otherwise are very close in what they say about that character. For example, Tacitus (*Hist.* 2:47) and Plutarch (*Otho* 15), who wrote at about the same time as Luke, closely agree in their biographies of Otho (Roman emperor, 69 CE) but give quite different accounts of his last speech. Even Josephus, who in his two major works often writes more than once about the same subject, puts two different speeches on Herod's lips (see *War* 1:19:4; *Ant.* 15:5:3). Similarly, Luke has Paul speak in his own

defense on two occasions, the first on the steps of the barracks in Jerusalem (22:1, 3–21), the second before Agrippa (26:2–23). As you read those speeches notice how Luke has varied what Paul says about himself as a Jew, about his experience on the road to Damascus (see 9:1–30), and about his persecution of Christians.

Speeches, then, an inherent part of ancient history writing, make a narrative vivid and dramatic; they are meant to be editorial comment that reveals the author's viewpoint, not part of historical tradition. Speeches comprise about a third of the history by Dionysius of Halicarnassus and a fifth of that by Thucydides. Similarly, about a third of Acts is speeches and dialogues. Although some scholars emphasize the historical aspect of the speeches more than others do, most agree that they are Lukan compositions. According to W. S. Kurz 1980, Luke argues "from premise to conclusion to prove . . . that Jesus is the Christ" according to the rules of Hellenistic rhetoric (the art of speaking). For example, "the Christ must suffer and rise [premise] and that (therefore) Jesus is the Christ [conclusion]." Through the speeches Luke gives meaning to the events being addressed. The speeches add intellectual and religious content to the narrative and give it vigor and depth. Acts without speeches would be like gospels without sayings of Jesus.

Peter has eight speeches in Acts, including one to his fellow disciples about the choice of Judas's successor (1:16–22), one to the crowd at Pentecost (2:14–36), one to the Sanhedrin (4:8–12), one to Cornelius and others (10:34–43), and one before the conference at Jerusalem (15:7–11). Not counting Paul's final speech to the Jews in Rome (28:17–20, 25–28), there are also eight speeches by Paul. Did Luke want to give equal speaking time to Peter and Paul? Paul's speeches include one to those in the synagogue at Antioch of Pisidia (13:16–41), one to the "Athenians" on the Areopagus (17:22–31), one to the elders of Ephesus (20:18–35), and those in his defense before the Jews in Jerusalem (22:1, 3–21), before Felix (24:10–21), and before Agrippa (26:2–23). Besides these there is Stephen's long speech before his martyrdom

(7:2–53) and two by James, one to the conference at Jerusalem (15:14–21) and one with the elders to advise Paul in Jerusalem (21:20–25).

People who are not Christians also speak in Acts. Gamaliel advises the Sanhedrin (5:35–39). The town clerk at Ephesus speaks to dismiss the crowd (19:35–40). Tertullus accuses Paul before Felix (24:2–8), and Festus summarizes Paul's case before Agrippa (25:14–21, 24–27). In addition to the speeches there are many dialogues, including that of Peter with Ananias and Sapphira (5:1–11), and Peter with Simon the magician (8:19–24).

For several reasons the speeches are usually thought to have been composed by Luke. The vocabulary and style are the same, no matter who is speaking; this is true for much of the form and the content as well. Compare, for example, Peter's speech at Pentecost (2:14–36) with Paul's speech in the synagogue at Antioch in Pisidia (13:16–41) and notice these common features in form and content: address to the crowd, "Men of . . ." (2:14, 22; 13:16) and "Men, brothers" (Greek; 2:29; 13:26); reference to scripture (2:16–21; 13:17–22); Jesus came as part of God's plan (2:22–23; 13:23–25); Jews responsible for Jesus' death (2:23; 13:27–29); God raised Jesus (2:31–33; 13:30–35); Ps 16:10 quoted with reference to Jesus (2:31; 13:35–36); and Jesus brings forgiveness (2:38; 13:38). There are exceptions, of course, necessitated by different circumstances and audiences, but generally the pattern of the speeches is the same in all of them, including literary style, form, and content. Part of the pattern is that there are three long speeches, five short ones, and then three long ones.

Now turn to Stephen's speech and notice that the story continues naturally from 6:15 and 7:55–60, and that the content of the speech has little to do with Stephen's martyrdom. The speech seems to be an insertion and was probably composed by Luke from passages in the Septuagint. The Septuagint (LXX), remember, is the OT in Greek and was used by Greek-speaking or Hellenistic Jews. Stephen's speech, then, reflects Christianity's movement from its beginning in Judaism to Hellenistic Judaism, as

well as the extreme hostility that was part of the process. It also sets the stage for Christianity's movement to Gentiles.

According to Acts, after Stephen's death, a Samaritan mission, and Paul's conversion (8–9), Cornelius becomes the first Gentile convert. Peter says in his speech at the time that God has approved a Gentile mission: "God shows no partiality, but in every nation anyone who fears him and does what is right is acceptable to him" (10:34–35). After Paul's speech in the synagogue at Antioch of Pisidia, "many Jews and devout converts to Judaism followed Paul and Barnabas," and "the next sabbath almost the whole city" came to hear them (13:16–43).

Next is Paul's speech at Athens (17:22–31). As the center of Greek philosophy, piety, wisdom, and religion, Athens typified the Hellenistic world. For Luke, though, Athens was symbolic of the confrontation between Christianity and Hellenism, and Paul's speech was meant to show that Christianity met the challenge.

On the steps of the Roman barracks in Jerusalem (22:3–21) Paul makes a "defense" (22:1). The Jews have accused him of bringing "Greeks [Gentiles] into the temple" and defiling "this holy place" (21:28). Paul really doesn't say a word in his defense, but rather explains his call to go to the Gentiles and says that it came to him in the temple (22:17–21). From the temple, God has sent Paul to preach to Gentiles, whose God he is also to be.

Finally, Paul's speech to Jews in Rome (28:17–20, 25–28) brings the second volume of Luke to a close on the same theme with which the first one began: Because the Jews rejected Jesus, Christians took their message to Gentiles. Remember that Luke places Jesus' rejection by his own people at Nazareth early in the gospel, in order to justify Jesus' preaching to non-Jews. And recall that only Luke continues the quotation from Isaiah to include the statement "All flesh shall see the salvation of God" (Luke 3:6). Luke has used the speeches in Acts as an important literary device in developing that theme. At the same time, the content of the speeches indicates what Luke, an intelligent Christian of the generation after the apostles, believed was the message preached by followers of Jesus as the church spread from Jews to Gentiles. (For the speeches in Acts, see H. J. Cadbury 1958:184–190; F. Veltman 1978; E. Schweizer 1980; W. Neil 1981:38–45; H. Conzelmann 1987:xliii–xlv.) For sources see C. H. H. Scobie 1979; for all points mentioned see especially J. A. Fitzmyer 1998.

LUKE AND PAUL

Of all the characters involved in the history of early Christianity, Paul is the one for whom Luke has a special fondness. Even Peter, to whom Luke devotes a lot of space, comes out second to Paul. Although Paul may have been a special hero for Luke, Paul must actually have been a man of unusual authority in the early church. Were that not true, Paul's letters would not be the oldest extant Christian writings. Recently, though, M. Goulder 1994 has uniquely argued that there never was one united church, even from earliest times. Instead, there was a mission in Jerusalem managed by Peter and James. At the same time, there was a mission by Paul conducted from various other cities and existed with that of Peter and James from the beginning. It was the mission of Paul that determined the writings of the NT. Therefore, the NT "is historically misleading" with respect to the importance of Peter's mission.

But did Luke actually know Paul, the authoritative person in the church? Several different answers to this question have been suggested. No real evidence exists that Luke ever read any of Paul's letters, but some people think Luke was familiar with one or more of them (see E. E. Ellis 1981:37–38, 51; J. Knox 1980). M. D. Goulder 1989:129–146 maintains that Luke knew at least 1 Thessalonians and 1 Corinthians. Others think that Luke knew Paul as a person because of ancient tradition that identified Luke as the companion of Paul and the one responsible for the "we sections." But the "we sections" nowhere name Luke as Paul's companion; therefore, some have argued that they came from the diary of someone other than Luke and that Luke inserted

them as a source, unchanged. Or perhaps Luke added the "we sections" to make it appear that he was an eyewitness of at least some of what he was narrating. If Luke were responsible for the "we sections," he would have been with Paul only for a short time and not when most of Paul's letters were written.

Three passages in letters from, or purporting to be from, Paul imply that Paul knew Luke: Col 4:14; 2 Tim 4:11; Phlm 24. However, many scholars no longer regard Colossians and 2 Timothy as authentic letters of Paul. But even if these passages are accepted as Pauline, there are several good reasons for believing that Luke did not know Paul, or certainly not very well. Luke says almost nothing about the important personal side of Paul's life—for example, Paul's stay in Arabia after his conversion (Gal 1:15–17; see also Acts 9). Acts portrays Paul as a persuasive public speaker before a variety of audiences—Jews (see, for example, 13:16–41; 22:1–21), Gentiles (14:15–17; 17:22–31), Roman officials (13:9–11; 24:10–21; 26:2–26), and philosophers (17:22–31)—and Paul always knows what to say. But Paul writes that, according to the Corinthians, "his [Paul's] bodily presence is weak, and his speech contemptible" (2 Cor 10:10).

Paul suffered countless beatings, many imprisonments, and other personal hardships (2 Cor 11:23–28; see also 4:7–12; 6:4–10; 1 Cor 4:9–13), and he experienced such trouble in Asia that he "despaired of life itself" (2 Cor 1:8; see also 2 Cor 7:5). But Luke does not mention any of this. Paul's statement that "the signs of a true apostle were performed among you . . . signs and wonders and mighty works" (2 Cor 12:12) probably refers to some kind of miraculous works as evidence of Paul's apostleship. Apparently Paul felt it necessary to make such a claim because his opponents had questioned that aspect of his authority (2 Cor 12:11), but it is the only reference to miracles of any kind in all of his letters. On the other hand, Acts portrays Paul as a fabulous miracle worker. Negatively, he blinds Elymas, the magician (13:8–12). Positively, he enables the cripple at Lystra to walk (14:8–10), rises from his own (seeming) death (14:19–20), and restores life to the young man Eutychus, who has dropped from the third story after falling asleep while listening to Paul speak (20:7–12). Even his handkerchief has such miraculous power that those who touch it are healed or cleansed of evil spirits (19:11–12). Little wonder that a viper's venom leaves him unharmed (28:3–6). Paul never refers to such miraculous feats either in defense of himself or in appealing to converts.

Perhaps the most important reason for questioning Luke's friendship with Paul is the account of Paul's religious experience on the way to Damascus. Given in three places (Acts 9:1–19; 22:6–16; 26:12–18), the details are different and contradictory. In each account there is a light and a voice, but not a word about Paul seeing the Lord or the Lord appearing to Paul. According to Paul, however, seeing the Lord is the one thing he feels is important. To the Corinthians he writes: "Have I not seen Jesus our Lord?" (1 Cor 9:1) and "Last of all . . . he [Jesus] appeared also to me" (1 Cor 15:8; see also Gal 1:11–12, 15–16; 2 Cor 12:1–5). It seems unlikely that if Luke knew Paul, he would fail to emphasize what for Paul is the only point worth stressing. For the relationship between Luke and Paul, see E. Haenchen 1971:112–116; J. A. Fitzmyer 1981:27–29, 47–51; W. Neil 1981:28–34; M. D. Goulder 1989:129–146; J. C. Lentz 1993; R. I. Pervo 1990; M. E. Rosenblatt 1995.

Recently J. D. Crossan 1998, using archaeological discoveries and literary and social-science criticism, attempts to throw new light on the decades after Jesus' death. As with his study of the gospels, Crossan finds early traditions in some apocryphal works.

We shall raise the question of the relationship between Luke and Paul again in our study of Galatians in Chapter 11 (see now Figures 11.1 and 11.2).

ORIGIN AND MEANING OF THE TERM "CHRISTIAN"

In Acts we discover the word "Christian" for the first time, and two of its three occurrences in the NT are in Acts (11:26; 26:28). Although the NT is a collection of Christian literature, the term "Christian" was just coming into use when some of the latest works were written. Apparently both Paul and the gospel writers were unaware of the word or purposely avoided using it. Luke reports that in Antioch "the disciples were first called 'Christians'" (11:26) and that Agrippa says to Paul, "Are you so quickly persuading me to become a Christian?" (26:28). Thus Luke attaches some significance to the term, but exactly what significance is uncertain. In 1 Pet 4:14–16 the word "Christian" is a term of reproach used during a time of persecution: "If you are reviled for the name of Christ, you are blessed. . . . Yet if any of you suffers as a Christian, do not consider it a disgrace, but glorify God because you bear this name." This passage implies that Christians were persecuted simply because they bore that name.

The writers of the NT did not refer to their readers as Christians, nor did Christians generally use the term in reference to themselves before the second century. Instead, they used a variety of terms, including "saints" (2 Cor 1:1; Rom 12:13; Acts 9:13, 32), "brothers" (1 Cor 1:10; Rom 1:13; Acts 1:16), "the believers" (Acts 10:45), "the Way" (Acts 9:2; 19:9, 23), "disciples" (often in gospels; Acts 6:1–2; 11:26), "the elect" (Mark 13:20; Matt 24:24; Rom 8:33), and "the church" (often in Paul; Acts 5:11; 8:3). Ignatius, an early bishop of Antioch, writes as though followers of Jesus accepted the name Christians and were using it among themselves. In his letter to the Romans, as he faces martyrdom (c. 112 CE), he asks them to pray that he "may not only be called a Christian but also be found to be one" (*To the Romans* 3:2).

Because the term "Christian" occurs so rarely in the NT, and because early followers of Jesus refer to themselves by other names, such as "saints" and "brothers," we must look elsewhere than to the Christians themselves for the origin of the term. The word "Christ" (*christos*) is the equivalent of the Hebrew word *messiah*, meaning "anointed one," and the Greek ending *ianos* means "followers of" or "partisans of." Since non-Christian Jews rejected Jesus as the Messiah, it is unlikely that they, even in irony, would have called followers of Jesus partisans of or followers of the Messiah, that is, Christians. According to

Acts, Jews referred to followers of Jesus as "the sect of the Nazarenes" (24:5) and "this sect" (28:22). The word "sect" is the same one Josephus uses when describing the Pharisees and other Jewish groups, so Acts 24:5 and 28:22 designate followers of Jesus as a Jewish group.

Tacitus, writing about Nero accusing Christians in order to dispel the rumor that he had set fire to Rome, says, "Nero falsely accused those . . . whom, hated for their shameful deeds, the people called Christians" (*Annals* 15:44:2). Tacitus may have learned the word "Christian" from the common people who associated it with the proper name Christ. In writing about Claudius expelling Jews from Rome, Suetonius says that "the Christians, a class of men of a new and evil superstition, were put to death" (*Nero* 16).

Now we can return to Agrippa's sarcastic use of the term "Christian" in Acts 26:28. Agrippa spent much of his life in Rome; and if Luke reports Agrippa's own words, Agrippa may have learned the word "Christian" there. But if Luke puts the words in Agrippa's mouth, then Luke was familiar with the derogatory use of the term that is reflected in the Roman writers Tacitus and Suetonius.

It seems, then, that the term "Christian" did not originate among Jews or Christians but among pagans either in Rome or Antioch. If current in Rome in Nero's time, it must have originated rather early. But if first applied to disciples of Jesus at Antioch, as Luke says, it may have been coined by Roman officials to distinguish the Christian group or new sect from Judaism, which was an approved religion in the Roman Empire. Or perhaps, as some believe, the word "Christian" was used to designate the Christian movement as hostile toward Agrippa, to whom Rome gave a kingdom around the sea of Galilee after c. 50 CE. At any rate, it was probably first used as a term of scorn, ridicule, or disdain, no matter when or where it originated.

At this point I want to suggest something further with respect to the origin of the term "Christian." I believe that Paul's conception of the phenomenon "in Christ" and "Christ in," as he taught it to his converts (see Chapter 9), gave rise to the designation "Christian." We learn especially from Romans 6 that after baptism converts were no longer to sin, not even so that God's grace might become effective (Rom 6:1–2). Immersion in water during baptism signifies the forgiveness of sins; and from the water, according to Paul, baptized persons rise to newness of life. They are no longer "slaves to impurity" but become "slaves to righteousness" (6:19; see all of Romans 6).

Paul also writes to the Roman converts that there is "no condemnation for those who are in Christ Jesus" (Rom 8:1). Such persons live "not according to the flesh but according to the Spirit" and "set their minds on the things of the Spirit" (Rom 8:4–5). If converts live according to the flesh, they "will die," but if by the Spirit they "put to death the deeds of the body," they "will live" (Rom 8:13). Paul writes to the Corinthians: "Come to a sober and right mind, and sin no more" (1 Cor 15:34). Of course, Paul wrote as he did because he believed that all would be repaid "according to each one's deeds," those who patiently do good will receive eternal life, but for those who do evil "there will be anguish and distress" (Rom 2:6–9; see also 2 Cor 5:10; Rom 14:10–12).

As with Paul (see Gal 2:20; Rom 9:1; 15:17), converts, after baptism, lived in a spiritual/moral relationship with the risen Jesus. They became partisans of the spiritual Christ for moral life. Because the idea of moral life became associated with the term "Christian," and because Christians took pride in the fact, "Christian" became a word of scorn on the lips of unbelievers. The only evidence for my view in the NT is the passage from 1 Pet 4:12–19, part of which was quoted above. It is the only place where the designation is given some characterization. The writer exhorts his readers to rejoice as they share in the fellowship of Christ's sufferings. If they are reviled for Christ's name, they are blessed because "the Spirit of God" rests on them. Then the writer continues: "But let none of you suffer as a murderer, a thief, a criminal, or even as a mischief maker. Yet if any of you suffers as a Christian, do not consider it a disgrace, but glorify God because you bear this name" (1 Pet 4:15–16).

Here Christian is placed in antithesis to immoral persons. This seems to me sufficient evidence that the term bore with it the stamp of moral character. The rest of 1 Pet 4:12–19 helps to confirm my suggestion. As I said, in Paul's time followers of the Jesus movement did not yet use the designation "Christian" to refer to themselves. But Paul, we can be sure, was largely responsible for having morality come to be associated with the designation.

Further evidence for my view is what Pliny says about the Christians in his letter to Emperor Trajan quoted in the Introduction. I quote it again:

> They were accustomed to meeting on a fixed day . . . and to singing in alternate verses a hymn to Christ as to a god, and bound themselves by a solemn oath not to do any wicked deeds, never to commit any fraud, theft, or adultery, never to falsify their word, nor break a

promise, nor deny a trust when called upon to make it good.

THE STRUCTURE OF ACTS

Remember that Acts is the second volume of a two-volume work, Luke-Acts. The basic thought-structure of the two volumes becomes clear from the partial outline displayed in Figure 8.1.

Although there is general agreement that Acts divides naturally into two rather distinct parts, not all agree about where the division occurs. Earlier scholars placed the division after 15:35, but recent scholars put the division at the end of chap. 12. This makes sense, since in the first part Peter is the main character, whereas in the second it is Paul. Yet this division is not wholly satisfactory, because Paul's vision comes in chap. 9, where Peter is central; and the conference at Jerusalem, in which Peter is prominent, comes in the second part, where Paul is central. This problem is alleviated by placing the division at the

---

F I G U R E 8 . 1   *Basic Thought-Structure of Luke and Acts*

Luke	Acts
Jesus is conceived by the Holy Spirit	The Holy Spirit comes upon the church
Holy Spirit descends upon Jesus at his baptism	The church is baptized with the Holy Spirit
"All flesh shall see the salvation of God"	"Men from every nation under heaven" experience the Spirit
Jesus is rejected by his own people	Jews challenge and are hostile to apostolic preaching
Jesus goes to the Gentiles through mission of the seventy	Mission to the Gentiles by Peter, Paul, and others
Jesus works miracles	Apostles duplicate Jesus' miracles
Jesus "set his face to go to Jerusalem"	Paul "must also see Rome"
"It is impossible for a prophet to be killed outside of Jerusalem"	Paul "must bear witness also in Rome"
The risen Jesus reminds the disciples that everything written about him in the law of Moses, the prophets, and the psalms had to be fulfilled	Paul testifies and tries to convince the Jews in Rome about Jesus, both from the law of Moses and the prophets
Jesus has overcome apparent defeat by the Jews	Paul preaches and teaches about Jesus "with all boldness and without hindrance"

end of chap. 9. The first part, then, deals with "The Mission in Palestine" and the second with "The Mission to the End of the Earth" (R. J. Dillon 1968:2:167–168; M. D. Goulder 1964 notes fourfold divisions in Acts).

The theme of Acts is the spread of Christianity from Jerusalem to Rome and from Jews to Gentiles through the apostles, who are under the guidance of the Holy Spirit. With that theme, the book divides naturally into six parts, with a summary after each part: (1) Christianity in Jerusalem and the work of Peter (1:1–6:7); (2) diffusion of Christianity in Judea, Galilee, and Samaria (6:8–9:31); (3) expansion of Christianity from Judea to Antioch in Syria (9:32–12:24); (4) diffusion of Christianity through Asia Minor (12:25–16:5); (5) advance of Christianity to Europe (16:6–19:20); and (6) establishment of Christianity in Rome (19:21–28:31). This is the basic structure of the outline and comments that follow.

Outline and Comments

I. *Christianity in Jerusalem and the work of Peter (1:1–6:7)*
  A. *The risen Jesus and his disciples (1:1–11)*
  B. *Replacement of Judas (1:12–26)*

The number twelve was symbolic of the church as the new Israel, so that number had to be restored. The eleven pray before the choice is made, as Jesus prayed in Luke (6:12) before he chose the twelve.

  C. *Pentecost: the descent of the Spirit (2:1–13)*

In 1:5 Luke described the coming of the Spirit as a baptism. As Jesus began his career with the experience of the Spirit (Luke 3:21–22; 4:18), so the church begins under the power of the Spirit. The people from every nation hearing and speaking in their own languages symbolize the universal mission of the church.

  D. *Peter's speech and dialogue (2:14–40)*
  E. *A major summary of the growth of the church and its communal nature (2:41–47)*

  F. *Lame man in the temple healed by Peter and John (3:1–11)*
  G. *Peter's speech to "you Israelites" (3:12–26)*
  H. *Apostles arrested, taken before the Sanhedrin, and released (4:1–22)*
  I. *Prayer of the apostles, then "all filled with the Holy Spirit" (4:23–31)*
  J. *Experiment in communal living unsuccessful because of one dishonest family (4:32–5:11)*
    1. *Summary of the growth of the church and its communal living (4:32–35)*
    2. *A good example: Joseph, called Barnabas (4:36–37)*
    3. *A bad example: Ananias and Sapphira (5:1–11)*
  K. *Many miracles of the apostles, who are brought before the Sanhedrin, beaten, and released (5:12–42)*
  L. *The Hellenists (6:1–6)*

This short section reflects three important aspects of the early church: better organization necessitated by growth in membership, the beginning of the Hellenistic Jewish Christian mission, which is at the same time a prelude to the future Gentile mission.

  M. *Summary at end of the first main section (6:7)*

"The number of the disciples increased greatly in Jerusalem, and a great many of the priests became obedient to the faith."

II. *Diffusion of Christianity in Judea, Samaria, and Galilee (6:8–9:31)*
  A. *The account of Stephen, his speech, and death (6:8–7:60)*

Stephen's speech explains the break between Hellenistic Jewish Christians and other Jewish Christians within Judaism.

  B. *Persecution and diffusion of Christians after Stephen's death (8:1–9:31)*
    1. *Persecution against the church, and the introduction of Saul/Paul (8:1–3)*

2. *Philip's preaching and work in Samaria and elsewhere (8:4–40)*

3. *Paul's experience on the road to Damascus and its sequels (9:1–30)*

The experience of Saul, also called Paul, reported here had significant results in his life and work. We discuss this experience in the next chapter on Paul.

C. Summary at end of second main section (9:31)

"The church throughout Judea, Galilee, and Samaria had peace and was built up. Living in the fear of the Lord and in the comfort of the Holy Spirit, it increased in numbers."

III. Expansion of Christianity from Judea to Antioch in Syria (9:32–12:24)

A. Stories of Peter's work and preaching, and their results (9:32–11:18)

Luke has introduced Paul, the ultimate hero-to-be of the Gentile mission, which is about to begin in chap. 10 and continues until the end of the book. In chaps. 10–11 Luke associates Peter with the mission to Gentiles as he has associated him with the Hellenistic Jewish mission. Thus, from the start, Luke brings the controversial factions of Jewish Christianity, under Peter's leadership, and Gentile Christianity, under Paul's leadership, into a harmonious relationship.

1. Peter's work at Lydda and Joppa (9:32–43)

Luke presents the apostles as imitating the work of Jesus in healing, casting out evil spirits, and raising people from the dead.

2. Peter and Cornelius, the first Gentile Christian (10:1–11:18)

Luke thinks this story is important because he devotes chap. 10 and much of chap. 11 to it, and alludes to it in chap. 15. He emphasizes the role of Peter, as head of the church, in admitting Gentiles to the church on equal status with Jews. Cornelius and Peter have visions (10:1–16), and the two men are brought together (10:17–33). In a speech, Peter declares that "God shows no partiality" and that "everyone who believes in him receives forgiveness of sins through his name" (10:34–43). Peter's Jewish Christian friends "were astounded that the gift of the Holy Spirit had been poured out even on the Gentiles" (10:44–48). Christians in Jerusalem criticize Peter for associating with Gentiles, and Peter defends himself by telling about his vision at Joppa (11:1–18).

B. Founding of the church in Antioch (11:19–30)

Jewish and Gentile Christianity converge at Antioch. The Jews send Barnabas from Jerusalem to Antioch, Barnabas brings Paul to Antioch, and the mission to Gentiles moves into full force. Antioch, not Jerusalem, now becomes the center of the church. Notice that unnamed people without approval from any authorities have already begun Christian communities "as far as Phoenicia, Cyprus, and Antioch" before the "big names" get there. Elsewhere, also, Luke indicates that not just major figures spread Christianity (8:4; 18:24–26).

C. Herod's (Agrippa I) persecution of Christians and his death (12:1–23)

D. Summary at the end of third main section (12:24)

"The word of God continued to advance and gain adherents."

IV. Diffusion of Christianity through Asia Minor (12:25–16:5)

The travel motif is especially marked in Luke's gospel from 9:51 to Jesus' arrival in Jerusalem. Luke shows his fondness for this motif also in Acts by presenting Paul's missionary work in three journeys (13:4–14:28; 15:36–18:22; 18:23–21:17). Paul was a traveling missionary, a fact confirmed by his letters as well as by Acts. But the journeys, along with the speeches, are probably more of a literary device for presenting Paul's work than a literal record of the sequence and chronology of his visits. Even so, the letters Paul wrote to Christian communities in cities he had previously visited confirm that he operated out of Antioch, was primarily concerned with Gentiles, and had the approval of the church.

A. First journey of Barnabas and Paul (12:25–14:28)

In accordance with Lukan theology, the journey is inspired by the Holy Spirit during worship and prayer (13:1–3). Each journey follows essentially the same pattern: visits to synagogues; speeches, dialogue, or even confrontation, with Jewish or Roman authorities; miraculous events of some kind; involvement of women in the movement; and success, in spite of opposition, because of the Holy Spirit. (See Figure 8.2.)

1. *The island of Cyprus (13:4–12)*
2. *Antioch in Pisidia (13:13–52)*
3. *Iconium (14:1–7)*
4. *Lystra (14:8–20a)*

Recall our discussion of the story of Lystra being inserted into the travel source between vv 7 and 20.

5. *Derbe and return to Antioch (14:20b–28)*

B. The conference at Jerusalem (15:1–35)

The first Christians were Jews who followed the law and worshiped in the temple and synagogue, but who accepted Jesus as the long-expected Messiah. The first Gentiles who became Christians probably had earlier been converted to Judaism and therefore had also been circumcised and taught Jewish law. But as greater numbers of Gentiles became Christians, many of them had never heard of the law of Moses and knew little about Judaism. Such converts were baptized, probably had to acknowledge faith in Jesus—perhaps as Lord—and were instructed in the Christian way of life.

Jews believed that they alone were God's people because of God's promise to Abraham that his descendants would be a great nation. In return, Abraham promised that every male among his descendants would be circumcised (Genesis 17). Circumcision, therefore, became the distinctive sign of the Jews as God's people. Those Jews who became Christians continued to believe that they were God's people and that Gentiles who became Christians should first become Jews by being circumcised and obeying Jewish law. Their position is stated in Acts 15:5: "It is necessary for them to be circumcised and ordered to keep the law of Moses." Jewish Christians even questioned whether they should eat with uncircumcised Gentile Christians. Thus a sharp controversy arose between Jewish Chris-

FIGURE 8.2   *Ruins of a beautiful street in ancient Perga, Asia Minor, with water pools in center.*

tians and Paul, who said that faith in Christ, not circumcision and such legal requirements as dietary regulations, was all that was required of converts. The struggle's intensity and Paul's position are clear from Paul's letters to the Galatians, especially chaps. 1–2.

Luke wrote after the major controversy was over and certainly did not want to intensify it. By putting the conciliatory positions in the mouths of the conservatives Peter and James, Luke reinterprets the issue for a later generation. The compromising decision is stated in Acts 15:20: Gentiles should "abstain only from things polluted by idols and from fornication and from whatever has been strangled and from blood."

The main problem for the historian today is that Paul never refers to the decision either in his discussion of eating meats offered to idols (1 Cor 8:1–13) or in his allusion to the conference at Jerusalem in Galatians 2. According to Galatians and Acts, Paul won out on the matter of circumcision. However, Galatians indicates that the point of compromise was that Paul and his party "remember the poor" Christians in Jerusalem. Paul says he is glad to do this (Gal 2:10; see also Rom 15:26). Gal 2:6–21 also seems to indicate that as the result of the conference the mission activity of the church was divided: Paul and his companions would go to the Gentiles; Peter and others in the church at Jerusalem would go to the Jews.

So since Paul never mentions the decision about foods (Acts 15:20, 29), many scholars believe that the decision as reported in Acts is an effort to solve a problem that resulted from—not during the time of—Paul's work among Gentiles. Paul's account of the controversy between Peter and him about eating with Gentiles indicates that in well-established churches there was the problem of Jewish Christians, who observed Jewish dietary regulations, and Gentile Christians, who did not, eating together. According to Galatians, the decision of the Jerusalem conference did not resolve that problem. The problem may have continued in many churches until after the destruction of Jerusalem in 70 CE, when the church there came to an end. Perhaps after that

the decision reported in Acts 15:19–29 compromised the problem of Jewish and Gentile Christians eating together. Now turn to Acts 21:17–26 and notice that when Paul returns to Jerusalem after his third journey, James reports the decision of the conference as though Paul has never before heard it.

Paul deals with the problem of eating "food sacrificed to idols" or, as Luke says, "things polluted by idols," in 1 Cor 8:1–13. In our discussion of that chapter we will consider the subject in more detail. The reference is to meat that the Jews thought was religiously contaminated because some of it had been used as a sacrifice in pagan ceremonies. From the Jews' point of view, eating meat dedicated to pagan gods violated their strict monotheism and condoned polytheism. "Fornication" is immoral behavior, especially illicit sexual relations. What is "strangled" and "blood" refer to the Mosaic prohibitions against eating meat from which the blood has not been properly drained. The Jews believed that the life-giving element of both humans and animals was in the blood, and that therefore even the blood of animals was sacred and not to be eaten (Lev 17:10–12; Deut 12:16, 23–25).

C. Second journey of Paul (15:36–16:5)
1. Disagreement and separation of Paul and Barnabas (15:36–39)

Barnabas takes Mark and goes to Cyprus; Paul chooses Silas and goes through Syria and Cilicia (check the map of Paul's journeys).

2. Churches established on first journey revisited (15:40–16:4)
3. Summary at the end of fourth main section (16:5)

"So the churches were strengthened in the faith and increased in numbers daily."

V. Advance of Christianity to Europe (16:6–19:20)
A. The guidance of the Spirit (16:6–10)

At this point, according to Acts, the Holy Spirit decides that Paul should give up the mission in

Asia and go to Europe. The pattern of Paul's visits remains the same and includes the Lukan themes of favorable response by Roman authorities and the guilt and hostility of Jews.

    B. *Philippi (16:11–40)*

    C. *Thessalonica (17:1–9)*

    D. *Beroea (17:10–15)*

    E. *Athens and Paul's speech on the Areopagus (17:16–34)*

    F. *Corinth (18:1–17)*

In contrast to Athens, a university city and cultural center, Corinth was a prosperous commercial metropolis.

    G. *Return to Antioch in Syria after a brief stop in Ephesus (18:18–22)*

    H. *Third journey of Paul in Galatia and Phrygia (18:23)*

    I. *Apollos from Alexandria in Ephesus and Achaia (18:24–28)*

    J. *Paul in Ephesus (19:1–19)*

Ephesus was the capital and largest city of the Roman province of Asia.

    K. *Summary at the end of the fifth main section (19:20)*

"The word of the Lord grew mightily and prevailed."

VI. *Christianity established in Rome (19:21–28:31)*

Acts 19:21 clearly marks the transition to the final main section in the narrative of the spread of Christianity from Jerusalem to Rome: "After these things had been accomplished, Paul resolved in the Spirit to go through Macedonia and Achaia, and then to Jerusalem. He said, 'After I have gone there, I must also see Rome.'" From this point on the travel motif focuses on Paul's journey to Rome, just as in Luke it had focused on Jesus' journey to Jerusalem. Luke clearly imposes the theme of the spread of Christianity from Jews to Gentiles in Paul's so-called defense speeches. There Paul begins his testimony with Jerusalem (22:3; 26:4) and concludes

with a reference to his Gentile mission (22:21; 26:20, 23). Indeed, the statement in 22:21—"I will send you far away to the Gentiles"—hints at Rome itself.

    A. *Still in Ephesus (19:21–20:1a; see Figure 8.3)*

    B. *Macedonia, Greece, Macedonia, Philippi, Troas (20:1b–6)*

    C. *Troas (20:7–12)*

    D. *Troas to Miletus (20:13–16)*

    E. *Miletus and speech to elders from Ephesus (20:17–38)*

    F. *Miletus to Jerusalem (21:1–15)*

    G. *Paul in Jerusalem (21:16–23:30)*

       1. Paul's report to James (21:16–26)

James advises Paul to purify himself in order to dispel Jewish suspicion that he does not obey the law.

       2. Paul's arrest by Jews (21:27–40)

Paul is accused of teaching people against the law and of taking a Gentile into the temple.

       3. Paul's defense on the steps of the tribune's barracks (22:1–21)

       4. Paul's dialogue with Roman authorities about his Roman citizenship (22:22–29)

       5. Before the Sanhedrin (22:30–23:10)

       6. The Jews' plot to kill Paul thwarted by his nephew, who reports to the tribune (23:11–22)

Acts 23:11 is an important transition in the travel motif. The Lord says to Paul, "Keep up your courage! For just as you have testified for me in Jerusalem, so you must bear witness also in Rome." This statement and the plot to kill Paul correspond to Herod's plan to kill Jesus and to Jesus' words in Luke 13:31–33 that a prophet cannot perish away from Jerusalem. Paul's witness in Jerusalem is finished, and his journey from Jerusalem to Rome is about to begin, but there are still exciting scenes in the last act of the drama.

FIGURE 8.3 *Statue of the goddess Artemis in the museum at Ephesus.*

7. Paul and the Roman authorities (23:23–30)

The tribune arranges for Paul to be taken to Felix, the Roman governor at Caesarea, and writes Felix a letter about Paul.

H. Paul taken to Caesarea (23:31–35)
I. Paul in Caesarea (24:1–26:32)
  1. Paul before Felix, and Paul's speech (24:1–21)
  2. Paul in prison (24:22–27)

3. Paul's appeal to Caesar (25:1–12)
4. Paul before Agrippa (25:13–27)

This Agrippa is Agrippa II. His father was Agrippa I, called Herod in Acts 12:1. Agrippa II was king of the territory in northeastern Palestine and of some of Syria, and his capital was at Caesarea Philippi. Bernice was Agrippa's sister. According to current gossip, he had an incestuous relationship with her.

5. Paul's speech before Agrippa (26:1–23)
6. Dialogue among Festus, Paul, and Agrippa (26:24–32)
J. Paul's journey to Rome (27:1–28:16)
  1. Departure for Rome (27:1–4)
  2. Dangerous and storm-tossed voyage at sea (27:5–26)

Paul encourages the crew because an angel has told him he "must stand before the emperor."

3. Adrift at sea and shipwrecked (27:27–44)
4. Winter on the island of Malta (28:1–10)
5. Arrival at Rome (28:11–16)
K. Paul in Rome (28:17–31)
  1. Paul's final witness before Jews (28:17–28)
  2. Final summary (28:30–31)

With the arrival of Paul at Rome and his witness there, the theme of Acts is brought to its climax: "He lived there two whole years . . . and welcomed all who came to him, proclaiming the kingdom of God and teaching about the Lord Jesus Christ with all boldness and without hindrance."

SUMMARY

Acts is a unique work in the NT because it gives a history of the early church, although not an impartial one. The author, Luke, who also wrote the gospel of Luke, had several historical and religious purposes for writing. He was especially committed to achieving for Christianity the status of a legal religion and to promoting an image of harmony between both Jewish and Gentile factions of early Christianity. The theme throughout Acts is the spread of Christianity from Jerusalem to Rome and from Jews to Gentiles by the apostles, who are under the guidance of the Holy Spirit. After presenting the activities of Peter and of early Jewish Christianity, which was centered around the temple in Jerusalem, Luke devotes the final sixteen chapters of Acts to Paul. According to Luke, the apostle Paul was the most influential person in the mission and expansion of Christianity from Jews to Gentiles.

Besides the works already cited, for further study of Acts see R. P. C. Hanson 1967; D. Juel 1983; R. J. Karris 1977, 1979; F. W. Danker 1976; D. L. Tiede 1980; D. J. Dupont 1979, 1964; H. J. Cadbury 1955; H. Conzelmann 1987; J. T. Sanders 1987; C. H. Talbert 1984; R. Maddox 1982; J. B. Tyson 1986; see also the works mentioned in our study of the gospel of Luke and C. S. C. Williams 1957; J. H. E. Hull 1967, for Spirit in Acts; M. Hengel 1980a; I. H. Marshall 1980; W. Neil 1981; D. J. Williams 1985; G. Luedemann 1988, 1989, Acts as history.

Regardless of whether Luke actually knew Paul as a person, Acts reflects Luke's admiration for Paul and helps us to understand Paul's life and work, which we will study in the next chapter.

CHAPTER 9

Paul the Apostle

ACCORDING TO ACTS, PAUL WAS A JEW who persecuted Christians. Then, while going to Damascus to seek out Christians, he had an experience that changed his life. He became a zealous Christian and traveled over most of the Mediterranean world as a missionary, trying to win converts to Christ and the Christian life. While on his travels, Paul wrote letters to communities of Christians that he and his companions had already established in certain cities. We do not know how many letters he wrote, but some were collected and incorporated into the NT.

Paul's letters are the earliest documents in the NT. The first three gospels reflect the earliest phase of the Christian religion in Palestine, but the earliest gospel was written after Paul's latest letter. Therefore, the churches to which Paul wrote had no other Christian writings. Being far removed from Palestine and from Jesus' first followers, people in Paul's churches probably had not heard of Jesus or his teachings before they met Paul or another Christian preacher.

The only passage in Paul's letters that provides a clue to the date of his career is 2 Cor 11:32, where Paul says that at Damascus the governor under the King Aretas guarded the city in order to seize him. That Aretas was probably Aretas IV, king of Nabatea—an Arab kingdom south and east of Palestine—who controlled Damascus from 34 to 39 CE. If Jesus' crucifixion took place c. 30 CE, Paul must have become a Christian less than a decade later; and according to Acts 18:12, Paul was in Corinth when Gallio was proconsul of Achaia, sometime between 51 and 53 CE. These dates, then, indicate that Paul's career as a convert to the Jesus movement began about the middle of the first century of the common era.

Paul and the main aspects of his thought have remained important up to the present. Paul was not only the first Christian whose writings became known to us, but he was also responsible for more than a third of the NT. Without Paul, Christianity may have continued as another sect within Judaism, and the Christian church may never have developed. When primitive Christianity was being forced to move from Palestine into

225

the Graeco-Roman world because of dissensions between Jewish and Gentile Christians, Paul, the Hellenistic Jew, appeared at the opportune time to expedite that move. Likewise, his writings inspired the great religious reformation of the sixteenth century, and Paul has profoundly influenced most Christian theologians since his time.

In this chapter we will study Paul as a person, including his occupation, personal traits, early relations with Christians, and the religious experience responsible for his becoming a Christian. We will also consider influences on Paul from Hellenism and Judaism. Then we will examine the main aspects of his thought, which developed from his basic belief that the death of Jesus made forgiveness of human sin possible. Because of Christ's death, according to Paul, forgiveness is made possible through God's righteousness, by which the person who has faith in Christ is justified—made righteous or forgiven—by God's grace. Symbolically, this occurs in baptism, after which the Christian is a different person, has a new existence "in Christ," and is obligated to live a moral and ethical life. These original Pauline contributions to Christian thought are summarized in this chapter and then discussed in connection with Paul's letters to the Galatians

and Romans in Chapter 11. At the end of this chapter are sections on recent works on Paul and on my views on Paul.

PAUL'S LIFE, NAME, OCCUPATION, AND PERSONAL TRAITS

There are two NT sources for the life and activity of Paul—the book of Acts and Paul's letters. What we learn about Paul in Acts, however, frequently does not coincide with information from his letters. The lists in Figure 9.1 show some typical similarities and differences.

According to Acts, Paul was known by two names, Saul and Paul, the former Hebrew and the latter Roman (Latin). Many Jews, especially those living in the Diaspora, did have more than one name. One of Paul's friends and companions, for example, was "John whose other name was Mark" (Acts 12:12). John was his Jewish name and Mark (Marcus) the Roman one (see Acts 1:23; Luke 22:3; Col 4:11). However, since in his letters Paul never uses the name Saul, it may be a fiction of the writer of Acts. On the other hand, because Paul's readers were mostly

---

FIGURE 9.1   *Similarities and Differences in Representing Paul*

Acts	Paul's Letters
Saul, a name for Paul	Never mentioned
Born in Tarsus in Cilicia, brought up in Jerusalem, studied under Gamaliel	None of this is mentioned
A Jew who lived as a strict Pharisee	Paul says the same thing about himself
Saul persecuted Christians	Paul lamentably admits this several times
Vision on the road to Damascus	Paul may allude to this experience
Preaching to Jews in Damascus	No reference to preaching in Damascus
God called Saul to preach to Gentiles and Jews, but it was necessary for Ananias to lay his hands on Paul and baptize him	Paul was called to preach to Gentiles and Jews, so his authority came only from God, not man; and Paul never even alludes to his baptism
At Corinth Paul meets Aquila and Priscilla, who set Apollos straight about the word of God	Aquila and Priscilla are Paul's helpers; Paul writes to Corinth, where Apollos competes with him

Gentiles, he may not have wanted to mention his Jewish name.

Whatever the truth about the real name of Paul, his becoming a Christian had nothing to do with his name. For Luke, the writer of Acts, however, the change from Saul to Paul is symbolic. The statement "Saul, also known as Paul" (Acts 13:9) is made precisely at that point in the narrative where the writer's attention turns to Paul's missionary activity in the Gentile world. As Paul begins his activity among Gentiles, the author shifts to the Roman name Paul.

According to Acts 18:3, Paul was a tentmaker. He probably learned how to make tents from leather as an apprentice with his father or someone else. Like many artisans of his time, Paul traveled from city to city. He would stay in the house of a new convert (Acts 16:15, 40; 17:5–7; Phlm 22) and work there or in a local shop (18:3, 11). When Paul reminds the Thessalonians of his "labor and toil . . . night and day" (1 Thess 2:9; see also 1 Cor 4:12; 9:6), he is saying that he worked hard all day long; this indicates that tentmaking was his full-time occupation. The workshop may often have provided the setting for his missionary preaching (1 Thess 4:10–12; See R. F. Hock 1980).

In Paul's letters, there are passages indicating that his personal presence was not very impressive. His critics say, "His letters are weighty and strong, but his bodily presence is weak, and his speech contemptible" (2 Cor 10:10). He reminds the Galatians that "it was because of a physical infirmity" that he preached the gospel to them at first and that his condition was a trial to them (Gal 4:13–14). Paul writes that to keep him from being too elated by the abundance of revelations, "a thorn was given me in the flesh, a messenger of Satan to torment me" (2 Cor 12:7–9). If this was a physical handicap, it was a chronic condition, probably ophthalmia—that is, weak or diseased eyes. In the same passage where Paul says that because of a physical infirmity he first preached to the Galatians, he also says, "Had it been possible, you would have torn out your eyes and given them to me." However, on the basis of 2 Cor 12:7–9, which has something of a theological tone, the thorn may have been Paul's receiving of mystic or spiritual revelations less frequently than he desired, rather than a physical handicap.

Paul displays a variety of emotions. Because the Corinthians distressed Paul, he writes "out of much distress and anguish of heart and with many tears" (2 Cor 2:4; see also Phil 3:18; 1 Cor 3:1–4). He shares the joys and sorrows of others (2 Cor 1:23–2:11). Sometimes he is tolerant and patient (1 Corinthians 8; Romans 14–15), sometimes intolerant, impatient, and even angry (Gal 1:1–24; 2:4; 4:16–17; 2 Cor 7:8–9) or ironic (1 Cor 2:1–10; 3:19–21; 4:8–13; 2 Corinthians 11). When dealing with his opponents, Paul's language is sometimes polemical and coarse (Gal 5:12; Phil 3:2, 18–19; 2 Cor 10:2; 11:12–15, 20; Rom 16:17–18). Yet Paul confronts the Corinthians "in weakness and in fear and in much trembling" (1 Cor 2:3), and the Corinthians say that Paul is humble when present but bold when absent (2 Cor 10:1). Paul was apparently emotionally strong, because he survived countless hardships and dangers besides being under "daily pressure" and "anxiety for all the churches" (2 Cor 11:23–28; see also 2 Cor 1:8; 4:7–12; 6:4–10; 7:5; 1 Cor 4:9–13; Phil 4:12; Acts 16:19–39).

PAUL AND JESUS

There is no solid evidence that Paul ever saw or knew the earthly Jesus. One passage that has led some scholars to argue that he had met Jesus is 2 Cor 5:16: "From now on, therefore, we regard no one from a human point of view; even though we once knew Christ from a human point of view, we know him no longer in that way." One interpretation of this verse is that Paul had once seen Jesus at Jerusalem or elsewhere. However, the context indicates that Paul is not talking about a relationship with the physical Jesus, but about the mystical or spiritual experience of Christ. The next verse confirms the point: "So if anyone is in Christ, there is a new creation: everything old has passed away; see everything has become new" (5:17). In other words, as a new creation after his vision, Paul sees Jesus from a different perspective than he did when he was persecuting Jesus' followers. Another passage mentioned in connection with Paul and Jesus is 1 Cor 15:8. In narrating the resurrection appearances of Jesus, Paul says, "Last of all, as to one untimely born, he appeared also to me." Here Paul is speaking about his experience on the road to Damascus (see also 1 Cor 9:1), not about an actual physical encounter with Jesus.

Paul does refer to incidents in Jesus' life that came to be recorded in the gospels. He says that Jesus was a descendant of David (Rom 1:3) and "born of woman, born under the law" (Gal 4:4). "Under the law" was an idiom meaning "to be a Jew." Paul also writes that he saw James, Jesus' brother (Gal 1:19; 2:9); and he mentions the night of Jesus' betrayal and the Lord's Supper, and quotes a version of Jesus' words on that occasion (1 Cor 11:23–26). He alludes to Jesus' sufferings (2 Cor 1:5; Phil 3:10) and often to his death and resurrection. Similarly, he mentions Jesus' burial (1 Cor 15:4) and says that the rulers of the age were responsible for Jesus' crucifixion (1 Cor 2:8).

Although aware of incidents in Jesus' life, Paul never quotes Jesus' words exactly as they are recorded in any of the gospels. The closest echoes of Jesus' words, as reported in the synoptic gospels, are in 1 Thess 5:15 and Rom 12:14–19, where Paul may allude to Jesus' Sermon on the Mount (Matt 5:43–46; Luke 6:27–28). Paul also alludes to Jesus' saying that "laborers deserve their food" or "his wages" (Greek; Matt 10:10; Luke 10:7): "In the same way, the Lord commanded that those who proclaim the gospel should get their living by the gospel" (1 Cor 9:14).

Similarities between Paul's words and Jesus' sayings must not be stressed too much (see D. J. Selby 1962:305–309, 339–345; D. L. Dungan 1971). Such similarities may be due to the common debt of Paul, Jesus, and the synoptists to Judaism, with its strong ethical tradition, rather than to Paul's acquaintance with Jesus' sayings or the synoptic tradition. Furthermore, the things Paul omits from Jesus' teachings are far more striking than the similarities between Jesus' teachings and Paul's writings. How could he have heard much of Jesus' teaching and never refer to a single parable? Likewise, in the synoptic gospels more verses of Jesus' teachings are on the kingdom of God than on any other subject. Yet Paul rarely mentions the kingdom of God; and when he does, there is little similarity between what he says and Jesus' teaching (see 1 Thess 2:12; 1 Cor 4:20; 6:9–10; 15:24, 50; Rom 14:17).

In contrast to those disciples of Jesus who disagreed with Paul about requirements for Gentile converts and who could appeal to their association with Jesus as the basis of their authority, Paul concentrated on Jesus' death and resurrection. As "Son of God . . . by resurrection from the dead" (Rom 1:4), Jesus was more than the earthly Messiah. Thus, Paul could defend his right to be an apostle on the basis of his having seen the risen Jesus: "Am I not an apostle? Have I not seen Jesus our Lord?" (1 Cor 9:1). This vision of the risen Jesus convinced Paul that he had greater authority as an apostle than his opponents did.

With respect to Paul and Jesus, R. A. Horsley 1997 carries his view of Jesus as a multiple revolutionary (see R. A. Horsley 1987 discussed in Chapter 3) over into the life of Paul. Jesus, John the Baptist, Paul, and early Christians were fighting not only a spiritual battle but also one against economic, cultural, and political dishevels and charges.

PAUL'S VISION ON THE DAMASCUS ROAD

According to Acts, Paul is introduced as a young man called Saul, at whose feet witnesses to the death of Stephen laid their garments (7:58): "And Saul approved of their killing him" (8:1). Immediately afterward he becomes a zealous persecutor of the Christians: "But Saul was ravaging the church by entering house after house; dragging off both men and women, he committed them to prison" (8:3).

Because belief in Jesus as the Messiah was not in itself sufficient reason for persecution of those who believed, the account in Acts 7:58–8:3 of Paul's presence at the death of Stephen and his subsequent persecution of Christians in Jerusalem is historically suspect. Paul himself says that he was unknown to the churches of Judea until after his successful missionary work in Syria and Cilicia (Gal 1:15–23). Although Paul never mentions any persecuting in Jerusalem, his ardent persecution of early Christians elsewhere left a lasting, lamentable impression upon him that he attests in his letters. He writes to the Galatians, "You have heard, no doubt, of my earlier life in Judaism. I was violently persecuting the church of God and was trying to destroy it" (1:13; see also 1:23), and to the Corinthians, "I am the least of the apostles, unfit to be called an apostle, because I persecuted the church of God" (1 Cor 15:9; see also Phil 3:6; Gal 1:23). Recall also Paul's defense speeches in Acts, and compare Gal 1:13–14 and Phil 3:5–6.

Very suddenly, in the midst of his persecutions, Paul turned from persecutor of Christians to missionary preacher of the new religion. This change—his conversion, so to speak—took place on the Damascus road. The term *conversion* is not the most apt for Paul's religious experience, since Paul never was converted in any modern sense of the term. He never really made a complete change either from no religion to religion or from one religion to another, not even from Judaism to Christianity. Paul never consciously forsook his Judaism, with its time-honored belief in the care and goodness of God, God's divine justice and mercy, and God's righteousness and wrath. There continued within his inner being a genuine conflict between the old ways of Judaism and the new Way of Christianity. Since Paul's Judaism is evident in his letters, the term "vision," rather than "conversion," is used for his transforming religious experience as reported in Acts and alluded to in Paul's letters.

Paul's vision on the road to Damascus was similar to the "calls" of the OT prophets Isaiah and Jeremiah. On the basis of his letters and Jeremiah 1, the following are common points:

both Jeremiah and Paul believed they were commissioned by God before birth (Jer 1:5; Gal 1:15); both spoke for the Lord (Jer 1:9; 1 Cor 7:10; see also 7:12, 25); both felt called to speak to the nations (Jer 1:5; Gal 1:16); and both felt inadequate for their tasks (Jer 1:6; 1 Cor 15:8–9). Moreover, the prophetic gifts of visions and ecstasy, experienced also by Paul, were common phenomena in Judaism before Paul's time, so they may have been a part of his religious experience even before he became a Christian.

According to Acts and Paul's letters, a divine influence changed Paul's attitude toward Jesus and the law (see, for example, Gal 1:15–16). That Paul accepted Jesus as the long-expected Jewish Messiah who had also become Lord is evident in his letters and Acts. Acts 17:2–3 reports that for three weeks in the synagogue at Thessalonica Paul argued from the scriptures with the Jews, "explaining and proving that it was necessary for the Messiah to suffer and to rise from the dead, and saying, 'This is the Messiah, Jesus whom I am proclaiming to you'" (see Acts 18:5, 28; 26:23).

In Paul's letters, as in Acts, Jesus became the Messiah through his suffering, death, and resurrection (see Rom 5:6–8; 6:4, 9; 1 Cor 1:23; Phil 2:8–11). Paul believed he shared in Jesus' crucifixion and resurrection by a kind of mystical union that is expressed with his phrases "in Christ" and "Christ in," Paul's most original and characteristic expressions (see below). Paul sums up his experience in Gal 2:20: "I have been crucified with Christ; and it is no longer I who live, but it is Christ who lives in me. And the life I now live . . . I live by faith in the Son of God" (see also Rom 8:10; Phil 3:8–14; 4:13; 2 Cor 12:9; 13:5). Paul, of course, does not mean that he was literally crucified with Christ. Rather, he is talking about a mystical or spiritual personal experience that is difficult to explain. Perhaps Paul is saying that Christ's death made it possible for him to share a spiritual fellowship with the risen Christ, who inspires his life in faith. As a result of his experience, Paul developed creative insight with respect to faith in Christ and living in the Christian Way. Paul the Jew had to die with

Christ in his own experience to become Paul the Jewish Christian, and Christ, whom Paul once rejected, became the focus of his changed life as a Christian.

Paul's vision of Christ also brought about a change in his attitude toward the Jewish law, although that change actually may have been developing before his vision. Even though Paul was circumcised (Phil 3:5) and advanced in Judaism beyond many of his own people (Gal 1:14), he lived and practiced his trade among Gentiles as well as Jews. When eating with Gentiles, he may not have been able to obey Jewish dietary laws. Even the conservative Jew Peter apparently found such observance impractical (Gal 2:11–14). Moreover, in Palestine as in the Diaspora, there were Jews—both individuals and groups—who disregarded external observances but kept other parts of the law. In situations where it was impractical or impossible to observe certain laws, those laws were no longer obeyed, and therefore it was easy to conclude that they were no longer valid. In short, as a Christian Paul concluded that living by the Spirit made the ceremonial aspects of the law, including dietary regulations and circumcision, unnecessary. "But now we are discharged from the law, dead to that which held us captive, so that we are slaves not under the old written code but in the new life of the Spirit" (Rom 7:6; see also Gal 5:18).

Eventually, after Paul met the challenge of the troublemakers at Galatia who insisted that Gentile Christians had to be circumcised and to obey the law, Paul had to rethink his position on the law also with respect to Gentiles. Before his vision, Paul had regarded the law as a barrier between Gentiles and Jews, but after his vision he believed the law should no longer be an obstacle to Jews or Gentiles who wanted to become Christians. Whereas the law had been central in his former life as a Jew, faith in Christ became central in his life as a Jewish Christian. The law should not prevent Jews or Gentiles who had faith in Christ from becoming a part of God's people in Christ, the church. Becoming Christians was the first step toward their ultimate salvation.

Paul, then, believed that his vision on the road to Damascus had been a personal encounter with the risen Jesus and had made him a distinctive person. After his vision, Paul apparently went into self-imposed exile for a number of years (see Gal 1:10–2:10). Then he began active mission work among Gentiles in Greece and Asia Minor (see Gal 2:1–10; Acts 12:25–28:31; see also Figures 11.1 and 11.2). But even after Paul became a convert, he remained a Jew living amid the Hellenism of the Roman Empire. Therefore, we will now consider possible Hellenistic influences on Paul, some of which doubtless were the result of his travels.

INFLUENCES ON PAUL FROM HIS TRAVELS

The writer of Acts presents Paul as traveling thousands of miles on land and sea, from city to city. Such travel was not unusual in the Roman world, and those who traveled included merchants, artisans, letter carriers, runaway slaves, athletes, teachers, students, government officials, and tourists. According to Acts, Paul traveled as an official (9:1–2), as a craftsman and preacher, as a pilgrim to a Jewish festival (20:16), and as a prisoner (27:1–28:14). Although conditions for travel in the Roman Empire were usually good, travelers faced delays and dangers. When traveling by sea, for example, they had to wait for a ship going in the right direction (Acts 21:1–2) and for favorable winds (Acts 27:4–24). Besides the dust and mud known to every ancient traveler, Paul faced hunger, thirst, cold, exposure, robbers, and shipwreck (2 Cor 11:25–27).

Paul sometimes speaks of his visit with the people to whom he is writing and sometimes makes plans for future visits. So the report in Acts that Paul was a traveling evangelist, going from one city to another, is confirmed in his letters. He wrote those letters because of his personal interest in the communities of believers that he had helped establish in various cities.

Paul's letters show that he was influenced by the city and by city life. Unlike Jesus' figures of speech which, according to the gospel writers, almost all concern the country and country life, Paul's mostly concern the city and city life. He speaks of athletes and games (1 Cor 9:24–26; Phil 3:14) and perhaps of the arena (1 Cor 4:9), and he uses figures pertaining to the military, such as soldiers, armor, and battle (1 Thess 5:8; 1 Cor 9:7; 14:8; 2 Cor 2:14; 10:3–6; Phil 2:25; Phlm 2).

Paul's letters also show influence from the institution of slavery, known in every city the world over and frequently encountered on his travels. Paul gives advice about relations between masters and slaves (Rom 14:4), and he speaks of himself and others figuratively as slaves of Christ (Rom 1:1; 1 Cor 7:22; 2 Cor 4:5; Gal 1:10; Phil 1:1). He speaks of being slaves of sin (Rom 6:17, 20) and says that Christ himself took the form of a slave (Phil 2:7). His most personal letter is written to the owner of a runaway slave; in it he pleads that the owner take back his slave "no longer as a slave but . . . a beloved brother" (Phlm 16). Little wonder Paul describes the community of believers in Galatia as one in which "there is no longer slave or free . . . for all of you are one in Christ Jesus" (Gal 3:28).

Paul shows acquaintance with legal practice and courts of law, as he encountered them on his travels. His vocabulary contains a wide range of legal terms: "law," "judgment," "judge," "acquit," "condemn," "just," "justice," "defend," "justification." Figures showing familiarity with the processes of building, crafts, commerce, and sea voyaging appear in Paul, since he had observed those things in his travels (Rom 9:21; 15:20; 1 Cor 3:10–15; 2 Cor 1:22; 5:1, 5; 11:25–26; Gal 2:18). He also speaks of authorities, powers, taxes, and revenue, all of which were so important in the cities he visited (Rom 13:1–7). Paul must have often seen or even visited public meat markets where Gentiles bought meat that had been dedicated to pagan deities. Eating such meat posed a real problem of conscience for some Christian Gentiles (1 Cor 8:7–10; 10:25–30; Rom 14:1–3). On his travels, Paul encountered opposition from clever itinerant orators and speech makers (1 Cor 1:12–20; 2:4, 13; 16:9; see also Acts 17:17–21). Among the throngs of the city were miracle workers, so common in the ancient world, and those seeking their signs (1 Cor 1:22; 12:10, 28–30; Gal 3:5). Paul had observed them all.

While traveling, Paul usually supported himself by practicing his trade; through it he made some converts and formed close friendships. At Corinth Paul stayed with Aquila and Priscilla because "he was of the same trade" (Acts 18:2–3, 18, 26), and they became his co-workers and once "risked their necks" for him (Rom 16:3–4).

That Paul traveled to many cities and established communities of believers in several of them is certain, and influence from the city life of his travels is evident in his letters. But that Paul traveled to exactly the same places and in a systematic fashion from Jerusalem to Rome, as portrayed in Acts, is doubtful. However, Paul did express a desire to visit Rome (Rom 1:8–15; 15:22–23), and according to tradition other than Acts, he did spend his final years there.

THE HELLENISM OF PAUL

To what extent Paul was influenced by Hellenism is debatable. In Acts Paul twice says that he is a citizen of Tarsus, once that he was born there. "I am a Jew, from Tarsus in Cilicia, a citizen of an important city . . . born in Tarsus in Cilicia" (21:39; 22:3; see also 9:11, 30; 11:25; 22:27–29). In his letters, however, Paul nowhere mentions Tarsus or refers to his Roman citizenship.

Although Tarsus became Hellenized, its population continued to be mixed Anatolian (eastern) with Greek, Roman, and Jewish communities. After Cilicia became a Roman province in 64 BCE, Tarsus was made its capital. The rich, fertile Cilician plains around Tarsus were conducive to general prosperity. Under Augustus, Tarsus was made a free city, became very influential as a center of learning, and remained unrivaled as a city until the third century. (See Figure 9.2.)

FIGURE 9.2
*Modern Tarsus, with
ancient wall and
archway to the north.*

Strabo describes the intellectual life in Tarsus:

> The people of Tarsus have become so zealous
> both for philosophy and the whole round of
> education that they have surpassed Athens,
> Alexandria, and any other place one might
> name where there have been schools and lec-
> tures of philosophers. . . . There are also all sorts
> of schools of rhetoric at Tarsus. [14:5:13]

Thus, Tarsus would have provided the kind of intellectual environment in which Paul could learn
to speak and write Greek. He would also have
had the opportunity there to hear and speak with
Stoics, Cynics, and other philosophers. Perhaps,
as some think, he even attended the famous university at Tarsus.

If Paul was a citizen of Tarsus, he was born a
Jew in Hellenistic surroundings. We assume,
then, that his friends were Hellenistic Jews or
Greeks, and Acts supports this assumption. Timothy was the son of a Greek father and Jewish
mother and was not circumcised until he met
Paul (Acts 16:1–3). Similarly, Titus was a Greek
and was not forced to be circumcised (Gal 2:3).
Probably the most Hellenistic of all Paul's friends

was Apollos, the eloquent Jew from Alexandria
(Acts 18:24). It is impossible to say, however,
how much Paul was influenced by the Hellenism
of his friends or his environment. From birth,
Paul and his friends belonged to that large group
of people who used two languages, Hebrew (Aramaic) and Greek, and who lived amid two cultures, Judaism and Hellenism. Such Jews would
speak Greek and were perhaps bilingual, and they
would be more familiar with Greek philosophy
and the many religious cults than Palestinian Jews
would. We know from Philo that Jews in the Diaspora had begun to question the superiority, validity, and relevance of their Mosaic law for the
Hellenistic communities in which they lived.

One way to determine a culture's influence on
writers is to look for quotations from the literature of that culture in their writings. Twice in
Acts Paul is reported as quoting from Greek literature, both times in his speech on the Areopagus in Athens. The first quotation, "In him we
live and move and have our being" (Acts 17:28),
is probably from Epimenides, a poet and prophet
from Crete (c. 600–500 BCE). The second, "for
we too are his offspring" (17:28), is an exact

quotation of five words from the *Phaenomena* of the Greek poet Aratus (born c. 310 BCE). The only direct quotation from a Greek writing in Paul's letters is in 1 Cor 15:33, where he quotes a line from the *Thais* of Menander, comic poet of Athens (c. 343–291 BCE): "Bad company ruins good morals." However, by Paul's time the saying probably was a proverbial expression, so it is quite conceivable that he never read or used Menander's work at all. (See F. W. Danker 1964 and A. J. Malherbe 1983:41–45.)

It is likely that if Paul really had a literary knowledge of Greek philosophical and religious thought, he would have quoted relevant passages more frequently to support particular points he was trying to make, especially when writing to Gentile converts. In Acts this is what he is reported to have done on the Areopagus, and in his letters he quotes many times from the Septuagint (see, for example, Rom 3:10–18; 2 Cor 6:2; Gal 3:11).

With respect to the quotations in Acts, recall that ancient writers frequently composed speeches and put them on the lips of characters in their narratives. So the quotations in Paul's speech at Athens do not show that Paul was familiar with Greek literature or philosophic thought. To be sure, however, there were many philosophical ideas in the air. Naturally, in his travels Paul encountered some aspects of Hellenistic culture that became his own, and at Tarsus or in his travels Paul was exposed to Stoics, Cynics, and other kinds of philosophic preachers. Indeed, his language and thought are closer to those of Stoicism than to any other aspect of Hellenistic culture.

Stoicism and Pauline Thought

Below are some interesting parallels between Paul and the Stoic writers Epictetus and Seneca, whose lives were roughly contemporary with Paul's. Topics from Stoicism are chosen at random from many possibilities and are not meant to be connected with each other.

Virtues and Vices. In their writings, both Stoic writers and Paul include lists of virtues and vices in human behavior. Similarly, both Stoics and Paul disdained wanton conduct.

> Their god is the belly; and their glory is in their shame. [Phil 3:19]

> One goes mad with lust, another serves his belly. [Seneca, *On Benefits* 7:26:4]

Although the language is similar, the thought behind each is different. Stoics despised such action because it was degrading to human dignity. But for Paul, such actions offended a moral God and were a sinful offense against the spiritual Christ living in the Christian.

Acting against One's Will.

> For I do not do what I want, but I do the very thing I hate. [Rom 7:15]

> What he wants he does not do and what he does not want he does. [Epictetus, *Dis.* 2:26:4]

Both writers are depicting the contradiction in human behavior when people do what they know they should not do. Paul is talking about himself or others who struggle to do God's will as revealed in the Jewish law but discover that they cannot do it. Epictetus, of course, does not have the same view in mind.

God and Spirit Within.

> God is in you. [from the Greek; 1 Cor 14:25]

> God is near you, he is with you, he is in you. [Seneca, *Mor. Ep.* 41:1]

> In each good man a god dwells, but what god is uncertain. [Seneca, *Mor. Ep.* 41:2]

> Do you not know that you are God's temple and that God's Spirit dwells in you? [1 Cor 3:16]

> Do you not know that your body is a temple of the Holy Spirit within you? [1 Cor 6:19]

> A holy spirit resides within us. [Seneca, *Mor. Ep.* 41:2]

In 1 Cor 14:25 the words are a familiar expression from the OT (Isa 45:14; 1 Kgs 18:39; Zech 8:23), and they refer to the one God of the Jews and Christians and no other. This distinguishes Paul's thought from that of Seneca, although the language is the same. In 1 Cor 3:16 Paul speaks of the whole Christian community of Corinth, and in 1 Cor 6:19 he is referring to the individual community members' bodies as temples of God. In contrast to the Spirit of God or the Holy Spirit of Paul, the holy spirit mentioned in Seneca's writing is probably best interpreted as reason. Again the thought is different in spite of the common literary expression.

Freedom.

For the law of the Spirit of life in Christ Jesus has set you free from the law of sin and of death. [Rom 8:2]

For you were called to freedom, brothers; only do not use your freedom as an opportunity for self-indulgence. [Gal 5:13]

Is freedom anything else than the right to spend our time as we wish? [Epictetus, *Dis.* 2:1:23]

He is free who lives as he wishes, who is not under compulsion, or hindrance, or force, whose choices are unhindered, whose desires are achieved, whose aversions are not diverted. [Epictetus, *Dis.* 4:1:14]

Paul's concept of freedom is close to that of the Stoics, if not borrowed from them, but there are differences between the two concepts. For Epictetus freedom sometimes involves only living as one wants under the Roman government; sometimes the concept also implies responsibility for right moral conduct by individuals and groups (see, for example, *Dis.* 1:12:9; 3:24:96–103). For Paul freedom comes from Christ: "For freedom Christ has set us free" (Gal 5:1). That means freedom to live a moral life by the Spirit (Gal 5:16, 25). However, for both Stoics and Paul freedom never means license to do as one pleases.

Conscience.

I am not lying; my conscience confirms it by the Holy Spirit. [Rom 9:1]

Nor can I consent to such things with a clear conscience. [Seneca, *Mor. Ep.* 117:1]

To the Cynic it is his conscience which gives him this power [to censure people]. [Epictetus, *Dis.* 3:22:94]

"Conscience" is a Pauline term sometimes attributed to Stoic influence. Not occurring at all in the thought of Plato and Aristotle, the concept of conscience came into Greek thought rather late. It may have originated among the Stoics, though its use is infrequent even among Stoics of Paul's time. There is no Hebrew word in the OT equivalent to the Greek term meaning "conscience," and the form occurs rarely in the Septuagint (Eccl 10:20; Wis 17:11; Sir 42:18). So Paul got the idea from his Greek rather than his Hebrew background.

Although these parallels show the similarity between the language of the Stoics and that of Paul, they do not prove that Paul was reproducing Stoic thought. On the surface, Paul's ideas may seem similar to those of the Stoics, but closer study shows that Paul reinterpreted whatever ideas he may have learned from Stoicism in light of his distinctive ideas about God, Christ, and the Spirit.

Clearly, however, Paul and the Stoics have several things in common. Paul's style often resembles that of the Stoic diatribe, a form of prolonged discussion or harangue often punctuated with short, brisk phrases or questions. Examples include "Do not be deceived" (Gal 6:7; 1 Cor 6:9); "You foolish Galatians!" (Gal 3:1); "What then?" (Rom 3:9); and "By no means!" (Rom 3:4, 6), an expression that occurs only in Paul and Epictetus (see, for example, *Dis.* 1:1:13; 1:2:35; 2:8:2; 3:1:42). Likewise, both Paul and the Stoics use imagery from athletics to illustrate a point. Paul writes that "in a race the runners all compete, but only one receives the prize. . . . Athletes exercise self-control in all things; they do it to receive a perishable wreath" (1 Cor 9:24–25; see also Gal 2:2; Phil 1:30; 2:16; 3:14; 1 Thess 2:2; Acts 20:24). Epictetus asks, "Do you want to win at Olympia?" Then he talks about the preparation for such a victory—discipline, strict diet, compulsory training—and says that in the contest athletes must play hard to win (*Manual* 29). Both Stoics and Paul exhort their readers to patient endurance, reverence for God, and moral behavior; and they emphasize the spiritual, not physical, aspects of life.

For a revival of the earlier view that Paul was greatly influenced by Hellenism, especially the mystery cults and Gnosticism, see H. Maccoby 1991; the older work by W. L. Knox 1944, still useful; for Paul and Gnosticism see E. H. Pagels 1975, 1979; W. Schmithals 1972.

Although we know that Hellenism greatly influenced Paul, it is difficult to identify that influence in Paul's writing. This is because Judaism, even in Palestine, had already felt the impact of Hellenism. All Judaism was certainly not Hellenistic, but there was no longer a sharp distinction between Palestinian Judaism and the Hellenistic Judaism of the Diaspora. Even in Palestine, little of Judaism was untouched by Hellenism. Consequently, it is often difficult to pinpoint aspects of Paul's thought that are derived from Judaism or Hellenism. But one thing is certain—Paul was a Jew and was strongly influenced by Judaism.

THE JUDAISM OF PAUL

Acts first introduces Paul in Jerusalem among other Jews participating in the persecution of Christians (7:58–8:3; 9:1–4, 21). Acts reports not only that Paul was a citizen of Tarsus but that he was a Jew, brought up in the city of Jerusalem "at the feet of Gamaliel, educated strictly according to" Jewish law (21:39–22:3). If Paul did study under Gamaliel, he had a distinguished teacher. Gamaliel was a descendant of Hillel, the famous teacher in the time of Herod the Great, and had become famous himself. However, there are reasons for doubting Paul's close association with Jerusalem and his study under Gamaliel.

Although Paul boasts several times of his Jewishness, he never mentions Gamaliel. Such study would have taken place in the temple at Jerusalem, but Paul never refers to any personal association with the temple. And in view of Acts 5:34–39, where Gamaliel advocates lenient treatment of Peter and other apostles, it seems odd that his pupil Paul would have become such a zealous persecutor of Christians. Some scholars, therefore, think that Paul's study under Gamaliel

in Jerusalem is a fiction of the writer of Acts, that Paul received his Jewish education in his native synagogue somewhere in the Diaspora, and that he was never in Jerusalem before he became a member of the Christian sect. On the other hand, some scholars have argued that Paul's use of the OT shows rabbinic influence and that he grew up in Jerusalem and went to rabbinic school there. Perhaps since Paul was writing to predominantly Gentile Christian groups, he thought it unnecessary or unwise to mention his study under Gamaliel or his early life in Jerusalem.

No matter where Paul grew up and was educated, the evidence of Paul's thorough Jewishness from Acts (21:39–22:3; 23:6; 26:4–5) is supported in his letters. Several times Paul writes, even boasts, about his Jewishness. To the Galatians he writes, "I advanced in Judaism beyond many contemporaries of my own people, being much more zealous for the traditions of my ancestors" (1:14; Greek). To the Philippians he says that he was "circumcised on the eighth day, a member of the people of Israel, of the tribe of Benjamin, a Hebrew born of Hebrews; as to the law, a Pharisee . . . as to righteousness under the law, blameless" (3:5–6; see also 2 Cor 11:22). But when Paul says he is a Pharisee, he doesn't tell us very much, although his belief in the resurrection of the body clearly distinguishes him as a Pharisee from the Sadducees, who rejected that doctrine.

Irrespective of where Paul was born and grew up, an early life in Jerusalem would not necessarily have precluded a Greek education. Palestine, including Jerusalem, was more Hellenized than scholars once thought. But there is no guarantee that Paul would have received a Greek education if he had spent his youth in Tarsus. Between the time of his conversion and his missionary travels there was plenty of time for Paul to have become familiar with aspects of Greek culture reflected in his letters.

The Law and the Synagogue

In all of Judaism, Torah—or law—was central, and its study and observance were the most important religious duties. The law occupied much of Paul's thought when he was a Pharisee and also after his vision. Because Sadducees did not adapt the law to changing circumstances, Paul was more likely as a Pharisee than he would have been as a Sadducee to adapt the law to changing circumstances and to his changing views as a Christian Jew.

Whether I was the first person to call Paul "a Christian Jew" I do not know, but I did so in the first edition of this book (1986). As is now again becoming more widely acknowledged, Paul never completely gave up his Judaism. So, even with that designation, the work *Christian* is valid only if we think of it in the original sense of "a partisan of Christ," that is, a follower of Jesus as the Messiah and his Way (see Acts 9:2; 18:25–26; 19:9, 23; 24:14, 22). "The Way" and "believers" (see 1 Thess 1:7; 2:10, 13; 1 Cor 6:8; 14:22; Gal 2:4; and often in Acts) were probably the earliest designations early followers of Jesus the Messiah used to refer to themselves. By force of habit I sometimes still use the term *Christian*, although it is anachronistic for persons who were in the period of transition from Judaism or paganism to the religion that only after Paul's time became known as Christianity (see end of this chapter).

B. H. Young 1997 calls Paul "the Jewish theologian" who never gave up thinking of himself as a Pharisee. Indeed, the crucial aspects of his teachings, such as grace, the law, faith, and love, are best understood in light of his Pharisaism. The model of love in 1 Corinthians 13 was the basis for mission work.

Paul's experience with the law as a Pharisee before he became a convert may be one reason for his diverse and contradictory statements about the law. He sometimes speaks out harshly against the law: "For the law brings wrath; but where there is no law, neither is there violation" (Rom 4:15). On the other hand, he says, "The law is holy, and the commandment is holy and just and good" (Rom 7:12; see also Rom 2:13; 3:28, 31).

It is certain that Paul never completely gave up all Jewish law. I have suggested (*The Apostle Paul*, pages 175–189) that Paul uses two words that give the best insight into what he means with respect to observance of the law. They are *dikaiōma* (plural, *dikaiōmata*), meaning "(just) requirement," "regulation," "commandment," or, best of all, "a righteous deed" (Rom 1:28–32; 2:25–28; 5:16–18; 8:1–4) and *entolē* (plural, *entolai*), meaning "command(ment)," "ordinance" (Rom 7:12; 13:8–10; 1 Cor 7:19; 14:37). Neither circumcision nor dietary regulations were law for Paul. But "the just requirement of God" (Rom 1:32; Greek), "the just requirements of the law" (Rom 2:26), "the just requirement of the law" (Rom 8:4), and "the commandments of God" (1 Cor 7:19) are the laws that, if observed, make the members of Paul's churches moral/ethical persons and prepare them for entrance into "the Israel of God" (Gal 6:16; see end of this chapter).

In light of these observations, Paul was his own distinctive person. This distinctive person's view of the law is best stated, perhaps, in 1 Cor 9:20–23. Please read those verses now. For Paul, then, the law of Christ and the experience of the Spirit make the ceremonial aspects of the Mosaic law unnecessary.

As a Jew, Paul may never have severed his relationship to the synagogue. It was very easy for him to keep in touch with the synagogue, but for information about Paul's relations with the synagogue we are dependent almost entirely upon Acts. Paul attended synagogues in many places, including Salamis on the island of Cyprus, Philippi, Thessalonica, Athens, Corinth, and Ephesus. Among such synagogues there would always be differences of opinion about theological questions and about messianic expectations, as well as disputes concerning the minutiae of the law and religious practices. Some people would have been ready to hear Paul present a new opinion on the Messiah. Apparently Paul was both respected and persuasive enough to win converts among his fellow Jews as well as among Gentiles (Acts 13:43; 14:1; 17:4, 11). But as the result of his preaching in the synagogue, some Jews became hostile and even incited riots (Acts 14:2; 17:5–7, 13). At the end of his third journey, Paul was apprehended by Jews while in the temple of Jerusalem (Acts 21:27–32). He remained under the discipline of the Sanhedrin even when being heard before Roman officials (21–26), but the Roman authorities released him when he appealed as a Roman citizen to the emperor (25:10–12, 21; 26:32).

At least one passage in Paul's letters indicates that he remained under the legal discipline of the synagogue: "Five times I have received from the Jews the forty lashes minus one" (2 Cor 11:24). According to the law in Deut 25:3, forty lashes was the punishment for various offenses. It was said that if the one inflicting the lashes exceeded forty, he was liable to a flogging himself, so he stopped at thirty-nine for fear of a miscount. Paul would not have been subject to such beatings had he been entirely dissociated from the synagogue.

Paul says nothing about his own relationship or that of his readers to the synagogue. He wrote his letters to groups of believers composed of both Jews and Gentiles. They shared a common bond, met in houses of members, and apparently were independent of the synagogue.

E. A. Judge 1960–1961:127 has suggested that it was only after Paul failed as a rabbi and was put out of synagogues that he became skilled in rhetoric "by hard experience rather than by training." This may be true, but as late in his career as when he had to deal with opposition at Corinth, Paul's speech was "contemptible" (2 Cor 10:10). Perhaps the Corinthians judged Paul in comparison with Apollos and others who were already more gifted in rhetoric than Paul was.

Use of the Old Testament

Paul's use of the OT most distinguishes him as a Jew. In his letters he quotes only one sentence from Greek literature—a popular proverb—but his acquaintance with the OT is evident in almost every chapter. For Paul, as for all Jews, the OT was the basis of authority for belief and practice. The words "it is written" and "the scripture says" were favorite authoritative formulae among Jews and Christians for introducing an appeal to

scripture. The principle for Paul is set forth in 1 Cor 4:6: "that you may learn through us not to go beyond what is written" (Greek), that is, in the scriptures. Of course, Paul brought his beliefs about Jesus to bear on his interpretation of the OT, but the scriptures retained the same basis of authority for him after he became a convert as they had before. He writes, "Christ died for our sins in accordance with the scriptures . . . he was buried . . . he was raised on the third day in accordance with the scriptures" (1 Cor 15:3–4).

For Paul, as for other NT writers and Hellenistic Jews, the version of the OT cited was usually the Septuagint. Not all of Paul's letters contain direct or literal quotations from the Septuagint, but in Romans, 1 and 2 Corinthians, and Galatians there are about eighty-eight direct quotations from about fifteen different books (for example, Prov 25:21–22 in Rom 12:20; Deut 25:4 in 1 Cor 9:9; Ps 112:9 in 2 Cor 9:9; Hab 2:4 in Gal 3:11). Fifty-three of Paul's quotations—almost two-thirds—are in the letter to the Romans, which is his classic work. In addition to the direct quotations, in the same letters and in Philippians there are many allusions to passages from many different OT books (for example, Exod 4:21 in Rom 9:18; Zech 8:17 in 1 Cor 13:5; Isa 49:13 in 2 Cor 7:6; Gen 16:15–16 in Gal 4:22–27; Job 13:16 in Phil 1:19). Such evidence of Paul's familiarity with the scriptures gives us the best insight into the depth of Paul's Jewishness. At the same time, his spiritual experience of Christ made him think of the scriptures in a new way. The righteousness of God was no longer made available through the scriptures but through Christ, so Paul used the scriptures to help clarify and confirm what God had done through Christ.

The Sect of Qumran

Paul's high regard for OT scriptures and his use of them to support his theological convictions is one of the ways he resembles the Sect of Qumran. Likewise, both the sect and Paul feel a sense of frustration with human sinfulness, and both think that humanity cannot escape from its sinful state except through forgiveness by God's grace. Although there are many similarities between the language and thought in Paul's writings and those of Qumran, there are important differences. Below are several subjects common to Paul and the sect; the quotations and the comments show the similarities and differences.

Justification of Sinners.   A cardinal doctrine of Paul in Galatians and Romans is faith in Christ, and the justification or forgiveness of sinners through that faith by God's grace. A key passage is Rom 3:21–24: "But now, apart from law, the righteousness [or justification] of God has been disclosed . . . the righteousness [or justification] of God through faith in Jesus Christ . . . they are now justified by his grace as a gift, through the redemption that is in Christ Jesus." A key passage in the Qumran Scrolls is 1QS 11:2–3, 5, 12–15: "As for me, my justification belongs to God . . . and by his righteousness my transgression is wiped out . . . and from the fountain of his righteousness comes my justification . . . and by his lovingkindness he will bring my justification. . . . He has justified me."

In both passages there is the idea of the justification of the sinner by God's righteousness. "His lovingkindness" in the Qumran passage corresponds to "his grace" in the passage from Romans. The phrases "through faith in Jesus Christ" and "through the redemption that is in Christ Jesus" are Paul's distinctive contributions to the idea of justification by God. For Paul, justification becomes effective through faith apart from works of the law. This is the distinctive difference between Paul and the Sect of Qumran.

The Holy Spirit Within.   Paul, the Stoics, and the Sect of Qumran speak of a Spirit or Holy Spirit dwelling within the body, which is sometimes thought of as a temple. Read again 1 Cor 3:16 and 6:19, quoted in our discussion of Paul and Stoicism, and compare them with these passages from Qumran: "The council of the community shall be established in truth, as a planting forever, a holy house [that is, temple] for Israel" (1QS 8:5) and "You [God] . . . have poured out

your Holy Spirit within me" (1QH 7:6). The community of Qumran thought of itself in various ways as a spiritual temple or holy house (see 1QS 5:6; 8:5–6; 9:6; 11:8), and the idea that a Holy Spirit resides within a person occurs frequently in the Qumran literature (see 1QH 12:11–12; 13:19; 16:11; 17:25–26).

Light and Darkness.

> For what partnership is there between righteousness and lawlessness? Or what fellowship is there between light and darkness? What agreement does Christ have with Belial? [2 Cor 6:14–15]

> All their guilty transgressions and their iniquities (which they committed) under the dominion of Belial. [1QS 1:23–24]

> From a spring of light come the generations of truth; but from a fountain of darkness come the generations of deceit. In the hand of the prince of lights is the dominion over all the sons of righteousness, and in the ways of light they walk. [1QS 3:19–20]

The antithesis of light and darkness occurs frequently in the scrolls from Qumran. Belial is the prince of evil or Satan, and his name is one of the scrolls' most characteristic terms. It occurs in the NT only in the passage quoted from Paul.

God Fashions His Creatures.

> But who indeed are you, a human being, to argue with God? Will what is molded say to the one who molds it, "Why have you made me like this?" Has the potter no right over the clay? . . . [Rom 9:20–21]

> What, indeed, is he, the son of man, amidst thy marvellous works? . . . Truly this man was shaped from dust . . . for he is something shaped, only fashioned clay. . . . What shall clay reply and that which is shaped by hand? [1QS 11:20–22]

Here both Paul and the writer from Qumran are saying that just as a potter molds the clay at will, so God is free to do what he wants with those he has created, and they have no more right to talk back to God than the clay to the potter. Several passages from the OT, such as Isa

29:16; 45:9–10; Jer 18:1–6; and Wis 12:12, have probably influenced both writers.

Messianic Community Meal.

> The Lord Jesus on the night when he was betrayed took a loaf of bread, and when he had given thanks, he broke it. . . . In the same way he took the cup also, after supper, saying, "This cup is the new covenant in my blood." [1 Cor 11:23–26]

> And when they are summoned to the table of the community to drink the wine and are arranged at the table of the community [and pour] the wine to drink, let no man put out his hand first [to take] the bread and the wine before the priest; for he is the one who blesses the first of the bread and the wine, and he puts his hand on the bread first of all. And afterwards the Messiah of Israel shall stretch out his hands on the bread. [1QSa 2:17–21]

The earliest record of the Lord's Supper is that of Paul quoted above. The Qumran community regularly held a messianic community meal with a blessing of the bread and wine; and the Christian community meal, which became known as the Lord's Supper, may have originated in some Jewish meal like that of Qumran. Even the words "new covenant," which also occur in Matthew's and Mark's accounts of the Lord's Supper, occur in the Qumran literature (see CD 8:15; 9:8).

Although Paul's language and thought are sometimes similar to those of the Sect of Qumran, this does not imply that Paul himself had been a member of that sect or that he was directly influenced by it. Instead, the similarities between Paul's language and thought and those of a Jewish sect of his time confirm Paul's strong Jewish background.

Finally, from Paul's Jewish background also comes his eschatology, which he shared with some of the Jews of his time, including those of Qumran. Paul accepted the Pharisaic idea of two ages, the present age and the age to come. Like Jews of his time, he believed that the present age was evil; but unlike Jews who were not Christians, he believed that the Messiah had come, in accordance with the will of God, to deliver people from that evil age (Gal 1:3–4). Paul often

implies that the present age is only temporary (Rom 12:2; 1 Cor 1:20; 2:6–8; 3:18–19). Like Jews of his time, he expected the end of this age soon and thought it might already be dawning (1 Cor 10:11). Indeed, he eagerly awaited that end, because for him as a Christian Jew it meant the coming again of Jesus (1 Thess 4:13–5:11; 1 Cor 1:7–8; 15:23–28).

PAUL AS A "CHRISTIAN" THINKER

Although both Judaism and Hellenism were influential in Paul's life, the most crucial event was his becoming a follower of the Jesus movement. After his religious experience on the road to Damascus, Paul, a devout Jew, became an ardent follower of Jesus as the Messiah, and he rethought all of his ideas from that perspective.

Although we use the term *thinker* with reference to Paul, his letters do not indicate that he had a superior education, possessed broad knowledge, or was intellectually perceptive. They reveal that Paul was profound in feeling, not in intellectual acumen. Nor was he a systematic theologian. In the words of one scholar, my beloved teacher: "If Paul had ever had to get up his own theology for examination purposes, he might have produced a unified system of Paulinism easier for us to grasp. Fortunately he left the whole wonderful muddle unarranged and alive, and we are the richer for it" (A. D. Nock 1972:2:928). The reason for this "wonderful muddle" is that, with the possible exception of Romans, no letter was carefully thought out, at least not in great detail, before Paul wrote it. His letters were written for specific occasions or to deal with specific questions or problems in the communities he was addressing. Therefore, they contain spontaneously and sometimes hastily dictated notes through which he shares his feelings and gives advice to converted Christians in communities he helped to establish.

The following are Paul's most important thoughts and feelings as a Christian Jew. Although after his experience on the Damascus road there were remarkable changes in his thinking and feeling about Christ, Christians (again, as often, the usual designation), and the law, Paul never believed that he was forsaking the Jews or Judaism. He believed that since Christ's coming Judaism had been an inauthentic religion, and he was inviting both fellow Jews and Gentiles to join him in the one authentic religion that was open to Jews and Gentiles alike—later known as Christianity.

Perhaps Phil 3:4–14 is the best passage for beginning to understand Paul as a Christian thinker. We have already read the first part of that passage, in which Paul boasts of his Jewishness. Read the rest of that passage now. There Paul gives the essence of both his Jewishness and his Christianity, but he places his life as a Christian above all else. As a Christian, Paul believes that whatever advantages he thought he had before his visionary experience are now disadvantages. The only thing that matters to him is his experience of the spiritual Christ. Through "faith in Christ," not through the law, he now experiences God's forgiveness. Here I retain the translation of Paul's Greek in Phil 3:9 and similar phrases elsewhere as "faith in Christ" (as does the *NSRV,* with the alternate translation "faith of Christ" given in the footnotes). An increasing number of scholars think the latter translation is the better choice for all or most of the passages where Paul uses the phrase (Gal 2:16, 20; 3:22; Rom 3:22, 26; Phil 3:9). The reasons for this view need not be discussed; but because I agree with it, I shall summarize my view in the discussion of Galatians, where the problem comes up for the first time.

Through sufferings like Christ's, Paul knows the meaning of Christ's resurrection and the hope for attaining a similar resurrection in the future. But Paul has not yet attained his final goal. In language of the athletic contest, he tells his readers that his experience is not total. He still presses on toward the goal of eternal life with God.

Justification by Faith, and "In Christ" and "Christ In"

Paul's best-known doctrine, though one very complicated and frequently overstressed, is that of justification by God's grace through faith in Christ, not by works of the law. Although not a central doctrine in Paul's letters, it is the best known because a Pauline quotation from the OT, "The righteous person shall live by faith" (Rom 1:17; Gal 3:11; my translation), became the watchword of Martin Luther, who led the religious reformation of the sixteenth century that gave rise to Protestantism (religion of Christian churches except Roman Catholic and Eastern Orthodox).

The basic form from which the idea of justification comes is the verb *dikaioō,* meaning "to make just" or "to make or declare righteous." Except for Romans and Galatians, this word occurs only in 1 Cor 4:4 and 6:11. The form Paul uses most often is the noun *dikaiosynē,* meaning "justice," "justness," or "righteousness"; it occurs mostly in Romans 1–10. The essence of Paul's doctrine is that sinners are justified or declared righteous—that is, forgiven before God—not by works of the law but by faith in Christ. For the Christian convert, this justification or forgiveness takes place symbolically through the rite of baptism, after which the Christian is obligated to live a moral life. This doctrine occurs only in Galatians and Romans. Since it originated in the controversy that occasioned the letter to the Galatians, we will discuss the doctrine when we turn to that letter.

Paul's most creative attempt to convey his new religious experience is through the expressions "in Christ," "Christ in," "in the Lord," and "with Christ." With those characteristic expressions Paul is trying to tell his readers about his spiritual relationship or fellowship with the risen Christ. They disclose the hidden mystery and meaning of Paul's religion, as he strives to bring it to the surface from the depths of his being. The following are key passages: "I have been crucified with Christ; and it is no longer I who live, but it is Christ who lives in me" (Gal 2:19–20). "I am speaking the truth in Christ— I am not lying" (Rom 9:1). "In Christ Jesus, then, I have reason to boast of my work for God" (Rom 15:17). They show that Christ has become the reason for Paul's mission work for God.

For Paul, "Lord" is an exalted title for the risen Jesus. Sometimes the Lord is the Spirit: "Now the Lord is the Spirit, and where the Spirit of the Lord is, there is freedom" (2 Cor 3:17). When Paul speaks of "Christ in" and "in Christ," he is also speaking of "the Spirit of the Lord" or the spiritual Christ mystically present in his life. Christ lives in Paul and Paul in him. He exists in such intimate fellowship with the spiritual presence of Christ that his whole life is in complete subjection to that presence. Paul speaks of the exalted or spiritual Christ in him and of himself in Christ, and that phenomenon is sometimes not distinguishable in his religious experience from the Spirit of God. Now read Rom 8:9, 11 and 1 Cor 2:14, 16, key passages for understanding Paul's view.

In Rom 11:34 and 1 Cor 2:16 "the mind of the Lord" is a quotation from Isa 40:13. Again, Paul's familiarity with the OT has provided the basis for creative Christian thought. The transfer from "the mind of the Lord" to "the mind of Christ" is natural for Paul. "But we have the mind of Christ" is another way of expressing his mystical experience of the spiritual Christ. The mind of Christ is the same as the Spirit of Christ, which in reality is the Spirit of God (see Rom 8:9; 1 Cor 3:16; Gal 4:6). This mind or spirit is part of the religious experience of those who share in the communion, or perhaps union, with the spiritual Christ. "But anyone united to the Lord becomes one spirit with him" (1 Cor 6:17). Paul is saying in a different way what he has said earlier in the same letter (1 Cor 2:12). To have the mind of Christ is to have the Spirit of God. To the Corinthians Paul also writes, "And I think that I too have the Spirit of God" (1 Cor 7:40). Paul does not try to distinguish among these various phenomena.

In a few passages (Rom 6:8; 8:32; 2 Cor 4:14; Phil 1:23; 1 Thess 4:17; 5:10) Paul also uses the phrases "with Christ," "with the Lord," and "with him" to express the Christian's fellowship with the spiritual Christ. Except for Rom 6:8, Paul writes in these verses about the relationship with Christ after death and in the resurrection—as, for example, in Phil 1:23, "My desire is to depart and be with Christ," and in 1 Thess 4:17,

"and so we will be with the Lord forever." Here, being "with Christ" or "with the Lord" is a higher future stage in religious experience, that of being with Christ in the resurrection.

Paul's characteristic expressions "in Christ" and "Christ in" indicate a kind of mystical experience of the spiritual Christ in his own life and the lives of Christians. That experience is to be enhanced in the resurrection, when Paul and other Christians will be with Christ. Paul believed that by the spiritual presence of Christ, he and the converts to whom he was writing were informed about morality and were transformed in order to live in accordance with that morality. Precisely here we have the clue to Paul's moral and ethical teachings. Ethical and moral acts are the outward manifestation of the experience of the spiritual Christ in life, and a moral demand is the consequence of being in Christ.

Moral/Ethical Teachings

Crucial to Paul's ethics is the idea that the right or wrong conduct of a person always places that person in a right or wrong relationship with a God who, Paul believes, is constantly concerned with human affairs. This is very important because it places Paul's ethics in the Jewish, not the Hellenistic, tradition. Paul was genuinely concerned with the right conduct and moral welfare of the people to whom he was writing. Since he was primarily a man of feeling and action, ethics (moral values and responsibilities, or right human character, aims, and actions) was uppermost in his mind. In his letters, as in Judaism, faith is never separated from ethics. For Paul, the belief that the end of the age is coming soon does not lessen ethical demand (V. P. Furnish 1968, 1979; J. T. Sanders 1975:47–90. W. Schrage 1988:163–239).

Paul's ethical teachings belong squarely with those of Judaism. From Judaism come his hatred of idolatry, sexual misconduct, and immorality of any kind. But because of Paul's new religious experience, the motivating force behind his ethical teachings is different; the teachings are the culmination of his experience of the Spirit of Christ in his life. Moral and ethical acts characterize those who live their lives under the influence of the Spirit and who are not under ceremonial laws. The experience of the Spirit brings the freedom to be morally responsible in personal and social life. The basis for such responsibility is love, as summed up in the Jewish command "You shall love your neighbor as yourself" (Gal 5:14; Rom 13:9). Gal 5:6, 13–26; 6:1–10; and Rom 13:8–14 are key passages showing that love is the basis of Paul's ethics (see also 1 Cor 6:9–20; 14:1; 2 Cor 8:7–8, 24; 1 Thess 5:12–22; Rom 8:12–17; 12:9–21).

In the context of Paul's ethical demands belong at least some of his references to the kingdom of God, although his ideas about the kingdom are not entirely consistent. Sometimes he speaks of the kingdom as a present possession, perhaps the equivalent of the forgiven state of the believer's life and religion. At other times, Paul writes as though the kingdom is something entirely of the future. In most cases, however, participation in the kingdom depends upon proper moral and ethical behavior. "For the kingdom of God is not food and drink but righteousness and peace and joy in the Holy Spirit" (Rom 14:17). Paul charges the Thessalonians to "lead a life worthy of God, who calls you into his own kingdom and glory" (1 Thess 2:12). He asks the Corinthians whether they do not know that "unrighteous persons [Greek] will not inherit the kingdom of God" (1 Cor 6:9; see also Gal 5:16–21). Then he tells them, "Fornicators, idolaters, adulterers, male prostitutes, sodomites, thieves, the greedy, drunkards, revilers, robbers—none of these will inherit the kingdom of God" (1 Cor 6:9–10). So for Paul, becoming a Christian by baptism and justification by faith through God's grace do not assure participation in the kingdom of God. That depends on right moral and ethical conduct, life worthy of the kingdom.

Theological Implications of Jesus' Death and Resurrection

Paul's thought on the kingdom of God, as all his thought, was influenced by his belief in the effi-

cacy of the death and resurrection of Jesus. As a Pharisee, Paul believed in the resurrection of the body, and Jesus was the first to rise from the dead. "But in fact Christ has been raised from the dead, the first fruits of those who have died" (1 Cor 15:20). From this basic conviction Paul developed a complicated doctrine that became central to his thinking.

Because God had raised Jesus from the dead, Paul believed that believers would also rise in the general resurrection. Several times he writes about how this will take place. In his earliest letter he uses apocalyptic terms in trying to assure the Thessalonians that their dead friends will not miss Jesus' second coming and the resurrection: "The dead in Christ will rise first. Then we who are alive, who are left, will be caught up in the clouds together with them to meet the Lord in the air; and so we will be with the Lord forever" (1 Thess 4:16–17; see also 2 Cor 4:14).

Paul's classic discussion of the resurrection is 1 Corinthians 15, in which he narrates resurrection appearances of Jesus, stresses the fact of Jesus' own resurrection, argues that because of it there will be a resurrection for his readers, and then discusses the nature of the resurrected body. Now read 1 Cor 15:42–44, 52–53. Here Paul exhibits his own creative blend of the Pharisaic idea of a resurrection of the physical body and the Greek concept of the immortality of the soul. He comes up with the immortality of a spiritual body. Paul wants to emphasize that the resurrected state will be a higher and better existence than earthly life.

For Paul, Jesus' resurrection is not only an event in history and a spiritual reality in the believer's life. It also has theological implications. Jesus was "raised on the third day in accordance with the scriptures" (1 Cor 15:4). This means that Jesus' resurrection didn't just happen but that God was responsible for it (Rom 4:24; 8:11; 10:9; 1 Cor 6:14; 2 Cor 4:14; 13:4; Gal 1:1); the resurrection means victory over death (1 Cor 15:54–57) and sin (Rom 6:10). For Paul, Jesus became the "Son of God with power . . . by resurrection from the dead" (Rom 1:4). Here Paul means that Jesus became a divine being with

God as a result of his resurrection. In the classic passage on baptism (Rom 6:1–10) Paul says that the baptized person shares metaphorically in Jesus' death, and so is dead to sin; that person also shares in Jesus' resurrection, and so is alive to God in Christ.

Sometimes Jesus' death is linked with the resurrection, as in some of the passages just listed; and like the resurrection, it has theological implications. For example, "Christ died for the ungodly" (Rom 5:6), that is, sinners. Christ's death was a sign of God's love (Rom 5:8) and of Christ's love (Gal 2:20); and through his death, Jesus showed his obedience (Rom 5:19; Phil 2:8). Sometimes Paul links the Spirit with Jesus' death and/or resurrection, as in Rom 8:11: "If the Spirit of him who raised Jesus from the dead dwells in you, he who raised Christ from the dead will give life to your mortal bodies also through his Spirit that dwells in you" (see Rom 1:3–4; 8:2–11; Gal 3:13–14).

Paul's ideas on Jesus' death and resurrection, and the implications of those ideas for his readers, are very complicated. Briefly, Paul was certain that Jesus, who had been crucified, was spiritually alive in his own life. The effect of Jesus' crucifixion and resurrection is the certainty of the sinner's justification before God, as summarized in Rom 4:25: "[Jesus] was handed over to death for our trespasses and was raised for our justification."

FINAL YEARS OF PAUL'S LIFE

Our knowledge from the NT about Paul as a traveling mission preacher and as a person ends with the account of his arrival at Rome and his stay there (Acts 28:14–31). Acts ends abruptly: "He lived there two whole years at his own expense and welcomed all who came to him, proclaiming the kingdom of God and teaching about the Lord Jesus Christ with all boldness and without hindrance" (28:30–31). Just that abruptly ends our knowledge of Paul's life! But why such an abrupt ending to such an unusual career? Was Paul ever brought to trial in Rome?

Was he released without trial? Was he acquitted? Was he martyred? In any case, why did the author of Acts not inform his readers?

Some scholars have attempted to show that Paul's imprisonment in Rome was terminated by his acquittal and release. They argue that Paul made a trip to Spain that could not have been made before his Roman imprisonment. In Rom 15:24, 28, Paul himself expresses a desire to see Spain: "I do hope to see you on my journey . . . by way of you to Spain." The earliest clear references to a journey to Spain are found in the Muratorian Fragment and in a work usually known as the *Acts of Peter*. The former says that Luke relates indirectly "the departure of Paul from the city [Rome] as he was proceeding to Spain." But this statement appears to be only a simple conclusion drawn by the author from the statement in Romans 15. The account in the *Acts of Peter* is clearly apocryphal and, like the Muratorian Fragment, mentions only Paul's departure from Rome for Spain, nothing about his trip or his arrival in Spain. Thus there is no evidence of Paul being in Spain, either in the church fathers (post-NT writers) of the second and third centuries or in the tradition of any Spanish church for centuries after Paul. On the contrary, most writers of the first centuries CE assumed that Paul had died in Rome.

The earliest extant reference to Paul's death is found in an early Christian writing known as *The First Epistle of Clement to the Corinthians*. The writer is not mentioned in the letter itself, but tradition has always identified him with a Clement whose name appears in lists of bishops as the third or fourth bishop of Rome toward the end of the first century. Clement merely alludes to Paul's death and gives no details with respect to time, place, or manner: "Having given testimony to the rulers, he then passed from the world and was taken up to the holy place, and became the greatest example of endurance" (5:7). Later Christian writers also say that Paul died as a martyr in Rome.

In the apocryphal *Acts of Paul*, the martyrdom of Paul is expanded and glorified. The story, though interesting, is not trustworthy. The writer tells of Nero's decree that Christians and soldiers of Christ be killed. When Paul is brought before the emperor after the decree, he is reported as saying: "Caesar, it is not for a little while that I live to my King. And if you cut off my head, this I will do—I will arise and appear before you and show you that I am not dead, but alive to my Lord Jesus Christ, who comes to judge the world." Then, when Paul's head is struck off, milk spurts upon the cloak of the soldier. When the soldier and all present see it, they marvel and they glorify God, who has given such glory to Paul. Then they report to Caesar what has happened. Many philosophers and the centurion are with Caesar, and Paul appears and says, "Caesar, behold, I Paul, the soldier of God, am not dead but live in my God." Having said that, Paul departs from him.

Although there is evidence for Paul's martyrdom, it is not conclusive. The nature of Paul's end is still a mystery, but his spirit lives on in his letters. To those who read them, in the words of Tertullian (Christian writer, c. 160–225), "he springs to life again."

SOME RECENT WORKS ON PAUL

Perhaps the most important emphasis in recent Pauline studies is the attempt to consider Paul as a creature of the first century CE and not of later centuries. Occasionally some scholars have treated Paul as though he were a person of modern times to be judged on the basis of modern sociology and psychology. Earlier we learned about the Jesus Seminar group of scholars concerned with discovering the real or historical Jesus. Encouraged by their work on that subject, the group has now turned their attention to the historical Paul. The results of their work are awaited. Meanwhile, many recent works on Paul have appeared that seek to get back to the historical Paul and his thought world. I mention several to illustrate different points of view.

J. Murphy-O'Connor 1996, in a critical (in the sense of careful and thorough) life of Paul, considers Paul's letters as primary in determining

his life and Acts as secondary. Utilizing historical, archaeological, and geographical information Murphy-O'Connor comes up with a detailed chronology of Paul's life and places his letters in the context of his ministry. Some of his views are criticized in a work the following year by M. Hengel and A. M. Schwemer 1997a. They are concerned with Paul's life during the time of his conversion on the way to Damascus and the beginning of his work in Antioch, "The Unknown Years." The prominent British literary critic A. N. Wilson 1997, writing from a literary editor's perspective, has expressed skepticism about some aspects of Paul's life and thought as generally understood. Wilson's skepticism is vigorously attacked by a fellow Briton, N.T. Wright 1997, who wrote about the historical Jesus. The title of Wright's book, *What Saint Paul Really Said,* gives a hint of his own more conservative views.

Those of you who become interested in learning more about the new search for the "real Paul" may find the work of B. Witherington 1998, *The Paul Quest: The Renewed Search for the Jew of Tarsus,* a good place to begin. He writes lucidly and is concerned with both method and content in the study of Paul. However, although Witherington aims to present Paul as a rabbi of the ancient Mediterranean world, he does not always escape the pitfalls of some whom he criticizes. Many scholars will disagree with his view that Paul actually wrote all the letters that bear his name, although probably with the help of a secretary. Nor will they agree with his extended chronology of Paul's life whereby he makes the events reported in Acts coincide with Paul's letters.

There has also been a renewed interest in Paul's moral/ethical teachings. The older studies of V. P. Furnish 1968, 1979 are noteworthy; however, his work is marred by an overemphasis on the grace and righteousness of God, to the neglect of righteousness on the part of believers themselves, and the doctrine of justification by faith. A more balanced treatment is that of the German scholar W. Schrage 1988:163–238, though, perhaps, he places too much stress on Paul's Christology and eschatology and not enough on his theology.

From the viewpoint of Paul as a man of his time, especially in light of his Hellenistic background, and his concern for morality, the works of W. A. Meeks 1983 (social world), 1986, 1993 (moral world of Paul) and A. J. Malherbe 1987, 1989 (Paul and the popular philosophers) are novel and significant. Malherbe calls attention to the similarities and differences between some of Paul's teachings and those of Stoics, Cynics, and other philosophers.

The subject of Paul's moral/ethical teachings is one to which, I think, I have contributed. In the conclusion to her review (*CBQ* 58:744–746) of my *Apostle Paul* 1994 R. A. Boisclair says: "Few scholars will be persuaded that F. has made it unnecessary to continue the perennial attempts to establish Paul's central message, but they will find many fresh insights and much to ponder."

THIS AUTHOR'S VIEWS ON PAUL

For most of this chapter I have discussed Paul and his thought along rather conventional lines. After decades of study and teaching, I have come to a different and, I think, better understanding of Paul. So, at the request of several readers over the years, using the moral/ethical approach I suggested in Chapter 2, I give some of my own views. (For details see E. D. Freed 1994. Translations of texts are mine.)

Although Paul became known as a Christian, he remained a Jew still utterly faithful to the only God he believed existed (see 1 Cor 8:4–6; 10:19–22; Gal 3:20; Rom 3:27–31). Paul's monotheism and his teaching were the antithesis of the pagan polytheism of the world of which he was a part. Paul's message was directed primarily to Gentiles, and conversion of Gentiles to Paul's God, to whom as a Jew he was still committed (see 1 Cor 8:4–6), was his primary effort. So to call persons converted by Paul Christians, at least in the modern sense of the term, is an anachronism, because, as we have learned, only after Paul's time did followers of Jesus refer to themselves with that designation.

In the same way, to refer to a group of converts as a "church" in the sense it came to have later, is not exactly appropriate either. As W. A. Meeks 1983:108, 230, n. 166 has shown, "church" is "not just the occasional gathering, but the group itself." In this way Paul's *ekklēsia* ("church") differed from the Greek town meeting, the name for which was *ekklēsia*, meaning "assembly." So, for Paul, the church was not an institution or a meeting, but the members of the assembly themselves. Such members were not Christians, but persons in transition from either Judaism or paganism to the religion that only later became known as Christianity.

The use of the term "Christianity" first occurs in the letter of Ignatius to the Magnesians (10:3), where it is used as a phenomenon different from Judaism. Ignatius was a bishop of Antioch and was martyred sometime early in the second century. He writes that "every tongue believing in God was brought together into it" (that is, Christianity). Notice that "believing in God" was apparently still the main criterion for entrance into the religion. This helps to support what I am about to say.

Paul uses four basic designations to refer to fellow converts: those called or chosen, brothers, those who believe or believers, and holy ones. (For evidence see *The Apostle Paul*, pages 123–128.) It was not just coincidence that "believers" and "holy ones" were among the first words used to designate members of the Jesus movement, referred to as "the Way" (recall discussion above) from others in the social world of the first century. From the beginning of the religion that came to be known as Christianity faithfulness toward God, certain beliefs about Jesus, and holiness of life were inseparably linked together. For these and other reasons, it is more appropriate to refer to the members of Paul's communities as believers or converts, designations that I now use interchangeably.

The basic text for an understanding of Paul's missionary activity is 1 Thess 1:8–9: "Your faith in God has gone forth everywhere . . . how you turned to God from idols to serve a living and true God." During a period of instruction in preparation for baptism converts were taught certain beliefs about Jesus, including the belief that he was the long-expected Messiah, that God raised him from the dead, that he became God's Son by virtue of his resurrection (Rom 1:3–4), and that he would come again. However, beliefs about Jesus were secondary to faithfulness toward God and the moral probity which that faithfulness demanded.

Paul believed that when persons became converted to faithfulness toward God they received the Holy Spirit given them by God. And Paul also believed that God called converts from immoral life to live in holiness. "Therefore," says Paul, "whoever disregards this disregards not humans but God, who gives his Holy Spirit to you" (1 Thess 4:7–8; see also 1 Cor 2:10–13; 3:16–17; 6:19; 2 Cor 1:22; 5:5; Gal 3:2–5; Rom 5:5; 8:9, 11).

Having received the Holy Spirit, converts were subjected to an intense period of moral instruction (*didachē*) to which they became committed (Rom 6:17; see also Rom 16:17-19). For converts' obedience and disobedience to that teaching see 2 Cor 2:9; 7:13–16; 10:5–6; Rom 16:9. Such teaching, I believe, was in preparation for baptism, whereby converts were acquitted (forgiven) of past sins and made righteous (*dikaioō*, Paul's word; recall discussion of Romans 6 above; see also 1 Cor 6:9–11).

Instead of still being among the unrighteous (*adikoi*), baptized converts were among the righteous (*dikaioi*). Paul links baptism, the converts, being made holy or righteous through baptism, and the forgiveness of *past* sins together ("such *were* some of you, *but*"; 1 Cor 6:11; emphasis mine). And not only that! Paul expected baptized converts to remain righteous or sinless. This becomes perfectly clear from Romans 6. Roman converts had heard about Paul and his coworkers being supercharged with the Spirit and living under its power, not under the law. But some mistook Paul's freedom from the law for license to do as they wanted and even said in slander that Paul had said, "Let us do evil in order that good may come" (Rom 3:8). Such converts thought that if God's grace was so effective for the forgiveness of sins they could continue to have a merry good time. If a little grace was good, more would only be better. Converts thought they could continue to sin and be forgiven all over again.

Paul responds to the Roman converts' slanderous remarks and other mistaken impressions by asking: "What shall we say then? Are we to continue in sin that grace may abound?" Paul's answer is a resounding, "No way! How can we who died to sin still live in it?" He goes on to explain that when converts are immersed in the water of baptism they share symbolically in Christ's death and thereby die to past sins. When they emerge from the water, they share symbolically in his resurrection. This happens so that just as Christ died and was raised, "we too might walk [metaphorically, "conduct one's life"] in newness of life." Converts who have died in baptism "have been acquitted (*dikaioō*) of sin. . . . So you must consider yourselves dead to sin but living to God in Christ Jesus" (Rom 6:7). And Paul exhorts his readers: "Do not, therefore, let sin rule in your mortal body to make you obey its passions. Do not yield your members as weapons of wickedness for sin, but offer yourselves to God . . . and your members to God as weapons of righteousness" (Rom 6:7, 12–13). Converts have it in their power not to sin, so Paul charges the Corinthian converts: "Be thoroughly sober in mind righteously [*dikaiōs*, adverb], and do not sin" (1 Cor 15:34).

According to Paul, baptized converts became members of a renewed covenant community of God (under influence from the OT), which in Gal 6:16 he calls "the Israel of God." Members lived a new life—life in Christ—under the power of the Holy Spirit, and their aim was complete moral probity. Converts in such communities were to strive to become "blameless in holiness" before God (1 Thess 3:13). Paul writes to the Corinthians: "Let us cleanse ourselves from every contamination of flesh (body) and spirit, making holiness perfect in the fear of God" (2 Cor 7:1). Moreover, converts must constantly be on their guard so that they do not revert to the sins of their previous, pagan immoral life when they did not know God (see 1 Thess 4:5; 1 Cor 12:2; Gal 4:8, 9). Final judgment and ultimate salvation are still to come: "The unrighteous (*adikoi*) will not inherit the kingdom of God" (1 Cor 6:9).

According to Paul, the wages of sin is still death for believers as for unbelievers. Eternal life is the free gift of God for those who live in Christ Jesus (Rom 6:23). But believers have to hold on to that gift. Paul said that through Christ "we have had access to this grace in which we stand, and we boast in hope of the glory of God" (Rom 5:2). That glory, however, is still only a hope, because the judgment and ultimate salvation lie ahead: "For we will all stand before the judgment seat of God. . . . So each one of us will be accountable to God" (Rom 14:10–12). A point too often overlooked is that, according to Paul, the goal for the lives of converts is not to have their "*faith* in Christ reckoned as righteousness before God at the last judgment" (against P. Stuhlmacher 1986:73), but their *deeds* (my emphasis): "according to what each has done in the body" (2 Cor 5:10). In Rom 2:6 Paul says: "He (God) will repay each person according to one's deeds" (see Rom 2:1–11).

Now that you have read some of my views on Paul and his thought, perhaps you want to discuss them with your instructor. Keep them in mind as you study Paul's letters in the next several chapters to see if you do or do not agree with some or all of what I have said. With respect to my views, I shall give you more to think about in the discussion of Galatians and Romans in Chapter 11. There I shall give what I believe is Paul's basic theological reason why God made it possible for converts to be forgiven of their past sins and come to new moral lives in Christ under the power of the Holy Spirit.

SUMMARY

In this chapter we have considered aspects of Paul's life, including his occupation as tentmaker, his personal traits, and his relationships to Jesus and his early followers. As a Hellenistic Jew, Paul was influenced by both Hellenism and Judaism. The greatest Hellenistic influences upon Paul appear in his use of Greek and in the similarities between his thought and language and those of the Stoics. As a Pharisaic Jew, Paul inherited a belief in scripture as an authoritative basis for faith and life, as well as a belief in the resurrection of the body. Paul also shared important ideas with the Jewish Sect of Qumran, including the sinfulness of humanity and forgiveness by God's grace.

In Acts we first meet Paul as a persecutor of Jesus' followers (those "who belonged to the Way"; Acts 9:2). However, an important visionary experience changed him from persecutor to ardent missionary. As the result of that experience, Paul not only accepted Jesus as the Jewish Messiah but also believed that Jesus had become the Son of God through his resurrection from the dead. To Paul, belief in Christ, not adherence to the Mosaic law, was necessary for the forgiveness of sins. Yet as a Jew, though he became a follower of Jesus, Paul remained a true monotheist faithful to his God. He wanted his converts to obey the just commandments of God, along with some teachings of Jesus' followers (*didachē*), that were the basis for moral life.

The basis of Paul's thought is his theological understanding of the death and resurrection of Jesus, and the significance of those events for faith and life. Christ's death brought the opportunity for justification or forgiveness of sins by the grace of God to all who have faith in Christ. The justified or forgiven person lives a new life in Christ; the spiritual Christ lives in the believer, and the believer is obligated to live a moral life based on love.

We learned about some recent works on Paul that presented different opinions with respect to determining the "real Paul," the Paul of history. Finally, we learned about some of my views reached by approaching Paul from his monotheism and his moral/ethical teachings.

For further study of Paul, you will find different approaches and emphases in the following works. For Paul in general see F. F. Bruce 1978b; G. Bornkamm 1971; S. Kim 1982; M. D. Hooker 1980; C. J. Roetzel 1991; A. J. Hultgren 1985;

S. Sandmel 1958, from Jewish perspective; G. Luedemann 1984; S. B. Marrow 1986; for theology see D. H. E. Whiteley 1964; J. A. Fitzmyer 1967b; H. Ridderbos 1975; J. C. Beker 1980, 1982; G. Theissen 1987, from psychological perspective; J. D. G. Dunn 1998; for the law see L. Gaston 1987; S. Westerholm 1988; E. P. Sanders 1983; C. J. Roetzel 1995; H. Huebner 1984; J. D. G. Dunn 1990; for Paul and Judaism see E. P. Sanders 1977; K. Stendahl 1976; F. Watson 1988; A. F. Segal 1990, from Jewish per-spective; P. Lapide 1984, from a Jewish and a Christian perspective.

In the next three chapters we will study the undisputed letters of Paul. They are called undisputed letters because they are generally accepted as authentic. The earliest of these seven undisputed letters—1 Thessalonians and 1 and 2 Corinthians—are the subjects of our next chapter. Later, in the final chapter of Part II, we will examine the three disputed letters of Paul.

CHAPTER 10

Undisputed Letters of Paul: 1 Thessalonians, 1 and 2 Corinthians

IN THIS CHAPTER WE WILL CONSIDER several matters that are important for understanding Paul's letters in general, including the Greek letter as a literary form. Paul's reasons for writing letters, and the sequence and authenticity of his letters follow. Then we will focus on Paul's earliest letters, with a brief description of the cities of Thessalonica and Corinth, the locations of the churches to which Paul wrote his first letters. We will consider the date and place of writing of these letters, as well as their purpose and content.

Paul wrote his letters, with the possible exception of Romans, to deal with specific problems. We will consider the problems at Thessalonica and Corinth and Paul's responses to them. The correspondence with Corinth presents special problems because, from the letters themselves, it seems clear that Paul wrote more letters to Corinth than the two included in the NT. Most likely, Paul wrote at least four letters to Corinth, including 1 Corinthians and three others, of which fragments have been put together in 2 Corinthians.

Finally, the chapter contains an outline of 1 Thessalonians and the Corinthian correspondence, with comments on important passages. These comments are intended as an aid to understanding Paul's responses to the situations in the churches of Thessalonica and Corinth. (Because many scholars think that Paul did not write 2 Thessalonians, it is discussed in Chapter 13 on disputed letters of Paul.)

THE LETTER AS A LITERARY FORM

In the Graeco-Roman world there were several kinds of letters, including private, personal letters and formal letters intended for the public. The latter frequently aimed to arouse publicity and to evoke a formal response to the authors' views. Paul's letters, however, are informal and were not intended to be made public or to gain publicity. With the possible exception of Romans, they are free, spontaneous, conversational compositions intended only for the people addressed. They are therefore not exactly public or private letters, but fall in between the two types.

Paul's letters generally follow the scheme of Hellenistic letters of his time. But because of his own creative ways of adapting each letter to the particular situation of the church he was addressing, his letters do not always follow the Greek style. Below is a translation of most of a letter sent from an Egyptian boy in the Roman navy to his father and family.

> Apion to Epimachus, his father and master, very many greetings. Before all things, I pray that you may be healthy and may always be well and prosper, along with my sister and her daughter and my brother. I give thanks to the lord Serapis that when I was in danger at sea he saved me immediately. . . . Greet Capiton many times and my brother and Serenilla and my friends. . . . I pray that you may be well. . . . Serenus, son of . . . greets you . . . and Turbo . . . to Epimachus from Apion his son. . . . [trans. from the Greek text in A. Deissmann 1927:179]

Now compare it with the following verses from the beginning and ending of Romans:

> Paul . . . called to be an apostle. . . . To all God's beloved in Rome. . . . Grace to you and peace from God our Father and the Lord Jesus Christ. First, I thank my God through Jesus Christ for all of you . . . I remember you always in my prayers. . . . Greet Prisca and Aquila, who work with me in Christ Jesus . . . greet also the church in their house. . . . Timothy, my co-worker, greets you; so do Lucius and Jason and Sosipater, my relatives.

Both letters include the writer's name, the people to whom the letter is addressed, and greetings. Paul expands this part to include a statement of his call to faith and a summary of his theology (see also 1 Cor 1:1–3; Gal 1:1–5; Phil 1:1–2). Paul's word "peace" represents the typical Jewish greeting "peace to you." "Grace" is probably derived directly from the usual word for greeting (*chairō*), meaning "rejoice." Paul uses it as a distinctive greeting, and it may have originated with him. Paul's words "grace to you and peace" are apparently a combination of his Jewish greeting "peace" and the greeting "grace," used by Jesus' followers, and indicate a religious content.

After the salutation, both letters have a short prayer of thanksgiving or a petition on behalf of those addressed. Both letters close with greetings from the writer and include greetings from other people. Paul sometimes expands the ending to include a statement of faith and a benediction (1 Cor 16:19–24; 2 Cor 13:11–14). Both Apion's letter and those of Paul include a request that the recipients give greetings from the sender to other people. Like Apion's letter, all of Paul's letters are in Greek; but unlike Apion's, Paul's letters are about as distinctive a contribution to literary types as the first gospels are. (For the letter as a literary form, see W. G. Doty 1973; J. L. White 1972, 1983; M. L. Stirewalt 1977.)

WHY DID PAUL WRITE LETTERS?

As Paul traveled from city to city, making new friends, winning converts to the developing new religion, and establishing churches, he was often separated from the people he had last met. Because the letter was the only form of long-distance communication, Paul wrote letters to communities he had previously visited. Although Paul was responsible for the content of his letters, he did not write them in his own hand but dictated them to a secretary, as we know from Rom 16:22: "I Tertius, the writer of this letter, greet you in the Lord." Sometimes Paul did add a personal note at the end, as in 1 Cor 16:21: "I, Paul, write this greeting with my own hand" (see also Gal 6:11–18; Phlm 19). This was a customary way of indicating that the letter was authentic. Paul's letters were delivered by messengers who traveled on land or sea.

Although Paul's letters are informal, they were not written just to extend greetings, to reminisce about old times, or to renew friendships. Instead, they are situational or occasional letters, that is, they address specific situations or occasions or deal with particular problems that have arisen in the communities addressed. In fact, it is only through Paul's responses to problems in his churches that we can determine his views. Moreover, if people in those churches had always agreed with Paul, we would not know very much about his thought, since he wrote in response to what they were thinking and doing. So Paul's letters, although incomplete, are intimate, mostly authentic, and first-hand information about his life and thought.

THE ORDER AND AUTHENTICITY OF PAUL'S LETTERS

Paul's letters in the NT are not arranged in the order in which they were originally written. So why were Paul's letters arranged in their present order? There is no certain answer to that question, but apparently the person who collected them placed the letters to churches first and then those to individuals, including the letters to Timothy and Titus. It seems that length also had something to do with the order. If we ignore the letters to Timothy and Titus, which were not included in the earliest list of Paul's letters, that of the heretic Marcion (c. 140 CE), the other ten letters are generally arranged from the longest to the shortest.

The Pauline correspondence is not usually discussed in the NT order for several reasons. Scholars generally agree that, because of its apocalyptic eschatology, 1 Thessalonians is the earliest of Paul's letters and that Romans is later. Moreover, 1 Thessalonians and the letters to Corinth could be the earliest because, with the exception of Philemon, they are the least theological. (For views about development in Paul's thought, see J. C. Hurd 1983:6–12.) The controversy concerning the requirements for Gentile converts at Galatia forced Paul, as both Jew and convert to Christ, for the first time to think out his own position on such requirements. Romans is Paul's attempt to state his position after the Galatian controversy, so without Galatians we might not have Romans. Therefore, Galatians and Romans are treated together after 1 Thessalonians and the Corinthian letters.

Some scholars have argued that the prison letters (Ephesians, Philippians, Colossians, and Philemon—so called because Paul wrote them while in prison) originated in some place other than Rome, the traditional site. If Rome is accepted as the place of Paul's imprisonment, then the prison letters would be the last written. However, if, as some think, Ephesus (see Chapter 12) was the city of Paul's imprisonment, then Philippians and/or Philemon could have been written close to the time of Corinthians and Galatians. It is impossible to determine precisely the sequence of the prison letters. Because there is considerable disagreement about the place and date of writing for Philippians and Philemon, they are discussed last among the undisputed letters.

Romans, 1 and 2 Corinthians, and Galatians are sometimes referred to as the "great letters" because of their length and importance for Christian teaching. Some scholars regard them as Paul's only authentic letters. At the other extreme, some scholars still accept ten or even thirteen letters as authentic. There is general agreement about the authenticity of the letters treated as undisputed (1 Thessalonians, 1 and 2 Corinthians, Galatians, Romans, Philemon, and Philippians), but beyond that there is wide difference of opinion. Although most scholars accept the authenticity of Philippians, many question its unity and think it consists of two or three fragments of Pauline letters. Because of the wide disagreement about the authenticity of 2 Thessalonians, Ephesians, and Colossians, they are dealt with separately as disputed letters of Paul. Most scholars regard the letters to Timothy and Titus as later than Paul, so they are not treated as letters of Paul.

1 THESSALONIANS

THESSALONICA

Because Thessalonica has been rebuilt at the same place after every disaster that befell it, most of its archaeological remains are buried under the present city. According to Strabo, Thessalonica was founded about 315 BCE by Cassander, general of Alexander the Great, who named it after his wife Thessalonike. Strabo says it was the metropolis of Macedonia and was more populous than any of the other cities. When Rome took over Macedonia in 168 BCE, Thessalonica became the capital of the second of its four districts. Then in 147 BCE, when Macedonia became a Roman province, Thessalonica became the chief city and the residence of the Roman governor. It supported Octavian and Antony against Brutus and Cassius in the battle of Philippi (42 BCE), and as a reward it was declared a free city.

As a free city Thessalonica had autonomy in all internal affairs, and its citizens could appoint their own magistrates. The writer of Acts (Greek) calls these magistrates "politarchs" (17:6, 8), the term for non-Roman rulers of a city. His use of the term "the people" (*dēmos*) seems to confirm the autonomy of the citizens whom the Jews have brought together, though probably not for a regular public meeting.

Before Paul's time Roman cults were established at Thessalonica. A temple honored Julius Caesar, and the image of Julius was printed on coins from the city. The emperor was worshiped, along with Oriental deities. Paul's converts turned from idols "to serve a living and true God" (1 Thess 1:9).

The Via Egnatia, the main road from Rome to the East, ran through Thessalonica. That road, along with the excellent harbor, made Thessalonica, with Corinth, a main trading center. At both the eastern and western entrances to the city it was spanned by Roman arches. An inscription on the arch at the western entrance is of special interest in Pauline studies. It begins with the words "In the time of the politarchs." Two other inscriptions from Thessalonica, one dated in the reign of Augustus and the other in that of Claudius, also use the word "politarchs." These inscriptions substantiate the use of the term by the writer of Acts.

How long Paul stayed in Thessalonica is not certain, but he was there long enough to develop a warm and affectionate relationship with those to whom he writes. He exhorts them "like a nurse tenderly caring for her own children" (1 Thess 2:7) and "like a father with his children" (1 Thess 2:11). In 1 Thessalonians Paul addresses his readers with the affectionate term "brothers" nineteen times, proportionately more than in any other letter.

THE SITUATION IN THE CHURCH AT THESSALONICA AND PAUL'S RESPONSE

There were Jews in Macedonia in the first century of the Christian era (Philo, *Embassy to Gaius* 36). Acts reports a synagogue in Thessalonica, and Paul began his mission preaching to the Jews and God-fearing pagans who came there. But some Jews made it rough for Paul and his companions (Acts 17:2–10). They were jealous because many devout Greeks and women attached to the synagogue had been converted to Christianity. This conversion led to much suffering among the new converts, suffering reflected in the strongly anti-Jewish passage in 1 Thess 2:14–16. Turn to it now.

This passage indicates that although the Jews had instigated the suffering at Thessalonica, the converts actually suffered at the hands of their fellow Gentiles in the mob (see also Acts 17:5). Paul's adversaries had associated him with the scores of other traveling salesmen for all sorts of religious cults and philosophies, who were out to make an easy living, whose rhetoric was beguiling, and for whom religion and morality were rarely connected. In 2:3–6 Paul defends himself against such charges brought against him in his absence and apparently reported to him by Timothy or in a letter from the Thessalonians.

As you read Thessalonians, you can see that the main concern of the Thessalonian Christians themselves was the time of Jesus' second coming. Like Paul (2:19), they believed Jesus was coming again, but they were worried that the faithful converts who had already died would miss his coming. Paul responds by saying they should "not grieve as others do who have no hope," and in vivid apocalyptic imagery he reassures them (1 Thess 4:13–18). The concern about Jesus' second coming gave rise to three groups that caused trouble in the Christian community at Thessalonica: the idlers, the faint hearted, and the weak (5:14). Paul writes to supply what is lacking in their faith (3:10) and to instruct them in the moral life (4–5).

DATE AND PLACE OF WRITING

From Thessalonica Paul and his friend Silas were hurried off to Beroea, but Jews from Thessalonica then came there and incited the people. So Paul was sent to Athens alone, and Silas and Timothy remained in Beroea. From Athens Paul went to Corinth where, according to Acts, Silas and Timothy joined him from Macedonia (Acts 17:10–15; 18:1, 5). Paul had sent Timothy, his co-worker, back to Thessalonica to establish the Thessalonians in their faith and exhort them (1 Thess 3:2). Timothy returned to Paul, perhaps at Athens (1 Thess 3:6). According to 2 Cor 1:19, which agrees with Acts 18:5, Silas and Timothy were with Paul in Corinth. Since Silas (Silvanus) and Timothy were with Paul when he wrote to the Thessalonians (1 Thess 1:1), it appears that Paul wrote from Corinth on his second journey, after Timothy returned with his report—or c. 51 CE. This date coincides with the consensus that Gallio, proconsul of Achaia when Paul visited Corinth (Acts 18:12–17), was in office for a year sometime between 51 and 53. Although this is the consensus of NT scholars, some think that 1 Thessalonians was written later and under different circumstances. For arguments pro and con, see W. G. Kuemmel 1975:257–260.

A. J. Malherbe 1983:23–27 maintains that Paul is not defending himself in 1 Thessalonians 1–3 and that those chapters "are paraenetic [exhortative] in function. They not only enable us to learn more about the Thessalonian church and Paul's relationship with it, but, through the self-description, they also establish the basis for the exhortation in chapters four and five. The antithetic style [written in opposition to] is not apologetic and is entirely appropriate in this type of writing," where Paul's style "is so heavily indebted to the popular philosophers." Like philosophers, Paul describes himself as being concerned with healing human souls (1 Thess 2:9). Part of this style is also to remind readers of what they already know, to encourage them to keep on doing what they are doing, and to exhort them to imitate others whose actions exemplify what is encouraged. But Paul "goes beyond the normal paraenetic style in not merely calling them to imitate him, but claiming that they have already done so." Keep these statements in mind to temper what you read in the comments that follow.

We turn now to the content of 1 Thessalonians. Below is an outline of the letter, with comments on important passages, to assist you in reading 1 Thessalonians.

Outline and Comments

I. Salutation (1:1)

II. Complimentary thanksgiving for the Thessalonians' acceptance and response to his message (1:2–10)

Paul talks about his relationship with the believers at Thessalonica when he established the community there and thanks God for their faithful response to his message. Their faith, love, and hope (1:3) have produced practical results. Paul is certain that God chose the Thessalonian converts because of the effectiveness of the gospel he preached "not in word only, but also in power and in the Holy Spirit and with full conviction" (1:5). Their conversion is verified by their becoming "imitators" of Paul and "of the Lord" and by their exemplary lives of "faith in God" (1:6–8). Recall comments in the last chapter on the importance of these verses for understanding Paul's mission efforts to convert Gentiles to faithfulness toward God and the moral life that faithfulness required.

That most of the converts at Thessalonica were Gentiles is clear from the words "you turned to God from idols, to serve a living and true God" (1:9). These words and those in 1:10—"and to wait for his Son from heaven, whom he raised from the dead—Jesus, who rescues us from the wrath that is coming"—are the essence of apostolic preaching to Gentiles, and combine Jewish polemic against idols with the Jewish-Christian eschatology. Converts give up the worship of idols, which have "no real existence" (my trans.) since "there is no God but one" (1 Cor 8:4), to serve a God that truly exists. To that monotheism is added the belief that Jesus is the Son of God, whom God raised from the dead, and the eschatological expectation that Jesus will return to deliver believers from the wrath to come—that is, the final judgment.

III. Paul's defense against the charges of his adversaries (2:1–12)

Paul's adversaries, who circulated charges against him, were not actually members of the believing community at Thessalonica. Paul develops the thought of 1:5, namely, that the power of God is at work in his ministry and that he and his companions are men whose motives are beyond reproach. The gospel message does not originate from "deceit or impure motives or trickery" (2:3). The words quoted imply the charges that Paul's preaching was wrong because it was deceitful, that his behavior was immoral, and that he was treacherously deluding others.

Verses 5 and 9 indicate that some thought Paul was a missionary who did not regard others and was greedy for money, but he reminds them that he has worked hard not to be dependent upon anyone for financial support. Paul also reminds the Thessalonians of his affectionate concern for them and of his teaching as evidence of his moral integrity and that of his companions. And he urges the Thessalonians to "lead a life worthy of God, who calls you into his own kingdom and glory" (2:12).

The last words quoted express what, in Paul's teaching, the goal of the Christian life was, but the meaning of the expression "kingdom" is not clear. Perhaps, as in the gospels, it means the new order that God offered humanity and that Jesus inaugurated. As such, its complete manifestation, its glory, would be revealed at the end of history with the return of Christ. Perhaps the kingdom and glory belong together and denote the eschatological society of the redeemed, over which God will reign in the future (see Gal 5:21; 1 Cor 6:9; Rom 14:17). The references listed tend to support the interpretation that the "kingdom and glory" here are the equivalent of the developing religion, into which the Thessalonians had just been taken as converts. Regardless of interpretation, morality and ethics are never to be excluded. This is clear from what immediately preceded, as well as from what follows in chaps. 4 and 5.

IV. A second thanksgiving, and condemnation of the sins of the Jews that caused the suffering of Thessalonian converts (2:13–16)

Because these verses contain a second thanksgiving and an anti-Jewish attitude not characteristic of Paul, some scholars regard them as a later insertion. They see a reference to the destruction of Jerusalem in the words "God's wrath has overtaken them." The verses would have been written, then, after 70 CE, too late to be from Paul. But if they are from Paul (see Phil 3:1–3), they repeat his gratitude for the faith of the Thessalonians even in time of suffering.

Those who regard vv 15–16 as Pauline have suggested that Paul had a specific historical event in mind when he said "God's wrath has overtaken them"—for example, the famine (Acts 11:28), Claudius's expulsion of the Jews from Rome (Acts 18:2), or the death of Agrippa I (Acts 12:21–23). Paul is speaking about the particular situation at Thessalonica, where some Jews outside the church have been causing problems. He speaks eschatologically and may mean that even before the impending judgment, the wrath of God has come upon those Jews because they refused to become converts, and also because they prevented some Gentiles from doing so.

V. Paul's relationship with the converts at Thessalonica after the church was established (2:17–3:13)

Paul explains his being unable to visit the Thessalonians as the work of Satan, and praises them affectionately (2:17–20). Timothy has been sent to strengthen their faith, that is, their perseverance in the moral way of life in time of affliction (3:1–5). Timothy returns with the good news of their faith, but Paul longs to see them again face to face to "restore whatever is lacking" in their faith (3:6–10). His exuberance over the Thessalonians' faith does not prevent him from realizing that among those converted from paganism there is always the risk of moral laxity. Paul prays that the Lord may make them "increase and abound in love for one another and for all" and that they may attain the goal of moral life, "blameless in holiness before our God and Father at the coming of our Lord Jesus" (3:11–13; Greek).

VI. *Advice and exhortation about concerns of the Thessalonians (4:1–5:22)*

The converts at Thessalonica are to conduct their lives as Paul has instructed them and to "do so more and more" (4:1–8). The expressions "in the Lord Jesus" and "through the Lord Jesus" imply that converts received systematic instruction in morality and ethics, perhaps based on oral teachings of Jesus. They were to abstain from sexual immorality, marry "in holiness and honor," and not have illicit sexual relations.

In pagan society in general, sexual immorality was not considered abnormal and wrong as it was in Jewish society, where matters of conduct were regulated by the Torah and disobedience was regarded as rejection of God. It must have been especially difficult for former pagans, therefore, to give up the habits of their earlier life for their new life as believers, but God had called them not "to impurity but in holiness." The Thessalonians were responsible to God, who had given them his Holy Spirit.

In 4:1–8 Paul uses a couple of words that may be taken to refer to specific sexual acts or to illicit sexual relationships in general. In 4:3 *porneia* may mean "fornication" (*NRSV*), because the men Paul is addressing apparently were not married. Paul wants each one to "know how to take a wife [footnote in *NRSV*] in holiness and honor, not with lustful passion, like the Gentiles who do not know God."

Some commentators (E. Best 1972, for example) think the words "no one wrong or exploit a brother" with respect to taking a wife refer to sexual misconduct within the community. If so, does Paul mean that one man sins against another if he has sexual relations with that man's wife? Or does Paul use "brother" with reference to a woman? If so, there were women in the community at Thessalonica, although never mentioned elsewhere in the letter. On the other hand, if Paul's language means a man should master his own body, then one has to come to a different conclusion.

No matter what view one takes of Paul's language, he surely wanted to stress that converts must not engage in the sexual immorality so characteristic of the pagan world. Converts were familiar with instances like those Paul knew so well (1 Cor 5:1; Gal 2:15). Among pagans there was no commandment or law forbidding adultery as that in Exod 20:14 and Deut 5:18.

It seems to me that the context, especially with the use of the word *porneia*, indicates Paul is concerned with men and their sex life. He is saying that a man should take a wife not because of his passionate desires, but with holy respect for the woman. Men converted to faithfulness toward God should not do as pagans who do not know God (4:5). If this interpretation is correct, then Paul not only exhorts men to behave with moral motives toward women, but he also shows an unusually great respect for women, a respect not generally thought to be characteristic of Paul. Instead, he is sometimes regarded as a misogynist of the worst kind.

At any rate, Paul was the first person who joined the Jesus movement to challenge the lurid sexual practices of the world around him. For him illicit sexual relationships of all kinds were wrong because they violated commandments of God. They were also wrong because they were in discord with the new life under the Spirit given by God. Paul had always believed that faithfulness toward God meant holiness of life in all its aspects. His new life in Christ under the power of the Spirit confirmed his Jewish belief.

Paul deals with the manner and time of Jesus' second coming, and the Thessalonians' responsibilities while awaiting it (4:13–5:22). The first converts believed that Jesus, who had ascended to heaven, would soon return and that they would be alive when he came (see, for example, Acts 1:1–11). But as time passed, more and more of them died, causing a problem for those still alive. Would those already dead miss the second coming of Jesus? No, says Paul, and he reassures them by saying that the dead will be the first to rise, and then those who are alive will join them to meet the returning Lord in the air (4:13–18).

How literally did Paul take what he was saying in his highly apocalyptic imagery? Would God himself blow the trumpet, or would there even be a trumpet (see 1 Cor 15:52; Matt 24:31)? If Paul is saying here that physical bodies will ascend heavenward, he has a different opinion in 1 Cor 15:50, where he says, "Flesh and blood cannot inherit the kingdom of God" (see 1 Cor 15:50; 2 Cor 5:1–5). Obviously Paul has never worked out a logical system of theology but is dealing with a specific situation at Thessalonica—the mistaken view that converts who had died would miss the second coming of Christ. In vivid imagery, he assures the Thessalonians that this will not happen.

Paul deals with the time of the Parousia in 5:1–11, where he says that the day of the Lord will come suddenly and unexpectedly, "like a thief in the night" (5:1–3). But unlike unbelievers, believers should not be surprised, because they belong to the forces of light, not darkness—that is, they are doing good, not evil. Recall that in Judaism, especially at Qumran, light and darkness had become opposing forces symbolic of good and evil, respectively.

Influenced by the OT conception of the armor of God (Isa 59:17; see also Wis 5:17–23), Paul uses the triad of faith, love, and hope again, as in 1:3. The redeeming character of Jesus' death delivers converts from the wrath of God that is to come upon his enemies (see 1:10). But they have not yet obtained complete salvation, something that is still a hope to be realized in the future. Converts must conform to the requirements for moral life, which are indicated in Paul's final exhortations (5:12–22).

All people are to respect their leaders and to be at peace among themselves. Paul is directing his remarks to three specific groups: the idle, faint hearted, and weak (5:14). The word "idle" (lit., "out of order") means either lazy or disorderly, and both meanings may apply to this group. Believing Paul that the End was near, they were inclined to loaf while waiting. But Paul was not in favor of loafing under any conditions, so he told the idle to mind their own affairs and to work with their hands (4:11). Paul shared the moral philosopher's idea that teachers should work manually to set examples for their pupils. In that way they would learn to "endure hardships" and experience "the pains of labor" without depending on others for help (A. J. Malherbe 1983:24).

The faint hearted were those depressed by their own afflictions (3:3–4) or with anxiety about the fate of their loved ones who had died (4:13–17), or perhaps about their own destiny (5:8–11). The weak were those not weak physically but morally, for whom the temptation to lapse into the immoral ways of their past was always strong (4:2–8).

In 5:15–18 Paul says God's will is that converts do good not only among themselves but to all people, with joy, prayer, and giving of thanks in all circumstances. He finally exhorts the believers at Thessalonica not to quench the Spirit when it is manifested in prophesying or in other ways. At the same time, they are to test all things for genuine manifestations (Paul does not say how) and then to "hold fast to what is good; abstain from every form of evil."

VII. Conclusion (5:23–28)

Paul prays that for each person at Thessalonica the whole human being may be sound and blameless at Jesus' return. He requests the Thessalonians to pray; exhorts them to greet each other with a kiss—a usual manner of extending greetings from an absent person to others; requests them to have the letter read to all; and gives a personal benediction, probably in his own hand.

SUMMARY

Even though it does not present any theological doctrine of Paul's that is worked out in detail or supported with argument, 1 Thessalonians is important. In an apocalyptic-eschatological style, it contains the germ of Paul's theology and moral and ethical teaching. "Jesus died and rose again. . . . For God has destined us not for wrath but for obtaining salvation through our Lord Jesus Christ, who died for us" (4:14; 5:9–10). But that salvation is not complete, because ultimate salvation comes at the end of time (5:9). The Thessalonians, however, are on the right track because they have been given the Holy Spirit, which they must not quench (5:19). Under its influence they must practice the moral way of life (4:1–8). That is Paul's final prayer for them: "May the God of peace himself sanctify you entirely; and may your spirit and soul and body be kept sound and blameless at the coming of our Lord Jesus Christ" (5:23).

For further study of 1 Thessalonians, see commentaries by E. J. Bicknell 1932; W. Neil 1950; J. T. Forestell 1968; J. M. Reese 1979; I. H. Marshall 1983; F. F. Bruce 1982b; E. Best 1972; see A. J. Malherbe 1987, social analysis of Paul's work; H. Boers 1975, form criticism; R. F. Collins 1984, various subjects; R. Jewett 1986, rhetorical and social criticism; H. L. Hendrix 1984, Roman cults; A. Smith, 1995, rhetorical argument and Paul's supposed audience.

Paul's basic ideas in 1 Thessalonians appear also in the Corinthian letters, the next ones he wrote. After a brief description of Corinth, we will examine the letters to the church in that city.

1 AND 2 CORINTHIANS

CORINTH

The history of Corinth goes back to very ancient times. By the seventh century BCE, Corinth had become a prosperous and powerful city that controlled the Italian and Adriatic trade routes. Its bronze and pottery were exported throughout the Mediterranean world. According to Jose-phus, one of the gates to the temple in Jerusalem was of Corinthian bronze, and it was far more valuable than the gates that were plated with silver and set in gold (*War* 5:5:3).

When Augustus made Achaia a senatorial province under a proconsul in 27 BCE, Corinth became the capital and the residence of the proconsul (Acts 18:12). It developed its industries and cultivated its arts. Strabo says, "Corinth is called 'wealthy' because of its place of trade, lying on the isthmus and being master of two harbors, of which one leads directly to Asia, and the other to Italy; and it makes easy the exchange of merchandise from both countries which are so far away from each other" (8:6:20). Ships from Egypt, Syria, and Asia Minor docked at the eastern port of Cenchreae (Acts 18:18; Rom 16:1), and those from Spain, Italy, and Sicily at the western port of Lechaeum. Goods were then transported from one port to the other; small boats were even dragged across the isthmus on a runway that Strabo calls a *diolkos* or "haul-across" (8:2:1).

In Paul's time Corinth spread over two levels of terrain, and in the background was a towering mountain, the Acrocorinthus. In the center of the city was the large agora, surrounded with colonnades and monuments. Shops stood along each side of the road leading there, with sidewalks on both sides. Perhaps Paul worked in one of those shops with Aquila and Priscilla (Acts 18:2–3). Just before the agora was the temple of Apollo, built in the sixth century BCE. Seven of its columns still stand (Figure 10.1). At the entrance to the agora was the famous fountain house of Peirene, the most important reservoir of ancient Corinth.

Entrance to the agora was through the *propylaea*, which consisted of a broad stairway surmounted by a splendid gateway. At the foot of the marble steps leading to the *propylaea* an inscription, "Synagogue of the Hebrews," was found on the lintel of a doorway. This inscription, though from a later time, may have marked the entrance to a synagogue like the one in which Paul spoke to Jews and Greeks (Acts 18:4). The large open space of the agora was divided into two levels, the upper level on the

FIGURE 10.1   *Temple of Apollo at Corinth, from the sixth century BCE.*

south and the lower level on the north. The two levels were divided by a long row of central shops, with the *bēma* extending from the upper into the lower level in the center. The *bēma* (see Figure 10.2) is of special interest because the writer of Acts (18:12–17) reports that the Jews brought Paul "before the tribunal" (*bēma*). It was a speaker's platform of blue and white marble, with benches behind it and on the sides. A large crowd could gather in front of it (see J. Finegan 1962; C. L. Thompson 1976; J. Murphy-O'Connor 1983, 1984).

In Paul's time temples and statues were everywhere. Besides the temple of Apollo, there was a "temple of the Isthmian Poseidon in the shade of a grove of pine trees, where the Corinthians used to celebrate the Isthmian games" (Strabo, 8:6:22). "Within the sanctuary of the god stand, on the one side, portrait statues of athletes who have won victories at the Isthmian games and, on the other side, pine trees growing in a row" (Pausanias, 1:7; see also 1 Cor. 9:24–27). In the center of the agora was a bronze Athena, and on the road to Lechaeum was a bronze image of a

seated Hermes and statues of other gods. There were also sanctuaries of the gods Isis and Serapis.

Near the north wall of the city was a temple of Asclepius, god of healing. Replicas of hands, feet, and other parts of the body found in the ruins of this temple indicate that patients coming to the shrine believed they were healed of various afflictions. Facilities for cooking and dining, as well as dining rooms with couches for reclining at meals, have also been discovered in the same area. The dining rooms in this and other areas had religious significance and were used for cultic meals.

Northwest of the city were two theaters. The smaller one was the Odeum or music hall. The larger was built on a hill; it had a large semicircle of seats facing a big stage and could seat eighteen thousand. Certainly Corinth in Paul's time was a very impressive city.

At Corinth Paul "discoursed in the synagogue every sabbath and persuaded Jews and Greeks" (Acts 18:4; Greek). At first he was well received, but then his fortune changed (18:6–8). In spite of difficulty, it was through the synagogue and

FIGURE 10.2
Bēma *or "tribunal"*
(Acts 18:12–17) at
Corinth.

the Jewish community that Paul began to establish a group of converts among Gentiles in Corinth. Titius Justus, as "a worshiper of God," was probably in some way associated with Judaism and the synagogue. Crispus, "the official of the synagogue," was one of the prominent men of the Jewish community and was respected by non-Jews as well. He was baptized by Paul himself (1 Cor 1:14–16).

The writer of Acts, in his usual fashion, says that Paul was given divine guidance at Corinth and makes it clear that Paul was not harmed, although the Jews did attack him and took him before Gallio the proconsul (18:9–16). It is impossible to say what the charge against Paul was, and whether it ran counter to Jewish or Roman law. The differences with the Jews may have arisen over Paul's claim that Jesus was the Christ, the Jewish Messiah, and his attempts to prove it from scripture. Despite problems, Paul's mission at Corinth must have been a success. He not only wrote several letters to the Christians there, but

wrote more letters from Corinth than from any other place. Romans, 1 Thessalonians, and perhaps Galatians were probably sent from Corinth.

THE SITUATION IN THE CHURCH AT CORINTH AND PAUL'S RESPONSE

It is clear from Acts and from Paul's letters that Paul had opponents in Corinth. They were mostly Jews who would not accept Paul's preaching "that the Messiah was Jesus" (Acts 18:5). Some scholars maintain that Paul's opponents were Jewish Christians from Judea who claimed, for example, that they had greater authority than Paul because they knew about the historical Jesus. Others have argued that Paul's opponents were Hellenistic Jews who imitated the traveling prophets, astrologers, magicians, and philosophers that were so numerous in the Hellenistic world. All of these people claimed special revelations from the gods and tried to prove it by miraculous acts. Recently some scholars have identified Paul's opponents as Gnostics (notably W. Schmithals 1971; see the review by G. W. MacRae 1972, who does not agree). They would have been converts who claimed that *gnōsis* (knowledge), rather than faith, was necessary for salvation. The term *gnōsis* does occur frequently in the Corinthian letters (fifteen times; for example, in 1 Cor 1:5; 8:1; 13:2, 8; 2 Cor 2:14; 4:6). Paul does not condemn such knowledge but stresses that it should be understood as a gift of God (1 Cor 1:5) and not used as an excuse for immoral behavior.

At Corinth the first serious divisions within the church developed, and reverence for others than Christ alone threatened its unity (1 Cor 1:10–17; 12:12–31). Chloe, a member of the church, reported to Paul that there were "divisions" among the members (1 Cor 1:10), and Paul refers to a report that at church meetings there were "divisions" among those attending (1 Cor 11:18; see also 12:14–26). Apparently there were several groups, each loyal to a different church leader who was perhaps revered equally with Christ. The groups were saying, "I belong to Paul," "I belong to Apollos," "I belong to Cephas," and "I belong to Christ" (1 Cor 1:12). Paul responded that the Corinthians should not be divided in their loyalty to Christ. Most of 2 Corinthians is Paul's defense of himself against his opponents (for example, 2 Cor 11:5, 12–15; 12:11).

The status of some women was also causing concern at Corinth. These women had joined the Jesus movement, apparently without their husbands' consent (1 Cor 7:13), and were sharing in such functions as prayer and prophecy (1 Cor 11:2–16). Obviously, such women were not conforming to what was usually expected of females in that day. This nonconformity in the church at Corinth may have been the first women's liberation movement in developing Christianity. Paul wrote to suggest a compromise for the situation, but what he wrote (1 Cor 7:1–40; 11:2–16; 14:33–36) raises many questions about how he actually felt.

Paul's response to the situation at Corinth was influenced by what was reported to him either orally or by letter. Paul usually begins discussing a matter about which the Corinthians have written to him (1 Cor 7:1) by using the formula "now concerning." But he does not always do this if all the following topics are discussed in reply to a letter: believers and marriage (7:1–16, 25–40), eating meat offered to idols (1 Cor 8:1–13; 10:14–30), behavior at public worship (1 Cor 11:3–16), spiritual gifts (1 Corinthians 12–14), the certainty of Jesus' resurrection and that of the believers of Corinth (1 Corinthians 15), the offering for the saints in Jerusalem (16:1–4), and brother Apollos (1 Cor 16:12). Note that "now concerning" appears with only some of these passages. Paul's response to these matters is usually organized and moderate, without criticism of past conduct. He shows understanding and concern, especially for weaker members, and appeals to sayings of Jesus, scripture, and his own authority as an apostle in order to convince his readers.

The following topics are discussed in response to oral reports to Paul by Chloe or others: divisions or cliques determined by preference for leaders (1 Cor 1:10–4:21), the incestuous man "living with his father's wife" (1 Cor 5:1–5), believers and courts of law (1 Cor 6:1–11), the body not being meant for immorality (1 Cor 6:12–20), and conduct at the Lord's Supper (1 Cor 11:17–34). Paul's tone on these matters is hostile and uncompromising—the incestuous man should be "removed from among you" (1 Cor 5:2). Paul cannot forget the past immoral behavior of the Corinthians as pagans and reminds them of it—"And such were some of you" (1 Cor 6:11; Greek). He speaks on his own authority, not appealing to anyone or anything else—"I do not commend you. . . . Shall I commend you in this? No, I will not" (1 Cor 11:17, 22; Greek). Concerning these matters, Paul does not write as though love is "patient" and "kind" (1 Cor 13:4).

Paul faced a tough situation when writing to the church at Corinth, not only because of opponents but also because there was always the danger that converts would lapse into the immoral ways of their pagan past. This danger was probably greater in Corinth than in any other city, because Corinth had a special reputation for revelry and immorality, especially in its seaports. The seaports were always temptations for athletes who came to Corinth from all over Greece for the Isthmian games, which were held every other spring, and for the many resident and itinerant sailors. Persons who wanted to could always find prostitutes, of whom, apparently, there was no short supply. Some ancient writers say that there were as many as one thousand temple-slaves (prostitutes) used in the worship of Aphrodite in the temple dedicated to her on the Acrocorinthus (see, for example, Strabo 8:6:20; 6: 2:6). Although such a figure may be an exaggeration, evidence indicates that the evil reputation of Corinth was well deserved. Little wonder, then, that moral problems among converts in Corinth caused Paul more concern than in any other city.

PAUL'S CORRESPONDENCE WITH THE CORINTHIANS

There are two letters to Corinth in the NT, and it is generally agreed that Paul wrote 1 Corinthians first and 2 Corinthians later. It is also generally agreed that 1 Corinthians is a unity, that it was not Paul's first letter to Corinth, and that 2 Corinthians is an editorial composition of two or more fragments of Corinthian correspondence. For different opinions on this point, see J. C. Hurd 1983:43–47. Some scholars defend the unity of 2 Corinthians (P. E. Hughes 1988; W. G. Kuemmel 1975:287–293; J. J. O'Rourke 1968; F. F. Bruce 1978a). F. W. Danker 1989: 19–20 cautions "against a too-ready adoption of partitionist hypotheses without some compelling modifications."

Although it is not easy to reconstruct Paul's correspondence with Corinth, we can begin by looking at 1 Cor 5:9–11. Obviously, if in 1 Corinthians Paul says "I *wrote* to you" (emphasis mine), it cannot be his first letter to Corinth. So we must try to discern the relationship between Paul and Corinth on the basis of Acts and 1 and

2 Corinthians in order to determine the sequence of the correspondence. We may assume that the following sequence of events approximates the sequence that elicited Paul's correspondence with Corinth.

Paul, Silas, and Timothy establish the church in Corinth (Acts 18:1–17; 1 Cor 3:6; 2 Cor 1:19; 10:14; 11:7).

Paul writes his first letter to Corinth (mentioned in 1 Cor 5:9–13); it is lost, unless 2 Cor 6:14–7:1 is part of it. It was probably written from Ephesus sometime between 53 and 56 CE.

Members of Chloe's household (1 Cor 1:11) and perhaps others report to Paul either orally (1 Cor 5:1) or by letter (1 Cor 7:1) about various subjects. Stephanas and others from Corinth visit Paul and bring a letter or oral reports (1 Cor 16:15–18).

Paul responds to the reports in a second letter to Corinth (1 Corinthians 1–16), probably written from Ephesus between 54 and 56 CE (1 Cor 16:8).

Paul sends Timothy to Corinth (1 Cor 4:17; Acts 19:22) and wants to send Apollos also (1 Cor 16:12). Paul intends to visit Corinth again (1 Cor 4:19; 11:34) via Macedonia (1 Cor 16:2–9; see also Acts 19:21) or by reverse route (2 Cor 1:15–16). A second visit is implied (2 Cor 2:1), then stated (2 Cor 13:2).

Paul writes a third letter to Corinth (2 Cor 2:3–4, 9; 7:6–9) "out of much distress and anguish of heart" (2 Cor 2:4; see also 7:8–12); it is lost, unless 2 Corinthians 10–13 is part of it. It was probably written from Ephesus between 54 and 56 CE.

2 Corinthians 10–13 is known as the "painful letter" because it seems to fit the description of such a letter in 2 Cor 2:4 and 7:8–12 (see 2 Cor 1:23; 2:1; 3:1), on the assumption that 2 Corinthians 1–9 was written after 2 Corinthians 10–13. Besides this, three pairs of cross-references are closely connected; each time the verb in the one from 2 Corinthians 10–13 is in the present tense, the one in the corresponding verse in 2 Corinthians 1–9 is in the past tense and seems, therefore, to refer to an earlier situation in 2 Corinthians 10–13. Notice the italicized words

---

FIGURE 10.3   *Contrast in Verb Tenses Between 2 Corinthians 10–13 and 1–9*

ready to punish every disobedience when your obedience is complete (2 Cor 10:6)	*I wrote* for this reason: to test you and to know whether you are obedient in everything (2 Cor 2:9)
if I come again, I will not be lenient (2 Cor 13:2)	it was to spare you that *I did not come* (2 Cor 1:23)
I *write* these things while I am away from you, so that *when I come,* I may not have to be severe (2 Cor 13:10)	And *I wrote* as I did, so that *when I came,* I might not suffer pain (2 Cor 2:3)

(italics mine) in the passages in Figure 10.3. Many scholars think that chaps. 10–13 of 2 Corinthians were written before chaps. 1–9 because the past tenses of the verbs probably indicate a later letter (1–9) and refer, in a gentler tone, to corresponding passages in the earlier letter (10–13).

Paul threatens a third visit to Corinth but does not carry it out (2 Cor 12:14; 13:1–2; see also 2 Cor 1:15–16, 23; 2:1, 3). He starts for Corinth via Macedonia (Acts 20:1; 2 Cor 2:12–13; 7:5). Titus returns from Corinth to Paul in Macedonia (2 Cor 7:5–7, 13).

Paul writes a fourth letter to Corinth from somewhere in Macedonia; it is lost, unless 2 Corinthians 1–9 (except 6:14–7:1) is a part of it. It was probably written between 54 and 56 CE. Perhaps, as some have suggested, 2 Corinthians 9 is a separate note about the offering for the saints in Jerusalem, since in 2 Cor 9:1 Paul seems to begin anew without referring to what he has said on the subject in chap. 8.

This outline of the sequence of events in the apostolic mission to Corinth and Paul's correspondence with the church there seems plausible for two main reasons. First, 1 Cor 5:9–11 clearly implies an earlier letter of Paul to Corinth, a fragment of which is perhaps preserved in 2 Cor 6:14–7:1, since the latter deals with the subject Paul says he addressed. Differences in tone between chaps. 1–9 and 10–13 probably result from parts of two separate letters being written at different times—each part coherent and well organized. Throughout chaps. 1–7, but especially in chap. 7, Paul seems greatly relieved that

a severe catastrophe has been averted at Corinth (see, for example, 2 Cor 7:4, 8–13). Chaps. 1–9, therefore, are best understood as the sequel to chaps. 10–13. This scheme of events is used in the outline and comments below.

C. K. Barrett 1973 accepts the view that 2 Corinthians 1–9 and 10–13 are separate letters, but maintains that 2 Corinthians 1–9 was written just a little before 2 Corinthians 10–13. See this work for comparisons between the two parts of the letter.

Outline and Comments

I. *Warning against association with immoral people (2 Cor 6:14–7:1)*

This is one of the passages that has caused problems with the unity of 2 Corinthians. We consider it before 1 Corinthians on the hypothesis that it is a fragment of Paul's first letter to Corinth. J. A. Fitzmyer 1961 presents evidence to show that this passage is a non-Pauline Christianized reworking of a paragraph from Qumran.

II. *Introduction to 1 Corinthians: greeting and thanksgiving (1 Cor 1:1–9)*

Notice how frequently the words "God," "Jesus Christ," and "Lord" occur. Paul realized that he was dealing with a community in which religious competition was keen, so he wanted to begin by putting the emphasis where it should be (see 1 Cor 8:4–6). Since Paul was forced to defend himself against "false apostles" and others, he immediately makes it clear that God himself is the basis of his authority (1:1)—"called by the will of God" to be an apostle.

The words "sanctified in Christ Jesus, called to be saints" (1:2) signify the essence of Pauline theology, mysticism, and morality. The word "sanctify" (*hagiazō*) is almost exclusively a biblical word and means to make holy or set apart for God or by God. As the result of baptism, converts are not only taken into the developing religion, but God becomes the source of their life in Christ (1:30). Paul sums it up in 6:11: "You were washed, you were sanctified, you were justified in the name of the Lord Jesus Christ and in the Spirit of our God." Through baptism, converts become saints. "Saints" was one of the earliest words for Christians (Acts 9:13, 32, 41; 26:10) and means "made holy" or "set apart as holy." The basic meaning is separation, and the moral and ethical implications are strong. Believers are to be different or apart from the world, not in the sense of aloofness but in the way they live. The Corinthians are not what they have been (6:9–11) because their lives are changed. Remember that "in Christ" is Paul's creative and favorite expression to indicate the unique and intimate experience of the believer with the spiritual Christ.

In 1:4–9 Paul gives thanks for speech, knowledge, and spiritual gifts, all of which become important in Paul's discussion later. Despite dissension and moral problems at Corinth, this passage is the only one (but see Rom 8:1) where Paul says that as believers "wait for the revealing of our Lord Jesus Christ," God will sustain them "to the end" so that they may be "blameless" (1:7–8). If this means their salvation is already obtained unconditionally because they are believers, it contradicts what Paul says many times elsewhere in Corinthians and in his other letters, where converts' ultimate salvation is dependent upon their continuing faith and moral and ethical behavior.

III. Response to quarreling and wisdom (1 Cor 1:10–4:21)

A. Divisions and request for unity (1:10–17)

Quarreling at Corinth led to dissensions, and it centered around several people. Perhaps the two major parties were those of Apollos, the Alexandrian Jew, "an eloquent man, well-versed in the scriptures . . . and burning in spirit" (Acts 18:24–25; Greek), and those of Paul, who perhaps had equal training, but whose "bodily presence is weak, and his speech contemptible" (2 Cor 10:10). Apollos would have appealed to the educated and intellectual minority of Corinthian converts and Paul to the uneducated and poor majority. This seems clear from Paul's argument against the emphasis on wisdom (1:10–4:21) and his reference to himself as "the rubbish of the world" (4:13).

B. Paul's preaching and wisdom (1:18–3:4)

Were the parties mentioned all insignificant compared with the real troublemakers, the "spiritualists" (see 2:15; 3:1; 14:37), those who claimed special revelations from Christ? Members of this group thought they possessed special wisdom; they looked down upon the weak and used their freedom to indulge in vices of all kinds. Paul responds to an overemphasis on wisdom throughout 1:18–3:4. The essence of his reply is in 1:18–31, where he deals with human wisdom. About such wisdom Paul comments elsewhere: "When I came to you, brothers and sisters, I did not come proclaiming the testimony of God to you in lofty words of wisdom. For I decided to know nothing among you except Jesus Christ, and him crucified" (2:1–2).

The words in 1:26 that not many are "wise by human standards" or "powerful" or of "noble birth" imply social differences in the church at Corinth. In the social makeup of that church, the majority belonged to the lower and poorer classes, but a group of wealthy and influential people may have been a dominant minority. Paul speaks primarily to that minority, which was ignoring the poorer majority.

In 2:6–3:4 Paul may be using his opponents' terminology to say that there are two kinds of wisdom, human and divine. Paul's opponents have only the former because they are immature (2:6) and "infants in Christ" (3:1). For Paul, the wisdom of God is to know "Jesus Christ, and him crucified" (2:2).

C. Apostolic preachers and the Corinthians (3:5–4:21)

Throughout the discussion on quarreling Paul has applied the same standards to himself as to others. Though he is unaware of anything against himself, he is not acquitted, since it is the Lord who judges him (4:1–7). Paul does not write to make the Corinthians ashamed but to admonish them as his beloved children and to urge them to imitate him.

Although the main point in the quarrel between Paul and the believers at Corinth (1:10–4:21) is the concept of wisdom, another factor—one not to be overstressed—entered into the quarrel: the view of baptism. Paul has raised the point earlier by saying that he baptized only a few of the Corinthians and that Christ did not send him to baptize but to preach the gospel (1:13–17). Apparently some people had developed a special attachment to—perhaps even an identification with—the person who baptized them. Some scholars see influence here from other religions, especially the mystery cults, in which the neophyte being prepared for initiation into the cult developed an intimate relationship with the tutor. Paul would have been opposed to this because he believed that the person baptized had a special relationship with Christ, not with the person who did the baptizing.

IV. Response to moral problems (1 Cor 5:1–6:20)

Paul begins his response to moral problems at Corinth by writing about incest (5:1–13). A Corinthian has had such a relationship with his stepmother, a relationship despised even by pagans. When Paul says the man is to be handed over "to Satan for the destruction of the flesh, so that his spirit may be saved in the day of the Lord" (5:5), he means the man is to be punished, perhaps excommunicated (5:2, 13). But what Paul means by Satan in this case and how the man is to be punished are uncertain. It is even more difficult to know what Paul means if we consider the contrast between flesh and spirit. This contrast reflects the typical Gnostic view that the flesh, or body, is evil and that only the

spirit is good. But Paul was not a Gnostic, and he does not even separate body and spirit in his discussion of the resurrection (1 Corinthians 15), where he talks about a "spiritual body." Like all Jews, Paul regarded the human being as a totality of body, soul, and spirit. It seems that Paul wanted the man accused of incest ultimately to be saved. Perhaps he meant that whatever action was taken against the man would cause him to repent and thus to be saved in the day of the Lord.

In 5:6–13 Paul deplores the boasting of some Corinthians, uses yeast as a metaphor for the penetrating and corrupting influence of a little evil in the community, and says that Christ's sacrificial death for the sins of others means that the Corinthians must rid their community of evil influence.

In chap. 6 Paul frequently uses the expression "Do you not know that?" (see also 1 Cor 3:16; 5:6; 9:13, 24; elsewhere in Paul's letters only Rom 6:16). After having discussed the wisdom of the Corinthians, Paul implies by this expression that they do not know the fundamentals of the developing religion.

Believers should settle grievances against their fellows among themselves, not before unrighteous pagans. Paul reminds the converts at Corinth that they once were immoral, like those who will not inherit the kingdom. They are, or should be, different now because they have been baptized and justified in Jesus' name.

Paul concludes his response to moral problems by declaring that the body is not meant for immorality because it is the temple of the Holy Spirit within (6:12–20). The bodies of believers belong to God. Perhaps by "you were bought with a price," Paul is saying that Jesus' death is what makes the believer's body belong to God (see Rom 3:24; Gal 3:13).

V. Problems raised in the letter and other reports from Corinth (1 Cor 7:1–16:4)

What Paul says here was influenced by his basic belief that the end of the world was coming soon. This is clear from the expressions "in view of the present crisis" (7:26) and "the appointed time has grown short" (7:29), which are eschatological. Everything must be put in the context of Paul's expectation of the End.

A. Marriage and divorce (7:1–40)

When Paul wrote to the Corinthians, he was not married (7:7–8), but we do not know whether he never married or whether he was a widower. He wishes all were unmarried like him. Yet he is not arguing the pros and cons of being married or unmarried, but saying that believers should remain in the state they were in when they became converts. Several verses throughout chap. 7 make this clear (for example, 7:17, 24). Within marriage, sexual intercourse should not be refused, because the man and wife owe it to each other. If both agree to abstain for a period of prayer, they should resume relations again afterward, lest they be tempted and lose self-control. If the unmarried cannot exercise self-control, they should marry.

On the subject of divorce (7:10–16), Paul says that believing partners should not separate, and his advice coincides with Jesus' teaching reported in Mark 10:1–12. If a person is married to an unbeliever and the unbelieving partner consents to live with the other, there should be no separation unless "the unbelieving partner separates." In baptism the unbelieving partner was sanctified or made holy (6:11), so in sexual union (that is, becoming one body) the unbelieving partner becomes sanctified through the believer in the same way that the person who has sexual relations with a prostitute becomes immoral.

In 7:25–38 Paul explains why it is better not to marry. First, because "the present form of this world is passing away" (7:31), it is better to remain unmarried; but if one marries, it is not wrong. Second, unmarried people are not so "anxious about the affairs of the world," so they can be more concerned with "the affairs of the Lord." Since marriage is such a close relationship, Paul assumes that each spouse might be more devoted to the other than to Christ. Third, a man and a woman who have agreed to live together without being married and without having sex may find that their "passions are strong," so it is all right to marry. Paul does not object to such an arrangement in principle, but he knows that it may become too difficult for the couple. His feelings are summed up in 7:38: "He who marries his fiancée (Greek, "virgin") does well; and he who refrains from marriage will do better"—especially, perhaps, since the end of the world is so near. (For the position of women in the Graeco-Roman world and in Paul's thought, see W. A. Meeks 1974. See also the section dealing with women in Chapter 3.)

B. Eating meats sacrificed to idols (8:1–11:1)

It was scarcely possible for a convert living in any Graeco-Roman city to avoid the problem of eating meat that had been offered to a deity. Such offerings often involved only the burning of some of the intestines, so the rest of the meat was fine for eating and could be bought in local shops. Many Corinthian converts had been pagans, and Paul had insisted upon a complete break with their pagan past. How could they do that and still eat meat, since almost all meat in the city butcher shops had been offered to pagan gods? Some people felt that such meat might be contaminated by association with idol worship, and that they would therefore be guilty of idolatry if they ate it. Here again, there may be social implications. The "weak," for example, were the poor, who rarely ate meat because they could not afford it. However, they would have eaten it at pagan festivals, where it was free; so after becoming believers, they found it hard to eat meat without associating it with those events. Their consciences would then bother them.

Paul's answer to the problem implies that some Corinthians who claimed "knowledge" that idols really had no existence were eating such meat without qualms concerning the feelings of others. He begins his response by stating the basic Jewish monotheistic view that there is only one God, so "no idol in the world really exists." If people have such knowledge, they can eat with a clear conscience. But if in eating idol-meats they cause a weak member who lacks that knowledge to feel guilty, they should not eat the meats.

Chap. 9 is sometimes regarded as a fragment of a separate letter. It may, however, be a digression in which Paul claims certain rights—such as financial support from other believers—as an authoritative apostle but rejects them for freedom in preaching the gospel (9:1–18). In doing so, he is free to adapt himself to all people. By becoming "all things to all people" he "might by all means save some" (9:19–23). Using well-known figures of speech from athletic contests, Paul urges the believers to use self-control to obtain the imperishable wreath as the crown of victory (9:24–27)—that is, a share in the blessings of the gospel (v 23).

In 10:1–13 Paul sees a prefiguration of the Lord's Supper in the "spiritual" drink and food provided by God to the Israelites in the desert (Exodus and Numbers). The rock from which God gave the Israelites water to drink was Christ, because even then Christ shared God's work. But the spiritual gifts of food and water did not save the Israelites because they misbehaved, and God was not pleased "with most of them." "Now these things occurred as examples," says Paul, for the Corinthians not to "desire evil as they [the Israelites] did." The Corinthians are not to worship idols, to have illicit sex, or to test the Lord's ability to provide power for resisting temptation.

After recalling the idolatry of the Israelites, Paul returns to the problem of eating meat sacrificed to idols. Believers who eat the Lord's Supper have communion with Christ, but not in such a way as to be freed from God's judgment. Although idols are nothing, those who eat meat offered to them have communion with the demons the idols represent. Here Paul introduces a new thought not in chap. 8. Although idols do not exist, he believes in the reality of demons. The Lord's Supper and demons do not go together—"You cannot partake of the table of the Lord and the table of demons" (10:14–22). Respecting the converts' concern for the good of their neighbors, the principle is "'All things are lawful,' but not all things are beneficial." Believers may eat anything at home or when invited out to dinner, unless in doing so they offend the consciences of others (10:23–11:1).

C. Conduct at worship and at the Lord's Supper (11:2–34)

On the theological principle that God created man first and then woman, Paul says that a woman who prays should have her head veiled, but a man should not cover his head. Paul has no reservations about women participating with men in worship, but he wants to make sure that their appearance is proper, probably in accordance with acceptable standards of his Jewish background, in contrast to the pagan customs at Corinth. (For hairstyles at Corinth, see C. L. Thompson 1988.) Does this make Paul sexist here, or does he just not want the sexes to be confused? Is the distinction between sexes to be kept even in outward appearance? For Paul the difference in sex is for the purpose of procreation, because "all things come from God" (11:2–16).

Division in the church at Corinth resulted in misconduct at the Lord's Supper, including excessive eating and drinking (11:17–34). Some people, perhaps the richer group, were humiliating the poorer group, "those who have nothing." Apparently the rich brought their own meal and thought that what they were eating was the Lord's Supper and need not be shared with others. This reflects an aspect of pagan society of Paul's time. Plutarch writes that at sacrifices and public banquets "the custom of an equal share for everyone was sometimes abandoned" and that "where each person has a private portion, fellowship is destroyed" (*Table Talk* 2:10:2). Paul cannot commend the believers at Corinth for such behavior at the Lord's Supper, and he stresses how shameful it is by reminding them of Jesus' words and action at the original supper with his disciples. Then Paul exhorts the Corinthians to examine themselves when participating in the supper. Only those who are morally and spiritually prepared should participate. Otherwise, participation will be ineffective and bring God's judgment.

D. Spiritual gifts (12:1–14:40)

The Holy Spirit, which the Corinthians received when baptized, makes possible the confession "Jesus is Lord" (12:1–3). (For interpretations of "Jesus be cursed!" see C. K. Barrett 1968:279–281.) People have various gifts, but all gifts come from the same Spirit and are to be used "for the common good" (12:4–12). By baptism converts are incorporated into the spiritual body of Christ, and believers at Corinth "are the body of Christ and individually members of it." As with the human body, "if one member suffers, all suffer together with it; if one member is honored, all rejoice together with it," so in a community of believers the individual member has to use his or her gifts and to accommodate his or her life to the welfare of the whole community (12:12–27).

E. S. Fiorenza 1999 follows the trend of trying to explain things in NT writings in terms of rhetorical and/or sociopolitical categories. There are correct observations about the egalitarianism in early churches—all persons are equal in status: Jew and Greek, slave and freed person, rich and poor, male and female. However, I do have doubts about thinking of Paul's term "body" (Greek, *sōma*; Latin, *corpus*) and Christians' "self-understanding" with the symbols "body/corporation of Christ/Messiah" and *ekklēsia* as "democratic assembly." According to Fiorenza, the messianic body must be understood in the language of the popular discussions of antiquity and the Greek *polis* ("city state") as "a body politic." Does the understanding of Paul's word "body" (*sōma*) in 1 Corinthians 12 as "corporation" best explain the sociopolitical language of the text? How "political" is the text?

In spite of arguments to the contrary, do the terms "corporation" and "political" not evoke images of modern corporations and political personalities whereby, as members of organizations that are far from egalitarian in nature, all are striving selfishly to get ahead, often with unethi-cal motives and without regard for the good of the whole body?

As we have learned, the most important difference between Greek political assemblies and Paul's churches is that for the Greeks the assembly was the town meeting, whereas an assembly of Paul was "not just the occasional gathering, but the group itself" (W. A. Meeks 1983:108). Moreover, the assemblies of Paul were hardly gathered to discuss secular corporate business matters or politics and government. Indeed, the underlying assumption of Paul's bodies of believers is stated in Rom 13:1–7, parts of which follow:

> Let every person be subject to the governing authorities; for there is no authority except from God, and those authorities that exist have been instituted by God. Therefore whoever resists authority resists what God has appointed, and those who resist will incur judgment.

On the basis of that assumption, it seems to me, highly unlikely that there were sociopolitical discussions in the assemblies of Paul. Evidence seems to indicate that members of his churches were not assembled to discuss politics but to learn how to become moral women and men, "blameless in holiness before our God and Father at the coming of our Lord Jesus" (1 Thess 3:13; my trans.). Paul concludes his discussion of the body and its members by saying that he will show them "a still more excellent way"—love (1 Cor 12:31). And Paul begins chapter 14 with the exhortation, "Pursue love." Moreover, "Those who prophesy build up the church" (14:4). Paul's word "build up" (*oikodomeō*) is used metaphorically and means "encourage moral and spiritual growth." Believers are "to strive to excel" in their "spiritual gifts" for "building up the church" (14:12, 26; see also 1 Thess 5:11). In truth, Paul's divine mission was for building up believers (2 Cor 12:19; 13:10).

Love is "a still more excellent way" than all gifts. Chap. 13 is sometimes regarded as an insertion by a later writer; however, it seems to be an integral part of Paul's argument. In 13:4–7 Paul politely describes qualities of love, which "builds up" (8:1) and which the Corinthians lack. In 13:8–12 love, which is perfect and eternal, is contrasted with spiritual gifts that are temporal and imperfect. In 13:13 love is said to be greater than faith or hope. In chap. 14 Paul places prophecy above speaking in tongues—that is, emotional utterances. He tells the Corinthians not to "forbid speaking in tongues" but "be eager to prophesy." "All things should be done decently and in order," and any gift should be used only to edify other worshipers. Prophecy can do this best because it is done with the power of the Spirit and therefore will edify all who hear.

Paul's statement that "women should be silent in the churches" (14:34–35) contradicts 11:2–6, where it is clearly implied that women properly veiled can participate in praying and prophesying at public worship. Because of this contradiction, because vv 33b–35 interrupt Paul's discussion about prophecy and speaking in tongues—which is resumed in v 37—and because the thought of those verses coincides with that of 1 Tim 2:11–12 and Eph 5:22, this may be a later interpolation. If the words are from Paul, he may have in mind a kind of meeting different from that in 11:2–6. Paul may have been influenced by the practice in Jewish synagogues, where women did not speak, or he may be trying to counter a strong feminist movement at Corinth that was contributing to disorder in worship. Or, Paul may want to ward off discussions between husbands and wives that might give the impression of insubordination of the wives to their husbands (see 14:34 and Gen 3:16).

E. The resurrection of the body (15:1–58)

Apparently some Corinthians were denying the resurrection, because Paul says, "How can some of you say there is no resurrection of the dead?" He replies by citing resurrection appearances of Jesus (15:1–11) and by saying that without Christ's resurrection, "the first fruits of those who have died," the apostolic preaching would be vain and faith fruitless (15:12–28). To support his argument Paul appeals to the Corinthian practice of being baptized "on behalf of the dead," which—whatever it means—implies some

kind of future existence, or else the practice would be useless. Paul himself would not submit to "danger every hour" if he did not expect to be raised from the dead (15:29–34).

Verses 35–58 deal with the questions of how the dead are raised and what kind of bodies they have. In answer to the first, Paul uses apocalyptic symbolism—or did he believe literally what he says in 15:51–52? The resurrected body, like a seed that is sown, does not consist of the same material it had when it was put into the ground. Paul's reply to the second question is the classic NT view of the resurrection. He combines his Pharisaic idea of a resurrection of the body with the Greek concept of the immortality of the soul. As a Jew, Paul could not think of a spiritual existence without some kind of bodily form, so he comes up with a spiritual body: "So is it with the resurrection of the dead. What is sown is perishable, what is raised is imperishable. . . . It is sown a physical body, it is raised a spiritual body" (1 Cor 15:42, 44).

F. The collection for the saints in Jerusalem (16:1–4)

The Corinthians are to save some money "on the first day of every week," that is, once a week, for the needy believers in Jerusalem. Paul will send their contribution to the needy, who are a special concern to him (see 2 Corinthians 8–9).

VI. Conclusion (1 Cor 16:5–24)

Paul plans to visit the Corinthians and advises them how to receive Timothy and Apollos when they come (16:5–12). He exhorts them: "Keep alert, stand firm in your faith, be courageous, be strong. Let all that you do be done in love" (16:13–14). And he commends certain Corinthians, sends greetings, and gives a benediction (16:15–24).

VII. Another letter of Paul to Corinth (2 Cor 10:1–13:14)

Paul is not weak but obeys Christ (10:1–18). God is the source of Paul's conduct and authority, and, unlike his opponents, Paul does not take credit for the Corinthians' conversion. Perhaps some new opponents had come to Corinth from somewhere else and were now causing trouble (11:1–15). Like his opponents, Paul is by nationality a Hebrew or Jew, but he is a better servant of Christ and has suffered far more. Although there is nothing to be gained by it, Paul must mention special spiritual experiences, "visions and revelations of the Lord." But to keep him "from being too elated" by the "exceptional character of the revelations," Paul says that a thorn was given him "in the flesh." All of these things make Paul strong in his weakness, so he is "not at all inferior to these super-apostles," his opponents (11:16–12:13).

Paul plans to visit Corinth for the third time. When he comes, there may still be quarreling, and there may be some who "have not repented of the impurity, sexual immorality, and licentiousness that they have practiced" (12:14–21). But when Paul arrives, he will deal with all problems by the power of Christ who speaks in him (13:1–4). Meanwhile, the Corinthians must examine themselves and mend their ways, agree with each other, and live in peace. Finally, Paul sends a greeting and gives a benediction (13:5–14).

VIII. Letter from somewhere in Macedonia (2 Cor 1:1–9:15, except 6:14–7:1)

According to Acts 20:1–2 (see also 2 Cor 2:12–13; 7:5), Paul left Ephesus for Macedonia and came to Greece, where he spent three months. In Greece, perhaps at Philippi, Paul probably wrote his last letter to Corinth. It is lost, unless 2 Corinthians 1–9 (except 6:14–7:1) is a part of it.

A. Introduction, greeting, and thanksgiving (1:1–11)

In 1 Cor 1:4–9 Paul is thankful for the Corinthians' progress in their enrichment in Christ. Here, in contrast, he is thankful for the strength God gave him to endure affliction.

B. Paul's relationship with the Corinthians and his defense of himself (1:12–2:17)

Paul has behaved toward the Corinthians "with holiness and godly sincerity, not by earthly wis-

dom but by the grace of God" (1:12–22). It was to spare the Corinthians that Paul did not visit them (1:23–2:11). Instead of a visit, he wrote a letter (2 Corinthians 10–13?) "out of much distress and anguish of heart and with many tears." Someone has offended Paul and the Corinthians somehow, but the offense has been dealt with and forgiven. Paul and his companions are "not peddlers of God's word like so many [for financial gain or other personal advantage]." Rather, "in Christ" they "speak as persons of sincerity, as persons sent from God" (2:12–17).

C. Paul's qualifications as an apostle (3:1–4:15)

The Corinthian believers are Paul's letter "of recommendation . . . written not with ink but with the Spirit of the living God" (3:1–3). Paul's authority is greater than that of Moses (3:4–11). God has qualified Paul as a minister "of a new covenant, not of letter [of law] but of Spirit; for the letter kills, but the Spirit gives life" (3:4–6). Here Paul brings out a major difference between Judaism (old covenant) and the developing religion (new covenant): the Spirit of God guides the inner life of all believers, not just apostles. All believers are being transformed into the likeness of the Lord "from one degree of glory to another." Unlike the law, from which the Jews could discover only what wrong they had done and the penalty for it, the Spirit can keep people from doing wrong. Unlike Moses, who had a veil to hide deficiencies and prevent direct contact with God, apostles preach openly by the light of God (3:12–4:6). Paul says that he suffers as Jesus did but that he is kept alive by the inner power of the living Christ (4:7–15).

D. The outer and inner natures (4:16–5:21)

Second Cor 4:16–5:10, especially 5:1–10, is difficult. In 4:16 Paul says, "Even though our outer nature is wasting away, our inner nature is being renewed day by day." In the verses that follow, Paul seems confident that this is part of the preparation for future eternal life (4:17–18). But in chap. 5 he seems to waver between the desire for and the fear of death. Yet Paul seems assured "that what is mortal" will "be swallowed up by life," because God has guaranteed this through the Spirit. In 5:6–8 Paul says that being "away from the body" (death) brings one "at home with the Lord"—that is, into the presence of Christ.

Perhaps, as 5:1 seems to indicate, Paul is trying to allay some Corinthians' fear of a future existence without a physical body: "For we know that if the earthly tent we live in is destroyed, we have a building from God, a house not made with hands, eternal in the heavens." Nevertheless, believers still have to aim to please God, for they must all "appear before the judgment seat of Christ, so that each may receive good or evil, according to what he has done in the body" (5:10; Greek). Paul and his companions are known to God and are controlled by the love of Christ, who died for all mankind (5:11–15). Believers can share in the experiences of Christ and become new creations in Christ (5:16–21).

The Greek verb for "reconcile" in 5:18–20 is *katallassō,* "to change thoroughly." Believers are changed to the extent that they are new creations. Paul means that he and his companions, as "ambassadors for Christ," are to change others as they themselves have been changed. As God worked through Christ to effect their reconciliation, so now God is working through them for the reconciliation of others. Paul beseeches the Corinthians to become new creations, to be both morally and spiritually reconciled to God. God made Jesus "to be sin who knew no sin, so that in him we might become the righteousness of God" (5:21).

Paul attempts to describe the unique life of a convert. How simple it would have been if he had been able to use the term "Christian," but that word had not yet become a part of Paul's vocabulary or that of his communities. Paul thinks of a converted person as a "new creation" (see Gal 6:15). Moffatt's translation brings out the thought here: "There is a new creation whenever a man comes to be in Christ." The expression "new creation" and similar ones were used among rabbis to describe a convert to Judaism,

who was regarded as a newborn child. Accordingly, God would not punish the convert for sins committed before conversion. These views are obviously reflected in Paul's words "The old has passed away, behold, the new has come" (Greek) and "not counting their trespasses against them."

E. Reconciliation between Paul and the Corinthians (6:1–13; 7:2–16)

The Corinthians are not to accept God's grace in vain by reverting to their former pagan ways. The apostles endured all sorts of hardships as servants of God. Accordingly, Paul asks the Corinthians to respond with their own affection (6:11–13; 7:2–4). Titus's return indicates that the Corinthians and Paul are completely reconciled (7:5–16).

F. The offering for the saints (8:1–9:15)

Paul urges the Corinthians to give generously because equality comes through sharing (8:1–15). Titus and others will come to collect (8:16–9:5). Generous gifts bring blessing from God (9:6–15).

For further study of the letters to Corinth, see J. Moffatt 1938; R. H. Strachan 1935; R. Kugelman 1968; M. E. Thrall 1965; J. S. Ruef 1971; W. F. Orr 1976; C. K. Barrett 1973; J. Hering 1962; J. Murphy-O'Connor 1982; V. P. Furnish 1984; D. Georgi 1976a, 1976b, 1986; see also bibliography at end of chapter.

SUMMARY

The letter was Paul's most direct and effective way of responding to problems in churches he had established earlier and could not revisit immediately. At Thessalonica the believers were concerned that their friends who had died would miss the Parousia. Paul reassures them by saying that those who are alive and those who have died will be caught up together to meet the Lord at his coming. At Corinth there was quarreling among factions that had become enthusiastic about different leaders in the church. Paul scolds them and says that believers should be united in their loyalty to Christ.

At Corinth, also, there were problems concerning behavior at the Lord's Supper, eating meat offered to pagan gods, illicit sexual relationships, and marital relations. The richer people were being inconsiderate of the poorer majority, especially in boasting about their wisdom and in their behavior at the Lord's Supper. Paul stresses the wisdom of God, which involves knowing the significance of Jesus' crucifixion; and he says that the Lord's Supper is a sacred occasion, not a time for feasting, carousing, and getting drunk. With respect to eating meat sacrificed to idols, the principle to keep in mind is consideration for the consciences of others. Some people know that an idol has no existence—and therefore is not God—and they eat such meat with a clear conscience. They should not eat the meat, however, if their eating offends the consciences of those who do not have the same knowledge. Paul's basic argument against immorality is that the bodies of believers belong to God and are temples of the Holy Spirit within.

For some later works and for advanced study see the following: commentaries: R. Bultmann 1985; C. H. Talbert 1987, literary and theological; G. D. Fee 1988; S. J. Kistemaker 1993, 1997; J. D. G. Dunn 1995b; G. F. Snyder 1992; K. Quast 1994; R. A. Horsley 1998; H. Conzelmann 1975; Corinth: J. Murphy-O'Connor 1983, 1984; O. Broneer 1951; V. P. Furnish 1988; ethics: V. P. Furnish 1968; B. S. Rosner 1995; introduction: F. F. Bruce 1978a; C. B. Puskas 1993; Pauline corpus: C. L. Mitton 1955; R. S. Ascouth 1998; man and woman: A. C. Wire 1990; N. Baumert 1996; marriage rules: O. L. Yarbrough 1985; ministry: T. B. Savage 1996; idol meat: W. L. Willis 1985; P. D. Gooch 1993; early Christian prophecy: T. W. Gillespie 1995; Paul's opponents: J. J. Gunther 1973; D. Georgi 1986; J. L. Sumney 1990; divisions of 2 Corinthians: H. D. Betz 1985b; Gnosticism: W. Schmithals 1971; rhetoric and theology: D. Litfin 1995; B. Witherington 1995a; M. M. DiCicco 1995.

In the next chapter we will study Paul's letters to the Galatians and Romans, written at the peak of his career. Again we will consider the situations that gave rise to those letters, along with Paul's responses.

CHAPTER 11

Undisputed Letters of Paul: Galatians and Romans

GALATIANS

GALATIA

The territory known as Galatia got its name from a people known as Galli or Gauls (often called Celts by the Greeks) who, in the third century BCE, invaded and conquered northeastern Phrygia in central Asia Minor. They established themselves as a robber state and for almost half a century were the scourge of Asia Minor. They controlled the great northern route from the Euphrates in the east to Ephesus in the west and collected tribute from all rulers north and west of the Taurus Mountains. The Gauls' chief cities were Ancyra and the trade centers of Pessinus and Tavium.

Neighboring powers forced the Gauls to settle permanently in the area that came to be named Galatia. In 189 BCE the Gauls were defeated by a Roman army; and except for a brief time later, their independence ended. In 25 BCE the Gauls' original territory was enlarged as a Roman province. Glance at the map of Paul's journeys (back endsheet) to see the boundaries and regions of the Roman province of Galatia.

DESTINATION OF GALATIANS AND PLACE AND DATE OF WRITING

There are two theories concerning the meaning of the terms "Galatian" and "Galatia" with respect to Paul's journeys and the destination of his letter to the Galatians. According to one theory, called the north Galatian theory, the term "Galatia" means Galatia proper, or the old Gallic kingdom. So when Paul was prevented by the Holy Spirit from speaking the word in Asia (Acts 16:6), he took a northern route, intending to visit Bithynia (Acts 16:7) and such well-known cities as Pessinus, Ancyra, and Tavium. It was to the converts of those and other cities in Galatia proper—Galatia in the narrower sense of the term—that Paul addressed his letter.

According to the other theory, the term "Galatia" means Galatia in the broader sense of the term, that is, the Roman province. On his second and third journeys Paul revisited the churches in Derbe, Lystra (Acts 16:1; 18:23), and presumably also Iconium (16:2) and Pisidian Antioch. It was to the converts of those cities in the southern part of the Roman province—Galatia—that Paul addressed his letter. This view is called the south Galatian theory.

Advocates of the north Galatian theory maintain that only native Gauls in northern Galatia were properly addressed as Galatians (Gal 3:1)—not the Phrygians or Lycaonians who lived in the Roman province of Galatia. On the other hand, Paul, unlike the writer of Acts, usually uses the official names of Roman provinces instead of names of countries. Today many scholars prefer the south Galatian theory, mainly because there is no evidence in Acts or in Paul's letters that Paul ever founded churches in northern Galatia (see W. G. Kuemmel 1975:295–298 and R. H. Fuller 1966:23–26).

Both the place and date of writing for Galatians are inevitably linked with the insoluble problems concerning Paul's travels (especially his trips to Jerusalem), the destination of the letter, and the interpretation of certain phrases in the letter itself. For example, if we knew how quickly "so quickly" (1:6) was, it would help us determine the interval between the founding of the churches and the time of writing. Because of insufficient information, Galatians has been considered the earliest and latest of Paul's letters, as well as one written sometime between the two extremes. If written to the churches at Antioch, Iconium, Lystra, and Derbe after the first missionary journey (Acts 13–14), it would be the earliest letter, as many today believe. It would have been written from Antioch in Syria or perhaps on the way to Jerusalem c. 48 CE, before the conference at Jerusalem (Acts 15).

If Paul founded churches in north Galatia on his second journey (Acts 16:6) and wrote to them after the initial visit, or if he wrote to the churches of south Galatia after a second visit, he could have written Galatians sometime on his second journey, probably from Corinth c. 51–52 or from Antioch at the journey's end, c. 52. Or if Paul wrote to churches in north Galatia and visited them a second time before he wrote, as some believe (Acts 18:23), he may have written from somewhere on his third journey, probably Ephesus c. 53–54, or even Corinth (Acts 20:3) the next year.

THE SITUATION IN THE CHURCHES OF GALATIA AND PAUL'S RESPONSE

After Paul established the churches of Galatia, others came there and caused problems (1:6–9). Although Paul does not name his opponents, the reference to James, Cephas, and John, all leaders in the Jewish community of converts in Jerusalem (2:9), may indicate that they were partly responsible for the trouble. The troublemakers wanted Gentile converts to be circumcised (5:2; 6:12–13) and to obey the Jewish law (3:2; 4:21; 5:4). Therefore, they are usually referred to as Judaizers, Jewish believers who wanted Gentiles to become Jews before becoming converts. Or the troublemakers could have been Gentile converts who were practicing some aspects of Judaism and wanted others to be like them. Most scholars, however, believe that Judaizers were the main problem at Galatia (for problems at Galatia, see G. Howard 1979).

Some scholars maintain that the words "My friends, if anyone is detected in a transgression, you who have received the Spirit should restore such a one in a spirit of gentleness" (6:1) indicate the existence of another group, because the words "you who have received the Spirit" (one word in Greek = "filled with the Spirit") indicate that others were opposing Paul. These others were radical freedom questers who opposed both Paul and the Judaizers. According to this view, Paul is attacking two groups, the Judaizers up to 5:12 and the radical freedom lovers with the hortatory section in 5:13–6:10. However, the word translated "you who have received the Spirit" (an adjective, *pneumatikos)* occurs in Galatians only in 6:1. We should never base a theory on the use of one word in only one passage. Furthermore, 6:1 is part of a passage dealing with the flesh and Spirit for those under pressure to be circumcised and obey Jewish law.

Just before 6:1 Paul says: "If we live by the Spirit, let us also be guided by the Spirit. Let us not become conceited, competing against one another, envying one another." Then he says what he does in 6:1. Paul's words "you who have received the Spirit" flow out of the context and mean "you who still live by the Spirit." Paul knows that even though converts have received the Spirit, some may lose it and do wrong while waiting for ultimate righteousness (5:5). So those who have forgotten God's grace, by which they received the Spirit, and now "want to be justified by the law" (5:4) are to be restored by those who have not lost the Spirit.

Another suggestion regarding troublemakers at Galatia is that they were Gnostics or at least had Gnostic tendencies (see especially W. Schmithals 1972:13–64 and the critique of his view by R. M. Wilson 1968b). Gal 4:8–9 is sometimes cited as evidence: "Formerly, when you did not know God. . . . Now, however, that you have come to know God, or rather to be known by God. . . ." Paul seems to be using Gnostic thought and language about knowing God against his opponents. However, the word "rather" shows that Paul shifts the emphasis from knowing God to being known by God. It has also been suggested that, since Paul speaks so much about the contrast between the flesh and the Spirit, the Gnostic Galatians had a real problem with the "flesh," which they regarded as evil. "Flesh" is a distinctive Pauline word and represents that part of the physical nature responsible for doing evil. In contrast, the "spirit" is responsible for doing good. Most of the relevant verses are in chaps. 5 and 6.

If you look at Gal 5:16–25 in its context, you will see that it is part of the section that begins with 5:1. Paul's language about flesh and the Spirit develops naturally out of the context. Believers in Galatia have been set free by Christ, so they are not to revert to their former life without the Spirit (5:1). By being circumcised they would be submitting again to that same kind of life (5:1–2). As believers they walk by the Spirit and do not gratify the desires of the flesh. "Flesh" represents life without the Spirit, and if the Galatian converts are "led by the Spirit," they "are not subject to the law" (5:18). For those who produce "the fruit of the Spirit . . . there is no law" (5:22–23). Those who live by the Spirit ought to behave accordingly and not revert to existence without the Spirit or to the ways of the flesh. To be circumcised and to follow the law would be of no help.

Paul is not arguing against Gnostics or freedom questers, but against those who want Gentile converts to be circumcised and to obey Jewish law. Paul responds to such Judaizers and their influence throughout the letter. The Galatians have received the Spirit by faith, not works of the law (3:2); they "desire to be subject to the law" (4:21); if they let themselves be circumcised, "Christ will be of no benefit" to them (5:2). Paul accuses the Judaizers of working "for no good purpose" (4:17), of not keeping the law themselves (2:14; 6:13), and even wishes that they "would castrate themselves!" (5:12). One of Paul's arguments is stated in Gal 2:15–16, which you should read very carefully now. This passage is crucial for understanding the problem in Galatia between the Gentile converts and the Judaizers, as well as for understanding Paul's thought in both Galatians and Romans that resulted from the problem.

We depend almost entirely on Acts for knowledge of the makeup of the churches in Galatia, but Galatians reflects that makeup. There were Jews and converts to Judaism who were becoming, or thinking of becoming, members of the Jesus movement (13:43). Jews believed that they were God's people and would inherit God's promise to Abraham that they would be a great nation (Gen 12:1–3, 7; 13:14–17; 17:18). Jews who became members of that movement also believed that it was only for Jews, and that if Gentiles wanted to become members they first had to become Jews by being circumcised and obeying the Jewish law. Paul writes emphatically to deny that position. Most converts in Galatia were Gentiles (13:48–49; 14:2, 27), who would not have been familiar with the Jewish concept of one God or the rigorous moral demands of Jewish law and Paul's teaching.

As in other communities of converts, all gathered in the members' houses (see Rom 16:5; 1 Cor 16:19; Phlm 2). We refer to those assemblies as house churches (from *ekklēsia*, meaning "assembly" or "church"), which were under the leadership of one or more members (recall comments on *ekklēsia* in Chapter 9). According to Acts 14:23, the apostles appointed elders in every church before they returned to Antioch after their mission. The groups of believers in Galatia may have developed into an inner-city community of inner-house churches. This would explain why Paul wrote one letter "to the churches of Galatia." In that community, which was comprised of Jews, Jewish proselytes, and Gentile converts, there were undoubtedly discussions about Jewish law. There would also be questions concerning circumcision and dietary laws as requirements for themselves and for new converts (Gal 2:3–14), as well as discussions about the function of the law as a religious institution.

In light of the moral and ethical teachings of Stoics and other moral philosophers of Paul's time, we must not assume that pagans were immoral. Yet with the new moral standards imposed upon them, there was always the temptation for Gentile converts to forget their new God (Acts 13:44–48) and revert to their former way of life. Paul writes emphatically about this to the Galatians: "Formerly, when you did not know God, you were enslaved to beings that by nature are not gods. Now, however, that you have come to know God, or rather to be known by God, how can you turn back again to the weak and beggarly elemental spirits? How can you want to be enslaved to them again?" (4:8–9). This is the point of chaps. 5 and 6. In other communities Gentile converts faced the same temptation to revert to former modes of behavior (see Rom 6:19–22; 1 Cor 6:9–11; 15:1; 2 Cor 12:19–21; 13:1–10; Phil 1:27–30). Paul offered all groups at Galatia a monotheism and a high morality

without circumcision, dietary laws, and other ritualistic demands.

Now observe the structure of Galatians, which divides naturally into three parts. After the autobiographical account and the defense of his position in chaps. 1 and 2, Paul is concerned with two matters regarding the converts in Galatia. First, he argues against those who threaten the gospel of Christ by stressing the law (3–4) and then against the idea that, if freedom under the Spirit has degenerated into license, being circumcised and obeying the law can replace life by the Spirit (5–6). This idea threatened the developing religion at Galatia as much as those who stressed the law did. Paul had already warned the Galatians that those who do the works of the flesh will not inherit the kingdom of God (5:19–21).

INFLUENCE OF GALATIA ON PAUL'S THOUGHT

Recall that one of Paul's main contributions to Christian thought is the idea that those who become converts are justified—that is, are declared righteous or have their sins forgiven—by God's grace through faith in Christ (see below), not through ceremonial laws. Recall also that after the rite of baptism, believers become new creations who live by the Spirit and are obligated to live moral lives. Before the crisis at Galatia, Paul's main concern was the moral and ethical lives of new converts as they faced the End. He encouraged those at Thessalonica in their suffering (1 Thess 3:1–5) and reminded them to "lead a life worthy of God" (1 Thess 2:12; see also 4:1–12). Anxiety over the Parousia was no excuse for moral laxity (4:13–5:23). Similarly, much of the Corinthian correspondence deals with moral and ethical problems.

Before the problem in Galatia concerning the law for Gentile converts, faith and works of the law were never placed in antithesis to each other, nor were they afterward, except in Romans. In fact, the word "law" (*nomos*) is not even mentioned in 1 (and 2) Thessalonians or 2 Corinthians. In 1 Corinthians Paul refers to the law only to support his own position on various matters (1 Cor 9:8–9, 20; 14:21, 34; see also 15:56). And except for Romans, after Galatians the word "law" appears in the undisputed letters only in Phil 3:5–9, where Paul boasts of his training in the law as a Pharisee. Except for Galatians and Romans, the term "justify" occurs only in 1 Cor 6:11, where it is used synonymously with words referring to baptism: "But you were washed, you were sanctified, you were justified in the name of the Lord Jesus Christ and in the Spirit of our God."

Paul's experience in becoming a convert to the Jesus movement convinced him that God by his grace (see 1 Cor 3:10; 15:10; 2 Cor 1:12) had opened the door not only to a new faith, but to a renewed moral and ethical life. This new life had been opened to Gentiles as well as Jews through the efficacy of Jesus' death and resurrection. The death and resurrection of Jesus were effective for justification apart from works of the law, but not for ultimate salvation apart from moral life. The fact that the words "save" and "salvation" occur nowhere in Galatians indicates that Paul had not yet worked out a new doctrine of salvation in relation to the Jewish law. At Galatia, Paul first developed his position that converts, Gentiles and Jews alike, are justified by faith, not by works of the law (Gal 5:4).

Through baptism converts become members of a community of believers. They receive a supernatural power—called variously the Spirit, the Spirit of Christ, the Spirit of God, or the Holy Spirit—as a gift from God that enables them to live new lives in Christ. Jews and Gentiles alike receive this gift: "As many of you as were baptized into Christ have clothed yourselves with Christ. There is no longer Jew or Greek" (Gal 3:27–28; see also 1 Cor 12:13). Here I have stated the usual view that "Christians" received the Holy Spirit when they were baptized. However, as I mentioned in Chapter 9, I now think that Paul believed God gave the Spirit when persons were converted to faithfulness toward God. The basic texts are 1 Thess 1:4–10 and 4:7–8. If I am correct, then instead of saying converts "receive" the Spirit at baptism, we should say that

their experience of the Spirit is intensified because they have been baptized into Christ and clothed themselves with Christ (see comments on Gal 3:27 below).

Baptism obliges converts to continue to behave morally both in their personal and social lives, in order to receive ultimate salvation (Galatians 5–6). This is the essence of Paul's conception of justification by faith, his idea of salvation (as worked out later in Romans), and his eschatology. Paul's ethics are inseparable from each of these concepts. Justification imposes upon the person justified a responsibility for moral behavior, which is demanded for ultimate salvation in the age to come (see esp. Gal 6:4–10).

Paul's word translated as "clothed yourselves" (*enduomai*) shows influence from the Hebrew scriptures. There putting on clothes is a metaphor for assuming inner moral or spiritual qualities or a different status in life. For example, "I put on righteousness and clothed myself with judgment like a mantle" (LXX Job 29:14) and "Your priests shall clothe themselves with righteousness" (LXX Ps 131:9; see also Ps 34:26). After being baptized naked or scantily clothed and dressing themselves again, converts share a new kind of moral and spiritual existence through life in Christ. They are now under the obligation to remain sinless. Remember that Paul says: "Should we continue in sin in order that grace may abound? By no means! How can we who died to sin go on living in it?" (Rom 6:1–2). In spite of all arguments to the contrary, should we not take Paul at his word?

PAULINE BIOGRAPHICAL MATERIAL IN GALATIANS AND ACTS

As far as events in Paul's life are concerned, it is impossible to reconcile completely the differences between Acts and Paul's writings. (On the harmonization of Acts and Galatians, see K. Lake 1933. For the accounts of Paul and Acts concerning Paul's visits to Jerusalem, see J. Knox

---

FIGURE 11.1   *Biographical Material about Paul in Galatians and Acts*

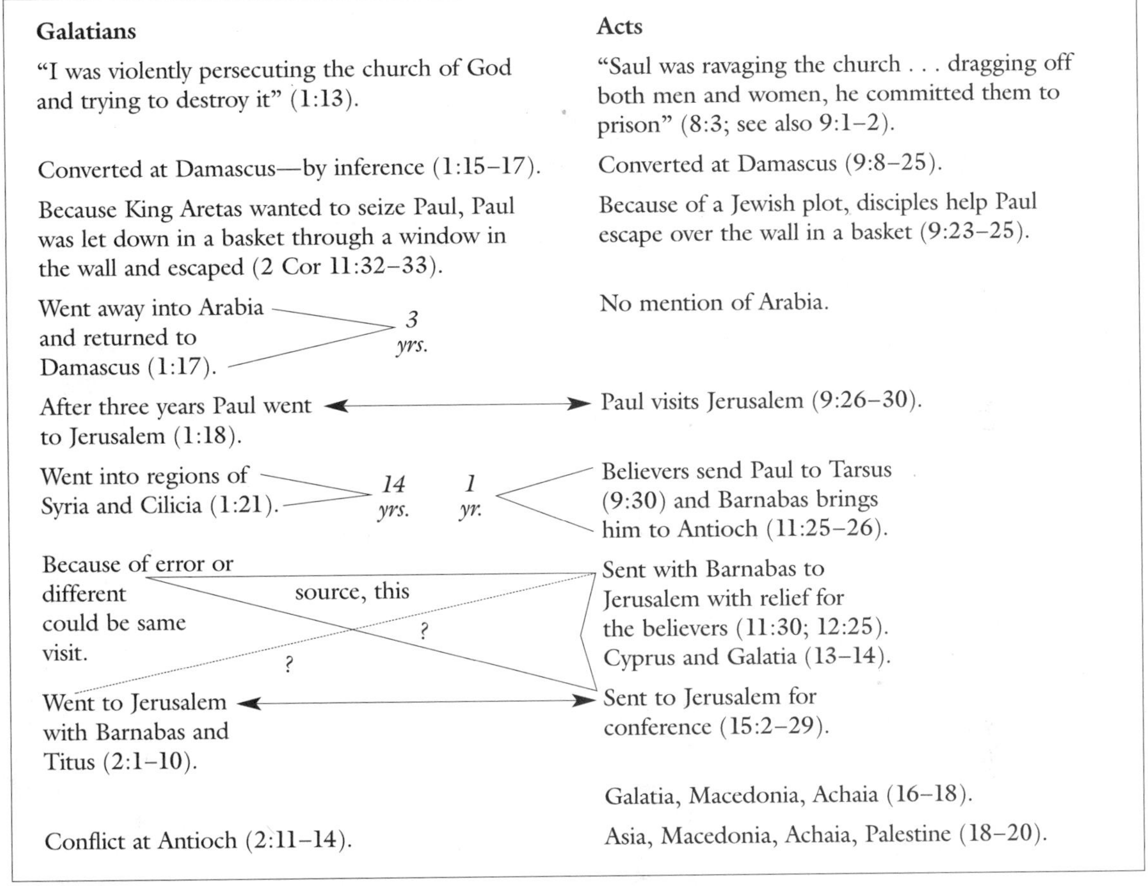

Galatians

"I was violently persecuting the church of God and trying to destroy it" (1:13).

Converted at Damascus—by inference (1:15–17).

Because King Aretas wanted to seize Paul, Paul was let down in a basket through a window in the wall and escaped (2 Cor 11:32–33).

Went away into Arabia and returned to Damascus (1:17).   *3 yrs.*

After three years Paul went to Jerusalem (1:18).

Went into regions of Syria and Cilicia (1:21).   *14 yrs.*   *1 yr.*

Because of error or different source, this could be same visit.   *?*   *?*

Went to Jerusalem with Barnabas and Titus (2:1–10).

Conflict at Antioch (2:11–14).

Acts

"Saul was ravaging the church . . . dragging off both men and women, he committed them to prison" (8:3; see also 9:1–2).

Converted at Damascus (9:8–25).

Because of a Jewish plot, disciples help Paul escape over the wall in a basket (9:23–25).

No mention of Arabia.

Paul visits Jerusalem (9:26–30).

Believers send Paul to Tarsus (9:30) and Barnabas brings him to Antioch (11:25–26).

Sent with Barnabas to Jerusalem with relief for the believers (11:30; 12:25). Cyprus and Galatia (13–14).

Sent to Jerusalem for conference (15:2–29).

Galatia, Macedonia, Achaia (16–18).

Asia, Macedonia, Achaia, Palestine (18–20).

1950.) One main problem appears when Paul's statements in Galatians 1–2 are compared with related statements in Acts. Some people think the two accounts can be harmonized somewhat as in Figure 11.1. On the other hand, G. H. C. Macgregor 1962 says that Paul's visits mentioned in Galatians 2 and Acts 15 cannot be reconciled without charging Paul with dishonesty or Luke with ignorance of facts about Paul. Again, on the other hand, B. Witherington 1998a:327–331 thinks the chronology of Acts and Paul can be reconciled.

In contrast to the similarities, the conflicting statements between Galatians and Acts shown in Figure 11.2 cannot be reconciled.

What did Paul do during the years he spent in Arabia, Syria, and Cilicia before he became attached to the church in Jerusalem? Acts is silent about those years, and Paul tells us nothing. Later church authorities write that he spent the years in solitude, meditating on his vision and preparing for his work. But in light of his emphasis on his call to preach to Gentiles, we may assume that he began that task immediately. (See here J. Murphy-O'Connor 1996 and M. Hengel 1997a, mentioned in Chapter 9, as well as B. Witherington 1998a referred to above.) No letters indicate success or failure in his first missionary work, but we do have a letter to the Galatians that deals with the problems Paul

---

FIGURE 11.2   *Conflicting Statements about Paul in Galatians and Acts*

Gal 1:18–24

I did go up to Jerusalem to visit Cephas and stayed with him fifteen days; but I did not see any other apostle except James the Lord's brother. In what I am writing to you, before God, I do not lie!

and I was still unknown by sight to the churches of Judea that are in Christ; they only heard it said, "The one who formerly was persecuting us is now proclaiming the faith he once tried to destroy." And they glorified God because of me.

Acts 9:26–29

When he had come to Jerusalem, he attempted to join the disciples; and they were all afraid of him, for they did not believe that he was a disciple. But Barnabas took him, brought him to the apostles, and described for them how on the road he had seen the Lord . . . and how in Damascus he had spoken boldly in the name of Jesus.

So he went in and out among them in Jerusalem, speaking boldly in the name of the Lord. He spoke and argued with the Hellenists; but they were attempting to kill him.

---

faced in Galatia. It is outlined, with comments, below.

Outline and Comments

I. *Autobiographical and historical material (1:1–2:21)*

Compared with the opening verses of Paul's other letters, Gal 1:1–5 is a harsh greeting. Paul defends himself immediately by saying that Christ and God, not men, are responsible for his apostleship, and he gives a concise statement of his message. Instead of thanksgiving for the faith and welfare of his readers, which Paul usually expresses at this point in his letters, he utters his disgust that the Galatians are so quickly deserting Christ and turning to a gospel preached by others. Let the persons proclaiming another gospel "be accursed!" (1:6–9).

Paul defends his gospel personally and historically by declaring that his apostleship is of divine and not human origin (1:10–24). He then admits his earlier persecution of believers. Like the prophet Jeremiah (1:4–10), he says that God set him apart before he was born and that through a revelation of his Son, God called him to preach Christ among the Gentiles. Paul's

gospel and work were approved by leaders in Jerusalem (2:1–10).

Gal 2:11–14 reflects the controversy that grew out of the successful mission to the Gentiles—whether converts who observed Jewish dietary laws should eat with those who did not. Paul accuses Peter of hypocrisy because at Antioch he ate with Gentiles until some conservative Jews came from Jerusalem. He reprimands Peter: "If you, though a Jew, live like a Gentile and not like a Jew, how can you compel the Gentiles to live like Jews?" In response to his own question to Peter, Paul concisely summarizes his view that in the process of becoming converts people need not be circumcised or observe dietary laws, but only have faith in Christ (2:15–21). The words "Jews . . . not Gentile sinners" and "we have come to believe in Christ Jesus, so that we might be justified by faith in Christ, and not by doing the works of the law" mean that Jews, who have the law, in contrast to Gentiles who do not, also must have faith in Christ to be regarded as righteous (= justified) and to become converts. Even though Jews had the law, they "have been found to be sinners," so if as believers they again submitted to the law, they would again be sinners.

In speaking about his own experience in becoming a convert, Paul says that "through the law" he "died to the law," that is, his life is no longer regulated by the law in order that he might "live to God." By sharing in Christ's crucifixion Paul does not live as he once did under the law and as a persecutor of believers. Rather, Christ lives in him and transforms even Paul's physical existence so he can "live by faith in the Son of God," who loved Paul and gave himself for him. Paul does not say how he shared Christ's crucifixion. Perhaps it was by being immersed in the waters of baptism (Romans 6) when he became a convert, or perhaps he meant by bearing the marks of Jesus on his body through suffering (2 Cor 11:23–28).

Please read now the discussion of the faithfulness of Christ at the end of the chapter.

II. Defense of Paul's view and refutation of opponents (3:1–4:31)

Paul defends his view that both Jews and Gentiles become acceptable to God by faith in Christ, not by works of the law, and uses scripture to refute his opponents' objections. He reminds the Galatians of their own reception of the Spirit by faith, not by works of the law (3:1–5).

Abraham is the first example of justification by faith. Paul quotes Gen 15:5–6 to show that Abraham, who was regarded as the father of many nations, was reckoned as righteous because of his faith. Abraham's faith, then, is an example of the gospel coming before the giving of the law, to show that "God would justify the Gentiles by faith." So all—including the Judaizers— who share in the promise that in Abraham all the nations would be blessed must also share his faith (3:6–9).

Through a series of OT quotations, Paul argues that those under the law who do not obey all things in the law face condemnation, because scripture (Hab 2:4) says that the righteous person shall live by faith. Christ brought redemption from law when he died on the cross. The promise to Abraham preceded the giving of the law. Abraham's true descendants are those who have faith and are not bound by the law, so Gentiles are included. Since a will or any other agreement cannot be altered unless all parties consent, the law does not annul the covenant with Abraham, since God does not consent (3:10–18).

Paul asks, "Why then the law?" The law was a temporary measure, a "disciplinarian" (*paidagōgos*), to make people aware of their faults until Christ came (3:19–22). A *paidagōgos* (lit., "boy-leader") was a freedman or slave who attended and protected boys on their way to and from school, and who was concerned also with their moral character until they were regarded as men. For believers the law as a disciplinarian is unnecessary, "for in Christ Jesus . . . you are all children of God through faith" (3:23–28). As children of God believers are free, and because they are free they know God intimately. Under the law, people are like heirs placed under a guardian and are no better than slaves. "But . . . God sent his Son . . . to redeem those who were under the law." As children of God, those freed from the law can know God intimately as *abba*, an Aramaic word equivalent to our affectionate term *daddy* (3:29–4:7).

Paul says Galatian converts must remain free, and he pleads with them not to return to their former state of bondage "to the weak and beggarly elemental spirits." This may be a reference to heavenly bodies that were regarded as demonic beings. It was a common Hellenistic belief that these beings influenced people's lives. The remark about days, months, and seasons is an indication of Jewish observances brought about by the Judaizers (4:8–11).

Paul appeals to the Galatians by recalling his visit with them and accuses his opponents of self-seeking motives (4:12–20). The allegory of Hagar and Sarah follows. Abraham had two sons, one by Hagar, Sarah's slave, the other by his wife Sarah, a free woman. The women represent two covenants. Hagar is the covenant of the law made at Sinai, a mountain in Arabia that represents "the present Jerusalem" under Roman rule in Paul's time. Sarah is the covenant of promise that was made to Abraham and represents the "Jerusalem above," or freedom. The Jews are linked with the son of Hagar, and so are slaves and will not share in the freedom. Believers are the children of promise fulfilled in Isaac, son of the free woman; they have freedom in Christ and are not under ritualistic requirements of the law (4:21–31).

III. Paul's description of Christian freedom in Christ (5:1–6:10)

Paul exhorts the Galatians to remain free in Christ and not to revert to a "yoke of slavery" by being circumcised and keeping the law. To do so would mean losing God's grace. "Through the Spirit, by faith," Paul and others wait for ultimate righteousness, that is, salvation. "For in Christ Jesus neither circumcision nor uncircumcision counts for anything; the only thing that counts is faith working through love" (5:1–6). Paul warns the Galatians not to yield to outside influence. They were doing well until the troublemakers came. But "a little yeast leavens the whole batch of dough"—a little Judaizing spreads its influence (5:7–12).

Paul gives instructions on how to retain freedom in Christ. He goes beyond the Stoic idea that freedom is doing what one wants so long as it does not harm another. Although Paul never defines what he means by "freedom," what follows helps to explain it. Faith working through love means that freedom is not license. It also means loving one's neighbor as oneself, living by the Spirit and not by "the desires of the flesh," correcting a person doing wrong, bearing one another's burdens by being helpful, and doing good to all people (5:13–6:10).

IV. Conclusion (6:11–18)

Paul takes the pen from his secretary, to whom he has dictated the letter, to attack his opponents a final time and to reiterate the main points he has made. The large letters are probably for emphasis.

For more detailed study of Galatians from various points of view, see three still useful older commentaries: J. B. Lightfoot 1974; W. M. Ramsay 1900; E. D. W. Burton 1920. See also J. A. Fitzmyer 1968b; F. F. Bruce 1982a; D. Guthrie 1981; H. D. Betz 1979; C. B. Cousar

1982; C. K. Barrett 1985. See additional bibliography at end of chapter.

ROMANS

ROME IN PAUL'S TIME

Rome was usually known as the city of seven hills. Many roads from all directions converged at its center, with the Tiber River flowing along its western edge. But Rome was much more than that. Magnificent public buildings, covered with marble in the time of Augustus, included public baths, theaters, amphitheaters, circuses (oval enclosures with seats on three sides), and temples. Rome, hub of the Roman Empire, was a great cosmopolitan city, with a population estimated at from one and a half to more than four million. Among its population were numerous foreigners from all parts of the world, including many Greek and Oriental slaves.

Foreigners usually settled in communities in special sections of the city and practiced their trades, arts, and crafts. They frequently formed clubs and associations, many of them religious in nature. There were also associations for occupations and trades, astrologers, athletes, teachers, philosophers, and rhetoricians; anyone who could pay, including slaves, was admitted to them. All of these groups were allowed to practice their own cults and to celebrate their own special festivals. Many also celebrated cults of the emperors, living and dead, by participating in sacrifices, games, and banquets.

Among foreign groups in Rome were Jews from Palestine and elsewhere. Like other foreigners, they were concentrated in special districts, formed religious associations, and maintained contact with the lands of their origins. There were Jewish quarters in several sections of the city, one west of the Tiber. Presumably the first converts in Rome were among Jews living in the Jewish quarters. The book of Acts ends with Paul in Rome, discoursing among Jewish leaders.

In the inner city the wealthy had elaborate palaces, gardens, and even parks of hundreds of acres. This reduced the space available for the poor and caused housing shortages for the ever-growing population. The rich, especially the ruling families, would spend a huge sum of money on a single banquet at which people would gorge themselves on pork, wines, and other delicacies until they were stuffed and drunk. In contrast, the poor were forced to live in cheap tenement housing, often several stories above the city shops, where conditions were crowded and generally terrible.

Sections of the city were so bad that Juvenal (satirist of the first century CE) writes about the constant dread of fire, the collapse of houses, and a thousand other dangers. Fires were Rome's greatest menace. Tacitus reports the terrible conflagration in Nero's time, which began among the shops with their inflammable wares, rapidly spread to the hills, and finally destroyed much of the city. To help remedy the drastic inner-city situation, Augustus added new buildings and colonies along three of the main roads, divided the city into fourteen regions (wards) governed by magistrates who were selected annually, instituted a police force, and developed professional firefighters known as *vigiles* (watchers).

The streets of Rome were narrow and curved. Carriages were not permitted inside the city, so most people walked from place to place. The wealthier rode horseback or were carried in sedan chairs. Those who ventured into the dark streets at night apparently took their lives into their own hands. According to Juvenal, people going out to supper without having made wills were remiss, because potsherds would fall upon their heads from windows. There were as many chances to be killed as there were open windows in the houses when people passed by. On the better side, the government provided and maintained aqueducts that carried good water into the city for public fountains, baths, and latrines.

The forum (see Figure 11.3) was the center of Roman social, legal, political, and commercial life and was surrounded by all kinds of shops, including those for banking. Military processions passed

FIGURE 11.3 *Ancient forum or marketplace in Rome.*

through the forum, and funeral processions paused there for the customary funeral orations. In the forum, as elsewhere in the city, were numerous altars and temples, including the temples of Castor and Pollux, Saturn, and the vestal virgins.

Many Romans were preoccupied with sports and other pleasures, especially on holidays, which numbered half the days of the year. People were entertained with three kinds of activities: horse races, theatrical performances, and gladiatorial contests. In Paul's time there were three theaters—those named after Pompey, Balbus, and Marcellus—which seated from eight to fourteen thousand people, and the large amphitheater in the Campus Martius. The most important structure, in which various spectacles were held, was the Circus Maximus, where people sat in three sections of seats separated from the arena by a wide channel of water that protected the people from the wild animals. It seated some 300,000 spectators.

Rome became a prominent religious center. There was a religious revival in the time of Augustus, who as emperor was the head of the state religion and had the title *Pontifex Maximus* (highest priest). He repaired temples and built a magnificent Temple of Apollo on the Palatine Hill. It was to be symbolic of present and future blessings. Although emperor worship was instituted in the provinces, Augustus did not accept divine honors in Rome. The state religion was highly organized under a college of priests over whom the *Pontifex Maximus* presided. These priests were responsible for all public religious ceremonies and for discovering the will of the gods through divination or consultation with the oracles. The state religion, of course, existed to serve the interests of the state and to inspire loyalty to the empire. In addition to the state religion, however, dozens of cults flourished. The religion of the Jews, with its worship of only one God and its strong moral and ethical laws, won many converts. But because Judaism excluded all other religious beliefs and practices, including the Roman state religion, it frequently encountered difficulty from Roman authorities. For the same reasons Jews were sometimes expelled from Rome.

With respect to sex, a double standard prevailed in much of the ancient world. It was taken for granted that the unmarried man would satisfy his sexual impulses, as long as the women of his choice were those whose reputations could not be spoiled. With no laws against prostitution, it was not difficult to find women of ill repute. Married men were expected to be faithful to their wives, but if they were not and did not become involved with another man's wife, their worst penalties were usually only quarrels with angry wives. Women were treated differently. If they were unfaithful to their husbands, they could be divorced immediately. However, many wives were respected as female heads of households, participated in social events with their husbands, and were usually respected on the streets. Although Augustus was responsible for laws intended to strengthen marriage, divorce was still frequent. Many wealthy men and women, especially in the ruling classes, often connived, to the point of murder, to be free to marry others.

Such was Rome when Paul wrote his letter to the converts who lived there and when he arrived c. 59 CE. (For more about Rome in the first century, read G. LaPiana 1927 and H. T. Rowell 1962, my main sources; see also R. E. Brown 1983; M. D. Nanos 1996.) But how did "Christianity" get started in Rome?

ORIGIN OF CHRISTIANITY IN ROME

There is no reference in the NT, even in Acts and Romans, to a founder of the church at Rome or to an initial Jesus mission in Rome. Paul had not visited Rome before the church was established. According to later tradition, Peter was the founder of the church in Rome, but it is unlikely that Paul thought this, because of the way he writes about Peter in Gal 2:7–8. Most modern scholars reject the Peter tradition, so we just do not know how Christianity got a foothold in Rome. It is likely, however, that the community there was established by converts who had come from Palestine, Syria, and other places in the Roman Empire. Among business people, soldiers, slaves, officials, students, and others who traveled to and from Rome, some took the developing religion there. Tacitus implies as much when he speaks about it in uncomplimentary terms: "This detestable superstition broke out . . . in Rome into which there flows all that is hideous and shameful in the whole world and finds many people to support it" (*Annals* 15:44).

In reporting the fire in Rome during the time of Nero, Tacitus says that Nero, wanting to free himself from blame, fixed the guilt upon a class called Christians. Suetonius, writing about Claudius and his expulsion of Jews from Rome, says that Jews were expelled because they caused disturbances in the name of Christ. The first converts in Rome were probably Jewish, were associated with synagogues, and were already present by the time of Claudius. If Claudius did expel "all Jews" (Acts 18:2), some Jewish converts could have returned again after his death in 54 CE. When Paul wrote his letter to Rome, there were also Gentile converts in Rome, as the following passage indicates: "I want you to know, brothers and sisters, that I have often intended to come to you . . . that I may reap some harvest among you as I have among the rest of the Gentiles" (1:13).

WHY DID PAUL WRITE ROMANS?

If we look at Romans itself, its immediate purpose seems clear. Paul had finished his work in the East and was about to take the offering to the saints in Jerusalem; then on the way to Spain he wanted to stop in Rome (15:17–29). Paul addresses the letter to "God's beloved in Rome" and says he longs to see them and preach the gospel in Rome (1:7–15). He is writing to prepare the Romans for his impending visit.

For several reasons, however, the answer to the question of why Paul wrote Romans is not that simple. First, many scholars think that chap. 16 (and perhaps 15 as well), although written by Paul, was not originally a part of Romans. One argument is that Paul would not have greeted so many people personally (16:3–15) in a letter to a church he had not visited. Therefore, chap. 16 may have been a separate letter of introduction for Phoebe (a deaconess of the church at Cenchreae, the port of Corinth) to some other church, perhaps the one at Ephesus, where Paul had many friends. On the other hand, some say that Paul may have made many friends in the provinces who later went to Rome, and that chap. 16 is therefore part of the original letter written to Rome. (See A. J. Malherbe 1983:65, n. 13.)

Second, because the doxology in 16:25–27 appears in some manuscripts after 15:33 or 14:23, or after both 14:23 and 16:23, there may have been three versions of Romans in the early church.

Third, in some manuscripts the words "in Rome" are lacking in 1:7, 15—evidence that originally Romans was not intended for a particular destination. For this and other reasons some scholars think Romans was written as a "circular letter," that is, one intended for several churches (M. S. Enslin 1938:262–272; others who hold this view are M. J. Suggs 1967; R. W. Funk 1967; J. Munck 1959). However, the authenticity of Romans—including chaps. 15 and 16, except for 16:25–27—is almost universally accepted.

"The Romans Debate"

Scholars differ widely about why Paul wrote Romans, and they refer to the discussion on the subject as "the Romans debate." A book with that title gives the views of several scholars. Some of those views and others follow.

Paul wrote to prepare the church at Rome for his future visit and to address the situation there (the view of many past and present scholars), and the purpose of Paul's letter and his visit are the same: to give the church an apostolic foundation because it had not been established by apostles (G. Klein 1977). Jerusalem, not Rome, was in Paul's mind when he wrote Romans; Romans is a speech intended to win the support of Gentile

Christians at Rome to help assure that Paul and the offering would be accepted by the church at Jerusalem (for example, J. Jervell 1977). Paul wrote to admonish Jewish or Gentile converts or both, either in Rome or elsewhere (the view of many past and present scholars). He wrote to resolve the conflict between "the weak" and "the strong" (14:1, 2, 21; 15:1), groups explained in different ways (for example, P. S. Minear 1971 and L. Morris 1970).

Romans is Paul's "last will and testament," which "arises from his own *past* experiences with his churches," in view of "the impending important meeting with the mother church in Jerusalem and the rounding off of his work as an apostle" (G. Bornkamm 1971:96; to some extent also W. G. Kuemmel 1975:312–313). Romans is a "letter-essay" like those written by ancient Greek authors, which were sent to specific people and were designed to supplement another writing by the same author or to take the place of a proposed work by him. As such it is, "the last will and testament of the Apostle Paul" (M. L. Stirewalt 1977). Clearly "the Romans debate" centers mainly on the issue of whether Paul wrote Romans to deal with a particular situation in Rome. Some scholars support a combination of the views presented (for example, R. H. Fuller 1966:53–54; W. Marxsen 1968:92–108; W. G. Kuemmel 1975:311–320).

Galatians and the Purpose of Romans

Remember that Paul wrote Galatians to deal with the question of whether Gentiles in the process of becoming converts should be circumcised and obey Jewish law. The situation at Galatia forced him to think seriously about the relationship between his new religious experience and the Jewish law. He never faced that question seriously before Galatia or after Romans, although Gal 2:11–14 gives a hint of the same problem with Peter and other Jews at Antioch. In writing Romans, as with Galatians, Paul is concerned not only with those who are becoming converts, but also with how they live once they are. Therefore, Romans, like Galatians, is divided into two main sections: how people become converts or believers (Galatians 3–4; Romans 1–11) and how they should behave once they are (Galatians 5–6; Romans 12–15). The theme of the first section is stated in 1:16–17, the theme of the second in 12:1–2.

Several other close affinities exist between Galatians and Romans. In Galatians 2–4 and Rom 3:21–8:11 Paul deals with these main subjects: justification by faith and not by works of the law, the faith of Abraham as an example, the law and its function, union with Christ, slavery and freedom, flesh and spirit, and the sending of God's Son in the flesh to deliver those under the law and make them children of God by the Spirit. Moreover, it seems that the summary of Paul's thought in Gal 2:15–21 is the outline from which Paul develops his views about justification by faith and not by works of the law in much of Romans 1–8.

There are other striking similarities between Galatians and Romans: the quotation from Hab 2:4 to support the argument of justification by faith (Gal 3:11; Rom 1:17), the reference to Lev 18:5 to show that those under the law are to live by the law (Gal 3:12; Rom 10:5), the idea that believers belong to the line of descendants reckoned through Sarah and Isaac (Gal 4:27–31; Rom 9:6–11), and the quotation from Lev 19:18, "You shall love your neighbor as yourself," as a summary of the whole law for believers (Gal 4:28–31; Rom 13:9).

All of these similarities indicate that in Romans Paul is elaborating themes touched on in Galatians. Romans is developed from Galatians, and without Galatians there would be no Romans. In Galatians Paul deals with believers whom the Judaizers urge to observe the law, but in Romans there is no reference to any opponents, and there are no answers to specific problems as there are in every other letter. In Romans Paul has one theme: the relationship between the believer and the law in light of his own struggle as a Jew and devotee to Christ. Since most Gentile converts came from the Jewish synagogue where they worshiped as God-fearers, Paul's message would apply to both Gentiles and Jews. In contrast to Galatians, here Paul has thought through his position and presents it calmly and objectively.

It seems reasonable to suppose that Paul wanted to share his message with as many communities of believers as possible. Because Romans contains no convincing evidence of opponents or of specific problems, and because chaps. 15–16 probably were not originally part of the letter—and therefore do not support the view that Paul wrote the letter to take the place of a visit—the theory that Paul first wrote Romans as a letter to be circulated among his churches is the best one.

Romans would have been appropriate for any church, especially the one in Ephesus, where opponents were making it difficult for believers. The original letter probably consisted of chaps. 1–14 and was meant for all churches in Asia Minor. In the copy sent to Ephesus, Paul added the introduction of Phoebe and the greetings to his friends at Ephesus (chap. 16). About the same time, he thought he should get in touch with Rome, since he hoped to do mission work in the West. He wanted to correct any wrong impressions or rumors believers there might have received. Paul could have not written a more fitting message than the carefully thought-out statement concerning the developing religion as he perceived it that is in the letter now known as Romans. In a subsequent copy he mentioned Rome specifically, added some encouragement for harmony among Christians, and stated clearly his reason for wanting to go to Rome (chap. 15; M. S. Enslin 1938:267–268).

Despite different opinions about why Paul wrote Romans, there is general agreement that he wrote it from Corinth while on his third journey, c. 55 CE. It is a complicated work, sometimes inconsistent and even contradictory. Read Romans and use the following outline and comments to help you understand it.

Outline and Comments

I. Greeting, thanksgiving, and desire to visit Rome (1:1–15)

II. The way people become believers (1:16–11:36)
   A. The way of God's justification by faith rejected (1:16–8:39)
      1. Justification and grace (1:16–3:31)

Rom 1:16–17 gives the theme of chaps. 1–11. The gospel makes justification possible by the righteousness of God for Jews and Gentiles who have faith (1:16–17). Recall the definition of "justification" or "righteousness." Two other important terms—"salvation" and "faith"—also need comment. (There is a lucid and thorough discussion of Pauline terms in E. D. W. Burton 1920:363–521.) When Paul uses "salvation," he always means ultimate salvation in the eschatological future. This is clear from two things: the force of the preposition "for" (v 16), which cannot be translated adequately with one word, and the words "will live" (v 17). This translation of v 16 conveys the meaning of the Greek very well: "For I am not ashamed of the Gospel, since it is the operation of God's power working towards salvation, effective for everyone who has faith—Jew first, and then the Gentile too" (C. K. Barrett 1957:27; I am much indebted to this commentary).

In the expression "the righteousness of God," is "the righteousness" only that of God, not of humans, because God is its source? Passages in Romans support this view (see, for example, 3:21–25; 10:3), but other passages indicate that the righteousness of God can become the righteousness of humans. In 2 Cor 5:17–21, as the result of a person's reconciliation to God, the righteousness of God—which makes one's reconciliation possible as a free gift when one becomes a believer—also becomes that person's righteousness: "For our sake he made him to be sin who knew no sin, so that in him we might become the righteousness of God." And in Rom 1:17 the epithet "righteous" is applied to the person who has faith, not to God.

It is difficult to tell what Paul means by the expression "through faith for faith" (lit., "from faith to faith," or perhaps "from one faith to another"). Paul certainly wants to stress the importance of faith. Perhaps he means that progress toward salvation is made effective by faith that continues after justification. Since most of Paul's ideas have several aspects, we must always try not to focus on just one. This is true for the quotation from Hab 2:4: "He who is righteous from faithfulness shall live" (my trans.).

Paul nowhere defines "faith," and many times, as here, he uses it absolutely (that is, without a stated object)—or as we might say, "faith, period!" There are other problems with the sentence. The Greek is ambiguous, so we do not know how to take the phrase "from faith." If we take it with "righteous," then we should translate as I do. If we take the phrase with "shall live," then it should be translated as in the NRSV: "The one who is righteous will live by faith." So what is Paul really saying? Does he mean that those who are made righteous by God as the result of their faith when they become converts will live in the future—that is, gain salvation? Or does he mean that those who are made righteous acquire a new kind of life by their faith? Or does Paul mean that converts should keep living by the faith they had before they became converts? Again, we should not stress one possibility but consider all of them, since Paul may not have intended only one meaning.

Gentiles who have not accepted the way of life necessary for becoming believers do not have righteousness, and by their unrighteousness they have incurred God's wrath. God is revealed in the works of his creation, but these Gentiles have chosen to worship idols instead of the Creator, so they deserve to die (1:19–32). Jews, also, who have not accepted the way of life necessary for becoming converts (2:1–29) will be judged according to their works. To those who do good, God will give eternal life, but for all who do evil, there will be tribulation. God will judge the Jews by their own law, but the Gentiles who do not have the Jewish law will be judged by their consciences, which serve as an unwritten moral law. Paul taunts the Jews in particular because they do not keep the law. For both uncircumcised Gentile and circumcised Jew, keeping the law is a matter of the spirit, not the letter (2:1–29; see 7:6).

Individuals are justified by the gift of God's grace "through the redemption that is in Christ Jesus, whom God put forward as a sacrifice of atonement by his blood, effective through faith" (3:1–31). Whatever Paul means here, this gift of grace is necessary for all people without distinction, "since all have sinned and fall short of the glory of God" (3:23). But what is Paul saying? Except for 1 Cor 6:11, Paul uses the word "justify" only in Galatians and Romans. In the Corinthian passage Paul speaks about pagan converts as "washed . . . sanctified . . . justified." This means that when converts are baptized they are acquitted of their past sins and are made righteous. Paul says this happens by God's grace as a gift.

"Redemption" (*apolutrōsis*), not a popular Pauline word (only Rom 3:24; 8:23; 1 Cor 1:30 in undisputed letters), originally referred to the freeing of a slave by his master. Paul uses it to say that converts, especially Gentiles, become freed from their pagan state of sin. This freedom was made possible by Jesus' sacrifice of atonement.

"Expiation" (*hilastērion*) occurs only in Rom 3:25 in Paul's letters and, with "by his blood," belongs to the terminology of religious sacrifices. Paul thought that Christ's blood was effective for the justification of sinners, but he does not say how. Is he speaking metaphorically? Perhaps a few verses from 4 Maccabees, a Jewish writing from close to Paul's time, will help clarify his thought: "These men, then, were sanctified by God. . . . They became, as it were, a ransom for the sin of the nation. It was through the blood of those righteous ones, and through the expiation of their death, that divine providence saved Israel" (17:20–22; my trans.). These words were written in praise of seven Jewish brothers who had given their lives for their religion. Notice the terms "sanctify," "ransom," "sin," "blood," "righteous ones," and "expiation," all of which were used in Judaism to describe the results of the merits of the righteous (W. D. Davies 1955:268–273). These people's merits were considered effective for other people. Similarly, Paul thinks Christ's death is effective for those who have faith.

Paul defends his view that those who become converts are justified by faith and not by works of the law. He ends chap. 3 by asking, "Do we then overthrow the law by this faith?" He answers:

"By no means! On the contrary, we uphold the law." Coming after what Paul has just said about the law, this statement is puzzling. It seems impossible to reconcile it (see Rom 7:12; 8:4) with the later statement "Christ is the end of the law so that there may be righteousness for everyone who believes" (10:4).

2. Justification and faith (4:1–5:21)

Paul uses the example of Abraham, whose faith preceded his obedience to God and his circumcision, to support his argument for justification by faith. Abraham's faith made him righteous, and he is the model for believers (4:1–25).

After their justification, believers "have peace with God" and can rejoice in the "hope of sharing the glory of God" (5:1–21). In chap. 5 Paul looks to the future. Now study carefully Rom 5:6–10. In this passage, being reconciled is synonymous with being justified, and the ideas of redemption and expiation from chap. 3 are also present. The main point is that before their conversion, converts were alienated from God by sin, but now they are reconciled to God by Christ's death. The ideas of being enemies of God (v 10) and expiation by death and blood have their roots in the OT (see Exod 23:22; Isa 1:24). In the OT, God is thought to be reconciled by the proper sacrifice, and in later Judaism through prayers, confession, or conversion.

Again, Paul's thought and Judaism are similar, as this sentence from 2 Maccabees (first century BCE) shows: "May he [God] hear your prayers and be reconciled to you" (1:5; see also 2 Macc 8:29). Paul, however, thinks that reconciliation with God was made possible by the expiating death and blood of Christ, but he never says how this happened. Perhaps he thought that Christ's blood had the same effect as the blood and death of sacrificial victims. The Jews believed that in sacrificial worship these victims took the place of the sacrificer's sins.

Rom 5:12–21 reflects the theological view that since Adam (Genesis 1–3) disobeyed God, sin and death came into the world and "spread to all because all have sinned." But according to Paul, the righteousness of Christ "leads to justification and life for all." This life overcomes the death that Adam brought about and has the potential for becoming eternal. In chap. 6, however, Paul dispels any notion that because converts have been justified and have the potential for eternal life through God's grace they can do as they please.

3. Justification and freedom from sin (6:1–23)

Justification or reconciliation to God frees believers from sin, and they are responsible for remaining free of sin. Some might think that since they were forgiven through God's grace, it would be all right to sin again so that God's grace might be the more effective. Paul emphatically rejects that idea, as is clear from vv 1–14.

Rom 6:1–14 is the classic NT statement on baptism and its meaning for moral life. Paul explains symbolically how justification or reconciliation becomes effective. The Greek word *baptizō* means "to dip" or "submerge." When converts are immersed in the water during baptism, they share symbolically in the death of Christ, and their past sins are forgiven through God's grace. When they come up from the water, they share symbolically in Jesus' resurrection, rise to newness of life, and are "alive to God in Christ Jesus" (see Gal 3:27). Baptism is inseparably connected with Paul's concepts of justification and salvation and must be understood in light of his eschatology. Converts can experience a resurrection in this age through baptism, but the ultimate experience comes in the next age. In this age they become members of God's people; in the age to come they will share in Christ's bodily resurrection (6:5). But baptism does not guarantee that ultimate experience, as the verses that follow make clear.

Justification, which is symbolized in the rite of baptism, brings forgiveness of sins. But this forgiveness is not automatic or magical, and converts are not relieved of future responsibility to lead moral lives. This responsibility is "the obedience of faith" Paul mentioned in 1:5. Becoming a convert means a complete break with one's past immoral life and the obligation to live free from sin and under grace "as slaves of righteousness" (6:18). But Paul, aware of the limitations of human life and the possibility that Gentile converts would revert to their former immoral ways, exhorts the Roman Christians not to sin (6:15–19).

In Rom 6:15–19 Paul recalls the nature of the readers' pagan life, thanks God that they have become sincerely obedient to the teaching to which they pledged themselves when they became believers, and reminds them of their present responsibility to be righteous. Paul is really saying that as pagans the Roman converts knew what they were doing, did it of their own free will, and were responsible for it. Now as believers they are responsible for following the instruction they received when they became believers.

The passage ends with the words "for sanctification," which occur also in v 22. The word "sanctification" (*hagiasmos*) derives from the verb *hagiazō*, meaning to "make holy" or "set apart as holy," and thus "sanctify." The preposition "for" here again means "for the purpose of" or "towards"—that is, moving toward a goal. The ending *asmos* on a Greek word means that the condition referred to by the word is not completed but still in process. The believer is still in the process of becoming *hagios* ("holy"). "Sanctification" has an ethical meaning (as in 1 Thess 4:1–7) because Paul has used it in direct contrast to "iniquity," which literally means "lawlessness," especially in the form of disobedience to God's will. Believers have become "enslaved to God," are in the process of becoming holy, and are moving toward their goal, "eternal life" (6:22–23).

Paul often makes clear that the ultimate salvation of believers lies in the future. Perhaps he does this because he wants to avoid giving any wrong impressions to Gentile converts who are familiar with the belief that initiation into the Graeco-Roman mystery cults confers upon initiates the certainty of salvation or eternal life. Among the mystery religions the initiation rites were themselves thought to be so sacramentally effective that initiates' pasts were completely atoned, initiates were provided comfort for the present, and they were guaranteed salvation for all time. Members of the mystery cults believed that as the result of their initiation they had beheld the revelation of an eternal god and that, like the god, they would not die but be eternally saved. The following quotations reflect these views:

> Be of good courage, ye initiates, because the God has been saved;
>
> To us also shall be salvation from woes.
>
> As truly as Osiris lives, he shall also live; as truly as Osiris is not dead, shall he not die; as truly as Osiris is not annihilated, shall he not be annihilated.
>
> Thrice blessed are they who have seen these rites and then go to the house of Hades, for they alone have life there; but all others have only woe. [M. S. Enslin 1930:47–48; I am indebted to this work for what I say here about the mystery cults.]

In the mystery cults salvation depended upon, and came as the result of, the magical efficacy of the sacramental rites of initiation. Rites, not what was right, were the important thing. The mystery cults did not usually even consider—much less insist upon—what was right in the sense of Paul's righteousness. Salvation was in no way dependent upon moral or righteous life.

For Paul, initiation through the rite of baptism was quite different. As the result of the initiates' faith, at baptism God justified them (that is, forgave their sins and saved them from continuing in lives of sin and death) by an act of his grace and bestowed upon them the gift of the Holy Spirit. But the converts' ultimate salvation depended upon their continuing life in or by the Spirit, a life of righteousness. Paul wanted to make certain that no new convert would mistakenly believe that baptism and justification had conferred the assurance of salvation apart from moral probity.

4. The law and the Spirit (7:1–8:39)

Paul returns to the subject of the law (7:1–25). What he says in 7:1–6 reflects the Jewish belief that as soon as a person died, that person was no longer bound by the law. Since in baptism believers share in the death of Christ, they are then freed from the law and live "in the new life of the Spirit."

After 7:7, chap. 7 is especially difficult because Paul says "I" so often. Is he speaking about himself, either before he became a convert or as a convert? Does he mean the Jewish people or mankind in general? Scholars do not agree on the answers to these questions. We must understand, though, that Paul is contrasting life "under the old written code" (the law) with "the new life of the Spirit" (7:6). He deals with the first way of life in chap. 7 and with the second in chap. 8.

Several times Paul has given the impression that the law is terrible, if not sinful (see, for example, 4:15; 5:13, 20; 6:14; 7:5). Now he gives the opposite impression: "The law is holy, and the commandment is holy and just and good" (7:12), apparently because God gave it. But because it only makes clear the distinction between right and wrong, the law is powerless in helping one do what is right. The law does not keep one from doing what is wrong.

In contrast to the law, the life-giving power of the Spirit frees believers from sin and death through God (or Christ) who loves them (8:1–39). God sent his son, who had the same human traits as everyone else, in order that those who live according to the Spirit might fulfill "the just requirement of the law." By "the just requirement of the law" Paul probably means what the law requires for righteous living, not the unimportant demands of the law, such as circumcision (8:1–11).

The Spirit serves as a kind of down payment for ultimate salvation. Believers are living in the interim between the experience of the Spirit and the experience of ultimate salvation. Meanwhile, when believers use the word *abba*—that is, "father"—they do so as "children of God." Use of this word is evidence that God has accepted them, but they must wait for their final adoption, the redemption of their bodies. Perhaps Paul was influenced by the thought of Lam 3:24–26: "'The Lord is my portion,' says my soul, 'therefore I will hope in him.' The Lord is good to those who wait for him, to the soul that seeks him. It is good that one should wait quietly for the salvation of the Lord." Paul asks whether any kind of suffering "will separate us from the love

of Christ." In responding, Paul concludes (8:37–39) the first major section of the letter with a triumphant and confident expression of faith.

B. God's rejection of Israel (9:1–11:36)

In dealing with God's rejection of Israel (the Jews), Paul does not want to appear as a Jew who has rejected his own religion because he preaches to Gentiles and accepts them. He is more worried about what people will think of God, who has made promises to Israel and now seems to be going back on his word. But the OT shows that God has a plan for the ultimate salvation of mankind.

1. Why God's justification did not come to the Jews (9:1–33)

If the Jews were God's chosen people and received his promises, then why didn't God's justification come to them? Paul laments the Jews' unbelief (9:1–5). God has always chosen whomever he wanted to be his people (9:6–29). God acts as a divine potter who molds his clay as he wills. When he does this, is God unrighteous? No, because out of his mercy he calls not only Jews but Gentiles. Israel, not God, is responsible for the lack of righteousness (= justification [9:30–33]). Why? Because Israel did not pursue "righteousness through faith" but through works of the law. Paul continues this theme into chap. 10.

2. What God does when people refuse to hear and heed the testimony of his preachers concerning faith (10:1–21)

Israel failed to acknowledge that "Christ is the end of the law so that there may be righteousness for everyone who believes" (10:1–4). Scripture itself says that being saved (= justified or becoming believers) is as easy as calling upon the name of the Lord. Paul's argument is in 10:5–13. For several reasons these verses are to be taken in the context of the justification of converts. First, in v 4 Paul says that Christ is the end of the law and that people are justified through faith. Second, the reference to confession is probably to that made at the time of baptism, when a convert's justification takes place. Third, the word "saved" in vv 9–10 is synonymous with "justified." Fourth, because these words are synonymous, faith is associated with the process of justification, not with ultimate salvation. This is also true elsewhere in Paul's writings.

Paul's language and thought show creative use of the OT. His statement about confession is influenced by Deut 30:14: "The word is very near to you; it is in your mouth and in your heart, for you to observe." For Paul, "the word" is "Jesus is Lord," one of the earliest formulations of believers' faith (see 1 Cor 12:3). He summarizes and concludes his argument with a quotation from Joel 2:32 that refers to the prophetic concept of "the great and terrible day of the Lord." The reference is to the end of the present age, when "everyone who calls on the name of the Lord shall be saved." The same idea is part of Paul's eschatological thought. For Paul, the justification of Gentiles is the fulfillment of Joel's prophecy. It is also a major step toward ultimate salvation in the age to come for all who believe and, according to Romans 12–15, continue to do what is expected of them. The rejection of the Jews is their own fault, not God's, because they have not listened to the prophets or to those who preach the gospel (10:14–20). But God still holds out his "hands to a disobedient and contrary people" (10:21).

3. The principle of justification by God's grace through faith, and its implications (11:1–36)

In chap. 11 Paul is concerned about the disbelief of the Jews and the faith of Gentiles (11:1–10). "Has God rejected his people?" As a Jew, Paul cannot accept that. Since some Jews are believers, God hasn't rejected all Jews. By his grace he has chosen a remnant. But as a whole, the Jews have rejected God's will, so by his grace God has also made it possible for Gentiles to become part of God's people.

In the rest of chap. 11 Paul deals with how God will act toward the Jews in particular and mankind in general (11:11–36). The Jews have made a mistake, but from their error good will result (11:11–12). Only because the Jews rejected Christ did the Gentiles have the opportunity to accept him. There would have been no mission to Gentiles if all Jews had accepted their Messiah. Acceptance by the Gentiles makes some Jews jealous, so eventually those Jews and all others will become members of God's people (11:15, 25–26, 30–31). As a missionary to Gentiles, Paul is also concerned about them, both for their own sake and—indirectly—for the Jews' sake as well (11:13–16).

Paul refers to the olive tree as he tries to explain what he means (11:17–24). His reference shows that Paul was a city person who knew nothing about the normal process of grafting fruit trees. However, for Paul the olive tree is the Jews, God's people, and God has had to break off some branches of Jews who did not believe. But God did not throw away those branches; instead, he saved them to use later. Into their places God grafted wild olive shoots—Gentiles. However, Gentiles should not boast but be on their guard, lest they slip from God's grace through loss of faith. Eventually the discarded branches will be grafted onto the tree again.

This is a lesson on "the kindness and the severity of God" (11:22), kindness to those who continue in his favor, severity to those who do not. Paul believes that God's kindness is greater than his severity. Verse 25 summarizes Paul's thought: part of Israel will not believe until all Gentiles become a part of God's people, and then all Jews will also be included (11:24–32). Paul is so happy at the thought of God's great mercy that he ends the section in poetic praise of God's great wisdom, and he includes words from the prophets (11:33–36). (For an analysis of Romans 9–11, see C. H. Giblin 1970.)

III. The way believers ought to behave (12:1–15:13)

A. Theme (12:1–2)

Rom 12:1–2 gives the theme of this section: the experience of God's justification or righteousness manifests itself in righteous living among fellow believers and others. Paul not only uses the word "sacrifice," but his vocabulary shows influence from the OT language of sacrifice. Observe the similarity between Paul's words that his readers should present their "bodies as a living sacrifice, holy and acceptable to God" and the OT legal requirements that the sin offering should be a lamb "without blemish" (Lev 4:32; Num 6:14) and that the lambs offered at the harvest Festival of Weeks should "be holy to the Lord" (Lev 23:20).

Believers are "living sacrifices" because they have received "newness of life" in Christ (Rom 6:4), so they are to live lives "holy and acceptable to God." Before the readers of the letter became converts, they conformed to the evil ways of the world because of their base minds and improper conduct (Rom 1:28). Their justification, then, means not only a transformation of their minds but of their whole persons; they now live moral and ethical lives in the community of believers.

B. Some general rules for all believers, not just the Romans (12:3–15:13)

Here Paul's teaching is closer to that of Jesus than in any other place. Believers are to be good citizens, "subject to the governing authorities," and "pay . . . what is due them—taxes to whom taxes are due, revenue to whom revenue is due, respect to whom respect is due, honor to whom honor is due" (13:1–7). Believers love their neighbors as themselves. This is the sum and substance of the law for moral living as believers approach the time of their ultimate salvation, which is nearer than when they first believed (13:8–14). Believers do not make hasty judgments about others who are too concerned with what they eat or with the observance of special days (14:1–23). The strong are to encourage the weak and keep in mind the good of others, in order that all may live in harmony with one another. In this way Jews and Gentiles together may glorify God under Jesus Christ (15:1–13).

IV. Conclusion (15:14–33)

Believers at Rome please Paul because they are "full of goodness, filled with all knowledge, and able to instruct one another." Paul expresses his strong desire to visit them.

V. Letter of recommendation for Phoebe (16:1–23)

Paul commends Phoebe to his readers and greets his friends. He also exhorts the brethren "to keep an eye on those who cause dissensions and offenses, in opposition to the teaching" they have been taught, and to be "wise in what is good and guileless in what is evil."

VI. Doxology (16:25–27)

THE FAITHFULNESS OF CHRIST

I have added this discussion to show you how one considers a section of a writing in more depth from a broader perspective than usual in the Outline and Comments and to present my view on the faithfulness of Christ. The translations are mine.

"Faith of Christ" is an alternative translation of Paul's Greek to "faith in Christ." Paul's word *pistis* is almost always translated as "faith," but I prefer "faithfulness" for the following reasons. It is a translation used many times, especially in the Septuagint. *Pistis* surely included intellectual assent to certain beliefs, such as "We believe that Jesus died and rose again" (1 Thess 4:14) and "Christ died for our sins according to the scriptures" (1 Cor 15:3). But, as Paul uses it, *pistis* is more than intellectual assent to certain abstract or philosophical propositions. Many times it is the equivalent of the Hebrew noun *emunah*, meaning loyalty or fidelity to the facts in one's behavior or to one's promises and, thus, "faithfulness." The psalmist writes: "The word of the Lord is upright (or righteous), and all his works are [done] in faithfulness" (Ps 33:4, Hebrew; LXX, *pistis*). Several times Paul writes that "God is faithful" in keeping his promises (1 Thess 5:24; 1 Cor 1:9; 10:13; 2 Cor 1:18).

In Isa 11:5 (Hebrew) we read: "And righteousness shall be the girdle of his loins and faithfulness the girdle of his hips." In Ps 33:4

uprightness or righteousness and faithfulness are attributes ascribed to God. In Isa 11:5 the same attributes are ascribed to the messianic figure predicted by the prophet Isaiah (Isa 11:1–10).

In the Septuagint passages the ideas of righteousness and faithfulness are in parallel. This means that the ideas they represent are inseparably linked together, with reference to God in the first passage and to the messianic ruler in the second. The same attributes are linked together also in a very popular Pauline passage: "The righteous person shall live on the basis of faithfulness" (Gal 3:11; Rom 1:17), a quotation from Hab 2:4.

Since Paul attributes the qualities of righteousness (1 Cor 1:30; Rom 5:12–21) and obedience (Rom 5:19; Phil 2:8) to Christ, and since he also attributes righteousness to converts (2 Cor 5:21), would it not be natural for him to think also of the faithfulness of Christ? This is the more likely in view of the quotation from Isa 11:5 where righteousness and faithfulness are attributes of the messianic figure predicted by the prophet. That Paul knew Isaiah 11 is clear from his quote from Isa 11:10 in Rom 15:12 as part of his proof from the scriptures that Christ became a minister to the circumcised (Jews) to confirm the promises of God to the patriarchs and for the hope of Gentiles.

In Gal 2:15–21 Paul says, "Christ lives in [Greek, *en*] me, and what I am now living in [Greek, *en*] the flesh, I live in [Greek, *en*] faithfulness, the faithfulness of the Son of God." I have translated the Greek preposition *en* as "in" every time. This translation conveys the idea that Paul believes he shares in the faithfulness of Jesus. Paul's sharing in Christ's faithfulness is a part of his mystical experience of the risen Christ, as with the phrases "in Christ" and "Christ in."

We should not overlook Paul's reference to "God is One" (Gal 3:30), the universal Jewish declaration of monotheistic belief (see Deut 6:4). For Paul, "there is no God but One" (1 Cor 8:4). And there is one God, the Father, compared with the many gods of the Gentiles, and one Lord, Jesus Christ, compared with the

Gentiles' many lords (1 Cor 8:5–6). Although he is a devotee of Christ, these passages clearly stress Paul's monotheism, and it is to be understood as the basic theological conviction behind all he writes. So the faithfulness of believers is believing something about Jesus, not in the person of Christ. To profess faith in Christ would fly in the face of all Paul, still a Jew, believed about the one God.

In Gal 2:15–21 Paul is arguing strongly against the Judaizers by saying that God by his grace (2:21) made possible the justification (literally, "righteousing") of Gentile converts by virtue of Christ's faithfulness and not on the basis of works of the law. Paul's commitment to the Way he formerly persecuted came about because he shared the faithfulness of the Son of God. In Gal 2:16 the "we" in the clause, "Even we came to believe in (*eis*) Christ Jesus," represents Paul and others, including Peter, who may well have shared Paul's ideas with respect to justification and the law. This is true because Paul reprimands Peter for being hypocritical (Gal 2:11–14). Paul's reprimand would be pointless if Peter had not at least partly shared his ideas, especially about food laws. Paul's words in Gal 2:12 that Peter feared the circumcision party may indicate that Peter himself was not fully committed to the position of the Judaizers. There is no indication that when Peter was entrusted with a mission to the Jews and Paul to the Gentiles (Gal 2:7–9) that the content of their mission preaching was different. In fact, Paul says that God was working through both of them (Gal 2:8). Only in retrospect does Paul say that he and other Jews, especially Peter, became converts in the first place in order to be made righteous (justified) by virtue of the faithfulness of Christ and not on the basis of the law. This coincides precisely with his statement, also made only in retrospect, that God had set him apart for mission work to the Gentiles even before he was born (Gal 1:15–16).

In light of Paul's comments in Galatians 2, I think that the words "we came to believe in [*eis*, literally, "with a view toward"] Christ Jesus" are to be understood in the sense of becoming converts to the belief that Jesus was the Messiah (Christ) and to the Jesus movement in order that they might be made righteous (justified) by virtue of the faithfulness of Jesus as the Christ and not on the basis of works of the law.

What Paul Does Not Say

Perhaps we can better understand Paul's thought from what he does not say. Several phrases in the disputed letters Ephesians and Colossians (see Chapter 13) help us to realize what Paul does not say. In Ephesians the author writes: "I have heard of your faith in [Greek *en*] the Lord Jesus" (Eph 1:15). Similarly, the writer of Colossians says that he has heard of the readers' "faith in [*en*] Christ Jesus" (Col 1:4) and speaks of "the bulwark" of their "faith in [*eis*] Christ" (Col 2:5; see also 1 Tim 1:14; 3:13; 2 Tim 1:13). Paul never writes about faith in or believing in Christ in the same way as the writers of Ephesians, Colossians, and the Pastoral Epistles do (see, for example, 1 Tim 1:16; 2 Tim 3:15). Nor, on the other hand, do those writers speak of the faithfulness of Jesus as Paul does.

There is, however, a single exception in Eph 3:1–13, where the writer conveys Paul's thought about the faithfulness of Jesus exactly. Writing in the name of Paul ("I, Paul"; 3:1) and speaking autobiographically, he writes about the grace of God given to him to preach the good news of the unsearchable riches of the Messiah. Then the writer continues: "In whom ["the Messiah, Jesus our Lord," the antecedent] we have boldness and access [to God] with confidence by virtue of his faithfulness" (*dia tēs pisteōs autou*; Eph 3:12). Here the author of Ephesians has conveyed Paul's idea of the faithfulness of Jesus precisely.

If someone should object to my view that Paul does not speak about faith in Jesus because it is an argument from silence, let me reply in the words of the Greek epigrammatist Palladas (c. 400 CE): "Silence is man's chief learning." Although we may not always understand what Paul says, sometimes what he does not say helps us to better understand what he does say, as well as what some other writers of the NT say. The si-

lence of Paul has been too long ignored in trying to understand his basic ideas.

More on Paul's Theological/ Christological Views

Now let me say something more about Paul's theological/christological views, especially in Galatians, as they relate to what we have been saying. Gal 1:1–4 gives a concise statement of the theological/christological foundation for Paul's own belief as a Jew committed to life in Christ. Paul's belief in the resurrection gave significance to the death of Jesus. However, the words "gave himself for our sins" (Gal 1:4; see also 1 Cor 15:3–4) should be taken with reference to sins committed before acquittal through baptism (see again Romans 6; see also 1 Cor 15:3, 17; 2 Cor 12:21; 13:2; Rom 3:25; 5:8). In all of these passages Paul is speaking about sins before baptism. He himself was not interested in the forgiveness of converts' sins after their baptism but in their not sinning again (recall Romans 6 and earlier comments on this point).

Furthermore, we must not overlook the moral purpose for Jesus' giving of himself: "in order to deliver us from the present evil [that is, immoral] age" (Gal 1:4). The words "according to the will of our God and Father" (Gal 1:4) indicate that Paul believed God was responsible for Christ's action (see also Gal 1:6).

Several passages in Ephesians and Colossians reveal how the ideas of the authors of those works, who surely were familiar with Paul's letters, differ from those of Paul himself. This is true especially with respect to Paul's ideas of grace and salvation. In Ephesians the word "save" occurs only twice (Eph 2:5, 8), where the phrases "by grace you have been saved" and "by grace you have been saved through faith" occur. In the undisputed letters of Paul there is nothing like that. Words for salvation occur only in Eph 1:13 ("gospel of your salvation"; see Rom 1:16 for the idea) and 6:17 ("helmet of salvation"). Neither "save" nor "salvation" occurs in Colossians.

The combination of being justified (made righteous) and believing or faithfulness is common in Galatians and Romans but not that of being saved and believing, as in the passage from Ephesians. Nor does the combination of being saved and grace ever occur in the undisputed letters of Paul. And only in Rom 8:24 does Paul, unlike the writer of Ephesians, use a past tense (*aorist*) when referring to salvation, but there it refers to the time when the readers became converts and is qualified by waiting and hoping for redemption that is still to come.

Paul's ideas of the justification or "righteousing" of converts and their ultimate salvation is linked with his belief in the efficacy of Jesus' death and resurrection. Paul thought of Jesus' resurrection as the confirmation of his Pharisaic belief in a general resurrection of the dead at the final judgment (1 Cor 15:20) and as the assurance that righteous converts would also rise in the general resurrection (1 Thess 4:13–17; 1 Corinthians 15; 2 Cor 4:14). But the resurrection of Jesus meant more than these things. It had theological implications for Paul. It did not just happen. God was responsible for it, and this idea is a frequently recurring theme in Paul's letters (see, for example, 1 Thess 1:10; 1 Cor 6:14; 15:4, 15; 2 Cor 4:14; 13:4; Gal 1:1; Rom 4:24; 8:11; 10:9). Jesus became the "Son of God in power . . . by his resurrection from the dead" (Rom 1:4).

Paul sometimes links Jesus' death with the resurrection, and his death also has theological implications. "Christ died on behalf of the impious" (Rom 5:6), and his death was a sign of God's love (Rom 5:8). The essence of Paul's belief in the death and resurrection of Jesus is that they made the justification or forgiveness of converts' past sins by the grace of God possible: Jesus "was handed over [for death] by virtue of our trespasses and raised for our justification" (Rom 4:25). But the justification of converts does not mean that they are assured of ultimate salvation. Ultimate salvation depends upon their continuing to live by the Spirit, that is, living moral lives free from sin (recall earlier comments on this point).

It is significant to observe that whereas believing or faithfulness is usually mentioned in con-

nection with, or as a requirement for, justification, believing is mentioned with salvation (*eis sōtērian,* "toward salvation") only in Rom 1:16 and believing with being saved only in Rom 10:9–10. In both of these passages Paul is clearly referring to the potential experience of converts, both Jews and Gentiles, who become justified or forgiven of their past sins. I believe it cannot be proven that Paul mentions faithfulness anywhere in Romans in connection with a convert's ultimate salvation. Equally significant is the fact that the word "grace" is not once used in any passage where the word "save" or "salvation" occurs.

Now I have briefly, and with only a few nontechnical details, presented some unconventional interpretations of Paul's thought with respect to faith(fullness), justification, grace, and salvation. Paul's theology may be summed up in one short sentence: Paul's theology is God-centered, not Christ-centered. Think about what I have said and discuss it with your instructor as you continue to study the undisputed and disputed letters of Paul.

For other views see J. M. G. Barclay 1991, Paul's ethics in Galatians; C. H. Cosgrove 1988, Paul's argument and theology in Galatians; J. D. G. Dunn 1990, the law; I. G. Wallis 1995, faith in and of Jesus.

SUMMARY AND OBSERVATIONS

In Galatians and Romans, as in all of his letters, Paul is not writing about Christians for all time. He believed the end of the world was coming in his own time or soon afterward. He was, therefore, writing to those who had recently converted to a developing religion, a religion in transition, that only after Paul's time became known as Christianity. They become converts by being justified by God through his grace or righteousness; the basis of justification is faith, not works of the law. Being justified (= reconciled, sanctified, and—sometimes—saved) involves a complete break with the sinful past and the acceptance of newness of life in Christ. The new life must be free of sin and lived under the influence of the Holy Spirit.

The change from the converts' pagan life of sin to life that is free of sin, is symbolized in the rite of baptism. When the converts are immersed into the water, their sins are forgiven; and when they come out of the water, they walk in newness of life, freed from sin. Converts are no longer slaves of sin but of righteousness and of God. They must therefore continue to live moral and ethical lives, because their ultimate salvation lies in the future.

After their justification, believers move toward ultimate salvation, but righteous conduct is necessary for that salvation. Faith or belief is usually mentioned in connection with, or as a requirement for, justification; but the word "faith" is mentioned with "salvation" only in Rom 1:16, and "believe" with "saved" only in Rom 10:9–10. According to 1:16 and 10:9, salvation lies in the future. In 10:10 "is saved" is synonymous with "is justified." Nowhere is faith mentioned in connection with converts' ultimate salvation, and the word "grace" is not once used in any passage where the words "save" or "salvation" occur.

In other words, Paul's position is that believers are justified by God's grace and through his righteousness, but faith alone does not guarantee ultimate salvation. Once the converts are believers, their ultimate salvation depends upon the continuation of their own righteous life in Christ, even when judging fellow believers. Near the end of Romans, Paul reminds his readers: "For we will all stand before the judgment seat of God. . . . So then, each of us will be accountable to God" (14:10–12; see also 2 Cor 5:10).

For further study of Galatians and Romans, see the following: Galatians—commentaries: R. Y. K. Fung 1988; J. A. Ziesler 1992; D. Luehrmann 1992; J. D. G. Dunn 1993a; C. R. Hume 1997; J. L. Martyn 1997; S. K. Williams 1997; B. Witherington 1988a; theology: V. P. Furnish 1968; J. A. Fitzmyer 1967b; J. D. G. Dunn 1993b; C. K. Barrett 1994; H. Boers 1994; law: N. T. Wright 1991; V. M. Smiles 1998; books mentioned in Chapter 9; Holy Spirit: D. J. Lull 1980; S. K. Williams 1987; Romans—commentaries: J. A. Fitzmyer 1993, superb in all aspects; C. H. Dodd 1932; E. Best 1967; E. H. Maly 1983; J. Murray 1987; L. Morris 1988; J. A. Ziesler 1989; R. Morgan 1993; R. H. Mounce 1995; L. T. Johnson 1997; baptism: P. L. Stepp 1996; law: S. Westerholm 1988; F. Thielman 1994; theology: D. Litfin 1994, 1995; ethics: V. P. Furnish 1968; B. S. Rosner 1995; Paul in general: S. Westerholm 1997; D. Wenham 1995; L. A. Jervis 1994; household, house churches, family life, education: C. Osiek 1997; Jews in Rome and background of Romans: R. E. Brown 1983; M. D. Nanos 1996.

CHAPTER 12

Undisputed Letters of Paul: Philippians and Philemon

PHILIPPIANS

THE CITY OF PHILIPPI

Philippi was originally a small town known as Krenides, which may refer to springs in the vicinity—from the Greek word *krēnē*, meaning "spring" or "well." Philippi was located in eastern Macedonia, so close to Thrace that it was sometimes regarded as a city of Thrace. Between 360 and 356 BCE Krenides was captured by Philip II, king of Macedonia, who renamed it Philippi. He added a large number of inhabitants to the city and made it a frontier stronghold against the neighboring Thracians. Present ruins of a wall around the city and up over the acropolis probably date from the time of Philip, as does a Greek theater lying below the acropolis. Philip greatly developed the gold mines of the region, and the gold coins he minted became widely known.

Philippi was enlarged again after the famous battle in 42 BCE. Antony settled some Roman soldiers in Philippi; and along with the territory eastward, including Neapolis, Philippi was designated a Roman colony (see Acts 16:12). Roman colonies were modeled on Rome herself, and Philippian colonists enjoyed the same rights as Roman citizens. Most remains of the city date from a period considerably later than Paul's time. However, a colonial archway on the western side of the city may date from his time; the Via Egnatia passed through that archway, and Paul probably went through the archway in going "outside the gate by the river" (Acts 16:13).

Inside the city was the Roman forum (Greek agora), which was the center of city life and could be entered through five porticoes on three sides. On the north side of the forum was a rectangular podium with steps leading up on both sides. It was a sort of tribunal for public speakers and magistrates engaged in dispensing justice. Paul and Silas were probably dragged to that tribunal before they were thrown into prison (Acts 16:19–24). The prison and other civic buildings, including a library, bordered the north and south sides of the forum, and at each end was a temple.

The populace of Philippi was mixed and included Thracians and Thasians indigenous to the area, as well as Greeks brought there by Philip of Macedon and Romans by Antony and Octavian. Peoples imported into Philippi spoke Greek, but most of the inscriptions from the city are in Latin. Coins also support the Latin element, including the Latin title for the city. These things indicate a more Roman character of the city than most other cities of Paul. Philippi was also different from other cities of Paul because it was an agricultural, rather than a trade, center. Farming around many small villages in the neighborhood of Philippi provided the economic base for the area (see W. A. Meeks 1983:45–46).

Because there is no conclusive evidence for a synagogue in Philippi, apparently not many Jews lived in Philippi. However, the word translated "place of prayer" (Acts 16:13) may be synonymous with "synagogue," since Philo and Josephus use those words synonymously.

As with the population, the religion of Philippi was also composite, including worship of old Anatolian (Eastern), Egyptian, Greek, and Roman deities. There were many religious associations and other aspects of religious worship and practice like those of Rome in Paul's time.

THE CHURCH AT PHILIPPI

Paul began his preaching at Philippi among a group of women who had gathered for worship. One of them was Lydia, "a worshiper of God" and "a dealer in purple cloth" (Acts 16:13–15). "A worshiper of God" indicates that Lydia was either a Jewess or Gentile who participated in synagogue worship. Because of her trade, she may have been one of the wealthier members of the group. She and her household were baptized, and then she invited the apostles to stay at her house. They visited her again before leaving Philippi.

It seems certain that in Philippi, as elsewhere, the church began within Jewish circles that included Gentile proselytes and God-fearers. Although the number of Jews in Philippi was apparently very small, Paul began his mission with the few Jewish worshipers and converts to Judaism who came to the place of prayer. Lydia may have become the leader of the community of believers at Philippi and her house a meeting place for the first Jewish converts. Paul, however, does not mention her in his letter to the Philippians.

In Acts 16:16–31, Paul and Silas are beaten and put into prison after they have cast the evil spirit out of a slave girl who makes money for her owners by telling fortunes. The prison becomes the setting for mission activity. As Paul and Silas are praying at midnight, their chains are miraculously unfastened, and the jailer, thinking the prisoners have escaped, wants to kill himself. When Paul tells him they are still there, the jailer is frightened and says, "Sirs, what must I do to be saved?" They answered, "Believe on the Lord Jesus, and you will be saved, you and your household." Paul and Silas then preach to the jailer and his family, and the family is baptized. The jailer takes Paul and Silas into his house, gets them a meal, and rejoices because he believes in God. Perhaps the jailer's house became a meeting place for the first Gentile converts at Philippi.

Although Paul's mission probably started in a Jewish group, such names in Philippians as Epaphroditus, Euodia, and Syntyche may indicate that the church in Philippi was predominantly Gentile. Because in Acts no men are mentioned in connection with the place of prayer, and because the presence of men was required for Jewish worship, some people maintain that the place of prayer was not a Jewish meeting place. Paul's use of the terms "bishops" and "deacons" (1:1) may indicate that the church at Philippi was more organized than the others to which he writes. Perhaps that is why the church there was among those that played a praiseworthy role in the collection for the saints in Jerusalem (2 Cor 8:1–5; Rom 15:26).

Converts in no other city gave Paul such feelings of satisfaction and joy as those at Philippi. In his letter he says that he yearns for them all "with the compassion of Christ Jesus" (1:8) and addresses them as "my brothers, whom I love and long for, my joy and crown" (4:1). On several occasions he shows his trust in them by accepting favors that he refused from other churches. Of the Philippians Paul says: "It was kind of you to share my distress. . . . No church shared with me in the matter of giving and receiving, except you alone" (4:14–15). Twice to Thessalonica and once to Corinth the Philippians sent gifts of appreciation to satisfy Paul's needs (4:16; 2 Cor 11:9). From Philippi Epaphroditus traveled over land and sea to take a gift to Paul in prison, for which Paul affectionately expresses his gratitude: "I have been paid in full and have more than enough; I am fully satisfied, now that I have received from Epaphroditus the gifts you sent, a fragrant offering, a sacrifice acceptable and pleasing to God" (4:18). Paul's experience at Philippi, however, was not entirely pleasant, since he (1 Thess 2:2; Phil 1:29–30) agrees with Acts (16:16–24) that he suffered persecution there. Philippians indicates, though, that the church at Philippi caused Paul the least trouble and gave him his greatest joy.

PURPOSE OF PHILIPPIANS AND DATE AND PLACE OF WRITING

If we consider the letter as a unit, its immediate purpose seems to be to thank the Philippians for their gifts while Paul was at Thessalonica (4:14–19). While Paul was in prison, Epaphroditus brought him another gift (2:25; 4:10, 18) and good news about the church at Philippi (1:15–18). Epaphroditus became ill, recovered, and wanted to return home to allay the concerns of the Philippians who had heard of his illness (2:26). So Paul sent Epaphroditus back to Philippi with the letter of sincere gratitude and affection.

The letter gives little indication of any major practical or theological problems. On the whole, the tone is gentle and joyful. The only exception is the attack against some Judaizers who had apparently appeared at Philippi as they had at other cities where there were Gentile churches: "Be-

ware of the dogs, beware of the evil workers, beware of those who mutilate the flesh!" (3:2; but see 1:28; 3:17–18). Some think Paul's opponents were Gnostics or "spirituals," as in Corinth and Galatia.

Several other verses also indicate that Philippi did not enjoy the perfect harmony that Paul desired (1:15–18; 2:1–2; 4:2–3). But either that lack of harmony and the problem with the Judaizers were not serious enough for Paul to deal with in more than passing fashion, or he was so overwhelmed with gratitude that he almost ignores them. Paul does write that some "proclaim Christ from envy and rivalry, but others from goodwill." But he goes on to say: "What then? Only that in every way, whether in pretense or in truth, Christ is proclaimed; and in that I rejoice" (1:15–18; RSV). It is difficult to imagine Paul writing in such gentle tones to the converts at Corinth or Galatia. It appears, then, that Paul's main reasons for writing the letter to the Philippians were to thank them for their gifts and to express his joy concerning the community at Philippi.

Paul was writing from someplace in prison (1:7, 13, 17), but the location of the prison is a matter for debate. The traditional site of Paul's imprisonment is Rome, from which Philippians and the other prison letters are thought to have been written. Here are some of the arguments for Rome as the place of writing. (1) This view has the weight of tradition behind it. (2) The term "imperial guard" (1:13) refers to the camp stationed outside Rome, and "the emperor's household" (4:22) refers to members of the emperor's staff. (3) Some passages (1:6, 20–23; 4:10) indicate that Paul is soon to face trial or even death, and this implies that Paul is in Rome near the end of his life. (4) The advanced Christology of Philippians—especially 2:5–11, with its ideas of the preexistence and incarnation of Christ—coincides with that of Ephesians and Colossians. Ephesians and Colossians were also written from Rome, where Paul was in prison. Most scholars, however, deny the authenticity of Ephesians and many deny that of Colossians also. Others believe that Phil 2:(5)6–11 is a pre-Pauline hymn that Paul incorporated into the letter. So according to these scholars, the fourth point is not valid.

Because, according to Acts 23–26, Paul was in prison at Caesarea for two years, a few scholars have defended it as the place of origin for Philippians. They say that in Phil 1:13–17 Paul writes as though the church in the city of his imprisonment was not founded by him. Moreover, they say that those in charge of soldiers in the capital of any Roman province could be referred to as the imperial guard. And since "imperial guard" is a translation of the Greek phrase meaning "in the whole praetorium," the "praetorium" (a building) could be the governor's residence, as in Acts 23:35 ("Herod's headquarters"). Those who defend Caesarea as the place of writing also say that the attack against the Judaizers in Philippians 3 fits in better with the time of the Gentile-Jewish controversy—a controversy we know of from the earlier letters Corinthians and Galatians—than with Paul's later letters Ephesians and Colossians.

Since about 1900, more and more scholars have argued that Ephesus was the place of Paul's imprisonment, even though Acts does not report that Paul was in prison there. They base their view on certain passages in the Corinthian letters. Paul writes about afflictions in Asia that were so bad he "despaired of life itself" (2 Cor 1:8–9), speaks of imprisonments (2 Cor 6:5), and boasts of "far more imprisonments" than his opponents (2 Cor 11:23). He also says, "I fought with wild animals at Ephesus" (1 Cor 15:32). These passages, say those arguing for an Ephesian imprisonment, imply that Paul was in prison many times and that one time was in Ephesus.

As usual there are counterarguments. Acts may not report everything that happened to Paul, including the number and places of his imprisonments. On the other hand, in the heat of debate with his adversaries, Paul may exaggerate the account of his sufferings. It has been suggested that the animals Paul fought "may well be human or demonic rather than zoological enemies" (J. L. Houlden 1977b:42). Although probably only prisoners were put into the arena with animals, we do not know whether Roman citizens were subjected to such treatment. If Paul did fight with wild animals, would he have lived to tell the tale?

Those who argue for an Ephesian imprisonment maintain that Paul wrote Philippians from Ephesus. The following points favor this view. (1) Inscriptions from Ephesus show that soldiers of the imperial guard did serve in Ephesus and that members of the emperor's family did reside there (J. A. Fitzmyer 1968c). Therefore, "imperial guard" (1:13) and "emperor's household" (4:22) do not necessarily indicate a Roman setting. (2) The letter indicates several round trips between Philippi and the place of Paul's imprisonment: Epaphroditus brings gifts; news of his illness gets back to the Philippians; Paul learns of their concern for Epaphroditus and sends him back to Philippi. Moreover, Paul wants to send Timothy to Philippi soon, and Paul himself intends to visit there shortly (2:19–24). All of this is more feasible in view of the shorter traveling time between Ephesus and Philippi than between Rome and Philippi. (3) The content and theology of Philippians are closer to Corinthians and Galatians than to Ephesians and Colossians. (4) Paul planned to visit Philippi soon, but from Rome, he wanted to go to Spain (Rom 15:24, 28); this implies a place of writing other than Rome.

The last two points have some counterarguments. There are parallels in language and thought between Philippians and all of Paul's letters, not just two or three (see C. L. Mitton 1951:330–332). And Paul could have changed his mind about going to Spain. Those who accept Pauline authorship of the pastoral epistles—1 and 2 Timothy and Titus—argue that Paul did just that. He was released from prison in Rome, did missionary work again in the East, and then was imprisoned in Rome a second time. So the argument about Spain is unimportant in defending Ephesus as the place of writing for Philippians.

The question of the place of writing naturally has a bearing on the time of writing. If the letter was written during Paul's imprisonment in Rome, then a date between 60 and 64 seems likely. If Paul wrote from Caesarea, the date would be c. 56–58, since Paul probably did not reach Rome before c. 59. Finally, if Paul wrote to Philippi from Ephesus about the time he wrote to Corinth, the date would be the mid-50s. Obviously, we cannot be certain about either the place or the date of the writing of Philippians.

THE UNITY OF PHILIPPIANS

Several aspects of the letter lead many scholars to believe that Philippians was not originally written as one letter. The most obvious are the use of "finally" twice (3:1; 4:8), which gives the impression of two endings, and the abrupt change in tone between 3:1 and 3:2. Actually, 4:4 would follow 3:1 naturally. Some think it strange that in a letter of thanks Paul waits until the end to get to the point. And 4:1–4 looks like an ending to a letter.

Such observations, along with the fact that Polycarp, bishop of Smyrna in Asia Minor (c. 70–156), says in his letter to the Philippians (3:2) that Paul "wrote letters to you," could indicate that Philippians is a composite of several Pauline fragments. But among those who hold this view there is considerable disagreement about what constitutes the fragments and why, when, and where they were written.

According to the older view (for example, E. J. Goodspeed 1937:90–96), Philippians consists of two letters. The earlier letter includes the material from 3:1 to 4:23—or perhaps only to 4:20, if vv 21–23 are put with the second letter. The later one includes 1:1–3:1, and perhaps also 4:21–23. The first was written to thank the Philippians for the gift Epaphroditus brought. Paul sent the second letter with Epaphroditus when he returned to Philippi; he wrote it to defend Epaphroditus from possible criticism for leaving him in prison and to arouse respect for Epaphroditus's work. Both were written from Rome c. 59–60.

However, most scholars who subscribe to the fragment hypothesis find three fragments in Philippians. F. W Beare 1959:4–5 divides the letter as follows: (1) a letter of thanks for the gift

Epaphroditus brought (4:10–20); (2) a letter sent to the Philippians with Epaphroditus, intended to make them respect Epaphroditus even more highly and to resolve the disagreement concerning Euodia and Syntyche (1:1–3:1; 4:2–9, 21–23); and (3) an interpolation "warning the readers against Jewish propaganda and against shameful self-indulgence" (3:2–4:1). Beare holds to the tradition that the letter was written in Rome between 60 and 64. (Beare's outline coincides with that of W Schmithals 1972:67–81; the same outline is given by K. Grayston 1967:3–4.)

B. D. Rahtjen 1960 agrees with others that 4:10–20 was written first, in response to Epaphroditus's gift. Paul wrote a second letter (1:1–2:30; 4:21–23) after Epaphroditus had returned to Philippi and was treated coolly and perhaps hostilely; he wanted to say he was content in his situation, to exhort the Philippians to behave, and to praise Epaphroditus. Finally, Paul wrote 3:1–4:9 as he was facing death in Rome "just after the beginning of the purge of Christians in Rome under Nero." "This letter follows the classical pattern of the Testament of a dying father to his children." B. S. Mackay 1961 criticizes Rahtjen's arguments and defends the unity of Philippians.

J. A. Fitzmyer 1968c divides the letter as follows: "*Letter A*, 1:1–2; 4:10–20 (a note in which Paul thanked the Philippians for their aid). *Letter B*, 1:3–3:1; 4:4–9, 21–23 (the letter in which Paul explained his personal situation, gave news of Epaphroditus and Timothy, and sent his instructions to the community). *Letter C*, 3:2–4:3 (a short note to warn the Philippians about the Judaizers)."

Because scholars disagree about possible fragments in Philippians, and for other reasons, some still support the unity of the letter. Here are some of the reasons: (1) Paul may have written more than one letter to Philippi; but if he did, those besides our Philippians are among Paul's lost letters. (2) The breaks in the continuity of the letter can be explained as frequent interruptions or as renewed feelings of intimacy and fond remembrance as Paul was writing—all of which prevented Paul from closing the letter after several tries (M. S. Enslin 1938:278). (3) The appeals to unity, Christian suffering, and joy are evident in all parts of the letter. (4) The change in tone in 3:2 is not lasting and is no different than similar outbursts of Pauline emotion elsewhere (Gal 3:1; 4:21; 5:12); changes of tone just as noticeable occur in 1 Cor 15:58; Rom 16:17–18; and Gal 6:10. Moreover, already in 1:28 Paul mentions opponents, and they can be taken to be the same as those in 3:2, 17–19. (5) The fragment theory is connected with specific reconstructions of Paul's relations with the church at Philippi; these reconstructions go beyond the evidence and thus become too hypothetical. (6) The assumption that Phil 2:5–11 is a pre-Pauline hymn cannot be proven. (For an outline of Paul's relationships with the Philippians, see R. H. Fuller 1966:37.)

Although there is general agreement that Paul wrote all of Philippians, there is wide disagreement about when, where, and why he wrote the whole or its parts. Scholars seem to be about equally divided in accepting or rejecting the unity of Philippians. Perhaps after considering a variety of the arguments, you can choose answers that you think are best supported by the evidence as you read Philippians with the following outline and comments.

For further study see W. G. Kuemmel 1975:320–335; G. B. Caird 1976:95–154; H. Koester 1976; R. P. Martin 1976c; J. F. Collange 1979. The last two books are especially useful because they provide a bibliography for each problem. Against Collange, who maintains that Philippians consists of three short letters of Paul, W. J. Dalton 1979:97–102 argues for the unity of the letter. See additional bibliography at end of chapter.

Outline and Comments

I. Introduction (1:1–11)

In 1:1–2 it is difficult to tell what significance the terms "bishops" and "deacons" have, since Paul does not use them in any other undisputed letter. The Greek term *episkopos* literally means "one who oversees" or "overseer," and *diakonos* means "waiter" or "servant." It is unlikely that the terms have the technical meaning they later had as official titles for church officers (see 1 Tim 3:2, 8, 12; Titus 1:7). Perhaps Paul is referring to a group of leaders and their helpers that was influential in the collection of funds for the church in Jerusalem and for him.

Paul thanks the Philippians for their "sharing in the gospel" (1:3–8). This means that the Philippian converts had a special role in Paul's larger mission of the church, including spiritual and financial support. Paul prays that the Philippians' "love may overflow more and more," that they "may approve what is excellent," and "be pure and blameless" for the day of Christ (1:9–11). The Greek words translated "what is excellent" derive from the verb meaning "to be different" or "to excel," and may also be translated as "the things that differ." Perhaps Paul intends something of both meanings. The Philippians are to distinguish between the things that are appropriate for believers and those that are not. The proper choice does make a difference in their lives. Although it was God "who began a good work" in them when they became converts, they must continue to be moral people.

II. Paul's concern for himself, his hopes, his plans, and exhortations to moral life (1:12–4:20)

These are the letter's subjects from the introduction to the final greeting. Paul's imprisonment has not impeded the gospel. No matter with what motives the gospel is preached, the fact that Christ is being preached makes Paul happy (1:12–18).

As Paul faces trial, he is torn between wanting to die and be with Christ, because that would be better than his present situation, and to remain alive to help the Philippians in their "progress and joy in faith" (1:19–26). No matter what might happen, Paul can confidently exclaim, "For to me, living is Christ and dying is gain" (1:21). For Paul, who already lives "in Christ," death can only lead to a higher existence.

The Philippians are to let their manner of life be "worthy of the gospel," "standing firm in one spirit" (be united) against their opponents (who are not specified), and be prepared not only to believe in Christ but also suffer for his sake (1:27–30). Following Christ, the supreme example of humility, Philippian believers are to be united and humble (2:1–11). They are to be of "the same mind," have "the same love," and "do nothing from selfish ambition or conceit, but in humility regard others as better than" themselves.

Because of the poetic qualities of the Greek text, 2:5–11 is generally regarded as a hymn or part of a creed, but there is a continuing debate over important questions. Is the hymn pre-Pauline? If so, where did it originate—in an early Jewish or Hellenistic setting? Where did Paul or whoever wrote the hymn find the precise vocabulary to express his thought? What do certain crucial expressions such as "form of God," "equality with God," and "human likeness" mean? Although these questions are too complicated for us to deal with in detail, we will briefly consider vv 6–11. Excellent discussions of these and related questions occur in most of the books already mentioned. In addition, see R. P. Martin 1976a; J. T. Sanders 1971; E. S. Fiorenza 1975: 17–41.

As vv 6–11 now stand, they are packed with Christology: Jesus preexisted with God and resembled God (2:6a); he chose to give up that status (2:6bc) to take the status of a slave as a human being (2:7); as a human being he humbled himself and was obedient (to his Master, God) to the point of death on the cross (2:8). For these reasons God greatly exalted Jesus and made him a person greater than any other person and gave him a name greater than any other name, so that through that special person with the special name everyone in the universe would worship God and confess that "Jesus Christ is Lord, to the Glory of God the Father" (2:9–11).

In this paraphrase I have tried to convey what I think the verses probably meant for Paul, regardless of their origin. I avoid the use of "form of God" and "equality with God" because Paul nowhere else equates Jesus with God. The special name is surely meant to be "Lord." In Jewish thought the name of a person represented that person, so I assume that Paul thought Jesus not only had a superior name, but was a superior person. The verse containing "every knee should bend" is an allusion to Isa 45:23, which Paul actually quotes in Rom 14:11: "As I live, says the Lord, every knee shall bow to me, and every tongue shall give praise to God." Therefore, in Phil 2:10–11 Paul has in mind worship of God, not worship of Jesus.

There are in Phil 2:6–11 many words, phrases, and ideas that do not occur elsewhere in Paul, and some, indeed, occur nowhere else in the NT. This could mean, as many argue, that Paul himself inserted these verses, possibly from a pre-Pauline hymn of Jewish origin. On the other hand, could they be a later interpotation by someone with a higher Christology? Verse 5 summarizes what goes before and makes a fine transition to the exhortation that follows in verse 12. Thus the omission of verses 6–11 leaves Paul's thought flowing smoothly with verse 12 following verse 5.

In 2:12–18 Paul exhorts the Philippians to work for the well-being of their church, to do things without grumbling, and to live moral lives in the midst of a pagan environment. As always, Paul reminds his newly converted readers that their progress toward ultimate salvation must be evident in their personal and social conduct (see 1:6, 9–11, 27). He hopes to send Timothy and to visit Philippi soon himself. He has sent, or is about to send, Epaphroditus, whom he hopes the Philippians will receive with joy and respect (2:19–3:1).

Paul reacts to some Jewish opponents in light of his own experience and faith (3:2–4:1), but it is hard to tell if he has these opponents in mind throughout. In attacking them, Paul boasts of his own Jewishness and says that he counts "everything as loss because of the surpassing value of knowing Christ Jesus" as his Lord (3:2–11). Paul clearly explains his present experience and future goal in 3:8–11. Here Paul summarizes his faith as developed in Galatians and Romans, where he argues that people become converts by God's righteousness through faith and that, as a result, God's righteousness becomes their righteousness also (see 2 Cor 5:21). Having submitted to God's righteousness through faith, not works of the law, Paul now wants to attain the ultimate goal of his faith—the resurrection from the dead.

Paul strives to attain his goal because he is not yet perfect (3:12–16). The word translated "have already been made perfect" means "to become full-grown or mature," or "completely good or perfect in character." What meaning does Paul intend here? Does the word refer to "the resurrection from the dead" of the previous verse, the resurrection Paul has not yet perfectly experienced? Or does the word echo the usage of the mystery cults in which the initiate who attained the highest rank was called "perfect"? If so, it is used here without any moral implications and may imply a higher state of being experienced through religious rites. Paul probably has in mind leaving this life to "be with Christ" (1:23), but Paul also may mean that he is not as mature a person in Christ as he wants to be. The verses that follow, especially 18–19, represent the contrast to what Paul is striving for. Paul's past as a Jew, and perhaps also as a person in Christ, is not good enough. As elsewhere (1 Cor 9:24–27; Gal 2:2), Paul compares the believer with a runner on the racetrack struggling to reach the tape.

Unlike what the "enemies of the cross of Christ" have, the believers' "commonwealth is in heaven" (3:17–4:1). It has been suggested that the "enemies" are "the evil workers" of 3:2—perhaps Gnostics, others who disagree with Paul, people who have not given up their pagan ways, converts who are no longer faithful, or converted freedom questers like those in Galatia. The word "commonwealth" (*politeuma*) occurs only here in the NT, and this is the only place in the undisputed letters of Paul where the word "Savior" occurs (elsewhere only Eph 5:23 and several times in the pastorals). *Politeuma* properly means "the way one lives as a citizen," but it can also mean "state" or "commonwealth." In the Greek, the "our" is emphatic. Does Paul have in mind the Roman colony at Philippi, of which the proud Gentile Christians were a part? If so, does Paul want to make the point "We are a colony of

heaven," that is, "*Our* Rome is heaven" (J. L. Houlden 1977b:104–105)?

In Phil 1:27 Paul uses the verbal form *politeuomai*, meaning "let your manner of life be." That word is used elsewhere in the NT only in Acts 23:1, where it has the same meaning. There Paul is saying to members of the Jewish Sanhedrin, "Brothers, up to this day I have lived my life with a clear conscience before God." If in Phil 3:20 Paul has in mind the same idea as in 1:27, the meaning of Paul's Greek would be, "The kind of life we now live as believers sets us apart as a community of heaven." In vv 20–21 both the present and the future are significant. Although believers are members of a heavenly community because of their changed manner of life, the full realization of such a status will come with the Parousia and the work of Christ as Savior. Christ's role as Savior is still awaited.

"Heaven" here is not only a place where believers expect to go, but also a place from which the second coming of Christ is awaited. If believers continue their present manner of life, Christ at his coming as Savior will change their physical bodies to conform to their spiritual nature, which will then be like the body of the exalted Lord (see 2:9) himself (see also 1 Cor 15:42–54). In realizing their ultimate salvation, believers will enter a higher state of existence, but one they have already begun to experience.

Paul not only entreats the women Euodia and Syntyche to agree, but also asks his "loyal companion" to help them agree. He exhorts the Philippians to rejoice, to have no anxiety, to pray, to think about what is true, honorable, just, pure, lovely, and gracious, and to do as they have learned and observed from him (4:2–9). Although Paul has learned to be content whatever his situation, he thanks the Philippians for their gifts (4:10–20).

Beginning with Lydia in Acts, and then with Euodia and Syntyche, who worked with Paul (4:2–3), women were active in the church at Philippi, and not as subordinates. This coincides with Paul's view in Gal 3:28 that among baptized converts there is no inequality between men and women. Paul's remark in Phil 4:2–3 also reflects the independent position and the initiative of women in Macedonian society, where they could become educated, engage in trade, hold political office, and enjoy many other privileges as the equals of men (see W. Tarn 1952:98–99).

III. Closing greeting (4:21–23)

PHILEMON

PURPOSE OF THE LETTER

The little letter to Philemon may have a significance for the study of Paul and the collection and publication of his letters far beyond that indicated by its size. This letter resembles one Pliny the Younger, Roman orator and letter writer (c. 61–114), wrote to a friend, begging him to pardon a former slave (*Letters* 9:21). It is a warm and personal letter addressed to Philemon, who apparently owned a house large enough for church meetings, since Paul refers to "the church in your [singular] house." Because Apphia and Archippus, usually assumed to be the wife and son of Philemon, are included in the address, and because the "you" and "your" in the greetings (3; 25) are plural, Paul must want the group to know what he is writing. In the same way, Paul addresses Philemon in the singular (21) and asks him to prepare a guest room (22a), but again the "your" and "you" in 22b are plural. So Philemon is a personal letter with a message intended for a group of believers meeting in Philemon's house. Moreover, Philemon may be the only letter in the NT in which a woman is included in the address (see 2 John 1:1).

Philemon, perhaps converted by Paul (17; 19), owned a slave named Onesimus. The slave ran away (11) and may have taken money or something else with him (18). Although we do not really know why or how, Onesimus got to Paul in prison. Perhaps trouble caught up with him and he was put into the same prison. Ordinarily a runaway slave would either be returned to his master or sold to someone else. If Onesimus was put into prison, he must have served his sentence, or Paul could not have sent him

back to his master—unless he was paroled on Paul's word that he would return. Or did Onesimus know where Paul was, so that he went to him intentionally? Perhaps Onesimus had heard Paul preach in his owner's house and had developed respect for Paul—if he had not actually been converted. However, Paul's words "whose father I have become during my imprisonment" (10) may imply that Onesimus became a convert only after meeting Paul in prison. At any rate, the two men apparently agreed that Onesimus should return to his master. Paul, therefore, wrote the letter to Philemon, appealing to him to take Onesimus back no longer as a slave but as a "beloved brother." Verses 15–17 indicate that this is the immediate purpose of the letter. A. D. Callahan 1997 maintains that Onesimus was a blood brother of Philemon, not his runaway slave. Paul wrote to reconcile the two men. I have not seen a response to his view.

Besides appealing to Philemon to take back Onesimus, Paul promises to repay any debt Onesimus owes his master and also asks Philemon to prepare a guest room for him. With the help of prayers from the church in Philemon's house, Paul hopes to visit the group soon and to stay with Philemon.

WHERE DID PHILEMON LIVE?

There is no concrete evidence to answer this question, but in Col 4:9 Onesimus is referred to as one of the Colossians, so presumably he lived at Colossae. The writer of Colossians closes with a word to Archippus (4:17), so assuming that Onesimus and Archippus are the same persons mentioned in the letter to Philemon, then Onesimus and probably also Archippus lived at Colossae. On this evidence, it has usually been assumed that Philemon also lived in Colossae, and that Paul sent the letter to Philemon with Onesimus when he sent Onesimus back to Colossae with Tychicus, the bearer of the letter to the Colossians (Col 4:7–9).

Since Acts does not report that Paul ever visited Colossae or any of its neighboring cities, and since Paul himself writes that the people there have not seen him (Col 2:1), Paul did not meet Philemon or Onesimus at Colossae. If Paul was a prisoner at Ephesus, perhaps Onesimus first met him there.

Another bit of evidence from Philemon and Colossians seems to indicate that Philemon's home was in Colossae and that Onesimus ran away from there. Besides Onesimus and Philemon, who are both mentioned in Philemon and Colossians, all the friends of Paul named in Philemon—except Apphia—are also included in Colossians. Timothy is with Paul when he writes both letters (Phlm 1; Col 1:1). Epaphras, founder of the church at Colossae (Col 1:7) and one of the Colossians (Col 4:12), is in prison with Paul when he writes Philemon. And Mark, Aristarchus, Demas, and Luke are mentioned in the closing greetings of Phlm 23 and Col 4:10–14. But then again, why would Paul add greetings from the same people in two letters sent to the same place (Colossae) at the same time? At any rate, nothing in Philemon indicates where Philemon or Onesimus lived or where the church mentioned was located.

In contrast to the usual interpretation, another view has been proposed by two American scholars. According to this view, Epaphras, founder of the church at Colossae, was succeeded by Philemon, who lived at Laodicea and not at Colossae. Archippus, on the other hand, lived at Colossae and owned Onesimus. Paul sent Onesimus back to his owner and asked not only that Onesimus be forgiven, but also that he be freed so he could do mission work. Paul sent Onesimus back to Archippus by way of Laodicea in order to gain the approval of Philemon, the leader of the church. Our letter to Philemon was then taken by Onesimus from Philemon at Laodicea to Archippus at Colossae, where it and the one to the Colossians were to be read in the church. Our letter to Philemon, therefore, is "the letter from Laodicea" referred to in Col 4:16, and "the task" that Archippus is asked to fulfill (Col 4:17) is exactly what Paul was requesting from the owner of Onesimus.

This is a combination of the views of E. J. Goodspeed 1933 and J. Knox 1960. For brief and lucid assessments of these views, see C. F. D.

Moule 1958:14–21; J. L. Houlden 1977:123–126; G. B. Caird 1976:217, 222. Houlden raises the question of two churches in Laodicea, one under the leadership of Philemon, the other under Nympha (see Col 4:15).

PLACE AND DATE OF WRITING

Like Philippians, Philemon was written while Paul was in prison (1; 9; 10; 23). But where was he in prison? The same problem exists here as with Philippians—Rome, Caesarea, or Ephesus? Most scholars favor either Rome or Ephesus. Here are some arguments in support of the various cities and some counterarguments.

According to Acts 28:30, in Rome Paul "welcomed all who came to him," so it would have been easy for Onesimus to get to Paul there. But the same was probably true for Caesarea, since Acts 24:23 reports that Felix, Roman governor of Judea, gave orders that Paul should have some freedom, and that none of his friends should be prevented from caring for his needs. So if Onesimus was intentionally looking for Paul, he probably could have visited him in Caesarea as well as in Rome.

According to Tacitus, every kind of evil was apt to find a place in Rome, so a runaway slave like Onesimus could easily become lost in the populace of Rome. Moreover, a large percentage of the population in Rome was slaves. Petronius, who was a satirist and a friend of Nero's, satirizes a wealthy Roman by saying that in the Roman's household there were so many slaves that only a tenth of them knew their master (*Satyricon* 37).

Paul expresses a desire to visit both the Philippians (2:4) and Philemon (22) soon. Philemon's home, whether in Colossae or Laodicea, was in the East, as was Philippi, but from Rome Paul intended to go to Spain. This is a point in favor of Ephesus and not Rome as the place of Paul's imprisonment, since Paul could make these visits while still in the East. At the same time, this would be a point against Caesarea, since Paul's intention while there, according to Acts, was to get to Rome (19:21; 23:11; 25:8–21; 26:32; 27:24). Moreover, Paul would hardly have wanted to be released soon in Caesarea, because he would have fallen victim to the Jewish mob (Acts 24:1–9; 25:2–4, 7). Because of the shorter distance, it would have been easier for Onesimus to get to Paul in either Ephesus or Caesarea than in Rome. Then again, he may have wanted to get to Rome in order to be as far away from his master as possible.

We learn from Phlm 24 and Col 4:10, 14 that among those with Paul when he wrote were Aristarchus and Luke. According to Acts, Aristarchus was with Paul at Ephesus (19:29), was with him later in Macedonia, and accompanied him to Rome (20:4; 27:2). If Luke was the author of the "we sections" in Acts, then he was also on the trip to Rome with Paul and arrived there with him (27:1–28:16). Since the "we source" does not include Paul's stay in Ephesus, all of this information seems to support Rome rather than Ephesus as the place of writing for Philemon and Colossians.

Again, as for Philippians, there are several possibilities for the place of writing for Philemon, and we cannot be certain about any one of them. Also as with Philippians, the date of Philemon depends on the place of writing. If Philemon was written from Ephesus, the date would be close to that of Philippians (if Philippians was written from Ephesus) and Corinthians, or the mid-50s. If written from Rome, its date would be c. 60–64; and if from Caesarea, c. 56–58.

Outline and Comments

I. Opening greetings (1–3)

II. Thanksgiving (4–7)

Paul thanks God not only for Philemon's love and faith toward the Lord Jesus, but also for the way Philemon's love has refreshed the hearts of others. That prepares Philemon psychologically for the request Paul is about to make—that Philemon take back his slave.

The meaning of v 6, "I pray that the sharing of your faith may become effective when you perceive all the good that we may do for Christ," is uncertain. The word translated "sharing" is *koinōnia,* and literally means "partnership," "contributory help," or "fellowship." Philemon is the subject and Onesimus the object in Paul's thinking. Paul is saying he hopes that when Philemon expresses his faith in dealing with Onesimus, this will have the effect (for the Greek word *energeō,* translated "promote") of making him realize all the good that is theirs as believers. Philemon's faith, active in love, has produced that effect in Paul's life; so Paul says, "I have indeed received much joy and encouragement from your love" (7).

III. Appeal to Philemon to take back Onesimus no longer as a slave, but as a beloved brother (8–22)

Despite his desire to keep Onesimus with him in prison, Paul offers to repay Philemon what Onesimus owes and expresses a hope to visit the church over which Philemon presides.

In the beginning of Philemon we become aware that it is a letter between unequals. Although Paul does not refer to himself as an apostle of Christ, he says he could "command" Philemon to do as requested. Philemon is in charge of the church in his house, but Paul has authority over Philemon's church and others. Paul makes his appeal "on the basis of love," but throughout the letter he reminds Philemon of his obligations to Paul (14; 19; 20; 21).

Verses 15–17 give the immediate purpose for writing. In v 11 there is a pun on the name Onesimus, for which the meaning of the Greek (*onēsimos*) is "useful." The name is contrasted with the adjective meaning "useless" (*achrēstos*) to describe Onesimus's former lack of service to his master. As a native of Colossae in ancient Phrygia, Onesimus would not have had a very good reputation to start with. Cicero (*Pro Flacco* 27) repeats a proverb that "a Phrygian is usually made better by a beating." But Onesimus has changed and now will be "useful" (*euchrēstos*). A clearer pun on the name Onesimus (*onēsimos*) is made in v 20 with the word meaning "benefit" (*onaimēn*) when Paul says, "Let me have this benefit from you in the Lord!" But what is the meaning of the pun? Does it mean, "If Onesimus now lives up to his name and is a *benefit* to his master, Philemon must in fair exchange be a *benefit* to Paul" (G. B. Caird 1976:223)? Or does it mean, "What he [Paul] wants to get out of the master is Onesimus himself; he wishes to be able to use the Useful One" (J. L. Houlden 1977:231)?

There is also a question about what Paul means when he remarks that Philemon "will do even more than" Paul asks. Besides asking Philemon to receive Onesimus as a beloved brother, is Paul also asking him to return Onesimus to him (see 13–14)? Or does Paul want him to do still more, that is, give Onesimus his freedom?

In writing to Philemon about his slave Onesimus, Paul makes no judgment on the institution of slavery as such. In both Hebrew and Graeco-Roman law, the right of human beings to own other humans was assumed, so slavery was an inherent part of the society in which Paul lived. Paul did not try to change the social structure of his time. Indeed, he realized that a runaway slave should be returned to his rightful owner, and Paul did that. But Paul's appeal "on the basis of love" (9) to Philemon is that he take Onesimus back "no longer as a slave but more than a slave, a beloved brother . . . in the Lord." Compare Gal 3:27–28: "As many of you as were baptized into Christ have clothed yourselves with Christ. There is no longer Jew or Greek, there is no longer slave or free, there is no longer male or female; for all of you are one in Christ Jesus."

IV. Closing greetings and blessing (23–25)

SUMMARY

Philippians and Philemon are distinctive letters of Paul. Philippians, along with Acts, reveals the active participation of women in the church at Philippi. That church had a special role in Paul's greater mission; consequently, Paul developed an unusually happy relationship with it. Philippians reveals that Gentile believers, as part of a minority, had to separate themselves from the majority in Philippi's Roman society, where life was less restricted than in the new society to which they now belonged. Philemon is distinctive in that it is Paul's most personal letter. Written to the owner of a runaway slave, it reveals, in a practical way, that in a society of believers even slaves are "brothers."

Most scholars agree on the following points concerning Paul and his letters. Paul's main background was Hellenistic Judaism. He did not write all of the letters attributed to him in the NT. His letters, not Acts, are the primary source for assessing Paul's life and work, and Acts must be disregarded for studying the content of Paul's preaching. The precise sequence of the letters cannot be determined. And even in letters that are universally regarded as authentic there may be some later non-Pauline interpolations.

Perhaps the most important things to remember when studying Paul and his letters are that his calling to preach the gospel to Gentiles (Gal 1:11–17) and the situations in the churches he established—insofar as they can be generally known—determined why, how, and what, including the theology, he wrote.

For further study of Philippians see commentaries by G. D. Fee 1995; F. Thielman 1995; M. Bockmuehl 1998; L. G. Bloomquist 1993, suffering in Philippians; C. S. Wansink 1996, Roman prisons; for Philemon see commentaries by E. Lohse 1971; R. P. Martin 1978; F. F. Bruce 1984; A. G. Patzia 1984; N. R. Petersen 1985, sociology.

In the next chapter we will discuss three of the most disputed letters among those purporting to be from Paul—Colossians, Ephesians, and 2 Thessalonians.

CHAPTER 13

Disputed Letters of Paul: Colossians, Ephesians, and 2 Thessalonians

IN THE STUDY OF PAUL IT IS IMPORTANT to try to determine if all letters purporting to be from Paul are authentic in order to determine as accurately as possible the bearing they might have on his life and work and the content of his theology. For literalists this is no problem because they accept everything in the Bible as written. However, most scholars today are willing to consider arguments on both sides of the question of authenticity, and that is what we do in this chapter. Here we will examine Colossians, Ephesians, and 2 Thessalonians, all of which purport to be from Paul. Because the two epistles to Timothy and the one to Titus also purport to be from Paul but are generally not thought to be authentic, they could also be discussed here. However, arguments for their inauthenticity seem to be stronger than those for some of the letters considered in this chapter. And they seem to reflect a time and circumstances in the church much later than the undisputed letters of Paul and probably later also than those discussed here. Therefore, the letters to Timothy and Titus are considered among the latest writings in the NT and are discussed in the last chapter.

Most scholars regard Colossians and 2 Thessalonians as authentic letters; and some, perhaps many, also regard Ephesians as genuine. However, an increasing number of scholars reject the authenticity of one or more of the three letters, particularly Ephesians.

M. Y MacDonald 1989 helps to confirm what I have said. She considers "the interplay between the ethos, ministry structures, ritual forms, and beliefs" of the Pauline and deutero-Pauline communities in order "to trace the process of institutionalization" in those communities. On the basis of work by other scholars, she assumes that Colossians was "written by a fellow worker or disciple of Paul" and that Ephesians is "dependent on Colossians" and "written by a close associate of Paul, probably fairly soon after Colossians." Because of the "late stage of church development they exhibit," the pastorals—1 Timothy, 2 Timothy, and Titus—date between 100–140. "Notoriously difficult problems of its dating and authorship make it [2 Thessalonians]—"virtually impossible" for its use in MacDonald's investigation.

There are affinities between the undisputed letters and Colossians, Ephesians, and 2 Thessalonians. If Paul did not write the three letters, he was at least indirectly responsible for them; therefore, some scholars prefer to call them deutero-Pauline letters, that is, letters that are secondary or are one step removed from Paul. In this book the term *disputed letters* is used because it is more neutral than *inauthentic letters* or *deutero-Pauline letters*. Likewise, the more neutral term *the writer*, rather than Paul, is used.

Before considering these letters, it is important to make several observations. First, 2 Thess 2:2 indicates that inauthentic letters were written in Paul's name. There the writer—no matter whether Paul or another person—begs the readers "not to be quickly shaken in mind or alarmed . . . by [a] letter, as though from us" (see 2 Thess 3:17). Second, it was not a violation of one's honor or integrity to affix someone else's name to a writing. Indeed, such action indirectly indicated the honor, respect, and authority of the person whose name was used. Finally, since there were no rights to one's own ideas or copyright laws, forgery was not a legal offense. Remember these points as we study the disputed letters of Paul in this chapter.

COLOSSIANS

THE CITY OF COLOSSAE

Colossae, Hierapolis, and Laodicea (Col 1:2; 2:1; 4:13, 15, 16; Rev 1:11) were neighboring cities in the Lycus River valley, which was in the Roman province Asia in Asia Minor (see map, "The Journeys of Paul"). During Roman times Colossae was inhabited by native Phrygians, Greek colonists, and Jews who were descendants of those settled in the region by Antiochus III and others. As in other cities in Asia Minor, the population was predominantly Gentile. (See Figure 13.1.)

Tacitus (*Annals* 14:27) says an earthquake destroyed Laodicea in 60–61, and Colossae may also have been destroyed then. Eusebius reports that in 63–64 the cities of Laodicea, Hierapolis, and Colossae were destroyed by an earthquake. There are no literary sources of information for Colossae after 61, but some coins from the second and third centuries CE indicate that the deities worshiped at Colossae included the Phrygian god Men and several gods and goddesses of the mystery cults.

There have been no excavations at Colossae, but the site has been identified since 1835, when a traveler named W J. Hamilton identified the city ruins. These included some marble stones from buildings, several stone seats from a theater, the acropolis, and some graves in the necropolis (lit., "city of the dead"; cemetery). Probably not much, if anything, will ever be known about the city of Colossae at the time a church was started there.

FOUNDING OF AND SITUATION IN THE CHURCH AT COLOSSAE AND THE WRITER'S RESPONSE

There is no evidence either in Acts or in Paul's letters that Paul ever visited Colossae, and the writer of Colossians indicates that he has not been to the church at Colossae. He says, "We have heard of your faith in Christ Jesus" (1:4) and "I am struggling for you, and for those in Laodicea, and for all who have not seen me face to face" (2:1). Apparently the Colossians had first learned of the gospel from Epaphras (1:7), a Colossian who had worked at Laodicea and Hierapolis (4:12–13). He reported the faith and love of the Colossian Christians to the writer of the letter (1:3–8).

Acts reports that during Paul's stay at Ephesus "all the residents of Asia, both Jews and Greeks, heard the word of the Lord" (19:10; see also 19:26). Perhaps among those who "heard the

FIGURE 13.1   *Remains of a very ancient church at Laodicea.*

word" were the converts in the three cities of the Lycus valley. Also, perhaps Epaphras—and maybe Philemon—came to Ephesus, was converted, and then returned to Colossae to establish the church there. In this way, then, Paul would have been indirectly responsible for founding the church at Colossae. These suggestions, of course, are only speculation.

Several times the writer of Colossians seems to be addressing Gentiles. He speaks of making known the mystery of Christ "among the Gentiles" (1:27), and the words "you who were once estranged and hostile in mind, doing evil deeds" (1:21) probably refer to Gentiles. The statement about being "circumcised with a circumcision made without hands" (2:11) and the remark about "festivals, new moons, or sabbaths" (2:16) indicate the presence also of Jews or of Gentile converts following Jewish practices.

We can begin to reconstruct the general situation in the church at Colossae by looking at two passages (2:4, 8). In 2:4 the writer says that he speaks about Christ as he does "so that no one may deceive you with plausible arguments." In 2:8 he warns the readers, "See to it that no one takes you captive through philosophy and empty deceit." These passages indicate that some false teachers, or "errorists" as they are sometimes called, were causing trouble for the Colossian converts with false teachings.

Scholars usually refer to the false teaching at Colossae as the Colossian heresy. Although the word *heresy* satisfactorily describes the general situation at Colossae, *religious syncretism* is more adequate. At Colossae, then, religious beliefs and practices other than the original ones the Colossians had been taught (2:7) were being introduced. The syncretists tended toward exclusiveness or snobbery, so the writer has to remind the readers that his teaching is for everyone. "Whom [Christ] we proclaim, warning everyone and teaching everyone in all wisdom, so that we may present everyone mature in Christ" (1:28).

There was "philosophy and empty deceit, according to human tradition, according to the elemental spirits of the universe, and not according to Christ" (2:8; see also 2:15, 20). Some of the syncretists did not regard Christ as superior to other forces or beings, and they advocated "worship of angels," subdeities, or other powers. But for the writer, Christ is the center of all things, and all things center in Christ, so the veneration of other beings or powers is useless. "For in him the whole fullness of deity dwells bodily" (2:9). The writer's reply to the situation at Colossae is summed up in the christological concept of Col 1:15–20.

There were questions of food and drink, festivals, new moon, and sabbaths" (2:16). Apparently some syncretists were insisting on the Jewish ritualistic observance of festivals and sabbaths. To them the writer replies: "These are only a shadow of what is to come, but the substance belongs to Christ" (2:17).

Some Colossians "submit to regulations, 'Do not handle, Do not taste, Do not touch'" (2:20–21). These words can be included with 2:16 and taken to mean that the syncretists are urging strict adherence to Jewish law. Or they may indicate an asceticism (aloofness from society, including self-denial or even self-imposed suffering) characteristic of Gnosticism, especially Jewish Gnosticism. According to the writer, these regulations perish as they are used and have "an appearance of wisdom in promoting self-imposed piety, humility, and severe treatment of the body, but they are of no value in checking self-indulgence" (2:22–23).

In Colossae, as in other early churches, there was the danger that Gentile converts, "who once were estranged and hostile in mind, doing evil deeds" (1:21), would revert to their pagan moral laxity. Such laxity would be more likely to occur among Gnostic than Jewish syncretists. For Gnostics, the body, which was composed of matter, was evil. With respect to morality, this idea led to one of two courses of action. In practicing asceticism, one could keep the body under control by denying it all pleasures. Or, at the other extreme, some Gnostics believed that one could use the body with unrestrained freedom because only the spirit was good. The writer may advise against the former action in 2:20–23 and exhort against the latter in 3:5.

Additional evidence indicates that the religious syncretism at Colossae included elements from Gnosticism that the writer opposes. Since, according to the Gnostics, the world is evil and God as spirit is entirely good, the world was not created by the true God but by some power hostile to him. To oppose that false doctrine the writer stresses the idea of Christ as an agent in creation (1:15–16). Certain Gnostics also believed that Christ himself was wholly spirit, that he never had existed in bodily form or died on the cross. Therefore, the writer reminds the readers that Christ has reconciled them "in his fleshly body through death" (1:22), thus stressing Jesus' physical nature. Similarly, for the Gnostics knowledge, not faith, was the way to salvation.

Therefore, the writer stresses the readers' faith: "We have heard of your faith in Christ" (1:4), and "the firmness of your faith in Christ" (2:5; see also 1:23).

Finally, words such as "fullness" (*plērōma*; 1:19; 2:9), "mystery" (*mystērion*; 1:26–27; 2:2; 4:3), and the word translated as "dwelling on visions" (*embateuō*; 2:18), which were used frequently in Gnosticism and the mystery religions, are also used by the writer to counter the syncretistic elements from those phenomena. However, those who reject the idea of such influence at Colossae say that the writer uses the words in his own way and gives them new meanings. (For the writer's response to possible elements from the mystery religions, see G. H. P. Thompson 1967:117–127. On this point and for the religious background of Colossians, see W. L. Knox 1939:146–181.)

Because the writer is more allusive than descriptive in his response, it is difficult to assess the situation at Colossae accurately, and there is no consensus about the nature of the religious syncretism there. Some scholars argue for a highly developed form of Gnosticism at Colossae, or at least an early form of Gnosticism or pre-Gnosticism. Others deny that there were any Gnostic elements at Colossae. Some scholars argue for the presence of a form of Jewish legalism like that at Qumran, a non-Jewish mystery cult from the East, Jewish Gnosticism, or Judaism like that in the wisdom literature and in Jewish speculation of the time—speculation like that in the Qumran Scrolls and apocalyptic writings (J. L. Houlden 1977: 193; see also W. G. Kuemmel 1975:339–340; G. Bornkamm 1975; G. H. P. Thompson 1967:117–127; C. F. D. Moule 1958:29–34; E. Lohse 1971).

That there were false teachers at Colossae is certain, but they did not attack the writer or other believers. Rather, they wanted to attach certain beliefs and practices to the original teaching. The syncretism perhaps developed naturally from the religious and intellectual atmosphere of the Graeco-Roman-Oriental world. Because of the nature of that syncretism, the letter to the

Colossians is difficult and more christologically advanced than the undisputed letters of Paul. This is one reason some scholars question its authenticity.

THE PROBLEM OF AUTHENTICITY

The letter to the Colossians purports to be written by Paul (1:1; 4:18), who is suffering (1:24) and in prison (4:3, 18). Epaphras, a Colossian (4:12) and the founder of the church (1:7), is with the author when he writes (4:12). Apparently Epaphras has brought good news about the Colossians' "faith in Christ," their love "for all the saints" (1:4), and their response to the gospel (1:6). In response to this good news, the writer wants to let the believers at Colossae know about his prayerful concern for them (1:9–14) and to express his joy at their good "morale and the firmness" of their "faith in Christ" (2:5). But because of the threat from the religious syncretism, the news is not all good, so the writer must warn the Colossians against the syncretism. But who is the writer? Although it is not generally agreed who wrote Colossians, Col 4:7–9 may indicate that Tychicus was the bearer of the letter.

Most scholars, including some who reject Pauline authorship of Ephesians, regard Colossians as a genuine letter of Paul. Some scholars accept parts of the letter as genuine, especially those coinciding with Philemon, and regard the rest as interpolations. Others reject Pauline authorship entirely, for reasons that follow.

Arguments against Authenticity

Vocabulary, Language, and Style. Colossians contains thirty-four words that occur nowhere else in the NT and twenty-five words and expressions that occur nowhere else in Paul. Examples are "inheritance" (1:12), "making peace through the blood of his cross" (1:20), "the whole fullness of deity" (2:9), "record" (2:14), "worship of angels" (2:18), and "seasoned with salt" (4:6). In contrast to the undisputed letters of Paul, Colossians is grammatically rough and contains an overabundance of words, including synonyms, infinitives, participles, and dependent clauses. Good examples of the cumbersome style are 1:9–12 and 1:24–27, each of which is one long sentence in Greek. Even in English we can recognize in the former passage "praying" and "asking," "wisdom and understanding," and endurance and patience as synonyms, and asking, bearing fruit, and increasing in the knowledge of God as participles strung together loosely.

Omission of Key Concepts. Concepts omitted include belief, law, justification, righteousness, saving, salvation, and revelation. Most significant, perhaps, in contrast to the Pauline letters, the word "Spirit" occurs in Colossians only in 1:8, and "baptism" is given a new meaning. In 2:11–12 the writer equates baptism with circumcision; this is in strong contrast to Romans 6, which says that in baptism converts die metaphorically to sin and rise to newness of life in Christ (see also Col 3:1). For Paul, circumcision is usually a meaningless Jewish rite not required of converts. The writer of Colossians does speak of "circumcision made without hands" (2:11), which is close to the concept in Rom 2:29, and Col 2:13–14 is close to Roman 6. But in Col 1:19–20 the writer uses a different word for "reconcile" than Paul does (Rom 5:11; 2 Cor 5:19). This makes a slight difference in the concept of reconciliation.

Advanced Christology. The key passage is 1:15–20. In 2 Cor 4:4 Paul says that Christ is "the image of God," and in Rom 8:29 predestined converts conform "to the image of his Son." But in Col 1:15 the writer refers to Christ as "the image of the invisible God, the firstborn of all creation." Here Christ makes God, who is invisible (see 1 Tim 1:17; Heb 11:27), visible. Christ is the first of God's creation and is the purpose of creation—"all things have been created through him and for him" (1:16). These ideas occur nowhere in Paul, and in 1 Cor 8:6 God himself is the reason for human existence— "for whom we exist." (For different interpretations of the Christology of Col 1:15–20, see G. B. Caird 1976:175–183.)

Ecclesiology (Doctrine of the Church). Christ as "the head of the body, the church" (1:18; see also 2:19) is a new concept and stands in contrast to 1 Cor 12:12–30, where believers are metaphorically "the body of Christ and individually members of it" (see also Rom 7:4; 12:5). Moreover, the use of the word *diakonos,* translated as "minister" or "servant" in Col 1:7, 23, 25 and 4:7, differs from the use in undisputed letters of Paul (but see 2 Cor 3:6). Here the term is closer to its use for a particular office in the church, as in 1 Tim 3:8, 12 and 4:6, and the usage indicates a development in church order later than Paul. This is true especially in Col 1:25, where the writer says he "became its servant according to God's commission" given to him.

Literary Dependence. There is considerable dependence on undisputed letters of Paul, especially in the first two chapters, which contain the greatest theological passages. The best explanation for this phenomenon is that a writer later than Paul who wanted to stress important theological issues used Paul's letters.

Arguments for Authenticity

Relationship to Philemon. Colossians has important similarities to Philemon, which is universally regarded as Pauline. In both, Paul is a prisoner with Timothy and mentions Onesimus, Archippus, Aristarchus, Mark, Epaphras, Demas, and Luke; in both, the writer mentions the sending of Onesimus; and in both, there is a special message for Archippus. However, the names of Mark and Aristarchus and Luke and Demas are given in reverse order in the two letters. And in Philemon, Epaphras is referred to as "my fellow prisoner," but in Colossians Aristarchus is the one so designated. These observations raise important questions. Why would the same writer mention so many of his friends in two letters to the same church, letters presumably written at the same time and delivered by the same person?

And how could the writer address a letter to a person thought to be the leader in the church at Colossae, and yet not even hint about the serious problem there? These are difficult questions.

Vocabulary, Language, and Style. The differences between Colossians and the undisputed letters can be explained by the fact that Paul is adapting his message to his Colossian readers. Paul is always able to suit his language and thought to the situation he addresses by saying new things in new ways. However, on the basis of language and style, scholars draw opposite conclusions. According to E. Schweizer 1982: 19, "The letter can neither have been written nor dictated by Paul," but according to W. G. Kuemmel 1975:342, "There is no reason to doubt the Pauline authorship of the letter."

Christology. Defenders of Pauline authorship maintain that differences in Christology can be explained in two main ways. As far as omission of key concepts is concerned, Paul never includes a discussion of all concepts in every letter. It would be ridiculous for him to do so, since he adapts his thought as well as his language to the context and develops them to meet new situations. The differences in thought between Colossians and the undisputed letters can be explained on the basis of a syncretistic Judaism, especially the theology of Jewish wisdom. Elements "present elsewhere in Paul but not prominently, here hold the centre of the stage," in the opinion of J. L. Houlden 1977:135 (see also G. H. P. Thompson 1967:107–110). The beginnings of the christological thought of Colossians appear in other letters of Paul (see Phil 2:5–11; 1 Cor 1:24; 8:6).

Ecclesiology. The germ of the Colossian ecclesiology also appears in other Pauline letters. The church is compared with a body in Rom 12:4–5 and 1 Cor 12:12–30. Paul seems to identify the church as Christ's body in 1 Cor 1:13; 12:12–13; and Gal 3:28, so there is no problem in understanding the statement that Christ "is the head of the body, the church" (Col 1:18). (For further defense of Pauline authorship of Colossians, see W. G. Kuemmel 1975:340–346.)

In sum, there are arguments for and against Paul's authorship. There are also two main theories regarding the author, if the author is not Paul. First, since most of the material that differs from Paul's writing in vocabulary, style, and thought occurs in the first two chapters, perhaps someone added numerous interpolations—especially from Ephesians—to a nucleus of Pauline material. Most scholars, however, now reject this view on the theory that Ephesians is based on Colossians rather than the other way around.

Second, perhaps one of Paul's close friends and disciples who was very familiar with his language and thought wrote Colossians. He may have taken material from the end of Philemon, imitated the opening verses in Paul's letters, and forged Paul's name. Such a theory accounts for both the likenesses and differences in style and thought between Colossians and the undisputed letters of Paul.

Thus, scholars draw different conclusions from the same data. Perhaps most are still convinced that Paul himself wrote all of Colossians. Some think Paul was directly or indirectly responsible for some of the material, and others think that Paul wrote none of it. I think the authorship of Colossians is still an open question.

PLACE AND DATE OF WRITING

If the connections between Philemon and Colossians are genuinely those of Paul, who was writing both letters from prison (4:3, 10, 18), the possible places of his imprisonment are Ephesus, Caesarea, and Rome. Arguments for and against each of these cities are the same as arguments concerning the places of writing of Philippians and Philemon. If Colossians was written by Paul from Ephesus, the date would be close to that of Corinthians, or the mid-50s; if from Caesarea, c. 56–58; and if from Rome, c. 60–64.

Several factors make dating Colossians even more complicated than dating Philemon. Based on the assumptions that there is a development in Paul's thought and that the Christology in Colossians is more advanced than that in 1 and 2 Corinthians, Galatians, and Romans, a late date from Rome is most plausible for Colossians. Then, because of the purported connections with Philemon, Philemon would also have to be assigned to the Roman period. However, if Philemon comes from Paul's Ephesian ministry, then Colossians, regardless of its affinities with Philemon, belongs in a post-Pauline period because of its advanced Christology.

If Colossae was destroyed by an earthquake sometime between 60 and 64, this raises questions about a post-Pauline author and date. A post-Pauline author would hardly have written before Paul's death and the earthquake. But is it conceivable that after the earthquake the author would say nothing at all about it? Were there even communities of believers in Laodicea, Hierapolis (Col 4:15–16), and Colossae after the earthquake? These questions and many others in the study of Colossians remain unanswerable. Think about them as you read Colossians with the following outline and comments.

Outline and Comments

I. Greeting, thanksgiving, and prayer (1:1–14)

Although the word "saints," used for believers, occurs in Paul's greetings (Rom 1:7; 1 Cor 1:2; Phil 1:1), the word "brothers" used in that way does not. Among greetings purporting to be from Paul, only in this greeting is the name of Christ not linked with that of God. In 1:3–8 the writer gives thanks for the Colossians' faith and love and for the fact that the gospel, as they have learned it from Epaphras, is bearing fruit among them. "Hope" (v 5) does not have the usual meaning of expectation that it has in Paul's letters; rather, hope is something reserved for the Colossians "in heaven." It is the same as "the inheritance of the saints in the light" in v 12. Is this hope the incentive for, or the consequence of, the faith and love mentioned?

The writer prays that the Colossians may be filled with the knowledge of God's "will in all spiritual wisdom and understanding." By using "spiritual wisdom," "understanding," and "knowledge," is the writer challenging Gnostics on their own terms? If so, God's will, which comes from proper knowledge, is the important thing. "Spiritual wisdom" may mean divine and not human wisdom, or it may be the wisdom of the believers, not of the syncretists. Such wisdom is not fully developed but must be increased so that believers can lead lives "worthy of the Lord" and "bear fruit in every good work" (1:9–10).

In 1:11–14 the writer prays that the Colossians may be strengthened and that they will thank God because he has qualified them to "share in the inheritance of the saints in the light." What this means is stated in vv 13–14: "He has rescued us from the power of darkness and transferred us into the kingdom of his beloved Son, in whom we have redemption, the forgiveness of sins." Perhaps we can best understand the theology and mythology behind the passage in light of Acts 26:18, where the writer depicts Paul reporting words that the risen Jesus spoke during Paul's vision on the Damascus road. Paul is to be sent to the Gentiles "to open their eyes, so that they may turn from darkness to light and from the power of Satan to God, so that they may receive forgiveness of sins and a place among those who are sanctified by faith" in Christ. This is precisely what has happened to the Gentile converts at Colossae. In ancient religions, light and darkness were widely used as symbols for the realms over which good and evil deities or powers presided, for good and evil in a moral sense, and for truth and falsehood. Precisely what the writer of Colossians means is uncertain.

II. Superiority of Christ in the universe and in the church (1:15–2:7)

The writer's prayer fades into a highly christological passage (1:15–20), one of the most difficult in the NT. Many scholars regard the passage as a hymn or liturgy based on the wisdom theology of the OT and on aspects of Graeco-Roman thought (for example, J. T. Sanders 1971:75–87; J. L. Houlden 1977:155–173; E. Kaesemann 1964:149–168; and G. B. Caird 1976:174–183). But there is no consensus as to whether the author himself wrote all or parts of it, whether the author adapted and incorporated a pre-Pauline hymn into his work, or whether someone else interpolated the passage. The essence of the writer's Christology is in 1:15–20, and many of the ideas here occur in other places in Colossians: the image of God (3:10), principalities and authorities (2:10, but translated differently), Christ as head (2:10, 19), fullness (2:10), creation (3:10), deity dwelling bodily in Christ (2:9), and reconciliation (1:22). These phrases indicate that the passage is an integral part of the letter.

The theme of 1:15–20 is the superiority of Jesus as Son of God (v 13) in all things, specifically in regard to his relationship to God, creation, the church, and his work of reconciliation (see also Heb 1:2–3). Several words and ideas in the passage may indicate that the writer was addressing people with at least quasi-Gnostic views. One of these words is *plērōma*, translated as "fullness" (1:19; 2:9). It was a key term among Gnostics and referred to all the heavenly powers and spiritual emanations, or to their dwelling place. Exactly what the writer means by it is difficult to say, but his readers would understand. Its meaning is clarified somewhat in 2:9, where the writer adds the terms "deity" and "bodily." So "in him all the fullness [of God—not in the Greek text] was pleased to dwell" (1:19) may mean "in him the whole fullness of deity dwells bodily." With these phrases the writer counters the view that Jesus was only one of many emanations from God to the world. Jesus was the unique and total revelation of God, and therefore made all other intermediaries between God and humans unnecessary.

With reference to quasi-Gnostics among the syncretists at Colossae who may have denied the physical existence of Jesus, the expressions (literally) "by the blood of his cross" (1:20), "body of flesh" (1:22), and "bodily" (2:9) are significant. They not only bring out the sacrificial aspect of Christ's death, but emphasize his human nature.

Verses 15–19 stress the divinity and preexistence of Jesus, but the writer also emphasizes Jesus' humanity. Jesus was not just a spiritual phantom; he had a real body. It was this Jesus through whom "all things, whether on earth or in heaven," were reconciled.

The word for "reconcile" here is *apokatallassō*, which means "to change thoroughly or completely," and so "to reconcile completely." It differs from the word used in undisputed letters of Paul, and elsewhere in the NT it occurs only in Eph 2:16. There are two main problems of interpretation here that we do not have in Paul's letters. First, who does the reconciling? Is God through Christ (a Pauline idea in 2 Cor 5:19) reconciling all things to himself? Or is Christ reconciling all things to himself? The Greek may be interpreted either way. Second, what is included in the expression "all things, whether on earth or in heaven"? Reconciliation is broadened to include creatures in addition to humans—or even the whole universe. The verb "reconcile" normally refers only to people, not things. The writer uses it that way in 1:21–22 (see also Eph 2:15–16), so the idea of "all things" remains difficult.

Perhaps the writer of Colossians was influenced by the Jewish book of *Jubilees* and other Jewish writings. According to *Jub.* 3:28–29, Adam's sin made all the other animals unable to speak, although previously they had spoken with one another in one language. Rabbis believed that when Adam sinned heavenly bodies lost their light, animals no longer obeyed man, the courses of the planets changed, and that everything would remain out of order until the Messiah came. Perhaps the writer of Colossians or of the hymn was saying that the reconciliation of Christ, like the sin of Adam, had cosmic effects.

In Col 1:21–23 the writer applies the idea of reconciliation to the readers, mostly Gentiles, "who were once estranged and hostile in mind, doing evil deeds." Their reconciliation, however, depends upon their remaining in "the faith," the meaning of which is uncertain. Perhaps "the faith" is the developing religion and includes both belief and behavior.

The writer talks about himself as a minister according to divine commission, thus defending his ministry in un-Pauline terms. He makes known the mystery (secret) of Christ among mankind, especially Gentiles, in order to make every person mature in Christ (1:24–29). But how could the writer, who has just said that in Christ "all the fullness of God was pleased to dwell," say that in his own sufferings he completes for the church "what is lacking in Christ's afflictions"? In 2:1–7 the writer's concern extends even to churches he has not visited. He asks that they may be "united in love" and experience the secret of Christ so that no one may delude them, and he rejoices at the firmness of their faith in Christ.

III. Warnings against false teaching and religious practices that do nothing to check sin (2:8–3:4)

The writer elaborates on the theme of the superiority of Christ, a superiority that leaves no room for "philosophy and empty deceit," "the elemental spirits of the universe" (either elementary doctrines, angels, and demons, or heavenly bodies), legal demands, questions of food and drink, and self-abasement. Recall our discussion of these topics earlier. Here the writer refutes the syncretists openly and on their own terms, except that for him Christ has triumphed over all opposing powers by his death on the cross (2:8–23). We might expect that, since the NT developed amid Graeco-Roman culture, the term "philosophy" would occur often in it. But it occurs only in Col 2:8, where the writer equates it with "empty deceit." Verse 23 probably means that the religious regulations mentioned are taken to be a sign of wisdom because they are voluntarily practiced to the extreme, but actually they are of no value in checking immorality.

Col 3:1–4 makes a transition between the doctrinal and ethical sections. Believers must seek nobler things because they "have been raised with Christ" so that they may also "be revealed with him in glory." Does the writer believe that the Colossian believers already share in Christ's resurrection, or is he speaking metaphorically, as Paul does in regard to the concept of baptism? "You have died" (v 3) cannot be taken literally, so it may refer to baptism.

IV. Exhortations for moral living (3:5–4:6)

The superiority of Christ brings the challenge to new life. Philosophical concepts (faith) must be matched with moral life. This means the elimination of the more obvious and the more subtle sins (3:5–11). In their place believers must put "compassion, kindness, humility, meekness, and patience," forgiveness, and above all, "love, which binds everything together in perfect harmony" (3:12–14). Colossian believers should do everything—teach, admonish one another, and worship—in the name of Jesus (3:15–17). Col 3:18–4:1 (see also Eph 5:21–6:9; 1 Pet 2:13–3:7) is an example of what German scholars have called *Haustafeln*—literally, "house tablets" (of rules). These rules deal with household members, including slaves and masters, and their relationships with each other. The emphasis is on doing one's duty, not on exercising one's rights. For household rules see E. G. Selwyn 1969: 419–439, especially 423; D. L. Balch 1988; C. A. Osiek 1997.

Lists of exhortations and warnings for people in various life situations were current in both Jewish and pagan Hellenistic writings. Such lists were widely used for moral teaching in the ancient world, where the family was regarded as a miniature of society. Proper behavior within families was thought to insure the welfare of society. It is likely that early believers used such lists and gradually sanctified them by adding catch phrases such as "in the Lord" (Col 3:18). Later believers altered the lists further as seemed practical (see 1 Pet 2:11–3:12). Within a church, then, order in the various families would guarantee harmony in the believing community as a whole.

The writer exhorts the Colossians to pray for themselves and for him and to give thanks to God. They are to conduct themselves "wisely toward outsiders" and let their "speech always be gracious, seasoned with salt" ("witty," "wholesome," "interesting," "not dry" are suggested

meanings). "Seasoned with salt" really seems to mean "have a ready response"; the idea is that the readers may know how to answer those who challenge them.

V. Closing greetings, signature, and blessing (4:7–18)

For further study of Colossians see commentaries by F. F. Bruce 1984; E. Schweizer 1982; R. P. Martin 1981; A. G. Patzia 1984; P. Pokorny 1991; for Paul's opponents see R. E. DeMaris 1994; J. D. G. Dunn 1995a; T. W. Martin 1996; C. E. Arnold 1996.

EPHESIANS

THE CITY OF EPHESUS

Ephesus was one of the most important places of Paul's work. It was the leading city in the district of Ionia, which was in the Roman province of Asia on the west coast of Asia Minor. Ephesus was on the main route between Rome and the East and was a hub where many secondary roads converged. Its location made Ephesus one of the greatest trade centers and, with Antioch in Syria and Alexandria, one of the greatest cities in the eastern Mediterranean world. In 133 BCE western Asia Minor became a Roman province, and except for a brief time, Ephesus remained subject to Rome. As a Roman city, along with Jerusalem, Antioch, and Rome herself, Ephesus became a capital city of the early first century CE. It remained a chief city of Asia Minor long after Paul's time.

J. T. Wood began excavations of Ephesus for the British Museum in 1863. He found a Roman inscription from the second century CE that told how, in celebration of the birthday of the goddess Artemis, several images of gold and silver (see Acts 19:24) were carried in procession from the temple to the theater. The inscription also said that the procession should enter the city by one gate and leave through another. Fortunately, Wood located the two city gates. He then followed

FIGURE 13.2
*Harbor street leading
to the theater in
Ephesus.*

the road through the gate and kept going until he came to the temple. Through Wood's work and that of others, we have learned about the main parts of the city in Paul's time, though most of the remains are from a later time.

The temple of Artemis was called the Artemision and stood until 262 CE, when it was destroyed by the Goths. It was more than 340 feet long and 160 feet wide, and had 100 columns about 60 feet high. Large white marble tiles covered the roof. The building was furnished with sculpture and paintings from famous artists of antiquity and decorated with gold leaf (Strabo, 14:1:23). The impressiveness of the temple may have suggested to Paul the figure of God's building in 1 Cor 3:9–16 (written from Ephesus); Paul concludes here by saying to the Corinthians, "Do you not know that you are God's temple and that God's Spirit dwells in you?"

From the Artemision a street ran west and slightly south for about a mile to one of the city gates. The first structure along the way was the ancient stadium, where races, athletic events, and gladiatorial contests were held. South of the stadium was the great theater (see Figure 13.2); located on the slope of a hill overlooking the city, it faced westward toward the harbor. The stage,

orchestra, and seating area for more than 24,500 people have been excavated, but the remains represent a period of construction later than Paul's time. According to Acts 19:23–41, the theater was the place of the near riot of the silversmiths and others instigated by Demetrius. He was protesting the effectiveness of Paul's preaching, which threatened the silversmiths' business and the worship of Artemis.

The main street of Ephesus was a beautiful thoroughfare of paved marble and led from the theater to the harbor. It was lined with stores and other buildings. Paul probably walked along a similar street to the center of the city and its many buildings, including baths, gymnasiums, and monuments. The agora of Paul's time was Roman and lay to the south of the theater, but present ruins are mostly from the early third century. The agora was a large, open, rectangular area enclosed by important public buildings and by colonnades through which one entered by beautiful gateways. Near the agora are remains of a library and other temples that probably date from the second century. (See Figure 13.3.) Although many of the present archaeological finds are later than Paul's time, the plan of the city and its important struc-

FIGURE 13.3   *Looking across marble street to temple of Hadrian in Ephesus.*

tures were probably about the same in his time as we have described them.

FOUNDING OF THE CHURCH AT EPHESUS

If Acts is trustworthy, Paul did not make the first converts at Ephesus, because when he arrived there, "he found some disciples" (19:1). They were not familiar with Paul's method of receiving converts. When Paul asked them if they had received the Holy Spirit when they believed, they said, "No, we have not even heard that there is a Holy Spirit." So Paul asked them what they had been baptized into, and they said into John's baptism. Paul then reminded them that John had baptized for repentance and had told people to believe in Jesus. Paul baptized the Ephesian disciples in the name of the Lord Jesus; and when he laid his hands on them, "the Holy Spirit came upon them" (Acts 19:1–6). Since the word "dis-

ciples" is used for followers of Jesus, its use here may mean that these people had become converts without any rite of initiation. Perhaps they, like Apollos, "had been instructed [orally] in the Way of the Lord" (18:24–25). These people became the nucleus of the church at Ephesus.

Paul entered the synagogue and tried to persuade Jews to follow Jesus; but they were as stubborn as Paul was eager, so his preaching was not successful (19:8–10). Perhaps the Ephesians regarded Paul as just another teacher of some new philosophical ideas, so he was permitted to use the hall of Tyrannus. Paul's public lectures were probably supplemented by private teaching in the homes of receptive listeners.

Although Paul stayed at Ephesus about three years, we know almost nothing of his activity there. The stories in Acts, though interesting, tell us little. Only indirectly from Paul's letters can we learn something about his work at Ephesus. According to 1 Cor 16:8–9, Paul was in Ephesus when he wrote to Corinth. He says, "But I will stay in Ephesus until Pentecost, for a wide door for effective work has opened to me, and there are many adversaries." Three things are clear: Paul was in Ephesus when he wrote 1 Corinthians, he had an opportunity for effective work there, and there was severe opposition to it.

Two other passages in Paul's letters give the impression that his work at Ephesus was carried on under difficulty. First, the passage in 1 Cor 15:32 about fighting with wild animals at Ephesus, whether taken literally or figuratively, indicates difficulty of some kind either in the arena with beasts or in the hall of public debate. Moral philosophers of Paul's time used the expression fighting "with wild animals" to describe their struggle against hedonistic society (A. J. Malherbe 1968), and perhaps Paul used it with reference to a group of hedonists at Ephesus. Second, in 2 Cor 1:8 Paul says, "We do not want you to be unaware, brothers, of the affliction we experienced in Asia; for we were so utterly, unbearably crushed that we despaired of life itself." If Paul is here referring to his experience at Ephesus, it must have been pretty bad.

On the basis of these passages, some scholars have concluded that Paul was in prison while in

Ephesus and that at least some of the prison letters were written from there. At any rate, Paul's situation at Ephesus may have been much worse than the writer of Acts implies, although the indirect evidence for Paul's work at Ephesus seems to indicate that it was successful. The church there originated under difficulty but grew into a central structure from which the developing religion spread to surrounding regions.

THE PROBLEM OF AUTHENTICITY

Ephesians purports to be from Paul (1:1; 3:1), and Paul's authorship was not questioned before the beginning of the nineteenth century. Since then, however, an increasing number of scholars, even many who regard Colossians as genuine, reject Paul's authorship. Here are their main arguments, with counterarguments by those who support Pauline authorship.

Words and Phrases

More than eighty words, such as *klydōnizō* (translated as "tossed to and fro"—4:14), "likeness" (4:24), and "debauchery" (5:18) occur nowhere in Paul's undisputed letters. And certain words such as "mystery," *oikonomia* (translated as "plan" in 1:10 and 3:9 and as "commission" in 3:2), and "fullness" are used in different senses in Ephesians. Defenders of Paul's authorship say these observations are misleading because a number of the words are closely related to words Paul uses and because many new words occur in only one letter or another. Moreover, they say it is silly to think Paul would use the same vocabulary in every letter, when in fact he frequently coins new words to express new ideas.

Style

In contrast to the undisputed letters, Ephesians is slow-moving and is encumbered with very long sentences (see, for example, 1:3–14; 1:15–23; 2:1–10), use of synonyms, participles, and relative clauses. Look at Eph 1:15–23 for a good example of the writer's long sentences, translated intact in the *RSV* but broken down into four in the *NRSV.* Other stylistic features are the use of cognate noun and verb (for example, "the great love with which he loved us" in 2:4); synonymous words connected by "and" (for example, "holy and blameless" in 1:4); and near synonyms, with the first followed by the genitive of the other (for example, "the praise of his glory" in 1:12). (For a nontechnical discussion of style, see H. J. Cadbury 1959:91–102; G. B. Caird 1976:15–17; M. Barth 1974:1:4–6.)

Certain stylistic traits of Paul, such as the use of questions, are noticeably lacking in Ephesians. In 8¾ pages of Greek text Ephesians has 1 question, compared with 92 in 26 pages of Romans, 100 in 24 pages of 1 Corinthians, 27 in 16¾ pages of 2 Corinthians, and 16 in 8¼ pages of Galatians (P. N. Harrison 1964:43). Defenders of Pauline authorship point out, however, that except for the argumentative sections in Paul's letters, there are also few questions. Furthermore, although the style of Ephesians does differ from that of Paul's letters, this is exactly what we should expect from a "great stylist" like Paul. All the stylistic traits of Ephesians, in fact, can be found in Paul's (other) letters. Moreover, Ephesians is a religious tract or meditation, not a letter quickly written to meet some problem demanding immediate response. In prison Paul had lots of time to think new thoughts and write in new ways.

Literary Relationships

There are close literary relationships between Ephesians and all of Paul's letters, but especially Colossians. We can observe the latter relationship even in English translation by comparing, for example, Eph 1:1 with Col 1:1–2; 1:4; and 1:22; 1:7 with 1:14 and 1:20; 2:5 with 2:13; and 4:2 with 3:12–13. Compare also Eph 1:11 with Rom 8:28, 30 and 1 Cor 12:6; Eph 3:8 with 1 Cor 15:9 and Gal 1:16; and Eph 3:12 with Rom 5:1–2 and 2 Cor 3:4, 12. Most scholars (exceptions are F. C. Synge 1959 and J. Coutts

1958) think the writer of Ephesians borrowed from Colossians, especially because more than a quarter of the words in Colossians reappear in Ephesians. However, a counterargument is that Col 4:7–9 and Eph 6:21–22 mention Tychicus as the bearer of both letters, so Ephesians was written about the time when Paul was thinking about similar things. The differences are due to Colossians being written to one church to deal with heresy and Ephesians being written to all of Paul's churches to tell about the sufficiency of Christ. The parallels of Ephesians with Pauline letters are given in English in E. J. Goodspeed 1956. Advanced readers should see C. L. Mitton 1951:55–110; his shorter commentary of 1973 is very helpful. For a list of topical parallels between Colossians and Ephesians see C. B. Puskas 1993:130–131; for an extensive list printed out see J. Moffatt 1918:375–381.

Eschatology

Expressions such as "in the ages to come" (2:7) and "to all generations" (3:21) indicate that the writer of Ephesians believed there would be a long time ahead, but Paul thought the End was coming soon. Defenders of Pauline authorship point out, though, that in Galatians there is only one reference to the End (5:5), and that in Romans 11 Paul says he expects all Jews and Gentiles to be saved.

Ecclesiology

The idea that the church is "built upon the foundation of the apostles and prophets" (2:20) contradicts Paul's statement in 1 Cor 3:11 that "no one can lay any foundation other than the one that has been laid; that foundation is Jesus Christ." The passage in Ephesians may mean that Paul and other early church leaders were dead. But some scholars contend that in Ephesians Paul is writing to combat the heretical teachers who were leaders of other religions; therefore, he wanted to emphasize proper apostleship and prophecy. Moreover, Paul uses metaphors differently in other letters. For ex-

ample, in 1 Cor 3:16 the Corinthians as a community "are God's temple," whereas in 1 Cor 6:19 the body of each Corinthian is "a temple of the Holy Spirit within you."

Theology

The expression "by grace you have been saved" (2:5, 8) occurs nowhere in Paul's letters, and the word "save" is used in past tenses, whereas Paul uses it with reference to the future. But some scholars argue that salvation for Paul is "a past fact, a present experience, and a future hope, and it requires all three tenses for its adequate expression" (G. B. Caird 1976:21).

Historical Situation

In Ephesians the church is an institution, the universal church, whereas for Paul it is a local community or congregation. Thus, Ephesians reflects a time later than Paul. But defenders of Pauline authorship reply that in a letter meant for all churches, Paul would naturally think of the church as an official body and of church officials in the life of the church.

Eph 2:11–12 (see also 3:2; 4:17) indicates that the work is addressed to Gentile converts. The controversy between Jewish and Gentile believers, so marked in Paul's letters, is over; this indicates a time later than Paul. Critics reply that Paul is concerned with theological and ecclesiastical matters for Gentile believers, not with Jewish attacks against Gentiles. Moreover, the "we" of 1:12 speaks for Jewish converts, and Paul writes of the union of Gentiles and Jews as a people and community of God in Christ (2:11–3:6).

Lack of Personal Touch

Ephesians is a very impersonal letter. There are no greetings, and only one name—Tychicus—is mentioned. Moreover, in 1:15 and 3:2 the writer speaks of having heard about the Ephesians' faith, and of them having heard about his "commission of God's grace." These passages imply a lack of personal contact between the writer and the people in a city where Paul had spent about three years. Supporters of Pauline authorship reply that the letter was meant to circulate widely, so personal greetings would naturally be lacking.

Having learned about the main arguments for and against the authenticity of Ephesians, what can we conclude about the authorship of Ephesians? There are several answers to this question.

AUTHORSHIP, PLACE OF WRITING, PURPOSE, AND DATE

Scholars who maintain that Paul wrote Ephesians accept the statements of Pauline authorship (1:1; 3:1) and of Paul's imprisonment (3:1; 4:1; 6:20). They believe that the likenesses and differences in language and thought reflect a person trying to remember what he had said before, but not one imitating Paul. No one else could have written so much like Paul and yet in such an original and different way. Although more developed in Ephesians than in other letters, the ideas are nevertheless Paul's own.

Many who regard Paul as the author of Ephesians think Ephesians was an encyclical letter, that is, one written for general circulation. In the oldest manuscripts of Ephesians, the words "in Ephesus," present in later manuscripts, are lacking in 1:1 (as in the *NRSV*; see note). The space was left blank so that the name of each church addressed could be added. But critics reply that there is no other evidence for that practice in antiquity. That the words "in Ephesus" are missing in the best manuscripts and that the letter is so impersonal support the view of an encyclical letter, whether written by Paul or someone else. If Ephesians is one of Paul's "prison letters," it was written either from Caesarea in the late 50s or from Rome in the early 60s.

Some scholars think evidence from language, style, and thought is insufficient to indicate that Ephesians was written after Paul's death. Although not written by Paul, they say, it was writ-

ten by someone devoted to Paul and thoroughly familiar with his vocabulary, style of speaking, and thought. It is usually suggested that this person traveled with Paul and wrote his letters. Paul told him the topics of the letter; then the person wrote up his own notes, which Paul approved and signed, and they sent out the letter.

Most scholars seem to regard the letter as pseudonymous, that is, written by someone later than Paul who used Paul's name. The most widely known pseudonymity theory is that of E. J. Goodspeed 1933:3–17, 1937:222–239 and J. Knox 1960. According to this theory, the letters of Paul had fallen into disuse, but the publication of Luke-Acts about 90 CE, by an author who did not know Paul's letters, brought about a renewed interest in the letters. One of Paul's friends who was thoroughly familiar with Colossians began a search for other letters. He visited the churches of Paul mentioned in Acts, collected some letters, and added them to Colossians and Philemon, which he already possessed. With Paul's letters in front of him, Onesimus, the runaway slave of Philemon, wrote Ephesians to serve as an introduction to the corpus (collection) of Paul's letters, which he wanted to share with others. Especially familiar with Colossians, Onesimus used much of its material with words and phrases from other letters. He was "the earliest student of the letters of Paul—indeed, we may truly say, the first interpreter of them. His own letter . . . is in a sense a commentary upon them." Ephesians served as "a stirring call to unity among the churches," which were threatened with heretical movements after the publication of Luke-Acts. Because Acts does not mention Colossae, a collector would not have gone there. So perhaps Ephesians was written from Ephesus, where Onesimus became bishop. Many scholars subscribe to Goodspeed and Knox's view either in whole or in part.

Some scholars strongly object to the views of Goodspeed and Knox because (1) they believe that Ephesians has its own themes and is not just a summary of Paul's ideas, (2) there is no evidence that it ever was first in the sequence of Paul's letters, and (3) Ephesians is not the only clue to the many questions concerning the collecting, editing, and distribution of Paul's letters. (For critical evaluations of Goodspeed's view, see C. L. Mitton 1951:45–54, 1955; and C. F. D. Moule 1958:14–21; for other possible purposes of Ephesians, see G. H. P. Thompson 1967:16–20. R. P. Martin 1968 suggests that, because of the similarities between Ephesians and Luke-Acts, Luke wrote Ephesians. E. Best 1997 suggests that the authors of Ephesians and Colossians belonged to the same Pauline school. That accounts for the likenesses and differences between the two letters. Perhaps the two authors had even discussed together Paul's theological views.

It is difficult to evaluate the arguments for and against the Pauline authorship of Ephesians. In light of present evidence, perhaps the most objective position is to leave the problem unsolved. We ask questions that the writers and readers of ancient documents could not even have understood, let alone answered. That makes our task more difficult. Well-informed students and scholars should never be embarrassed to say that they cannot decide. After all, it is not easy to decide between Paul, who diverges from his own style only a little, and an imitator who reproduces most of Paul's style. In your mind, try to compare Ephesians with the undisputed letters of Paul as you read it now.

Outline and Comments

I. Greeting, blessing, and thanksgiving prayer (1:1–23)

After the greeting (1:1–2), there is a blessing (1:3–14) like that of a Jewish *berakah* ("blessing," as in 2 Cor 1:3–4; in a *berakah* a person praises God for something the person has done or desires). The writer continues this mood until the end of chap. 3. He praises God for redemption, which had been planned before creation so that the readers might be "holy and blameless" before God. To this end, they were destined by God "for adoption as his children" and to be redeemed through Christ's blood (1:3–8).

Through Christ God purposed to unite all people (1:9–10), and this is the theme of most of the letter. Through Christ, Jews first became believers, and that blessing has been extended also to Gentiles under the guarantee of the Holy Spirit (1:11–14). "The gospel of your salvation" (v 13) refers to the divine favor bestowed upon the readers as Gentiles, who were given the opportunity to hear the good news of salvation.

The writer thanks God for the Ephesians' faith and prays that they may know God, know the hope for the future (judgment), appreciate their present status, and know the power of God in Christ through Christ's resurrection and his superiority "over all things for the church, which is his body" (1:15–23). The words "wisdom," "revelation," and "know" (v 17) would be familiar not only to Gnostics, but also to Jews familiar with the OT and with first-century Judaism. "The eyes of your heart enlightened" may seem strange. In biblical thought the heart signifies the whole inner being, including understanding and will. In this expression the writer may have in mind the readers' spiritual enlightenment, or perhaps their baptism. The words translated "the working of his great power" (1:19–20) do not convey the writer's style. The Greek words are *energeian*, a noun, and *enērgēsen*, a verb; the verb picks up the sound and sense of the noun. The equivalent in English would be "the energy that he energized."

II. Gentile converts and God's grace (2:1–3:21)

A. Their salvation by grace (2:1–10)

The pagan life of the Gentiles is expressed in moral and mythological imagery. Before becoming converts, the Gentiles lived immoral lives. "Walked" (Greek) is a common Jewish expression for "conducted their lives." "Sons of disobedience" (Greek) is an idiom meaning "disobedient people" (see "children of wrath"). "The ruler of the power of the air" reflects the current cosmology (doctrine of the world) and mythology, and is probably a title for Satan. The "air" was the layer of the cosmos next to the earth in which demons ruled by Satan lived. The writer may be speaking metaphorically of the immoral conditions from which mankind wants to be saved. From these conditions "we"—meaning Jews as well as Gentiles—were saved by God's great love or grace.

The combination of "grace," "save," and "faith" does not occur in undisputed letters of Paul. The combinations of "justify" and "grace" and "justify" and "faith" do occur in Paul (see, for example, Rom 3:24, 28), but not the combination "to be saved" and "faith" and "grace," as here. So we could substitute "justified" for "saved" and have Paul's meaning precisely. In fact, the writer may replace Paul's characteristic term "to justify," which does not occur in Ephesians, with "to save." The use of the past tense ("saved") with reference to salvation is quite unlike Paul. He prefers the future or present passive ("being saved") in order to represent salvation as a continuing process that will culminate in the future.

B. Their pagan state, their reconciliation through Christ and what it means (2:11–22)

The theme of this section is that Gentile as well as Jewish believers now belong to the people of God (the church). Jews thought the human race was divided into two groups, the Jews and the rest of mankind. The covenant of circumcision—traditionally a Jewish rite since Abraham—dietary laws, sabbath observance, and the hatred of idols set Jews apart from non-Jews. Jews referred to non-Jews as Gentiles, or "the nations," and the "uncircumcision." Circumcision and other "commandments and ordinances" (2:15) had strengthened the Jews' conviction that they were God's special people, "the commonwealth of Israel" (2:12), and therefore different from others. At the same time, that conviction caused anti-Jewish feelings among Gentiles.

In Ephesians 2 the writer thinks of his religious experience during which the seemingly irresoluble hostility between Jews and Gentiles has been overcome. For the first time in history, Christ has made that possible by "putting to death that hostility" (2:16). That hostility, one of

the most intense in the ancient world, separated not only Jew and Gentile from one another, but also, according to the writer of Ephesians, both from God. Now all are "members of the household of God [the church] . . . with Christ Jesus himself as the cornerstone" (2:19–20).

The words "the dividing wall" (lit., "the wall between") may allude to the stone wall that set off the inner part of the temple, into which only Jews could go, from the outer court. Gentiles were permitted in the outer court, but if they went beyond it they faced the threat of death. Josephus writes that stone slabs with Greek and Latin inscriptions warned foreigners that, because of the law of purification, they were not permitted to enter the holy place (*War* 5:5:2; *Ant.* 15:11:5). One of those slabs was discovered in the last century and is now in a museum in Istanbul. The Greek inscription reads: "No foreigner is to enter within the restraining railing around the sanctuary. Whoever is apprehended will have himself to blame for his death which follows."

The words "brought near" and "peace to you who were far off and peace to those who were near" (2:13, 17) show influence from Judaism, going back to Isaiah. With Eph 2:13, 17 compare Isa 57:19: "Peace, peace, to the far and to the near, says the Lord; and I will heal them." Isaiah was referring to Jews of the Diaspora, who were far from or near to Jerusalem. In Judaism the expressions "to be far from" and "to bring near" were sometimes used with reference to sinners who were far from God but brought themselves near to God when they repented.

Although the writer of Ephesians was probably a Jew who was influenced by the language and thought of Judaism, he had something special as a convert: the experience of Christ in his life, which he believed was made possible "by the blood of Christ . . . through the cross" (2:13, 16). The idea of atonement through blood was itself a Jewish concept (see Eph 1:7).

With the expressions "both groups into one" (2:14) and "one new humanity in place of the two" (2:15) the writer says that Jews and Gentiles share a new unity without distinction. This is the result of Christ's work with respect to the law, which he abolished "in his flesh"—perhaps by his manner of life as well as by his death. Paul speaks of the individual believer as a "new creation" (2 Cor 5:17), but in Ephesians the transformation is applied to the community of believers as a whole, in which Jews and Gentiles share a new relationship yet retain their separate identities as persons—"in the flesh" (2:11). This relationship is a triangular one in which Jews and Gentiles have been reconciled not only to each other but to God—"both groups to God in one body" (2:16).

The word for "reconcile" is the same as that in Col 1:20, 22 (*apokatallassō*) and means "to change thoroughly" or "to reconcile completely." Although both Jews and Gentiles retain separate identities as persons, they have become so reconciled through Christ that they both "have access in one Spirit to the Father" (2:18). The word "access" (*prosagōgē*) is forceful and means the act of bringing someone to someone else or of introducing one person to another. It was used especially for presenting a person to a monarch. Christ has provided those who are reconciled to each other the necessary introductions to God.

In the final verses of chap. 2 the writer's thought comes to a climax. The community of believers is "one new humanity," "the household of God" (the church); united in Christ, it "grows into a holy temple in the Lord . . . into a dwelling place for God" (2:20–22).

C. The writer's part in bringing Christ to the Gentiles, a prayer, and a doxology (3:1–21)

The writer ("Paul," in 3:1) received a revelation that Gentiles were to be "fellow heirs [with Jews], members of the same body." In mythological terms the writer says that even "the rulers and authorities" (see 1:21; 6:12) should become aware of the mystery of Christ through the church (3:1–13). Perhaps the "rulers and authorities" were good and evil beings thought to reside above the earth, forces opposed to the welfare of humans, or heavenly bodies—all of which the ancients thought had some control over human lives. In 3:14–19 the writer prays that God may give the readers spiritual strength, that Christ may dwell in their hearts, and that they may know God's limitless love. Verses 20–21 are a doxology (a giving of glory to God).

III. Exhortations for moral living (4:1–6:20)
A. Exhortation to lead lives "worthy of the calling" that believers have received (4:1–16)

Moral life can be achieved through patience, meekness, and love. The objective is unity of the Spirit in the ministry for Christ. Verse 8 is an inaccurate quotation from Ps 68:18 and does not seem to fit the context. Several interpretations have been given for vv 9–10: "the descent of Christ to the place of the dead between his crucifixion and resurrection" (see Rom 10:7; 1 Pet 4:6), "the earth itself," "an assurance of the reality of the incarnation," and the return of Christ after his ascension "at Pentecost to bestow his spiritual gifts upon the Church" (J. L. Houlden 1977:310–311).

B. Exhortation not to live like pagan Gentiles (4:17–5:2)

Verses 22–24 say it all: "You were taught to put away your former way of life, your old self, corrupt and deluded by its lusts, and to be renewed in the spirit of your minds, and to clothe yourselves with the new self, created according to the likeness of God in true righteousness and holiness" (see also 5:1–2). This renewal is made possible by following the teaching of Jesus referred to in vv 20–21.

C. Exhortation to avoid immorality, silly talk, deceiving words, and drunkenness, and to practice what is pleasing to God (5:3–20)

Eph 5:14 may come from a hymn, perhaps from one of those referred to in v 19 (see also 1 Tim 3:16). Perhaps the hymn was used in baptism liturgies, since in baptism converts died and rose symbolically with Christ. The use of "shine on you" may be symbolic of good, and "awake" may then refer to the passing from the old life into the new. The following verse—which begins, "Be careful then how you live"—seems to support this interpretation.

> D. *Exhortation to practice the family virtues (5:21–6:9)*
>
> E. *Exhortation to put on the armor of God (6:10–17)*

Believers are to prepare for spiritual warfare, not against human foes but against spiritual powers and cosmic forces. These forces are "the wiles of the devil" and all of his allies. The imagery for the armor is derived from Jewish wisdom sources (see Isa 59:17; Wis 5:17–20; Sir 46:6).

> F. *Exhortation to pray for themselves and the author and to be alert (6:18–20)*
>
> IV. *Commendation of Tychicus and benediction (6:21–24)*

For further study of Ephesians see commentaries by C. L. Mitton 1973; A. T. Lincoln 1990; M. Barth 1974; L. Kreitzer 1997; P. Perkins 1997; W. L. Liefeld 1996; E. Best 1998; H. Koester 1995, for religious cults.

2 THESSALONIANS

THE PROBLEM OF AUTHENTICITY

Most scholars think Paul wrote 2 Thessalonians, but because some reject its authenticity, we will treat it as a disputed letter of Paul. The debate centers around one important question: How could the same person write a letter so similar to and yet so different from one he wrote to the same church? Various answers to the question are based on the following points.

Words and Phrases

About 146 words are common to 1 and 2 Thessalonians, and there are many parallel phrases.

Notice these parallels: the opening greetings are closer than those in any other two letters—"We must always give thanks to God for you" (2 Thess 1:3) and "We always give thanks to God for all of you" (1 Thess 1:2); "work of faith" (2 Thess 1:11; 1 Thess 1:3); "who do not know God" (2 Thess 1:8; 1 Thess 4:5); "obtaining the glory of our Lord Jesus Christ" (2 Thess 2:14) and "obtain salvation through our Lord Jesus Christ" (1 Thess 5:9); "with toil and labor we worked night and day, so that we might not burden any of you" (2 Thess 3:8; 1 Thess 2:9); and "for even when we were with you" (2 Thess 3:10; 1 Thess 3:4). On the other hand, in 2 Thessalonians there are many words and phrases that occur nowhere else in Paul. Expressions such as "we must always give thanks" (1:3; 2:13), "shaken in mind" (2:2), "believed the truth" (2:12), and "spread rapidly" (3:1) are non-Pauline. Those who reject Pauline authorship of 2 Thessalonians say the parallels mentioned prove a literary dependence on 1 Thessalonians.

Defenders of Pauline authorship respond that the parallels prove nothing, that they reflect Paul writing two letters to the same church after only a short interval, and that many of the same or similar expressions are found elsewhere in Paul's letters. Moreover, critics point out that of the 146 common words, all but four appear in the "great letters" of Paul, that two of the four appear in the prison epistles, and that one of the other two is "Thessalonians." And every letter contains some words not found elsewhere in Paul. In fact, about 88 percent of the words in both 1 and 2 Thessalonians are Pauline if the two letters are compared with the other eight letters.

Style

The letter lacks warmth and affection and is cold and formal. Formal expressions such as "we must always give thanks" (1:3) and "as is right" (1:3) are not characteristic of Paul. But defenders of Pauline authorship reply that if we ignore Paul's defense of himself in 1 Thess 2:1–12, the difference in tone is insignificant; 2 Thessalonians is equally warm and even more tactful. The writer refers to the readers as "brothers," asks for their prayers (3:1–2), and is polite and mild in dealing with the situation (3:6–16), especially with offenders. Compared with 1 Thess 2:16, 2 Thess 3:15 is mild.

References to Another Letter (2 Thess 2:2, 15; 3:14, 17)

These references are suspect for three reasons, not counting the grammatical difficulties involved. First, it is unlikely that forged letters would appear in Paul's lifetime (2:2). Second, the signature in 3:17 is a fake intended to give the impression of authenticity and would be more appropriate in a first than in a second letter. Third, if Paul had already written to the Thessalonians, they would recognize his writing. The only valid reply to all of this seems to be that in both Gal 6:11 and 2 Thess 3:17 the author uses the same expression, "with my own hand," to confirm his identity.

Structure

The writer follows the structure or outline of 1 Thessalonians so closely that clearly he was using it as a model. For example, "we must always give thanks" in 2 Thess 2:13 repeats 2 Thess 1:3 in the same way that 1 Thess 2:13 repeats 1 Thess 1:2. Defenders of Paul's authorship reply that in 1 Thessalonians there are three thanksgivings (1:2; 2:13; 3:9) but only two in 2 Thessalonians (1:3; 2:13). And there are two prayers in 1 Thessalonians (3:11–13; 5:23) but three in 2 Thessalonians (2:16–17; 3:5, 16). These examples and others like them raise the question of why there would be such noticeable differences if a writer were following 1 Thessalonians as a model.

Eschatology

The differing eschatologies of the two letters are a major reason for regarding 2 Thessalonians as non-Pauline. In 1 Thess 5:1–10 "the day of the Lord" (Parousia) will come suddenly—"like a thief in the night"—so the readers must behave properly and not be unprepared. But according to 2 Thess 2:1–12 there will be a series of events before that day comes, so the readers cannot be unprepared. Such a delay conflicts with Paul's thought not only in 1 Thess 4:15–17 and 5:1–4, but also in 1 Cor 7:29; Phil 4:5; and Rom 13:11–12, where the End is near. But as some suggest, Paul could have changed his mind between the times he wrote. But then why, in later dealing with eschatological expectations in 1 Corinthians, Romans, and Philippians, would Paul write as in 1 Thessalonians and not as in 2 Thessalonians? He could have changed his mind again, but that is not a satisfactory explanation. A better explanation is that Paul did not write 2 Thessalonians.

The concepts of "the rebellion"—whatever is meant—"the man of lawlessness," "restraining him," and "the son of destruction" occur nowhere in Paul's letters. The last three expressions may refer to the Antichrist, a mythological creature that will appear before the Parousia to oppress believers but will be destroyed by Christ when Christ returns. Or they may reflect the belief current in the Roman world that the dead Nero would return as an even more wicked character. Both ideas reflect a time later than Paul.

Defenders of Paul's authorship, however, find evidence to refute the arguments from eschatology. The differences in the concepts, they say, are more apparent than real. For example, in 1 Thess 5:1 Paul uses "the times and the seasons" as a technical term familiar to the readers. This refers to a series of events, not just one, and shows that Paul had taught his readers about events that would happen before the Parousia. So in 2 Thess 2:1–12 Paul only reminds the readers of those events. Some people had become overeager about the End, so Paul had to calm them down by emphasizing signs. Actually, the words "the mystery of lawlessness is already at work" (2 Thess 2:7) indicate that the escalator is moving as in 1 Thessalonians, but just a little slower. Moreover, the common point in the letters is that God alone determines the time of the End (1 Thess 5:9; 2 Thess 2:11). In apocalyptic thought, the ideas of suddenness and signs are combined, as in Mark 13:32–36 and 13:5–23, for example. With respect to "the man of lawlessness," defenders of Pauline authorship point out that such a figure was a part of apocalyptic thought before Paul. And of course they deny that there is any reference to the idea of Nero's return, simply because of the lack of evidence.

Theology

In Paul's letters the concept of the Spirit is always prominent, but in 2 Thessalonians it rarely appears, and it never has the same meaning as for Paul. In "by spirit or by word" (2:2), "spirit" may mean a "prophetic pronouncement" or "rumor" or "report." In 2:8 it has its basic meaning of "breath." And it is difficult to tell whether in 2:13, in "sanctification by the Spirit" (lit., "sanctification of spirit"), "spirit" is that of humans or of God (in contrast, see 1 Thess 1:5–6; 4:8; 5:19).

The most important Pauline doctrine is that of the death and resurrection of Jesus. Although in 1 Thessalonians the only reference to it is in the early formulation "we believe that Jesus died and rose again" (4:14), there is no reference to Jesus' death and resurrection in 2 Thessalonians. It is difficult to explain this. However, some respond by saying that Paul was not addressing a theological controversy but a mistaken view about "the day of the Lord."

Finally, the writer of 2 Thessalonians sometimes replaces the word God in 1 Thessalonians with the title "Lord" to refer to Jesus. The best example is 2 Thess 2:13, where "beloved by God" from 1 Thess 1:4 is "beloved by the Lord." This may reflect a liturgical development later than Paul's time.

AUTHORSHIP AND PURPOSE

Who wrote 2 Thessalonians and why? The usual view is that Paul wrote the letter after someone brought him a second report from Thessalonica. Although there is no reference to the weak and faint hearted (1 Thess 5:14) in 2 Thessalonians, and although 2 Thess 1:3—"your faith is growing abundantly"—shows an improvement over 1 Thessalonians, the first letter had not accomplished all Paul intended. On the basis of the letter itself, a threefold purpose emerges: to encourage those who were suffering (1:4), to correct a distorted view of the Parousia (2:1–2), and to admonish the idle or disorderly (3:6, 11). The writer's responses are "It is indeed just of God to repay with affliction those who afflict you" (1:6); "that day will not come unless the rebellion comes first . . ." (2:3); and "Anyone unwilling to work should not eat" (3:10).

Realizing the difficulties in ascribing 2 Thessalonians to Paul, those who maintain his authorship do so in various ways. Some say that Paul kept a customary rough draft of the first letter to the Thessalonians and then used it when he wrote the second. But others say there is no evidence for such a practice. Some say the difficulties can be lessened, if not resolved, by reversing the sequence of the letters. For example, they suggest that 1 Thess 5:1—"you do not need to have anything written to you"—makes better sense if the readers had already read 2 Thess 2:3–10. Also, the emphasis on genuineness in 2 Thess 3:17 is more fitting in a first letter. But defenders of the present sequence reply, for example, that the reference to spiritual growth in 2 Thess 1:3 implies that 2 Thessalonians is a later letter, and that 2 Thess 2:2, 15 implies an earlier letter. Of course, those who would reverse the sequence say that 2 Thess 2:2, 15 refer to a lost letter.

A few scholars have subscribed to the view that Paul wrote letters at about the same time to two different groups, one Gentiles, the other Jews. The groups may have been in Thessalonica, or perhaps in Philippi or Beroea. One Thess 1:9 indicates that only Gentiles are addressed, but 2 Thessalonians is meant for Jews (see 1:6–10; 2:1–12). The ones chosen "from the beginning" (2 Thess 2:13), the first converts, include Jews. And the remark in 1 Thess 5:27 that the letter is to "be read to all the brothers" implies more than one group.

Those who reject the suggestion of two different groups reply, for example, that both letters are addressed to "the church [singular] of the Thessalonians" and that "all the brothers" means the whole church, not separate churches. Moreover, the expressions "our being gathered together" in 2 Thess 2:1 and "God did not call us" in 1 Thess 4:7 are similar and could not refer to congregations in different cities. And the idea that Paul would write letters to two different groups at the same place strongly conflicts with his view elsewhere that "there is no longer Jew or Greek" (Gal 3:28; see also 1 Cor 12:13; Rom 10:12).

Perhaps I can best summarize the views of those who maintain Pauline authorship in this way. Paul wrote every letter to meet a specific situation—Corinthians to correct wrong practices, Galatians to resolve the trouble with the Judaizers, Romans to delineate the Christian religion. He wrote 2 Thessalonians to inform a new church that was facing persecution, differences of opinion, and improper conduct. Changing and developing his ideas to meet new situations, Paul wrote to Thessalonica to address the situation there, not to reveal the state of his own theology. His language and style were also determined by the situation.

R. Jewett 1986 has considered arguments against Pauline authorship of 2 Thessalonians; he counters the arguments and asserts the authenticity of the letter because of weaknesses in the arguments against it. Jewett maintains that "the marks of authentic use of Pauline vocabulary, style and argumentative form are sufficiently extensive that any forgery hypothesis is hard to sustain" (17). Now read again what M. Y. MacDonald 1989 says about the authenticity of several of Paul's letters, including 2 Thessalonians, in the beginning of this chapter.

Those who reject Pauline authorship cannot be sure who wrote 2 Thessalonians; some say Silvanus, Timothy, or another of Paul's close friends. M. J. J. Menken 1994 defends the view that 2 Thessalonians was written pseudonymously but that the author was dependent on 1 Thessalonians literarily. The author's purpose was to refute the belief that the day of the Lord had already come.

It is equally difficult to determine the author's purpose for writing. Several have been suggested: to admonish a community that had gotten lazy either because it thought the End was soon coming or because it was influenced by the Hellenistic notion that citizens did not engage in physical labor; to refute Gnostic ideas that the day of the Lord had already come and that therefore one could do as one pleased; and to explain why the day of the Lord had not come (see 2 Pet 3:3–10).

PLACE AND DATE OF WRITING

If Paul wrote 2 Thessalonians, he was still at Corinth, and the date would be c. 51–52 CE. If Paul did not write the letter, we cannot be certain about either the place or date of writing. If "the temple of God" in 2:4 refers to the temple in Jerusalem, then the date must be before 70 CE. But in apocalyptic writing, things may exist in imagination but not in reality, so that reference is not a reliable clue to the date.

Some passages suggest a date about the time of Paul. There is no reference to leaders or other officials among the readers, as there is in 1 Thess 5:12. It is hard to explain why there is no such reference if the letter is much later than Paul's time. Two Thess 2:15 and 3:10 refer to traditions and teaching, but there is no reference to their transmission as in the pastorals, which were written later.

Perhaps the best answer that those who reject Pauline authorship of 2 Thessalonians can propose concerning the place and date of writing is that 2 Thessalonians was probably written near the end of the first century or the beginning of the second, after Paul's death. I think the evidence supports post-Pauline authorship, and I think that who wrote 2 Thessalonians, or when and where it was written, will never be known for certain. We can determine the purpose for writing only on the basis of internal evidence. The letter seems to have been written to encourage those suffering, to deal with the question of the Parousia, and to admonish the idle. Notice these things as you read the letter.

Outline and Comments

I. Greeting (1:1–2)

II. Thanksgiving and prayer (1:3–12)

Verses 3–10 are one long Greek sentence that is hard to break into clear divisions. But in 1:3–5 the writer thanks God for the Thessalonians' faith, which is "growing abundantly," and for their "steadfastness and faith" in the "persecutions and the afflictions" they are enduring. Then in 1:6–10 the writer assures the readers that God is just in repaying "with affliction those who afflict you." This echoes the OT law of an "eye for eye, tooth for tooth" (Exod 21:24; Lev 24:20), that is, equal retaliation for wrongdoing. The writer's language and thought are influenced by Jewish apocalyptic imagery from the OT and later Jewish literature. With Jesus' revelation "from heaven with his mighty angels in flaming fire" (v 7), compare "The angel of the Lord appeared to him [Moses] in a flame of fire" (Exod 3:2). Compare also Isa 66:4, 15–16; Jer 10:25; Isa 2:10–11 with 1:8–10. Verses 11–12 are a prayer that the faithful may be worthy of God's call and be rewarded accordingly.

III. The day of the Lord and signs of its coming (2:1–12)

The Thessalonians must not be deceived by those who say that "the day of the Lord is already here" (2:1–2). Its coming will be preceded by certain events, including "the rebellion" and the coming of "the lawless one," "the son of destruction." He will be restrained for a while, "whom the Lord Jesus will destroy with the breath of his mouth" (2:3–8). A final thrust of power by Satan will deceive some "who are perishing, because they refused to love the truth and so be saved." God will rightfully condemn them (2:9–12). Some scholars think these verses are an allusion to the destruction of Jerusalem in

70 CE. If this is true, then Paul could not have written them. Perhaps, as some suggest, they are an interpolation into an original letter of Paul.

Apparently the readers understood the writer's apocalyptic terminology, but we do not. It is influenced by descriptions of tyrants in the OT (see Daniel 10–12; Isa 14:12–21; Ezek 28:2–10) and elsewhere. Compare "declaring himself to be God" (v 4) with Ezekiel's words about "the prince of Tyre," who "compares his mind with the mind of a god" and who says, "I am a god." And with "the lawless one," compare the account of Pompey capturing Jerusalem (63 BCE) by the writer of the *Psalms of Solomon*: "When the sinful man became proud, with a battering ram he threw down fortified walls, and you did not restrain him" (2:1). "Restraining" (2:6–7) may allude to the Roman Empire and the emperor, or to some supernatural power, perhaps Satan. The words "you know" (v 6) indicate that the readers knew what the writer was talking about.

IV. Thanksgivings, prayers, and exhortations (2:13–3:15)

In 2:13–15 the writer gives thanks that God has chosen the Thessalonians "for salvation through sanctification by the Spirit." We cannot be sure whether "spirit" here should be capitalized to indicate the Holy Spirit, or whether it should not be, in order to indicate the human spirit. Perhaps it is an allusion to baptism, which conferred the Spirit. "The truth" in vv 10 and 13 probably means the gospel or instruction in the developing religion.

The writer prays that God may comfort the readers and "strengthen them in every good work and word" (2:16–17). Then he asks them to pray for him, expresses his confidence in them, and prays that they may love God and be loyal to Christ (3:1–5). Finally, he exhorts them to "keep away from every brother who is living in idleness" and commands that anyone who will not work shall not eat. The Thessalonians, however, are not to treat the person who does not obey what the writer says "as an enemy," but to "warn him as a brother" (3:6–15; Greek).

V. Benediction, signature, and final blessing
(3:16–18)

For various aspects of this discussion, consult E. J. Bicknell 1932; W. Neil 1950; E. Best 1972; W. G. Kuemmel 1975:262–269; I. H. Marshall 1983; J. M. Reese 1979. For further study of 2 Thessalonians see C. H. Giblin 1967, faith; J. A. Bailey 1978, authorship; F. F. Bruce 1982b, commentary; F. W. Hughes 1989, rhetoric; R. Jewett 1986, form, rhetoric, piety; A. J. Malherbe 1987, philosophy; M. J. J. Menken 1994, commentary.

SUMMARY

This chapter on Colossians, Ephesians, and 2 Thessalonians concludes Part II of our study of the NT, in which we have examined Acts and Paul and his letters. Both Acts and Paul's letters are important documents for our knowledge of the earliest phase of developing Christianity after Jesus' death. This is true even of Colossians, Ephesians, and 2 Thessalonians, although they may not be authentic letters of Paul. On the basis of vocabulary and style, theological viewpoint, and ecclesiological developments, these three letters may best be ascribed to different friends of Paul who were influenced by his life and work. 2 Thessalonians, however, may be even later and may have been written by an imitator of Paul rather than by a friend or disciple.

Colossians is important for showing how a religious syncretism of many facets had penetrated developing Christianity in a particular community. The author writes to convince his readers that Christ is the center of all things and that all things center in Christ. No other beings or powers are necessary, therefore, for faith and worship. The dependency of Ephesians on Colossians and its close relationship to undisputed letters of Paul may indicate that it was written by a follower of Paul as a cover letter for the corpus of Paul's letters before their publication. As an encyclical letter, Ephesians is a semirepresentation of Paul's thought and is intended to encourage unity in the church. As an institution in the world, the church must take the whole armor of God—truth, righteousness, peace, faith, the Spirit—in order to maintain its faith throughout a long struggle before the End.

The relationship of 2 Thessalonians to the undisputed letters of Paul is the most difficult to determine. Through an apocalyptic mythology unlike anything in Paul's letters, the author assures his readers that they need not worry about the coming of the End so long as they live in accordance with the moral and ethical tradition they have received. Indeed, the three letters discussed in this chapter, like those of Paul, stress the necessity for moral and ethical probity in a community of converts amidst a pagan environment.

The next chapter brings us to the final major section of this book. Part III deals with post-Pauline writings from times of oppression by opponents and of controversy among believers. The Gospel of John, Hebrews, Revelation, and 1 Peter, writings representing different literary types and theological points of view, will be the focus of the next two chapters.

PART III

Writings from Times of Oppression and Controversy

CHAPTER 14

The Gospel of John

PART III OF THIS BOOK PRESENTS THE conglomeration of post-Pauline writings of different literary types and various theological and christological viewpoints that make up the remainder of the NT. Scholars generally agree that these writings—including the letters to Timothy and Titus, which purport to be from Paul—reflect christological and ecclesiastical developments after Paul's time. The church's growing pains are evident in the differences in beliefs and practices that appear within and among the writings. Yet even though the writings represent different literary types and diverse viewpoints, they all reflect some kind of persecution of believers by nonbelievers or controversy among believers themselves. They are therefore treated together.

With respect to problems of critical investigation, including authorship, place of writing, background, structure, sources, literary style, and the relationship to the synoptic gospels, the gospel of John, also known as the fourth gospel, is one of the greatest enigmas in the whole field of NT study. It is a subtle blend of fact, faith, and fiction. But one thing becomes increasingly clear from recent Johannine studies: the author represents a community of believers in controversy with several other groups who had differing theologies and with the Jews. The latter may also represent several groups whose views concerning Jesus differed. Some Jews were so proud of their ancestral attachment to Abraham that they did not understand Jesus (8:31–59). Others refused to follow Jesus because they were disciples of Moses (9:38–39).

That the prevailing mood in John is one of controversy and criticism is evident from the beginning. Jesus "came to his own, and his own people did not receive him, but all who did receive him, to them he gave power to become children of God, to those who believe in his name" (1:11–12; my trans.). This passage indicates that in John's community among Jesus' own people, the Jews, there was a group who accepted Jesus and believed something about him and a group who rejected him. The group of Jews who did not accept or believe in Jesus belonged to the synagogue and wanted to put anyone who confessed Jesus as the Messiah out of the synagogue (9:22). This clearly implies that within the synagogue there were some Jews whose faith in Jesus at least included an acknowledgment of his messiahship (see also 12:42; 16:2).

Some Jews, and perhaps some non-Jews as well, believed in Jesus because of the "signs" (healings and other miracles) he did (2:23; 6:2; 7:31). There may have been several groups of such believers, some of whom could not be trusted because of latent hostility (2:24). Because of his signs some accepted Jesus as the prophet who was to come into the world (6:14). Did Nicodemus, and perhaps Joseph of Arimathea, belong to that group (3:1–3; 7:50; 19:38–39)? This group or others who believed because of Jesus' signs were at least open to further belief in Jesus (6:26–34). Perhaps it was primarily this group to whom the author wrote that these signs "are written so that you may come to believe that Jesus is the Christ, the Son of God, and that through believing you may have life in his name" (20:30–31). Did the author think that this was the minimum belief required of Jews who wanted to become converts?

Apparently some who believed because of Jesus' signs were hostile to more advanced christological faith in Jesus as Son of God or as God (10:31–39) or to the view of the Eucharist presented in John 6:52–59 or to the idea of Jesus' preexistence (8:48–59). On the other hand, some included those things as part of their faith in Jesus or else John would not have written about them (see also 1:1; 3:13; 6:62; 20:28).

Besides the various groups, whether Jews or believers, just mentioned, there were Samaritans who may have accepted a variety of beliefs about Jesus, including Jesus as the source of eternal life (4:13–15), Jesus as prophet (4:19), as the Savior of the world (4:42), and perhaps as Messiah (4:25–26, 29).

Although we cannot be sure what groups of believers are intended by John's figurative references to "fold" and "sheep fold" who are and are not of the fold, they are further evidence of disharmony among believing groups with whom John was familiar (10:1–18).

There is also something unique about the social and religious background of the gospel of John that differs from the general nature of other early groups of believers. The problem is to identify that uniqueness precisely. One aspect of it is that the people or community behind the gospel thought they were associated with the historical Jesus through someone in the gospel known as "the disciple whom Jesus loved" (John 13:23; 19:26; 20:2; see below).

Many unanswered questions remain with respect to the various groups of Jews and believers and their beliefs with which John was concerned when he wrote his gospel. The lack of answers does show, however, that the gospel of John belongs with those other writings of the NT that grew out of times of oppression and controversy in the church at the end of the first or the beginning of the second century. The letters of John (Chapter 16) provide further evidence of such times of controversy within the early church. For a detailed analysis of groups of believers in the Johannine church, see R. E. Brown 1979; R. T. Fortna 1988:294–341.

This evidence in the gospel of John of controversy within the church of the author's time—around the start of the second century—is one of the main reasons why I discuss John here and not after the study of the first three gospels. Moreover, in spite of the similarities between John and the synoptics, the whole atmosphere of John is different. And in John's presentation of Jesus there are major differences compared with the synoptics: no short sayings like those in the Sermon on the Mount, no parables, no association with outcasts and sinners, no healing of demoniacs, and no teaching about the kingdom of God. It might be argued, I suppose, that Jesus was teaching about the kingdom of God in the reported discourse between him and Nicodemus (John 3:1–5).

When you read a few verses of the gospel of John, you notice immediately a difference between it and the first three gospels. But if you continue reading, you notice, too, that by the end of the first chapter John seems similar to the other gospels. The similarities and differences between John and the synoptics is one of the reasons why the critical study of John is both interesting and difficult.

In this chapter we will consider the authorship, date, and place of writing, structure, and sources of the fourth gospel. We will examine the diverse Judaic and Hellenistic backgrounds of the gospel of John to gain insight into the nature of the author and his gospel. We will also study the author's unique presentation of Jesus, his peculiar literary style, and other features that distinguish his gospel from the other three.

AUTHORSHIP, PLACE OF WRITING, AND DATE

As with the other gospels, the Greek title is "according to John" or "gospel according to John." Four people in the NT are called John: John the Baptist; the son of Zebedee (see, for example, Mark 1:19, 29; Matt 4:21; Luke 5:10; 8:51; Acts 3:1, 4; Gal 2:9); John Mark (see, for example, Acts 12:12, 25); and the writer of Revelation, who calls himself John (1:1, 4, 9; 22:8). Was one of these people the author of the fourth gospel?

Because four other works in the NT are attributed to a man named John—1, 2, and 3 John and the book of Revelation—the problem of authorship becomes even more complicated. Were some or all of the five Johannine works written by the same John? The author of Revelation is the only one to refer to himself by name; the author of 2 and 3 John calls himself "the elder" (2 John 1; 3 John 1). The Greek word for elder, *presbyteros*, means "old man." It was also used as a title of honor among Jews (see, for example, Mark 8:31 = Matt 16:21; Luke 9:22) and as a title of an official of a Christian community or church (see, for example, Acts 11:30; 20:17; 1 Tim 5:17; Jas 5:14). So was the author of 2 and 3 John an old man or a church officer or both? And what was the relationship between him and

the author or authors of the other Johannine literature?

In John there are references to a "disciple whom Jesus loved" (13:23; 19:26; 20:2; 21:7, 20) and to "another disciple" (18:15–16; 20: 2–4, 8). The two people seem to be identified in 20:2: "the other disciple, the one whom Jesus loved." Was that person the author of the gospel who concealed his identity by using such veiled designations? At the end of the gospel there is another mysterious reference: "This is the disciple who is testifying to these things and has written them" (21:24; see also 19:35). Is the witness the same as the disciple whom Jesus loved, and thus the author of the gospel? John 20:30–31 seems to be another ending to the gospel, so did the witness write only chapter 21 and someone else the rest of the gospel? Or did the same author add chapter 21 later, so that the witness was the author of the whole gospel?

Evidence within the gospel raises more questions than it answers with respect to authorship. Nothing in the gospel indicates who wrote it and where it was written. For possible answers to these questions, therefore, we will consider evidence from early Christian tradition. The oldest tradition, that of Papias, is preserved in Eusebius (*Hist.* 3.39:4). It is the hardest to interpret:

> If ever anyone came who had followed the elders, I inquired about the words of the elders—what Andrew or Peter or Philip or Thomas or James or what John or Matthew or what any other of the Lord's disciples said, and what Aristion and the elder John, the Lord's disciples were saying.

According to this statement, there was an elder John, but where he lived is not stated. And whether he is the same person as the John mentioned earlier in the passage we cannot say, because the meaning of the text is uncertain.

Two passages from Irenaeus, also quoted in Eusebius (5:8:4; 3:23:3–4), are important. The first reads, "Then John, the disciple of the Lord, who reclined on his breast [see John 13:23; 21:20], also himself gave out the gospel, while he was spending time in Asia." The second passage states that John, the disciple, remained in Ephesus in Asia until the time of Trajan (98–117). The evidence of Irenaeus is clear: the author of John was the disciple whom Jesus loved; he lived in Ephesus as an old man, and from there "he gave out" (wrote or published?) the gospel. But these passages have caused endless debate among scholars for several reasons, one of which is evidence that John died as a martyr in the mid–60s.

Traditions about John's gospel grew. Clement of Alexandria (150–220) says that John wrote last of all: "Aware that the bodily facts had been disclosed in the [other] gospels, and urged by his pupils and divinely moved by the Spirit, he wrote a spiritual gospel." According to the Muratorian Canon, John was urged to write a gospel; and after a three-day fast, Andrew received a revelation that, indeed, John should write in his own name. Moved by the Spirit, he then also wrote the letters of John. Gradually tradition ascribed all five Johannine works to John the disciple.

Some scholars (notably L. Morris 1969:139–292, 1971:8–30) still hold the traditional view that John the beloved disciple wrote the gospel. Others believe that John, the son of Zebedee, was the authority behind the gospel: although he was not the author, a pupil or disciple wrote later under his influence (see J. A. Grassi 1992). D. Wenham 1997 says that the author's claim that the beloved disciple was the eyewitness behind his gospel should be given greater acknowledgment than it sometimes has.

These views take the references to the witness and the tradition of Irenaeus seriously in associating the gospel with the beloved disciple, albeit not directly (see especially R. E. Brown 1966: lxxxvii-cii and R. Schnackenburg 1980: 75–104). According to the second view, the gospel developed in several stages. The first stage was the "memoirs" of an eyewitness, known as "the witness" or "the disciple whom Jesus loved." In a second stage someone, usually referred to as "the evangelist," wrote the gospel on the basis of the information from the eyewitness. In later stages a redactor or two produced the final work. Defenders of these two views hold to the tradi-

tion of Ephesus as the place of the final stage in the gospel's composition.

Some scholars think that neither the internal evidence nor the tradition is strong enough to support Johannine authorship, so they suggest other views. Among these is the view that, since in the early church John the disciple was confused with John Mark from Acts, the latter was really the author (J. N. Sanders 1968:29–52). According to this view, Lazarus, not John, was the beloved disciple because only he is definitely identified as the one whom Jesus loved (11:5, 36). Also according to this view, it is unlikely that the fisherman from Galilee (John the disciple) would be known to the high priest (18:15–16). John Mark got the notes of Lazarus, and on that basis wrote the gospel. Later he was exiled to Patmos (see Rev 1:9), and there wrote Revelation. Released from Patmos, he went to Ephesus, where he then wrote 1 John as an introduction to the gospel and later also 2 and 3 John.

Other scholars believe that the author of John is anonymous (see J. Marsh 1968:20–25; B. Lindars 1972:28–34). Most seem to agree that the beloved disciple was a real person but that his identity is unknown. However, what role, if any, he played in the composition of the gospel is uncertain. For these scholars the gospel reflects the situation of the community in which it was written more than a specific apostolic tradition.

Finally, there is increasing support for the view that the fourth gospel originated among a specific group of believers, variously referred to as a circle, school, or community (O. Cullmann 1976; J. L. Martyn 1978, 1979; R. A. Culpepper 1975; R. E. Brown 1979). Several passages in 1 John seem to indicate such a group, for example, "We declare to you what we have seen and heard so that you also may have fellowship with us" (1:3; see also 2:19–24; 4:6). M. Hengel 1989 has suggested that John the Elder, who knew Jesus, revered the beloved disciple, and became the leader of a school in his honor, was the author of the gospel. J. H. Charlesworth 1995 has argued for Thomas as the author.

This view usually posits an early community of Jewish believers in or near Palestine who were under the leadership of the disciple John. As the community grew, it included Gentiles and moved to some Gentile environment, perhaps Ephesus. From this diverse community of people with different backgrounds and theological perspectives emerged the gospel of John in one or more revised editions that reflect the different views of the changing community. From the community came the letters of John and perhaps also the book of Revelation, although the latter is not given equal consideration with the others. That early Christians believed all five Johannine works were related is clear because the same name was associated with each. The view of a Johannine school or community perhaps best explains the similarities and differences in both literary style and theological viewpoint among the five works.

In sum, a few scholars think John wrote the five works, but otherwise there is a wide variety of opinion. Those who believe John wrote some or all of the literature tend to favor Ephesus as the place of writing. Those who support anonymity tend to leave the question of place open, though Ephesus, Antioch, and Alexandria are suggested. Most scholars think that the gospel and Revelation are not the work of the same person and that 1 John and the gospel are more closely related than any two of the other writings. Some think all three letters were written by the same person, some think they were written by two or three different persons, and some think 2 and 3 John were written by the same author (see R. E. Brown 1982:3–35).

The discovery of several papyri of John makes it possible to fix a probable date beyond which the gospel was not written. One of these papyri is a fragment of John 18:31–33, 37–38 and can be dated between c. 135 and 150. Another papyrus, written c. 150, shows dependence on John and the synoptics. Assuming that a period of time elapsed between the actual writing of the gospel and the publication of these papyri, scholars generally agree on a date no later than c. 120. It is generally agreed that the reference to being put out of the synagogue in John 9:22 (see also 9:34–35) reflects a Jewish benediction intro-

duced into the synagogue service. Drawn up c. 85–90, the benediction was intended to exclude heretics, including Jewish believers, from belonging to the synagogue. Therefore, the gospel was probably not written before c. 90, and we can fix the date for the writing of John from c. 90 to 120.

JOHN AND THE SYNOPTICS

The relationship between John and the first three gospels is a mysterious one. There are similarities and differences, yet even within the similarities there are significant differences, as the following examples show. The synoptics and John both report a ministry of John the Baptist. In the former, John is imprisoned before Jesus begins his ministry; in the latter, Jesus and the Baptist work at the same time. Again, in both John and the synoptics first disciples are mentioned. In the synoptics, Jesus invites them to follow him; but in John they come to Jesus without being invited, and one of the first four is Nathanael, a person not mentioned in the synoptics (1:35–49). The following incidents common to John and the synoptics also have differences: feeding of the five thousand, the only miracle in all four gospels; Jesus' walking on the water; Jesus' entry into Jerusalem; last supper with disciples; announcement of Jesus' betrayal and arrest; Peter's resistance; trials before the Sanhedrin and Pilate; choice of Barabbas instead of Jesus; crucifixion and burial; and the empty tomb and resurrection.

The following important incidents are peculiar to John: four miracles—turning water into wine (2:1–12), the lame man at Beth-zatha (5:1–18), man born blind (9:1–41), and the raising of Lazarus (11:1–41); the stories of Nicodemus (3:1–15) and the woman of Samaria (4:1–26); Jesus' discourses (see, for example, 5:19–47); and some aspects of the passion—the visit of the Greeks (12:20–22), Jesus' washing of the disciples' feet (13:1–20), a trial before Annas (18:12–24), the visit of Peter and "the other disciple" to the tomb (20:1–10), and Jesus' appearance to Thomas (20:26–29).

FIGURE 14.1   *Sea of Galilee, with Jordan River flowing out of the south end.*

Many things in the synoptics are not in John, among which are these: actual baptism of Jesus, birth narratives and genealogy, Jesus' temptations and transfiguration, institution of the Lord's Supper, and suffering in Gethsemane. Besides these, several differences between John and the synoptics are crucial in the study of Jesus. There are three chronological differences concerning Jesus' career. First, in John's gospel Jesus attends three Passovers (2:13; 6:4; 11:55), whereas in the synoptics he attends only the one before his death. So according to John, Jesus' ministry lasted at least two years and perhaps longer. Second, Jesus' first public act in John is the cleansing of the temple, but the synoptics place this event in the last week of Jesus' life. Third, in John the crucifixion takes place before the Passover meal is to be eaten, but in the synoptics Jesus eats the Passover meal with his disciples. So in John, Jesus is dying on the cross as the Passover lambs are being killed in the temple.

There is no certain explanation for these major differences. The question arises as to whether they are to be explained historically or theologi-

cally, since, for example, only in John is Jesus called "the Lamb of God" (1:29, 36). In other words, did John indicate the correct time of the crucifixion, or was his reference to the time of that event determined by his theological conviction that Jesus was the real sacrificial Lamb?

We should note here that John's stated purpose is theological (see John 20:30–31 and below). If John believed that Jesus was the lamb of God, then, for John, Jesus had to die as Passover lambs were being sacrificed, regardless of the actual time of the crucifixion. Ancient writers often combined faith and history when reporting historical events, so for them what they were saying was an interaction between faith and history, not a contradiction.

In the synoptics, Jesus begins his ministry in Galilee (see Figure 14.1) and then journeys to Jerusalem, where he spends the final week of his life. But in John Jesus travels back and forth between Galilee and Judea, and he frequently spends time in Jerusalem disputing with the Jews. Was this the actual pattern of Jesus' ministry, and was he active so much longer than the synoptics say he was? If Jesus had been in Jerusalem only once, the Jews could have replied to John's charges that they had rejected Jesus by saying that Jesus had not been around long enough for them even to know him, let alone reject him. In John's account, the clue to the length and locale of Jesus' ministry may be in 15:22: "If I had not come and spoken to them, they would not have sin; but now they have no excuse for their sin."

There are also other important differences between John and the synoptics. Short, pithy sayings of Jesus, like those in the Sermon on the Mount, and parables are conspicuously absent in John. In the synoptic gospels, the main subject of Jesus' teaching is the kingdom of God. In John, however, Jesus refers to the kingdom of God only twice (3:3, 5) and in a different way than the synoptics do. In John, Jesus never associates with outcasts and sinners, and he never heals a demoniac. John's whole portrayal of Jesus, beginning with the first verse, is radically different from that of the synoptists. All these differences between John and the synoptics raise serious questions about the historical value of John as a source for the study of Jesus, although, of course, the synoptic writers, like John, were not primarily concerned with writing history. But with what, then, was John primarily concerned?

PURPOSES AND SITUATION OF JOHN

Mark reveals his theological motive for writing in his first verse: "The beginning of the gospel of Jesus Christ, the Son of God." But we must turn to the end of John's gospel to discover his primary motive. There Thomas says to the risen Jesus, "My Lord and my God!" And Jesus says to him: "Have you believed because you have seen me? Blessed are those who have not seen and yet have come to believe." Then the writer adds, "But these [signs] are written so that you may come to believe that Jesus is the Christ, the Son of God, and that through believing you may have life in his name" (20:28–31). Here John is speaking to those who, unlike Thomas, do not have physical proof of Jesus' existence. They are living at a time later than Thomas's, and John writes to inspire or renew their faith in Jesus as the Christ and Son of God. Such faith will assure them of an abundant life now (10:10) and eternal life in the future (3:16; 10:28).

If we turn to the first verses of John's gospel, we can see how theological beliefs are combined with the practical situation behind the gospel. John's first verse reads, "In the beginning was the Word, and the Word was with God, and the Word was God." The word translated here as "Word" is *logos* and means word as the expression of a thought. *Logos* embodies a conception or idea that evolves from the processes of reasoning. The Stoics speak of God as reason (*logos*) that permeates the universe. Philo, the Jewish philosopher of Alexandria, uses *logos* in various senses, usually with reference to God and his activities. Thus, Jews and Gentiles living in the Hellenistic world would be familiar with the concept of *logos*. For them it would be easy to grasp the idea of Jesus as the Word (*logos*), and by it the writer adapted his gospel to a setting somewhere in the world of Hellenism.

For John, however, Jesus as the Word did not remain in the world of conception. He became a part of the world of perception—"The Word became flesh and lived among us" (1:14). As a human being, Jesus "came to what was his own, and his own people did not accept him" (1:11). Jesus' own people are those Jews who reject him, and throughout the gospel they are categorized as "the Jews." Thus, we move from the world of philosophical thought in the Hellenistic culture of John's own time to the world of Jesus and the Jews. The gospel originated, then, in a situation of conflict between believers and Jews, and even the situation of Jesus and the Jews in John's gospel reflects John's own time as much as it does the time of Jesus. For example, according to John (9:22; see also 12:42; 16:2), Jews who confessed Jesus as the Christ were to "be put out of the synagogue." Since in Jesus' own time people who followed Jesus would not be excluded from the synagogue, John 9:22 reflects a time after the

Jews introduced the benediction against heretics into the synagogue service. At the same time, however, the writer reports the tradition of Jesus' healing activity and thus reflects the time of Jesus himself.

In reporting the traditional conflict of Jesus with Jewish authorities, John reveals the conflict of his own community with "the Jews" and the synagogue even more clearly than Matthew reveals a similar conflict of his day. Although the term "the Jews" may not always mean precisely the same thing, in general it represents opponents of Jesus and opponents of John and his community who do not share John's views about Jesus. Within the general purpose of addressing Jewish opposition to Jesus and to John's community of Christians, there are related purposes, one of which is to counteract a group of John the Baptist's followers.

The author of John emphasizes the inferiority of the Baptist to Jesus. As in the synoptics, the Baptist says he is not worthy to untie the sandals of the one who comes after him (1:27). But in John, the Baptist also proclaims Jesus as "the Lamb of God who takes away the sin of the world" (1:29; see also 1:36), and he says that Jesus must increase and that he must decrease (3:30). In John the ministries of the Baptist and Jesus overlap, and two of the Baptist's disciples leave him to follow Jesus (1:35–37). Perhaps the author of the fourth gospel subordinates the Baptist to Jesus because a Baptist sect was competing with the Jesus movement. One of John's purposes, then, would be to win followers to the Jesus movement from the Baptist sect.

By the time John wrote, believers held diverse views about Jesus. Some doubted that he had ever been truly human, with the weaknesses and emotions of human beings. John writes to reassure these people of the reality of Jesus' human existence. In contrast to Matthew and Luke, who tend to eliminate from Mark the human traits of Jesus, John emphasizes his human qualities. In John, Jesus participates in a wedding (2:1–11), where he seems to rebuke his mother (2:4). He makes a whip and drives people and animals out of the temple (2:13–15). He gets tired and asks a

woman to get him a drink (4:6–7). Jesus has a discussion with his brothers about going to Jerusalem, says he is not going, and then later goes (7:1–10). Only John reports that Jesus loved someone—"Jesus loved Martha and her sister and Lazarus" (11:5; see also 11:3, 36; 13:23; 15:9). And Jesus speaks of others loving him (14:15, 21, 23–24; 21:15–16). Jesus weeps at the death of his friend Lazarus (11:35), and he thirsts on the cross (19:28). (For a study on the humanity of Jesus, see M. M. Thompson 1988.)

John also presents Jesus as a divine figure by using a variety of literary expressions. Jesus is not only the Son of God, as in the synoptics, but also God (1:1). Jesus is confessed as God in the Johannine community, as the words put on the lips of Thomas make clear: "My Lord and my God!" (20:28); the confession is meant to strengthen the faith of doubting members. There are more subtle implications of the deity of Jesus in such passages as "The Father and I are one" (10:30) and "Whoever has seen me has seen the Father" (14:9).

John's interest in Jesus as one with God begins in the first verse of the gospel with Jesus as the Word (*logos*). To begin with a genealogy (Matthew) or birth narrative (Luke) would be to present Jesus as a figure too mundane for John's readers. As the *logos,* Jesus was "with God," "was God," and was "in the beginning with God" as an agent in the creation of the world. Jesus always existed (the preexistence of Jesus), so a narrative of his birth would be out of place. Nevertheless, "The Word became flesh and lived among us, and we have seen his glory full of grace and truth . . ." (1:14). Subtle implications like this, rather than direct narrative, make it difficult to understand fully John's portrayal of Jesus, a subject to which we now turn.

JOHN'S PRESENTATION OF JESUS

Recall the theme stated at the end of the gospel: believe in Jesus the Christ, the Son of God, that you may have life. This theme is repeated with variations again and again as the characters from "this world" appear on the stage of John's drama to meet the leading character, the divine Son of God, who is "not of this world" (8:23). Those who respond by believing in him experience life that has already become eternal (see, for example, 5:24; 11:25–26). In the synoptics Jesus always directs attention from himself to God. Only once does he mention belief in him (Mark 9:42 = Matt 18:6), and that is in a saying attributed to the tradition, not to Jesus. By contrast, John constantly presents Jesus as directing attention toward himself and asking for belief in him. Indeed, we could call John the "I and me gospel" because of the way John presents Jesus as referring to himself.

Jesus as "I Am"

Notice how often Jesus uses "I am" (*egō eimi* in Greek), an expression almost peculiar to John, who puts it on the lips of Jesus with reference to himself in two ways. First, it is used absolutely—that is, without a predicate—in such expressions as "You will die in your sins unless you believe that I am" (8:24) and "Before Abraham was, I am" (8:58; see also 8:28; 13:19). Most scholars think that such passages show influence from the OT Hebrew expression "I am he," spoken by God and usually translated as *egō eimi* in the Septuagint, especially in Isaiah (see, for example, 43:25; 45:18; 51:12; 52:6). Consequently, they regard the Johannine usage of *egō eimi* ("I am") as a formula equivalent to the divine name Yahweh (YHWH) or to the divine presence itself. Second, eleven times Jesus uses "I am" with an expressed predicate—for example, "I am the bread of life" (6:35), "I am the way, and the truth, and the life" (14:6), and "I am the good shepherd" (10:11, 14; see also 6:51; 8:12; 10:7, 9; 11:25).

The meaning of the sayings using "I am" with a predicate is usually clear from the context, but the use of the expression without a predicate causes problems of interpretation. John may indeed have used the expression to convey his understanding of the deity of Jesus or the unity of Jesus with God. However, another plausible interpretation is that the words "I am" represent

John's attempt to explain his unique conception of Jesus as the Christ, the Son of God.

The body of the gospel begins with the Baptist's emphatic denial that he is the Christ. When Jews ask him who he is, he confesses, "I am not the Christ" (1:20; see also 3:28). The negative form of the expression translated "I am" is used here. Then in 4:26 Jesus positively confesses that he is the Christ in response to the Samaritan woman's remark about the Messiah coming. To her Jesus says (lit.), "I am [he], the one who is speaking to you." Thus, in contrast to the Baptist, Jesus affirms that he is the Christ by the use of "I am" (see Mark 13:6 and Matt 24:5). Moreover, it makes good Johannine sense to understand "the Christ" with "I am" when the latter is used without a predicate. For example, "You will die in your sins unless you believe that I am" the Christ, the Son of God (8:24). This ties in with John's stated purpose for writing in 20:30–31. And if we understand "the Christ" with "I am" in 8:58, Jesus' saying means, "Before Abraham was, I the Christ existed," and it ties in with the writer's thought in 1:1 that the Word was in the beginning with God.

By the use of "I am," then, John attempts to explain to his readers his conception of Jesus as the Christ, the Son of God. Therefore, "I am" is synonymous with other christological titles for Jesus—which are also synonymous with each other—including Son of God, Son, and Son of Man. The use of "I am" with a predicate gives substance to Jesus as "I am" for a generation of Christians who, not having seen Jesus, are to believe (20:27–31). By the use of "I am" John describes Jesus as the giver of life ("bread of life"—first use of "I am" with a predicate in 6:35) in a variety of images. Thus, John portrays Jesus as the Christ who has a relationship with believers of his own time. Jesus makes life for them more meaningful (10:10). As "I am," Jesus is present as the light of the world during controversy with the Jews (8:12–59). He has an abiding and saving relationship with the sheep (some Christians) of the fold (the church or some faction of it [10:11–18]) and with the branches of the vine (15:1–8). Jesus is here and now the resurrection and the life, so that those who believe in him will not die (11:25–26); and except through him "no one comes to the Father" (14:6). As "I am," Jesus' own relationship with the Father is unique.

In discussing the gospel of John and the other NT literature in this section, it becomes more appropriate to use the term "Christians" as a designation for members of churches than in discussing the letters of Paul. Why? Because by the end of the first century CE the religion in transition in many places had all but become independent of Judaism.

For Son of Man in John see E. D. Freed 1967; F. J. Moloney 1978; D. Burkett 1991; for "I am" see D. M. Ball 1996.

Jesus and the Father

Although in John Jesus is always talking about himself, much of that talk is about himself in relationship to God as his Father. The following are main ideas that express Jesus' relationship with the Father and are repeated with variations throughout the gospel.

Jesus came from the Father and will return to him: "I came from the Father and have come into the world; again, I am leaving the world and am going to the Father" (16:28; see also 8:14, 42; 13:1–3; 14:2, 28; 16:10, 17). The Father sent the Son (3:17, 34; 5:36; 6:57; 7:29; 10:36; 11:42; 17:18) and has borne witness to him. Jesus appeals to his works as evidence of his being sent by God: "The very works that I am doing, testify on my behalf that the Father has sent me" (5:36–37; see also 3:16–17, 34; 5:43; 6:44, 57; 7:28; 10:36; 14:24; 17:25; 20:21). Jesus not only does the work of his Father, but also says what the Father tells him. "My Father is still working, and I also am working" (5:17; see also 8:28; 10:25, 32). "I do as the Father has commanded me" (14:31). "For I have not spoken on my own, but the Father who sent me has himself given me a commandment about what to say and what to speak. . . . What I speak, therefore, I speak just as the Father has told me" (12:49–50).

"The Father loves the Son" (3:35; see also 5:20; 10:17; 15:9), and the Son loves the Father: "I do as the Father has commanded me, so that the world may know that I love the Father" (14:31). Only Jesus has seen the Father: "Not that anyone has seen the Father except the one who is from God; he has seen the Father" (6:46; see also 8:38). The Father glorifies Jesus: "If I glorify myself, my glory is nothing. It is my Father who glorifies me" (8:54; see also 11:4; 13:31–32; 17:5). Jesus knows the Father, and the Father knows him: "as the Father knows me and I know the Father" (10:15; see also 7:29; 17:25). There is a oneness or unity between Father and Son: "The Father and I are one" (10:30; see also 5:18). "The Father is in me and I am in the Father" (10:38; see also 14:20; 17:21, 24). "Whoever has seen me has seen the Father. . . . Do you not believe that I am in the Father and the Father is in me?" (14:9–11).

Jesus as a Person of Glory and as a Doer of Signs and Works

The glorification of Jesus is one of the main themes of John. Jesus' glory had already been seen by Isaiah the prophet: "Isaiah . . . saw his glory and spoke about him" (12:41). This is an allusion to Isaiah's vision of the Lord in the temple and the voice saying that "the whole earth is full of his glory" (6:3). Thus, for John, Jesus had a kind of preexistent glory that soon became apparent, as is evident already in the prologue to the gospel: "And the Word became flesh and . . . we have seen his glory, the glory as of a father's only son" (1:14). This glory is sometimes evident in Jesus' earthly life. Twice John says that Jesus is currently glorified by his miracles. After Jesus' first sign at Cana, Jesus "revealed his glory" (2:11). And at the beginning of the story of Lazarus, the writer says that Lazarus's illness was "for God's glory, so that the Son of God may be glorified through it." By raising Lazarus from the dead, Jesus is glorified and also brings glory to God (11:4, 40).

Sometimes Jesus' present glorification is combined with glory still anticipated. After Andrew and Philip tell Jesus that some Greeks want to see him, Jesus says, "The hour has come for the Son of Man to be glorified" (12:23). The "hour" is John's special way of referring to Jesus' being lifted up on the cross, which is his special exaltation or glorification. So the passage quoted seems to be a transition between Jesus' present and future glorification (see 13:30–32).

Sometimes Jesus' glorification is said to be entirely in the future and is associated with his death and/or resurrection. In 7:39 the writer says that the Spirit had not yet been given "because Jesus was not yet glorified" (see 12:16). In Jesus' prayer in chapter 17, John brings all the variations on the theme of glory together as Jesus still prays for glory: "Glorify your Son so that the Son may glorify you. . . . I glorified you on earth . . . glorify me in your own presence with the glory in your presence that I had before the world existed. . . . I have been glorified in them" (that is, the disciples).

Jesus was currently glorified on earth through the "signs" he did. "Sign" (sēmeion) is a distinctive word for a miracle. For John, a sign is a miracle performed by a person who is superhuman, the purpose of which is to inspire faith in that person. This idea is put in the words of Nicodemus, perhaps a secret follower of Jesus: "No one can do these signs that you do apart from the presence of God" (3:2).

Four of Jesus' miracles are specifically called signs: the changing of water into wine (2:1–11), after which "his disciples believed in him"; the healing of the official's son (4:46–54); the feeding of the five thousand (6:1–14), after which Jesus is acclaimed as a prophet; and the raising of Lazarus (11:38–44), as the result of which many Jews believed in him. Indeed, Jesus' signs are the main concern of his Jewish adversaries: "This man is performing many signs. If we let him go on like this, everyone will believe in him" (11:47–48). At other times also, there are references to Jesus' signs in general as evoking faith (2:23; 4:48; 7:31). Thus, John uses Jesus' signs to promote faith in Jesus. This contrasts with the synoptics where, when faith is mentioned in connection with one of Jesus' miracles,

it always precedes the miracle. Remember that John says the signs "are written so that you may come to believe that Jesus is the Christ, the son of God" (20:31).

An even more distinctive Johannine word for what Jesus does, including his miracles, is "work" (ergon), usually used in the plural, "works" (erga). Jesus works as his Father is working (5:17) and works the works of him who sent him (9:4; see 4:34; 5:36; 10:37). Jesus' testimony to himself is greater than that of the Baptist, "the works that the Father has given me to complete, the very works that I am doing, testify on my behalf that the Father has sent me" (5:36; see also 10:25). Only in John does Jesus appeal to his works as a reason for people to have faith in him: "Believe me that I am in the Father and the Father is in me; but if you do not, then believe me because of the works themselves" (14:11; see also 10:37–38). Those who believe in Jesus will also do the works that he does, and greater works, because he is going to the Father (14:12). The disciples are to carry on Jesus' work, that is, "bear much fruit" (15:5) and keep his commandments (15:10). Jesus' greatest work is the giving of eternal life, a unique concept in John.

Jesus as Bringer of Eternal Life and Judgment

The Pharisees, Jesus, Paul, and the early church believed that a final judgment lay in the future. Those who survived the judgment would then begin eternal life. The whole process has six stages: this life, death, the grave, resurrection, judgment, and eternal life or eternal punishment. This view is known as future or final eschatology, and in certain passages John shares it. Jesus tells the Jews, "The hour is coming when all who are in their graves will . . . come out—those who have done good, to the resurrection of life, and those who have done evil, to the resurrection of condemnation" (5:28–29; see also 11:23–24).

In other passages, sometimes in the same context as those mentioned, John introduces a unique concept of eternal life and judgment. According to this view, the one who believes in Jesus or God begins to experience eternal life on this earth and will not face future judgment. For the believer, then, physical death is simply a passing from this life into the next. On the other hand, those who do not believe in Jesus are already judged by their disbelief. This view is known as present or realized eschatology. Here are some passages that illustrate it: "Anyone who hears my word and believes him who sent me, has eternal life, and does not come under judgment, but has passed from death to life" (5:24). "Those who believe in him [the Son] are not condemned [or judged; same Greek word]; but those who do not believe are condemned [or judged] already, because they have not believed in the name of the only Son of God" (3:18). "Whoever believes in the Son has eternal life; whoever disobeys the Son will not see life, but must endure God's wrath" (3:36). "I am the resurrection and the life. Those who believe in me, even though they die, will live, and everyone who lives and believes in me will never die" (11:25–26). Again, in typical fashion, John repeats the same theme with variations: those who believe in Jesus begin to experience eternal life already and do not come into future judgment. Those who do not believe are already judged. Such variations are typical of John's style.

Let me point out that in John's presentation of Jesus conversing with women, the women are all given a positive role in promoting faith. After an initial rebuke of his mother—not so unnaturally, perhaps—he performs his first sign at her request: "Do whatever he tells you" (2:5). The Samaritan woman comprehends Jesus in progressive stages of faithfulness: the giver of eternal life (4:13–15); a prophet (4:19); and the Messiah (4:25–26), in spite of her doubt (4:28–29). Because of her initial testimony, many other Samaritans not only believed in Jesus but also acknowledged him as "the Savior of the world" (4:39–42).

The later insertion in John 7:53–8:11 is consistent with the presentation of Jesus as forgiving a sinful woman in Mark 7:37–39, when he says to the woman: "Go . . . and from now on do not sin again" (see John 5:13–14). Mary venerates

Jesus by anointing him (11:2; 12:3–8). Martha first confesses her faith in Jesus' saving presence and in the resurrection and then becomes the first woman to confess that Jesus is the Messiah, the Son of God (11:20–27).

Mary likewise reverences Jesus and acknowledges her faith in him (11:32). So Mary and Martha emerge as women of great faith, in spite of personal loss. And only in John does Mary Magdalene become the only woman to confront the resurrected Jesus, acknowledge him as "Teacher," and later refer to him as "Lord" in the presence of the disciples (20:1–18).

VOCABULARY AND STYLE OF JOHN

In contrast to the vocabularies of most NT writers, John's is small, yet he uses about seventy words that occur nowhere else in the NT. John prefers to use a smaller number of words again and again. Here are some of his favorites (numbers represent Mark, Matthew, Luke, and John, respectively): "Father"—of God (4, 45, 17, 118), "world" (3, 9, 3, 78), "Jew" and "the Jews" (6, 5, 5, 71), "know" (*ginōskō* [12, 20, 28, 57]), "know" (*oida* [21, 24, 25, 84]), "work" (noun [2, 6, 2, 27]), "witness" (noun [3, 0, 1, 14]), "I am" (4, 14, 16, 54), "true" and "truth" (4, 2, 4, 48), "love" (verb, *agapaō*, and noun, *agapē* [5, 9, 14, 44]), "life" (4, 7, 5, 36), "send" (*pempō* [1, 4, 10, 32]), "light" (1, 7, 7, 23), "love" (verb, *phileō* [1, 5, 2, 13]), "judge" (verb [0, 6, 6, 19]), and "believe" (*pisteuō* [14, 11, 9, 98]).

The most characteristic feature of John's literary style is variation in both language and thought. This is more evident, of course, in the Greek text than in English translation, but the examples of variation (in Figure 14.2) among synonyms will illustrate the point.

There are dozens of variations in phrasing, such as "see the kingdom of God" (3:3) and "enter the kingdom of God" (3:5), "bread of life" (6:35) and "living bread" (6:51). Read through chapter 6 and notice in how many different ways John describes Jesus as the bread. John also likes to vary

FIGURE 14.2   *Variation Among Synonyms in Gospel of John*

See	Know	Send	Love
horaō (1:18)	*oida* (1:33)	*apostellō* (1:19)	*phileō* (11:3)
blepō (1:29)	*ginōskō* (1:48)	*pempō* (1:22)	*agapaō* (11:5)
theaomai (1:32)	*ginōskō* (4:1)	*apostellō* (5:36)	*phileō* (15:17)
theaomai (1:38)	*oida* (4:10)	*pempō* (5:37)	*agapaō* (15:19)
theōreō (2:23)	*ginōskō* (5:6)		*agapaō* (21:15)
ide (5:14)	*oida* (5:13)		*phileō* (21:15)
blepō (5:19)	*ginōskō* (6:44)		*agapaō* (21:16)
theaomai (6:5)	*oida* (6:64)		*phileō* (21:16)
theōreō (6:14)			
horaō (6:36)			
blepō (11:9)			
ide (11:36)			

the way he uses proper names (Greek text): "Judas the son of Simon Iscariot" (6:71), "Judas Iscariot" (12:4), "Judas Iscariot, Simon's son" (13:2); "Andrew, Simon Peter's brother" (1:40), "Andrew" (1:44), "Andrew, Simon Peter's brother" (6:8), "Andrew" (12:22); "a woman of Samaria" (4:7), "the Samaritan woman" (4.9), "a woman of Samaria" (4.9), "the woman" (4:11). John also sometimes says the same thing in two or more different ways; for example, "living water" is *hudōr zōn* (4: 10) and *to hudōr to zōn* (4:11).

There are also many variations in the writer's thought on main ideas, even to the point of contradiction. We have already seen how the theme of Jesus' glory and glorification is varied. Here are two other themes with variations—judgment and truth. "God did not send the Son into the world to condemn [judge] the world" (3:17). "The Father judges no one but has given all judgment to the Son" (5:22). "I judge no one. Yet even if I do judge, my judgment is valid; for it is not I alone who judge, but I and the Father who sent me" (8:15–16). "I came into this world for judgment" (9:39). "I do not judge anyone who hears my words and does not keep them, for I came not to judge the world, but to save the world" (12:47). Notice other variations on this theme as you read the gospel.

Truth is one of the most complicated and difficult themes in the fourth gospel. The Word was "full of grace and truth" (1:14), and "grace and truth came through Jesus Christ" (1:17). "Those who do what is true come to the light" (3:21). "The true worshipers will worship the Father in spirit and truth" (4:23–24). The Baptist "testified to the truth" (5:33). To some Jews who have believed in Jesus, Jesus says that if they continue in his word, they will know the truth and the truth will make them free (8:31–32). Jesus accuses the Jews of seeking to kill him, "a man who has told you the truth that I heard from God" (8:40). Then he says that they are of their father the devil, who "does not stand in the truth, because there is no truth in him" (8:44), and he asks why they do not believe if he tells them the truth (8:46; see also 16:7). Jesus not only tells the truth; he is the truth (14:6). When the Spirit of truth, the Counselor (14:17; 15:26), comes, "he will guide you into all the truth" (16:13). Jesus prays that the Father may sanctify his followers in the truth, for his "word is truth" (17:17, 19). Jesus tells Pilate that he came into the world "to testify to the truth" and that "everyone who belongs to the truth" hears his voice (18:37). Then Pilate asks, "What is truth?" (18:38).

There are so many variations on the theme of truth that we cannot be certain what "truth" means. We are left to ask "What is truth?" in John's gospel. Such variations in the writer's thought present the most difficult problem in the study of the gospel. Scholars have suggested that the variations may be due to different sources, used without changes, or to different editors with widely diverse points of view. Perhaps the gospel represents a community of believers in the developing church at a time when many different points of view were discussed and became incorporated into the gospel. But without more evidence, we cannot explain the variations, and we must study many themes in John in darkness while searching for light.

"Light" is a favorite word in John's vocabulary, and it is an often overlooked theme in the gospel. The noun *phōs* ("light") occurs twenty-three times in John, compared with one in Mark and seven in each of Matthew and Luke. "Light" (*phōs*), not "Word" (*logos*), is the prevailing theme in the Prologue (1:1–18). *Logos* does not occur once elsewhere in the gospel with the christological meaning it has in the Prologue. On the other hand, the themes of light and darkness, with Jesus as the Light, are an inherent part of the rest of the gospel. Here are two examples: "I am the light of the world. Whoever follows me will never walk in darkness but will have the light of life" (8:12) and "The light is with you for a little longer. Walk while you have the light, so that the darkness may not overtake you" (12:35; see also 9:5; 12:46). It is never reported that Jesus refers to himself as the *Logos*.

Another aspect of John's style, not readily observed in English translation, is poetry. The poetic sections in the gospel and even that Jesus spoke in poetic form were noted long ago (C. F. Burney 1925). Poetry is especially evident in the Prologue. Take the first two verses, for example:

In the beginning was the Word,
and the Word was with God,
and the Word was God.
He was in the beginning with God.

Compare John 8:12:

I am the light of the World.
Whoever follows me will
never walk in darkness
but will have the light of life.

These examples are similar to, but not exactly the same as, a form of Hebrew poetry known as synonymous parallelism, whereby the same idea is repeated in another way in one or more lines. John's poetry is especially marked by rhythm, lines about the same length, and a beat or accent unlike Greek prose. In this respect the lines quoted are different from the prose sections in the gospel. For parallelism in John see, for example, 3:11; 4:36; 6:35, 55; 7:34; 13:6. A good place to begin studying the subject is R. E. Brown 1966:cxxxii–cxxxv, 1970:748–751.

Some scholars have become interested in various aspects of literary analysis of the fourth gospel. R. A. Culpepper 1983 was the first to turn his attention away from the usual historical, sociological, and theological concerns "to expose the Fourth Gospel's rhetorical power to analysis by studying the literary elements of its 'anatomy.'" This is to help in "understanding the gospel as a narrative text, what it is, and how it works." The method differs "from reading the gospel *looking for* particular kinds of historical evidence." The unique literary unity of the gospel is due to "the effect it achieves through thematic development, the spectrum of characters, and the implicit commentary conveyed through irony and symbolism." For other works concerned with literary aspects of the gospel of John, see P. F. Ellis 1984; L. W. Countryman 1987; J. L. Staley 1988. For all topics see bibliography at end of chapter.

JOHN'S SOURCES

There is a relationship between John and the synoptics, but there is little agreement about what the relationship is. Most scholars think John did not use the synoptics in the way Matthew and Luke used Mark. And most believe that John used an oral tradition similar to the synoptics—but not the synoptics themselves—and that this best explains the likenesses and differences between the first three gospels and the fourth. (Among the exceptions to this consensus are C. K. Barrett 1978:15–21, 42–46; F. Neirynck 1977, 1984; M. Sabbe 1977.) As we learned in our study of Luke, there is a possible common tradition between Luke and John (see again Figure 6.1).

I remain convinced that John did know and use the synoptic gospels but in a very creative way as he used the OT (see below). Eusebius (*Hist.* 3:24:7, 13) writes that John, "it is said, used all the time a message [*kērygma*] not written down and finally got to writing." Then Eusebius continues: "The three gospels that had already been written down before were distributed to all and to him" (John). Seeing that those gospels lacked certain things, John then began to write his gospel. According to Eusebius, "It is reasonable to think that John was satisfied to remain silent about the genealogy of our Savior according to the flesh because it had earlier been written by Matthew and Luke."

We have, then, the tradition reported by Eusebius that John used an oral tradition for his gospel and that he also had the earlier three gospels before him when he wrote his own. Is there a better reason for believing that John did not use one or all of those three gospels than that he did?

It is virtually impossible to identify the sources John may have used. There is a growing consensus, however, that he used a signs source for his treatment of Jesus' miracles, but not all agree that such a source was a kind of "minigospel" or "gospel in the narrower sense." This is the view of R. T Fortna 1970, for whom the source consists of material on the Baptist, the call of disciples, seven miracles, including the catch of fish in chapter 21, the story of the Samaritan woman, and the passion narrative (see also H. M. Teeple 1974:30–51; R. Kysar 1975:13–37).

Occasionally other sources have been suggested, such as a sayings source for Jesus' teachings. And a narrative-discourse source has been proposed for the "core" of John's gospel (S. Temple 1975:255–282). According to this view, a narrative of an incident from Jesus' life is followed by a discourse. In chapter 6, for example, vv 1–35, 41–51, 60, and 66–70 are the chapter's core source, and vv 36–40 and 61–65 are the writer's own expansion of the source as he incorporated it into the gospel. These examples of attempts to discern sources behind the fourth gospel have not yet produced a consensus of opinion like that with respect to the sources of Matthew and Luke.

THE JUDAIC BACKGROUND

Among NT writers, John's intellectual background is one of the most diverse, but we can isolate several strands from the Judaism and Hellenism of his time. The aspect of Judaism easiest to detect is the OT, which John knew well enough to quote when he wanted to support a theological idea.

The Old Testament

Although John uses fewer direct quotations from the OT than other gospel writers do, they are especially significant. Unlike the synoptists, John uses proof texts not to show that Jesus was the expected Messiah, but to aid in the development of his unique conception of Jesus as the Christ, the Son of God, as the following examples show.

A quotation made up from several OT texts (Ps 78:24; Exod 16:4, 15) is a key passage in John's portrayal of Jesus as the bread of life. The quotation is put on the lips of Jews who have asked Jesus what sign he will do that they might see and believe. They say, "Our ancestors ate the manna in the wilderness; as it is written, 'He gave them bread from heaven to eat'" (6:31). This refers to the manna that God gave the Israelites in the desert during Moses' time. John uses the quotation to set the context for his presentation of Jesus as the bread of life, which follows. Jesus is "the bread of life," "the bread that came down from heaven," and which is "for the life of the world" (6:35, 41, 51). Jesus is "the living bread," and "whoever eats of this bread will live forever" (6:51). Thus, Jesus is placed in strong contrast to Moses, the hero of the Jews. The Jews looked upon Moses as their deliverer and the giver of the manna that their ancestors ate, but that manna did not provide eternal life (6:49; see W. A. Meeks 1967).

During the last supper of Jesus with his disciples he says, "I know whom I have chosen. But it is to fulfill the scripture, 'The one who ate my bread has lifted his heel against me'" (13:18, from Ps 41:9). In the psalm quoted, the psalmist is lamenting his betrayal by an intimate friend. John takes the quotation as a prediction and puts it on the lips of Jesus to show that it is fulfilled in Jesus' own betrayal by Judas. Like the synoptists, John says that at the supper Jesus predicted the betrayal by Judas. But unlike the synoptists, John does not leave the identity of the traitor in doubt. Jesus took the morsel and "gave it to Judas" (13:26) who, as Jesus already knew, would betray him to fulfill the scripture. As an intimate friend and dining companion, Judas had already been predestined to betray Jesus (13:2).

John associates the prediction of Jesus' betrayal by Judas with the glorification of Jesus and uses it as a transition between Jesus' present glorification and his future glorification through his death and resurrection. John says that Judas, "after receiving the piece of bread . . . went out. And it was night." Night symbolizes the end of Jesus' work (9:4; 11:10; 12:35). When Judas goes out, Jesus says, "Now the Son of man has been glorified, and God has been glorified in him. If God has been glorified in him, God will also glorify him in himself" (13:31–32). John stresses the betrayal by Judas as a necessary step toward Jesus' ultimate glorification through his death and resurrection, which result from the betrayal. John found a passage in the OT that he thought was fulfilled in Judas' action.

Another example of John's use of the OT to support his theological view of Jesus is the quotation in 19:36b to fulfill scripture: "None of his bones shall be broken." John has reported that the soldiers broke the legs of the criminals crucified with Jesus. Archaeological evidence confirms that the legs of those crucified were broken, apparently to hasten death (J. A. Fitzmyer 1978). But John says that Jesus' legs were not broken because he was already dead. He says that the soldiers pierced Jesus' side with a spear because the scripture says, "They will look on the one whom they have pierced" (19:34, 37). Although

we cannot be certain of the precise passage John had in mind, the reference is to the lamb to be sacrificed during Passover in celebration of the Israelites' deliverance from Egypt (Exod 12:10, LXX, 46; Num 9:12). According to OT law, not a bone of that lamb was to be broken, so that it would be a perfect sacrifice.

The Baptist had pointed out Jesus as "the Lamb of God who takes away the sin of the world" (1:29); and in John, the time of Jesus' crucifixion coincides with the killing of the Passover lambs. It seems clear, therefore, that the reason Jesus' legs were not broken was that he was the perfect sacrificial victim for mankind's sin. Again, John knew the OT well enough to find a quotation to support his theological view.

Besides specific quotations, dozens of allusions to the OT in John show that it was a part of the writer's intellectual background. This is true in many places where the average reader is unaware of it. For example, John always uses the word "law" as in the Septuagint for the meanings of the Hebrew word *torah,* concepts not included in the usual meaning of the Greek word *nomos* (law). And the key concepts that Jesus is the giver of light and life have their basis in the OT idea that God is the source of light and life, for example, in Ps 36:9: "For with you is the fountain of life; in your light we see light."

The OT is the only obvious and indisputable source John used. The most significant point about its use is that in all but one or two instances the source of the quotation can be positively identified. Therefore the quotations provide good insight into how John probably dealt with any source he used. He was not bound to any OT text he used but adapted each one to its context in the gospel, his peculiar literary style, and his theological/christological views. It appears that John was concerned primarily with theological motives and ideas and with writing a literary composition rather than a historical account. Moreover, the changes John makes in the quotations reveal a creative hand at work that we may assume was operative also in whatever sources he used, including the synoptic gospels.

Qumran

The thought of John has important affinities with that of Qumran (see, for example, J. H. Charlesworth 1972). The antithesis of the forces of light and darkness—symbolic of good and evil, respectively—is present in both Qumran and John. With John 3:19–21, compare 1QS 1:9: "love all the sons of light . . . but hate all the sons of darkness" (see also 1QS 1:5). The expression "sons of light" occurs only in John 12:36 in the NT. And the exhortation to "love all the sons of light"—that is, the members of the Qumran Sect—corresponds to Jesus' command that his disciples "love one another" (13:34; 15:17; 1 John 3:23; 4:11; 2 John 5). In 1QS 3:17–26 there are several ideas close to those in John. The writer talks about "the spirits of light and darkness" and also calls them "the spirits of truth and error." Compare "the Spirit of truth" in John 14:17; 15:26; and 16:13 and "the spirit of truth and the spirit of error" in 1 John 4:6. The "Spirit of truth" in John is the Counselor promised by Jesus in chaps. 14–16 and is described in various ways. "Counselor" translates the Greek *paraklētos,* which occurs in the NT only in John's gospel and 1 John 2:1. It can also be translated as "helper," "comforter," or "advocate." In 1QS 3:24 we read, "The God of Israel and his angel of truth have helped all the sons of light," and in 1QM 13:10, "You appointed in former times the prince of light as our helper." The ideas are very similar.

Now compare the passages below, the first from Qumran, the second from John.

> In a fountain of light are the origins of truth, and from a fountain of darkness are the origins of error. In the hand of the prince of lights is the rule over all the sons of righteousness; in the ways of light they walk. And in the hand of the angel of darkness is all the rule over the sons of error; and in the ways of darkness they walk. [1QS 3:19–21]

> The light is with you for a little longer. Walk while you have the light, so that the darkness may not overtake you. If you walk in the darkness, you do not know where you are going. While you have the light, believe in the light, so that you may become children of light. [John 12:35–36]

The dualism of light and darkness is similar in Qumran and John. For John, Jesus the light has already appeared, and believing in the light makes people children of light (see 1QS 3:7 and John 8:12).

For both Qumran and John "truth" is a key word, and on this subject the two are sometimes very close. The expression "do or practice the truth" occurs only in John and 1 John in the NT. John 3:20–21 (lit.) reads: "Every one who does evil hates the light and does not come to the light, that his deeds may not be exposed. But he who does the truth comes to the light, that his deeds may be manifest that they have been done in God." The writer of Qumran exhorts the members of the sect to "cling to all good works and to do truth and righteousness and justice on earth" (1QS 1:5; see also 5:3–4; 8:2). Similar ideas occur in 1 John 1:6: "If we say that we have fellowship with him while we are walking in darkness, we lie and [lit.] do not do the truth."

Walking in the (spirit of) truth is an idea shared by Qumran (1QS 4:6, 15) and 2 John 4 and 3 John 3. In the NT the concept of witnessing to the truth occurs only in John 5:33 and 18:37. In the former passage, the Baptist bears such witness, and in the latter, Jesus tells Pilate that he came into the world "to bear witness to the truth." The members of the Sect of Qumran are called "witnesses of truth" (1QS 8:6). This witnessing to the truth, whatever the truth is, makes a difference in the lives of those who do the truth in the community of Qumran and in John's community. "According as every man shares in truth and righteousness, so he hates evil; but according to his share of perversity and evil in him, so he detests truth" (1QS 4:24; see also John 3:20–21, quoted above).

Both Qumran and John present truth as a means of cleansing or sanctification. "Then God will cleanse by his truth all the works of a man . . . to cleanse him through a holy spirit from all wicked deeds, sprinkling upon him a spirit of truth as water of purification" (1QS 4:20–21). Compare John 17:17–19: "Sanctify them in the truth. . . . For their sake I sanctify myself, so that they also may be sanctified in truth."

Both Qumran and John emphasize unity in the community. Members of the Sect of Qumran actually join the "oneness" or "union," usually translated as "community" (1QS 5:7). With John's phrases "that they may be one" (17:11, 21) and "may become completely one" (17:23), compare "to become a oneness in Torah" (1QS 5:2). The closest verbal parallel is that between John 1:3 and 1QS 11:11. In John, "All things came into being through him, and without him not one thing came into being." The latter reads, "By his knowledge everything comes into being, and everything that is, by his purpose he establishes, and except for him nothing is made."

There are differences of opinion about the importance of the parallels between Qumran and John. Many of the same parallels also occur in the OT and in later Jewish literature. The most important difference between Qumran and John, of course, is John's concern for belief in Christ. John was not a member of Qumran, and members of Qumran were not Christians, but it is clear that there is much in common between the thought of John and that of Qumran. This helps to confirm the Jewish background of the gospel.

Messianic Ideas

Several distinctive ideas regarding messianic belief occur only in the fourth gospel. Although John added his own creative touch to most of them, some reflect messianic thought in current Jewish apocalyptic writings or foreshadow that in later rabbinic literature.

John is the only NT writer to use the Greek term *messias,* a transliteration of the Hebrew or Aramaic *messiah.* When Andrew tells his brother Simon Peter about Jesus (1:41), he says, "We have found the Messiah [*messias*]." John adds, "(which means Christ)." The translation "Christ" (Greek, *christos*) was the title used in Christian tradition. Since John's usage indicates a Hebrew or Aramaic original, it did not come from Christian tradition, where *christos* was used for the Messiah, as John's translation, "which means Christ," makes clear. So Andrew's word *messias* represents the Jewish usage of John's time (see *Pss. Sol.* 17:36).

A contemporary Jewish view of the Messiah is also reflected in the Jews' comment, "When the Christ comes, no one will know where he is from" (7:27). According to later Jewish belief, when the Messiah appeared, he would be concealed until God decided to reveal him. A similar view is reflected in 2 Esdr 13:52, written near the time of John: "Just as no one can explore or know what is in the depths of the sea, so no one on earth can see my Son . . . except in the time of his day." For John, of course, the Messiah has come, but the Jews do not accept him.

In at least two other passages John reflects views of the Messiah that were current in his day. The first is, "When the Christ comes, will he do more signs than this man has done?" (7:31). Although there is almost nothing in Jewish sources that concerns miracles to be performed by the Messiah, the Jews' question indicates that the Jewish circles of John's time expected the Messiah to perform miracles. The second is John 12:34: "We have heard from the law that the Christ remains forever." Jesus has just spoken about his coming death on the cross, but for the Jews a crucified Messiah is inconceivable. In contrast, for John, Jesus' death is his exaltation and his final glorification. In presenting Jesus as the Messiah, however, John reveals messianic beliefs current in the Judaism of his time (see C. H. Dodd 1953:87–93 and M. de Jonge 1977:77–116).

THE HELLENISTIC BACKGROUND

Although John was influenced by elements from Hellenistic culture, when compared with the evidence from Judaism, the evidence for Hellenistic influence is uncertain and illusive. The reason for this is that the intellectual world of the first century was so syncretistic.

Jewish Wisdom, Philo of Alexandria, and Plato

Much debate on the background of the gospel has centered on the concept of the Word (*logos*) in the Prologue. Studies have sometimes stressed influence from the Stoic idea of *logos*. Current scholarship emphasizes the influence of the Jewish notion of wisdom on John's prologue. Wisdom was present with the Most High (God) and came forth from his mouth (Sir 24:2–3). Like the Word, wisdom is divine, "a breath of the power of God, and a pure emanation of the glory [see John 1:14] of the Almighty . . . a reflection of eternal light [see John 1:4–5] . . . and . . . can do all things" (Wis 7:25–27). Wisdom, like the Word, was present at the creation (Wis 9:9) and was not accepted by "sinners" (Sir 15:7; see R. E. Brown 1966:519–534).

Philo speaks of the *logos* hundreds of times and in various complicated ways. Sometimes his concepts are close to those of John; for example, *logos* is "the first-born son" of God. Although it occurs in a context where *logos* is not used, divine beings become humans in one passage of Philo. Of the visitors who came to Abraham to tell him that his wife would bear a son through whom Abraham's descendants would be a mighty nation (Gen 18:1–21), Philo says, "being incorporeal [lit., "without bodies"] they received human form to do kindness to the worthy person" (*On Abraham* 23; see also John 1:14).

The biggest difference between John's *logos* and Philo's is that Philo's *logos* never descends from the world above—the world of the mind—into the world below, that of the senses. Philo's *logos* never becomes flesh. As *logos*, Jesus becomes a part of history; Philo's *logos* does not. Some scholars think that in the *logos* concept John adapted a basic Hellenistic Jewish idea in a Greek mode of expression, combining the ideas of wisdom, word of God, and Torah (see C. H. Dodd 1953:278; R. Schnackenburg 1980:1:493; P. Borgen 1983a, 1987).

In 1 John 2:1 the term *paraklētos* is translated as "advocate" (= intercessor): "If any one does sin, we have an advocate with the Father, Jesus Christ the righteous." In speaking about God's mercy toward the Israelites, Philo says, "They have three intercessors [*paraklētois*] to reconcile them with the Father" (*On Rewards and Punishments* 29). The use of the term *paraklētos* in Philo is exactly like that of 1 John. But John's in-

tellectual world also has other things in common with Philo's (C. H. Dodd 1953:54–73; R. E. Brown 1966:lvii–lviii).

Perhaps some passages in John show the influence of Plato's theory of ideas. Plato makes a sharp distinction between the material world, perceived by the senses, and the real world, comprehended by reason. The real world is eternal and invisible; the material world is temporary and is a poor copy of the real world. True reality exists only in the supersensory world of ideas. For example, the chair on which you are sitting is just a copy of the real chair, which existed only in the mind of the craftsperson who made it. Everything around us is subordinate to and results from the world of ideas. The mind, to which the body is inferior, contemplates ideas; and all ideas are subordinate to and become focused on the highest idea, the Idea of the Good, God.

When John presents Jesus as the "true light" (1:9), "true bread" (6:32), and "true vine" (15:1), "true" has the meaning "real" or "genuine." The implication is that Jesus is "real" or "ideal," and that compared with him others are imperfect copies. In this respect Jesus is also like God, because God who sent Jesus is "true" (7:28; 17:3). Several passages reflect the Platonic notion of two worlds, again with reference to Jesus. "The one who comes from above is above all; the one who is of the earth belongs to the earth. . . . The one who comes from heaven is above all" (3:31). The Jews are "from below" and Jesus is "from above"; they are "of this world"; he is "not of this world" (8:23; see also Jesus' prayer in chap. 17).

Gnosticism

As we have learned, the intellectual world of John's time was one of philosophic-religious syncretism. Some scholars see Gnostic rather than Platonic or Jewish influence on such dualisms as light and darkness, the world above and the world below, and flesh and spirit. The debate about Gnostic influence on John has also centered upon the Johannine Son of Man, the incarnation of Jesus (1:14), and the "I am" (see R. Kysar 1975:111–122).

Although Gnosticism as a system of thought developed fully only after John's time, John's frequent use of "to know" echoes that concept in Gnosticism. Remember that the Gnostics believed one gained salvation by knowledge, not faith. Strangely enough, however, John uses neither the noun "knowledge" nor "faith." By avoiding those terms and by using "believe," and especially "know," was he fighting Gnostics partially on their own terms? The statement in 17:3, "This is eternal life, that they know you, the only true God, and Jesus Christ whom you have sent" (see 8:32; 16:3), is close to the Gnostic idea of salvation. That statement and the emphasis on the unity of Christians with each other and with God (17:20–23) have led some scholars to think that John lived in an environment in which Gnosticism was developing (see E. Kaesemann 1968).

On the basis of several documents from the texts of Nag Hammadi, other scholars suggest possible influence from Gnosticism on "the language and imagery of the Johannine prologue," the "genre of revelation discourse," "patterns of Gnostic and Johannine Christology and soteriology," the "theme of becoming children of the Father," "possible Gnostic interaction of the Johannine Christians who were rejected by the author of the First Epistle of John" (G. W. MacRae 1986), on the "controversy traditions in John 8:12–59" (H. Koester 1986), and on the "I am" (G. W. MacRae 1970). C. A. Evans 1993 argues against any Gnostic influence on the gospel of John.

For the relationship between Johannine Christianity and Gnosticism, especially for influence of the former on the latter, see E. H. Pagels 1973 and P. Perkins 1980. For parallels among John, the synoptic gospels, and noncanonical early Christian literature, see R. W. Funk 1985.

John breathed in deeply the intellectual syncretistic atmosphere of his time, especially that of Judaism. He also absorbed much from Hellenistic and Oriental cultures. All of this means that any discussion of John's background must always be open to new and changing insights based on a continually expanding body of knowledge.

THE STRUCTURE OF JOHN

For the gospel of John more than for any other writing in the NT, we can use a key word or two as clues to the content of each chapter: (1) word and disciples, (2) wine and temple, (3) birth, (4) water, (5) work and witness, (6) bread, (7) feast and controversy, (8) feast and controversy, (9) sight, (10) shepherd and sheep, (11) life, (12) anointing and glory, (13) supper and service, (14) mansions and Counselor, (15) vine, (16) Counselor, (17) prayer, (18) arrest and trial, (19) cross and crown, (20) resurrection, and (21) fishing with Peter.

The gospel divides naturally at the end of chapter 12. The first part, after an introduction, presents Jesus' public life, and the second part his life alone with the disciples. The first part is often referred to as the book of signs and the second as the book of the passion or the book of glory with an epilogue. If we separate the passion narrative from the book of glory, there is a natural five-fold division: introduction (1:1–51), Jesus' public life (2:1–12:50), Jesus alone with his disciples (13:1–17:26), passion narrative (18:1–20:29), and epilogue (21:1–25). This is the basis of the outline and comments that follow. Refer to them as you read through the gospel of John.

Outline and Comments

1. Introduction (1:1–51)
   A. Prologue (1:1–18)

The verses about the Word were probably added to adapt the gospel to a particular environment. *Logos* is not used in the same way elsewhere in the gospel. Light becomes a main theme of the Prologue and is a main theme in the rest of the gospel. As the eschatological and ethical light of the world, Jesus came to save people from the darkness of sin and death (3:19–21; 8:12; 9:5; 11:9–10; 12:35–36, 46)

   B. Jesus and the Baptist (1:19–51)

The Baptist and disciples testify to Jesus in a summary of John's Christology: Jesus is the

Lamb of God, Son of God, Teacher, Messiah (Christ), King of Israel, and Son of Man.

II. Jesus' public life, one of controversy with the Jews (2:1–12:50)

A. First sign: water to wine (2:1–11)

With this sign, we must face the question of whether John was writing fact, faith, or fiction. Did Jesus really turn about 150 gallons of water into wine, or did John create a symbolic story to show that Christianity (wine) was superior to Judaism (water)? Remember that John wrote to promote faith in Jesus as the Christ. This was Jesus' first manifestation of his glory, "and his disciples believed in him" (2:11).

B. Jesus in Capernaum (2:12)

C. First Passover: cleansing of the temple (2:13–22)

The temple, the main symbol of the old order, Judaism, is replaced by Jesus' resurrection, which also elicits the response of faith (2:22).

D. Reaction: belief of some Jews (2:23–25)

E. Jesus and Nicodemus (3:1–21)

Jesus speaks with Nicodemus, a representative of Judaism and "a teacher of Israel," who sees Jesus only as a "teacher who has come from God." "Born from above" picks up the idea of being born of God, from the Prologue. As Son of Man, Jesus descended from heaven to be lifted up (= crucified and glorified). Whoever believes in him escapes judgment and does good deeds.

F. The Baptist's final witness to Jesus (3:22–30)

G. Return to discourse (3:31–36)

H. Jesus in Judea, Galilee, and Samaria (4:1–6)

I. Jesus and the Samaritan woman (4:7–42)

Jesus gives living water, that is, eternal life. The discourse is intended to win Samaritans as well as Jews to the new religion. True worship is not a matter of place, either in Samaria, the seat of the Samaritan cult, or in Jerusalem, the center of Judaism. It is a matter of the spirit. Jesus is not the special figure expected by either Jews or Samaritans. He is the Savior of the world.

J. Jesus in Galilee (4:43–45)

K. Second sign: official's son healed (4:46–54)

L. Jesus at Jerusalem for a feast of the Jews (5:1–47)
1. Healing at Beth-zatha (5:1–16)
2. Discourse on Jesus' work (5:17–47)

The sabbath is the Jews' most holy day. God decreed that on it "you shall not do any work" (Exod 20:10; Deut 5:14). In the synoptics Jesus' healing and the disciples' plucking of grain on the sabbath leads to a discussion of what work is permitted on the sabbath. Here the discourse centers on Jesus working as God works, that is, to judge and give eternal life. As a Son of God and one equal to God, Jesus can do this.

M. Jesus in Galilee or at second Passover (6:1–71)

The reference to the Passover in v 4 is confusing, but apparently Galilee (6:1–3) is the setting for what follows.

1. Feeding of the five thousand and walking on the water (6:1–21)
2. Discourse with the Jews who come to Jesus (6:22–34)

Jesus is the bread from heaven that gives life to the world. This contrasts sharply with the manna in the wilderness (Exod 16:13–36), which did not bring the Jews the same kind of life (see 6:58).

3. Discourse on the bread of life (6:35–59)

There may be a reference here to the bread of the Lord's Supper as a symbol of Jesus' life-giving power.

4. Reaction to the discourse (6:60–71)

N. Jesus at the feast of Tabernacles (7:1–8:59)

Originally a harvest festival, Tabernacles, or Booths, commemorated the Israelites' wandering in the wilderness after the Exodus from Egypt; during this wandering they had lived in booths. Two aspects of the temple ritual were water libations and lighting of the women's court. During the libations the words of Isa 12:3 were recited: "With joy you will draw water from the wells of salvation." As the Messiah, Jesus is the source of living water (7:37–39) and the light of the world (8:12), and replaces the ritual of Tabernacles.

1. *Jesus' discourse with his brothers (7:1–13)*
2. *Discourse with the Jews in the middle of the feast (7:14–36)*

Jesus' authority to heal, even on the sabbath, comes from God (7:14–24). Some people in Jerusalem acknowledge Jesus' signs and wonder if he is really the Christ (7:25–31). Jesus' remark that he is going away introduces the theme of his death (7:32–36).

3. *Discourse on the last day of the feast (7:37–53)*

Jesus is the source of living water (7:37–39). The Jews are divided over the question of whether Jesus is the Christ (7:40–53).

4. *More discourses (8:12–59)*

Behind these discourses we can discern the writer's feeling about Jesus' rejection by the Jews. Some Jews had accepted Jesus (8:31); others were responsible for his death. In the same way, the church of John's time was partially successful in its mission to Jews, perhaps mostly among Greek-speaking Jews in the Diaspora (7:35–36). Jesus' proclamation of himself as the light of the world leads to a debate with the Jews that ends with their wanting to stone him. Jesus is greater than Abraham, the father of the Jewish people. "Before Abraham was, I am" (8:58) harks back to the idea of Jesus' preexistence in the prologue.

O. *Sight given to the man born blind (9:1–41)*

John continues the themes of Jesus doing the Father's works (4:34; 5:17, 36; 6:28) and of Jesus as the light of the world (1:4, 9; 8:12; 9:5). Notice how cleverly John portrays the blind man's ever-deepening insight into who Jesus is: "the man called Jesus" (9:11); "He is a prophet" (9:17); Jesus is not a sinner but comes from God (9:31, 33); the man believes in Jesus as Son of Man and addresses him as Lord (9:35–38); and finally he worships Jesus (9:38). The man's views represent those of members of the church and synagogue of John's community who were debating the meaning of Jesus and belief in him as a requirement for becoming Christians. Similarly, John portrays the Jews as becoming increasingly hostile to Jesus, and the way he does it reflects the historical situation both of Jesus' time and of his own.

1. *The healing miracle (9:1–7)*

Jesus' actions arouse the innocent curiosity of his fellow Jews.

2. *Discussions following the healing (9:8–41)*

The neighbors question the man about his healing (9:8–12), and then there is a discussion between the man and the Pharisees (9:13–17). Historically, Jesus was opposed by Jewish authorities who were partially responsible for his death, but here the Pharisees also represent Jewish authorities of John's time who were responsible for excluding Jewish Christians from the synagogue. In the discussion between the Jews and the man's parents (9:18–23), the Jews represent nonbelieving Jews not only of Jesus' time but also of John's time. The comment that if anyone confessed Jesus to be the Messiah (Christ), he should be put out of the synagogue (9:22) reflects the synagogue benediction against Christians and heretics that was drawn up c. 85 CE. So the parents represent Jews of John's time who wanted to believe in Jesus as the Christ but did not want to be excommunicated from the synagogue. In the discussion between the Jews and the man healed (9:24–34), the casting out of the man represents the fate of those Jews who, having become Christians, were put out of the synagogue. Perhaps John and some of his friends had experienced the same fate. The final discussion involves the Jews, the man, and Jesus (9:35–41). The man joins the community of Christians who confess Jesus as Lord and worship him. Jesus' words reflect the writer's view that disbelief brings judgment upon those who disbelieve (see J. L. Martyn 1979).

P. The shepherd and the sheep (10:1–21)

The Jews' remark in v 21 ties this story in with what precedes. The story is a complicated allegory in which Jesus is first the shepherd, then the door to the sheep pen, and then the good shepherd. We cannot be certain of what some of the imagery represents, but divisions between Jews and Christians are clearly represented, and perhaps also different Christian groups.

1. Jesus as shepherd and door (10:1–18)

This section reflects competition between those who follow Jesus and those who follow leaders who are out of favor with the first group. Compared with other leaders, Jesus is the good shepherd because he gives his life for his followers. Verse 16 is a key verse, but what does it mean? Perhaps "this fold" is Christianity and "other sheep" are Gentiles, or perhaps other Jews who are being sought as converts. Perhaps "this fold" represents John's community of Christians and "other sheep" represents Christians of another community—Christians whom John wants to be brought into, or back into, his community. The point is that there is to be unity in the community: "There will be one flock, one shepherd" (10:16).

2. Differences of opinion among Jews (10:19–21)

Q. Jesus at the feast of Dedication (10:22–39)

Dedication, or Hanukkah, celebrates the cleansing and dedication of the temple in 165 BCE, after its pollution by Antiochus IV. Verse 27 ties the section in with what precedes.

1. Jesus as shepherd (10:22–31)

Jesus gives eternal life to his followers.

2. Jesus as Son of God (10:32–39)

Jesus' works as Son of God make him one with the Father. As the temple was dedicated, so the Father consecrated Jesus and sent him into the world.

R. A summary of Jesus' success (10:40–42)

In spite of attempts on Jesus' life (10:31, 39), "many believed in him." The verses in 10:40–42, with those in 1:29–34, frame the section of the gospel dealing with Jesus' public life and his controversy with the Jews. Chaps. 11–12 form the conclusion to that section and serve as the introduction to the next section.

S. A foreshadowing of Jesus' death and glorification (11:1–12:50)
1. The raising of Lazarus (11:1–44)

Luke tells essentially the same story of Mary and Martha, but he says nothing about Lazarus as their brother (Luke 10:38–42). The synoptics do not report any miracle resembling this one in John. Therefore, we must again raise the question of fact, faith, or fiction in the writing of the fourth gospel. John was writing primarily to promote faith in Jesus, not to record what actually happened. The story of the man born blind illustrates Jesus' claim to being the light of the world. Now the raising of Lazarus gives John's readers a vivid illustration of why John believes that Jesus is the good shepherd who does give eternal life to his sheep (10:28; 11:25–26), that is, those who believe (20:30–31). The story is also an important step in the development of John's theme of the glorification of Jesus (11:4, 40). Does all this mean that the story of the raising of Lazarus is just that—a story—and that, therefore, Lazarus was not actually resuscitated? What do you think?

2. Jesus condemned to death by the Sanhedrin (11:45–53)

The decision of the Sanhedrin is theological, not historical, as the words of the high priest Caiaphas show. Jesus must die not only for the Jews but also for the Gentiles so the children of God may be one (11:52).

3. Jesus in Ephraim (11:54–57)

The Jews plan to arrest Jesus if he goes to Jerusalem for the Passover.

4. Jesus anointed at Bethany (12:1–8)

This act prepares Jesus for his burial.

5. Jesus in Jerusalem (12:9–36)

Jesus is acclaimed by the crowds (12:9–19), and some Greeks want to see him (12:20–36). Jesus' entry into Jerusalem marks the beginning of the gathering of the children of God into one (11:52) and moves the drama of Jesus' approaching death nearer to its climax. The meaning of Jesus' death is explained in vv 23–36.

6. A summary conclusion to Jesus' public life and a review of his message (12:37–50)

III. Jesus alone with his disciples (13:1–17:26)

A. John's version of the Last Supper, the footwashing, and the prediction of Jesus' betrayal (13:1–30)

B. Jesus' last discourses (13:31–17:26)

It is difficult to outline these discourses satisfactorily because of the blending of new themes with old ones, but the following is an attempt to convey John's main thought.

1. Jesus going away and coming again, and the responsibility of discipleship (13:31–14:31)

John seems to be trying to convey to his readers the nature of the relationship between believers and the glorified Christ. Disciples must keep the new commandment to love one another, and they must do the works that Jesus does. The Counselor (*paraklētos*), described as the Spirit of truth and the Holy Spirit, will help them. The *paraklete* represents the spiritual presence of the glorified or risen Christ with believers.

2. The relationship of Christ with his disciples as they encounter the world without his physical presence (15:1–17:26)

Believers abide (remain) in Jesus as branches on the vine, and like the branches they must bear fruit (15:1–11). Believers must love one another (15:12–17). Believers do not "belong to the world" but will suffer in the world (15:18–16:4). What John means here is uncertain. He does not say that believers should separate themselves from the world, but they are different, as Jesus was different. They will experience the same kind of suffering Jesus did. For John, Christians have already suffered.

The theme of Jesus going away and coming again (16:16–33) is followed with Jesus' prayer (17:1–26). Jesus' prayer is the writer's summary of the meaning of Jesus for believers. Jesus prays for his ultimate glorification in his death (17:1–5), for believers who still have to bear witness in the world (17:6–19), and for the unity of all believers with the Father, with the Son, and with each other in love (17:20–26).

IV. Passion narrative (18:1–20:29)

With a few exceptions, John's account closely follows Mark's. Beginning with Nathanael's confession of Jesus as King of Israel (1:49), John has presented Jesus as King (6:14–15; 12:12–19), a theme that reaches its climax in the passion narrative. In the synoptics, Jesus is referred to as a king only in mockery, but in John Pilate himself writes the title over the cross, "Jesus of Nazareth, the King of the Jews" (19:19), refuses to change it when asked (19:19–21), and says, "What I have written, I have written" (19:22). Ironically, neither Pilate nor the Jews understand Jesus' claim to kingship. For John, Jesus' kingdom is not of this world (18:36), but is a spiritual kingdom that believers can experience without its worldly Jewish messianic implications.

A special feature of John's passion account is the use of OT quotations that he believes were fulfilled in Jesus. The synoptic accounts of Jesus' death are marked with allusions to OT scripture, but there is no direct quotation, nor is there any mention of fulfillment. Although we cannot always be sure of the passage cited, John believes four were fulfilled in incidents connected with Jesus' death. Two are the soldiers' dividing of

Jesus' clothes (19:23–24) and Jesus' thirst while on the cross (19:28). The others are more closely related. We have learned that Jesus' legs were not broken so that, like the Passover lambs, he would be a perfect sacrifice. On the other hand, Jesus' side was pierced so that the scripture "When they look on the one whom they have pierced" (Zech 12:10) might be fulfilled (19:37). These quotations give the death of Jesus a more theological significance in John than in the synoptics.

Finally, the introduction of "another disciple" (18:15–16; 20:2–4, 8) is a new feature in John's passion narrative. Known to the high priest, that disciple brings Peter into the courtyard where Peter then denies Jesus. In 20:2 that disciple is identified as the one whom Jesus loved, and he and Peter run to the tomb to find it empty, as Mary Magdalene has reported. After that there is reference only to the disciple whom Jesus loved.

A. Jesus' betrayal and arrest (18:1–12)

B. Jesus before the high priest, and Peter's denial (18:13–27)

Caiaphas, the high priest, represents the people for whom, according to Caiaphas's words (11:49–51; 19:14), Jesus is to die. So for John, Caiaphas has symbolic, not historical, significance.

C. Jesus before Pilate (18:28–19:16)

As in Luke, Pilate is innocent of Jesus' death, so the Jews alone are responsible for it. Three times Pilate says, "I find no case against him" (18:38; 19:4, 6; see also Luke 23:4, 22). Perhaps as a Jew, John is revealing his own sensitivity to the Jews' rejection of Jesus. Like Matthew, also a Jew, John emphasizes the Jews' rejection of Jesus: "Away with him! Away with him! Crucify him!" (19:15; Matt 27:25).

D. Crucifixion and burial (19:17–42)

E. Resurrection of Jesus (20:1–29)

The sequence of incidents in John is the empty tomb (20:1–10), appearance to Mary Magdalene (20:11–18), appearance to the disciples with Thomas absent (20:19–25), and the appearance to the disciples with Thomas present (20:26–29). Like Thomas, the readers of John's gospel were not present when Jesus first appeared to the disciples. Thomas represents the skepticism and doubt of those readers who refused to believe what they were being told about Jesus. But Thomas also represents those who have the potential for rising above the point of doubt, not only to faith but also to confession with the church that Jesus is Lord and God. Using Thomas symbolically as the link between the experience of Jesus' first followers and those of his own time, John assures his readers that they are at no disadvantage for not having seen Jesus. "Those who have not seen and yet have come to believe" are equally blessed (20:29).

V. Statement of purpose (20:30–31)

VI. Epilogue (21:1–25)

Although most scholars agree that chap. 21 was not part of the first edition of the gospel, they do not agree about its author or purpose. There is not much difference in style between it and the rest of the gospel, and some of the same ideas appear—for example, Jesus as the shepherd with his sheep, and the disciple whom Jesus loved.

Several purposes of chap. 21 are clear. The writer wanted to supplement the tradition of Jesus' resurrection appearances in Jerusalem with one also in Galilee (21:1–14), which he knew from another tradition (see Luke 5:1–11). He wanted to reinstate Peter in the church's favor after his denial (21:15–19) and to correct a mistaken tradition that Jesus had said that the disciple whom he loved would not die. That disciple did die, so the effort was made to show that Jesus' words had been misunderstood (21:20–23). The author of chap. 21 wanted to make clear that the "beloved disciple," perhaps alluded to in 19:35, wrote the gospel (21:24). Verse 25 is therefore an expansion of 20:30.

SUMMARY

From beginning to end, the fourth gospel differs from the first three in concept, content, and structure. The background of John is diverse, but it has strong affinities with Judaism, as the use of the OT, the similarities with writings from Qumran, and messianic ideas clearly show. At the same time, there are influences from the syncretism of the Hellenistic world, including popular Platonism, incipient Gnosticism, Jewish wisdom, and Philo.

The anonymous author states clearly that he writes to promote faith in Jesus as the Christ, the Son of God, and to assure those who believe in Jesus that they have eternal life, which begins already with their faith in Jesus. Although in general John's story of Jesus is the same as that of the synoptists, his presentation of Jesus differs radically from theirs. For John, Jesus is not only the Christ, the Son of God, and Son of Man, but also the "I am." This is the writer's unique concept of Jesus as the Christ, whose spiritual presence as "the resurrection and the life," for example, can be experienced in the lives of believers. Also for John, Jesus is uniquely a figure of glory, whose glorification began with the signs he performed, reached its climax in his death and resurrection, and continues in the unification of his followers.

In contrast to the synoptics, in John the primary locale of Jesus' ministry is Jerusalem, where Jesus is presented in conflict with "the Jews." This conflict reflects the historical controversy between Jesus and the Jewish authorities, but it also mirrors the conflict between the writer's Christian community and the synagogue of his time. In sharp contrast to the unanimous portrayal of Jesus in the synoptics, Jesus' association with outcasts and sinners is conspicuously absent from John, and in Jesus' teaching there are no parables or actual teachings about the kingdom of God, both of which are so prominent in the synoptic story of Jesus.

Obviously, John is even less concerned with the historical Jesus of Nazareth than the synoptic writers are. In his own creative way, John presents Jesus as a person whose spiritual presence can be experienced by those who already believe or who are to believe in the future. In this way the author tries to strengthen the faith of believing and doubting members of his own Christian community as opponents in the Jewish community of his time confront them with rejection and hostility. John's unique interest in promoting faith through the person of Jesus makes him one of the three greatest NT theologians, along with Paul and the writer of Hebrews.

For further study of various issues in John see the following. *Background*: D. M. Smith 1984; B. J. Malina 1993, 1996; D. J. Hawkin 1996; R. C. Hill 1996. *OT in John*: E. D. Freed 1965; M. J. J. Menken 1996. *Interpretation*: R. H. Strachan 1943; E. C. Hoskyns 1947; C. H. Dodd 1953; J. C. Fenton 1970; L. Morris 1971; C. K. Barrett 1978, 1982a; P. Perkins 1978; G. W. MacRae 1978; J. Painter 1980, 1993; R. A. Whitacre 1982; J. Jervell 1984; R. Kysar 1984, 1986a; J. R. Michaels 1984, 1989; D. M. Smith 1984, 1995a, 1995b; G. R. Beasley-Murray 1987; D. Rensberger 1988; C. H. Talbert 1994b; J. Ashton 1997; H. Ridderbos 1997; S. S. Smalley 1998. *John and Synoptics*: D. L. Dungan 1990; D. M. Smith 1980, 1992; E. D. Freed 1992. *Wisdom*: M. Scott 1992; M. E. Willett 1992; R. C. Hill 1996. *Messiah*: L. Morris 1989; J. Painter 1993. *Passion*: D. P. Senior 1991; R. E. Brown 1994, for bibliography, 104–106. *Love*: F. F. Segovia 1982. *"I am"*: D. M. Ball 1996. *Conflict in John*: D. B. Woll 1981. *Son of Man*: F. J. Moloney 1978; D. Burkett 1991; E. D. Freed 1967. *Structure*: D. M. Smith 1965; B. Olsson 1974; G. H. Ostenstad 1998. *Prologue*: C. A. Evans 1993; E. Harris 1994. *Social Science Perspective*: J. H. Neyrey 1988; N. R. Petersen 1993; B. J. Malina 1998. *Symbolism*: D. A. Lee 1994; C. R. Koester 1995. *Irony*: P. D. Duke 1985; G. R. O'Day 1986. *Style*: D. W. Weed 1970. *Rhetoric*: J. L. Staley 1988; M. Davies 1992. *Narrative*: M. W. G. Stibbe 1992, 1993. *Research*: R. Kysar 1975, 1983; G. S. Sloyan 1991. *Mysticism*: L. W. Countryman 1987. *Christology*: T. E. Pollard 1970. *Priority of John*: J. A. T. Robinson 1985.

In the next chapter we will consider Hebrews, along with Revelation and 1 Peter, works that, like John, reveal times of oppression and controversy.

CHAPTER 15

Hebrews, Revelation, and 1 Peter

IN THIS CHAPTER WE WILL STUDY HE-brews, Revelation, and 1 Peter. Although these writings differ in literary type, theology, and style of writing, we will study them together because of their common purpose of encouraging their Christian readers, in a time of suffering, to remain faithful and obedient to what they have been taught.

HEBREWS

For centuries, those who have studied Hebrews have had to consider the following questions: Who was the author, and why did he write? Who were his intended readers—Jewish or Gentile Christians? What is the religious-historical background of the work? And what type of writing is Hebrews? In the following pages we will consider suggested answers to these questions.

WHO WROTE HEBREWS?

Even Christian writers of the second and third centuries didn't agree about who wrote Hebrews. Irenaeus knew the work but did not think Paul wrote it. Tertullian (*On Modesty* 20) mentioned "an Epistle to the Hebrews under the name of Barnabas," friend and companion of Paul. Since the author of Hebrews writes a lot about the priesthood and about Jesus as a priest, and because Barnabas was a Levite (that is, a member of the priestly family of Jews), Barnabas was a natural choice as author. But according to Eusebius (*Hist.* 6:14:2–4), Clement of Alexandria thought Paul had written Hebrews and that Luke had translated it for Greek-speaking Christians. Clement also says that Paul did not affix his name to the writing because the Jews were prejudiced against him as an apostle to Gentiles. So in order not to offend the Jews, for the sake of modesty, and "to give due honor to the Lord," Paul left Hebrews nameless. Also, according to Eusebius (*Hist.* 6:25:11–14), Origen (Christian scholar and writer of Alexandria c. 185–250) said that anyone who accepted "this epistle as Paul's was to be commended." Origen believed that the thoughts were Paul's and that "the style and composition" were those of someone who had recalled the apostle's teachings and then written them down, "but who wrote the epistle, truly God knows." By the middle of the fourth century, however, Hebrews was universally accepted as a letter of Paul.

The mention of "brother Timothy" in 13:23 obviously was intended to suggest Paul's authorship. But the writer's statement in 2:3 that the Lord's message of salvation "was attested to us by those who heard him" contradicts Paul's affirmation that he did not receive the gospel he preached from man but "through a revelation of Jesus Christ" directly (Gal 1:10–12). Thus the writer seems to belong to a generation of Christians later than Paul, and the writer's failure to include a salutation with his name and a reference to the recipients of the letter is contrary to Paul's practice.

There are other reasons for doubting Paul's authorship of Hebrews. Origen realized that the style of Hebrews "does not have the commonplace language of the apostle" and that the work is written in better Greek. In fact, the Greek of Hebrews is excellent, and the writer's acquaintance with current philosophical thought indicates that he was familiar with Hellenism. But the writer also has a Jewish background, as his familiarity with the OT and the Hebrew covenant, priesthood, sacrificial system, and concept of creation clearly show. The writer may therefore have been a Diaspora Jew like Paul.

Scholars today agree with Origen's assessment of the writer's Greek and style. In general, the literary style of Hebrews is distinct from that of any other NT writing. Except for the passages quoted from the Septuagint, the Greek is classical, formal, literary, refined, and lacks the emotional tones of Paul. It has little of the *koinē* (common Greek), so called because it was the Greek used by the common people. Paul's style, on the other hand, is spontaneous and informal,

the result of his hasty responses to specific problems. The writer of Hebrews, however, deals with a single theme—Christ as the superior revelation of God—in a carefully planned and systematic manner.

Scholars do not agree with Origen that "the thoughts are the apostle's," even though they are, in Origen's words, "admirable." They lack the most important Pauline conceptions, such as the Christian as a new creation in Christ, justification by faith, and the idea of the Holy Spirit dwelling in Christians (but see Heb 6:4). Although "faith" is a keyword in Paul's letters and Hebrews, the meaning of the term differs in each; and the priesthood of Christ, the central theme of Hebrews, is not even suggested by Paul.

Thus, because the writer of Hebrews belongs to a generation of Christians later than Paul, and because his style and thought differ from Paul's, the author of Hebrews was not Paul. Who, then, did write Hebrews?

Apollos, the Christian Jew from Alexandria, is sometimes suggested as the author. H. W Montefiore 1979:9–11 has given arguments in support of this view, including the following. Apollos was a Jew (Acts 18:24), and the author of Hebrews was surely a Jew. He was "an eloquent man, well-versed in the scriptures" (Acts 18:24), and both those qualities fit the author of Hebrews. Apollos "had been instructed in the Way of the Lord" (Acts 18:25), and the writer of Hebrews gives a synopsis of Jesus' life, referring to his birth, baptism, temptations, suffering in Gethsemane, death, and resurrection. However, these comparisons, though interesting, do not prove that Apollos wrote Hebrews.

Scholars have often argued that the writer, if not Apollos, must have been another Alexandrian, since his thought shows affinities with that of Philo. Both, for example, stress that Melchizedek, king of Salem (Gen 14:18), is "king of righteousness" and of peace (Philo, *Alleg. Inter.* 3:25; Heb 7:2). In addition to a common interest in Melchizedek, Hebrews (5:11–6:1) and Philo (*The Preliminary Studies* 3–5) both talk about milk and solid food with respect to instruction. But Hebrews refers to instruction in the Christian religion, whereas Philo speaks of music, rhetoric, grammar, and other branches of intellectual studies. (For different points of view about the relationship between Hebrews and Philo, see R. Williamson 1970; L. K. K. Dey 1975; H. W. Montefiore 1979:6–8.) Like the suggestions about Apollos as the author of Hebrews, those about Philo are interesting but lack proof.

As early as 1900 the German scholar A. Harnack considered it a probability that Priscilla, along with her husband Aquila (see Acts 18:2, 18, 26; 1 Cor 16:19; Rom 16:19; Rom 16:3; 2 Tim 4:19) in a secondary role, wrote Hebrews. That view has been argued by S. Terrien 1985, whose thesis is that, according to biblical theology, woman is the crown of creation. I am unaware of anyone who agrees with Terrien about Priscilla's authorship of Hebrews.

H. W. Attridge 1989:5 says that "inferences can be made from the character of Hebrews about the type of individual who composed it." He was well educated with training in rhetoric, had some knowledge of the categories of Greek philosophy, "and extensive experience in the exegesis of Jewish scriptures in a Greek form." He was probably a Jew who came to accept Jesus as the Messiah. "He himself was not an eyewitness to the ministry of Jesus (2:3), but stands within an ecclesiastical tradition . . . generally associated with the radical Gentile-oriented wing of the early church to which, of course, Paul belonged." If the reference to Timothy (13:23) is to Paul's friend, then the author may have been loosely associated with the Pauline school.

In sum, we cannot be certain about who wrote Hebrews; so—to paraphrase Origen—who wrote Hebrews, only God knows.

PURPOSE OF WRITING AND THE RECIPIENTS OF HEBREWS

The author of Hebrews seems to have several reasons for writing. According to 10:32–34 (see

also 12:4), some readers, after they became believers, "endured a hard struggle with sufferings, sometimes being publicly exposed to abuse and persecution, and . . . accepted the plundering of . . . possessions." The author writes to encourage them not to give up their confidence but to endure, so that when they "have done the will of God," they "may receive what was promised" (10:35–36). Perhaps because of their suffering, some recipients of Hebrews were losing interest in and loyalty to their new religion, and were therefore likely to revert to their status as Jews or pagans, or to no religion at all. The author writes to revive the diligence and loyalty of such people, who are to pay closer attention to what they have heard and not "drift away from it" (2:2) and not "turn away from the living God" (3:12; see also 5:11–6:8; 12:12–13). By enduring for a while longer, they will succeed in reaching heaven, the destination of Christians.

Perhaps the readers were in danger of relapsing into Judaism, because the writer's theological purpose is clear throughout. He wants to persuade his readers that Jesus is the supreme revelation of God and that Christianity is superior to and therefore replaces Judaism. Several passages indicate that the author also has an ethical purpose for writing. He writes not only to strengthen the readers' faith in the living God and their loyalty to what they have been taught, but also to remind them that their hearts are to be "clean from an evil conscience" and thus to encourage them "to provoke one another to love and good deeds" (10:22–24; also chaps. 12–13).

The readers were in danger not only of neglecting what they had heard (2:2), but also of being "carried away by all kinds of strange teachings" (13:9). The references in 13:10–13 to foods, the altar, Jewish tabernacle (tent for worship during the Israelite wanderings), and Jewish worship seem to indicate that there was some controversy among the letter's recipients over a syncretism of dietary laws and other Jewish elements and Christian practices. The recipients were also in danger of losing their faith because of some crisis involving suffering and loss of property. But who were the recipients of the letter?

The title "To Hebrews" was meant to designate the readers as Jewish Christians in general, or perhaps Palestinian Jewish Christians in particular. However, since the title was not added before the third century, it has only caused confusion about the original recipients. The title is one of the reasons some people have suggested that the addressees were Jewish Christians in Palestine who, as the result of the Roman conquest in 70 CE, were in danger of lapsing into Judaism. This view, however, is usually rejected for several reasons. The church in Jerusalem no longer existed after 70. The readers are not addressed specifically as either Jews or Christians, nor does the writer allude to the fall of Jerusalem or to the temple. And the words "You need some one to teach you again the basic elements of the oracles of God" (5:12) are not appropriate for Christians of Jerusalem, since they were Christians from firsthand experience.

That the readers were on the verge of turning, if not reverting, to Judaism from Christianity seems clear from the writer's argument that Christianity had replaced Judaism. This explains his severe warning that if the readers become unfaithful, they "are crucifying again the Son of God" (6:6), a clear allusion to the early Christian view that the Jews were responsible for Jesus' death. Moreover, the writing presupposes a more intimate and thorough knowledge of Judaism with respect to the scriptures, the covenant, the priesthood and sacrificial system, and the Day of Atonement (most sacred holy day of the Jews) than Gentile converts to Judaism could have gained. The expression "transgressions under the first covenant" (9:15) would be more meaningful to Jews by birth than to Gentiles. Also, Jews would be more likely than Gentiles to relate to an idea of "perfection . . . attainable through the levitical priesthood" (7:11). More specifically, P. E. Hughes 1977:10–15 has suggested that Hebrews was written to oppose a general Essenism attested at Qumran. Jewish Christians opposed by non-Christian Jews were faced with reverting to a Judaism like that at Qumran.

Finally, according to the view that the recipients were Jewish Christians, the writer's use of the OT is significant. By quoting the OT he assumes that the readers regard it as authoritative and did so as Jews before they became Christians. If, then, they reverted to Judaism, the readers would continue to regard the OT as authoritative. On the other hand, Gentile converts, although they would regard the OT as sacred while they were Christians, would not do so if they gave up their Christianity. Thus, the writer's arguments from scripture would lose their effectiveness with Gentile Christians.

Despite strong arguments that the recipients of Hebrews were Jewish, some scholars have maintained that they were Gentile. Gentile Christians would be familiar with the Greek OT, which was "the Bible" of all Christians; and like Jewish Christians, they would know about the covenant with Israel, the Mosaic law, the priesthood, and other aspects of Judaism mentioned by the writer. Although the writer presents Judaism as superseded by Christianity, he does not refer to Judaism as the readers' former religion, nor does he imply that the readers' loss of faith would be a reversion. Moreover, a reversion to Judaism would not mean turning away from the living God (3:12), the God they would continue to worship as Jews. Although there were exceptions, Jews were known the world over for their high moral and ethical standards; so the exhortations to pursue holiness (12:14) and to keep marriages undefiled, as well as the references to immorality and adultery (13:4), were most likely addressed to Gentiles.

Thus, the recipients of Hebrews could have been either Jewish or Gentile Christians. Or perhaps the readers were neither Jewish nor Gentile Christians, but were Jews who were not Christians. A reason for this view is that one of the writer's favorite expressions, "draw near" (Greek; 4:16; 7:19, 25; 10:1, 22; 11:6), was used with reference to converts to Judaism. Perhaps the writer is using this terminology with reference to Jews who were on the verge of becoming Christians. Such Jews would understand that by the use of the words "draw near" they were being invited to become Christians. The writer's purpose, then, would be to encourage those Jews to become

Christians, rather than to keep them from reverting to Judaism in the face of oppression.

THE RECIPIENTS' COMMUNITY AND THE DATE OF HEBREWS

Some scholars have suggested that the recipients were Jewish Christians living in Jerusalem during the time of the war with Rome, c. 70 CE. Others have specified that they were a group of priests in Jerusalem from that great number who "became obedient to the faith" (Acts 6:7). Still other scholars have suggested that Hebrews was intended for a community of Jewish Christians who had been Essenes, perhaps even from the community at Qumran. Certain common themes and practices of the Sect of Qumran and Hebrews, such as belief in angels, the expectation of two Messiahs—one a priest, the other a royal figure—rejection of sacrifice in the temple, interest in the obscure figure Melchizedek, belonging to a new covenant, and an assembly of people destined for heaven, support this view. More specifically, compare Heb 6:4–8 with 1QS 2:11–17, where the person who sins and forsakes God is without forgiveness and will be burned in eternal destruction. On the other hand, nothing in Hebrews corresponds to the sect's fanatical devotion to Jewish law. Many of the themes in Hebrews also occur in other Jewish literature, of the time, so it is not certain that Hebrews was addressed to Essene converts.

Since angels, Jewish dietary observances, and the superiority of Christ are also discussed in Colossians, some scholars have suggested the Christians at Colossae, Laodicea, and Hierapolis (Col 1:2; 4:13) as the recipients of Hebrews. Others suggest Rome as their residence because Rome may be inferred from the words in 13:24: "Those from Italy send you greetings." This greeting seems to imply that Christians not living in Italy send greetings to their fellow Christians in Italy (Rome ?). There were, of course, Jewish and Gentile Christians in Rome, so Hebrews could have been intended for one of those groups. And the fact that Clement of Rome quotes Hebrews in his letter to the Corinthians indicates that the work was known in Rome and may therefore have originally been sent there, or even have originated there. Two other cities have been mentioned as the residence of the recipients of Hebrews: Alexandria and Corinth.

G. W Buchanan 1972:255–256 suggests that Hebrews was intended for a group of migrants to Jerusalem whom the writer describes as those who "have come to Mount Zion and to the city of the living God, the heavenly Jerusalem" (12:22). They arrived there too late to have met Jesus personally, but they received "the message of salvation secondhand from those who heard it from Jesus himself" (2:3). One criticism of this view, which Buchanan acknowledges, is that the author may be speaking metaphorically, not literally. However, assuming that the recipients of Hebrews were actually migrants to Jerusalem, Buchanan says that Hebrews was written to them "sometime after the death of Jesus (A.D. 26–36) and before the destruction of the temple (A.D. 70)."

Scholars generally agree that the recipients of Hebrews were only a small group within a larger Christian community, a conclusion supported by several passages. According to 10:25, for example, some Christians were not meeting to worship with others. And the words "Greet all your leaders and all the saints" in 13:24 imply that only some people were directly addressed and that they were not the leaders of their community. But insurmountable difficulties make it impossible to identify a specific group of Christians in Jerusalem, Rome, Alexandria, Corinth, or elsewhere as the recipients of Hebrews.

Like the question of the residence of the recipients of Hebrews, the date of writing is also complicated and is usually determined on the basis of passages in the work itself. Some scholars argue that since references to the priesthood are in the present tense, the sacrificial system was still operative in the temple, so the date would have to be before 70 CE. But such an interpretation may be incorrect, because the writer is speaking about the tabernacle during the Israelites' wanderings before entering Canaan, the promised land, and not about the temple.

Since Clement of Rome quotes Hebrews, the time he wrote provides a clue to the latest possible date for the work. It is usually assumed that the words with which Clement begins, "sudden and repeated misfortunes and calamities which have happened to us," refer to the persecution under Domitian (81–96). The date of Clement would then be c. 96, so Hebrews would have been written sometime before that. However, some scholars have asserted that Clement's letter to Corinth should be dated early in 70, because "calamities" refers to the persecution by Nero (54–68); therefore, Hebrews should be dated prior to 70. Other scholars, realizing that evidence for the persecution Clement refers to is slight, and that the persecution is perhaps even a figment of his Christian imagination and only an excuse for his procrastination, fix the date of Clement c. 120 and the date for Hebrews, then, c. 110. This date is also based on the view that the separation of the group addressed from the other Christians referred to, the reference to "earlier days" (10:32), and other internal evidence imply a considerable lapse of time after Paul's letters.

Apart from the dating of Clement's letter, other data support a date near the end of the first century. The readers clearly belong to a generation of Christians that learned its religion secondhand (2:3). They are mature Christians, so the writer warns them that if they become unfaithful, there can be no repentance (6:4–8; 10:26–31; 12:17). The reference to oppression in 10:32–34 fits with Tacitus's description of persecution in Rome under Nero in the 60s, but the reference has the character of reminiscence, not of recent experience. And references to suffering in the future (10:36; 12:3–11; 13:7) are like those in Revelation and 1 Peter, and therefore seem to place Hebrews, like those writings, in the time of Domitian's oppression of Christians. Considering the evidence presented, though it is very tenuous, we can date Hebrews sometime between c. 60 and 110.

LITERARY STYLE AND STRUCTURE OF HEBREWS

When turning to Hebrews after studying Paul's letters, it is natural, perhaps, to think of it as an-

other letter. Indeed, from ancient times to the present, Hebrews has been regarded as a letter. The word "letter" does not occur in the Greek title, which is simply "To Hebrews"; but in the *NRSV* the title is "The Letter to the Hebrews," and modern commentators refer to Hebrews as such. Although the work does end like a letter, it does not begin like one, since it lacks the usual greeting with the name of the sender and a reference to the recipients. The ending, as some think, may have been added to the work later by someone wanting to give it the appearance of a letter and thus to adapt it to a wider audience than was originally intended.

On the other hand, some who regard Hebrews as a letter think it had an epistolary beginning that, according to J. Moffatt 1924:xxviii, "may have been lost by accident, in the tear and wear of the manuscript." Present manuscripts provide no evidence for either the view that the ending has been added or the beginning lost. Hebrews is an uncommon literary form that has been called "the riddle of the New Testament," and scholars try to solve the riddle in various ways.

In 13:22 the writer refers to his work as a "word of exhortation." The last word is *paraklēsis* in Greek and has many meanings, including "consolation," "exhortation," "intercession," and "imploring." Because all of these meanings pertain to aspects of preachers' sermons; because the writer addresses his readers personally and directly as "brothers" (3:1, 12; so also in speeches in Acts) and "you" (5:11–12; 12:4–5); because he alludes to himself, as preachers often do (5:11; 6:9–12); because he refers to himself as speaking (2:5; 6:9; 8:1), rather than writing; and because, like a preacher, he quotes a passage of scripture and then explains it, Hebrews has been regarded as a sermon or homily. Moreover, the writer's "word of exhortation" corresponds exactly to the invitation by the rulers of the synagogue in Antioch of Pisidia to Paul and his friends to speak: "If you have any word of exhortation for the people, give it" (Acts 13:15). Paul responded with a long sermon. For these reasons most scholars think Hebrews was originally a sermon written for a particular community and then sent as a letter with an appropriate conclusion. It is thus almost always referred to as "the epistle to the Hebrews."

G. W. Buchanan 1972 has suggested that Hebrews is a *midrash* (pl., *midrashim*) on Psalm 110 (see also R. H. Fuller 1977:1–27). The word *midrash* is derived from the Hebrew *darash,* meaning "seek," "examine," or "ask." The Hebrew noun *midhrash* means "explanation" or "commentary," so a *midrash* is really a commentary on a passage of scripture, written by a person who has studied the passage to determine its true meaning. According to this view, Hebrews is a midrash on Psalm 110 and interprets the psalm as explaining the priesthood of Christ. Actually, within the whole midrash are smaller midrashim. For example, 3:7–4:11 is a midrash on Psalm 95 and is used to explain the superiority of Christ to Joshua, who succeeded Moses as leader of the Israelites,

Whether Hebrews is a midrash or not, one of its characteristic features is the use of the OT. Besides about eighty allusions, there are more OT quotations in Hebrews than in any other book in the NT. These include about an equal number (eleven or twelve) from the Pentateuch and from Psalms, and several from other OT books. The writer usually quotes from the Septuagint, and this indicates that he comes from a Jewish Greek-speaking background. He uses the OT in several ways. His favorite OT text, of course, is Psalm 110, from which he cites different parts at different times to support a point he is making. Sometimes he cites an OT passage in its entirety, as he does, for example, with Jeremiah's text on the new covenant in chap. 8. At other times he strings a lot of passages together, as he does in 1:5–13 to show that Jesus is superior to angels. Sometimes the writer focuses on a longer text but interposes passages from other sources, as in 3:7–4:11, where he centers on Psalm 95 but interposes passages from Numbers 14 and Genesis 2. Frequently the writer cites a verse or part of a verse, especially from the Psalms or the Pentateuch. This practice is evident throughout the work.

The writer of Hebrews was the first Christian to use a thoroughly typological explanation of OT passages. Typology (from the Greek *typos,* "impression" or "pattern") is a method of exegesis (critical interpretation) whereby people or events in the OT are taken as prototypes or foreshadowings of people or events in the NT. For example, in 7:1–3 Melchizedek is presented as a type of true priest and the prototype of Christ. In contrast, Philo allegorizes Melchizedek as mind (*Alleg. Inter.* 3:79). In Hebrews also, the Israelites' wanderings—which the Israelites continued despite their unbelief and hardships—are a foreshadowing of Christians as God's people on the way to their future destination with Christ.

In the more technical aspects of his literary style, the writer of Hebrews displays his skill in several ways, as, for example, when he engages in wordplay or uses synonyms that begin in the same way. One of the writer's favorite literary devices is inclusion (from Latin *inclusio,* "shutting up"). This device involves enclosing a unit of material by using the same word or words at the end as at the beginning. An excellent example of inclusion is 3:1–4:16, where the words "Jesus," "high priest," and "confession" are used in 3:1 and 4:14.

In discussing Jesus as priest, the author argues his point by using comparisons with Judaism, so he often uses the comparative degree followed later by "therefore" or "then" to introduce an exhortation. Here are two good examples: Jesus is "much superior to angels. . . . Therefore we must pay greater attention to what we have heard" (1:4; 2:1). And "Jesus is worthy of more glory than Moses. . . . Let us then with confidence draw near to the throne of grace, that we may receive mercy" (3:3; 4:16; Greek).

Another of the author's literary devices is the use of key words to end one section and begin another. For example, in 1:4 he concludes his introduction by saying that Jesus became "much superior to angels"; and then in 1:5, which begins the next section (1:5–2:18), he asks, "For to which of the angels did God ever say . . . ?" (see also 3:15 and 3:16; 4:10 and 4:11). All of these things provide clues to the structure of the work.

Taking into consideration inclusion, key words that introduce new subjects and sections, catchwords, and other devices of the writer,

A. Vanhoye 1989 has analyzed the structure of Hebrews into five main parts: (1) 1:5–2:18; (2) 3:1–5:10; (3) 5:11–10:39; (4) 11:1–12:13; and (5) 12:14–13:19. There are also an introduction (1:1–4), conclusion (13:20–21), and a parting word (13:22–25). J. H. Davies 1967:15 analyzes the structure of Hebrews according to "doctrinal exposition and practical exhortation" as follows (exhortation in parentheses): 1:1–14; (2:1–4); 2:5–3:6; (3:7–4:13); 4:14–5:10; (5:11–6:20); 7:1–10:22; (10:23–39); 11:1–12:2; (12:3–17); 12:18–29; (13:1–25).

In sum, throughout the work the writer of Hebrews treats the sole theme of Jesus as superior to Jewish phenomena, leaders, and institutions. In presenting his case, the author closely intertwines argument—mostly from scripture—and exhortation. He uses comparisons to introduce many of his arguments, and catchwords such as "therefore" and "then" to introduce his exhortations. And he often makes transitions by repeating a key word or words from the end of one section in the first lines of the next section. By intertwining argument and exhortation the author is not like Paul, who presents his doctrinal arguments first and then his exhortations. Keep all of these things in mind as you study Hebrews with the outline and comments below.

Outline and Comments

I. Theological introduction (1:1–4)

In 1:2–4 the author states the essence of his Christology. As Son of God Jesus is God's greatest revelation. In Hebrew society inheritance and sonship were closely related; but unlike an ordinary son, who inherited only earthly possessions, as "heir of all things" Jesus received from God the universe and the world to come (see Ps 8:2). Jesus was an agent in creation (see John 1:1–3; Col 1:16–17) and is like God in that he reveals his presence, wisdom, holiness, and character. As Son, Jesus not only inherited all things, but he controls them with the power of his word (see Col 1:17). After he made atonement for human sin, Jesus was exalted to the presence of God (see Acts 7:56); that made him superior to angels, with Son as a name more excellent than theirs (see Eph 1:20–21).

II. Jesus, as Son of God, superior to angels (1:5–2:18)

Argument: The writer quotes a series of OT passages to show that Jesus is superior to angels because he is God's Son. Angels worship him; his Sonship is eternal; his kingdom is one of righteousness; as Lord, he is Creator, but angels were created; only the Son was invited by God to sit in the place of honor at his right hand, whereas angels are only servants of God (1:5–14).

Exhortation: Because of Jesus' superiority as God's Son, readers must heed what they have been taught about the salvation they are to obtain in the future and not "drift away," or they will be punished (2:1, 3).

Argument: The message of salvation brought by Jesus, God's supreme revelation, was attested by Jesus' followers, miracles, and gifts of the Holy Spirit. For a while Jesus was a little lower than angels (Ps 8:4–6) that he might become perfect through suffering (2:2–16).

Transition: By becoming human, being tempted, and suffering like his fellow humans, Jesus became a merciful high priest, sympathetic and forgiving of human sin (2:17–18).

III. Jesus as superior high priest, and his qualifications (3:1–10:39)

Exhortation: Fellow Christians must appreciate Jesus as high priest and apostle (lit., "one sent") of God as they confess their faith (3:1).

A. Superior to Moses (3:2–4:16)

Argument: Like Moses, Jesus was faithful to God who appointed him. Moses was faithful in his relationship to the people of Israel as a servant, but Jesus is superior to Moses because he is faithful in his relationship to Christians, the new community of God (3:2–11).

Exhortation: In order to have fellowship with Christ (3:12–15), fellow Christians must be faithful and not sin in rebellion, as the Israelites did (Ps 95:7–11).

Argument: In spite of their deliverance from Egypt, some Israelites were unfaithful and rebelled against God (Num 14:26–35; Deut 32–20). Therefore, they did not enter the promised land (3:16–19).

Exhortation: Fellow Christians must be careful that they do not fail to reach their rest (4:1). What "rest" means is uncertain, but it may mean a blissful experience as Christians in the present or in the future, perhaps in heaven.

Argument: The readers had the message of salvation taught to them just as the Israelites did, but the Israelites did not respond in faith (Ps 95:7–11). Christians should not make the same mistake; they still can attain their goal (4:2–10).

Transitional exhortation and argument: Again the writer exhorts the readers to strive for their goal (rest). God has offered the goal to everyone through his word, which penetrates to the inmost being (4:11–13). Jesus, as a high priest greater than Moses and as Son of God, has experienced God's rest—that is, he "has passed through the heavens." Although tempted, he did not sin, so he brings the opportunity for mercy and grace to those who "with boldness" draw near to "the throne of grace," that is, to God (4:14–16).

B. In the order of Melchizedek (5:1–7:22)

Argument: Here we have the essence of the writer's view. All high priests are chosen by God and are to act for humans in relation to God by offering gifts and sacrifices for sins. As humans, then, they share human weaknesses and must make sacrifices for their own sins. Jesus was appointed by God as Son after the order of Melchizedek. As a human he offered prayers to God, who heard him because he became obedient through suffering. Being made perfect, Jesus "became the source of eternal salvation for all who obey him" (5:1–10).

Perhaps a document from Qumran (11QMelch) is most useful for providing a background against which to understand the writer's designation of Christ as "a priest forever, according to the order of Melchizedek" (5:6). It reveals a tradition about Melchizedek known to some Palestinian Jews close to the time of Hebrews. All the descriptive phrases, except "resembling

the Son of God" (Heb 7:3), can now be explained in light of 11QMelch (see A. S. van der Woude 1976; J. A. Fitzmyer 1967a).

Exhortation and warning: The writer wants to say more about the priesthood of Christ after the order of Melchizedek, but the readers are indifferent and spiritually immature, when they should be teaching others. Readers should become mature Christians by giving up elementary doctrines, by refraining from evil deeds for which there is no repentance, and by continuing their faith in God. They must also give up elementary religious ceremonies involving baptisms and commissioning of church officers (for the OT background see Lev 1:4 and Num 27:18, where those who make sacrifices place a hand on the head of the animal, and where Moses lays his hand on his successor Joshua), and inadequate or mistaken conceptions of the resurrection and future judgment. Having been familiar with these things from Judaism, the readers gained new insights through what they were taught about Christ's message of salvation. So the writer warns them that they must mature in the experience of Christian baptism, the Holy Spirit, and the word of God, and gain a foretaste of the age to come. If they relapse and become unfaithful instead, repentance will not be effective. The writer, however, still has hope for his readers, since God in his justice will not overlook their good work and love toward fellow Christians. But they must not be sluggish; rather, they must grow in faith and patience to inherit God's promises (5:11–6:12).

Argument: God confirmed his promise of blessing and many descendants to Abraham because Abraham was faithful (Gen 22:15–19). People make oaths by someone greater than themselves. For example, when Hebrews took oaths, they said, "As the Lord lives." But there is no one greater than God by whom he can swear, so God guaranteed his promise with an oath. Those two things, a promise and an oath, are the basis of Christian hope through Christ as high priest in the order of Melchizedek. In the tabernacle "the inner shrine behind the curtain" (6:19), where the presence of God was thought to dwell, was separated from the worshipers by a curtain. By removing that barrier, Christ has now made it possible for all faithful Christians who "seize the hope" to experience the presence of God (6:13–20).

Repeating the catchword "Melchizedek" from the preceding verse, the writer gives a midrash on the story of Melchizedek and Abraham in Gen 14:17–20, in order to explain later the significance of Christ as the eternal priest in the order of Melchizedek. The name Melchizedek is composed of two parts, *melek*, "king," and *zedek*, "righteousness." "Salem" comes from the Hebrew word *shalom*, "peace," so Melchizedek was simultaneously king of righteousness and of peace. Since there is no record of Melchizedek's birth, genealogy, or death, the writer says that Melchizedek continues as a priest forever (7:1–3). Then, in a complicated way that was understood by his readers, the writer shows that Melchizedek was superior to Abraham and Aaron (the brother of Moses), as well as to Aaron's descendants, the levitical priests, who were familiar to the readers. But because they were mortal, perfection did not come with those priests, so the priesthood changed whenever one died. The Lord Jesus, however, was from the tribe of Judah, which was not connected with the priesthood (7:4–14).

The old priesthood was imperfect and ineffective in bringing people to God because the priests were mortal, because they got their office through "physical descent"—that is, through the priestly family line of Levi—and because they took office without an oath. But Jesus, as a priest in the order of Melchizedek, supersedes all other priests. This is true, according to the writer, because Jesus became priest not by physical descent "but through the power of an indestructible life," and because his office was confirmed by an oath, as Ps 110:4 shows (7:15–21).

Transition: Because of these qualifications, Jesus is the surety of a better covenant (7:22).

C. Surety of a better covenant (7:23–10:39)

Argument: Jesus' priesthood, unlike that of earlier priests, is eternal because he lives forever, so he is always available to save those who approach God through him. Because of his sinless character, Jesus, unlike other priests, does not have to offer sacrifice for his own sins and for those of the people. As God's Son, he did that "once for all when he offered himself" (7:23–28). Jesus' ministry of atonement under a better covenant is "more excellent" than the old ministry by former priests because it takes place in heaven, the true sanctuary. The old covenant has become obsolete by the realization of the new covenant predicted by Jeremiah (8:1–13).

The writer describes worship as conducted under the old covenant by the levitical priests in the tabernacle. The tabernacle was divided into two parts, an outer part and an inner part, separated by a curtain. The outer part was called "the Holy Place" and the inner part "the Holy of Holies." The inner part contained the ark of the covenant (a wooden chest that served as a symbol), over which were spread the wings of two cherubim (a cherub was a winged creature of some sort). Above the ark and beneath the outstretched wings of the cherubim, the Presence of God was thought to dwell. This made the Holy of Holies the more sacred of the two parts of the tabernacle, and for that reason no one was permitted to enter it except the high priest. He entered the Holy of Holies only once a year, on the Day of Atonement, to perform a special blood ritual in which he asked for forgiveness for himself and for the nation (9:1–5).

Next, the writer says that this limited access to the Holy of Holies indicates that people were not yet free under the old system to approach God's presence, and the priest's offerings would not make the worshipers' consciences perfect (9:6–10). But when Christ appeared, he gave his own blood, which, unlike that of bulls and goats, does purify the "conscience from dead works to worship the living God!" (9:11–14). Since Jesus was "the mediator of a new covenant," his self-sacrifice was eternally effective for forgiveness of sins and replaced the Jewish rituals of the Day of Atonement (Leviticus 16; Numbers 19), rituals that were only temporarily effective at best. Those rituals had to be repeated and took place on earth, although they were a foreshadowing of the heavenly sanctuary. Jesus' sacrifice, however, took place only once and became effective for all time because Jesus entered into heaven itself and came before God as mediator on behalf of humanity. Since Jesus' sacrifice was eternally effective, he will not have to deal with sin when he comes again, when he will "save those who are eagerly waiting for him" (9:28)—that is, those who have kept their confidence and hope (3:6; 6:11), even the hope of drawing near to God (7:19). They will then enter the "rest" (4:1, 11) that they have been promised (9:15–28).

In 10:1–18 the author reiterates his point that under the law, "only a shadow of the good things to come," sacrifices were ineffective and had to be repeated every year, and thus reminded worshipers of their sin year after year. "For it is impossible for the blood of bulls and goats to take away sins" (10:4). Moreover, such sacrifices were not pleasing to God (Ps 40:6–8). But "by a single offering he [Christ] has perfected for all time those who are sanctified" (10:14). The Holy Spirit bears witness to Christ's work under the new covenant (Jer 31:33–34), so offerings for sin are unnecessary.

Exhortation and warning: In view of what Christ has done for them, readers are exhorted to draw near to God in worship with their consciences cleansed in baptism, to maintain their hope and faith, and to encourage each other "to love and good deeds" (10:19–25), because the day they await is near. The writer warns the readers that for those who "sin deliberately (Greek) after having received the knowledge of the truth, there no longer remains a sacrifice for sins, but a fearful prospect of judgment, and a fury of fire that will consume the adversaries" (10:26–27). To "sin deliberately" corresponds to the OT concept of sinning "with a high hand," for which there was no forgiveness (Num 15:30–31). It is even worse to spurn the Son of God and the Spirit of grace. God's wrath on those who sin, according to the author, is as furious as his love is gracious to those who obey (10:28–31; see also Deut 32:35–36; Isa 26:20, LXX). Finally, the readers are encouraged to recall their severe sufferings after becoming Christians ("enlight-

ened" in 10:32 refers to their baptism) and to endure so that they, "having done the will of God, may receive what was promised" and not lose faith (10:32–38; see also Hab 2:3–4).

Transition: The writer and readers are not among those who shrink back (a gentle warning) and are destroyed, "but among those who have faith [a gentle reminder] and so are saved" (10:39).

IV. OT witnesses through faith (11:1–12:29)

The author could have concluded his exhortation in 10:39 by proceeding to 12:1, "Therefore . . . let us also lay aside every weight and the sin. . . ." Instead, he uses the catchword "faith" from 10:39 in 11:1 to give a definition of faith (11:1), and then to show how such faith was exemplified in the lives of OT heroes. They had only God's promises, no visible evidence on which to fix their hope. They believed that what they hoped for would happen and therefore acted accordingly (11:1–40). For comparable praise for Jewish heroes, though unnamed, see Wis 10:1–21; see also Sirach 44–50.

Exhortation: The readers must look to Jesus, "the pioneer and perfecter" of their faith, for perseverance and strength (12:1–3).

Argument: Jesus, like many of the heroes in the OT, suffered death, but the readers have not yet resisted their oppression to the point of death. They must also remember that by their suffering, God, like an earthly father, is disciplining them as sons (Prov 3:11–12) for their own good moral character (12:4–11).

Exhortation: Therefore, readers are to strengthen their morality, "pursue peace with everyone, and the holiness without which no one will see the Lord." They are not to be bitter and cause trouble, or they will fail "to obtain the grace of God" (12:12–17).

Argument: The receiving of the law on Mt. Sinai (Exod 19:12–22; 20:18–21; Deut 4:11–12; 5:22–27; 9:19) was a fearful experience because of the unapproachableness of God. In contrast, as converts to Christianity, the readers have come to Jerusalem, "the city of the living God." With the imagery of coming to Jerusalem, "angels in festal gathering" (12:22–23), and "Jesus, the mediator of a new covenant," the writer is saying that as Christians the readers are already experiencing what is to be consummated in the future (12:18–24).

Exhortation and warning: "Do not refuse the one [God] who is speaking." The Israelites did not escape punishment when they disobeyed God after receiving the law, so "much less" shall the readers escape if they "reject the one who warns from heaven!" (12:25).

Argument: At Sinai God's voice shook the earth (Exod 19:18), and he will once more shake both earth and heaven (Hag 2:6). This will take place on the last day, when "what cannot be shaken may remain" (12:26–27), that is, those who are faithful.

Final exhortation and warning: The writer exhorts his readers to be grateful for "receiving a kingdom that cannot be shaken" and to "offer to God an acceptable worship with reverence and awe." Then he warns that "God is a consuming fire" (12:28–29).

V. General exhortations (13:1–19)

The author has ended his discussion through argument and exhortation with the words in 12:28–29, and he could have concluded his work with them. In fact, some scholars think that the general exhortations in chap. 13, which are characteristic of epistolary endings, were added to give the work the appearance of a letter, perhaps even one from Paul. Others think that chap. 13, with the exception, perhaps, of vv 22–25, is an integral part of the work. Verses 9–14 are the most difficult, and refer to Jewish practices concerning food (see Col 2:16, 21–23; 1 Cor 8:8). The heart is strengthened by God's grace, not by rules about what to eat.

"Altar" in v 10 is symbolic of "sacrifice," and those who serve in the priesthood cannot participate in sacrifice, since they still follow prescribed rituals and reject Christ. On the Day of Atonement, blood from the animals sacrificed was taken into the sanctuary, but the animals were burned outside (Lev 16:27). Jesus was crucified outside Jerusalem; that is, he was rejected by those for whom Jerusalem was sacred—the Jews. Outside Jerusalem Jesus sanctified the people (Gentiles ?) with his blood. Because the readers seek the city of the future, the heavenly Jerusalem, they must be prepared to suffer as Jesus did. The readers also must make sacrifices that please God by acknowledging his name, by doing good, and by sharing what they have.

VI. Benediction and closing greetings (13:20–25)

The writer prays that God may bless the readers with everything good for doing God's will, and expresses his desire to see them soon.

SUMMARY

The Christology of Hebrews is unique. As high priest in the order of Melchizedek, Jesus is superior to all who preceded him because he was appointed by God as Son. Moreover, Christ is king of righteousness and peace, and his ministry is eternal because of his indestructible life. By his self-sacrifice, which is effective for all time, he was exalted to heaven, the true sanctuary. There he makes the experience of God possible to all who accept the salvation that God worked through Jesus. As minister of a new covenant, Jesus superseded the priesthood and sacrificial cultus under the old covenant, although they foreshadowed what was to come in Christ. Jesus' sacrifice of his own blood put an end to all the sacrifices of blood required by the law.

Those who belong to the new covenant, who are enlightened about God's gift of salvation, and who experience the Holy Spirit after baptism, cannot repent if they "have fallen away" (6:4–6). The words "fallen away" translate one Greek word that literally means "fall back," in the sense of becoming unfaithful and living godless lives. The writer, therefore, constantly exhorts his readers to remain faithful to the living God and not to relapse. They are to live in such a way as to maintain their hope for the perfect experience of the eternal rest that God has promised.

For further study of Hebrews see the following: P. E. Hughes 1977; D. A. Hagner 1983; D. Guthrie 1983; L. H. Evans 1985; H. W. Attridge 1989; F. F. Bruce 1990; L. D. Hurst 1990, thought background; W. L. Lane 1991; P. Ellingworth 1991, 1993; F. T. Gench 1996; D. A. de Silva 1996, sociology; V. C. Pfitzner 1997.

We turn now to Revelation, a literary work very different from Hebrews, though also written to strengthen the faith of Christians who were suffering.

REVELATION

No book of the NT has provoked so much discussion and been so misunderstood as Revelation. One of the reasons people misunderstand the book is that they think its cryptic language is prophetic. Therefore, they either try to unravel the book's secrets and apply them to their own times, or they ignore the work as unworthy of consideration. Jerome (348–420 CE), for example, one of the most scholarly church fathers, wrote that the Revelation of John had about as many secrets as words (*Epistles* 53:9), and Martin Luther said that he could not fit his spirit into the book because Christ was not taught or known in it (*Second Preface to Revelation*).

In the OT the book of Daniel is a classical apocalypse, and apocalyptic sections are Isaiah 24–27; 56–66; Ezekiel 34–48; and Zechariah 9–14. Most apocalyptic literature is to be found outside the OT scriptures (see the *NRSV*; J. H. Charlesworth 1983, 1985), of which these are examples: *4 Ezra, 1 and 2 Enoch, 2 Baruch*. The main difference between Jewish apocalypses and Revelation is that the coming of Jesus was thought to be the beginning of a new age in history. Christians continued to write apocalypses after NT times, for example, *Shepherd of Hermas, Apocryphon of John,* and *Apocalypse of Peter.*

As with apocalypses in the OT, many passages in Revelation are impossible to understand because we are so far removed from the circumstances under which it was written, but we can learn why we do not understand them. It is especially important to learn that Revelation, like every other work in the NT, is situational; that is, it grew out of a specific situation in NT times and was addressed to readers of those times, not to future readers. We will begin by discussing apocalypse as a literary genre and then discuss Revelation, an apocalypse that developed out of the religious situation confronting the writer.

LITERARY TYPE, STRUCTURE, AND STYLE

The Greek title reads "Apocalypse of John," and the first word in the Greek text is "apocalypse," which means "uncovering" or "revelation." Thus, Revelation does not belong to the literary types of gospel, history, letter, sermon, or essay, but to the literary genre known as apocalypse, which flourished as a type of Jewish literature from c. 200 BCE to c. 100 CE.

Apocalypses in general are written in cryptic language, which only those familiar with the situations under which they are written can understand. Apocalypses abound in symbolism, often of a grotesque kind, and they include dreams, visions, angels, and frequently numerical schemes. All of these are included in Revelation, in addition to such symbols as the following: horns as a symbol for power—especially of men (12:3; 13:1; 17:3)—eyes for knowledge (2:18; 4:6), a sharp sword for the word of God (2:12, 16; 19:21), white robes for glory and purity (6:11; 7:9), black for famine and death (6:5, 12), crowns for victory and dominion (2:10; 3:11; 14:14), and horses of various colors for different calamities (6:2–8). Such symbolism adds to the mystery of apocalypse for modern readers.

Apocalypses often use the device of prediction, but sometimes the predictions are deceiving because they may actually be allusions to events of the past or present yet they make it appear as though the events are to happen in the future. Apocalypses originate during times of persecution and are intended to boost morale and strengthen faith. They deal with two ages, the present evil age and a future age in which the forces of good will triumph over evil. Apocalypses also include a doctrine of the resurrection, at least of the righteous dead. Thus, dualism is a feature of apocalypse, but the dualism of apocalypse pertains to history and the world. It is not the Gnostic dualism between matter and spirit or the Pauline dualism between spirit and flesh.

Perhaps the dominant feature of John's apocalypse is a dualism between two ages, this age and the age to come. This age, which is only temporary, is under the control of Satan, whose demonic forces and evil human agents torment the righteous. But it will soon end with a cataclysmic upheaval during which Satan and his forces will be defeated by God and his forces, and Christ will return as judge. The new age, with a new heaven and a new earth, will be eternal, with everlasting happiness for the righteous. Then God will rule in the world, not from above it, and all will have happened in accordance with the divine plan.

Numbers and numerical schemes play a big part in John's composition, which is the result of a highly imaginative mind. He uses 1260 days (11:3; 12:6) and forty-two months (13:5), which both come out to three and a half years, and he mentions a beast whose number is 666 (13:18). His favorite numbers are twelve (twenty-three times), used for the faithful of the twelve tribes of Israel at the end of time; four (nineteen times), for all the parts of the world; and three (eleven times) and ten (nine times), the symbolism of which is uncertain. But John uses seven (fifty-five times) much more than any other number; it probably symbolizes completeness or perfection. He describes things in sevens and seems to structure his book around the number seven, as the following outline shows.

I. *Prologue (1)*

II. *Letters to seven churches (2–3)*

III. *The apocalypse proper (4:1–22:5)*
   A. *Introductory visions (4–5)*
   B. *Visions of seven seals and their opening (6:1–8:1)*
   C. *Visions of seven trumpets and their blowing (8:2–11:19)*
   D. *Seven visions of the dragon, woman, and beasts (12:1–13:18)*
   E. *Seven visions of the lamb and angels (14:1–20)*
   F. *Visions of the seven bowls of the wrath of God (15:1–16:21)*
   G. *Seven visions of the fall of "Babylon" (17:1–19:10)*
   H. *Seven visions of the end of the age of Satan and the final victory of Christ (19:11–22:5)*

IV. *Epilogue (22:6–21)*

Since it is difficult to find seven visions in several of the series, it has been suggested that originally there were six series of six things. However, the seven series is used in the outline and comments below because of John's special interest in the number seven and because the seven series may be closer to the writer's original plan, especially since John uses the number six only once (4:8). But like all apocalypses, Revelation lacks coherence, so a completely coherent outline of the structure is not possible.

Almost every commentator has a different opinion of the structure of Revelation and a specific method for determining it. C. R. Smith 1994, for example, uses the phrase "in the Spirit" to help determine where sections begin (see that author and E. S. Fiorenza 1985:159–180 for theories of structure).

As in Hebrews, a chief feature is the writer's use of the OT, but John uses it in a very different way. Whereas Hebrews has many exact quotations and clear allusions, there is not one literal quotation in Revelation. However, there is an average of one echo or allusion to the OT for every other verse, with more than four hundred allusions in chaps. 4–22. The author's use of the OT is one of the factors indicating that originally Revelation may have been a Jewish work. Unlike the excellent Greek of Hebrews, that of Revelation is the worst in the NT, perhaps because the author is translating into Greek from a Hebrew text. He translates Hebrew idioms literally and uses Greek grammar very loosely, sometimes even incorrectly. In this respect, Revelation is a very unconventional work.

Besides the Hebraistic style, if the frequent reference to the lamb (see, for example, 5:6; 6:1; 7:10; 13:8; 14:1) is to the lamb of Jewish apocalypses and not to a christological title for Jesus, then there is really nothing specifically Christian in the body of the work (4:1–22:5). This contrasts sharply with chaps. 1–3 and 22:16a, 20b–21, which are definitely Christian in origin and could have been added to a Jewish apocalyptic work. However, many scholars dispute this point and argue that "the lamb" is a christological title for Jesus and that the work, therefore, is Christian throughout. They also believe that on the basis of language and style, chaps. 1–3 are an integral part of the work, which is a unity. According to these scholars, then, Revelation was originally a Christian book, not a Jewish one with Christian additions.

Because Revelation is apocalypse and not history, it is written in the language of imagery and myth and has a combination of symbolism and visions throughout most of the work. The author uses materials from the OT, Jewish apocalyptic thought, mythology, and Christian traditions in such a way that there are gaps and repetitions in his thought and language. Even so, features of the writer's style, including repetitions, unity of style, careful organization, and consistency of phrasing, give the work coherence. Although the grammar is bad (in that respect the work is unparalleled in the NT), the consistency of the writer's usage gives his Greek a certain clarity, simplicity, and evenness. For example, the writer uses possessive pronouns ("my," "our," "your," and so on) more than one hundred times, and he never separates them from the nouns they modify. He also repeats word combinations and phrases—for example, "flashes of lightning, and rumblings and peals of thunder" (4:5; 11:19; 16:18). In sum, Revelation is an unconventional but creative work by a person who calls himself John.

E. S. Fiorenza 1985:181–203 is concerned with the author's portrayal of women as perceived through his use of symbolism and other imagery and with finding an appropriate response. The affinities between John and Revelation and a Johannine school are assumed, so a literary interrelationship between the two no longer has to be defended. However, "a dialectical exchange of theological thought between their respective schools and traditions" is assumed. Revelation is "a particular rhetorical response to the social-political and religious situation of the churches in Asia Minor."

Revelation arouses the imagination of contemporary readers "to perceive women in terms of good or evil, pure or impure, heavenly or destructive, helpless or powerful, bride or temptress, wife or whore." Its "symbolic action," therefore, "can perpetrate prejudice and injustice if it is not 'translated' into a contemporary 'rhetorical situation' to which it can be a 'fitting' rhetorical response."

Before you read this section read again the discussion of the authorship of the gospel of John in Chapter 14.

AUTHORSHIP

In the first and last chapters of his book, the author shares common beliefs that people sleeping or having visions or revelations were told to write something (Rev 1:1, 11, 19; 10:4; 21:5), that the writing was in response to the request of a deity (Rev 22:6, 16), and that nothing should be added or removed from the book. Artemidorus says that he wrote his treatise "out of obedience to Apollo." With the writer of Revelation's admonition not to add to his words or take away from them (Rev 22:18–19), compare Artemidorus's request that those who read his books are "not to add or remove anything from the present contents." Artemidorus also says that if some things seem superfluous readers should use only what pleases them but not discard the rest. After all, they should realize that "it was out of obedience to Apollo . . . that I undertook this treatise." Perhaps as you read Revelation you will think that is good advice for you also. (R. J. White, 1975:137; see also Plato, *Phaedo* 60E–61B).

Because the writer refers to himself as John early Christian writers since the second century ascribed Revelation, along with the other Johannine writings, to the apostle John. But scholars today generally agree that the author was not the apostle. He never calls himself an apostle, and 18:20 seems to imply that he was not an apostle. Moreover, the reference in 21:14 to "the twelve names of the twelve apostles of the Lamb" on the foundations of the wall of Jerusalem indicates that the apostolic age is over and the apostles dead. And the writer never even alludes to a single incident in Jesus' life, as would be natural for one who knew Jesus.

Although the author nowhere calls himself a prophet, he refers to his work as a prophecy (1:3; 22:7, 10, 18–19). There are similarities between prophecy and apocalypse, but there are also crucial differences between John's work and the prophetic books of the OT. Like the prophets, John believed that Israel was God's chosen people and that God would redeem his people at the end of history. Similarly, John is concerned with the future, especially the end of the present age. But here is a crucial difference. The OT prophets' main concern was life in their own times, including present political, social, and economic issues. John, however, is concerned with the present only as it leads to the future, which he thinks about in otherworldly terms. In Revelation, as in apocalypse in general, the reader passes from the concrete imagery of prophecy to the mysterious, symbolic, mythical atmosphere of speculation. Revelation is not a prophetic book, although the author refers to it as "the words of the prophecy" (1:3). R. H. Charles 1920:1:xxxviii–1 argues that Revelation was written by "John the prophet—a Palestinian Jew, who late in life migrated to Asia Minor," the traditional site of the publication of the Johannine literature. D. E. Aune 1983:207–208 considers early Christian prophecy and John as a prophet.

Scholars agree universally that the gospel of John and Revelation were not written by the same person, but there are some interesting similarities between the two works. Both use "lamb" as a christological title for Jesus (John 1:29, 36; Rev 14:1), although the Greek words are different—an insignificant fact since the two are synonymous. Both works use several of the same expressions (Greek), for example, "you cannot bear" (John 16:12; Rev 2:2), "living water" (John 4:10–11; Rev 7:17), and "let him who is thirsty come" (John 7:27; Rev 22:17). And certain words and phrases occur in the NT only in John and Revelation, including "speak to" (see, for example, John 9:37; Rev 1:12) in the same Greek form, "to keep the word or words" (see, for example, John 8:51; Rev 3:8), and "a little longer" (John 12:35; Rev 20:3).

There are also common ideas in Revelation and the gospel of John. Here are some of them: "the beginning" (John 1:1; 8:25; Rev 3:14; 21:6), Jesus as "I am" (see Chapter 14; Rev 1:8, 17; 2:23), the devil (Satan) as a chief adversary (John 6:70; 8:44; 13:2, 27; Rev 2: 9, 13, 24), end of the Jewish temple (John 2:19–21; 4:21; Rev 21:22), "woman" used to refer to Jesus' mother (John 2:4; 19:26; Rev 12:1–2, 4, 13), "Jews" spoken of disparagingly (often in John: Rev 2:9; 3:9), beholding Christ as one pierced (John 19:37; Rev 1:7), and Jesus as witness or testifying (John 3:11; 5:31; 7:7; 8:14; Rev 1:5; 3:14).

Some parallels also occur between Revelation and the letters of John: God as light (Rev 21:23–24; 22:5; 1 John 1:5), a church represented by a woman and her children (Rev 12:17; 2 John 1, 13), the coming of antichrist (Rev 13:11, without the use of the word; 1 John 2:18–19, 22), and false prophets (1 John 4:1) or prophetess (Rev 2:20).

In spite of similarities between the gospel and Revelation, there are striking differences, the major one being that the gospel is the least apocalyptic NT writing. The works have great differences in grammar and style, and certain favorite words of one author are used little or not at all by the other. For example, "faith" (four times) and "faithful" (eight times) occur in Revelation, but "faith" does not occur in the gospel, and "faithful" occurs only once. "Faith" occurs once in 1 John and "faithful" once in 1 John and once in 3 John. On the other hand, a common word in the gospel is "believe" (ninety-eight times), but it does not occur in Revelation. "Believe" occurs nine times in 1 John but not in 2 John or 3 John. The words "truth," *alētheia* (twenty-five), and "true," *alēthēs* (fourteen) in John also do not appear in Revelation. The former occurs nine times in 1 John, five times in 2 John, and six times in 3 John, the latter twice in 1 John and once in 3 John. Similarly, two verbs for "love," *agapaō* (thirty-seven) and *phileō* (thirteen), are common in the gospel, but the former occurs only four times and the latter twice in Revelation. The noun "love" (*agapē*) occurs seven times in John but only twice in Revelation. "Love" is a theme of 1 John, *agapaō* occurring twenty-eight times but only twice in 2 John and once in 3 John. Similarly, *agapē* occurs eighteen times in 1 John but only twice in 2 John and once in 3 John. The word for "world" (*kosmos*) appears seventy-eight times in the gospel but only three times in Revelation. In the gospel it is used of the world opposed to God its Creator, frequently referring to the world of human beings in a bad sense, but in Revelation it refers to the created world. *Kosmos* is used twenty-three times in 1 John and used as in John, once in 2 John, as in John, but not in 3 John.

These examples indicate that the gospel and the apocalypse probably were not written by the same person. They also indicate that John and 1 John have much in common, as we learned in our study of the gospel. And they have more in common than either has with Revelation.

In our study of the fourth gospel, we learned of a tradition that an "elder John" lived near the end of the first century CE. Some scholars think he wrote Revelation, while others maintain that John the Baptist was responsible for some of it. J. M. Ford 1975:4–5, 28–37, following several others, argues that chaps. 4–11 originated among the Baptist's followers before they came to know Jesus, and that the chapters were written during "the time of the Baptist" and before the ministry of Jesus. Chaps. 12–22 are later, but still came from the Baptist's disciples, "who may or may not have converted to Christianity." Those chapters were written before the fall of Jerusalem in 70 CE, or in the mid-60s. Chaps. 1–3 and 22:16a, 20b–21 "were added later by a Jewish Christian disciple, perhaps one who had come to know Jesus Christ more accurately, like the disciples of the Baptist at Ephesus in Acts 19:1–7 or the Scripture scholar Apollos in Acts 18:24–28."

Attempts to solve the riddle of the authorship of Revelation through the reference to John can only be intelligent guesses based on external evidence, although internal evidence indicates that the author and his background were Jewish. From Revelation itself we learn that John, whoever he was, was a Christian who had been exiled to Patmos, an island off the west coast of Asia Minor. There he was moved, as he says, "in the Spirit" (1:9–10), to write down "the revelation of Jesus Christ." But why and to whom did he write?

PURPOSE, RECIPIENTS, AND DATE

It is clear that the writer had some connection with seven churches in the Roman province of Asia, since he sent his work to them (1:4, 20–3:22). The words "Blessed is the one who reads" (1:3) and "I warn everyone who hears" (22:18) show that the author intended the book to be read aloud in the churches addressed. From the messages to those churches, it is also clear that the churches were threatened by false teachers from within (2:2, 6, 13–15, 20–23; 3:4, 8–10) and oppression from without (1:9; 2:10). The author writes to encourage Christians confronted with those circumstances to be patient and faithful, and to stand firm. To those challenged by false teaching his repeated advice is "To everyone who conquers, I will give permission . . ." (2:7, 11, 17, 26; 3:5, 12, 21). He writes to encourage and warn those oppressed to be faithful: "Do not fear what you are about to suffer. . . . Be faithful until death, and I will give you the crown of life" (2:10).

In the apocalypse proper there are several allusions to the recipients' suffering (6:9; 12:7–8; 17:6). The author writes to remind all who are suffering that they can do little to improve their lot. Things might even get worse, but meantime the recipients must remain faithful to God and loyal to their religion, and await God's own intervention from his heavenly throne. Such suffering most likely occurred in the time of Nero (54–68) or Domitian (81–96).

We have learned that, according to Tacitus, some Christians in Rome were persecuted by Nero, and that Clement of Rome refers to oppressions, perhaps also those during Nero's time. Several passages in Revelation may allude to beliefs or incidents associated with Nero. After his death, two phases of a myth that Nero would return developed. According to the first phase, Nero had not actually died but had gone to the East to lead the Parthians, Rome's enemy, against Rome. According to the second phase, Nero had died but would be revived (Nero *redivivus*) and return. The author of Revelation may reflect his awareness of the Nero myth when he writes, for example, that the beast's "mortal wound had been healed" (13:3) and that the beast that "was, and is not" still has authority (17:8–12). The Nero myth did not develop until the end of the first century, so according to this evidence Revelation could not have been written before then.

In 17:10 the author writes that there are "seven kings, of whom five have fallen, one is living, and the other has not yet come; and when he comes, he must remain only a little while." These cryptic words may refer to the tumultuous times after Nero's death. Since Nero was the fifth emperor, the writer is aware of his death and knows that his successor Galba (68 CE) is in power. The writer thinks that Galba will not be in power very long. In fact, Galba was succeeded by Otho and Vitellius in the same year. So on this evidence, the author wrote soon after Nero's suicide in 68. However, if 666, the number of the beast in 13:18, refers to Nero, as is frequently assumed, then Nero may still have been alive when Revelation was written—unless, of course, the writer believed that Nero would return. At any rate, the evidence that Revelation was written in or near the time of Nero is tenuous, somewhat contradictory, and certainly inconclusive.

If the "ten diadems" in 13:1 refer to ten emperors, then Revelation would have been written in the time of Titus (79–81), the tenth emperor. Other evidence may indicate a date even later, perhaps during the time of Domitian, who decreed that all official proclamations should begin with "Our Lord and God orders." Domitian commanded his family to address him as "our Lord and God"; he had his niece Domitilla banished and her husband, Flavius Clemens, and others executed as "atheists" in 95 because they did not take part in the emperor cult.

Words like "They worshiped the dragon" (13:4; see also 4:8, 11–18) may refer to the cult of emperor worship, and it is usually assumed that the words "the souls of those who had been slaughtered for the word of God and for the testimony they had given" (6:9) refer to Christians who refused to participate in the emperor cult. Domitian was the first emperor to encourage that cult in the East. Therefore, there may have been some capricious persecution of Christians in Asia Minor near the end of his reign, although there is no direct evidence for it.

In 92 CE Domitian ordered that half the vineyards in the provinces be destroyed to increase the acreage for grain, presumably to help vineyard owners in Italy. The words "A quart of wheat for a day's pay, and three quarts of barley for a day's pay" in 6:6 may allude to Domitian's order. Already in the second century, Irenaeus (*Her.* 5:30:3) thought Revelation had been written near the end of Domitian's reign, and most scholars still prefer that date.

Evidence of another kind throws light on the date of Revelation. Excepting Philemon, the author quotes phrases from both the undisputed and disputed letters of Paul, including Ephesians, which may have been the cover letter of the Pauline corpus. Therefore, since the writer probably knew Paul's letters as a collection, Revelation was not written before the end of the first century after Paul's letters had been published as a group.

In conclusion, sometime between c. 68 and 96, a Christian wrote to urge fellow Christians living in the Roman province of Asia to remain faithful, patient, and courageous when confronted with false teachers within the church and persecution from Rome. The worst is yet to come, the writer says, but in the end right will win out, Rome will fall, all wickedness will cease, and the righteous will be eternally rewarded and the wicked eternally punished. The writer stresses at the beginning and end of his work that he is writing about "what must soon take place" (1:1; 22:6). Thus, he was writing for his own time, not for future times; and in doing so, he chose to use the cryptic and symbolic language characteristic of the literary genre known as apocalypse. That is why so much of his language and imagery is unintelligible to modern readers. We will look now at the theology and moral teachings of Revelation.

THEOLOGY OF REVELATION

Let me say, first of all, that several theological terms prominent in some NT writings are absent in Revelation. The word "grace" (Greek, *charis*; Hebrew, *hesed*) occurs only in the salutation (1:4) and the benediction (22:21). From a literary perspective these passages set off the whole work as an *inclusio*. The concept of grace, however, may be symbolized by the rainbow in 4:3 (see Gen 9:12–17). The words "save" and "savior" do not occur, nor do the words for "mercy" and "forgiveness." "Salvation" occurs only three times (7:10; 12:10; 19:1), and it comes from God and/or the Lamb (Christ). The writer does not use the usual word for "redemption." His word is *agorazō*, literally "buy," "purchase," the meaning it always has in the gospel of John (4:8; 6:5; 13:29; not used in letters of John). In the *NRSV agorazō* is translated that way in 3:18; 13:17; and 18:11; as "ransomed" in 5:9; and "redeemed" in 14:3–5 (appropriate translations), where it is used with reference to those who "are blameless" morally.

The best way to learn about the theology of Revelation is to observe what the writer actually says. God is the Creator: "You created all things, and by your will they existed and were created" (4:11; see John 1:1–3, where creating activity is ascribed to Jesus as "the Word"). Rev 14:7 is a desperate plea of the writer for all peoples to "fear God and give him glory, for the hour of his judgment has come; and worship him who made heaven and earth, the sea and the springs of water."

God is Father (1:6; 2:28; 3:5, 21), "the Alpha and the Omega" (1:8; 21:6; 22:13), "who is and

who was and who is to come, the Almighty" (1:8; 4:8; 11:17; 15:3; 16:7, 14; 19:6, 15; 21:22). As the Almighty, God is judge, his ways "just and true" (15:3–4), and his "judgments are true and just" (16:7; 19:2).

For the prophet Isaiah God as "the Holy One of Israel" is a key theological concept (see, for example, Isa 1:4; 5:19, 24). In Revelation God is also the Holy One, though sometimes the attribute is transferred to Jesus, as in Rev 3:7. Elsewhere God is the Holy One (4:8; 6:10; 15:4; 16:5).

The writer of Revelation has a theology of history rather than a philosophy of history. God is the beginning and the end of history (21:6; 22:13), expressed through the manner of thinking and the symbolism of OT prophecy and Jewish apocalypses. God is the Master of history, perceived in terms of action and concreteness rather than in abstract concepts. He will bring ultimate redemption to those who remain faithful and endure to the end (2:9–17; 3:11–13; 11:16–19; 20:1–21:4).

God's sovereignty is portrayed through the visions of his throne in heaven (4:1–5:14) and his transcendence by the "sea of glass" in front of it (4:1–6; 15:1–4). The omniscience of God is symbolized by his seven spirits "sent out into all the earth" (5:6). The ultimate salvation of God for "those who are written in the Lamb's book of life" (21:27) is symbolized by God's gift of drinking "from the spring of the water of life" (21:6) and eating fruit "from the tree of life that is in the paradise of God" (2:7). But all the while the reader can never forget the inevitable wrath of God. The writer asks: "Sovereign Lord, holy and true, how long will it be before you judge and avenge our blood on the inhabitants of the earth?" (6:10).

The wrath of God and the Lamb (Christ) is expressed through vivid imagery, for example, in the opening of the sixth seal (6:12–17). The writer leaves no doubt about the guilt of the inhabitants of the earth and the unbelievable consequences of it. According to 14:9–11, vengeance will be especially terrible upon "Babylon" (Rome) and her people and "those who worship the beast [the emperor] and its image."

Please read now Rev 14:9–11 for an example of apocalyptic literary excellence even though the thoughts may be objectionable when judged by some standards. Theologically, the passage is "a call for the endurance of the saints (holy ones), those who keep the commandments of God and hold fast to the faith of Jesus." The reward is that those who "die in the Lord . . . will rest from their labors, for their deeds follow them" (14:12–13).

Forgiveness and mercy, attributes of God in the OT, are conspicuously absent in Revelation. The writer, who has a vengeful spirit, can ask how long until the martyrs' blood will be avenged (6:10, quoted above). God's ways are just and true, but there is no mention of forgiveness or mercy. Repentance (verb) is mentioned several times and may imply that it would bring forgiveness. Apart from repentance, destruction is certain. The church in Ephesus is told: "Repent, and do the works you did at first. If not, I will come to you and remove your lampstand from its place, unless you repent" (2:5; see also 2:16–22; 3:3, 19; 9:20–21). Elsewhere also there is an emphasis on repentance for misdeeds with an implied reward for good works (16:8–11; see 14:13, quoted above).

It is paradoxical that, in spite of the vindictive vengeance of God's wrath portrayed in 14:8–11 and elsewhere, there is a mollifying view in the vision of the new Jerusalem (21:22–27). There "the nations will walk" by the light of the Lamb, "and the kings of the earth will bring their glory into it." However, there will be no entrance into the city for immoral persons "but only those who are written in the Lamb's book of life." There are actually no resolutions of these paradoxes.

MORAL TEACHINGS OF REVELATION

We may be overwhelmed by the symbolism of the writer's apocalyptic language and, therefore, miss a significant aspect of his message. The theme of Revelation, as we have learned, is stated in 2:10–11: "Do not fear what you are about to suffer. Beware, the devil is about to throw some

of you into prison so that you may be tested. . . . Be faithful until death, and I will give you the crown of life. . . . Whoever conquers will not be harmed by the second death." As you will see, "faithful" is meant to be expressed actively by living moral lives, including good works, and abstaining from evil. In the beginning the writer tells his readers that "those who hear and who keep [that is, "do"] what is written" will be blessed (1:1–3). Throughout his book he reminds them of their moral responsibility and of the consequences of disobedience.

The basic message of the letters to the seven churches is that the members will be rewarded or punished according to their deeds. That message is conveyed vividly in the symbolism of the apocalypse proper that follows in 4:1–22:5. Persecution and suffering are not excuses for wrongdoing.

The writer often uses the word "conquer" (*nikaō*) but never explains what he means by it. Enduring suffering as Christ did is surely part of it, but it just as surely has moral implications, sometimes stated explicitly. With it he often uses the words "hear," "keep," and "listen." The moral demand is quite explicit in 2:26: "To everyone who conquers and continues to do my [Christ's] works to the end, I will give authority over the nations." In the vision of the new Jerusalem and the new earth those who conquer will inherit the gift of the water of life. They are contrasted to the cowardly, faithless, polluted, murderers, and other immoral persons who will end up in the lake of fire (21:5–8).

The author writes to the church in Ephesus: "I know your works, your toil and your patient endurance. I know that you cannot tolerate evildoers; you have tested those who [falsely] claim to be apostles but are not. . . . But I have this against you, that you have abandoned the love you had at first. Remember then from what you have fallen; repent, and do the works you did at first" (2:2–5). The Ephesians are commended because they "hate the works of the Nicolaitans" (2:6), a sect that paid little attention to rules and regulations in life. Apparently they confused Christian freedom with non-Christian license (see 2:14–16). The readers who conquer their present improper manner of life will "eat from the tree of life that is in the paradise of God" (2:7).

Please read now the writer's praise and rebuke for right or wrong conduct accordingly for members in the churches of Smyrna, Pergamum, Thyatira, Sardis, Philadelphia, and Laodicea. Pay special attention to Rev 2:13, 19–26; 3:1–4, 21.

In the complicated visions of the apocalypse proper the central theme concerns those who are worthy to do something in the unfolding of the visions or to receive something in the life portrayed in the visions. For example, "Who is worthy to open the scroll and break its seals?" (5:2). And: "I saw under the altar the souls of those who had been slaughtered for the word of God and for the testimony they had given" (6:9). The point seems to be that future position is determined by past action. And the degree to which the readers understood the message of the apocalypse was depended upon their perception of the moral, spiritual, and ethical qualities necessary to comprehend the mysteries of the visions.

At one point in the vision of the trumpets, the center of the book (6:6–11:19), the writer seems to break into the apocalypse to make his point perfectly clear. "The rest of humankind . . . did not repent of the works of their hands or give up worshiping demons and idols. . . . And they did not repent of their murders or their sorceries or their fornication [immorality] or their thefts" (9:20). They were so hardened in their wickedness that they did not repent even after seeing the rest of humankind killed (see also 16:9–11).

Elsewhere the writer interjects a sentence or two to emphasize proper conduct for ultimate reward: "The dragon was angry with the woman [mother of the Messiah; see also Rev 12:1–2; LXX Isa 26:14; 54:1], and went off to make war on the rest of her children, those who keep the commandments of God and hold the testimony of Jesus" (12:17; see also 14:12–13). Apparently this is intended to signify that Christians everywhere who keep God's commandments may have to endure persecution. "These who have not defiled themselves with women . . . follow the Lamb wherever he goes . . . have been redeemed

from humankind as first fruits for God and the Lamb, and in their mouth no lie was found; they are blameless" (14:4–5).

In 14:14–20 the figure of the harvest of the earth symbolizes the complete judgment upon the wicked. Notice especially the wickedness of Babylon [Rome] and her doom (17:1–19:21). "God has remembered her iniquities" (18:5). She will be repaid as she has acted but double her deeds. The bride of the Lamb [Christ] is clothed "with fine linen, bright and pure," which is symbolic of "the righteous deeds of the saints" (19:8; see also 19:11–21).

In the last judgment (20:1–15) "the dead were judged according to their works, as recorded in the books" (20:12–13). No matter how or when persons died, they must rise for judgment before God, who will reward or punish all according to their deeds. This much of the apocalyptist's language is always absolutely clear.

In the vision of the new heaven and the new earth God will be the God of those who conquer, and they will be God's children (21:7). "But as for the cowardly, the faithless, the polluted, the murderers, the fornicators [the sexually immoral], the sorcerers, the idolaters, and all liars, their place will be in the lake that burns with fire" (21:8). In the new Jerusalem "nothing unclean will enter it, nor anyone who practices abomination or falsehood, but only those who are written in the Lamb's book of life" (21:27).

The writer concludes with emphasis on the nearness of the time when what he has been talking about will come to pass. There is a final contrast between the doers of good and the doers of evil, with contrasting recompense as well. The final trial is about to come upon all (22:10–11). "See, I am coming soon; my reward is with me, to repay according to everyone's work. . . . Blessed are those who wash their robes [do the commandments], so that they will have the right to the tree of life and may enter the city. . . . Outside are the dogs and sorcerers and fornicators and murderers and idolaters, and everyone who loves and practices falsehood" (22:12–15).

The writer's view with respect to the theme of right and wrong, with reward and punishment accordingly, in the scheme of his apocalypse is clear. He does, however, leave room for repentance, which, if necessary, is a condition for having one's name in the book of life. I think there is no place where the writer says that it is necessary for those who obey God's commandments to repent. You better check me on this point, though.

Consider what I have said about theology and morality in Revelation as you study the book with the outline and comments that follow. Again, do you usually agree or not with what I have said? Why? These would be good topics for discussion with your instructor.

Outline and Comments

I. *Prologue (1:1–20)*
   A. *Superscription (1:1–3)*

The writer says that his "revelation" came to him from God through Christ by an angel sent to deliver the message. The person who reads the message aloud and those who hear and observe it will be blessed. Martin Luther wondered how those who heard, let alone "observed," what was written in Revelation were to be blessed, since no one could understand it. Perhaps many of the first hearers also did not understand what they heard. But many Jewish Christians who heard the message would have been familiar with apocalyptic thought, and the person who read the work aloud probably helped the hearers understand the writer's message.

   B. *Epistolary greeting and theological summary (1:4–8)*

Perhaps John's greeting to seven churches should not be taken literally, since in the ancient world the number seven symbolized perfection or completeness. So for John, seven may symbolize completeness, that is, all churches. Similarly, the seven spirits before God's throne symbolize the perfection and completeness of God's power.

As in the first verses of Hebrews, a lot of theology is packed into several verses: God is eternal and is about to enter the scene of history; Christ is a faithful witness, whose suffering can give the

readers comfort; he is the first person to have risen from the dead; and he has power over human rulers. The last two characteristics are the fulfillment of the psalmist's words about the Davidic Messiah: "I will make him the firstborn, the highest of the kings of the earth" (Ps 89:27). The writer reminds his readers that through his love (see Ps 89:28) Christ forgave their sins and made them "priests serving his God and Father." With the last expression (see also Exod 19:6; 1 Pet 2:9), the author shares the view of some other NT writers that Christians are the new people of God. Christ will return again (see Dan 7:13), and then those who crucified him (see Zech 12:10; John 19:37) will lament for what they did. But it is uncertain whether wailing on his account means that these people will be avenged for their deed or that all who have rejected the Christian faith will be judged accordingly.

   C. *Initial vision (1:9–20)*

In 1:10 the sabbath is referred to as "the Lord's day," the only occurrence of the expression in the NT. Perhaps the writer intended to contrast the sabbath with the day of the week known as "emperor's day," also called "the lord's day." Using language from Daniel 7 and names of equipment of the temple and priesthood, such as the girdle priests wore and the lampstands, the author describes his overwhelming vision of the exalted Christ in heaven, the Christ by whom he was commissioned to write to the churches. Although it is impossible to explain all the symbolism as we proceed, the white hair and the sharp sword, for example, symbolize the purity and the powerful (effective) word of Christ, before whom the writer falls in awe (see Ezek 1:28; Isa 6:5). Notice how frequently the number seven has already occurred. The angels of the churches are the guardian angels that were thought to represent the churches in heaven, or perhaps they are the ministers of the churches.

II. *Letters to the seven churches in Asia (2:1–3:22)*

These letters all follow the same format: an introductory formula ("I know your . . .") to

FIGURE 15.1
*Asclepium, ancient
health center, in
Pergamum, Asia
Minor.*

describe the church's condition; a compliment and then a warning; a promise to those who remain firm in time of oppression; and the exhortation to all the churches, usually at the end— "Let anyone who has an ear listen to what the Spirit is saying to the churches."

The references to the Nicolaitans in Ephesus, "a synagogue of Satan" in Smyrna and Philadelphia, the teaching of Balaam and the Nicolaitans at Pergamum (see Figure 15.1), Jezebel in Thyatira, and unsoiled garments in Sardis all indicate some threat to Christian faith either by Jews or Gentiles. Smyrna and Philadelphia are praised the most; Laodicea is reproved the most; Sardis is strongly rebuked; and Ephesus, Pergamum, and Thyatira are commended but criticized. So in times of crisis because of false teachers within the church and oppression from without, some churches are loyal to their religion and others are lukewarm or lose faith. The writer's message to the churches in chaps. 2–3 becomes a message for the whole church in the rest of the book, and it ties the letters to the churches in with the body of the apocalypse. The church must be unified within and firm in its faith when oppressed, and then Christ himself will soon come to save it.

Apparently the author knew each city in which a church was located. See the classic work by

W. M. Ramsay 1904, revised by M. W. Wilson 1994; see also C. J. Hemer 1986.

III. The apocalypse proper (4:1–22:5)

The drama of Revelation unfolds with scenes from earth and heaven placed side by side, history—which wavers between past, present, and future—and prophecy.

A. Introductory visions (4:1–5:14)

The writer returns to his vision or revelation by describing a scene in heaven. There, as in a large courtroom, God sits on his throne. Modeled on Ezek 1:4–28 and 2:9–10 and other OT passages (see also 1 Kgs 19:22–23; Isa 6:1–8; Ps 33:3; 141:2; 47:2–9), the description seems incoherent and obscure to modern readers. But John's readers, familiar with apocalypse in general and with the OT passages on which these chapters are based, would find the description less obscure. The torches, elders, trumpet, singing, and incense are symbols from Jewish liturgy. The beautiful and precious stones are symbolic of God's sovereignty on his throne, and perhaps the writer is contrasting God's throne to the throne of Rome and the emperor's sovereignty.

The point of chap. 4 seems to be that as creator of all things, God is worthy "to receive glory and honor and power" (4:11). The point of chap. 5 is that the Messiah of David (5:5), by his redeeming death, became worthy as "the Lamb" to receive and open the seven-sealed scroll. The Lamb, of course, is Christ.

B. Visions of seven seals and their opening (6:1–8:1)

By opening the seven seals, the Lamb displays his power as the eschatological figure who rules the world and brings on the sufferings that are signs of the End and the judgment. Again, the composition is based on passages from the OT. The four horses, for example, which symbolize war, rebellion or civil strife, famine, and death, may come from Zech 1:8–11, where they are symbolic of the four winds. Based on many sources, which are obviously woven into the apocalypse, Revelation stresses the consequences of yielding to false teaching or to the emperor cult. John would rather that his readers died than yielded.

In chap. 6 we may have examples of a primary characteristic of apocalypse: past history written in the future tense. The Parthians, famous bowmen (6:2a), were Rome's enemy in the East and defeated a Roman army in 62 CE. The writer may be alluding to that incident. Or, since the Roman army was conquering the world, and since its officers rode white horses after victories, he may be alluding to Roman conquests (6:2b). The red horse, symbolic of rebellion or civil strife, may allude to the civil wars that took place in Rome for a century before Augustus became the first emperor. The black horse, symbolic of famine, may allude to the shortage of grain in the time of Domitian, when, as usual, barley was the poor person's food.

In 6:9–17 are some of the most vengeful and uncharacteristic verses in the Bible (see, for example, Ps 79:5). The writer sees those in heaven rejoicing at the suffering of sinners on earth. Basing his words on the prophets' bitter exhortations (for example, Joel 2: 10–11; Amos 5:18–20; Hos 10:8) and using their images of terror, the writer wants to warn those still alive.

Chap. 7 is an interlude before the opening of the seventh seal. The two visions are intended to contrast the bliss of the elect in heaven with the consternation of "the kings of the earth and the magnates and the generals" and others at "the wrath of the Lamb" (6:12–17)—that is, the judgment to come. God's people will not escape the suffering, but they will survive. The opening of the seventh seal is a prelude to the seven trumpets (8:1). The opening is followed by silence in heaven, which precedes the storm of the following chapters.

C. Visions of seven trumpets and their blowing (8:2–11:19)

The seven trumpets represent the wrath of God in world upheavals that precede the new exodus of God's people from the powers of the earth. The scene opens (8:1–6) with imagery from the temple (altar, incense, prayer), recast in heaven with the heavenly host. There prayer is a sacrifice to God (Ps 141:2) and serves to unleash the catastrophes that follow (8:7–9:21). Each trumpet signals an attack on a different part of the world, but the destruction, which is not total (9:18), is only a foretaste of that to come for those who do not repent.

In 10:1–11:14 there is a double interlude between the sixth and seventh trumpets, as there was between the sixth and seventh seals. The writer shifts the scene from heaven to earth in order to comfort and encourage his faithful readers. Much of the imagery, based on numerous OT passages (for example, Dan 12:4–9; Ezek 1:28; 2:9–3:3; 40:3–6; Ps 29:1–10; Amos 7:7–9; Zech 2:1–2; Deut 19:15), defies interpretation, although we can guess at some of it. For example, the angel with one foot on the sea and the other on land (10: 2) symbolizes the universal message of the writer.

In chap. 11 the author focuses on Jerusalem, which has been destroyed (11:2). He also focuses on the temple, in the sense that Christians are a temple of God (see also 1 Cor 3:16–17; 2 Cor 6:16; Eph 2:19–21; 1 Pet 2:5). The two witnesses are Moses (Exod 7:14–21) and Elijah (1 Kgs 17–19; 2 Kgs 1:9–10), representatives of the law and prophecy in which the coming of the Messiah was predicted. According to Jewish tradition, those two men were expected to return before the Messiah came (Deut 18:15–18; Mal 3:22–24). The beast from the bottomless pit (11:7), like the dragon in 12:3 and the beasts in 13:1 and 17:3, is symbolic of total opposition to God.

The seventh trumpet takes the readers' imagination back to heaven for a preview of the conflict to come and the glory that is to follow (11:15–19). The author is so sure that God is in control that he writes about the coming kingdom in the past tense: "The kingdom of the world has become the kingdom of our Lord and of his Messiah" (11:15).

D. Seven visions of the woman, dragon, and beasts (12:1–13:18)

According to myths from Babylonia, Egypt, and Greece, a goddess who was to bear a savior-king would be pursued by a terrible monster waiting to devour the child at birth. But the child was born safely and later killed the monster, the personification of evil. John may have used parts of such myths in the story of the woman and the child in chap. 12. John's child, Jesus, does not destroy the monster but "was snatched away and taken to God and to his throne" (12:5), and John shifts attention from the child to the woman. In the past, commentators have identified the woman with the church or Mary, the mother of Jesus. Modern interpreters, however, generally think the woman represents the Jewish people from whom the Messiah came. In the rest of chap. 12 she personifies the suffering and resistance that ultimately bring salvation to those "who keep the commandments of God and hold the testimony of Jesus" (12:17).

In chap. 13, which is based on Dan 7:4–7, the beasts are the agents of the dragon, or Satan, on earth. Most scholars think these beasts represent the Roman Empire and emperors, and especially the imperial cult. The writer urges his readers to resist the forces that bring blasphemies against God (13:6) and to choose death instead (13:15).

In 13:18 the beast is said to be a human, and the number of its name is 666. Since every letter in Hebrew and Greek names had a numerical equivalent, the number 666 has led to endless speculation about the person intended. Here are some proposed solutions: Nero, written in the Hebrew form *nrwn qsr* = 666; *lateinos* (= "The Roman"), written in Greek = 666; and the number 616, a textual variant, can be gotten from Gaius Caesar or "Caesar god" written in Greek. Most scholars prefer the name of Nero because it best fits the context; but an objection to this view is that the text of Revelation was written in Greek, not Hebrew, so the name should not be converted into Hebrew. Because we do not have the key to unlock the numerical secret of 666, we cannot solve the apocalyptic riddle.

E. Seven visions of the Lamb and angels (14:1–20)

Influenced by OT conceptions of a remnant of the faithful (1 Kgs 19:18; Isa 4:2–6; 10: 19–23; Zeph 2:7–9), the writer again reminds his readers of the bliss in heaven for those who have remained true to God and his Son. Those who have remained true are in heaven because they did not succumb to immorality and because they followed Christ (14:1–7). Convinced of the fall of Rome (= Babylon, as in some other apocalyptic writings), the author writes in the past tense to anticipate for the readers what is to be described in chap. 18 (14:8).

Again, the author expresses his vengeful feelings in a manner characteristic of apocalypse (14:9–11) and anticipates the expressions of God's wrath in chaps. 15–16. Compare Rev 14:10–12 with 2 Esdr 7:36–38: "The pit of torment shall appear, and opposite it shall be the place of rest; and the furnace of hell shall be disclosed, and opposite it the paradise of delight. . . . 'Look on this side and on that; here are delight and rest, and there are fire and torments.'" Recall the parable of the rich man and Lazarus (Luke 16:19–31). Again, John has used strong language to warn his readers to remain faithful. If they do, they can look forward to a blessed life in heaven because "their deeds follow them!" (14:12–13). Notice that, for John, it is by their deeds that they pass the test of faith.

In 14:14–20 the writer shows strong influence from the OT symbolism of the harvest and vintage for God's judgment (Hos 6:11; Lam 1:15; Isa 63:1–6; Joel 3:2, 12–13). The "one like the Son of Man" (= Christ ?) and his angels are sent to reap the harvest (see also Matt 13:24–30, 36–43). The son of man reaps those on the way to salvation, the angels those on the way to hell.

F. Visions of seven bowls of the wrath of God (15:1–16:21)

With the restatement of his recurring theme that those who remain faithful to God and live moral lives will be rewarded and others punished (chap. 14), John could have concluded his work. From there on most is anticlimactic and repeats symbolically the final catastrophes upon earth that result from God's wrath. Much of chaps. 15–16 is an Exodus typology of Moses, the Israelites, and the plagues on Egypt (see Exod 7:20–10:29; Rev 16:2–21). "The kings from the east" (16:12) may be the Parthian rulers whom, according to the Nero myth, Nero would lead against Rome. Rome is referred to as "the great city" and "Babylon" in 16:19.

G. Seven visions of the fall of "Babylon" (17:1–19:10)

The "great city" of 16:19 becomes "the great whore" (Rome) in 17:1–6. In the OT cities were called harlots—for example, Nineveh (Nah 3:4), Tyre (Isa 23:16–17), and Jerusalem (Isa 1:21; Ezek 16:16). The author may have had Messalina, wife of the emperor Claudius, as his model (see Juvenal, *Satire* 6:114–132). The harlot is the counterpart of the bride of the Lamb (19:7), symbol of the new Jerusalem (21:2, 9). So the author places the beast and the harlot that represent Rome in contrast to the Lamb and his bride, who represent the new Jerusalem.

The attack against Rome (the harlot) by the beast that "was, and is not" (Nero returned ?) and his allies is described in 17:7–18. Then the author describes the fall of the magnificent city as past history, and the lamentations that follow (18:1–24). He also records the joyful songs in heaven over the doom of the city (19:1–8) and the symbolic marriage of the Lamb with the righteous who are invited (19:9–10).

H. Seven visions of the end of the age of Satan, and the final victory of Christ (19:11–22:5)

In this section John has been influenced by OT and later Jewish eschatology (for example, Ezekiel 38–48; Joel 3:1–16; 2 *Bar* 40:3; 2 Esdr 7:27–29; *Enoch* 93:3–10). As the final scene of the drama unfolds, there are no more secrets to be revealed. Jesus is depicted as an army general riding on a white horse to victory over the beast and the false prophet (introduced in 16:13), who are thrown into the lake of fire (19:11–21). Unexpectedly, and unlike any other NT passages dealing with Jesus' second coming, Jesus reigns for a thousand years. After a first resurrection, those who "had not worshiped the beast or its image," along with those who died for their faith, reign with Christ (20:1–6). Satan is released from prison (see 20:2–3) and thrown into the lake of fire (20:7–10). Then there is a general resurrection when God judges all people according to the record of "what they had done" (20:11–15; see also Exod 32:32–33; Ps 69:28; Isa 4:3; Dan 7:10; *Enoch* 90:20; 2 *Bar* 24:1; 2 Esdr 6:20).

After describing the judgment, the writer presents his vision (21:1–8) of the new heaven and the new earth (see also Isaiah 65–66; *Enoch* 45; 72; 2 *Bar* 32:6), with the new Jerusalem (Isa 60:11–22; Ezekiel 40; 48), where God dwells with the faithful as the prophets predicted (Lev 26:11–12; Jer 31:33–34; Ezek 37:26–28; Zech 2:11–12; 8:7–8). Then the author describes the new Jerusalem as the bride of the Lamb (see 19:7; 21:2); as such, it is in sharp contrast to the city of Rome ("Babylon") in chap. 18 (21:9–22:4). And, after all the visions, seals, trumpets, bowls, beasts, the harlot, and other images of horror—which contrast sharply to the author's magnificent description of God's new creation—the author sounds a final note of hope and comfort for his faithful readers (see 2:10): "And there will be no more night; they need no light of lamp or sun, for the Lord God will be their light, and they will reign for ever and ever" (22:5).

IV. Epilogue (22: 6–21)

The Revelation of John ends with an anticlimactic series of disconnected and repetitious exhortations and warnings. Although some of vv 6–21 may not have been written by the person who wrote the apocalypse proper, their theme is that the readers are to stand firm in the face of suffering and the imminent coming of Christ. In fact, the time is so near that the scroll, unlike one written for the distant future, is not to be sealed (22:10).

SUMMARY

The apocalypse of John, like all apocalypses, is not to be taken literally or as a prediction for a time beyond that of his readers. In the province of Asia, some Christians who acclaimed Christ as their "Lord and God" were persecuted for refusing to participate in the emperor cult being enforced by Domitian, who claimed to be "Lord and God." At the same time, those Christians were being oppressed by false teachers within the church. Under such circumstances, the faith of Christians would be challenged and threatened, and it would be tempting for some to give up their faith. A person who calls himself John wrote to exhort and warn such Christians to remain faithful, behave properly, and wait for the imminent return of Christ. Using his vivid imagination and an abundance of exaggerated symbols typical of the literary genre of apocalypse— symbols used to stress his message—the writer has created a work that differs both in literary style and content from any other in the NT.

For further study of Revelation, see the books already mentioned plus A. Farrer 1963; T. F. Glasson 1965; G. B. Caird 1966; R. H. Mounce 1998; G. R. Beasley-Murray 1981; J. M. Court 1979; E. S. Fiorenza 1985; A. Y. Collins 1983, 1984, 1986; E. Corsini 1983; J. M. P. Sweet 1979. For different approaches see also G. Krodel 1989; P. E. Hughes 1990; G. W. Buchanan 1993; B. M. Metzger 1993; J. Roloff 1993; C. H. Talbert 1994a; B. J. Malina 1995; J. N. Kraybill 1996; D. E. Aune 1997; J. R. Michaels 1997; L. L. Thompson 1997; J. L. Resseguie 1998.

We turn now to 1 Peter, a work of a very different sort, though occasioned by circumstances similar to those of Revelation.

1 PETER

The writings known as the "catholic" (= universal) or "general epistles" include 1 and 2 Peter, 1, 2, and 3 John, James, and Jude. They were named catholic because they were intended for the whole church—not individual churches, as were Paul's letters. In contrast to Paul's letters, which were named from their recipients, the catholic epistles were named from their reputed authors.

AUTHORSHIP OF 1 PETER

The letter claims to be written by "Peter, an apostle of Jesus Christ" (1:1). The writer also refers to himself as "an elder myself and a witness of the sufferings of Christ" (5:1). However, since the nineteenth century, Peter's authorship has been disputed for several reasons.

The Greek in 1 Peter is some of the best in the NT, both in vocabulary and natural manner of writing, so the fisherman and "uneducated" (Acts 4:13) Peter could not have written it. Moreover, according to Papias, Peter used Mark as his interpreter when he was in Greek lands, so how could Peter, who spoke Aramaic, write such excellent Greek? The usual response to this point by those who defend Peter's authorship is that the author says, "Through Silvanus . . . I have written this short letter to encourage you" (5:12). This means that Silvanus (1 Thess 1:1; 2 Thess 1:1; 2 Cor 1:19) or Silas (Acts 15:22, 27, 32; 17:4), the companion of Paul, actually wrote what Peter dictated. Thus, Peter was responsible for the content of the letter and Silvanus for the vocabulary and literary style.

Another objection to Peter's authorship is that the quotations from the OT are based on the Septuagint, not the Hebrew text familiar to the Palestinian Jew Peter. Some argue, however, that Peter would have used direct quotations from the version familiar to his Greek readers. But critics of this response say that the writer's allusions to the OT show that he thought in Greek, not Hebrew. For example, in 3:10–15, a quotation from Ps 34:12–16 and an allusion to Isa 8:12–13 are so naturally woven into the writer's argument that many readers would be unaware that he was using the OT at all.

Those who reject Petrine authorship point out that 1 Peter shows familiarity with the thought, vocabulary, and phraseology of several of Paul's letters—especially Romans, and also Ephesians, which is widely regarded as a cover letter for the Pauline corpus. Here are some examples. The expression "do not be conformed to" occurs only in 1 Pet 1:14 and Rom 12:2. Except for Jas 1:25 and 2:12, the Pauline word "freedom" (for example, in Rom 8:21; Gal 2:4; 1 Cor 10:29) occurs only in 1 Pet 2:16 and 2 Pet 2:19. Paul's favorite phrase, "in Christ," is used in 1 Pet 3:16; 5:10; and 5:14, and the author's reference to himself as a servant and apostle of Jesus Christ (1:1) is like that of Paul in Rom 1:1. Both writers talk about sacrifice pleasing to God (1 Pet 2:5; Rom 12:1) and sharing in Christ's suffering (1 Pet 5:1; Rom 8:17). The idea of Christians as children of Sarah occurs only in Gal 4:24–28 and 1 Pet 3:5–6. The author's acquaintance with both the undisputed and disputed letters of Paul is taken by those who reject the authenticity of 1 Peter as indicating the writer's familiarity with Paul's letters as a collection. Therefore, Peter, the contemporary of Paul, could not have written the letter purporting to be from him.

Those who support Peter's authorship, however, point out that similarities between 1 Peter, 1 and 2 Thessalonians, James, and the pastorals indicate a common tradition or a school. From that tradition, the writers of these works drew material used for instruction and in liturgies—for example, the liturgical phrase "at the right hand of God" (1 Pet 3:22; Rom 8:34). For parallels between 1 Peter and James see, for example (1 Peter first), 1:6 and 1:2; 1:23 and 1:18; 1:24 and 1:10; 2:1 and 1:21; 5:8–9 and 4:7. For main parallels between 1 Peter and other NT writings see J. N. D. Kelly 1969:11–12.

But another argument against Peter's authorship is that not a single passage indicates that the author had seen or heard Jesus. Although the writer urges his readers to follow Jesus' steps (2:21), he does not refer to Jesus' words about following him or about discipleship. Nor does the author allude to any of Jesus' parables or miracles, or to any incident in which Peter was involved with Jesus (see, for example, Mark 14:66–72; Matt 16:16–23).

On the other hand, supporters of Petrine authorship say that the words "a witness of the sufferings of Christ" and "one who shares in the glory to be revealed" (5:1) prove the author's association with Jesus. The first expression is taken as Peter's testimony to the crucifixion of Jesus and the second as a reference to Jesus' transfiguration, at which Peter was present (Mark 9:2–8). But those who reject Peter's authorship point out that, after his denial of Jesus, Peter is never mentioned in the gospel narratives in connection with Jesus' death, so there is really no evidence that Peter witnessed Jesus' death. The expression may also be taken to mean that the writer shares the sufferings of his readers, sufferings for Christ. The reference to glory is not to that of the transfiguration but to Jesus' eschatological glory, which Christians will share at the Parousia. It has also been argued that the expressions in 5:1 are a faked attempt by the writer to give the impression that Peter was the author.

Although the writer never introduces them as sayings, as does Paul (see, for example, 1 Cor 7:10, 12, 25), some passages in 1 Peter seem to reflect sayings of Jesus (compare, for example, 1:13 with Luke 12:35; 2:12 with Matt 5:16; 3:9 with Matt 5:44; 3:14 with Matt 5:10; 4:14 with Luke 6:22). Scholars use such parallels to sayings of Jesus to support opposing points of view. Some point out that there are no clear allusions to Mark's gospel, for which Peter was the traditional authority. This is true in spite of the author's reference to Mark as "my son" (5:13). So the allusions to words and phrases from a tradition of Jesus' sayings do not indicate that the author of 1 Peter was acquainted with Jesus himself. On the other hand, some think that this is enough evidence to prove that a tradition for Jesus' sayings exists in 1 Peter—a tradition originating from Peter's association with Jesus. (To study further the points we have been considering concerning authorship of 1 Peter, see E. G. Selwyn 1969:7–38; F. W Beare 1958:9–31; E. Best 1982.)

On the basis of these examples of the kinds of evidence that must be considered in trying to determine who wrote 1 Peter, scholars arrive at two main views concerning authorship. Some believe that if Peter did not actually write the letter, Silvanus, his secretary, wrote what he dictated. Thus, they argue that the content is Peter's but that the excellent Greek is that of Silvanus. Other scholars think that 1 Peter is pseudonymous and comes from a time after Peter's death. For lack of positive evidence supporting Silvanus's author-

ship, E. Best 1982:49–63 concludes that 1 Peter "was pseudonymous but emerged from a Petrine school." But other factors, such as the recipients of the letter, the purpose, the place of writing, and the date, also have a bearing on the question of authorship.

RECIPIENTS, PURPOSE, PLACE OF WRITING, AND DATE

"The exiles of the Dispersion in Pontus, Galatia, Cappadocia [see Figure 15.2], Asia, and Bithynia" are the intended audience of 1 Peter. "Dispersion" does not refer to the Diaspora of the Jews, but to Christians living in the Roman provinces the author names. The author's expressions about their former ignorance (1:14), "you were ransomed from the futile ways inherited from your ancestors" (1:18), and "You have already spent enough time in doing what the Gentiles like to do" (4:3) indicate that the recipients are Gentile Christians who, according to the author, have become a part of "God's own people"

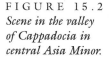

FIGURE 15.2
Scene in the valley of Cappadocia in central Asia Minor.

(2:9–10). It is uncertain whether these people were converted by Paul or other missionaries, but the words "the things that have now been announced to you through those who brought you good news" (1:12) make it certain that the writer himself did not establish churches among the recipients.

It is clear that, like the recipients of Hebrews and Revelation, those of 1 Peter were being oppressed and were perhaps suffering persecution. But since the writer advises obedience to "every human institution, whether of the emperor as supreme" (2:13), it is equally clear that they are not being systematically and officially persecuted by Roman authorities. The nature of their suffering is different in the two main parts of the letter. Up to 4:11, it is anticipated: "though now for a little while you may have to suffer various trials" (1:6); "even if you do [lit., 'if you were to'] suffer for righteousness' sake" (3:14); and "It is better to suffer for doing right, if that should be God's will, than for doing wrong" (3:17). After 4:11, the suffering is spoken of as a "fiery ordeal" that *is* happening. The writer's remark about "something strange" and the words that follow seem to indicate that his readers are already suffering just because they are Christians (4:12–16).

The Christians to whom the author writes are "a chosen race, a royal priesthood, a holy nation, God's own people" who have "received mercy" (2:9–10). The true test of their status as Christians, as God's people, is suffering, and through it all they must remain faithful to God and do what is right. This is the theme of the letter. The author also writes to exhort, encourage, and give the readers hope, and "to testify that this is the true grace of God" (5:12). Various trials test the genuineness of the readers' faith (1:6–7), but they are to be holy as he who called them is holy (1:15). The writer asks, "Now who will harm you if you are eager to do what is good?" (3:13) and then says that if they suffer as Christians they should not be ashamed, but they are not to suffer as wrongdoers (4:13–16). The readers of the letter are being abused verbally by their neighbors because they do not join them in their immoral conduct (4:4). In times of verbal abuse

and physical suffering, the readers' faith and hope must never wane.

But when were the readers suffering? Christians anywhere might experience oppressions such as being maligned (2:12), reviled (3:9), troubled (3:14), abused (4:3), and reproached (4:14). Such oppressions do not imply any persecution initiated by Rome. But according to some scholars, the words "reviled for the name of Christ" (4:14) and "if any of you suffers as a Christian" (4:16) imply that some people were punished by Roman authorities because they were Christians. Scholars who maintain that the letter was written by Peter argue that these passages refer to the persecution by Nero, and that 1 Peter was therefore written before Peter's death in the Neronian persecution of 64 CE. But as others point out, Christians who died under Nero served as scapegoats to shift the blame for the fire in Rome from himself. There is no evidence that they were punished as criminals just because they were Christians who refused to participate in the imperial cult.

In 1 Pet 4:14–15, being a Christian is included with being a murderer, thief, wrongdoer, and mischief-maker. It seems clear, therefore, that being a Christian was the equivalent of committing a crime. Many, if not most, scholars today think that such a situation did not exist in Roman provinces before the time of Domitian (81–96), and probably not before Trajan (98–117; see the correspondence between Trajan and Pliny mentioned in the Introduction to this book). So if the recipients of 1 Peter lived in the provinces mentioned in 1:1 during the time of Domitian or Trajan, where was the author living when he wrote to them?

There is only one clue to the place of writing—the greeting in 5:13 (Greek), where the writer says, "She who is at Babylon . . . sends you greetings." Here, as in Revelation, Babylon is a cryptic metaphor for Rome, so the greeting could mean that the church in Rome sends greetings. On the other hand, Rome (Babylon) as the place of writing may be implied only to give the impression that Peter is the writer, since tradition already associated him with Rome. The reference to governors sent by the emperor to punish wrongdoers seems to imply that the writer was living in a Roman province under a governor. So the letter may have been written by a church officer who calls himself "an elder myself" (5:1) and who lived in one of the provinces to which the letter is addressed.

The fact that the author refers to himself as an elder must also be considered in trying to determine the date of 1 Peter. There is no evidence that elders, or presbyters, were officers in the churches of Paul before the time of Luke-Acts and the pastoral epistles—that is, near the end of the first century. We have already mentioned that the author knew several of Paul's letters and Ephesians, and we have said that the writer's references to the readers' sufferings in 4:12–19 fit with the situation under Domitian, or perhaps that under Trajan. In addition, 1 Peter was first known to the author of 2 Peter, who mentions the Pauline corpus (3:15–16), and to Polycarp, who quotes from 1 Peter (*Epistle to the Philippians* 1:3; 2:1–2, for example), sometime between 120 and 130. Also, Babylon as a cryptic reference for Rome was not used in Jewish literature before the fall of Jerusalem in 70 CE. It is unlikely, therefore, that Christians would have used Babylon for Rome, either, before 70 CE. Taking all of this into consideration, it appears that 1 Peter was written by an unknown Christian living in a Roman province in Asia Minor sometime between c. 70 and 115.

UNITY AND STRUCTURE OF 1 PETER

Because of the hortatory nature of 1 Peter, it is difficult to outline its contents. There seems to be a natural break at 4:11; but in spite of that, many scholars regard 1 Peter as a unity. Because of that break, however, others think the letter is composed of two or more sections written at different times, and perhaps by different authors. Since there appear to be a number of references to baptism in the first part (1:3, 18, 22–23; 2:2–3, 9–10, 21, 24–25; 3:21), several scholars have

suggested that 1 Pet 1:3–4:11 was originally a baptismal sermon or homily preached to new converts. Some passages seem to be addressed to recent converts. For example, the word "now" is often used: "Baptism . . . now saves you" (3:21) and "Once you were not a people but now you are God's people" (2:10). To the baptismal sermon, then, were added 1:1–2 and 4:12–5:14 to give the work the form of a letter to churches in Asia Minor.

Some scholars divide the first part into one or more hymns (for example, 1:3–5; 2:21–24; 3:18–22) and credal confessions (for example, 1:18–21; 3:18–19, 22). Although many scholars recognize the composite nature of 1 Peter, they generally agree that the same person wrote the whole work, since the same style, fondness for concrete imagery, and manner of using the OT appear throughout.

Perhaps an important argument in favor of two different authors is the change in attitude toward Rome in 2:13–17 and 5:13. In the former, the author urges respect for Rome, but in the latter Rome is described as "Babylon," a derogatory term. Indeed, it may be, as A. E. Barnett 1958:209, 202 has suggested, that most of 1 Peter was written "in the name of the Roman church to disavow the bitterness of Revelation," as shown in Rev 18:2–24, for example. Revelation would have encouraged a revolutionary attitude that the writer of 1 Pet 3:11–17 and 4:12–19 tried to counteract.

Whether or not 1 Peter was originally a unity, as it now stands it has the form of a letter, with an opening formula and a closing greeting. Since it was meant for a wide circle of readers, it is impersonal; and with the exception of Mark, no one is mentioned in the greeting. Mark's name was probably inserted to associate the letter with Peter, for whom, traditionally, Mark served as interpreter.

Some scholars (for example, F. L. Cross 1954) have argued that 1 Peter is a baptismal liturgy associated with the early Christian festival of Easter and therefore not a letter. The references to suffering do not refer to persecution but are a play on the words *paschō*, "to suffer," and the festival *pascha* (see 1 Cor 5:7). As usual, other scholars have reacted strongly to that view, especially to the idea of wordplay. The consensus is that 1 Peter is a letter and that it was written for Gentile Christians later than the time of the apostles Peter and James.

The theme of the letter is that the readers must remain faithful to God and do what is right during their suffering; this is the true test of their faith as Christians. In emphasizing his theme, the writer mixes theology and exhortation (see 5:12) in a way that makes it difficult to make a clear and logical outline with headings and subheadings. So in the outline and comments that follow, the work is divided only into several main sections.

Outline and Comments

I. *The writer begins with a greeting and benediction (1:1–2)*

The words "exiles" (1:1) and "aliens" (2:11) may have social rather than geographical implications. As recent Gentile converts (2:12; 4:3) who have adopted a different lifestyle, the readers feel like social outcasts in their pagan environment (see 1:17). As chosen and destined (lit., "foreknown") by God and "sanctified by the Spirit to be obedient to Jesus Christ," Christians, like the Israelites (Hos 11:1; Isa 41:8–9; 51:2; Ps 105:43; Ezek 20:5), are conscious of being God's people and are obligated to do right. "Sprinkled with his blood" may be an allusion to the making of the Israelite covenant (Exod 24:3–8), when the people of Israel promised to be obedient to God's commands. "Blood" may refer to the death of Christ, through which a new relationship between God and humankind was made possible.

II. *The writer praises God for the readers' new birth as Christians, which brings hope for salvation (1:3–12)*

God is responsible for the new spiritual experience through Jesus' resurrection, but for a while the readers may have to suffer so that their faith may be tested and refined, as gold is by the fire (1:3–9). The prophets foresaw the future glory of the readers, when their faith would ultimately be rewarded (1:10–12).

III. *Being "a chosen race, a royal priesthood, a holy nation, God's own people" demands expression in moral lives (1:13–2:10)*

God's demand "Be holy, for I am holy" (Lev 11:44–45) takes on new meaning because Christ ransomed the readers from their former futile, sinful ways. At the eschatological judgment, people will be judged impartially according to their deeds (1:13–21). The new birth as Christians is expressed in love for one another (1:22–25); so, as newly baptized people, the readers must not sin against each other but must mature in their spiritual life to attain salvation (2:1–3). As God's special people, they can do this by becoming a temple of God (see 1 Cor 3:16–17; 2 Cor 6:16; Eph 2:21–22; 1QS 8:4–8) with "living stones"; they are no longer representatives of pagan temples with lifeless stones. Spiritual union with Christ, the cornerstone of their new lives (see Ps 118:22; Isa 8:14–15; 28:16), inspires spiritual sacrifices—that is, devout lives and helpful deeds (2:4–10; see also Rom 12:1; Heb 13:15–16; Isa 1:11; Hos 6:6; Mic 6:6–8; Ps 50:14–15, 23; 51:17; 1QS 9:3–6).

IV. *The author gives directions for living in a pagan society (2:11–3:12)*

The word translated as "Gentiles" in 2:12 and 4:3 is translated as "pagans" in 1 Cor 12:2, and that is probably the meaning intended here. Thus far the writer has described the nature of Christian life in general, but now he gives concrete rules of conduct for Christians among pagans and among themselves. The recipients of 1 Peter were oppressed more for social than for official or legal reasons because they were causing suspicion among their pagan neighbors. But as social aliens and exiles, Christians must maintain good conduct, not only for their own sakes as Christians but also in the hope of making converts (2:11–12). They must also obey Roman authorities "for the Lord's sake" and by doing right silence their oppressors (2:13–17).

In 2:18–3:12 the rules for family households, usually referred to as *Haustafeln* (see comments on Col 3:18–4:1 and the reference to Selwyn 1969 above; for families see H. Moxnes 1997), apply to the whole Christian community thought of as a brotherhood (2:17; 5:9) in which all members must live in unity and peace (see also Rom 12:10, 14–15; 15:5; 1 Cor 4:12; 12:26; Phil 2:2; Matt 5:43–44; Luke 6:27–28). This section (2:18–3:12) gives an insight into the social nature of a Christian community within a society that misunderstood and was suspicious of it.

V. The author gives advice about how to react to undeserved suffering (3:13–4:11)

Reverence Christ and do what is right, for it is better to suffer for doing right than for doing wrong (3:13–17). Christ is the readers' example, and they will triumph as he did because baptism is their guarantee. Just as Noah survived the flood (Genesis 6–9), the recipients of 1 Peter have survived by going through the water of baptism (3:18–22).

The words that Jesus was made alive in the Spirit "in which also he went and made a proclamation to the spirits in prison, who in former times did not obey, when God waited patiently in the days of Noah" (3:19–20) are difficult, and no one knows for sure what they mean. Perhaps they mean that between his death and resurrection Jesus went to the underworld, Hades, to preach to the sinful generation of Noah (see Gen 6:1–8) and others. This view gave rise to the credal statement about Jesus' descent into Hell, or Hades. If "the spirits" are not the same as "the dead" in 4:6, then the reference may be to the angelic prisoners in the second heaven or elsewhere, who did not obey God's commands (see *2 Enoch* 7:1–5; *Enoch* 6; 10:4–6, 11–14, 17–19; 21:1–7; *Jub.* 5:6).

Although the writer (3:18–20) does not say where the spirits were when Jesus went to preach to them, the idea of Jesus' descent into the underworld may reflect a Christianized form of redemption myths in Oriental religions—for example, the story of the descent of Ishtar to the lower world. Several Greek myths, such as those of Orpheus and Eurydice and Heracles and Alcestis, reflect the same idea. Recently, several scholars have taken the following view: "The risen Christ proclaimed his triumph to the imprisoned spirits as he passed through the heavens to his exaltation" (J. A. Fitzmyer 1968a:366–367).

Readers should give up their evil ways even though they may have to face suffering. Suffering like Christ means living by the will of God, which brings cessation from sin (4:1–6; see also Rom 6:1–10). "The dead" in 4:5–6 are probably believers who had died before the letter was written. The End is near, so act graciously toward each other (4:7–11).

VI. The writer advises those actually being persecuted (4:12–5:11)

Rejoice because you share Christ's suffering (see Rom 8:17), do not do wrong, and entrust yourselves to God (4:12–19). Like administrators, teachers, preachers (1 Tim 5:17), and pastoral leaders in the churches (Jas 5:14), the elders are to perform their duties eagerly, willingly, humbly, and without desire for material gain (5:1–5). The writer exhorts his readers to resist the devil, described as "a roaring lion" seeking its prey, by standing firm in their faith. The language the author uses here is symbolic of the Roman persecutors. Persecutions will bring suffering for a little while, but then God will "restore, support, strengthen, and establish" the readers (5:6–11).

VII. The writer closes with a greeting and benediction (5:12–14)

These verses were either written by the person who dictated the letter to Silvanus or were added by someone who wanted to ascribe the work to Peter. The words "the true grace of God" refer to the message of the whole letter, but especially to 5:10 (see also 1:3–12; 2:4–10; 3:13–4:7). For further study of 1 Peter, see A. R. C. Leaney 1967; G. Krodel 1977; J. N. D. Kelly 1969; G. R. Beasley-Murray 1965; J. Moffatt 1928; J. H. Elliott 1990; D. P. Senior 1980. See, more recently, D. L. Balch 1981; R. A. Martin 1982; L. Goppelt 1993; R. P. Martin 1994; P. Perkins 1995; P. J. Achtemeier 1996.

SUMMARY

Hebrews, Revelation, and 1 Peter, though very different works, are all addressed to those confronted with oppression, sometimes even persecution, by non-Christians. Each work was written to encourage the readers to remain faithful to the Christian religion.

The author of Hebrews, a religious essay or tract, wrote to encourage his readers not to revert to their former religion of Judaism or to paganism. If they remain faithful, in spite of difficulty, they will reach their eternal rest guaranteed by Jesus, the superior high priest. The writer of Revelation, a work representing a unique form of Jewish-Christian literature called apocalypse, exhorts his readers to remain faithful, and warns that if they do not do so there will be terrible consequences. Although the worst is yet to come, those who remain faithful will receive the crown of life; and the agents of Rome, along with Satan and his evil followers, will be eternally punished.

Though it is in the form of a letter, 1 Peter may originally have been a sermon or homily for recently baptized converts who were suffering ridicule and rebuke and some persecution just because they were Christians. The author wrote to exhort them to look to the suffering of Christ as an example, to consider their suffering as a test of their faith, and to be sure always to do right, never wrong. The author may also have written to counteract the vengeful and revolutionary attitude in Revelation. If the recipients of 1 Peter do right and entrust their souls to God, they "will win the crown of glory that never fades away."

A group of NT writings known as the catholic or general epistles was introduced to us in 1 Peter. In the next chapter we will examine the rest of those epistles—the letters of John, James, Jude, and 2 Peter.

CHAPTER 16

Letters of John, James, Jude, and 2 Peter

THE LETTERS TREATED IN THIS CHAPTER, like 1 Peter, belong to that group of writings known as the catholic or general epistles because they were intended for the whole church, not individual churches. Generally, they reflect universal problems in the church caused by the delay of the Parousia and by false teachers. The letters' authors share the purpose of refuting false teaching and exhorting their readers to right moral and ethical living as they await the Parousia.

A common thread tying these letters together is the idea that opposition to Christians comes from "the world" (1 Pet 5:9; 2 Pet 1:4; 2:20; 1 John 2:15–17; 4:1–5; 5:4–5; 2 John 7; Jas 1:27; 4:4; Jude 19), which is the source of various trials before the End (1 Pet 1:6; 2 Pet 2:9; Jas 1:2, 12; 1 John 2:8, 18–28; Jude 18). Such trials are a test of faith, so Christians must respond with patience, courage, and especially good behavior if they are to face suffering and perhaps even death.

The general epistles provide insight into the piety and everyday life of Christians as a minority group facing the social, political, and economic challenges from the majority. As in the time of Paul, congregations did not own buildings used for worship, so Christians met in the homes of church members. Christians meeting in such homes thought of themselves as a brotherhood (1 Pet 2:17; 5:9) in which the chief virtues were love of the members (1 Pet 4:8; 5:14; 1 John 2:5; 4:7, 17–21; 2 John 3; 6; 2 Pet 1:7; Jude 2; 21) and hospitality to traveling Christians (1 Pet 4:9; Jas 2:1–9; 4:11; 2 John 9–12; 3 John 3; 5–10).

1 JOHN

The three letters 1, 2, and 3 John, along with the gospel of John and Revelation, belong to a group of writings known as the Johannine literature because tradition ascribed all of them to the apostle John. The three letters share some vocabulary and have the same style, so they are closely related to each other. One John has more in common with the fourth gospel than do the other two letters, and there is general agreement that none of the letters is related to Revelation. However, see parallels in Chapter 15.

Although the author of each letter is nameless, the writer of 2 and 3 John calls himself "the elder"; this may indicate, as most scholars believe, that the two letters were written by the same person. Moreover, the words "I have written something to the church" in 3 John 9 may be an allusion to 1 or 2 John. Opinion about whether the author of 2 and 3 John also wrote 1 John is divided, as is opinion about the authorship of 1 John and the gospel. All agree, however, that the gospel and 1 John are closely related. (Review my discussion of the gospel of John and see R. E. Brown 1982:5–35 for a discussion of authorship.)

RELATIONSHIP BETWEEN 1 JOHN AND THE GOSPEL OF JOHN

That 1 John and the gospel are closely related is clear from the similarities in vocabulary, phraseology, and thought. More than fifty words and phrases in the NT occur only in John and 1 John, including the following—from the Greek text (first references are to gospel): *paraklētos* ("counselor," 14:16, 26; "advocate," 2:1); *logos* ("word," used of Jesus; 1:1; 1:1); "murderer" (8:44; 3:15); "children," as a form of address (21:5; 2:14, 18); "to see" (two different words) and "bear witness to" (1:32, 34; 1:2; 4:14); "filled with joy" (3:29; 1:4); "do the truth" (3:21; 1:6); "take away sin" (1:29; 3:5); "believe in the name of Jesus" (1:12; 5:13); "have sin" (9:41; 1:8); "the world did not know him" (1:10; 3:1); "keep Jesus' word" (8:51; 2:5); "have life" (3:36; 5:12); "the world hates you" (15:18; 3:13); "a new commandment" (13:34; 2:7); "savior of the world" (4:42; 4:14); and "to overcome the world" (16:33; 5:5).

Besides similarities in vocabulary and phraseology, certain ideas are the same. Jesus was a human being (1:14; 4:2). He was "the life" (5:26; 11:25; 1:1, 2) and the source of life for others (1:4; 6:33, 35; 5:11). Believers remain or abide in Christ (6:56; 14:20; 2:24; 5:20), and God's word abides in them (5:38; 2:14). Because of his love, God sent his only Son (3:16; 4:9). Jesus commanded believers, who are "of" or "from" God (8:47; 3:10), to love one another (13:34; 3:23). Similarly, several pairs of opposites in both works are striking: light and darkness, life and death, love and hate, truth and falsehood, the Father and the world, to be of the world and to be not of the world, God and the devil, to know and not to know God, to have seen and not to have seen God, and to have and not to have life. (This list and the preceding one are from A. E. Brooke 1912:viii–ix.)

Despite striking similarities between John and 1 John in vocabulary, phraseology, and thought, there are also significant differences. Most of the differences in vocabulary, such as key words in the gospel omitted in the epistle, reflect different occasions for writing. But there are differences in thought that are difficult to explain. Things attributed to Jesus in 1 John are attributed to God in the gospel: Christ/God is light (1:4; 8:12; 1:5); Christ/God is the life (11:25; 14:6; 5:20); believers abide in Christ/God (6:56; 15:4–5; 2:6; 3:24; 4:13); Christ/God abides in believers (6:56; 15:4–5; 3:24; 4:12–13); the word of Christ/God (5:24; 8:31; 1:10; 2:14); the commandment(s) of Christ/God (13:34; 14:15, 21; 15:10, 12, 14, 17; 2:3–4; 3:22–24; 4:21; 5:2–3); Christ/God in believers overcomes the world (16:33; 5:4); and believers relate to God through Christ in John (1:12; 14:6, 20–21; 17:21, 23, 25–26) but directly to God in 1 John (1:6; 2:6, 29; 3:1, 9–10; 4:4, 6–7; 5:1, 4, 18–19).

The writer of John stresses the glory and glorifying of Jesus, the culmination of which is his death. But the words "glory" and "glorify," which occur thirty-nine times in John, never appear in the epistles. In 1 John the death of Jesus has sacrificial and atoning significance (1:7; 2:2; 3:16; 4:10; see also John 1:29). Although both writers use the term *paraklētos*, it is never applied to Jesus in John, but in 1 John 2:1 it is applied to Jesus and has the meaning "advocate." In John, on the other hand, it is the peculiar designation for the Holy Spirit or Spirit of truth (14:17, 26; 15:26). Although 1 John never uses the term

"Holy Spirit," there are clear references to the Spirit in 1 John 3:24; 4:13; 5:6, 8. Use of the word "spirit" in the antithesis between the spirit of truth and the spirit of error in 1 John 4:1–6 is unlike the use of "the Spirit" in the gospel. Another important difference between John and 1 John is that there are no quotations from the OT in 1 John, and only one allusion to it (3:12), whereas there are many quotations and allusions in John. The absence of polemic against "the Jews" in 1 John may account for the lack of OT quotation. For similarities between John and letters of John see R. E. Brown 1982: 755–759; K. Grayston 1984; R. A. Culpepper 1998.

There are important similarities and differences, then, in both literary features and thought between John and 1 John. This problem defies solution, but several answers have been suggested. One view is that both works were written by the same person but at different times and under different circumstances. Another possibility is that 1 John was written by a follower or pupil of the gospel writer, or by an editor of the gospel who perhaps also wrote John 21, the appendix to the gospel. Both writings, according to yet another view, come from a Johannine school or circle. Recently, some scholars have suggested that 1 John was written because a group of Christians had separated themselves from the Johannine community. The Johannine community was responsible for the gospel and was represented by the author of 1 John and probably also of 2 and 3 John. According to this view, the relationship between the gospel and epistles is best explained on the hypothesis that the group represented by the author of the epistle(s) and that represented by the recipients of the epistle(s) both knew the Christianity of the gospel, if not the gospel itself. As with authorship, there are varying ideas about the recipients of the Johannine epistles.

RECIPIENTS OF 1 JOHN AND THE AUTHOR'S PURPOSE

From 1 John 2:19 (see also 4:1–2; 2 John 7) it is clear that some people had left the community of Christians represented by the author: "They went out from us, but they did not belong to us; for if they had belonged to us, they would have remained with us." But we do not know what motivated the withdrawal of the separatists. It seems, however, that in 1:3 the writer is inviting them to come back—"so that you also may have fellowship with us."

By reading between the lines in the epistle(s), we can discover several theological and moral differences that seem to be the root of the problem between the separatists and the writer. In a very unsystematic and incoherent way, the author writes to defend his views, which are clear from his response to the views of his opponents. The separatists claimed to have fellowship with God as light and to be sinless (1:6, 8–10). The writer seems to accuse them of walking in darkness—that is, not behaving properly—and therefore of lying when they say they have no sin. At the same time, the separatists seem to ignore the atoning death of Jesus—a view not mentioned in the fourth gospel, except possibly in 1:29. The epistle writer, however, stresses the atonement of Jesus (1:7; 2:1–2; 3:5; 5:6). The separatists were saying, "I have come to know him [God or Christ]," "I abide in him" (2:6), "I am in the light" (2:9), and "I love God" (4:20), but not obeying his commandments. According to the writer, this is a contradiction, because "Whoever says, 'I have come to know him' but does not obey his commandments, is a liar" (2:4) and "We may be sure that we know him, if we obey his commandments" (2:3).

Apparently the separatists were also claiming to love God while, at the same time, not getting along well with fellow believers (2:10–11; 4:20–21). The writer is emphatic, using the expression "hates his brother" (2:9, 11; 3:15; 4:20; Greek), which shows the intensity of the schism in the Johannine community. The bulk of the letter, therefore, deals with the proper love relationship between believers and God and among believers themselves.

Christologically, the separatists were denying that Jesus was the Christ (2:22) and the Son of God (2:23; 3:23; 4:15; 5:5) and that Jesus had come in the flesh—that he had been human (4:2; 2 John 7). These denials were the teachings of the "antichrist" (2:18, 22; 4:3; 2 John 7) and "false prophets" (4:1), who for true believers were a sign that the End was near (2:18). Such negative teachings were the germ that grew into the fully developed Gnosticism of the second century. But the "gnosticism" of the writer is entirely positive: "we know" God or Christ (2:3), "we know love" (3:16), "we are from the truth" (3:19; see also 2 John 1), "he abides in us" (3:24), "we abide in him" (4:13), "believe the love that God has for us" (4:16), and "we love the children of God, when we love God and obey his commandments" (5:2). The writer reminds his readers that by confessing "that Jesus Christ has come in the flesh" (4:2) they can "know the Father" (2:14) and "him who is from the beginning" (2:14)—that is, Jesus as a preexistent being—and the Spirit of God.

Evidence indicates that the author of 1 John wrote to counter the christological views and ethical differences between his followers and the separatists. The Johannine community, which produced the fourth gospel, was falling apart. The author of 1 John wrote not so much to promote faith in Jesus as the Christ—that by believing, readers might have life (John 20:31)—as to encourage those who already "believe in the name of the Son of God" to be confident that they had eternal life (5:13–14; see also 5:11; John 3:36; 5:24; 6:40, 47; 10: 28). He says he writes "not because you do not know the truth, but because you know it" (2:21).

LITERARY FORM, STYLE, AND STRUCTURE OF 1 JOHN

Although the author frequently says he is writing (thirteen times), 1 John has no epistolary introduction or concluding greeting, so it is not a letter. Perhaps the author had intended to write a letter but got so carried away that he substituted a theological prologue—comparable to that of John—and a conclusion for the customary beginning and ending of a letter. The author alternates between theological statements and ethical exhortations, and this gives the work the nature of a sermon, essay, or religious tract.

In contrast to the Greek of the fourth gospel, which is usually clear and easy to translate, that of 1 John is often vague and difficult to translate. The writer has a limited vocabulary, which he uses over and over. A casual reading reveals immediately that he speaks often about God, the Father, the Son, and love, and statistics support this (numbers in parentheses are for 1, 2, and 3 John, respectively): "God" (62,2,3); "Father" (12,4,0); "Son" (22,2,0); "love," *agapaō*, verb (28,2,1); "love," *agapē*, noun (18,2,1); and "beloved" (6,0,4). Other favorite words are "know," *ginōskō* (25,1,0) and *oida* (15,0,1); "have" (28,4,2); "world" (23,1,0); "truth" (9,5,6); and "all" or "every," *pas* (27,2,2).

Because the style of 1 John is rambling and repetitious, with unclear transitions, the writer's manner of thinking and writing has been called "spiral." According to R. Law 1968:5, "The course of thought does not move from point to point in a straight line. It is like a winding staircase—always revolving around the same centre, always recurring to the same topics, but at a higher level" (for examples, see 2–4, 7–24). Although the writer of 1 John does not quote the OT, his style is sometimes remarkably like that of the parallel passages in Hebrew poetry. Here are examples:

Whoever has the Son has life;
Whoever does not have the Son of God does
   not have life [5:12].

No one who abides in him sins;
No one who sins has either seen him or known
   him [3:6].

This poetic style of much of 1 John is closely related to the complicated problem of the letter's structure (for various suggestions, see I. H. Marshall 1978a:22–27). J. C. O'Neill 1966 has suggested that the structure consists of a prologue and twelve separate poetic admonitions. Actually, 1 John does not seem to be organized in a particular pattern or around a special theme, but 3:23 is close to being the theme of the work: "And this is his commandment, that we should believe in the name of his Son Jesus Christ and love one another, just as he has commanded us." Notice how this theme occurs in 1 John as you study the following outline and comments.

Outline and Comments

I. Prologue (1:1–4)

The writer seems to be interpreting the prologue of John's gospel. Although Jesus existed from the time of creation, he became a real flesh and blood person who could be seen, heard, and touched. He was a human being who brought eternal life, which is fellowship with God and with his Son Jesus Christ.

II. Walking in the light (1:5–2:2)

"God is light," and to have fellowship with God means walking in the light, which is symbolic of moral goodness, not in darkness, which is symbolic of moral corruption. To have fellowship with God also means to "do the truth," that is, practice fully the will of God as revealed through Christ. This kind of Christian response distinguishes the author's "My little children" (2:1), as true believers, from the "antichrists" (2:18) and "false prophets" (4:1) among the separatists. Walking in the light, or being in fellowship with God, also means recognition of sin and forgiveness through Jesus his Son.

III. Keeping God's commandments (2:3–11)

Those who keep God's commandments know God. When the author writes about people who say they know God but disobey his commandments, he is reproving those separatists who hold the Gnostic idea that knowledge of God does not necessitate moral conduct (2:3–6). Keeping the commandments and walking in the light also mean loving one's brother (2:7–11).

IV. True believers and the world (2:12–17)

The various groups among the author's followers, who as true believers had their sins forgiven, must be on their guard against the wiles of the world, which is beginning to pass away.

V. Warning against those opposing Christ (2:18–29)

As the End approaches, watch out for the antichrists, who are a sign of the last hour (2:18). The term "antichrist" occurs only in 1 John 2:18, 22; 4:3; and 2 John 7. It represents an early Christian belief that there would be a final force or person (see "man of lawlessness" in 2 Thess 2:1–12 and "the beast" in Rev 13:1–18) opposed to God and Christ. The view is a summation of several pagan and Jewish myths concerning the monster from the sea (Isa 27:1; 30:7; 51:9; Job 3:8; 7:12; 26:12; Pss 74:13–14; 89:8–10) and Satan (lit., "adversary") as an angelic being in heaven opposing God and accusing humans (Gen 3:1–15; Dan 10:13; 12:1; *Jub.* 1:20; Wis 2:24; 1QS 1:18–24; 2:4–5; 3:20–21; *Enoch* 6–16; 1QM 1:1–2). The concept of Satan appears in the NT as "the ruler of this world" (John 12:31; 14:30; 16:11; see also Eph 2:2; 6:12) and "Belial" or Beliar (2 Cor 6:15). Other forms of the myth involved evil being embodied in a human ruler—for example, Antiochus IV as "the Prince of princes" (Dan 8:25) and a mortal equal to God (2 Macc 9:12), the Roman rulers in Revelation, and the false prophet or prophets who lead people astray (Deut 13:1–5; 18:20; Mark 13:22; Matt 24:11, 24; 1 John 4:1; Rev 16:13; 19:20; 20:10; 2 Pet 2:1).

For the writer(s) of the Johannine epistles, the antichrists are those separatists who deny that Jesus was the Christ (2:22) and that he was human (2 John 7). The true believers are to remain firm and abide in Jesus. The source of their strength is the Spirit, which they received in baptism (2:26–29; see also 3:24).

VI. True believers as children of God (3:1–4:6)

By repeating the same idea several times, the writer stresses that as children of God now and as people who will be like God when the End comes, true believers must keep pure from sin and not be children of the devil by committing sin and disobeying God's commandments (3:1–10). The statements that "no one who abides in him sins" (3:6) and "Those who have been born of God do not sin" (3:9) contradict the earlier statements that "if we say that we have no sin, we deceive ourselves" (1:8) and "If we say that we have not sinned . . . his word is not in us" (1:10; see also 2:1–2). Perhaps the best explanation is that in 1:5–2:2 the writer is speaking about the separatists who, though walking in darkness, were claiming to be free from sin. But the writer's concept of sin is so difficult and illusive that there is no completely satisfactory explanation for it (see C. H. Dodd 1946:68–81 and I. H. Marshall 1978a:175–184).

True believers express their love by helping fellow Christians and by keeping God's commandments, not in speaking. By doing these things they can have confidence that God will hear their prayers (3:11–24). True Christians confess that Jesus came in the flesh, and so are children of God. They must be on their guard against those who, by denying that Jesus came in the flesh, are not of God but represent the forces of the world or evil (4:1–6).

The denial that Jesus came in the flesh developed into a phenomenon known as Docetism, an aspect of Gnosticism. *Docetism* is derived from the Greek word *dokeō*, meaning "to seem or appear." As Gnostics, the Docetists believed that Jesus was only spirit and did not have a body, which as matter was evil. Thus, without a physical body, Jesus only seemed to be human, to suffer, and to die. Later a Gnostic known as Cerinthus (see Irenaeus, *Her.* 1:26:1) maintained that Jesus, born of Joseph and Mary, and therefore human like all other children, became divine only after his baptism, when the spiritual being—the Christ—descended upon him as a dove. Then after preaching about God and performing miracles, the spiritual Christ withdrew from Jesus, who therefore did not really suffer and die. Because the separatists, whom the writer of 1 John is opposing, were denying Jesus' physical existence, the writer begins his work by defending the physical nature of Jesus.

VII. God's love and human love (4:7–5:12)

The theme that those who believe Jesus is the Christ love God and one another and keep God's commandments is repeated, and the three subjects of the theme are interwoven. By loving each other, believers know God, who is love and who abides in them to perfect their love (4:7–12). Because believers have the Spirit, confess Jesus as the Son of God, and love one another, they have the assurance of God's abiding love (4:13–21). Love for God is manifested by keeping his commandments (5:1–3). Faith in Jesus as the Son of God means victory over the world and eternal life, assurances the separatists do not have (5:4–12).

The words about water, blood, and the Spirit in 5:6–8 are probably the most obscure in 1 John. The author may be refuting an early form of the Docetic belief about the baptism and death of Jesus. He is saying that, as the Christ, Jesus was really baptized in water and then received the Spirit, and that he also really did bleed in his death on the cross. As a flesh and blood person, Jesus appeared "not with the water only but with the water [baptism] and the blood" (death; 5:6). For the writer, Jesus was truly human, but he was also the divine Son of God. So it was the total person, Jesus Christ, who received the Spirit at his baptism and died on the cross. Through this total person, Jesus Christ, the Son of God, God gave eternal life to believers (5:11–12; see R. E. Brown 1982: 572–587).

VIII. Conclusion (5:13–21)

The writer gives final assurance to his followers as children of God and summarizes his arguments. In 5:16–17 there is a new thought: by praying, Christians can secure God's forgiveness for the sins of fellow Christians, except for "mortal sin" (lit., "sin unto death"). What the writer means by such sin is uncertain. Perhaps he means a sin so unusual and so terrible that it is impossible, "morally speaking," to comprehend forgiveness. The complicated, even contradictory, doctrine of sin in 1 John is not even mentioned in 2 and 3 John, to which we now turn.

2 AND 3 JOHN

These writings are definitely letters and are so closely related that they probably come from the same unknown author, who calls himself "the elder." The words "I have written" in 3 John 9 may refer to 2 John, and therefore imply common authorship. Although the words "the elect lady" in 2 John 1 may refer to an individual Christian, they are usually taken as a personification of a Christian community. Indeed, the closing greeting, "The children of your elect sister greet you" (2 John 13; Greek), confirms this view. Why would the children of the "elect sister," and not the sister herself, send greetings to "the elect lady" if an individual were meant?

The references to many deceivers gone out into the world (2 John 7) presuppose separatists from the writer's community who deny Jesus' humanity. The purposes of 2 John are to remind the readers that the teaching they received is "the truth" (4) and to warn them not to welcome those teaching other doctrines (9–10). Those who do so share in their wicked work (11).

Three John is addressed to Gaius, an individual. The author praises him and Demetrius but severely criticizes Diotrephes, who challenges the author's authority. The author writes to encourage the welcoming of traveling orthodox missionaries and even strangers as a religious duty. These travelers are being sent by the author. The letter may reflect a situation in early Christianity toward the end of the first century, when area churches were united around their own local officers, who were beginning to rival the traveling missionary preachers of earlier times. Three John, then, could have been written by the same writer as 2 John—or by another—to correct a possible misimpression given by 2 John that such missionaries were no longer to be welcomed for fear they might be false teachers.

Although 2 John appears to be addressed to a specific church and 3 John to a particular individual, these addresses may be fictitious. If they are, then 2 and 3 John, like 1 John, were intended to be catholic or general epistles.

For further study of the letters of John, see especially R. E. Brown 1982 and the extensive bibliography throughout that volume. See also J. L. Houlden 1973; I. H. Marshall 1978a; K. Grayston 1984; R. Kysar 1986b; D. M. Smith 1991; R. Schnackenburg 1992; R. B. Edwards 1996; G. Strecker 1996, advanced redaction criticism; D. Rensberger 1997.

JAMES

BACKGROUND IN JUDAISM, HELLENISM, AND CHRISTIANITY

A truly general epistle is that of James. Like the letters of John, it is a puzzle, especially the background out of which it developed. If we take out the references to the Lord Jesus Christ in 1:1 and 2:1, the work is thoroughly Jewish. In fact, it has been suggested that James was originally a completely Jewish work and was touched up with those references and then published by a Christian writer. There is much in James to support that view. In saying to his readers that they do well if they believe that God is one (2:19), the writer echoes the basic doctrine of Jewish belief. Similarly, when he says that "Whoever keeps the whole law but fails in one point has become accountable for all of it" (2:10), and when he speaks about the law as perfect (1:25), he shares the views of many Jews of his time, especially those of Qumran (see, for example, 1QS 1:1, 16–20; 5:1, 7–10, 21–22; 8:15–16). Jews would also agree that those who do what the law requires will save their souls (1:21) and be blessed (1:25; see also 2:8–12; 4:11–12). The writer, however, never says what law he is talking about. No Jew would disagree with the writer's comment on religion: "Religion that is pure and undefiled before God, the Father, is this: to care for orphans and widows in their distress, and to keep oneself unstained by the world" (1:27). Another important Jewish idea in James is that God, in whose likeness humans were created (3:9), is one (2:19), is free from temptation (1:13), and gives good gifts to humans (1:5, 17). God brings judgment under the law, yet shows mercy (3:12–13) and will forgive the person who prays (5:15). The writer refers to God as "the Lord of hosts" (5:4), a distinctly Jewish title, and uses the Jewish term "Gehenna" for the place of punishment (3:6).

Ideas very similar to those of the Jewish wisdom writings of Proverbs, Sirach, Wisdom, and the *Testaments of the Twelve Patriarchs* occur in

James. The following are interesting parallels (references to James are first): 4:6, quoting Prov 3:34; fruit of righteousness (3:18; Prov 11:30); blaming God (1:13; Prov 19:3; Sir 15:11–20); not knowing about tomorrow (4:13–14; Prov 27:1); being slow to speak (1:19; Prov 29:20); a wicked tongue (3:5–10; Sir 19:6–12; 20:5–8; 22:27; 28:13–26); beasts controlled by humans, who are made in God's likeness (3:7, 9; Sir 17:3–4); speaking evil against another (4:11; 5:9; Wis 1:11); life vanishing as a mist (4:14; Wis 2:4); oppressing the poor (2:6; Wis 2:10–20); trials as tests sent by God (1:2–3, 12–13; Wis 3:4–6); riches fading away (1:10–12; Wis 4:8–9); the tongue used for blessing and cursing (3:9–10; *T Benj.* 6:5); obeying God making the devil flee (4:7; *T Naph.* 8:4); and drawing near to God (4:8; *T Dan* 6:2). Perhaps Jewish wisdom is the most influential background of James and may be the best clue for understanding its relationship to Paul's thought (see below).

Although there are many parallels in language and thought between James and Jewish writings, certain primary concerns of Judaism, such as circumcision, sabbath observance, dietary and ritual purity laws, and temple worship, are absent in James. In light of the Jewishness of James, it is difficult to explain such omissions, unless perhaps the writer took these concerns for granted and thought it unnecessary to mention them.

In addition to being familiar with Jewish thought, the writer of James seems to be equally influenced by Hellenism—especially Stoicism, with its short, crisp form of speaking and writing known as the diatribe. Among the characteristics of the diatribe are debate with an imaginary speaker and short questions and answers, of which Jas 2:18–20 is a good example: "But someone will say. . . . Do you want to be shown . . . that faith apart from works is barren?" (see also 2:21–24; 5:13–14). Quite characteristic also are short phrases (Greek), such as "Do not be deceived" (1:16), "Know this" (1:19), "You see" (2:22, 24), "Be patient" (5:7), and "But above all" (5:12). Rhetorical questions, such as "Who is wise and understanding among you?"

(3:13; see also 2:4–5; 4:4–5), and imperatives, such as "Do not swear" (5:12) and "Come now" (5:1), are very common, as they are in the works of Stoic philosophers. As in the Greek diatribes, James even uses derogatory speech, such as "you senseless person" (2:20; see also 4:4). Analogies involving the bridles of horses, rudders of ships, and forest fire (3:2–5) are common to James and to Greek writers.

In our discussion of the apostle Paul, we learned about parallels in language and thought between Paul and the Stoic writers Seneca (*Ep.*) and Epictetus (*Dis.*). Among the similarities between James and those writers are the expression "friend of God" (2:24; *Dis.* 4:3:9), the similes of the mirror (1:23; *Dis.* 2:14:21) and the fig tree and olives (3:12; *Ep.* 87:25), and the idea of joy in times of adversity (1:2; *Ep.* 23:2).

That James shows influence from Judaism and Hellenism is certain, but his influence from early Christianity is a matter of debate, especially concerning his possible acquaintance with Paul's letters. Some scholars see a literary acquaintance in the expressions "doers of the word" (1:22) and "doers of the law" (Rom 2:13), the idea of rejoicing in suffering that produces endurance (1:2–4; Rom 5:3–4), and the phrases "transgressor of the law" and "apart from works," which occur in the NT only in Jas 2:9, 11, 18 and Rom 2:25, 27; 3:28. Other scholars, however, reject even these close parallels as insufficient evidence for literary acquaintance.

There seem to be close parallels between James and the teachings of Jesus in the synoptic tradition on the following points: ask and it will be given (1:5; Matt 7:7; Luke 11:9), good gifts from the Father (1:17; Matt 7:11), the poor as those who receive the kingdom (2:5; Matt 5:3; Luke 6:20), and peacemaking (3:18; Matt 5:9). The most obvious parallel is between Jas 5:12 and Matt 5:33–37, on the subject of taking oaths. (For a Jesus tradition common to Matthew and James see R. E. Brown 1997:734–735.) But these ideas, as well as James's strong insistence on doing rather than hearing or saying, were all current in Judaism, from which they got into the

Christian tradition, so they prove nothing about James's acquaintance with sayings of Jesus.

Perhaps James has more in common with 1 Peter than with any other NT work. Both are addressed to those in the "Dispersion" (1:1; 1 Pet 1:1) who are suffering "trials" for their faith (1:2–3, 12; 1 Pet 1:6). Both speak of humans as created by God's word (1:18; 1 Pet 1:23), have the idea that love covers "a multitude of sins" (5:20; 1 Pet 4:8), and use the metaphor of the passions at war with the body (4:1; 1 Pet 2:11). Both have a warning to be humble, a quotation from Prov 3:34, and a plea to resist the devil all in one context (4:6–10; 1 Pet 5:5–9). But even such close parallels do not prove a literary dependence of one writer upon the other.

In strong contrast to most NT writers, James never refers to Jesus' death or resurrection, or to the gift and efficacy of the Holy Spirit. Such omissions only make it more difficult to understand this enigmatic writing and its relationship to early Christianity.

AUTHORSHIP, DATE, AND PURPOSE OF JAMES

The author calls himself "James, a servant of God and of the Lord Jesus Christ" (1:1). The word "servant," Jude's reference to himself as "brother of James" (1:1), and the authoritative tone of James indicate that the author was a well-known official and authority in the church. Tradition has found such an authority in "James the Lord's brother" (Gal 1:19) and a leader of Jewish Christianity in Jerusalem (Gal 2:9, 12; Acts 12:17; 15:13; 21:18; 1 Cor 15:7; Mark 6:3; Matt 13:55). This is about all of the evidence supporting the tradition that the author was James, Jesus' brother. For a defense of James the brother of Jesus as the author see P. A. Bernheim 1997.

On the other hand, there are several reasons for believing that the work was not written by that James. The Greek, which is classed with that of Hebrews, is so good that it could not have been written by an unlearned Palestinian Jew. It is clear, moreover, from his allusions and quota-

tions (for example, 1:10–11 reflects Isa 40:6–7; 2:22 quotes Gen 15:6; and 5:11 alludes to Ps 103:8) that the writer knew and used the Greek OT. However, those who uphold the traditional view of authorship reply to the objection based on the Greek of James with two arguments. One is that James, like Paul, used a Greek-speaking secretary to write what he dictated. But in contrast to Paul's letters, there is no evidence in James that the writer used a secretary. The other argument, perhaps more plausible, is that the work represents sermons of James that were collected, edited, and sent out as a general letter by someone who wrote good Greek (see P. H. Davids 1983:20).

A second objection to James's authorship is that it is unlikely that, as a brother of Jesus, James would never refer to his personal relationship with Jesus. Another argument against the traditional view is that the letter of James did not get into the Canon before the third century; therefore, the tradition that James was written by Jesus' brother did not develop very early. Against this objection, defenders of the traditional view reply that the type of Jewish Christianity reflected in James must have originated before 70 CE and that the more orthodox Pauline Gentile Christianity would not quickly have acknowledged such a work by James, the venerated leader of Jewish Christianity.

Finally, the discussion about faith and works in Jas 2:14–26 presupposes an awareness of the Pauline emphasis on justification by faith and not works, and therefore indicates an author later than Paul. However, Paul writes about "works of the law" (Rom 3:20; Gal 2:16; 3:5, 10), such as circumcision and dietary regulations, which separate Jews and Gentiles, while James talks about deeds of mercy. The writer's failure to debate with Paul on the law itself and to understand that Paul also stressed moral and ethical conduct seems to indicate that Paul's teaching has been misunderstood. So the writer's awareness of Paul's teaching was not directly derived from Paul's letters but was learned secondhand. The work of James, therefore, was written long enough after Paul's death for Paul's views to be misunderstood by an anonymous person who used the name of James to give his work authority. This seems to be the prevailing view among scholars although some, especially Roman Catholic scholars, subscribe to the traditional view.

The date and place of writing of James are as uncertain as the authorship. Scholars who maintain that the work was written by James, the brother of Jesus, usually suggest some Palestinian city, such as Jerusalem or Caesarea, as the place of origin. If the work was written by James, the date would have to be sometime before c. 62 CE, the traditional date for his martyrdom. Scholars who think the work is anonymous have suggested Galilee, Syria, and Rome as places of origin, and a date near the end of the first century. James, therefore, is post-Pauline; it was written after the controversy between Jewish and Gentile Christianity, so marked in Paul's letters and Acts, had subsided.

Of NT writers only the author of James refers to a Christian meeting for worship—if, indeed, it is a Christian service—as a synagogue (= "your assembly," 2:2). This may indicate that the author was a Jew writing especially for Jewish Christians. However, as with place of origin and date, we cannot be certain about this.

The work is addressed "to the twelve tribes in the Dispersion," symbolic of Christians everywhere as God's people. This indicates that the writer was not concerned with a particular church, crisis, or occasion, but intended to edify readers anywhere who happened to read his work. James, therefore, is a truly general work. The central purpose seems to be to oppose strongly the superficialities of religion expressed in pious words, and to encourage righteous deeds. The hortatory purpose and theme of James are summed up in 1:22: "Be doers of the word, and not merely hearers."

FORM, LITERARY STYLE, AND STRUCTURE OF JAMES

With only the slightest opening salutation and greeting, and no epistolary conclusion, James is really not a letter. It may perhaps best be described as an ethical tract or religious essay. The writer's diatribe style was familiar to all who heard the moral speeches delivered on the streets of Hellenistic cities. Part of this style is the imperative or command, and in James there are about sixty in a total of 108 verses. The words are usually simple, and the sentences are not long or complex. In sum, the writer's style is direct and vivid, as we can observe even in English translation. According to M. Dibelius 1976:3, James is best described as "*paraenesis* . . . a text which strings together admonitions of general ethical content." This, I think, is a valid assessment.

Despite the simple literary style and method, it is impossible to construct a logical outline of James. Not counting the opening address (1:1), we can divide the work into twelve parts, as in the outline and comments below.

Outline and Comments

I. *Trials, the rich and the poor, and God's gifts (1:2–18)*

Christians everywhere, not just those of a particular community, should be glad for various trials because they test faith and produce endurance and sound character (1:2–4). Wisdom comes from God through prayer "never doubting" (1:5–8). The next verses reflect a time in the church when there were social distinctions between the rich and the poor. Riches may fade away, but poverty is a permanent blessing (1:9–11). Temptations come from human lust, not divine initiative; those who resist temptations will receive the crown of life, but there is no such reward for the person who sins. Good gifts come from God (1:12–18).

II. *Hearing and doing the word of God (1:19–27)*

Readers must listen rather than speak, but above all they must do the word of God; this includes being careful in speaking (1:19–26). In 1:27 the writer states his view of religion, quoted earlier. As in the Johannine literature, "the world" represents opposition to God.

III. The sin of partiality to the rich (2:1–13)

Merciful deeds are useless if readers favor the rich (see Sir 11:2–6), who are actually their oppressors, and neglect the poor, who are the heirs of God's kingdom. People who favor the rich and neglect the poor do not obey the law to love their neighbors as themselves. They therefore break the whole law.

IV. Faith and works (2:14–26)

The thesis of James, anticipated in 1:22–25, is set forth in this section. Faith, which is strengthened through testing and shows no partiality, is useless without good deeds. Even demons believe in the oneness of God, but they do not do his will. Abraham and Rahab were justified by their works, not by their faith, because their faith was "justified by works."

V. Control of the tongue (3:1–12)

Although the idea that proper conduct includes appropriate speech as well as proper action was a common theme in Judaism (see Prov 15:1–4, 7, 23, 26, 28; Sir 5:11–6:1; 19:16; 28:13–26; 1QS 7:1–5; 10:6, 21), James is the only NT writer to stress the same theme with respect to Christian conduct (see also Rom 3:13; 14:11; 1 Pet 3:10). The dangers of the tongue are introduced with a warning to teachers, including himself, whose position in the church is important and respected (see Acts 13:1–3; 1 Cor 12:28; Eph 4:11). Since teachers must speak, James warns them about their speech and illustrates what he means with the metaphors of the horses' bits and the rudder.

VI. Heavenly and earthly wisdom (3:13–18)

The discussion of wisdom was anticipated in 1:5, 16–17 and harks back to the teachers in the previous section. In Judaism "the wise man" and teacher are closely associated. Wisdom, which comes "down from above," is manifested in generous good works performed in meekness

and not in selfish ambition, which is earthly and unspiritual.

VII. Worldly desires and their consequences (4:1–12)

Hostilities that spring from worldly desires and disrupt Christian communities are denounced. Readers can resist such desires by drawing near to God, who will then draw near to them (4:1–10). Anyone who speaks evil against another disobeys the commandment to love one's neighbor as oneself (see 2:8), and therefore is judged by that law (4:11–12).

VIII. Uncertainty about the future (4:13–17)

Those who are arrogantly overconfident about the future are like merchants who travel abroad without considering God's will (4:13–17). This passage reflects the trading class in the society of every large city in the Hellenistic world from Jerusalem to Rome. It also reflects the distrust of the mercantile class evidenced in the OT (for example, in Prov 20:23; Amos 8:4–6; Ezek 27:3–36; Sir 26:29–27:2; see also Rev 18:1–19).

IX. Another denunciation of the rich (5:1–6)

In light of "the miseries that are coming" upon them, the writer offers no consolation for the rich. James's view reflects a time when the wealthy social classes in Hellenistic cities had become influential in Christian society.

X. The coming End (5:7–12)

Following the examples of the patience and suffering of the OT prophets and Job, readers should "be patient . . . until the coming of the Lord," when they will be rewarded by his compassion and mercy (5:7–11). In 5:12 the author inserts a disconnected prohibition against oath taking (see 5:9; Matt 5:33–37).

XI. Advice for people in various situations in life (5:13–18)

The prayers of Elijah are evidence that prayer is effective for healing the sick and for the forgiveness of sins (see Sir 38:9–10). If anyone is cheerful, let him sing praise.

XII. *Restoring erring members (5:19–20)*

Those who restore an erring member will be blessed. The expression "cover a multitude of sins" occurs also in 1 Pet 4:8 and the OT (Prov 10:12; Ps 31:1) and means that the sins are forgiven. Without a formal conclusion, James ends very abruptly with the assurance of forgiveness for errant members of Christian communities dispersed throughout the Roman world.

For further study of James, see M. Dibelius 1976; S. Laws 1980; T. W. Leahy 1968a; R. R. Williams 1965; J. Moffatt 1928; G. R. Beasley-Murray 1965; P. H. Davids 1982; R. P. Martin 1988; J. B. Adamson 1989; F. T. Gench 1996; D. P. Nystrom 1997; P. W. Wall 1997.

JUDE

Jude is treated next, between James and 2 Peter, because its author claims to be a "brother of James," presumably the writer of James. Moreover, most scholars agree that Jude was used by the author of 2 Peter.

AUTHORSHIP, DATE, PURPOSE, AND RECIPIENTS

The author calls himself "Judas [trans. "Jude"], a servant of Jesus Christ and brother of James." This Judas has generally been taken as the brother not only of James, but also of Jesus (see Mark 6:3; Matt 13:55). However, certain statements in Jude itself seem to preclude authorship by a brother of Jesus or even by Judas, the disciple of Jesus (see Luke 6:16; John 14:22). For example, in v 17 the writer says, "Remember the predictions of the apostles of our Lord Jesus Christ." This verse sets the writer apart from the apostles and puts him at a time after the apostolic age. The same is true when he refers, in the past tense, to "the faith that was once for all en-

trusted to the saints" and says "long ago" (3–4; see also 14–15).

Because of the verses cited, because the work is first referred to in the Muratorian Canon (c. 180 CE), and because of its good Greek style, most scholars think Jude was not written by a brother of Jesus or by the disciple Judas. Most agree that Jude was written pseudonymously sometime in the first half of the second century. Because of the good Greek and the citation of the Jewish works *Assumption of Moses* (9) and *Enoch* (14–15), Jude may have been written by a Hellenistic Jewish Christian. We do not know where it was written.

R. J. Bauckham 1983 bucks the trend by arguing negatively against current positions and concludes that Jude may have been written by the brother of James in the 50s. See the same author 1990:134–178 for a summary of research on Jude. J. H. Neyrey 1993 studies the "social location" of the author, outlines its rhetorical structure, and suggests Alexandria as the place of origin in the early second century.

The purpose of Jude is perfectly clear. It is a strong warning to readers "to contend for the faith that was once for all entrusted to the saints" (3) against false teachers "who pervert the grace of our God into licentiousness and deny our only Master and Lord, Jesus Christ" (4). The words "For certain intruders have stolen in among you" (4) and "hidden rocks [trans. "blemishes"] on your love-feasts" (12) indicate that the false teachers were not openly hostile to the Christian faith but were working underhandedly in the church. Who were these false teachers?

Several characterizations in Jude reflect the Gnosticism of the second century. The words "deny our only Master and Lord, Jesus Christ" (4) probably reflect the Docetic idea that the spiritual Christ was different from the human Jesus. The charges of "licentiousness" (4), "indulged in sexual immorality and pursued unnatural lust" (7), "defile the flesh" (8), "indulging their own ungodly lusts" (18), and others indicate that those against whom the letter is directed behaved in grossly immoral and unnatural ways. Although the heretics were of the worst kind, the writer seems to think that some, who were not thoroughly convinced about what they were doing, were worth trying to save (22–23).

At least two other characterizations lead some scholars to believe that the false teachers were Gnostics. The words "reject authority" (8) and "slander whatever they do not understand" (10) may be taken as references to the OT, which Christians regarded as authoritative but Gnostics rejected. And the characterizations "worldly people (*psychikoi*), devoid of the Spirit" may be taken as Gnostic accusations against ordinary people, who in the Gnostics' view were without the true spirit claimed by the Gnostics. This is plausible because the Gnostics used the terms *psychikos* and *pneumatikos* to designate certain categories. Jude is writing to the "worldly people," ordinary people in the eyes of the Gnostics, and accusing the heretics of being "devoid of the Spirit."

Although the address, "To those who are called . . ." gives the work a general character, the work may have been intended for particular communities in one area where the specific false teaching was prevalent. The kind of unrestrained conduct that the writer describes points to a Gentile environment of the readers. On the other hand, the references to the OT and other Jewish writings indicate that the readers were Jewish. So the recipients were probably Jewish Christians who could have been living in almost any city in the Hellenistic world.

LITERARY FORM AND OUTLINE OF JUDE

The epistolary beginning and the benedictory ending make the work in its present form a letter, but these may be only the usual literary devices to assure the work a wide reading. In reality, Jude seems to be an apocalyptic tract, written in the harsh, uncompromising style of apocalypse, yet unlike the apocalypse of Revelation.

Although very brief, Jude is the most severe attack against false teachers in the NT. After the salutary greeting (1–2), the writer appeals to the readers to defend the Christian faith against the false teachers who deny the "Master and Lord,

Jesus Christ" (3–4). God will take vengeance upon them for their disbelief and disgraceful conduct, as he did upon the faithless Israelites, whom he had previously delivered from Egypt (Num 14:1–38; Ps 95:7–11), the "sons of God" (angels) who misbehaved (Gen 6:1–4), and the immoral cities (Gen 19:1–25) Sodom and Gomorrah (5–7).

In 8–16 the false teachers are described. They are "dreamers," in the sense that their thinking is muddled; they are also guilty of immorality, and they defy recognized authorities (8). Even the archangel Michael (Dan 10:13, 21; 12:1; 1QM 9:15–16; 17:6–9; *Enoch* 20:5; 40:4–9; Rev 12:7) was not so despicable in dealing with the devil (9–10). Like Cain, who according to Jewish literature (see, for example, Josephus, *Ant.* 1:1:4–2:1–2) was the embodiment of depravity, greed, and lust, the heretics are described with vivid imagery from nature (11–13). Enoch, God's friend (Gen 5:21–24; *Enoch* 1:9), prophesied their coming and their impending judgment (14–16).

In 17–23 the author reminds the readers that the apostles predicted the coming of scoffers in the last days, and warns them to remain obedient to their teaching and to show compassion to those who are threatened by the false teaching. Then the writer ends his work with a doxology (24–25), instead of with the more usual closing greeting.

2 PETER

Jude is closely related to 2 Peter in vocabulary, phrasing, content, and sequence of ideas. If you compare Jude 4–16 with 2 Pet 2:1–18, and Jude 17–18 with 2 Pet 3:1–3, you will notice the unusual similarities. In fact, the two works are so similar that there is obviously a literary dependence of one on the other (for a list of parallels, see A. R. C. Leaney 1967). In such a situation there are three possibilities: Jude copied from Peter, Peter copied from Jude, or each copied from the same source. For many reasons, including the idea that the author of 2 Peter would be more likely to drop the quotation from *Enoch*

(Jude 14) than Jude would be to insert it into the context of 2 Peter, most scholars agree that the author of 2 Peter copied from Jude (see J. N. D. Kelly 1969:225–227). However, some think that the likenesses and differences between the two works can best be explained on the theory that both authors drew from a common source, perhaps a sermon that had become a model for resisting heretics in the church (see B. Reicke 1964:189–190).

AUTHORSHIP AND DATE OF 2 PETER

The author claims to be "an apostle of Jesus Christ," and even uses the Aramaic name Simeon with the Greek name Peter. That the author wants to be identified with the apostle Peter and as the writer also of 1 Peter is clear from his allusion to 1 Peter in 3:1, his claiming to be present at the transfiguration (1:16–18), his reference to Paul as "our beloved brother" (3:15), his pretending to be about ready to die (1:13–15) as Jesus predicted (John 21:18–19), and his professing to be an eyewitness to Jesus (1:16).

In spite of the author's strong claims, scholars almost unanimously agree that 2 Peter is a pseudonymous work and one of the latest in the NT. But for arguments in defense of Peter's authorship, see C. Bigg 1905:242–247. By his words "ever since our ancestors died" (3:4), the author inadvertently reveals that he belongs to a time after that of the apostles. Likewise, the reference to the collected letters of Paul, which have the same authority as "the other scriptures" (3:15–16), makes a date before early in the second century virtually impossible. The writer is also concerned with an interpretation of scripture (1:20–21; 3:15–16), with "the holy prophets, and the commandment of the Lord and Savior," and with apostolic tradition (3:2) in a way more characteristic of a period of developing orthodoxy than of the time of Peter.

On external grounds, the use of Jude (a work recognized as late by most scholars), the reluctance of the church to accept 2 Peter as authentic, and the Gnosticizing teachings of the heretics support a date not earlier than c. 100–125. Moreover, it is generally agreed that the two "letters of Peter" come from different authors. Not only the vocabulary (2 Peter has many more hapaxlegomena, that is, words occurring only once in the NT) and style, but also the ideas of 2 Peter differ from those of 1 Peter. One noticeable difference, for example, is the use of "the salvation of your souls" (1 Pet 1:9) and "entry into the eternal kingdom of our Lord and Savior Jesus Christ" (2 Pet 1:11) to refer to the reward of those who remain obedient to Christian teaching. Such differences make it unlikely that 2 Peter was written by the same author as 1 Peter, no matter what the date of the latter. Most scholars today accept a date between c. 100 and 125 for 2 Peter.

R. J. Bauckham 1983 says that, unlike Jude, 2 Peter is a pseudonymous work. Because its language and thought show affinities to those of *1 Clement* and *Hermas,* Roman works, the author of 2 Peter was a leader in the church at Rome. Jude is to be dated between 80 and 90.

PURPOSES, RECIPIENTS, AND LITERARY FORM OF 2 PETER

The writer of 2 Peter clearly has two purposes. His primary one is to explain the delay of the Parousia to those readers challenged by the scoffers' question: "Where is the promise of his coming?" (3:4). The writer replies that the divine calculation of time differs from that of humans, and alludes to Ps 90:4: "With the Lord one day is like a thousand years, and a thousand years are like one day" (3:8). He then gives a theological reason for the delay of the Parousia: God is not slow about his promise, just delaying in order to give all people time to repent (3:9). "But the day of the Lord will come" (3:10). The author also writes to warn his readers against "false teachers" who "secretly bring in destructive opinions," deny the Master, and malign "the way of truth" (2:1–2). The author takes over Jude's tirade and reworks it to apply to the opponents of his own readers, whom he admonishes to be morally "without spot or blemish" (3:14).

The opponents were essentially like the rabble-rousing, dissipating false teachers of Jude. Besides this, they have followed the way of Balaam (Num 22–24), presumably the same heresy referred to in Rev 2:14. They were also teaching "cleverly devised myths" with respect to "the power and coming" of Jesus (1:16). All of these things, along with the author's intimation that the real "knowledge" is knowledge of Christ (1:2–3, 8; 2:20), indicate that the recipients were being confronted by people who, in typical Gnostic fashion, were misconstruing traditional teachings of the early church. J. H. Neyrey 1993 suggests, unconvincingly to most scholars, that the adversaries in 2 Peter were Epicureans.

The recipients of 2 Peter are addressed as "those who have received a faith as precious as" that of the writer (1:1). This is a very general address and may indicate that the writer intended his work for the whole church. However, by alluding to 1 Peter (3:1), the writer may have been indicating that the work was intended for the "exiles" in Asia Minor, who are referred to in 1 Pet 1:1. Thus, the destination could have been churches in the regions listed in that passage. The writer probably lived in one of those areas. However, since the author wrote in the name of Peter, he must have wanted to link his work with Rome, so that his readers would think it had the authority of the church at Rome behind it.

That the readers were Gentiles seems clear not only from the nature of the false teaching addressed, but also from the writer's Hellenistic expressions. Although he speaks of "entry into the eternal kingdom of our Lord" (1:11) in terms of traditional Jewish-Christian eschatology, he talks about the readers becoming "participants of the divine nature" (1:4)—a Greek, not biblical, idea. The words translated as "godliness" (1:3, 6–7; 3:11) and "goodness" (1:5) are *eusebeia* and *aretē*, respectively, words frequently used by Stoics and Jewish wisdom writers (see, for example, Epictetus, *Dis.* 2:20:22–23; 1:4:5–10; Wis 4:1; 5:13; 10:12; Sir 49:3) to mean "piety" and "virtue." The idea that the world would be destroyed in a final conflagration (3:7, 10–12) is also Stoic. Only Gentiles or Hellenistic Jews living in a Hellenistic environment would be likely to understand such language and thought. For rhetorical criticism of 2 Peter see D. F. Watson 1988.

With respect to the writer's language, the epistolary opening is mere formality. Since the writer presents Peter as about to die (1:13–15), the work is actually a kind of farewell speech or last will and testament, a well-known literary form in antiquity, especially among Jews. Traces of this form appear in Jesus' farewell discourse in John 13–17, in Acts 20:17–38, and in the pastoral epistles (see, for example, 2 Tim 4:6). That the work is a farewell testament may account for its stiff, formal style. Sentences are long, unbalanced, and often unclear. Perhaps the most noticeable aspect of the writer's style is his application of vivid metaphors to the heretics: "irrational animals," "waterless springs and mists driven by a storm" (2:12, 17).

Outline and Comments

I. *Salutation (1:1–2)*

II. *Exhortation to Christian hope and virtue (1:3–21)*

God has made Christian life possible (1:3–4), so make every effort to move up from the virtue of faith to love, the greatest of all virtues (1:5–8). Whoever lacks these virtues has forgotten the forgiveness received in baptism (1:9). The exhortation to stand firmly committed to the Christian religion, with the "kingdom of our Lord and Savior Jesus Christ" as a reward, is the thesis of the work (1:10–11).

A statement of the author's motive for writing (1:12–15) is followed by two reasons that readers should remain faithful and virtuous. Jesus' transfiguration, which was witnessed by apostles, is a guarantee of his return (1:16–18). And scriptures, written by people whom the Holy Spirit moved, also assure the Parousia (1:19–21).

III. *Tirade against false teachers (2:1–22)*

There is precedent for the presence of false teachers and their following (2:1–3), but examples from the OT prove that God punishes the wicked and rewards the righteous (2:4–9).

In malicious metaphorical language, the writer condemns the heretics because they are grossly immoral, defy authority, "entice unsteady souls," are greedy, and promise freedom from moral restraints (2:10–19). But because they once experienced knowledge of Christ and then reverted to their heretical and immoral ways, they will be more severely punished than if they had never "known the way of righteousness" (2:20–22; see also Matt 12:45; Luke 11:26).

IV. Delay of the Parousia explained (3:1–16)

Readers are to remember what they learned through the predictions of the prophets and the commands of Jesus as taught by their apostles (3:1–2). Scoffers, skeptical about the Parousia, will appear in the last days (3:3–4). In saying that "all things continue as they were from the beginning of creation," they ignore the ideas that God's first creation was destroyed by the flood (Genesis 6–9) and that the present world will be consumed by fire (3:5–7). Readers must also remember that God's reckoning of time differs from that of the heretics, and that all people therefore have time to repent before the End comes suddenly and terribly (3:8–10). Prepare, then, for the day of the Lord by living "lives of holiness and godliness . . . at peace, without spot or blemish" (3:11–16).

V. Final warning and benediction (3:17–18)

Readers must not yield to the errors of the false teachers, "but grow in the grace and knowledge of our Lord and Savior Jesus Christ."

For further study of Jude and 2 Peter see T. W. Leahy 1968a, 1968b, 1968c; D. P. Senior 1980; E. M. Sidebottom 1982; J. Knight 1995.

SUMMARY

The "letters" of John, James, Jude, and 2 Peter are called general or catholic epistles because, with the possible exceptions of 2 and 3 John, they were intended for wide circulation or even for the whole church, not just specific churches. Although diverse in nature, they share the common purposes of warning their readers against false teachers—who are like Gnostics in their denial of the humanity of Jesus and their indifference to or rejection of Christian moral standards—and exhorting them to moral behavior. At the same time, each writing has a distinctive emphasis.

The emphasis in the letters of John is on love for God and fellow believers, because God is love. James stresses that faith without deeds of mercy is useless, and both Jude and 2 Peter warn their readers to remain firm in their faith and true to their moral commitment while under pressure from scoffers who have secretly entered the church. But 2 Peter has an additional emphasis on godliness and virtue as readers await the Parousia. According to God's calculation of time, the Parousia is near, although it has been delayed to give everyone an opportunity to repent.

In the final chapter of this book we will examine the three letters known as the pastoral epistles, 1 and 2 Timothy and Titus. Like the general epistles, they originated from times of controversy and false teaching within the church. But unlike the general letters—and even Paul's letters—they are addressed to specific individuals.

CHAPTER 17

1 and 2 Timothy and Titus

AS EARLY AS THE THIRTEENTH OR THE fourteenth century, the letters to Timothy and Titus were called "pastoral epistles" because they contained instructions to their recipients concerning their duties as pastors (from Latin *pastor,* "herdsman," "shepherd") in Christian congregations. Although these letters purport to be written by Paul, we deal with them here because most scholars believe they are post-Pauline—even later than Colossians, Ephesians, and 2 Thessalonians.

Timothy was Paul's most important associate (Acts 16:1–3; 17:14–15; 18:5; 19:22) and conducted Christian missions at Thessalonica (1 Thess 3:2) and Corinth (1 Cor 4:17). As a "co-worker" (Rom 16:21), "beloved and faithful" (1 Cor 4:17), Timothy is included in the salutations of 1 Thess 1:1; 2 Cor 1:1; Phil 1:1; and Phlm 1:1, as well as those of Col 1:1 and 2 Thess 1:1. Titus is not so well known, but apparently he was a convert from paganism and joined Paul soon after his conversion (Gal 2:1–5). Titus was most closely associated with Paul in his work with the Corinthians, to whom he was Paul's envoy (2 Cor 8:16–24; 12:18) and from whom he brought good news to Paul (1 Cor 7:6–7, 13–14).

AUTHORSHIP AND PURPOSES OF WRITING

There is no evidence that the pastorals ever circulated as separate letters, so they were probably written as a group by the same person and circulated as a corpus from the beginning. This is clear from their common vocabulary, style, and content. More than 175 words in 1 Timothy, 2 Timothy, and Titus occur nowhere else in the NT, including the phrases "the saying is sure" (1 Tim 1:15; 3:1; 4:9; 2 Tim 2:11; Titus 3:8) and "sound teaching" (1 Tim 1:10; 2 Tim 4:3; Titus 1:9; 2:1). Moreover, the writings have the same purposes. The addressees, living in a pagan environment, are to preserve traditional doctrines of the faith, to select morally responsible and qualified church officials, to preserve order in the church and regulate worship, to urge believers to live godly lives such as those they see exemplified in their leaders, and to reject all false teachers and teachings. Words from 1 Tim 3:15 state the general purpose of the letters: "that . . . you may know how one ought to behave in the household of God, which is the church of the living God." In Titus 2:11–14 the moral purpose is stated similarly, but with a reminder of Christ's saving work as the incentive for good deeds. Thus, it seems certain that the pastorals were written by one person, but was Paul that person?

Question of Pauline Authorship

In addition to the declaration of Pauline authorship in each salutation, certain references make it seem as though Paul himself is speaking. A good example of this is "the glorious gospel of the blessed God, which he entrusted to me" (1 Tim 1:11). Yet, if you compare that statement with those about Paul and the gospel in undisputed letters, you will notice that the latter are much shorter and are less adorned, for example, "set apart for the gospel of God" (Rom 1:1; see also 15:19; 1 Cor 15:1). Differences like these have led scholars to question Paul's authorship of the pastorals. The main arguments against Pauline authorship, with counterarguments, follow.

Vocabulary and Style. More than three hundred words in the pastorals are not in either the undisputed or disputed letters of Paul. In 1 Tim 1:3–7 the language already sounds different from that of Paul. The following words and phrases in those verses occur in none of the ten Pauline letters: "teach any different doctrine" (one word in Greek; 1:3; see also 6:3), "occupy themselves" (1:4; see also 3:8; 4:1, 13; Titus 1:14), "myths and endless genealogies" (1:4; see also 4:7; 2 Tim 4:4; Titus 1:14; 3:9), "speculations" (1:4), "pure heart" (1:5; see also 2 Tim 2:22), "good conscience" (1:5; see also 1:19), "sincere faith" (1:5; see also 2 Tim 1:5), "deviated from" (1:6; see also 6:12; 2 Tim 2:18), "turned to" (1:6; see also 5:15; 6:20; 2 Tim 4:4), "meaningless talk" (1:6), "teachers of the law" (one word; 1:7), and "make assertions"

(1:7; see also Titus 3:8). The references in parentheses show that the same Greek words occur elsewhere in the pastorals. The important word (*eusebeia*) translated "godliness" occurs ten times, but not once in any other letter purporting to be from Paul.

Just as important as the use of non-Pauline vocabulary are the absence of favorite Pauline words and expressions, and the presence of Pauline terms that are used in a different sense. Here are some important examples. "Spirit" and "Holy Spirit" occur 120 times in the undisputed letters of Paul, but "spirit" occurs only seven times in the pastorals, in which "Holy Spirit" is used only twice (2 Tim 1:14; Titus 3:5). Similarly, Paul's most characteristic expressions "in Christ" and "Christ in" do not occur in the pastorals. Paul's distinctive words "justify" (twenty-five times) and "justification" (fifty) occur seven times, but except in Titus 3:7, never with the meaning they have in Paul. Paul uses the word "good" (seventeen times) mostly as a noun—"the good" or "right" (for example, in Rom 7:21; 12:17; 2 Cor 13:7). The writer of the pastorals uses it (twenty-four) mostly as an adjective, especially with "works"—that is, "good works" (for example, in 1 Tim 5:10, 25; 6:18; Titus 2:7, 14; Greek), an expression that does not appear in Paul.

Defenders of the traditional view point out parallels in language (Greek), for example, "the law is good" (Rom 7:16; 1 Tim 1:8), "I thank God whom I serve" (2 Tim 1:3; Rom 1:8), and "I am telling the truth, I am not lying" (1 Tim 2:7; Rom 9:1). Although there are variations in the nuances intended in language and thought (see esp. 2 Tim 1:10), these parallels, according to traditionalists, support Pauline authorship. (For other parallels between the pastorals and Paul's undisputed letters, compare these passages: 1 Tim 6:12 and Phil 3:12–14; 2 Tim 1:6–9 and Rom 8:12–17; 2 Tim 3:16–17 and Rom 15:4–6; 2 Tim 4:6–8 and Phil 2:16–17; and see A. T. Hanson 1982:28–31.)

The literary style of the pastorals also differs markedly from that of Paul. Paul writes in the Greek of the common person (*koinē*), whereas the pastorals are written in Hellenistic Greek at a more sophisticated level. Besides this, the most noticeable difference in style is the pastorals' lack of arguments to support positions—arguments that in Paul are often long, involved, and emotional. And Paul's fast-moving, vivacious, ecstatic language is entirely absent from the pastorals, as is the angry, frustrated, despairing language, with its drama and metaphor.

The evidence from vocabulary and style is striking and provides the strongest argument against Pauline authorship of the pastorals. Yet those who defend Paul's authorship reply that Paul was addressing situations that necessitated different vocabulary, that every letter has peculiar linguistic traits, that the different subjects addressed necessitated different styles, that Paul was writing as an old man, less vigorous and dramatic, or that a secretary had complete freedom and therefore used Paul's own vocabulary and style.

Theology.   Paul's writings and the pastorals have a basic difference in the concept of faith. In Paul's works "faith" is the means to relate to God or Christ, but in the pastorals "the faith" (1 Tim 3:9; 4:1; Titus 1:13) is the doctrines of the church or is Christianity itself. In the following passages the change in emphasis is clear. "The Spirit expressly says that in later times some will renounce the faith by paying attention to deceitful spirits" (1 Tim 4:1). The writer urges the readers to "fight the good fight of the faith" (1 Tim 6:12) and has "Paul" say, "I have kept the faith" (2 Tim 4:7). These are signs of an orthodoxy in Christianity later than Paul's time. The same is true for the writer's expressions "knowledge of the truth" (1 Tim 2:4; 2 Tim 3:7; Titus 1:1), "sound teaching" (1 Tim 1:10; 2 Tim 4:3; Titus 1:9; 2:1), and "sound words" (1 Tim 6:3; 2 Tim 1:13), which represent orthodox Christian beliefs. In the church, the bastion of "the truth" (1 Tim 3:15), credal confessions had become a part of worship (1 Tim 3:16; 6:12–16; 2 Tim 2:8).

We have already mentioned the absence of the Pauline concepts of justification, the Spirit, and the spiritual experience of Christ in the pastorals, as well as the pastorals' emphasis on the Hellenistic term "godliness," which is lacking in Paul's vocabulary. Absent from the pastorals also is Paul's emphasis on Jesus' crucifixion and resurrection.

Scholars who uphold the traditional view of authorship maintain that a nucleus of Pauline ideas is present. Among these are the idea that "Christ Jesus came into the world to save sinners" (1 Tim 1:15), that people are "justified by his grace" (Titus 3:7; see also 3:4–8), and that eternal life lies in the future but is at present enjoyed by the elect (1 Tim 6:12; 2 Tim 1:1; Titus 1:2–3; 3:7).

Biographical Information.   The information about Paul in the pastorals does not coincide with that in Paul's letters and Acts. For example, we cannot tally the account of Paul and Timothy at Ephesus in 1 and 2 Timothy with the account in Acts, and neither Paul nor Acts mentions a visit of Paul to Crete as reported in Titus 1:5. Those who defend Paul's authorship, however, assume that Paul was released from prison in Rome and returned to the East for another period of missionary activity. This missionary activity is reported in the pastorals.

The Situation in the Church.   The concern with bishops, elders, deacons, and widows in the pastorals reflects an organizational development later than Paul's time. The church is no longer run by volunteer, spiritually enlightened leaders. Although the writer speaks of the coming of the End (1 Tim 6:15; 2 Tim 3:1), he assumes that the church will continue (1 Tim 3:1–4:16). Moreover, the gospel of Luke (10:7) has the status of scripture in the church and is cited as such, along with Deut 25:4, in 1 Tim 5:18. "The books" and "the parchments" in 2 Tim 4:13 may refer to other Christian writings that were considered scripture. All of this implies a time considerably later than Paul.

The Heresies.   Many complexities of the thought and life of the Mediterranean world are reflected in the pastoral epistles. This makes it impossible to determine the true nature of the false teachings so strongly castigated. Statements such as "forbid marriage and demand abstinence from foods" (1 Tim 4:3), "those of the circumcision" (Titus 1:10), "Jewish myths" (Titus 1:14), and "quarrels about the law" (Titus 3:9) indicate a Jewish-Christian heresy. Dietary regulations are typically Jewish, and the forbidding of marriage could show Essene influence. Of course, some Christian group, perhaps influenced by Paul in 1 Cor 7:8, for example, could have advocated celibacy.

Some scholars think that the problems mentioned in the pastorals are similar to those in the letters of John, Jude, and 2 Peter, and therefore reflect a Gnostic heresy. One of the pertinent arguments in the letters against Gnostic beliefs is "Everything created by God is good" (1 Tim 4:4), which refutes the Gnostic idea that the world as matter is evil. Likewise, God as Creator (1 Tim 4:3–4) and as Savior (1 Tim 1:1; 2:3; Titus 1:3; 2:10; 3:4) and the statement "There is one God" (1 Tim 2:5) refute the Gnostic concept of two gods, a lower one as creator and a higher one as savior. "The word of God" (1 Tim 4:5) and references to prophecy (1 Tim 1:18; 4:14) refer to the OT, which was regarded as scripture (2 Tim 3:15–16), but which the Gnostics rejected.

Gnostic Christians rejected early Christian eschatology, including the ideas of a Parousia and future resurrection. Although Christ will come "at the right time" (1 Tim 6:14–15), his coming is no longer imminent. The End, nevertheless, will come (Titus 2:13), and then Christ will judge "the living and the dead" (2 Tim 4:1). The heretics who hold that "the resurrection has already taken place" have "swerved from the truth" (2 Tim 2:17–18). Such statements are directed against the Gnostic denials. Finally, the reference to Christ Jesus as "himself human" (1 Tim 2:5) and the confession "He was revealed in the flesh" (1 Tim 3:16) refute the Gnostic denial of the humanity of Christ. (For a discussion of heresy in the pastorals, see F. D. Gealy 1955.)

Most scholars believe that the heresies attacked in the pastorals come from a time later than Paul. Some also believe that the writer's ter-

minology reveals an underlying challenge to the emperor cult. In the Hellenistic world "savior" was a title applied to gods and humans. Asclepius was recognized as savior, in the East Nero and other emperors were acknowledged as "savior of the world," and the combination "god and savior" was applied to Augustus. It is significant that the author of the pastorals uses the term "savior" of both God and Christ (1 Tim 1:1; 2:3; 2 Tim 1:10; Titus 1:3, 4; 2:10; 3:6) and that, except for 2 Pet 1:1, the combination "God and Savior" occurs only in his writings (Titus 2:13). Paul uses the term "Savior" of Christ only in Phil 3:20 (see also Eph 5:23). The author of the pastorals may be saying that God/Christ, not the emperor, is the true God.

The terms "appear" (*epiphainō*) and "appearance" or "appearing" (*epiphaneia*) were used of the emperors. For example, an inscription contains the words "in the first year of the appearance of Gaius Caesar," and a coin struck in honor of Hadrian reads, "appearance of Augustus" (see A. Deissmann 1927:344 n. 5, 363–365, 371 n. 1, 373). Significantly, the terms "appear" and "appearing" or "appearance," used with reference to the coming of Jesus, occur only in the pastorals. In Titus 2:11 we read, "the grace of God has appeared, bringing salvation to all." Compare this with the inscription "the grace of Gaius Caesar" and with the one about the emperor Galba (68 CE), "he who has lightened upon us, the benefactor for the salvation of the entire human race" (A. T Hanson 1982:187; see also Titus 3:4 and A. Deissmann 1927:371, 373).

Both the past and future coming of Jesus are referred to as "the appearing." The grace of God in Christ was "revealed through the appearing of our Savior Christ Jesus" (2 Tim 1:10; see also 4:1, 8). Readers are to remain "without spot or blame until the manifestation of our Lord Jesus Christ" (1 Tim 6:14; see also Titus 2:13). The writer of the pastorals, more than any other NT writer, apparently uses the terminology of the imperial cult to oppose it. Such opposition does not appear in Paul's letters, and is therefore a basic reason for thinking that the pastorals are among the latest writings in the NT.

Internal Inconsistencies. Several passages make it clear that the real Paul would not write to the real Timothy as the author does. Paul would not need to inform Timothy, an associate during his whole career, that he "was appointed a herald and an apostle" and then clinch the fact by saying that he is "telling the truth" and "not lying" (1 Tim 2:7; see also 2 Tim 1:11–12). And surely neither Timothy nor Titus needed to be exhorted to "know how one ought to behave in the household of God" (1 Tim 3:15) or to "teach what is consistent with sound doctrine" (Titus 2:1).

Two Tim 4:6–8 is "Paul's" last testament, yet the writer refers to Timothy as an inexperienced youth (1 Tim 4:12) who must "shun youthful passions and pursue righteousness" (2 Tim 2:22). Similarly, the writer instructs Titus in an unnatural and elementary way about his duties at Crete (Titus 1:5–9). The real Paul would hardly write these kinds of things to his long-time, tried and true associates.

Theories of Authorship

Because of internal inconsistencies, the nature of the false teachings attacked—especially those reflecting Gnosticizing tendencies and the imperial cult—and the differences in vocabulary and style, most scholars believe the pastorals are entirely pseudonymous and post-Pauline. The letters have little, if any, Pauline material in them, and were composed by someone using Paul's name to give them authority. (Among supporters of this view are B. S. Easton 1947; F. D. Gealy 1955; M. S. Enslin 1963; A. T. Hanson 1982.) But those who reject Paul's authorship do not agree about how well the author knew Paul and his letters. Some think the author knew Paul well and wrote soon after his death. Others think the pastorals were composed by one of Marcion's contemporaries. Marcion was the heretic in Rome whose canon (c. 140 CE) contained only ten letters of Paul.

Some scholars maintain the traditional view of authorship, which takes two main forms. According to one view, Paul himself wrote the actual words of the letters, as he did with every one of his

others. These scholars resolve the inconsistencies by arguing that the vocabulary and style, for example, are different because of the situation: Paul was writing to associates in charge of churches, as he had done with Philemon. Other inconsistencies are explained by the fact that Paul was writing as an old man in prison (2 Tim 1:8, 12; 2:9; 4:6–7) and was about to die (2 Tim 4:6–8) after severe suffering (2 Tim 1:11–12). Paul had lost his fighting spirit but had kept the faith (2 Tim 4:7). Meanwhile, he had come to appreciate Hellenistic philosophy and had given up the idea that the Parousia was near. (Defenders of the traditional view are W. Lock 1924; J. N. D. Kelly 1963; G. A. Denzer 1968; D. Guthrie 1957.)

According to the other main view of traditional authorship, a secretary, not necessarily the same one every time, wrote the pastorals. He expressed Paul's thought in his own way and was responsible for non-Pauline material; but Paul, of course, was responsible for what seems Pauline. Occasionally scholars have suggested a specific person as the secretary—for example, Tychicus, a "beloved brother" of Paul's (see Eph 6:21; Col 4:7; see also Acts 20:4; 2 Tim 4:12; Titus 3:12), and Luke (S. G. Wilson 1979; G. W. Knight 1992). Perhaps this is the easiest way to solve the problems connected with the pastorals, but a difficulty with this theory is knowing how much to attribute to the secretary.

Another theory, closely related to the theory of a secretary, is known as the "fragment hypothesis." According to the hypothesis, a later Christian writer found some fragments of letters by Paul, perhaps addressed to Timothy and Titus, and composed the pastorals with those fragments as a nucleus. The fragments usually suggested are 2 Tim 1:15–18, with parts of chaps. 3 and 4; 2 Tim 4:9–15 or 4:6–22; and Titus 3:12–15 (P. N. Harrison 1964). Supporters of this hypothesis try to find genuine Pauline material in the pastorals, but it is impossible to be certain that a given piece of material is Pauline. A basic problem with the hypothesis is determining how the fragments survived.

Two other views are notable. According to J. D. Miller 1997, the pastorals are composite documents for which no one author was responsible. They are the results of a compiler rather than an author, but based on genuine notes of Paul written to the pastors.

The view of D. R. MacDonald 1983 is entirely different. It is argued that the author of the pastorals wrote under the name of Paul in order to refute the portrayal of him in the oral legends that developed behind the apocryphal *Acts of Paul*. The legends were reported by women in order to defend their own work as celibate storytellers in Asia Minor in the second century. They did their work apart from male authority and family and social relationships. Thus there were several competing legends about Paul, so the tradition about Paul is not just a single line of development from the apostle to the pastorals.

One thing is certain, though, it seems to me, on the basis of evidence in the pastorals. The authority of Paul was assumed by the author or authors who wrote out of respect for the apostle rather than to correct wrong impressions of him. "Timothy" is to instruct others "not to teach any different doctrine" (1 Tim 1:3; see also 3:14–16; 2 Tim 2:1–3; 3:10–15; Titus 1:4).

DATE, PLACE OF ORIGIN, AND FORM OF THE PASTORALS

Several factors bearing on the date of the letters have already been discussed. If Paul wrote them, they must date from the early 60s. Those who believe that internal evidence suggests a development in the church later than Paul—when church organization was being established, hymns and creeds were being developed (1 Tim 2:5; 3:14–16; 6:12; 2 Tim 2:8), and the church was becoming the guardian of "the faith" (orthodoxy)—date the pastorals between 100 and 180.

The letters contain some clues to possible places of origin. In 2 Tim 1:8, 12; 2:9; and 4:6–7 the writer refers to his imprisonment, so if Paul is speaking, the cities suggested for his imprisonment—Rome, Ephesus, Caesarea—are likely choices, especially Rome or Ephesus. References to Ephesus (1 Tim 1:3; 2 Tim 1:18; 4:12), Asia

(2 Tim 1:15), and Crete (Titus 1:5) imply that the letters were written for churches in Asia. They may therefore also have been written in Asia, perhaps in Ephesus, as many scholars suggest. Or perhaps as other scholars suggest, they were written from Philippi, in Macedonia, as may be implied from 1 Tim 1:3. Rome has also been suggested by some scholars who think the letters are pseudonymous, as well as by some who hold the traditional view of authorship.

In their present form the pastorals are letters with the customary opening salutations and closing greetings. They are naturally regarded as letters by those who uphold Pauline authorship. But those who regard the works as pseudonymous say the pastorals are not to be taken as letters in any sense of the word. Timothy and Titus are fictitious people used by the writer to express his views about the kind of instruction he wants certain churches to receive. It is clear that the writer is especially interested in church officials and their duties and in worship services. For that reason the works have been described as primitive church manuals or treatises in the form of advice to church leaders. This makes the pastorals a distinctive type of writing in the NT, as you will see when you read them with the outlines and comments below.

Outline and Comments: 1 Timothy

I. Salutation (1:1–2)

The idea that Paul's authority came from God occurs in most of his salutations, but here the idea is stated differently. Paul usually writes "by the will of God" (1 Cor 1:1; 2 Cor 1:1; see also Eph 1:1; Col 1:1; 2 Tim 1:1), so "the command of God" (1 Tim 1:1) is non-Pauline—as it probably also is in Rom 16:26, a passage that most scholars agree is not by Paul. Nowhere in the Pauline corpus does Paul call God "Savior," and he uses that designation for Christ only in Phil 3:20 (see also Eph 5:23). So the language in the salutation is uncharacteristic of Paul. Although the letter is purportedly addressed to Timothy, the writer intends his work for church officials. Timothy serves as the fictitious means of communication.

II. Attack on false teaching and false teachers (1:3–20)

False teaching is not only doctrinally unsound, but corrupts morals. Paul may have shared this idea, but the writer expresses it in quite un-Pauline terms. Because the writer condemns the heretics' teaching without describing it, we cannot be sure what the teaching really is. The doctrines referred to are probably a syncretism of Jewish and Gnostic elements. "Myths" and "genealogies" could refer to some of the stories and genealogical lists of Genesis (for example, 2:4–5:32; 10–11). Or they could refer to current Jewish interpretations of Genesis stories, as in the book of *Jubilees*. "Genealogies," especially, could refer to the hierarchy of heavenly beings in the Gnostics' religious systems.

No matter what the origin of the heresy, the writer rebukes its proponents. They are only would-be teachers of the law who don't know what they are talking about, nor do they understand the passages they are teaching. These Jewish teachers (Titus 1:14; 3:9) are not like the Judaizers at Galatia, who certainly knew the law, so perhaps they are Jewish Gnostics who misinterpret the OT (1:3–7). The purpose of the law is to keep people from immoral deeds (see 1QS 4:2–11), which are contrary to the sound doctrine of the gospel (1:8–11).

In 1:12–17 the writer gives his view of Paul's persecution of Christians and his "conversion" (see Eph 3:7–12). Again, the un-Pauline language betrays the author. For example, Paul's word for "I thank" is always *eucharisteō*, a word not used in the pastorals, instead of *charin echō*, the words used here. The real Paul never makes excuses for his persecution of Christians (1 Cor 15–9; Gal 1:13), but the writer defends Paul by saying that he "acted ignorantly in unbelief." Indeed, for Paul ignorance is no excuse for unbelief (Rom 1:18–21; but see also 10:1–3). However, the ideas that Paul was sinful before his conversion and that God acted with grace and love toward him are Pauline (1 Cor 15:9–10; Rom 5:8).

It is very unlikely that Paul would be discussing his conversion with his old friend Timothy so long after the event. For the writer, Paul is the foremost example for all future believers. Verse 17 is a liturgical formula used to close the section, which is followed by a charge to the readers to remain faithful and to learn from the fate of certain false teachers (1:18–20).

III. Instructions for the churches (2:1–3:16)

The theme of this section, and of the pastorals as a group, is that "you may know how one ought to behave in the household of God, which is the church" (3:15). At public worship one should pray for all people, because God desires all to be saved through Christ, who gave himself to redeem all (2:1–6, 8; see also Rom 3:29–32; 11:25–32). Because of God's desire that all be saved, "Paul" was appointed as preacher, apostle, and teacher for the Gentiles (1:7).

Again, the vocabulary is un-Pauline. Paul never uses the word "appointed" with reference to God's action toward him, but "called" (Rom 9:24; 1 Cor 7:15; Gal 1:15; 1 Thess 4:7; see also 2 Tim 1:9) or "set apart" (Rom 1:1; Gal 1:15). "Appointed" reflects the selection of church officials in the writer's own time (see 1 Cor 12:28). Similarly, "preacher" (*NRSV*, "herald") is never used by Paul and is used only in the pastorals to refer to an office in the church (1 Tim 2:7; 2 Tim 1:11). The "kings" in 2:2 are the emperors *for* whom Christians are to pray; Christians are not to pray *to* them, as participants in the imperial cult do. Finally, "mediator" is used of Christ only here and in Hebrews. Christ as the "one mediator between God and humankind" (2:5) excludes Jewish mediators, such as Moses (Gal 3:19–20), angels (Col 2:18), and high priests (Heb 8:6; 9:15), as well as the "aeons"—the hierarchies of being in the universe, such as "mind," "word," and "wisdom" of the Gnostic systems.

In 2:9–15 the writer deals with the dress and behavior of women when they are praying in public. They should be more concerned with good deeds than with expensive clothing or jewelry, "as befits women who profess religion." "Religion" (*theosebeia*) was one of the most common words in the paganism of the writer's time, but it is never used by Paul or any other NT writer. The idea that women should not speak in church coincides with Paul's even harsher view in 1 Cor 14:34–35, which many believe is a non-Pauline insertion. In 1 Cor 11:2–16 Paul says only that women should be veiled when praying or prophesying in public worship.

The passage in 1 Timothy may reflect a later, more conservative reactionary view to the freedom of women in Pauline circles. Paul bases his view of the subordination of women in 1 Cor 11:2–16 on the story in Gen 2:18–23 about Eve, the woman, being made from and for Adam, the man. The writer of 1 Timothy defends the superiority of men with the idea that Adam was created first and that Eve, not Adam, was deceived by the serpent (see Gen 2:7, 21–22; 3:1–6). In Gen 3:16 childbearing is Eve's punishment, but in 1 Tim 2:15 it is the means of woman's salvation, if "they continue in faith and love and holiness, with modesty." "They" may indicate that the writer is combating false teachers who "forbid marriage" (4:3).

It is all right to seek church offices, but those who do so must be above reproach morally, effective in the management of their households, and respected by those outside the church (3:1–13). The terms "bishop" (*episkopos*) and "deacon" (*diakonos*) come from either Greek or Jewish secular usage and were used without religious significance. *Episkopos* means "overseer," and was used for anyone in charge of overseeing others or of inspecting things. *Diakonos* means "servant" or "waiter," and was used of anyone who served in a subordinate capacity. In Phil 1:1, Paul mentions bishops and deacons along with "all the saints" (the members of the church at Philippi), but he uses the term "bishop" nowhere else in the undisputed letters (see Eph 3:7; 6:21; Col 1:7, 23, 25; 4:7). Paul uses the word *diakonos* with the meaning of "servant" in, for example, Rom 13:4; 15:8; 1 Cor 3:5; and 2 Cor 6:4, and the feminine form with reference to Phoebe, "a deaconess of the church at Cenchreae" (Rom 16:1). In the pastorals, the titles "bishop" and "deacon," along with "elder" (*presbyteros*; 1 Tim

5:17, 19; Titus 1:5), a term not used by Paul, represent administrative offices. In 1 Cor 12:28 Paul lists administration (*kybernēsis*) last in a group of seven church offices.

Contrary to some other scholars, J. H. Stiefel 1995 argues that "women likewise" (1 Tim 3:11) is not to be understood as deacons' wives but as women who themselves were deacons (see footnote in the *NRSV*).

The author closes the section (2:1–3:16) with a statement of his purpose for writing and with a fragment of a liturgical hymn or creed (3:14–16).

IV. False teachings and the proper response (4:1–16)

The writer castigates the false teachings about abstinence from certain foods and marriage, teachings that are motivated by evil spirits appearing in the last days. These prohibitions are typical of second-century Gnosticism (Irenaeus, *Her.* 1:28), although Paul had to deal with the issue of foods (Romans 14). The writer believes that since all foods are a part of God's creation, they may be eaten if received with thanks and prayer, which are elements of Jewish-Christian practice before meals (4:1–5).

As a representative of orthodoxy, the church minister (Greek, "deacon") is to warn his members against the "profane myths" of the heretics and to exhort them to train themselves in "godliness" (4:6–10). Although the writer never defines "godliness," it is the distinctive Christian piety that is the best defense against the impiety of false teachers. Unlike bodily training, which is effective only in the present life, godliness is effective also for the life to come. The words "train," "nourish," and "follow," as well as "godliness," belonged to the vocabulary of the Stoics. The reference to bodily training may echo the Stoics' criticism of the strenuous training of athletes. The reference to God as "the Savior of all people, especially of those who believe," may be directed against the Gnostic idea that salvation is attained through knowledge, not faith.

The church leader is to be an example in speech and conduct, and to perform the duties of public worship (4:11–16). The word "prophecy" means that the church leader was guided into his office by Christian prophets under the influence of the Spirit (see Acts 13:1–3). The laying on of hands was part of the ceremony whereby the leader was inducted into his office (see Acts 8:18; 2 Tim 1:6; Heb 6:2).

V. Dealing with various groups in Christian communities (5:1–6:2)

The writer thinks of the church as a big family, "the household of God" (3:15). The idea that older people should be treated as parents and younger people as brothers and sisters (5:1–2) shows influence from pagan literature (see, for example, Plato, *Republic* 5:463C). As in Judaism (see, for example, Deut 10:18; 24:17; Isa 1:17), there is special concern for widows (5:3–8). There were established orders of widows, with specific regulations for each order (5:9–16). "Elders" (presbyters), a title derived from Judaism, are to be respected and fairly paid for their work, punished if evidence warrants, and removed from office if unworthy (5:17–25). Slaves should honor their masters, and if their masters are Christians, the slaves must not expect special favors because they are fellow Christians (6:1–2).

VI. Attack on false teachers, and exhortations (6:3–19)

This attack repeats most of the one in 1:3–20. Here, however, the heretics think of their work as "godliness" deserving financial gain. The writer replies that there is a spiritual reward for godliness that is content with the necessities of life (6:3–10). Leaders in the church must shun the greed of the false teachers, keep "the faith" (that is, orthodox teaching), and be morally above reproach (6:11–16). They must charge the rich not to be haughty or to set their hope on uncertain riches, but on God, and to be rich in good deeds, which are the foundation for the life to come (6:17–19).

VII. Conclusion (6:20–21)

The author finally charges church officials to preserve orthodox Christianity and to shun heresy, especially the "falsely called knowledge" of Gnostic teaching. In the benediction "Grace be with you," the "you" is plural. This indicates that the work was intended not for Timothy but for a group of church officials, and through them for the whole church.

Outline and Comments: 2 Timothy

I. Salutation (1:1–2)

Instead of "the command of God" in 1 Tim 1:1, the author uses the Pauline "by the will of God." The phrase "in Christ Jesus" is probably not to be taken in the Pauline sense of the spiritual or mystical experience, which is represented by the expression "in Christ." The fact that the pastorals never mention people as being "in Christ," in contrast to Paul (see, for example, Rom 16:9–10; 1 Cor 4:15; 15:18; 2 Cor 1:21; 2:17; 5:17; Gal 1:6; 3:28; Phil 1:1), supports this view. On the other hand, the phrase "in Christ Jesus" may be the same as Paul's phrase "in Christ," as some commentators maintain. The fact that Paul occasionally mentions things as being in Christ (see, for example, Rom 3:24; 6:23; Phil 2:1, 5; 1 Thess 2:14), as the pastorals always do, supports the view that the phrases are equivalent in the two works.

II. Thanksgiving (1:3–5)

Unlike 1 Timothy and Titus, 2 Timothy contains a thanksgiving similar to some in Paul's letters; it includes statements about prayer and about remembering the readers and their faith (see also 1 Thess 1:2–3; Phil 1:3–11; Phlm 4–6).

III. Exhortations (1:6–2:13)

After the ceremony of induction into their offices (see 1 Tim 4:14), to which they were called by God's purpose and grace, church officials must be courageous and use their power in love and self-control. They must not be ashamed to testify to the Lord, must be prepared to suffer for the gospel, and should follow the example of the writer in these respects (1:6–14). Some have become disloyal, but others have remained faithful (1:15–18).

The official is to communicate what he has learned to others, who will do likewise (2:1–2). Like the good soldier, the church leader must be prepared to suffer; like the athlete, he must obey the rules; and like the farmer, he must work hard if he is to achieve results (2:3–7). Possibly by the use of fragments of a preaching formula (2:8) or early creed (2:11–13), the writer warns church leaders to stand firm and be faithful so that they may "obtain the salvation that is in Christ Jesus" (2:8–13).

IV. *Warning against false teachers (2:14–3:9)*

Church leaders must warn against heresies, which are as penetrating as gangrene, and they themselves must be effective and honest in conveying orthodox doctrine. The Lord can identify his true workers, who refrain from evil, as two allusions to the OT (see Num 16:5; LXX, Lev 24:16; Isa 26:13) prove (2:14–19). Members of the church are like vessels in a house. Faithful Christians, like gold and silver vessels, serve a noble purpose; faithless Christians, like wood and ceramic utensils, are less useful (2:20–21). "The Lord's servant" must shun youthful passions and heretical teaching, and must not be quarrelsome but kind to everyone and easy on opponents (2:22–26). In the last days faithless and evil people will appear, even in the church, and will corrupt weaker members. But like the magicians Jannes and Jambres of Jewish tradition, who opposed Moses in Egypt (Exod 7:11), they will not succeed (3:1–9).

V. *More exhortations (3:10–4:5)*

Writing in the manner of Paul, and appealing to his own faith, patience, love, and persecutions, the author exhorts church leaders to continue in their faith and teaching; he also exhorts them to seek guidance in the scriptures for their teaching and training in righteousness and good works (3:11–17). In spite of increasing heresy, church leaders must continue to preach the word of sound teaching (4:1–5).

VI. *The writer's farewell and instructions (4:6–18)*

Although the farewell testament, a characteristic of the pastorals, may actually have begun in 3:10, the verses in 4:6–8 are emphatically that. Verses 9–21 are difficult for several reasons. They seem inconsistent with what has preceded. For example, "Paul" has encouraged "Timothy" to continue his work at Ephesus, but now he wants "Timothy" to come to him soon. Why would Paul at the point of death (4:6) want Timothy to bring Mark, who is useful in serving Paul (4:11)? Moreover, most of the people listed are not mentioned in undisputed letters of Paul. These observations add to the difficulty of regarding the pastorals as authentic letters of Paul. However, because Demas, Titus, and Mark are mentioned in undisputed letters, and because some scholars find ways of reconciling the difficulties, they regard the verses as Pauline. Other scholars think that the verses may be a Pauline fragment of a lost letter. Some who consider the pastorals pseudonymous think the writer may have had some information about Paul's travels, his coworkers, and his last days; they think what the writer says about Paul's approaching death is fiction, and that in reality Paul had long been dead.

The reference to books and parchments is a curious phenomenon, especially "parchments," which occurs only here in the NT, and about which "Paul" is especially concerned. The books were probably rolls of papyrus, a writing material made from the plant of the same name. Parchment was an expensive writing material made from the skins of sheep or goats and was more valuable than papyrus. But what, if anything, was written in the books and parchments? The books could have been writings of many kinds, or even blank rolls for future use. Most scholars seem to think the parchments were the Greek OT or parts of it. Others have suggested legal documents of some sort, including the evidence for Paul's Roman citizenship, Paul's letters, records of sayings of Jesus, and other Christian writings.

VII. *Closing greetings and blessing (4:19–22)*

This is rather anticlimactic after the "Amen" of v 18. The "your" in "The Lord be with your Spirit," a benediction that resembles those of Paul (Gal 6:18; Phil 4:23; Phlm 25), is singular. But the "you" in "Grace be with you" is plural, as in 1 Tim 6:22 and Phlm 25, and indicates that the writing was intended for more people than just "Timothy."

Outline and Comments: Titus

I. Salutation (1:1–4)

The real Paul never refers to himself as "a servant of God" (see Jas 1:1) but as a "servant of Christ" (Rom 1:1; Phil 1:1). This is the longest salutation in the pastorals. Church officials are to promote the faith and knowledge of orthodox Christianity and godliness in the hope of eternal life, which God promised and has shown in his word as preached by the apostles.

II. Advice for church officials (1:5–9)

We know nothing about Crete, a large island in the Mediterranean Sea southeast of Greece, at the time the pastorals were written. According to Acts 27:7–21, Paul sailed along its shores on the way to Rome. Although we cannot fit Crete into the life and work of Paul as we know them from Acts and his letters, we may assume that the writer of Titus was concerned about conditions in the church there. Compare the list of qualifications for church officials with those in 1 Tim 3:1–12 and 2 Tim 2:24–26.

III. Condemnation of false teachings (1:10–16)

The heresies described are essentially the same as those mentioned elsewhere (see 1 Tim 1:3–10; 4:1–10; 6:3–10; 2 Tim 2:14–18, 23; 3:2–5). But at Crete they are accentuated because the Cretans are by nature "always liars, vicious brutes, lazy gluttons." The saying quoted was attributed to Epimenides, a half-mythical Cretan poet of the sixth century BCE, and it may have become proverbial. But why would a writer include such a harsh saying in an actual letter meant for Crete? Wouldn't the elders and bishops to be appointed have been Cretans? Did the writer use the saying just to condemn the heretics, or was the letter strictly personal and addressed to "Titus," a non-Cretan, by a writer who was insensitive to the severity of his accusation? We really cannot answer these questions, but most scholars think Paul would not have written like this.

IV. Instructions about how to deal with different social groups (2:1–15)

Church officials must teach orthodox doctrine when guiding older men and women, younger people, and slaves and their masters in their relationships with each other. At the same time, church leaders, in order to preserve their authority, must be models in speech and conduct, which are to be based on the faith that the grace of God appeared in Jesus Christ for the salvation of all people.

V. Christian conduct in a pagan environment (3:1–7)

Church officials must teach church members obedience to political authorities. They must also teach them the desire for kind deeds, so that the members may offset their abominable actions before they became Christians through the loving kindness of God in their baptism. Words such as "rebirth" and "renewal," used with reference to becoming Christians, belonged to pagan religious vocabulary, especially that of the Stoics.

VI. Advice for dealing with heretics (3:8–11)

Good deeds are the best defense against false teaching, and the disobedient must be admonished, perhaps even put out of the church.

VII. Conclusion (3:12–15)

The writer plans his future and makes a final appeal to "our people" (3:14; Greek)—the "all of you" for whom the letter was really intended—to do good deeds.

SUMMARY

Little clues like "our people" and "all of you" are among many indicating that the pastorals are pseudonymous works not intended for only one person. The common vocabulary and style, as well as the similarity in the heresies dealt with, indicate a single author writing at one time in the history of the church. Although the precise time is uncertain, the author wrote when orthodox or catholic Christianity was emerging and was threatened with incipient Gnosticism and other false teachings. This was all occurring in the post-apostolic age when apocalyptic expectations had faded. The purpose of the letters was to advise, warn, and instruct church leaders as they taught "the faith" and selected qualified officials to conduct worship and maintain discipline. Above all, church leaders were to be models in speech and conduct and to exhort their members to good deeds of love and kindness, which were the best defense against heretics and false teaching.

For further study of the pastorals, see the books referred to in the course of our discussion, as well as D. C. Verner 1983, social world of pastorals; G. D. Fee 1984; J. D. Quinn 1990, Titus; G. W. Knight 1992; M. P. Prior 1989, Paul and 2 Timothy; C. S. Keener 1992 and H. S. Baldwin 1995, women in 1 Timothy; F. M. Young 1994, theology of pastorals; M. Harding 1998, rhetorical approach.

Concluding Summary

THE NT, COMPRISING TWENTY-SEVEN writings of diverse literary types and theological views, has its setting in Roman provinces east and north of the Mediterranean Sea. The Hellenistic culture of those lands was syncretistic, and the NT reflects the political, social, and economic life of that culture and reveals influence from Judaism and Hellenism. However, we cannot be entirely certain about specific elements of influence from either culture, because by the time of Jesus Hellenism had influenced many aspects of Judaism. Affinities of Christianity with Judaism seem closest in the use of OT scriptures, Essenism, especially as represented by the Sect of Qumran, and Jewish wisdom. NT writers—with few, if any, exceptions—used the Greek language, the language used in most mission preaching. To some degree, early Christian writers were influenced by Greek philosophy, especially Stoicism. How much several NT writers were influenced by the developing syncretistic phenomenon known as Gnosticism is still a debatable issue.

The NT reflects, throughout the diversity of its writings, which are often more theological than historical in nature, the inspiration of the historical person known as Jesus of Nazareth.

Jesus, a Jew in Palestine, became the teacher of a small group of Jewish disciples who came to regard him as the expected Messiah. Jesus' teachings are different from those of Judaism not in content, but in their radical moral and ethical demands. Some Hellenistic Jews and Gentiles also became followers of Jesus and formed Christian communities, first within Judaism in Palestine and then in lands north of the Mediterranean—even in Rome. Christians within those communities produced the literature of the NT for people living in similar communities, in order to propagate the Christian faith and to provide instruction in moral and social life.

Jesus' life ended in crucifixion on a Roman cross and did not bring the expected redemption of the Jews. Jesus' followers were not prepared to accept a crucified Messiah, but they became convinced of his resurrection from the dead. They also came to believe that he had predicted his own passion—that is, his suffering, death, and resurrection—and attempted to find evidence for his predictions in OT scriptures. And early Christians also came to believe that Jesus' death had occurred for the forgiveness of their own past sins.

Some scholars have proposed that Christianity began as a millenarian movement, at the center of which stood Jesus in the image of a prophet who challenged traditional assumptions about values. Christianity failed as a millenarian movement because the new world order did not appear. But Christianity succeeded because of its radical sense of community without social distinctions and its concern for all aspects of believers' lives.

As Christianity developed as a separate sect within Judaism and eventually became a Gentile religion, some Christians suffered oppression from some Jews and non-Jews alike. In such situations, Christians generally came to believe that Jesus had not only predicted his own suffering but their own as well. Rather than resist persecution, Christians viewed their own cross-bearing as a mark of Christian self-identity and looked to the example of Jesus for perseverance in the present and hope for the future. Good citizenship in the Roman Empire involved being "subject to the governing authorities" (Rom 13:1). And good citizenship also meant living a sound moral life, knowing that "it is better to suffer for doing good . . . than to suffer for doing evil," entrusting "themselves to a faithful Creator" (1 Pet 3:17; 4:19).

The literature of the NT divides naturally into three parts: the gospels, Acts and Paul's letters, and the other writings. Neither histories nor biographies, the gospels are a distinctive literary type and provide the only record of the life, work, and teaching of Jesus. Written after the letters of Paul and after the earliest phase of Christianity, which is reflected in Acts, the material in the gospels had been shaped by oral tradition and earlier sources. That material was shaped further through each writer's redaction, which involved his individual literary style, special interests, emphases, and theological concerns. Therefore, it is necessary to study the gospels critically to try to distinguish what is historical from what is theological. The historical-critical method, with the techniques of literary, form, and redaction criticism, is especially helpful in this process.

The first three gospels are known as synoptic gospels because they are closely related in content as well as in style. Most scholars still subscribe to the two-source theory, that is, that in the composition of their gospels, Matthew and Luke each used Mark, the earliest gospel, and another common source named Q. The independence of Q as a source continues to be challenged, and a number of scholars ardently defend the hypothesis that Matthew is the earliest gospel, Luke the second, and Mark an abbreviation of both Matthew and Luke. Perhaps one of the strongest arguments for this hypothesis is the remarkably large number of agreements between Matthew and Luke as against Mark. On the other hand, if, as maintained by this hypothesis, Mark is a condensation of Matthew and Luke, scholars ask, among other questions, for what sound reasons would Mark omit the birth narratives, most of the Sermon on the Mount, and the resurrection appearances of Jesus?

The fourth gospel, John, is an enigma in many ways. The author of John wrote primarily to inspire faith in Jesus as the unique Son of God, and to assure his readers that the spiritual presence of Jesus could provide strength and courage for facing opposition from the Jewish synagogue. Evidence in the gospel, with the epistles of John, indicates that the writers of these works, or the circle or school responsible for them, wrote in opposition to the Jews but also to certain Christian groups with whom there were theological differences.

The conspicuous absence in John of sayings by Jesus like those in the Sermon on the Mount, parables, teaching about the kingdom of God, Jesus' association with outcasts and sinners, and healing of demoniacs, as well as other major differences between John and the synoptics, make the fourth gospel even more suspect as a historical source than the other gospels are. The whole gospel must be understood basically as a theological work in light of its purpose to inspire faith in Jesus as "the Christ, the Son of God" (20:30–31).

Although some scholars stress the importance of the Nag Hammadi gospels for the study of Jesus' sayings and the gospels, others maintain that they are of little or no value for such study. The radical differences between those gospels and the canonical gospels and the great uncertainty about dates and milieus of the Gnostic gospels make it difficult to make a positive judgment about their value for NT study.

An increasing number of women are involved in NT studies, and from their perspectives women played a much more influential role among Jesus' followers and in the early church than male scholars have heretofore acknowledged. Sometimes passages that appear to be unfavorable toward women are explained by exegesis and interpretation of cultural context to show that women were not given a lower status than men. By including all kinds of persons, Christianity brought about a different idea of God, a God of goodness who accepts everyone without exception.

The book of Acts was written partly to reconcile the conflict between Judaism and emerging Christianity, as it was spreading to Gentiles, and especially to deal with the problem of requirements for Gentile converts. Written also to win Rome's favor toward Christianity as it spread throughout the Roman Empire, Acts is the first history of the church. It provides an introduction to the life and work of Paul, a converted Jew who was very influential in spreading Christianity to Gentiles. He is the first Christian thinker whose works have survived. Under his leadership, Christianity, which was at first a Jewish sect, became a worldwide religion. In the arrangement of the NT, Acts serves as a link between the gospels and the letters of Paul.

Although I continue to follow the custom of referring to Paul as a Christian, we should remember that the use of that term during the time of Paul is an anachronism and that the religion of the Jesus movement during Paul's time was not known as Christianity. That religion was a developing religion, a religion in transition either from Judaism or paganism to the religion that only after Paul's time became known as Christianity. And when we think of Paul's so-called "doctrine" of justification by faith, faith may, perhaps, be more accurately understood as that "of Jesus" rather than faith "in Jesus" (recall our discussion of that point).

Paul wrote each of his letters to deal with specific problems in local churches. The church members, living in a pagan environment, faced challenges to their developing Christian faith, including strict moral and ethical demands. One Thessalonians, Corinthians, Galatians, Romans, Philippians, and Philemon are universally regarded as genuine, but the authenticity of Colossians, Ephesians, and 2 Thessalonians is disputed. Among Paul's letters, Galatians and Romans are distinctive in that they emphasize Paul's conviction that the basic requirements of the Christian religion are faith in Christ and a moral and ethical life, not the circumcision and dietary regulations of the Jewish law. The letters of Paul, therefore, provide valuable information about the life and vicissitudes of early Christian communities as they developed into a universal church in the Roman Empire.

The writings in the NT placed after those of Paul also are a distinctive group because of the circumstances from which they originated. Although these writings are traditionally ascribed to prominent people in the church, most scholars regard them as either anonymous or pseudonymous. As the various churches throughout the Roman world developed into the universal or catholic church, doctrinal differences became more acute within the church, and persecutions threatened from without. The diverse literary and religious writings from Hebrews to Revelation emerged in times of controversy among Christians and oppression by non-Christians.

Although distinctive in literary type and religious thought, Hebrews, Revelation, and 1 Peter all exhort their readers, in a time of persecution, to be firm in their faith so that they will be rewarded in the future life. The letters of

John reflect separation and controversy in the community that produced the Johannine literature. The purpose of those letters was to defend the more orthodox faith of the original community, to encourage unity through love for God/Christ and for fellow Christians, and to warn against the Docetic teachings of some Gnosticizing heretics.

James, perhaps unique in its influence from the religious syncretism of its time, especially from Judaic and Stoic aspects, is an ethical tract or religious essay. It reflects social problems in the church caused by the presence of rich members, and it stresses that religious faith without works of mercy is vain. Jude and 2 Peter were written to warn against heresy in the church, but the writer of 2 Peter also had to deal with skepticism resulting from the delay of the Parousia.

Although purporting to be written by Paul, the letters to Timothy and Titus are generally regarded as pseudonymous. They are called pastoral epistles because they were written by a church leader to other church leaders. Basic differences—especially in literary style, content, and theological views—the church organization presupposed, and the nature of the heresies addressed indicate a time of origin later than Paul, perhaps even in the early part of the second century. The main purpose of the pastorals, all thought to be written by the same person, was to exhort church leaders to proper behavior in "the household of God, which is the church of the living God," as they ministered to church members confronted with false teachers.

The early church survived not only severe controversy because of heresies from within, but also persecution by non-Christians. This persecution arose because of social conflict and because of the imperial cult. During the first centuries of the Christian era, hundreds of Christian writings—which originated within the church—were collected, sorted, and edited. One collection became known as the NT and was regarded as scripture inspired by God; it was therefore considered equal if not superior in authority to the OT, the scriptures of early Christians. The two Testaments were eventually placed together in a work known in much of the world as the Bible.

The preface to this book states that the aim of our study is to inform, not to convert, and to educate, not to indoctrinate. There also the hope is expressed that, through a critical study of the NT, readers may become informed and enlightened about both certainties and uncertainties on subjects about which certainty is too often assumed.

Throughout this book we have illustrated approaches and techniques used to evaluate the evidence objectively; this objectivity is essential in a critical study of the NT. The conclusions resulting from such study are often only tentative at best, and this is true for the conclusions in the chapters of this book. So thoughtful and open-minded readers will, naturally, still be uncertain about many of the NT issues we have examined. For all of us, then, Pilate's question to Jesus, "What is truth?" (John 18:38), can be the challenge for further critical study of that part of the Bible known as the New Testament.

Bibliography

Achtemeier, P. J. 1970. "Toward the Isolation of Pre-Markan Miracle Catenae." In *JBL* 99:265–291. 1975. *Mark*. Philadelphia: Fortress. 1978. "The Lukan Perspective on the Miracles of Jesus: A Preliminary Sketch." In *Perspectives on Luke-Acts,* 153–167, ed. C. H. Talbert. Danville, VA: ABPR. 1987. *The Quest for Unity in the New Testament Church*. Philadelphia: Fortress. 1996. *1 Peter*. Minneapolis: Fortress.

Adamson, J. B. 1989. *James the Man and His Message*. Grand Rapids: Eerdmans.

Alexander, L. 1993. *The Preface to Luke's Gospel*. Cambridge: University.

Allison, D. C. 1985. *The End of the Ages Has Come: An Early Interpretation of the Passion and Resurrection of Jesus*. Philadelphia: Fortress. 1993. *The New Moses*. Minneapolis: Fortress.

Argyle, A. W. 1963. *The Gospel According to Matthew*. Cambridge: University.

Arlandson, J. M. 1997. *Women, Class, and Society in Early Christianity*. Peabody, MA: Hendrickson.

Arnold, C. E. 1996. *The Colossian Syncretism*. Grand Rapids: Baker.

Ascouth, R. S. 1998. *The Formation of the Pauline Corpus*. New York: Paulist.

Ashton, J. 1991. *Understanding the Fourth Gospel*. Oxford: Clarendon. Ed. 1997. *The Interpretation of John*. Edinburgh: Clark.

Attridge, H. W. 1989. *The Epistle to the Hebrews*. Philadelphia: Fortress.

Aune, D. E. 1981. "The Problem of the Genre of the Gospels: A Critique of C. H. Talbert's *What Is a Gospel?*" In *Gospel Perspectives,* 2:9–60, ed. R. T. France and D. Wenham. Sheffield: JSOT. 1983. *Prophecy in Early Christianity and the Ancient Mediterranean World*. Grand Rapids: Eerdmans. 1986. "The Apocalypse of John and the Problem of Genre." In *Semeia* 36:65–96. Ed. 1988. *Greco-Roman Literature and the New Testament*. Atlanta: Scholars. 1997. *Revelation 1–5*. Dallas: Word.

Bacon, B. W. 1930. *Studies in Matthew*. New York: Holt.

Bailey, J. A. 1963. *The Traditions Common to the Gospels of Luke and John*. Leiden: Brill. 1978. "Who Wrote II Thessalonians?" In *NTS* 25: 131–145.

Bailey, J. L. and L. D. Vander Broek. 1992. *Literary Forms in the New Testament: A Handbook*. Louisville: W/K.

Balch, D. L. 1981. *Let Wives Be Submissive: The Domestic Code in 1 Peter.* Chico: Scholars. 1988. "Household Codes." In *Greco-Roman Literature and the New Testament,* 25–50, ed. D. E. Aune. Atlanta: Scholars.

Baldwin, H. S. 1995. *Women in the Church: A Fresh Analysis of 1 Timothy 2:11–15.* Grand Rapids: Baker.

Ball, D. M. 1996. *"I AM" in John's Gospel.* Sheffield: Academic.

Bammel, E., ed. 1970. *The Trial of Jesus.* London: SCM.

Banks, R. 1980. *Paul's Idea of Community.* Grand Rapids: Eerdmans.

Barbour, R. S. 1972. *Traditio-Historical Criticism of the Gospels.* London: SPCK.

Barclay, J. M. G. 1991. *Obeying the Truth: Paul's Ethics in Galatians.* Minneapolis: Fortress. 1997. *Colossians and Philemon.* Sheffield: Academic.

Barnett, A. E. 1958. *The New Testament: Its Making and Meaning.* New York: Abingdon.

Barrett, C. K. 1957. *A Commentary on the Epistle to the Romans.* New York: Harper. 1961. *Luke the Historian in Recent Study.* London: Epworth. 1968. *A Commentary on the First Epistle to the Corinthians.* New York: Harper & Row. 1973. *A Commentary on the Second Epistle to the Corinthians.* New York: Harper & Row. 1975. *The Gospel of John and Judaism.* Philadelphia: Fortress. 1978. *The Gospel According to St. John.* Philadelphia: Westminster. 1982a. *Essays on John.* Philadelphia: Fortress. 1982b. *Essays on Paul.* Philadelphia: Fortress. 1985. *Freedom and Obligation: A Study of the Epistle to the Galatians.* Philadelphia: Westminster. 1987. *The New Testament Background.* London: SPCK. 1994. *Paul: An Introduction to His Thought.* Louisville: W/K.

Barth, G. 1963. "Matthew's Understanding of the Law." In *Tradition and Interpretation in Matthew,* 58–164, ed. G. Bornkamm et al. Philadelphia: Westminster.

Barth, M. 1974. *Ephesians.* 2 vols. Garden City, NY: Doubleday.

Bauckham, R. J. 1983. *Jude, 2 Peter.* Waco: Word. 1990. *Jude and the Relatives of Jesus in the Early Church.* Edinburgh: Clark.

Bauer, D. R. 1988. *The Structure of Matthew's Gospel.* Sheffield: Almond.

Baumert, N. 1996. *Woman and Man in Paul.* Collegeville, MN: Liturgical.

Beardslee, W. A. 1970. *Literary Criticism of the New Testament.* Philadelphia: Fortress. 1989. "Recent Literary Criticism." In *The New Testament and Its Modern Interpreters,* 175–198, ed. E. J. Epp and G. W. MacRae. Philadelphia: Fortress.

Beare, F. W. 1958. *The First Epistle of Peter.* Oxford: Blackwell. 1959. *A Commentary on the Epistle to the Philippians.* New York: Harper. 1981. *The Gospel According to Matthew.* San Francisco: Harper & Row.

Beasley-Murray, G. R. 1965. *The General Epistles James, 1 Peter, Jude, 2 Peter.* New York: Abingdon. 1981. *The Book of Revelation.* Grand Rapids: Eerdmans. 1986. *Jesus and the Kingdom of God.* Grand Rapids: Eerdmans. 1987. *John.* Waco: Word.

Beker, J. C. 1980. *Paul the Apostle.* Philadelphia: Fortress. 1982. *Paul's Apocalyptic Gospel.* Philadelphia: Fortress.

Bellinzoni, A. J. 1987. "Extra-Canonical Literature and the Synoptic Problem." In *Jesus, the Gospels, and the Church,* 3–15, ed. E. P. Sanders. Macon: Mercer.

Bellinzoni, A. J., J. B. Tyson, and W. O. Walker, eds. 1985. *The Two-Source Hypothesis: A Critical Appraisal.* Macon: Mercer.

Bernheim, P. A. 1997. *James, Brother of Jesus.* London: SCM.

Best, E. A. 1967. *The Letter of Paul to the Romans.* Cambridge: University. 1972. *A Commentary on the First and Second Epistles to the Thessalonians.* New York: Harper & Row. 1977. "The Role of the Disciples in Mark." In *NTS* 23:377–401. 1981. *Following Jesus.* Sheffield: JSOT. 1982. *1 Peter.* Grand Rapids: Eerdmans. 1997. "Who Used Whom?: The Relationship of Ephesians and Colossians." In *NTS* 43:72–96. 1998. *A Critical and Exegetical Commentary on Ephesians.* Edinburgh: Clark.

Betz, H. D. 1979. *Galatians.* Philadelphia: Fortress. 1985a. *Essays on the Sermon on the Mount.* Philadelphia: Fortress. 1985b. *2 Corinthians 8 and 9.* Philadelphia: Fortress. 1995. *The Sermon on the Mount.* Minneapolis: Fortress.

Bicknell, E. J. 1932. *The First and Second Epistles to the Thessalonians.* London: Methuen.

Bigg, C. 1905. *The Epistles of St. Peter and St. Jude.* New York: Scribners.

Blinzler, J. 1959. *The Trial of Jesus*. Westminster, MD: Newman.

Blomberg, C. L. 1990. *Interpreting the Parables*. Downers Grove, IL: InterVarsity.

Bloomquist, L. G. 1993. *The Function of Suffering in Philippians*. Sheffield: JSOT.

Bockmuehl, M. 1998. *The Epistle to the Philippians*. Peabody, MA: Hendrickson.

Boers, H. 1975. "The Form-Critical Study of Paul's Letters: 1 Thessalonians as a Case Study." In *NTS* 22:140–158.   1994. *The Justification of the Gentiles: Paul's Letters to the Galatians and Romans*. Peabody, MA: Hendrickson.

Boisclair, R. A., 1996. Review of E. D. Freid 1994. In *CBS* 58:744–746.

Booth, W. 1983. *The Rhetoric of Fiction*. Chicago: University.

Borg, M. J. 1987. *Jesus, A New Vision*. San Francisco: Harper.   1994a. *Jesus in Contemporary Scholarship*. Valley Forge: Trinity.   1994b. *Meeting Jesus Again for the First Time*. San Francisco: Harper Collins.   1998. *Conflict, Holiness and Politics in the Teaching of Jesus*. Harrisburg, PA: Trinity.   And N. T. Wright 1998. *The Meaning of Jesus*. San Francisco: Harper.

Borgen, P. 1983a. *Logos Was the True Light and Other Essays on the Gospel of John*. Trondheim: Tapir.   1983b. *Paul Preaches Circumcision and Pleases Men and Other Essays on Christian Origins*. Trondheim: Tapir.   1987. *Philo, John and Paul*. Atlanta: Scholars.

Boring, M. E. 1973. "What Are We Looking For? Toward a Definition of the Term 'Christian Prophet.'" In *SBLSP* 142–154.   1976. "Christian Prophecy and Matt 10:23: A Test Exegesis." In *SBLSP* 127–133.   1977. "The Paucity of Sayings in Mark." In *SBLSP* 371–377.   1992. *The Continuing Voice of Jesus*. Louisville: W/K.   Et al. 1995. *Hellenistic Commentary to the New Testament*. Nashville: Abingdon.

Bornkamm, G. 1959. *Jesus of Nazareth*. New York: Harper.   1963. *Tradition and Interpretation in Matthew*. Philadelphia: Westminster.   1971. *Paul*. New York: Harper & Row.   1975. "The Heresy of Colossians." In *Conflict at Colossae*, 123–145, ed. F. O. Francis and W. A. Meeks. Missoula, MT: Scholars.

Boslooper, T. 1962. *The Virgin Birth*. Philadelphia: Westminster.

Boucher, M. 1977. *The Mysterious Parable*. Washington: CBAA.

Bradley, D. G. 1953. "The *Topos* as Form in the Pauline Paraenesis." In *JBL* 72:238–246.

Brawley, R. L. 1987. *Luke-Acts and the Jews*. Atlanta: Scholars.

Breech, E. 1978. "Kingdom of God and the Parables of Jesus." In *Semeia* 12:15–40.

Broneer, O. 1951. "Corinth: Center of Paul's Missionary Work in Greece." In *BA* 14: 78–96.

Brooke, A. E. 1912. *The Johannine Epistles*. New York: Scribners.

Brooten, B. J. 1982. *Women Leaders in the Ancient Synagogues*. Chico: Scholars.

Brown, C. 1984. *Miracles and the Critical Mind*. Grand Rapids: Eerdmans.

Brown, R. E. 1966, 1970. *The Gospel according to John*. 2 vols. Garden City, NY: Doubleday.   And J. A. Fitzmyer and R. E. Murphy, eds. 1968. *The Jerome Biblical Commentary*. 2 vols. in one. Englewood Cliffs: Prentice Hall.   1977. *The Birth of the Messiah*. Garden City, NY: Doubleday. 1979. *The Community of the Beloved Disciple*. New York: Paulist.   1980. "The Christians Who Lost Out." Review of E. Pagels, *The Gnostic Gospels*. New York Times Book Review (Jan. 20):3, 33. 1982. *The Epistles of John*. Garden City, NY: Doubleday.   And J. P. Meier. 1983. *Antioch and Rome*. New York: Paulist.   1984. *The Churches the Apostles Left Behind*. New York: Paulist.   1987. "The Gospel of Peter and Canonical Gospel Priority." In *NTS* 33:321–343.   1994. *The Death of the Messiah*, 2 vols. New York: Doubleday. 1997. *An Introduction to the New Testament*. New York: Doubleday.

Brown, S. 1978. "The Role of the Prologue in Determining the Purpose of Luke-Acts." In *Perspectives on Luke-Acts*, 99–111, ed. C. H. Talbert. Danville, VA: ABPR.

Bruce, F. F. 1972. *New Testament History*. Garden City, NY: Doubleday.   1978a. *1 and 2 Corinthians*. Grand Rapids: Eerdmans.   1978b. *Paul: Apostle of the Heart Set Free*. Grand Rapids: Eerdmans.   1979. *The Epistles of John*. Grand Rapids: Eerdmans.   1982a. *The Epistle to the Galatians*. Grand Rapids: Eerdmans.   1982b. *1 and 2 Thessalonians*. Waco: Word.   1983a. *The Gospel of John*. Grand Rapids: Eerdmans.   1983b. *Philippians*. Grand Rapids: Eerdmans.   1984. *The Epistles to the Colossians, to Philemon, and to the Ephesians*. Grand Rapids: Eerdmans.   1988. *The Canon of Scripture*. Downers Grove, IL:

InterVarsity. 1990. *The Epistle to the Hebrews.* Grand Rapids: Eerdmans.

Brunt, J. C. 1985. "More on *Topos* as a New Testament Form." In *JBL* 104:495–500.

Bryan, C. A. 1993. *A Preface to Mark.* New York: Oxford.

Buchanan, G. W. 1972. *To the Hebrews.* Garden City, NY: Doubleday. 1984. *Jesus the King and His Kingdom.* Macon: Mercer. 1993. *The Book of Revelation.* Lewiston, NY: Mellen.

Bultmann, R. 1951, 1955. *Theology of the New Testament.* 2 vols. New York: Scribners. 1960. *Jesus Christ and Mythology.* London: SCM. 1961. "New Testament and Mythology." In *Kerygma and Myth,* 1–44, ed. H. W. Bartsch. New York: Harper & Row. 1963. *The History of the Synoptic Tradition.* New York: Harper & Row. 1971. *The Gospel of John.* Philadelphia: Westminster. 1985. *The Second Letter to the Corinthians.* Minneapolis: Augsburg.

Burkert, W. 1985. *Greek Religions.* Cambridge: Harvard. 1987. *Ancient Mystery Cults.* Cambridge: Harvard.

Burkett, D. 1991. *The Son of Man in the Gospel of John.* Sheffield: JSOT.

Burney, C. F. 1925. *The Poetry of Our Lord.* Oxford: Clarendon.

Burton, E. D. 1920. *The Epistle to the Galatians.* New York: Scribners.

Buttrick, G. A. et al., eds. 1951–1957. *The Interpreter's Bible.* 12 vols. New York: Abingdon. Et al., eds. 1962. *The Interpreter's Dictionary of the Bible.* 4 vols. New York: Abingdon.

Cadbury, H. J. 1920. *The Style and Literary Method of Luke.* Cambridge: Harvard. 1947. *Jesus What Manner of Man?* New York: Macmillan. 1955. *The Book of Acts in History.* New York: Harper. 1958. *The Making of Luke-Acts.* London: SPCK. 1959. "The Dilemma of Ephesians." In *NTS* 5:91–102.

Caird, G. B. 1963. *The Gospel of St. Luke.* Baltimore: Penguin. 1966. *A Commentary on the Revelation of St. John the Divine.* New York: Harper & Row. 1976. *Paul's Letters from Prison.* Oxford: University.

Callahan, A. D. 1997. *Embassy of Onesimus: The Letter of Paul to Philemon.* Valley Forge: Trinity.

Calloud, J. 1976. *Structural Analysis of Narrative.* Philadelphia: Fortress.

Cameron, R., ed. 1982. *The Other Gospels: Non-Canonical Gospel Texts.* Philadelphia: Westminster.

Carlston, C. E. 1968. "The Things that Defile (Mk VII:14) and the Law in Matthew and Mark." In *NTS* 15:75–96. 1975. *The Parables of the Triple Tradition.* Philadelphia: Fortress.

Carson, D. A. 1994. "Five Gospels, No Christ." In *Christianity Today,* 1994:30–33.

Carter, W. 1994. *What Are They Saying about Matthew's Sermon on the Mount?* New York: Paulist.

Cartlidge, D. A. and D. L. Dungan. 1994. *Documents for the Study of the Gospels.* Minneapolis: Fortress.

Case, S. J. 1923. *The Social Origins of Christianity.* Chicago: University.

Casey, M. 1998. "Where Wright is Wrong: A Critical Review of Wright's *Jesus and the Victory of God.* In *JSNT* 69:95–103.

Catchpole, D. R. 1976. "Trial of Jesus." In *IDB,* Supp. Vol., 917–919.

Charles, R. H. 1920. *The Revelation of St. John.* 2 vols. New York: Scribners.

Charlesworth, J. H., ed. 1972. *John and Qumran.* London: Chapman. 1983, 1985. *The Old Testament Pseudepigrapha.* 2 vols. Garden City, NY: Doubleday. 1987. *The Old Testament Pseudepigrapha and the New Testament.* Cambridge: University. 1988. *Jesus Within Judaism.* New York: Doubleday. Et al., eds. 1992. *The Messiah: Developments in Earliest Judaism and Christianity.* Minneapolis: Fortress. 1995. *The Beloved Disciple.* Valley Forge: Trinity.

Childs, B. 1979. *Introduction to the Old Testament as Scripture.* Philadelphia: Fortress. 1984. *The New Testament as Canon: An Introduction.* Philadelphia: Fortress.

Chilton, B. D. 1979. *God in Strength: Jesus' Announcement of the Kingdom.* Freistadt: Ploechl. Ed. 1984. *The Kingdom of God in the Teaching of Jesus.* Philadelphia: Fortress. And J. I. H. McDonald. 1987. *Jesus and the Ethics of the Kingdom.* Grand Rapids: Eerdmans. And C. A. Evans. 1994. *Studying the Historical Jesus.* Leiden: Brill.

Coleridge, M. 1993. *The Birth of the Lukan Narrative: Narrative as Christology in Luke 1–2.* Sheffield: JSOT.

Collange, J. F. 1979. *The Epistle of Saint Paul to the Philippians.* London: Epworth.

Collins, A. Y. 1983. *The Apocalypse.* Wilmington: Glazier. 1984. *Crisis and Catharsis: The Power of the Apocalypse.* Philadelphia: Westminster. 1986. "Early Christian Apocalypticism: Genre and Social Setting." In *Semeia* 36:1–11. 1992. *The*

Beginning of the Gospel: Probings of Mark in Context. Minneapolis: Fortress.

Collins, J. J. 1986. *Between Athens and Jerusalem: Jewish Identity in the Hellenistic Diaspora*. New York: Crossroad.

Collins, R. F. 1983. *Introduction to the New Testament*. Garden City, NY: Doubleday. 1984. *Studies on the First Letter to the Thessalonians*. Leuven: University. 1993. *The Birth of the New Testament*. New York: Crossroad.

Conybeare, F. C. 1912. Trans. of *Philostratus: The Life of Apollonius of Tyana*. 2 vols. Loeb Classical Library. Cambridge: Harvard.

Conzelmann, H. 1960. *The Theology of St. Luke*. New York: Harper & Row. 1975. *1 Corinthians*. Philadelphia: Fortress. 1987. *Acts of the Apostles*. Philadelphia: Fortress.

Cook, J. G. 1996. *The Structure and Persuasive Power of Mark: A Linguistic Approach*. Atlanta: Scholars.

Cope, O. L. 1976. *Matthew: A Scribe Trained for the Kingdom of Heaven*. Washington: CBAA.

Corsini, E. 1983. *The Apocalypse*. Ed., F. J. Moloney. Wilmington: Glazier.

Cosgrove, C. H. 1988. *The Cross and the Spirit: A Study in the Argument and Theology of Galatians*. Macon: Mercer.

Countryman, L. W. 1987. *The Mystical Way in the Fourth Gospel*. Philadelphia: Fortress.

Court, J. M. 1979. *Myth and History in the Book of Revelation*. Atlanta: Knox.

Cousar, C. B. 1982. *Galatians*. Atlanta: Knox.

Coutts, J. 1958. "The Relationship of Ephesians and Colossians." In *NTS* 4:201–207.

Cox, P. 1983. *Biography in Late Antiquity: A Quest for the Holy Man*. Berkeley: University of California.

Cranfield, C. E. B. 1975. *The Epistle to the Romans*. 2 vols. Edinburgh: Clark.

Creed, J. M. 1942. *The Gospel according to St. Luke*. London: Macmillan.

Cribbs, F. L. 1971. "St. Luke and the Johannine Tradition." In *JBL* 90:422–450. 1978. "The Agreements That Exist between John and Acts." In *Perspectives on Luke-Acts*, 40–61, ed. C. H. Talbert. Danville, VA: ABPR.

Crim, K. et al., eds. 1976. *The Interpreter's Dictionary of the Bible*. Supplementary Volume. Nashville: Abingdon.

Cross, F. L. 1954. *1 Peter: A Paschal Liturgy*. London: Mowbray.

Cross, F. M. 1961. *The Ancient Library of Qumran and Modern Biblical Studies*. Garden City, NY: Doubleday.

Crossan, J. D. 1973. *In Parables*. New York: Harper & Row. 1974. "A Structuralist Approach to the Parables." In *Semeia* 1:1–278. 1985. *Four Other Gospels*. Minneapolis: Winston. 1986. *Sayings Parallels: A Workbook for the Jesus Tradition*. Philadelphia: Fortress. 1988. *The Cross that Spoke: The Origins of the Passion Narrative*. San Francisco: Harper. 1991. *The Historical Jesus: The Life of a Mediterranean Jewish Peasant*. San Francisco: Harper. 1994. *Jesus a Revolutionary Biography*. San Francisco: Harper. 1998. *The Birth of Christianity*. San Francisco: Harper.

Crump, D. M. 1992. *Jesus the Intercessor: Prayer and Christology in Luke-Acts*. Tuebingen: Mohr.

Cullmann, O. 1962. *Peter—Disciple, Apostle, Martyr*. Philadelphia: Westminster. 1976. *The Johannine Circle*. Philadelphia: Westminster.

Culpepper, R. A. 1975. *The Johannine School*. Missoula, MT: Scholars. 1983. *Anatomy of the Fourth Gospel: A Study in Literary Design*. Philadelphia: Fortress. 1998. *The Gospel and Letters of John*. Nashville: Abingdon.

Cumont, F. 1956. *The Mysteries of Mithra*. New York: Dover.

Cunningham, A., ed. 1982. *The Early Church and the State*. Philadelphia: Fortress.

Dahl, N. A. 1977. *Studies in Paul*. Minneapolis: Augsburg.

Dalton, W. J. 1979. "The Integrity of Philippians." In *Biblica* 60:97–102.

Danker, F. W. 1964. "Menander and the New Testament." In *NTS* 10:365–368. 1976. *Luke*. Philadelphia: Fortress. 1988. *Jesus and the New Age: A Commentary on St. Luke's Gospel*. Philadelphia: Fortress. 1989. *II Corinthians*. Minneapolis: Augsburg.

Dart, J. 1988. *The Jesus of Heresy and History: The Discovery and Meaning of the Nag Hammadi Library*. San Francisco: Harper.

Davids, P. H. 1982. *The Epistle of James*. Grand Rapids: Eerdmans. 1983. *James*. San Francisco: Harper.

Davies, J. H. 1967. *A Letter to Hebrews*. Cambridge: University.

Davies, M. 1992. *Rhetoric and Reference in the Fourth Gospel*. Sheffield: JSOT.

Davies, W. D. 1955. *Paul and Rabbinic Judaism*. London: SPCK. 1964. *The Setting of the Sermon on the Mount*. Cambridge: University. 1984. *Jewish and Pauline Studies*. Philadelphia: Fortress.

Davison, J. E. 1985. "*Anomia* and the Question of Antinomian Polemic in Matthew." In *JBL* 104:617–635.

Deissmann, A. 1927. *Light from the Ancient East*. New York: Doran. 1957. *Paul*. New York: Harper.

de Jonge, M. 1977. *Jesus: Stranger from Heaven and Son of God*. Missoula, MT: Scholars. 1988. *Christology in Context: The Earliest Christian Response to Jesus*. Philadelphia: Westminster. 1991. *Jesus, the Servant Messiah*. New Haven: Yale.

DeMaris, R. E. 1994. *The Colossian Controversy*. Sheffield: Academic.

Denzer, G. A. 1968. "The Pastoral Letters." In *JBC* 2:350–361.

de Silva, D. A. 1996. *Despising Shame: Honor Discourse and Community Maintenance in the Epistle to the Hebrews*. Atlanta: Scholars.

Dewey, J. 1997. "Women in the Synoptic Gospels: Seen but Not Heard." In *BTB* 27:53–60.

Dey, L. K. K. 1975. *The Intermediary World and Patterns of Perfection in Philo and Hebrews*. Missoula, MT: Scholars.

Dibelius, M. 1935. *From Tradition to Gospel*. New York: Scribners. 1956. *Studies in the Acts of the Apostles*. London: SCM. 1976. *A Commentary on the Epistle of James*. Philadelphia: Fortress.

DiCicco, M. M. 1995. *Paul's Use of Ethos, Pathos, and Logos in 2 Corinthians 10–13*. Lewiston: Mellen.

Dickerson, P. L. 1997. "The New Character Narratives in Luke-Acts and the Synoptic Problem." In *JBL* 116:291–312.

Dillon, J. T. 1995. *Jesus as a Teacher: A Multidisciplinary Case Study*. Bethesda, MD: International Scholars.

Dillon, R. J. and J. A. Fitzmyer. 1968. "Acts of the Apostles." In *JBC* 2:165–214.

Dodd, C. H. 1932. *The Epistle of Paul to the Romans*. New York: Harper & Row. 1936. *The Apostolic Preaching and Its Development*. New York: Harper. 1946. *The Johannine Epistles*. New York: Harper. 1953. *The Interpretation of the Fourth Gospel*. Cambridge: University. 1961. *The Parables of the Kingdom*. New York: Scribners. 1963. *Historical Tradition in the Fourth Gospel*. Cambridge: University.

Donahue, J. R. 1973. *Are You the Christ?* Missoula, MT: Scholars. 1988. *The Gospel in Parable: Metaphor, Narrative, and Theology in the Synoptic Gospels*. Philadelphia: Fortress.

Doty, W. G. 1973. *Letters in Primitive Christianity*. Philadelphia: Fortress.

Downing, F. G. 1992. *Cynics and Christian Origins*. Edinburgh: Clark.

Drury, J. 1977. *Tradition and Design in Luke's Gospel*. Atlanta: Knox. 1989. *The Parables in the Gospels*. New York: Crossroad.

Duke, P. D. 1985. *Irony in the Fourth Gospel*. Atlanta: Knox.

Duncan, G. S. n.d. *The Epistle of Paul to the Galatians*. New York: Harper.

Dungan, D. L. 1971. *The Sayings of Jesus in the Churches of Paul*. Philadelphia: Fortress. Ed. 1990. *The Interrelations of the Gospels*. Leuven: University.

Dunn, J. D. G. 1975. *Jesus and the Spirit*. Philadelphia: Westminster. 1977. *Unity and Diversity in the New Testament*. Philadelphia: Westminster. 1988. *Romans*. 2 vols. Dallas: Waco. 1990. *Jesus, Paul and the Law*. Louisville: W/K. 1993a. *The Epistle to the Galatians*. London: Black. 1993b. *The Theology of Paul's Letter to the Galatians*. Cambridge: University. 1995a. "The Colossian Philosophy: A Confident Jewish Apologia." In *Biblica* 76:153–181. 1995b. *1 Corinthians*. Sheffield: Academic. 1996. *The Epistles to the Colossians and to Philemon*. Grand Rapids: Eerdmans. 1998. *The Theology of Paul the Apostle*. Grand Rapids: Eerdmans.

Dupont, D. J. 1964. *The Sources of Acts*. London: Darton, Longmann & Todd. 1979. *The Salvation of Gentiles*. New York: Paulist.

Dupont-Sommer, A. 1962. *The Essene Writings from Qumran*. Trans. G. Vermes. Cleveland: World.

Easton, B. S. 1947. *The Pastoral Epistles*. New York: Scribners.

Edwards, R. A. 1976a. "Christian Prophecy and the Q Tradition." In *SBLSP* 119–126. 1976b. *A Theology of Q*. Philadelphia: Fortress. 1985. *Matthew's Story of Jesus*. Philadelphia: Fortress.

Edwards, R. B. 1996. *The Johannine Epistles*. Sheffield: Academic.

Eisenman, R. and M. Wise. 1993. *The Dead Sea Scrolls Uncovered*. New York: Penguin.

Ellingworth, P. 1991. *The Epistle to the Hebrews*. London: Epworth. 1993. *The Epistle to the Hebrews*. Grand Rapids: Eerdmans.

Elliott, J. H. 1986. "Social-Scientific Criticism of the New Testament and Its Social World." In *Semeia* 35. 1990. *A Home for the Homeless: A Social-Scientific Criticism of 1 Peter, Its Situation and Strategy*. Minneapolis: Fortress. 1993. *What Is Social-Scientific Criticism?* Minneapolis: Fortress.

Elliott, J. K. 1982. *Questioning Christian Origins.* London: SCM.   Ed. 1993. *The Language and Style of Mark.* Leiden: Brill.   And I. Moir. 1995. *Manuscripts and the Text of the New Testament.* Edinburgh: Clark.

Ellis, E. E. 1978. *Prophecy and Hermeneutic in Early Christianity.* Grand Rapids: Eerdmans.   1981. *The Gospel of Luke.* Grand Rapids: Eerdmans.

Ellis, P. F. 1984. *The Genius of John: A Composition-Critical Commentary on the Fourth Gospel.* Minneapolis: Liturgical.

Enslin, M. S. 1930. *The Ethics of Paul.* New York: Harper.   1938. *Christian Beginnings.* New York: Harper.   1963. *Letters to the Churches.* New York: Abingdon.

Esler, P. F. 1994. *The First Christians in their Social Worlds.* London: Routledge.

Evans, C. A. 1992. *Noncanonical Writings and New Testament Interpretation.* Peabody, MA: Hendrickson.   1993. *Word and Glory.* Sheffield: JSOT.

Evans, L. H. 1985. *Hebrews.* Waco: Word.

Farmer, W. R. 1964. *The Synoptic Problem.* New York: Macmillan.   1982. *Jesus and the Gospel.* Philadelphia: Fortress.   1983. *New Synoptic Studies.* Macon: Mercer.

Farrer, A. 1955. "On Dispensing with Q." In *Studies in the Gospels,* 55–86, ed. D. E. Nineham. Oxford: Blackwell.   1963. *A Rebirth of Images.* Boston: Beacon.

Fee, G. D. 1984. *1 and 2 Timothy, Titus.* San Francisco: Harper.   1988. *The First Epistle to the Corinthians.* Grand Rapids: Eerdmans.   1995. *Paul's Letter to the Philippians.* Grand Rapids: Eerdmans.

Fenton, J. C. 1963. *The Gospel of St. Matthew.* Baltimore: Penguin.   1970. *The Gospel according to John.* Oxford: Clarendon.

Ferguson, E. 1993. *Background of Early Christianity.* Grand Rapids: Eerdmans.

Finegan, J. 1962. "Corinth." In *IDB* 1:683–684.   1989. *Myth and Mystery: An Introduction to the Pagan Religions of the Biblical World.* Grand Rapids: Baker.

Fiorenza, E. S. 1975. "Wisdom Mythology and the Christological Hymns in the New Testament." In *Aspects of Wisdom in Judaism and Early Christianity,* 17–41, ed. R. L. Wilken. Notre Dame: University.   1983. *In Memory of Her: A Feminist Theological Reconstruction of Christian Origins.* New York: Crossroad.   1985. *The Book*

of Revelation. Philadelphia: Fortress.   Ed. 1994. *Searching the Scriptures: A Feminist Commentary.* New York: Crossroad.   1999. *Sharing Her Word: Feminist Biblical Interpretation in Context.* Boston: Beacon.

Fitzmyer, J. A. 1961. "Qumran and the Interpolated Paragraph in 2 Cor 6:14–7:1." In *CBQ* 23:271–280.   1967a. "Further Light on Melchizedek from Qumran Cave 11." In *JBL* 86:25–41.   1967b. *Pauline Theology: A Brief Sketch.* Englewood Cliffs: Prentice Hall.   1968a. "The First Epistle of Peter." In *JBC* 2:362–368.   1968b. "The Letter to the Galatians." In *JBC* 2:236–246.   1968c. "The Letter to the Philippians." In *JBC* 2:247–253.   1970. "The Priority of Mark and the 'Q' Source in Luke." In *Jesus and Man's Hope,* 1:131–170, ed. D. G. Buttrick and J. M. Bald. Pittsburgh: Pickwick.   1976. "The Matthean Divorce Texts and Some New Palestinian Evidence." In *TS* 37:197–226.   1978. "Crucifixion in Ancient Palestine, Qumran Literature, and the New Testament." In *CBQ* 40:493–513.   1980. "The Gnostic Gospels according to Pagels." In *America* 123:122–124.   1981, 1985. *The Gospel according to Luke.* 2 vols. Garden City, NY: Doubleday.   1989. *Luke the Theologian.* New York: Paulist.   1993. *Romans.* New York: Doubleday.   1997. *The Semitic Background of the New Testament.* Grand Rapids: Eerdmans.   1998. *The Acts of the Apostles.* New York: Doubleday.

Ford, J. M. 1975. *Revelation.* Garden City, NY: Doubleday.

Forestell, J. T. 1968. "The Letters to the Thessalonians." In *JBC* 2:227–235.

Fortna, R. T. 1970. *The Gospel of Signs.* Cambridge: University.   1988. *The Fourth Gospel and Its Predecessor.* Philadelphia: Fortress.

France, R. T. 1980. "Mark and the Teaching of Jesus." In *Gospel Perspectives* 1:101–136, ed. R. T. France and D. Wenham. Sheffield: JSOT.   And D. Wenham, eds. 1980, 1981. *Gospel Perspectives.* 2 vols. Sheffield: JSOT.   1998. *Matthew: Evangelist and Teacher.* Downers Grove, IL: InterVarsity.

Franklin, E. 1975. *Christ the Lord.* Philadelphia: Westminster.

Fredriksen, P. 1988. *From Jesus to Christ.* New Haven: Yale.

Freed, E. D. 1965. *Old Testament Quotations in the Gospel of John.* Leiden: Brill.   1967. "The Son of Man in the Fourth Gospel." In *JBL* 86:402–

409. 1987. "The Parable of the Judge and the Widow (Luke 18:1–8)." In *NTS* 33:38–60. 1992. "Jn 1, 19–27 in Light of Related Passages in John, the Synoptics, and Acts." In *The Four Gospels*, 1943–1961, ed. F. Van Segbroeck. Leuven: University. 1994. *The Apostle Paul*. Lanham, MD: University Press of America. Forthcoming. *The Stories of Jesus' Birth: A Critical Introduction*.

Fridrichsen, A. 1972. *The Problem of Miracle in Primitive Christianity*. Minneapolis: Augsburg.

Frye, R. M. 1970. "A Literary Perspective for the Criticism of the Gospels." In *Jesus and Man's Hope*, 2:193–221, ed. D. G. Miller and D. Y. Hadidan. Pittsburgh: Pickwick.

Fuller, R. H. 1963. *Interpreting the Miracles*. London: SCM. 1966. *A Critical Introduction to the New Testament*. London: Duckworth. 1971. *The Formation of the Resurrection Narratives*. New York: Macmillan. 1977. *The Letter to the Hebrews*. Philadelphia: Fortress.

Fung, R. Y. K. 1988. *The Epistle to the Galatians*. Grand Rapids: Eerdmans

Funk, R. W. 1966. *Language, Hermeneutic and Word of God*. New York: Harper & Row. 1967. "The Apostolic Parousia: Form and Significance." In *Christian History and Interpretation*, 249–268, ed. W. R. Farmer et al. Cambridge: University. Ed. 1974. "The Good Samaritan." In *Semeia* 2:1–193. Et al. 1982. *Parables and Presence*. Philadelphia: Fortress. Ed. 1985. *New Gospel Parallels*. 2 vols. Philadelphia: Fortress. 1993. *The Five Gospels: The Search for the Authentic Words of Jesus*. New York: Macmillan.

Furnish, V. P. 1968. *Theology and Ethics in Paul*. Nashville: Abingdon. 1979. *The Moral Teaching of Paul*. Nashville: Abingdon. 1984. *II Corinthians*. Garden City, NY: Doubleday. 1988. "Corinth in Paul's Time." In *BAR* 15:14–27.

Gager, J. G. 1975. *Kingdom and Community: The Social World of Early Christianity*. Englewood Cliffs: Prentice Hall.

Gamble, H. Y. 1985. *The New Testament Canon*. Philadelphia: Fortress.

Gardner-Smith, P. 1938. *Saint John and the Synoptic Gospels*. Cambridge: University.

Gaston, L. 1987. *Paul and the Torah*. Vancouver: University of British Columbia.

Gealy, F. D. 1955. "The First and Second Epistles to Timothy and The Epistle to Titus." In *IB* 11:343–551.

Gench, F. T. 1996. *Hebrews and James*. Louisville: W/K.

Georgi, D. 1976a. "Corinthians, First Letter to the." In *IDB*, Suppl. Vol., 180–183. 1976b. "Corinthians, Second Letter to the." In *IDB*, Suppl. Vol., 183–186. 1986. *The Opponents of Paul in Second Corinthians*. Philadelphia: Fortress.

Gerhardsson, B. 1964a. *Memory and Manuscript: Oral Tradition and Written Transmission in Rabbinic Judaism and Early Christianity*. Lund: Gleerup. 1964b. *Tradition and Transmission in Early Christianity*. Lund: Gleerup. 1979. *The Origins of Gospel Traditions*. Philadelphia: Fortress.

Giblin, C. H. 1967. *The Threat to Faith: An Exegetical and Theological Re-Examination of 2 Thessalonians*. Rome: Pontifical Biblical Institute. 1970. *In Hope of God's Glory. Pauline Theological Perspectives*. New York: Herder.

Gillespie, T. W. 1995. *The First Theologians: A Study in Early Christian Prophecy*. Grand Rapids: Eerdmans.

Glasson, T. F. 1965. *The Revelation of John*. Cambridge: University.

Godwin, J. 1981. *Mystery Religions in the Ancient World*. San Francisco: Harper.

Gooch, P. D. 1993. *Dangerous Food*. Waterloo, Ont.: Laurier Un.

Goodenough, E. R. 1986. *An Introduction to Philo Judaeus*. Lanham, MD: University Press of America.

Goodspeed, E. J. 1933. *The Meaning of Ephesians*. Chicago: University. 1937. *An Introduction to the New Testament*. Chicago: University. 1956. *The Key to Ephesians*. Chicago: University.

Goppelt, L. 1993. *A Commentary on 1 Peter*. Grand Rapids: Eerdmans.

Goulder, M. D. 1964. *Type and History in Acts*. London: SPCK. 1974. *Midrash and Lection in Matthew*. London: SPCK. 1989. *Luke A New Paradigm*. 2 Vols. Sheffield: JSOT. 1994. *A Tale of Two Missions*. London: SCM.

Graf, F. 1997. *Magic in the Ancient World*. Cambridge: Harvard.

Grant, F. C., ed. 1953. *Hellenistic Religions*. New York: Liberal Arts. Ed. 1957. *Ancient Roman Religion*. New York: Liberal Arts.

Grant, R. M. 1961. *Gnosticism*. New York: Harper. 1966. *Gnosticism and Early Christianity*. New York: Harper & Row.

Grassi, J. A. 1992. *The Secret Identity of the Beloved Disciple*. New York: Paulist.

Grayston, K. 1967. *The Letters of Paul to the Philippians and to the Thessalonians.* Cambridge: University.   1984. *The Johannine Epistles.* Grand Rapids: Eerdmans.

Green, J. B. 1997. *The Gospel of Luke.* Grand Rapids: Eerdmans.

Greenlee, J. H. 1995. *Introduction to New Testament Textual Criticism.* Peabody, MA: Hendrickson.

Guelich, R. A. 1982. *The Sermon on the Mount.* Waco: Word.

Gundry, R. H. 1982. *Matthew.* Grand Rapids: Eerdmans.

Gunther, J. J. 1973. *Paul's Opponents and Their Background.* Leiden: Brill.

Guthrie, D. 1957. *The Pastoral Epistles.* Grand Rapids: Eerdmans.   1981. *Galatians.* Grand Rapids: Eerdmans.   1983. *The Letter to the Hebrews.* Grand Rapids: Eerdmans.   1990. *New Testament Introduction.* Downers Grove, IL: InterVarsity.

Guettgemanns, E. 1979. *Candid Questions Concerning Gospel Form Criticism.* Pittsburgh: Pickwick.

Hadas, M. and M. Smith. 1965. *Heroes and Gods: Spiritual Biographies in Antiquity.* New York: Harper & Row.

Haenchen, E. 1971. *The Acts of the Apostles.* Philadelphia: Westminster.   1984. *A Commentary on the Gospel of John.* 2 vols. Philadelphia: Fortress.

Hagner, D. A. 1983. *Hebrews.* San Francisco: Harper.

Hagner, D. A. and M. J. Harris, eds. 1980. *Pauline Studies.* Grand Rapids: Eerdmans.

Hanson, A. T. 1982. *The Pastoral Epistles.* Grand Rapids: Eerdmans.

Hanson, K. C. and D. E. Oakman. 1998. *Palestine in the Time of Jesus: Social Structures and Social Conflicts.* Minneapolis: Fortress.

Hanson, R. P. C. 1967. *The Acts.* Oxford: Clarendon.

Harding, M. 1998. *Tradition and Rhetoric in the Pastoral Epistles.* New York: Lang.

Harnack, A. 1907. *Luke the Physician.* New York: Putnam.   1909. The *Acts of the Apostles.* New York: Putnam.

Harris, E. 1994. *Prologue and Gospel.* Sheffield: Academic.

Harrison, P. N. 1964. *Paulines and Pastorals.* London: Villiers.

Havener, I. 1987. *Q: The Sayings of Jesus.* Collegeville, MN: Liturgical.

Hawkin, D. J. 1996. *The Johannine World.* Albany: SUNY.

Hawkins, J. C. 1968. *Horae Synopticae.* Grand Rapids: Baker.

Hawthorne, G. F. 1975. "Christian Prophecy and the Sayings of Jesus: Evidence of and Criteria for." In *SBLSP* 2:105–129.

Hayes, J. H. and S. R. Mandell. 1998. *The Jewish People in Classical Antiquity.* Louisville: W/K.

Hedrick, C. W., ed. 1988. "The Historical Jesus and the Rejected Gospels." In *Semeia* 44.

Hedrick, C. W. and R. Hodgson, eds. 1986. *Nag Hammadi, Gnosticism, and Early Christianity.* Peabody, MA: Hendrickson.

Heil, J. P. 1979. "Significant Aspects of the Healing Miracles in Matthew." In *CBQ* 41:274–287.

Held, H. J. 1963. "Matthew as Interpreter of the Miracle Stories." In *Tradition and Interpretation in Matthew,* 165–299, ed. G. Bornkamm, G. Barth, and H. J. Held. Philadelphia: Westminster.

Hemer, C. J. 1986. *The Letters to the Seven Churches of Asia in Their Social Setting.* Sheffield: JSOT.

Hendrickx, H. 1987. *The Miracle Stories of the Synoptic Gospels.* London: Chapman.

Hendrix, H. L. 1984. *Thessalonicans Honor Romans.* Cambridge: Harvard.

Hengel, M. 1974. *Judaism and Christianity.* 2 vols. Philadelphia: Fortress.   1977. *Crucifixion.* Philadelphia: Fortress.   1980a. *Acts and the History of Earliest Christianity.* Philadelphia: Fortress.   1980b. *Jews, Greeks and Barbarians.* Philadelphia: Fortress.   1981a. *The Charismatic Leader and His Followers.* New York: Crossroad. 1981b. *Judaism and Hellenism.* Philadelphia: Fortress.   1983. *Between Jesus and Paul.* Philadelphia: Fortress.   1985. *Studies in the Gospel of Mark.* Philadelphia: Fortress.   1989. *The Johannine Question.* Philadelphia: Trinity.   And A.M. Schwemer. 1997a. *Paul Between Damascus and Antioch: The Unknown Years.* Louisville: W/K.   1997b. *The Zealots.* Edinburgh: Clark.

Hering, J. 1962. *The First Epistle of Saint Paul to the Corinthians.* London: Epworth.

Higgins, A. J. B. 1980. *The Son of Man in the Teaching of Jesus.* Cambridge: University.

Hill, D. 1979. *New Testament Prophecy.* Atlanta: Knox.

Hill, R. C. 1996. *Wisdom's Many Faces.* Collegeville, MN: Liturgical.

Hobart, W. K. 1954. *The Medical Language of St. Luke.* Grand Rapids: Baker. First published in 1882.

Hock, R. F. 1980. *The Social Context of Paul's Ministry.* Philadelphia: Fortress.

Hogan, A. H. B. 1996. *Gnostic Truth and Christian Heresy: A Study in the History of Gnosticism.* Peabody, MA: Hendrickson.

Holladay, C. R. 1977. *THEIOS ANER in Hellenistic-Judaism: A Critique of the Use of This Category in New Testament Christology.* Missoula, MT: Scholars. 1983–1996. *Fragments from Hellenistic Jewish Authors,* 4 vols. Atlanta: Scholars.

Holmberg, B. 1990. *Sociology and the New Testament.* Minneapolis: Fortress.

Hong, G. 1993. *The Law in Galatians.* Sheffield: JSOT.

Hooker, M. D. 1967. *The Son of Man in Mark.* London: SPCK. 1972. "On Using the Wrong Tool." In *Theology* 75:570–581. 1980. *A Preface to Paul.* New York: Oxford. 1982a. *Studying the New Testament.* Minneapolis: Augsburg. And S. G. Wilson, eds. 1982b. *Paul and Paulinism.* London: SPCK.

Horsley, G. H. R. et al., eds. 1981–1987. *New Documents Illustrating Early Christianity,* 4 vols. North Ryde, Australia: Macquarie University.

Horsley, R. A. 1984. "Popular Messianic Movements around the Time of Jesus." In *CBQ* 46:471–495. And J. S. Hanson. 1985. *Bandits, Prophets, and Messiahs: Popular Movements at the Time of Jesus.* San Francisco: Harper. 1987. *Jesus and the Spiral of Violence.* San Francisco: Harper. 1989a. *The Liberation of Christmas: The Infancy Narratives in Social Context.* New York: Crossroad. 1989b. *Sociology and the Jesus Movement.* New York: Crossroad. And N. A. Silberman. 1997. *The Message and the Kingdom; How Jesus and Paul Ignited a Revolution and Transformed the Ancient World.* New York: Grosset/Putnam. 1998. *1 Corinthians.* Nashville: Abingdon.

Hoskyns, E. C. 1947. *The Fourth Gospel.* Ed. F. N. Davey. London: Faber.

Houlden, J. L. 1973. *A Commentary on the Johannine Epistles.* New York: Harper & Row. 1977. *Paul's Letters from Prison.* Philadelphia: Westminster. 1987. *Backward into Light: The Passion and Resurrection of Jesus according to Matthew and Mark.* London: SCM.

Howard, G. 1979. *Paul: Crisis in Galatia.* Cambridge: University.

Huebner, H. 1984. *Law in Paul's Thought.* Edinburgh: Clark.

Hughes, F. W. 1989. *Early Christian Rhetoric and 2 Thessalonians.* Sheffield: JSOT.

Hughes, P. E. 1977. *A Commentary on the Epistle to the Hebrews.* Grand Rapids: Eerdmans. 1988. *Paul's Second Epistle to the Corinthians.* Grand Rapids: Eerdmans. 1990. *The Book of Revelation: A Commentary.* Grand Rapids: Eerdmans.

Hull, J. H. E. 1967. *The Holy Spirit in the Acts of the Apostles.* London: Lutterworth.

Hull, J. M. 1974. *Hellenistic Magic and the Synoptic Tradition.* London: SCM.

Hultgren, A. J. 1979. *Jesus and His Adversaries.* Minneapolis: Augsburg. 1985. *Paul's Gospel and Mission.* Philadelphia: Fortress.

Hume, C. R. 1997. *Reading Through Galatians.* London: SCM.

Hunt, L. D. 1990. *The Epistle to the Hebrews: Its Background of Thought.* Cambridge: University.

Hurd, J. C. 1983. *The Origin of l Corinthians.* Macon: Mercer.

Hurst, L. D. 1990. *The Epistle to the Hebrews: Its Background of Thought.* Cambridge: University.

Hurtado, L. W. 1983. *Mark.* San Francisco: Harper.

The Interpreter's Bible. 1951–1957. Ed. G. A. Buttrick et al. 12 vols. New York: Abingdon.

The Interpreter's Dictionary of the Bible. 1962. Ed. G. A. Buttrick et al. 4 vols. New York: Abingdon. *Supplementary Volume.* 1976. Ed. K. Crim et al. Nashville: Abingdon.

Jeremias, J. 1963. *The Parables of Jesus.* New York: Scribners. 1971. *New Testament Theology.* New York: Scribners. *The Jerome Biblical Commentary.* 1968. Ed. R. E. Brown et al. 2 vols. in one. Englewood Cliffs: Prentice Hall.

Jervell, J. 1972. *Luke and the People of God.* Minneapolis: Augsburg. 1977. "The Letter to Jerusalem." In *The Romans Debate,* 61–74, ed. K. P. Donfried. Minneapolis: Augsburg. 1984. *Jesus in the Gospel of John.* Minneapolis: Augsburg.

Jervis, L. A. and P. Richardson. 1994. *Studies on Corinthians, Romans and Galatians for Richard N. Longenecker.* Sheffield: Academic.

Jewett, R. 1986. *The Thessalonian Correspondence: Pauline Rhetoric and Millenarian Piety.* Philadelphia: Fortress.

Johnson, L. T. 1995. *The Real Jesus.* San Francisco: Harper. 1997. *Reading Romans.* New York: Crossroad.

Jonas, H. 1963. *The Gnostic Religion.* Boston: Beacon.

Judge, E. A. 1960–1961. "The Early Christians as a Scholastic Community." In *Journal of Religious History 1.* 1960. *The Social Pattern of Christian Groups in the First Century.* London: Tyndale.

Juel, D. 1977. *Messiah and Temple*. Missoula, MT: Scholars.   1983. *Luke-Acts*. Atlanta: Knox.

Juelicher, A. 1910. *Die Gleichnisreden Jesu*. (Eng. meaning, "the parables of Jesus"). Tuebingen: Mohr.

Kaehler, M. 1964. *The So-Called Historical Jesus and the Historic Biblical Christ*. Philadelphia: Fortress.

Kaesemann, E. 1964. *Essays on New Testament Themes*. London: SCM.   1968. *The Testament of Jesus: A Study of the Gospel of John in the Light of Chapter 17*. Philadelphia: Fortress.   1969a. *New Testament Questions of Today*. Philadelphia: Fortress.   1969b. *Perspectives on Paul*. Philadelphia: Fortress.   1980. *Commentary on Romans*. Ed. G. W. Bromiley. Grand Rapids: Eerdmans.   1984. *The Wandering People of God: An Investigation of the Letter to the Hebrews*. Minneapolis: Augsburg.

Karris, R. J. 1977. *Invitation to Luke*. Garden City, NY: Doubleday.   1979. "Missionary Communities: A New Paradigm for the Study of Luke-Acts." In *CBQ* 41:80–97.   1986. "Luke 23:47 and the Lucan View of Jesus' Death." In *JBL* 105:65–74.   1994. "Women and Discipleship in Luke." In *CBQ* 56:1–20.

Kaylor, R. D. 1988. *Paul's Covenant Community: Jew and Gentile in Romans*. Atlanta: Knox.

Kealy, S. P. 1982. *Mark's Gospel: A History of Its Interpretation*. New York: Paulist.

Keck, L. E. 1988. *Paul and His Letters*. Philadelphia: Fortress.

Kee, H. C. 1977a. *Community of the New Age: Studies in Mark's Gospel*. Philadelphia: Westminster.   1977b. *Jesus in History*. New York: Harcourt Brace Jovanovich.   1980. *Christian Origins in Sociological Perspective*. Philadelphia: Westminster.   1983. *Miracle in the Early Christian World*. New Haven: Yale.   1986. *Medicine, Miracle, and Magic in New Testament Times*. Cambridge: University.   1989. *Knowing the Truth: A Sociological Approach to New Testament Interpretation*. Minneapolis: Fortress.   1990. "The Transformation of the Synagogue after 70 CE: Its Import for Early Christianity." In *NTS* 36:1–24.

Keener, C. S. 1992. *Paul, Women and Wives*. Peabody, MA: Hendrickson.   1996. *3 Crucial Questions about the Holy Spirit*. Grand Rapids: Baker.   1997a. *Matthew*. Downers Grove, IL: InterVarsity.   1997b. *The Spirit in the Gospels and Acts*. Peabody, MA: Hendrickson.

Kelber, W. 1974. *The Kingdom in Mark*. Philadelphia: Fortress.   Ed. 1976. *The Passion in Mark*. Philadelphia: Fortress.   1979. *Mark's Story of Jesus*. Philadelphia: Fortress.   1983. *The Oral and the Written Gospel*. Philadelphia: Fortress.

Keller, E. and M. 1969. *Miracles in Dispute*. Philadelphia: Fortress.

Kelly, J. N. D. 1963. *A Commentary on the Pastoral Epistles*. New York: Harper & Row.   1969. *A Commentary on the Epistles of Peter and Jude*. New York: Harper & Row.

Kennedy, G. A. 1984. *New Testament Interpretation Through Rhetorical Criticism*. Chapel Hill: University of North Carolina.

Kim, S. 1982. *The Origin of Paul's Gospel*. Grand Rapids: Eerdmans.   1985. *"The Son of Man" as the Son of God*. Grand Rapids: Eerdmans.

Kingsbury, J. D. 1969. *The Parables of Jesus in Matthew 13*. London: SPCK.   1975. *Matthew: Structure, Christology, Kingdom*. Philadelphia: Fortress.   1977. *Matthew*. Philadelphia: Fortress. 1978. "Observations on the 'Miracle Chapters' of Matthew 8–9." In *CBQ* 40:559–573.   1981. *Jesus Christ in Matthew, Mark, and Luke*. Philadelphia: Fortress.   1983. *The Christology of Mark's Gospel*. Philadelphia: Fortress.   1986. "The Parable of the Wicked Husbandmen and the Secret of Jesus' Divine Sonship in Matthew: Some Literary-Critical Observations." In *JBL* 105:643–655.   1988. *Matthew As Story*. Philadelphia: Fortress.   1989. *Conflict in Mark*. Minneapolis: Fortress.   Ed. 1997. *Gospel Interpretation: Narrative-Critical and Social-Scientific Approaches*. Harrisburg, PA: Trinity.

Kirk, A. 1994. "Examining Priorities: Another Look at the *Gospel of Peter's* Relationship to the New Testament Gospels." In *NTS* 40: 572–595.

Kissinger, W. S. 1979. *The Parables of Jesus: A History of Interpretation and Bibliography*. Metuchen: Scarecrow.

Kistemaker, S. J. 1993. *Exposition of the First Epistle to the Corinthians*. Grand Rapids: Baker.   1997. *Exposition of the Second Epistle to the Corinthians*. Grand Rapids: Baker.

Klein, G. 1977. "Paul's Purpose in Writing the Epistle to the Romans." In *The Romans Debate*, 32–49, ed. K. P. Donfried. Minneapolis: Augsburg.

Kloppenborg, J. S. 1987. *The Formation of Q*. Philadelphia: Fortress.   And L. E. Vaage, eds. 1992. *Early Christianity, Q and Jesus*. In *Semeia* 55. Atlanta: Scholars.

Knight, G. W. 1992. *The Pastoral Epistles.* Grand Rapids: Eerdmans.

Knight, J. 1995. *2 Peter and Jude.* Sheffield: Academic. 1998. *Luke's Gospel.* New York: Routledge.

Knox, J. 1950. *Chapters in a Life of Paul.* Nashville: Abingdon. 1959. *Philemon among the Letters of Paul.* London: Collins. 1980. "Acts and the Pauline Letter Corpus." In *Studies in Luke-Acts,* 279–287, ed. L. E. Keck and J. L. Martyn. Philadelphia: Fortress.

Knox, W. L. 1939. *St. Paul and the Church of the Gentiles.* Cambridge: University. 1944. *Some Hellenistic Elements in Primitive Christianity.* London: Oxford.

Koester, C. R. 1995. *Symbolism in the Fourth Gospel.* Minneapolis: Fortress.

Koester, H. 1976. "Philippians, Letter to the." In *IDB,* Suppl. Vol., 665–666. 1982. *Introduction to the New Testament.* 2 vols. Philadelphia: Fortress. 1983. "History and Development of Mark's Gospel (From Mark to Secret Mark and 'Canonical' Mark)." In *Colloquy on New Testament Studies,* 35–57, ed. B. Corley. Macon: Mercer. 1986. "Gnostic Sayings and Controversy Traditions in John 8:12–59." In *Nag Hammadi, Gnostics, and Early Christianity,* 97–110, ed. C. W. Hedrick and R. Hodgson. Peabody, MA: Hendrickson. 1989. "From the Kerygma-Gospel to Written Gospels." In *NTS* 35:361–381. 1995. *Ephesus: Metropolis of Asia.* Valley Forge: Trinity.

Kraemer, R. S. 1988. *Maenads, Martyrs, Matrons, Monastics.* Philadelphia: Fortress.

Kraybill, J. N. 1996. *Imperial Cult and Commerce in John's Apocalypse.* Sheffield: Academic.

Kreitzer, L. 1997. *The Epistle to the Ephesians.* London: Epworth.

Krodel, G. 1977. *The First Letter of Peter.* Philadelphia: Fortress. 1981. *Acts.* Philadelphia: Fortress. 1989. *Revelation.* Minneapolis: Fortress.

Kroeger, C. C. et al., eds. 1995. *Study Bible for Women: The New Testament.* Grand Rapids: Baker.

Kuemmel, W. G. 1961. *Promise and Fulfilment: The Eschatological Message of Jesus.* London: SCM. 1975. *Introduction to the New Testament.* Nashville: Abingdon.

Kugelman, R. 1968. "The First Letter to the Corinthians." In *JBC* 2:234–275.

Kurz, W. S. 1980. "Hellenistic Rhetoric in the Christological Proof of Luke-Acts." In *CBQ* 42:171–195.

Kysar, R. 1975. *The Fourth Evangelist and His Gospel.* Minneapolis: Augsburg. 1983. "The Gospel of John in Current Research." In *RSR* 9:314–323. 1984. *John's Story of Jesus.* Philadelphia: Fortress. 1986a. *John.* Minneapolis: Augsburg. 1986b. *I, II, III John.* Minneapolis: Augsburg. 1993. *John, the Maverick Gospel.* Louisville: W/K.

Laato, T. 1995. *Paul and Judaism: An Anthropological Approach.* Atlanta: Scholars.

Ladd, G. E. 1967. *The New Testament and Criticism.* Grand Rapids: Eerdmans. 1974. *A Theology of the New Testament.* Grand Rapids: Eerdmans.

Lake, K. 1933. "The Conversion of Paul and the Events Immediately Following It." In *The Beginnings of Christianity,* 5:188–195, ed. F. J. F. Jackson and K. Lake. 5 vols. London: Macmillan.

Lambrecht, J. 1981. *Once More Astonished: The Parables of Jesus.* New York: Crossroad.

Lane, W. L. 1991. *Hebrews.* 2 vols. Waco/Dallas: Word.

LaPiana, G. 1927. "Foreign Groups in Rome during the First Centuries of the Empire." In *HTR* 20:183–403.

Lapide, P. and P. Stuhlmacher. 1984. *Paul: Rabbi and Apostle.* Minneapolis: Augsburg.

LaPorte, J. 1982. *The Role of Women in Early Christianity.* New York: Mellen.

LaSor, W. S. 1972. *The Dead Sea Scrolls and the New Testament.* Grand Rapids: Eerdmans.

Law, R. 1968. *The Tests of Life: A Study of the First Epistle of St. John.* Grand Rapids: Baker.

Laws, S. 1980. *A Commentary on the Epistle of James.* San Francisco: Harper.

Leahy, T. W. 1968a. "The Epistle of James." In *JBC* 2:369–377. 1968b. "The Epistle of Jude." In *JBC* 2:378–380. 1968c. "The Second Epistle of Peter." In *JBC* 2:494–498.

Leaney, A. R. C. 1967. *The Letters of Peter and Jude.* Cambridge: University. 1984. *The Jewish and Christian World, 200 BC–AD 70.* Cambridge: University.

Lee, D. A. 1994. *The Symbolic Narratives of the Fourth Gospel.* Sheffield: JSOT.

Légasse, S. 1997. *The Trial of Jesus.* London: SCM.

Lentz, J. C. 1993. *Luke's Portrait of Paul.* Cambridge: University.

Liefeld, W. L. 1996. *Ephesians.* Downers Grove, IL: InterVarsity.

Lightfoot, J. B. 1974. *The Epistle of St. Paul to the Galatians.* Grand Rapids: Zondervan.

Lightfoot, R. H. 1934. *History and Interpretation in the Gospels*. New York: Harper.

Lincoln, A. T. 1990. *Ephesians*. Waco: Word.

Lindars, B. 1972. *The Gospel of John*. London: Oliphants.   1983. *Jesus Son of Man*. London: SPCK.

Linnemann, E. 1966. *Jesus of the Parables*. New York: Harper & Row.

Litfin, D. 1994. *St. Paul's Theology of Proclamation*. Cambridge: University.   1995. *St. Paul's Theology of Rhetorical Style*. Cambridge: University.

Lock, W. 1924. *The Pastoral Epistles*. New York: Scribners.

Logan, A. H. B. and A. J. Widderburn, eds. 1983. *The New Testament Gnosis*. Edinburgh: Clark. 1996. *Gnostic Truth and Christian Heresy*. Edinburgh: Clark.

Lohse, E. 1971. *Colossians and Philemon*. Philadelphia: Fortress.

Long, A. A. 1986. *Hellenistic Philosophy*. London: Duckworth.

Loos, H. V. D. 1968. *The Miracles of Jesus*. Leiden: Brill.

Luedemann, G. 1984. *Paul*. Philadelphia: Fortress. 1988. "Acts of the Apostles as a Historical Source." In *The Social World of Formative Christianity and Judaism*, 109–125, ed. J. Neusner, et al. Philadelphia: Fortress.   1989. *Early Christianity according to the Traditions in Acts*. Minneapolis: Fortress.   1994. *The Resurrection of Jesus*. Minneapolis: Fortress. 1999. *The Great Deception. And What Jesus Really Said and Did*. London: SCM.

Luehrmann, D. 1992. *Galatians: A Continental Commentary*. Minneapolis: Fortress.

Lull, D. J. 1980. *The Spirit in Galatia*. Chico: Scholars.

McArthur, H. K., ed. 1969. *In Search of the Historical Jesus*. New York: Scribners.   1973. "Son of Mary." In *NovT* 15:38–58.

Maccoby, H. 1991. *Paul and Hellenism*. London: SCM.

MacDonald, D. R. 1983. *The Legend and the Apostle*. Philadelphia: Westminster.

McDonald, L. M. 1988. *The Formation of the Christian Biblical Canon*. Nashville: Abingdon.

MacDonald, M. Y. 1989. *The Pauline Churches: A Socio-historical Study of Institutionalization in the Pauline and Deutero-Pauline Writings*. New York: Cambridge.

Macgregor, G. H. C. 1962. "Acts." In *IB* 9:3–352.

McHaffie, B. 1986. *Her Story: Women in Christian Tradition*. Philadelphia: Fortress.

Machen, J. 1932. *The Virgin Birth of Christ*. New York: Harper.

Mack, B. L. 1988. *A Myth of Innocence: Mark and Christian Origins*. Philadelphia: Fortress.

Mackay, B. S. 1961. "Further Thoughts on Philippians." In *NTS* 7:161–170.

McKenzie, J. L. 1968. "The Gospel according to Matthew." In *JBC* 2:62–114.

McKnight, E. V. 1969. *What Is Form Criticism?* Philadelphia: Fortress.

MacMullen, R. 1974. *Roman Social Relations*. New Haven: Yale.   1981. *Paganism in the Roman Empire*. New Haven: Yale.

McNeile, A. H. 1952. *The Gospel according to Matthew*. London: Macmillan.

McNicol, A. J. 1987. "The Two Gospel Hypothesis Under Scrutiny: A Response to C. M. Tuckett's Analysis of Recent Neo-Griesbachian Gospel Criticism." In *Perkins Journal* 40:5–13.

MacRae, G. W. 1970. "The Ego-Proclamation in Gnostic Sources." In *The Trial of Jesus*, 122–134, ed. E. Bammel. Naperville, IL: Allenson.   1972. Review of *Gnosticism in Corinth*, by W. Schmithals. In *Interpretation* 26:489–491. 1978. *Invitation to John*. Garden City, NY: Doubleday.   1986. "Gnosticism and the Church of John's Gospel." In *Nag Hammadi and Early Christianity*, 89–96, ed. C. W. Hedrick and R. Hodgson. Peabody, MA: Hendrickson.

Maddox, R. 1982. *The Purpose of Luke-Acts*. Edinburgh: Clark.

Maier, G. 1977. *The End of the Historical-Critical Method*. St. Louis: Concordia.

Malbon, E. S. 1986. *Narrative Space and Mythic Meaning in Mark*. San Francisco: Harper.   And E. V. McKnight, eds. 1994. *The New Literary Criticism and the New Testament*. Sheffield: JSOT.

Malherbe, A. J. 1968. "The Beasts at Ephesus." In *JBL* 87:71–80.   1983. *Social Aspects of Early Christianity*. Philadelphia: Fortress.   1987. *Paul and the Thessalonians*. Philadelphia: Fortress. 1989. *Paul and the Popular Philosophers*. Minneapolis: Fortress.

Malina, B. J. 1992. *Social Science Commentary on the Synoptic Gospels*. Minneapolis: Fortress.   1993. *Windows on the World of Jesus*. Louisville: W/K.

1995. *On the Genre and Message of Revelation.* Peabody, MA: Hendrickson. 1996. *The Social World of Jesus and the Gospels.* London: Routledge. And R. L. Rohrbaugh. 1998. *Social Science Commentary on the Gospel of John.* Minneapolis: Fortress.

Mally, E. J. 1968. "The Gospel According to Mark." In *JBC* 2:21–61.

Maly, E. H. 1983. *Romans.* Wilmington: Glazier.

Mann, C. S. 1986. *Mark.* Garden City, NY: Doubleday.

Manson, T. W. 1945. *The Teaching of Jesus.* Cambridge: University.

Manson, W. 1930. *The Gospel of Luke.* New York: Harper. 1946. *Jesus the Messiah.* Philadelphia: Westminster.

Marrou, H. I. 1956. *History of Education in Antiquity.* London: Sheed and Ward.

Marrow, S. B. 1986. *Paul: His Letters and His Theology.* New York: Paulist. 1995. *The Gospel of John.* New York: Paulist.

Marsh, J. 1968. *The Gospel of St. John.* Baltimore: Penguin.

Marshall, I. H. 1971. *Luke: Historian and Theologian.* Grand Rapids: Zondervan. 1978a. *The Epistles of John.* Grand Rapids: Eerdmans. 1978b. *The Gospel of Luke.* Grand Rapids: Eerdmans. 1980. *The Acts of the Apostles.* Grand Rapids: Eerdmans. 1983. *1 and 2 Thessalonians.* Grand Rapids: Eerdmans.

Martin, L. H. 1987. *Hellenistic Religions.* New York: Oxford.

Martin, R. A. 1982. *James, I–II Peter/Jude.* Minneapolis: Augsburg.

Martin, R. P. 1968. "An Epistle in Search of a Life-Setting." In *Expository Times.* 79:297–302. 1976a. *Carmen Christi: Philippians ii.5–11 in Recent Interpretation and in the Setting of Early Christian Worship.* Cambridge: University. 1976b. *Mark: Evangelist and Theologian.* Grand Rapids: Zondervan. 1976c. *Philippians.* Grand Rapids: Eerdmans. 1981. *Colossians and Philemon.* Grand Rapids: Eerdmans. 1988. *James.* Waco: Word. 1994. *1 Peter.* Cambridge: University.

Martin, T. W. 1996. *By Philosophy and Empty Deceit: Colossians as Response to a Cynic Critique.* Sheffield: Academic.

Martyn, J. L. 1978. *The Gospel of John in Christian History.* New York: Paulist. 1979. *History and Theology in the Fourth Gospel.* Nashville: Abingdon. 1997. *Galatians.* New York: Doubleday.

Marxsen, W. 1968. *Introduction to the New Testament.* Philadelphia: Fortress. 1969. *Mark the Evangelist.* Nashville: Abingdon. 1970. *The Resurrection of Jesus of Nazareth.* Philadelphia: Fortress.

Mattingly, H. M. 1959. *Roman Imperial Civilization.* Garden City, NY: Doubleday.

Meeks, W. A. 1967. *The Prophet-King: Moses Traditions and the Johannine Christology.* Leiden: Brill. Ed. 1972. *The Writings of St. Paul.* New York: Norton. 1974. "The Image of the Androgyne: Some Uses of a Symbol in Earliest Christianity." In *History of Religions* 13:165–208. 1983. *The First Urban Christians: The Social World of the Apostle Paul.* New Haven: Yale. 1986. *The Moral World of the First Christians.* Philadelphia: Westminster. 1993. *The Origins of Christian Morality.* New Haven: Yale.

Meier, J. P. 1979. *The Vision of Matthew.* New York: Paulist. 1983. *Matthew.* Wilmington: Glazier. 1991. *A Marginal Jew. Rethinking the Historical Jesus.* Vol. 1: *The Roots of the Problem and the Person.* New York: Doubleday. 1994. Vol. 2: *Mentor, Message, and Miracles.* New York: Doubleday. 1996. "Dividing Lines on Jesus Research Today." In *Interpretation* 50:355–372.

Menken, M. J. J. 1994. *2 Thessalonians.* New York: Routledge. 1996. *Old Testament Quotations in the Fourth Gospel.* Kampen: Kok Pharos.

Menzies, R. P. 1991. *The Development of Early Christian Pneumatology, with Special Reference to Luke-Acts.* Sheffield: JSOT.

Metzger, B. M. 1993. *Breaking the Code.* Nashville: Abingdon. 1994. *A Textual Commentary on the Greek New Testament.* Stuttgart: United Bible Societies. 1997. *The Canon of the New Testament: Its Origin, Development, and Significance.* New York: Oxford.

Meyer, B. F. 1994. *Reality and Illusion in New Testament Scholarship.* Collegeville, MN: Liturgical.

Meyer, M. W., ed. 1987. *The Ancient Mysteries: A Sourcebook.* San Francisco: Harper.

Michaels, J. R. 1976. "Christian Prophecy and Matthew 23:8–12: A Test Exegesis." In *SBLSP* 305–310. 1984. *John.* San Francisco: Harper. 1989. *John.* Peabody, MA: Hendrickson. 1997. *Revelation.* Downers Grove, IL: InterVarsity.

Miethe, T. L., ed. 1987. *Did Jesus Rise from the Dead?* San Francisco: Harper.

Miller, D. G. and D. Y. Hadidian, eds. 1971. *Jesus and Man's Hope II*. Pittsburgh: Pickwick.

Miller, J. D. 1997. *The Pastoral Letters as Composite Documents*. New York: Cambridge.

Minear, P. S. 1971. *The Obedience of Faith: The Purpose of Paul in the Epistle to the Romans*. London: SCM.

Mitton, C. L. 1951. *The Epistle to the Ephesians*. Oxford: Clarendon.   1955. *The Formation of the Pauline Corpus*. London: Epworth.   1973. *Ephesians*. Grand Rapids: Eerdmans.

Moessner, D. P. 1988. "And Once Again, What Sort of 'Essence?': A Response to Charles Talbert." In *Semeia* 43:75–84.

Moffatt, J. 1918. *An Introduction to the Literature of the New Testament*. Edinburgh: Clark.   1924. *The Epistle to the Hebrews*. New York: Scribners. 1928. *The General Epistles James, Peter, and Judas*. London: Hodder and Stoughton.   1938. *The First Epistle of Paul to the Corinthians*. New York: Harper.

Moloney, F. J. 1978. *The Johannine Son of Man*. Rome: Salesianum.

Montefiore, H. W. 1979. *A Commentary on the Epistle to the Hebrews*. London: Black.

Moore, C. A. 1977. *Daniel, Esther, and Jeremiah: The Additions*. Garden City, NY: Doubleday.

Morgan, R. 1993. *Romans*. Sheffield: Academic.

Morris, L. 1969. *Studies in the Fourth Gospel*. Grand Rapids: Eerdmans.   1970. "The Theme of Romans." In *Apostolic History and the Gospel*, 249–263, ed. W. W. Gasque and R. P. Martin. Grand Rapids: Eerdmans.   1971. *The Gospel according to John*. Grand Rapids: Eerdmans. 1988. *The Epistle to the Romans*. Grand Rapids: Eerdmans.   1989. *Jesus Is the Christ: Studies in the Theology of John*. Grand Rapids: Eerdmans.

Moule, C. F. D. 1958. *The Epistles of Paul the Apostle to the Colossians and to Philemon*. Cambridge: University.   1965a. *The Gospel according to Mark*. Cambridge: University.   Ed. 1965b. *Miracles*. London: Mowbray.   1967. *The Phenomenon of the New Testament*. London: SCM.   Ed. 1968. *The Significance of the Message of the Resurrection for Faith in Jesus Christ*. London: SCM.

Mounce, R. H. 1995. *Romans*. Nashville: Broadman and Holman.   1998. *The Book of Revelation*. Grand Rapids: Eerdmans.

Moxnes, H. 1988. *The Economy of the Kingdom: Social Conflict and Economic Relations in Luke's Gospel*. Philadelphia: Fortress.   Ed. 1997. *Constructing Early Christian Families*. New York: Routledge.

Moyise, S. 1995. *The Old Testament in the Book of Revelation*. Sheffield: Academic.

Mullins, T. Y. 1980. "Topos as a New Testament Form." In *JBL* 99:541–547.

Munck, J. 1959. *Paul and the Salvation of Mankind*. Richmond: Knox.

Munro, W. 1982. "Women Disciples in Mark?" In *CBQ* 44:225–241.   1998. *Jesus Born of a Slave: The Social and Economic Origin of Jesus' Message*. New York: E. Mellen.

Murphy, F. J. 1991. *The Religious World of Jesus*. Nashville: Abingdon.

Murphy-O'Connor, J. 1982. *1 Corinthians*. Wilmington: Glazier.   1983. *St. Paul's Corinth*. Wilmington: Glazier.   1984. "The Corinth that Saint Paul Saw." In *BA* 47:147–159.   1996. *Paul: A Critical Life*. New York: Oxford.

Murray, J. 1987. *The Epistle to the Romans*. Grand Rapids: Eerdmans.

Nanos, M. D. 1996. *The Mystery of Romans: The Jewish Context of Paul's Letter*. Minneapolis: Fortress.

Neil, W. 1950. *The Epistle of Paul to the Thessalonians*. London: Hodder and Stoughton.   1981. *Acts*. Grand Rapids: Eerdmans.

Neirynck, F. 1974. *The Minor Agreements of Matthew and Luke Against Mark with a Cumulative List*. Leuven: University.   1977. "John and the Synoptics." In *L'Evangile de Jean*, 73–106, ed. M. de Jonge. Leuven: University.   1984. "John and the Synoptics: The Empty Tomb Stories." In *NTS* 30:161–187.

Neusner, J. et al. 1975. *Christianity, Judaism and Other Greco-Roman Cults*, 3 vols. Leiden: Brill.

Neusner, J. 1984. *Judaism in the Beginning of Christianity*. Philadelphia: Fortress.   With W. S. Green and E. Frerichs, eds. 1987. *Judaisms and Their Messiahs at the Turn of the Christian Era*. New York: Cambridge.   With P. Borgen et al. eds. 1988. *The Social World of Formative Christianity and Judaism*. Philadelphia: Fortress.

Neyrey, J. H. 1988. *An Ideology of Revolt: John's Christology in Social-Science Perspective*. Philadelphia: Fortress.   1993. *2 Peter, Jude*. New York: Doubleday.

Nilsson, M. P. 1961. *Greek Folk Religion*. New York: Harper.   1962. *Imperial Rome*. New York: Schocken.

Nineham, D. E., ed. 1955. *Studies in the Gospels*. Oxford: Blackwell.   1963. *The Gospel of St. Mark*. Baltimore: Penguin.

Nock, A. D. 1933a. *Conversion*. Oxford: Clarendon. 1933b. "The Vocabulary of the New Testament." In *JBL* 52:131–139.   1964. *Early Gentile Christianity and Its Hellenistic Background*. New York: Harper & Row.   1972. "'Son of God' in Pauline and Hellenistic Thought." In *Essays on Religion and the Ancient World*, 2:928–939. Ed. Z. Stewart. 2 vols. Cambridge: Harvard.

Nystrom, D. P. 1997. *James*. Grand Rapids: Zondervan.

O'Day, G. R. 1986. *Revelation in the Fourth Gospel: Narrative Mode and Theological Claim*. Philadelphia: Fortress.

Olsson, B. 1974. *Structure and Meaning of the Fourth Gospel*. Lund: Gleerup.

O'Neill, J. C. 1966. *The Puzzle of 1 John*. London: SPCK.

O'Rourke, J. J. 1968. "The Second Letter to the Corinthians." In *JBC* 2:276–290.

Orr, W. F. and J. A. Walther. 1976. *1 Corinthians*. Garden City, NY: Doubleday.

Osiek, C. A. 1984. *What Are They Saying about the Social Setting of the New Testament?* New York: Paulist.   1985. "The Feminist and the Bible: Hermeneutical Alternatives." In *Feminist Perspectives on Biblical Scholarship*, 93–105, ed. A. Y. Collins. Chico: Scholars.   1989. "The New Handmaid: The Bible and the Social Sciences." In *TS* 50:260–278.   1997. *Families in the New Testament World: Households and House Churches*. Louisville: W/K.

Ostenstad, G. H. 1998. *Patterns of Redemption in the Fourth Gospel*. United Kingdom: Mellen.

Overman, J. A. 1990. *Matthew's Gospel and Formative Judaism*. Minneapolis: Fortress.

Pagels, E. H. 1973. *The Johannine Gospel in Gnostic Exegesis*. Nashville: Abingdon.   1975. *The Gnostic Paul*. Philadelphia: Fortress.   1979. *The Gnostic Gospels*. New York: Random House.

Painter, J. 1980. *Reading John's Gospel Today*. Atlanta: Knox.   1993. *The Quest for the Messiah: The History, Literature and Theology of the Johannine Community*. Nashville: Abingdon.   1997. *Mark's Gospel: Worlds in Conflict*. New York: Routledge.

Parker, P. 1953. *The Gospel before Mark*. Chicago: University.   1981. "A Second Look at The Gospel before Mark." In *JBL* 100:389–413.

Parsons, M. C. and R. I. Pervo. 1993. *Rethinking the Unity of Luke and Acts*. Minneapolis: Fortress.

Patte, D. 1976a. Ed. *Semiology and Parables: Exploration of the Possibilities Offered by Structuralism for Exegesis*. Pittsburgh: Pickwick. 1976b. *What Is Structural Exegesis?* Philadelphia: Fortress.   1983. *Paul's Faith and the Power of the Gospel*. Philadelphia: Fortress.   1990. *Structural Exegesis for New Testament Critics*. Minneapolis: Fortress.   1996. *The Gospel According to Matthew: A Structural Commentary on Matthew's Faith*. Valley Forge: Trinity.

Patzia, A. G. 1984. *Colossians, Philemon, Ephesians*. San Francisco: Harper.

Peabody, D. B. 1983. "The Late Secondary Redaction of Mark's Gospel and the Griesbach Hypothesis: A Response to Helmut Koester." In *Colloquy on New Testament Studies*, 87–132, ed. B. C. Corley. Macon: Mercer.   1987. *Mark as Composer*. Macon: Mercer.

Perkins, P. 1978. *The Gospel according to St. John*. Chicago: Franciscan Herald.   1980. *The Gnostic Dialogue*. New York: Paulist.   1981. *Hearing the Parables of Jesus*. New York: Paulist.   1984. *Resurrection: New Testament Witness and Contemporary Reflection*. London: Chapman. 1995. *First and Second Peter, James, and Jude*. Louisville: W/K.   1997. *Ephesians*. Nashville: Abingdon.

Perrin, N. 1963. *The Kingdom of God in the Teaching of Jesus*. Philadelphia: Westminster.   1967. *Rediscovering the Teaching of Jesus*. New York: Harper & Row.   1969. *What Is Redaction Criticism?* Philadelphia: Fortress.   1974. *A Modern Pilgrimage in New Testament Christology*. Philadelphia: Fortress.   1976. *Jesus and the Language of the Kingdom*. Philadelphia: Fortress.

Pervo, R. I. 1990. *Luke's Story of Paul*. Minneapolis: Fortress.

Petersen, N. R. 1978. *Literary Criticism for New Testament Critics*. Philadelphia: Fortress.   Ed. 1980. *Perspectives on Mark's Gospel*. In *Semeia* 16. 1985. *Rediscovering Paul: Philemon and the Society of Paul's Narrative*. Philadelphia: Fortress. 1993. *The Gospel of John and the Sociology of Light: Language and Characterization in the Fourth Gospel*. Valley Forge: Trinity.

Pfeiffer, R. H. 1949. *History of New Testament Times with an Introduction to the Apocrypha*. New York: Harper.

Pfitzner, V. C. 1997. *Hebrews*. Nashville: Abingdon.

Pilch, J. J. 1998. "Appearances of the Risen Jesus in Cultural Context: Experiences of Alternate Reality." In *BTB* 28:52–60.

Plymale, S. F. 1991. *The Prayer Texts of Luke-Acts*. New York: Lang.

Pokorny, P. 1987. *The Genesis of Christology*. Edinburgh: Clark.   1991. *Colossians: A Commentary*. Peabody, MA: Hendrickson.

Pollard, T. E. 1970. *Johannine Christology and the Early Church*. Cambridge: University.

Polzin, R. M. 1977. *Biblical Structuralism: Method and Subjectivity in the Study of Ancient Texts*. Missoula, MT: Scholars.

Porter, S. E. and C. A. Evans, eds. 1995. *The Johannine Writings*. Sheffield: Academic. Eds. 1995. *The Pauline Writings*. Sheffield: Academic.

Porter, S. E. and T. H. Olbricht, eds. 1993. *Rhetoric and the New Testament*. Sheffield: JSOT.

Porter, S. E. and D. Tombs, eds. 1995. *Approaches to New Testament Study*. Sheffield: JSOT.

Powell, M. A. 1990. *What Is Narrative Criticism?* Minneapolis: Fortress.

Prior, M. P. 1989. *Paul the Letter-Writer and the Second Letter to Timothy*. Sheffield: JSOT.

Puskas, C. B. 1993. *The Letters of Paul: An Introduction*. Collegeville, MN: Liturgical.

Quast, K. 1994. *Reading the Corinthian Correspondence*. New York: Paulist.

Quinn, J. D. 1990. *Titus*. New York: Doubleday.

Rahtjen, B. D. 1960. "The Three Letters of Paul to the Philippians." In *NTS* 6:167–173.

Räisänen, H. 1986. *Paul and the Law*. Philadelphia: Fortress.

Rajak, T. 1984. *Josephus the Historian and His Society*. Philadelphia: Fortress.

Ramsay, W. M. 1900. *A Historical Commentary on St. Paul's Epistle to the Galatians*. London: Hodder and Stoughton.   1904. *The Letters to the Seven Churches*. Rev. ed. M. W. Wilson.   1994. Peabody, MA: Hendrickson.

Reese, J. M. 1979. *1 and 2 Thessalonians*. Wilmington: Glazier.

Reicke, B. 1964. *The Epistles of James, Peter, and Jude*. Garden City, NY: Doubleday.

Reid, B. E. 1996. *Choosing the Better Part? Women in the Gospel of Luke*. Collegeville, MN: Liturgical.

Rensberger, D. 1988. *Johannine Faith and Liberating Community*. Philadelphia: Westminster.   1997. *1 John, 2 John, 3 John*. Nashville: Abingdon.

Resseguie, J. L. 1998. *Revelation Unsealed: A Narrative Critical Approach to John's Apocalypse*. Leiden: Brill.

Reumann, J. 1991. *Variety and Unity in New Testament Thought*. Oxford: University.

Rhoads, D. 1976. *Israel in Revolution 6–74 C.E.* Philadelphia: Fortress.   Et al. 1999. *Mark as Story*. Philadelphia: Fortress.

Rice, D. G. and J. E. Stambaugh. 1979. *Sources for the Study of Greek Religion*. Missoula: Scholars.

Richardson, A. 1941. *The Miracle Stories of the Gospels*. London: SCM. Reprint 1991.

Ridderbos, H. 1975. *Paul: An Outline of His Theology*. Grand Rapids: Eerdmans.   1997. *The Gospel according to John*. Grand Rapids: Eerdmans.

Riesenfeld, H. 1970. *The Gospel Tradition*. Philadelphia: Fortress.

Ringgren, H. 1963. *The Faith of Qumran*. Philadelphia: Fortress.

Robbins, V. K. 1975. "The We-Passages in Acts and Ancient Sea Voyages." In *Biblical Research* 20:1–14.   1978. "By Land and by Sea." In *Perspectives on Luke-Acts*, 215–242, ed. C. H. Talbert. Danville, VA: ABPR.   1984. *Jesus the Teacher: A Socio-Rhetorical Interpretation of Mark*. Philadelphia: Fortress.

Robinson, J. A. T. 1976. *Redating the New Testament*. Philadelphia: Westminster.   1985. *The Priority of John*, ed. J. F. Coakley. London: SCM.

Robinson, J. M., ed. 1988. *The Nag Hammadi Library in English*. San Francisco: Harper.

Roetzel, C. J. 1985. *The World That Shaped the New Testament*. Atlanta: Knox.   1991. *The Letters of Paul*. Louisville: W/K.   1995. "Paul and the Law: Whence and Wither?" In *CRBS* 3:249–275.

Rohde, J. 1968. *Rediscovering the Teaching of the Evangelists*. London: SCM.

Roloff, J. 1993. *The Revelation of John*. Minneapolis: Fortress.

Rose, H. R. 1959. *Religion in Greece and Rome*. New York: Harper.

Rosenblatt, M. E. 1995. *Paul the Accused: Portrait in the Acts of the Apostles*. Collegeville, MN: Liturgical.

Rosner, B. S., ed. 1995. *Understanding Paul's Ethics; Twentieth-Century Approaches*. Grand Rapids: Eerdmans.

Rowell, H. T. 1962. *Rome in the Augustan Age.* Norman: University of Oklahoma.

Rudolph, K. 1983. *Gnosis.* Edinburgh: Clark.

Ruef, J. S. 1971. *Paul's First Letter to Corinth.* Baltimore: Penguin.

Ruether, R. and E. McLaughlin, eds. 1979. *Women of Spirit: Female Leadership in the Jewish and Christian Traditions.* New York: Simon and Schuster.

Ryan, R. 1985. "The Women from Galilee and Discipleship in Luke." In *BTB* 15:56–59.

Sabbe, M. 1977. "The Arrest of Jesus in Jn 18, 1–11 and Its Relation to the Synoptic Gospels." In *L'Evangile de Jean*, 203–234, ed. M. de Jonge. Leuven: University.

Saldarini, A. J. 1988. *Pharisees, Scribes and Sadducees in Palestinian Society.* Wilmington: Glazier.

Sanders, E. P. 1977. *Paul and Palestinian Judaism.* Philadelphia: Fortress. 1983. *Paul, the Law, and the Jewish People.* Philadelphia: Fortress. 1985. *Jesus and Judaism.* Philadelphia: Fortress. 1992. *Judaism: Practice and Belief 63 BCE–66 CE.* London: SCM.

Sanders, J. A. 1972. *Torah and Canon.* Philadelphia: Fortress. 1984. *Canon and Community: A Guide to Canonical Criticism.* Philadelphia: Fortress.

Sanders, J. N. and B. A. Mastin. 1968. *A Commentary on the Gospel according to St. John.* New York: Harper & Row.

Sanders, J. T. 1971. *The New Testament Christological Hymns.* Cambridge: University. 1975. *Ethics in the New Testament.* Philadelphia: Fortress. 1987. *The Jews in Luke-Acts.* Philadelphia: Fortress.

Sandmel, S. 1958. *The Genius of Paul.* New York: Farrar, Straus & Cudahy. 1967. *Herod: Profile of a Tyrant.* Philadelphia: Lippincott. 1969. *The First Christian Century in Judaism and Christianity.* New York: Oxford. 1979. *Philo of Alexandria.* New York: Oxford.

Savage, T. B. 1996. *Power Through Weakness: Paul's Understanding of the Christian Ministry in 2 Corinthians.* Cambridge: University.

Schaberg, J. 1987. *The Illegitimacy of Jesus.* San Francisco: Harper. 1997. "Feminist Interpretations of the Infancy Narrative of Matthew." In *Journal of Feminist Studies in Religion* 13:35–62.

Schiffman, L. H. 1975. *The Halakkah at Qumran.* Leiden: Brill.

Schmeichel, W. 1976. "Christian Prophecy in Lukan Thought: Luke 4:16–30." In *SBLSP* 293–304.

Schmidt, K. L. 1919. *Der Rahmen der Geschichte Jesu.* (Eng. meaning, "the framework of the story of Jesus"). Berlin: Trowitsch & Sohn.

Schmithals, W. 1971. *Gnosticism in Corinth.* Nashville: Abingdon. 1972. *Paul and the Gnostics.* Nashville: Abingdon.

Schnackenburg, R. 1980–1982. *The Gospel according to St. John.* 3 vols. New York: Seabury. 1991. *The Epistle to the Ephesians.* Edinburgh: Clark. 1992. *The Johannine Epistles.* New York: Crossroad.

Schottroff, L. 1993. *Let the Oppressed Go Free: Feminist Perspectives on the New Testament.* Louisville: W/K. 1995. *Lydia's Impatient Sisters: A Feminist Social History of Early Christianity.* Louisville: W/K.

Schrage, W. 1988. *The Ethics of the New Testament.* Philadelphia: Fortress.

Schuerer, E. 1973–1987. *The History of the Jewish People in the Age of Jesus Christ (175 B.C.–A.D. 135).* 4 vols. Rev. and ed. G. Vermes et al. Edinburgh: Clark.

Schweitzer, A. 1945. *The Quest of the Historical Jesus.* London: Black.

Schweizer, E. 1975. *The Good News according to Matthew.* Atlanta: Knox. 1976. *The Good News according to Mark.* Atlanta: Knox. 1980. "Concerning the Speeches in Acts." In *Studies in Luke-Acts*, 208–216, ed. L. E. Keck and J. L. Martyn. Philadelphia: Fortress. 1982. *The Letter to the Colossians.* Minneapolis: Augsburg. 1984. *The Good News according to Luke.* Atlanta: Knox.

Scobie, C. H. H. 1979. "The Use of Source Material in the Speeches of Acts III and VII." In *NTS* 25:399–421.

Scott, B. B. 1989. *Hear Then the Parables.* Philadelphia: Fortress.

Scott, M. 1992. *Sophia and the Johannine Jesus.* Sheffield: JSOT.

Scroggs, R. 1980. "The Sociological Interpretation of the New Testament: The Present State of Research." In *NTS* 26:164–179.

Segal, A. F. 1986. *Rebecca's Children: Judaism and Christianity in the Roman World.* Cambridge: Harvard. 1990. *Paul the Convert.* New Haven: Yale.

Segovia, F. F. 1982. *Love Relationships in the Johannine Tradition.* Chico: Scholars.

Selby, D. J. 1962. *Toward the Understanding of St. Paul.* Englewood Cliffs: Prentice Hall.

Selwyn, E. G. 1969. *The First Epistle of St. Peter.* London: Macmillan.

Senior, D. P. 1977. *Invitation to Matthew.* Garden City, NY: Doubleday.   1980. *1 and 2 Peter.* Wilmington: Glazier.   1983. *What Are They Saying about Matthew?* New York: Paulist.   1984. *The Passion of Jesus in the Gospel of Mark.* Wilmington: Glazier.   1985. *The Passion of Jesus in the Gospel of Matthew.* Wilmington: Glazier.   1991. *The Passion of Jesus in the Gospel of John.* Wilmington: Glazier.

Setzer, C. 1997. "Excellent Women: Female Witness to the Resurrection." In *JBL* 116:259–272.

Shelton, J. 1988. *As the Romans Did: A Sourcebook in Roman Social History.* New York: Oxford.

Shuler, P. L. 1982. *A Genre for the Gospels.* Philadelphia: Fortress.

Sidebottom, E. M. 1982. *James, Jude, 2 Peter.* Grand Rapids: Eerdmans.

Sloyan, G. S. 1991. *What Are They Saying about John?* New York: Paulist.

Smalley, S. S. 1998. *John: Evangelist and Interpreter.* Downers Grove, IL: InterVarsity.

Smallwood, E. M. 1976. *The Jews Under Roman Rule.* Leiden: Brill.

Smiles, V. M. 1998. *The Gospel and Law in Galatia.* Collegeville, MN: Liturgical.

Smith, A. 1995. *Comfort One Another: Reconstructing the Rhetoric and Audience of 1 Thessalonians.* Louisville: W/K.

Smith, B. T. D. 1937. *The Parables of the Synoptic Gospels.* Cambridge: University.

Smith, C. R. 1994. "The Structure of the Book of Revelation in Light of Apocalyptic Literary Conventions." In *NovT* 36:373–393.

Smith, C. W. F. 1975. *The Jesus of the Parables.* Philadelphia: United Church.

Smith, D. M. 1965. *The Composition and Order of the Fourth Gospel.* New Haven: Yale.   1980. "John and the Synoptics: Some Dimensions of the Problem." In *NTS* 26:425–444.   1984. *Johannine Christianity: Essays on Its Setting, Sources, and Theology.* Columbia, SC: University of South Carolina.   1991. *First, Second, and Third John.* Louisville: Knox.   1992. *John among the Gospels: The Relationship in Twentieth-Century Research.* Minneapolis: Fortress. 1995a. *John.* Philadelphia: Fortress.   1995b. *The Theology of the Gospel of John.* New York: Cambridge.

Smith, M. 1973a. *Clement of Alexandria and a Secret Gospel of Mark.* Cambridge: Harvard.   1973b. *The Secret Gospel.* New York: Harper.   1978. *Jesus the Magician.* San Francisco: Harper.   1982. "Clement of Alexandria and Secret Mark: The Score at the End of the First Decade." In *HTR* 75:449–461.

Snyder, G. F. 1992. *First Corinthians.* Macon: Mercer.

Stagg, E. and F. 1978. *Women in the World of Jesus.* Philadelphia: Westminster.

Staley, J. L. 1988. *The Print's First Kiss: A Rhetorical Investigation of the Implied Reader in the Fourth Gospel.* Atlanta: Scholars.

Stambaugh, J. E. and D. L. Balch. 1986. *The New Testament in Its Social Environment.* Philadelphia: Westminster.

Stanton, G. N. 1983. Ed. *The Interpretation of Matthew.* Philadelphia: Fortress.   1989. *The Gospels and Jesus.* Macon: Mercer.   1992. *A Gospel for a New People: Studies in Matthew.* Edinburgh: Clark.   1995. *Gospel Truth?* Valley Forge: Trinity.

Stauffer, E. 1960. *Jesus and His Story.* New York: Knopf.

Stegemann, W. 1997. "Women in the Jesus Movement in Social-Scientific Perspective." In *Listening* 32:8–21.

Stein, R. H. 1980. "The 'Criteria' for Authenticity." In *Gospel Perspectives,* 1:225–263, ed. R. T. France and D. Wenham. Sheffield: JSOT.   1981. *An Introduction to the Parables of Jesus.* Philadelphia: Westminster.

Stemberger, G. 1995. *Jewish Contemporaries of Jesus.* Minneapolis: Fortress.

Stendahl, K., ed. 1957. *The Scrolls and the New Testament.* New York: Harper.   1976. *Paul among Jews and Gentiles.* Philadelphia: Fortress.

Stepp, P. L. 1996. *The Believer's Participation in the Death of Christ.* Lewiston, NY: Mellen.

Stibbe, M. W. G. 1992. *John as Storyteller: Narrative Criticism and the Fourth Gospel.* Cambridge: University.   Ed. 1993. *The Gospel of John as Literature.* Leiden: Brill.

Stiefel, J. H. 1995. "Women Deacons in 1 Timothy. . . ." In *NTS* 41:442–457.

Stirewalt, M. L. 1977. "The Form and Function of the Greek Letter-Essay." In *The Romans Debate,* 175–206, ed. K. P. Donfried. Minneapolis: Augsburg.

Stoldt, H. 1980. *History and Criticism of the Marcan Hypothesis.* Macon: Mercer.

Stonehouse, N. B. 1963. *Origins of the Synoptic Gospels*. Grand Rapids: Eerdmans.

Strachan, R. H. 1935. *The Second Epistle of Paul to the Corinthians*. New York: Harper. 1943. *The Fourth Gospel*. London: SPCK.

Strauss, D. F. 1972. *The Life of Jesus Critically Examined*. Reprint ed. P. C. Hodgson. Philadelphia: Fortress.

Strecker, G. 1988. *The Sermon on the Mount*. Nashville: Abingdon. 1996. *The Johannine Letters*. Ed. H. Attridge. Minneapolis: Fortress.

Streeter, B. H. 1951. *The Four Gospels*. London: Macmillan.

Stuhlmacher, P. 1986. *Reconciliation, Law, and Righteousness*. Philadelphia: Fortress.

Stuhlmueller, C. 1968. "The Gospel According to Luke." In *JBC* 2:115–164.

Suggs, M. J. 1967. "'The Word is Near You': Romans 10:6–10 within the Purpose of the Letter." In *Christian History and Interpretation*, 289–312, ed. W. R. Farmer et al. Cambridge: University.

Sumney, J. L. 1990. *Identifying Paul's Opponents*. Sheffield: Academic.

Sweet, J. M. P. 1979. *Revelation*. Philadelphia: Westminster.

Synge, F. C. 1959. *St. Paul's Epistle to the Ephesians*. London: Macmillan.

Talbert, C. H. 1970. "The Redaction Critical Quest for Luke the Theologian." In *Jesus and Man's Hope*, 1:171–222, ed. D. G. Miller and D. Y. Hadidian. Pittsburgh: Pickwick. And E. V. McKnight. 1972. "Can the Griesbach Hypothesis Be Falsified?" In *JBL* 91:338–368. 1974. *Literary Patterns, Theological Themes, and the Genre of Luke-Acts*. Missoula, MT: Scholars. 1977. *What Is a Gospel? The Genre of the Canonical Gospels*. Philadelphia: Fortress. Ed. 1978. *Perspectives on Luke-Acts*. Danville, VA: ABPR. 1982. *Reading Luke: A Literary and Theological Commentary on the Third Gospel*. New York: Crossroad. Ed. 1984. *Luke-Acts*. New York: Crossroad. 1987. *Reading Corinthians*. New York: Crossroad. 1988. "Once Again: Gospel Genre." In *Semeia* 43:53–73. 1994a. *The Apocalypse*. Louisville: W/K. 1994b. *Reading John*. New York: Crossroad. 1997. *Reading Acts*. New York: Crossroad.

Tannehill, R. C. 1986. *The Narrative Unity of Luke-Acts*. Philadelphia: Fortress.

Tarn, W. and G. T. Griffith. 1952. *Hellenistic Civilization*. London: Arnold.

Taylor, V. 1957. *The Gospel according to St. Mark*. London: Macmillan. 1960. *The Formation of the Gospel Tradition*. London: Macmillan.

Tcherikover, V. 1966. *Hellenistic Civilization and the Jews*. Philadelphia: Jewish Publication Society.

Tcherikover, V. and A. Fuks et al., eds. 1957–1964. *Corpus Papyrorum Judaicarum*. 3 vols. Cambridge: Harvard.

Teeple, H. M. 1974. *The Literary Origin of the Gospel of John*. Evanston: Religion and Ethics Institute.

Telford, W., ed. 1985. *The Interpretation of Mark*. Philadelphia: Fortress.

Temple, S. 1975. *The Core of the Fourth Gospel*. London: Mowbray.

Terrien, S. 1985. *Till the Heart Sings: A Biblical Theology of Manhood and Womanhood*. Philadelphia: Fortress.

Tetlow, E. M. 1980. *Women and Ministry in the New Testament*. Lanham, MD: University Press of America.

Thackeray, H. S. 1967. *Josephus the Man and the Historian*. New York: KTAV.

Theissen, G. 1978. *Sociology of Early Palestinian Christianity*. Philadelphia: Fortress. 1982. *The Social Setting of Pauline Christianity*. Philadelphia: Fortress. 1987. *Psychological Aspects of Pauline Theology*. Philadelphia: Fortress. 1992. *Social Reality and the Early Christians*. Minneapolis: Fortress. And A. Merz. 1998. *The Historical Jesus: A Comprehensive Guide*. Minneapolis: Fortress.

Thielman, F. 1994. *Paul and the Law*. Downers Grove, IL: InterVarsity. 1995. *Philippians*. Grand Rapids: Zondervan.

Thompson, C. L. 1976. "Corinth." In *IDB*, Suppl. Vol., 179–180. 1988. "Hairstyles, Head-coverings, and St. Paul: Portraits from Roman Corinth." In *BA* 51:99–115.

Thompson, G. H. P. 1967. *The Letters of Paul to the Ephesians, to the Colossians, and to Philemon*. Cambridge: University.

Thompson, L. 1986. "A Sociological Analysis of Tribulation in the Apocalypse of John." In *Semeia* 36:147–174. 1997. *The Book of Revelation: Apocalypse and Empire*. New York: Oxford.

Thompson, M. M. 1988. *The Humanity of Jesus in the Fourth Gospel*. Philadelphia: Fortress.

Thrall, M. E. 1965. *The First and Second Letters of Paul to the Corinthians*. Cambridge: University.

Thurston, B. B. 1989. *The Widows: A Women's Ministry in the Early Church*. Minneapolis: Fortress.

Tidball, D. 1983. *An Introduction to the Sociology of the New Testament*. Exeter: Paternoster.

Tiede, D. L. 1972. *The Charismatic Figure as Miracle Worker*. Missoula, MT: University of Montana.   1980. *Prophecy and History in Luke-Acts*. Philadelphia: Fortress.   1988. *Luke*. Minneapolis: Augsburg.

Tinsley, E. J. 1965. *The Gospel according to Luke*. Cambridge: University.

Toedt, H. E. 1965. *The Son of Man in the Synoptic Tradition*. Philadelphia: Westminster.

Tolbert, M. A. 1979. *Perspectives on the Parables*. Philadelphia: Fortress.   1989. *Sowing the Gospel: Mark's World in Literary-Historical Perspective*. Minneapolis: Fortress.

Trocme, E. 1975. *The Formation of the Gospel according to Mark*. Philadelphia: Westminster.

Tuckett, C. M. 1983a. *The Revival of the Griesbach Hypothesis: An Analysis and Appraisal*. New York: Cambridge.   Ed. 1983b. *The Messianic Secret*. Philadelphia: Fortress.   Ed. 1984. *Synoptic Studies. The Ampleforth Conferences of 1982 and 1983*. Sheffield: JSOT.   1986. *Nag Hammadi and the Gospel Tradition*. Edinburgh: Clark. 1987. *Reading the New Testament: Methods of Interpretation*. Philadelphia: Fortress.

Turcan, R. 1996. *The Cults of the Roman Empire*. Oxford: Blackwell.

Tyson, J. B. 1986. *The Death of Jesus in Luke-Acts*. Columbia, SC: University of South Carolina. Ed. 1988. *Luke-Acts and the Jewish People*. Minneapolis: Augsburg.   1992. *Images of Judaism in Luke-Acts*. Columbia, SC: University of South Carolina.

Vanhoye, A. 1989. *Structure and Message of the Epistle to the Hebrews*. Ed. J. Swetnam. Rome: Pontifical Biblical Institute.

Veltman, F. 1978. "The Defense Speeches of Paul in Acts." In *Perspectives on Luke-Acts*, 243–256, ed. C. H. Talbert. Danville, VA: ABPR.

Vermes, G. 1973. *Jesus the Jew*. London: Collins. 1981. *The Dead Sea Scrolls: Qumran in Perspective*. Philadelphia: Fortress.   1983. *Jesus and the World of Judaism*. Philadelphia: Fortress. 1993. *The Religion of Jesus the Jew*. Minneapolis:

Fortress.   1994. *The Complete Dead Sea Scrolls in English*. New York: Lane/Penguin.

Verner, D. C. 1983. *The Household of God: The Social World of the Pastoral Epistles*. Chico: Scholars.

Veyne, P. 1988. *Did the Greeks Believe in Their Myths?* Chicago: University.

Via, D. O. 1967. *The Parables*. Philadelphia: Fortress. 1976. "The Parable of the Unjust Judge: A Metaphor of the Unrealized Self." In *Semiology and Parables*, 1–32, ed. D. Patte. Pittsburgh: Pickwick.   1985. *The Ethics of Mark's Gospel*. Philadelphia: Fortress.

Waetjen, H. C. 1989. *Recording of Power: A Sociopolitical Reading of Mark's Gospel*. Minneapolis: Fortress.

Walbank, F. W. 1982. *The Hellenistic World*. Cambridge, MA: Harvard.

Walker, W. O., ed. 1978. *The Relationships among the Gospels*. San Antonio: Trinity University.

Wall, P. W. 1997. *Community of the Wise: The Letter of James*. Valley Forge: Trinity.

Wallis, I. G. 1995. *The Faith of Jesus Christ in Early Christian Traditions*. New York: Cambridge.

Wansink, C. S. 1996. *Imprisonment for the Gospel*. Sheffield: Academic.

Watson, D. F. 1988. *Invention, Arrangement, and Style: Rhetorical Criticism of Jude and 2 Peter*. Atlanta: Scholars.

Watson, F. 1988. *Paul, Judaism and the Gentiles*. Cambridge: University.

Weed, D. W. 1970. *The Literary Devices in John's Gospel*. Basel: Reinhardt.

Weeden, T. J. 1971. *Mark—Traditions in Conflict*. Philadelphia: Fortress.

Wenham, D. 1989. *The Parables of Jesus*. Downers Grove, IL: InterVarsity.   1995. *Paul: Follower of Jesus or Founder of Christianity?* Grand Rapids: Eerdmans.   1997. "The Enigma of the Fourth Gospel: Another Look." In *Tyndale Bulletin* 48:149–178.

Wensinck, A. J. 1921. *Tree and Bud as Cosmological Symbols in Western Asia*. Amsterdam: Muller.

Westerholm, S. 1988. *Israel's Law and the Church's Faith: Paul and His Recent Interpreters*. Grand Rapids: Eerdmans.   1997. *Preface to the Study of Paul*. Grand Rapids: Eerdmans.

Westermann, C. 1990. *The Parables of Jesus in Light of the Old Testament*. Edinburgh: Clark.

Whitacre, R. A. 1982. *Johannine Polemic: The Role of Tradition and Theology*. Chico: Scholars.

White, J. L. 1972. *The Form and Structure of the Official Petition*. Missoula, MT: University of Montana.   1983. "Saint Paul and the Apostolic Letter." In *CBQ* 45:433–444.

White, L. M. and O. L. Yarbrough, eds. 1995. *The Social World of the First Christians*. Minneapolis: Fortress.

White, R. J. 1975. *Artemidorus, The Interpretation of Dreams—Oneirocritica Trans. and Commentary*. Park Ridge, NJ: Noyes.

Whiteley, D. H. E. 1964. *The Theology of St. Paul*. Philadelphia: Fortress.

Wilckens, U. 1978. *Resurrection*. Atlanta: Knox.

Wilder, A. N. 1950. *Eschatology and Ethics in the Teaching of Jesus*. New York: Harper.   1978. *Early Christian Rhetoric: The Language of the Gospel*. Cambridge: Harvard.   1982. *Jesus' Parables and the War of Myths*. Philadelphia: Fortress.

Willett, M. E. 1992. *Wisdom Christology and the Fourth Gospel*. San Francisco: Mellen.

Williams, C. S. C. 1957. *A Commentary on the Acts of the Apostles*. New York: Harper.

Williams, D. J. 1985. *Acts*. San Francisco: Harper.

Williams, J. F. 1994. *Other Followers of Jesus*. Sheffield: JSOT.

Williams, R. R. 1965. *The Letters of John and James*. Cambridge: University.

Williams, S. K. 1987. "Justification and the Spirit in Galatians." In *JSNT* 29:91–100.   1997. *Galatians*. Nashville: Abingdon.

Williamson, R. 1970. *Philo and the Epistle to the Hebrews*. Leiden: Brill.

Willis, W. L. 1985. *Idol Meat in Corinth*. Chico: Scholars.

Wilson, A. N. 1997. *Paul: The Mind of the Apostle*. New York: Norton.

Wilson, I. 1997. *Jesus: The Evidence, the Latest Research and Discoveries*. San Francisco: Harper Collins.

Wilson, R. M. 1958. *The Gnostic Problem*. London: Mowbray.   1968a. *Gnosis and the New Testament*. Philadelphia: Fortress.   1968b. "Gnostics in Galatia." In *Studia Evangelica* 4:358–364. Berlin: Akademic.

Wilson, S. G. 1979. *Luke and the Pastoral Epistles*. London: SPCK.

Wilson, W. R. 1970. *The Execution of Jesus*. New York: Scribners.

Winter, P. 1974. *On the Trial of Jesus,* ed. T. A. Burkill and G. Vermes. New York: De Gruyter.

Wire, A. C. 1990. *The Corinthian Women Prophets*. Minneapolis: Fortress.

Witherington, B. 1985. *Women in the Ministry of Jesus*. Cambridge: University.   1988. *Women in the Earliest Churches*. Cambridge: University.   1994. *Jesus the Sage: The Pilgrimage of Wisdom*. Minneapolis: Fortress.   1995a. *Conflict and Community in Corinth: A Socio-Rhetorical Commentary on 1 and 2 Corinthians*. Grand Rapids: Eerdmans.   1995b. *The Jesus Quest: The Third Search for the Jew of Nazareth*. Downers Grove, IL: InterVarsity.   1998a. *Grace in Galatia: A Commentary on St Paul's Letter to the Galatians*. Grand Rapids: Eerdmans.   1998b. *The Paul Quest: The Renewed Search for the Jew of Tarsus*. Downers Grove, IL: InterVarsity.

Wolfson, H. A. 1947. *Philo*. 2 vols. Cambridge, MA: Harvard.

Woll, D. B. 1981. *Johannine Christianity in Conflict*. Chico: Scholars.

Woude, A. S. van der. 1976. "Melchizedek." In *IDB,* Suppl. Vol., 585–586.

Wrede, W. 1971. *The Messianic Secret*. London: Clarke. German ed. 1901.

Wright, C. J. 1930. *Miracle in History and in Modern Thought*. New York: Holt.

Wright, N. T. 1991. *The Climax of the Covenant: Christ and the Law in Pauline Theology*. Edinburgh: Clark.   1992. *Who Was Jesus?* Grand Rapids: Eerdmans.   1996a. *Jesus and the Victory of God*. Minneapolis: Fortress.   1996b. *The Original Jesus: The Life and Vision of a Revolutionary*. Grand Rapids: Eerdmans.   1997. *What Saint Paul Really Said*. Grand Rapids: Eerdmans.

Wuellner, W. 1987. "Where Is Rhetorical Criticism Taking Us?" In *CBQ* 49:448–463.

Yadin, Y. 1957. *The Message of the Scrolls*. New York: Simon and Schuster.   1963. *The Finds from the Bar Kokhba Period in the Cave of Letters*. Jerusalem: Israel Exploration Society.   1971. *Masada*. New York: Random House.

Yamauchi, E. 1983. *Pre-Christian Gnosticism*. Grand Rapids: Eerdmans.

Yarbrough, O. L. 1985. *Not Like the Gentiles: Marriage Rules in the Letters of Paul*. Atlanta: Scholars.

Yonge, C. D. 1993. *The Works of Philo*. Peabody, MA: Hendrickson.

Young, B. H. 1989. *Jesus and His Jewish Parables*. New York: Paulist.   1997. *Paul the Jewish*

Theologian: A Pharisee among Christians, Jews, and Gentiles. Peabody, MA: Hendrickson.

Young, F. M. 1994. *The Theology of the Pastoral Letters.* New York: Cambridge.

Zeitlin, S. 1962–1978. *The Rise and Fall of the Judaean State.* 3 vols. Philadelphia: Jewish Publication Society.   1964. *Who Crucified Jesus?* New York: Bloch.

Ziesler, J. A. 1983. *Pauline Christianity.* Oxford: University.   1989. *Paul's Letter to the Romans.* London: SCM.   1992. *The Epistle to the Galatians.* London: Epworth.

Author Index

Subject Index

Abraham, 50, 153, 210, 220
  in Hebrews, 369
  in John, 334, 342, 355
  in narratives of Jesus' birth, 175, 176, 180
  in Paul, 274, 279, 287
Achaia, 165, 222
Acts of the Apostles, 208–24. *See also* Luke, gospel of.
  outline and comments, 218–23
  and Paul, 226, 230–31
  purposes, 209–11, 424
  sources for, 211–12
  speeches in, 212–14
  structure, 217–18
  summary, 223–24
  term Christian in, 215–17
  travels of Paul in, 210, 230
Acts of Paul, 243
Acts of Peter, 243
Adam
  in genealogy in Luke, 180
  in Paul, 287
Adversaries
  of Jesus, 24, 128
  of Paul, 252, 254, 259–60, 278–80, 300,
    302–3, 319
Agrippa 1. *See* Herod, Agrippa I.
Agrippa H. *See* Herod, Agrippa II.
Alexander the Great, 4, 10, 47, 252
Alexandria, 3, 4, 45, 48, 50, 338, 364
Allegory, 189
Almsgiving, 155
Ananias, 198, 209
Andrew, disciple of Jesus, 337, 343, 351
Angel(s)
  in Hebrews, 364, 366
  in Judaism, 18, 20, 24, 26
  in Luke, 90, 168, 169, 174–75
Anna, 170
Annas, 165
Antioch, in Pisidia, 212, 213
Antioch, in Syria, 4, 124, 142, 143. *See also* Syria.
  center for Gentile Christianity, 209–11
  founding of church in, 219
  home of Luke, 164, 165

  origin of term Christian in, 215–16
  as possible place of origin for John's gospel, 338
  for source of Acts, 212
  for synoptic material, 65, 67, 124
Antiochus III, 4, 309
Antiochus IV, 5, 137
Antipas. *See* Herod, Antipas.
Antitheses in Matthew, 68
Antony, 252, 296, 297
Apocalypse, 20
  of John, 372–86
  as literary type, 1, 19–20, 78, 124, 138, 372–73
  and prophecy, 375
Apocalyptic thought, 19, 22, 78. *See also*
    Eschatology.
  Christian, 98–99, 114–15, 124, 126
  of Jesus, 93, 98–99, 121–22, 137–38, 149, 161,
    186
  Jewish, 19–21
  of Jude, 406
  of Paul, 242, 251, 253, 256, 268
  of Revelation, 372–75, 380
Apocrypha, 3, 25, 243
Apollo, 41, 42, 257, 258, 259, 282
Apollonius of Tyana, 3, 45, 114, 201, 202–3
Apollos of Alexandria, 222, 226, 232, 237, 260, 261,
    263, 268, 361–62
Apostle
  James. *See also* James, son of Zebedee.
  John, 336–38. *See also* John, disciple of Jesus.
  Paul, 1, 8, 33, 35, 36, 37, 39, 40, 41, 50, 75, 78,
    102, 105, 106, 116–17, 118–19, 120–21,
    132, 225–48
  Peter, 144, 145, 146, 152. *See also* Peter.
Apostles, 54, 75, 102, 105, 106, 114, 119
  Acts of the, 208–24
Apostleship
  of Paul, 214, 269, 278
Apostolic age, 54
Apphia, 304, 305
Aquila, 231, 257, 362
Aramaic, 10
  in Mark, 61
Aratus, 233

457

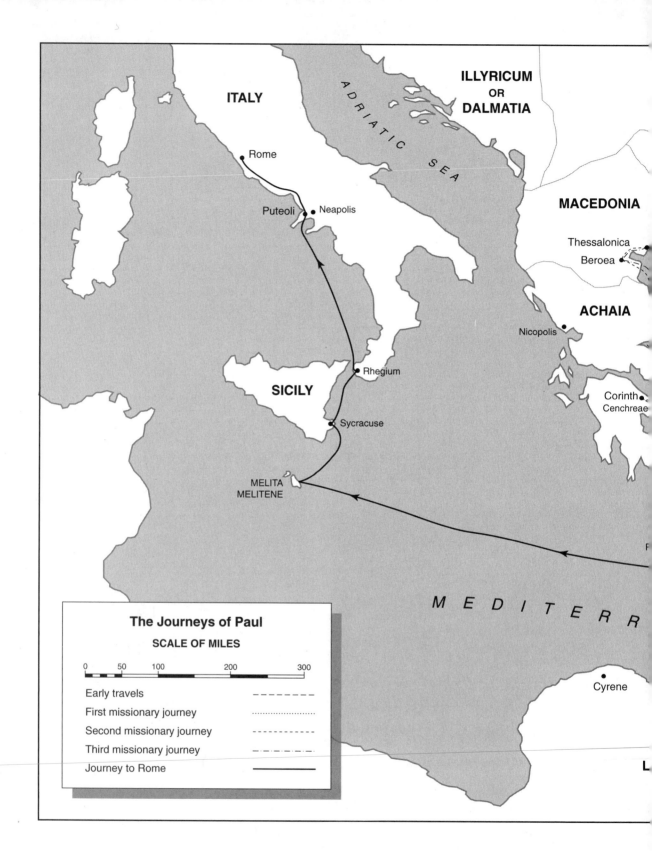

ITALY

ADRIATIC SEA

ILLYRICUM
OR
DALMATIA

Rome

Puteoli   • Neapolis

MACEDONIA

Thessalonica
Beroea

ACHAIA

Nicopolis

Rhegium

SICILY

Corinth
Cenchreae

Sycracuse

MELITA
MELITENE

MEDITERR

Cyrene

The Journeys of Paul

SCALE OF MILES

0   50   100   200   300

Early travels   – – – – – – –

First missionary journey   ....

Second missionary journey   – – – – – –

Third missionary journey   –·–·–·–·–

Journey to Rome   ————

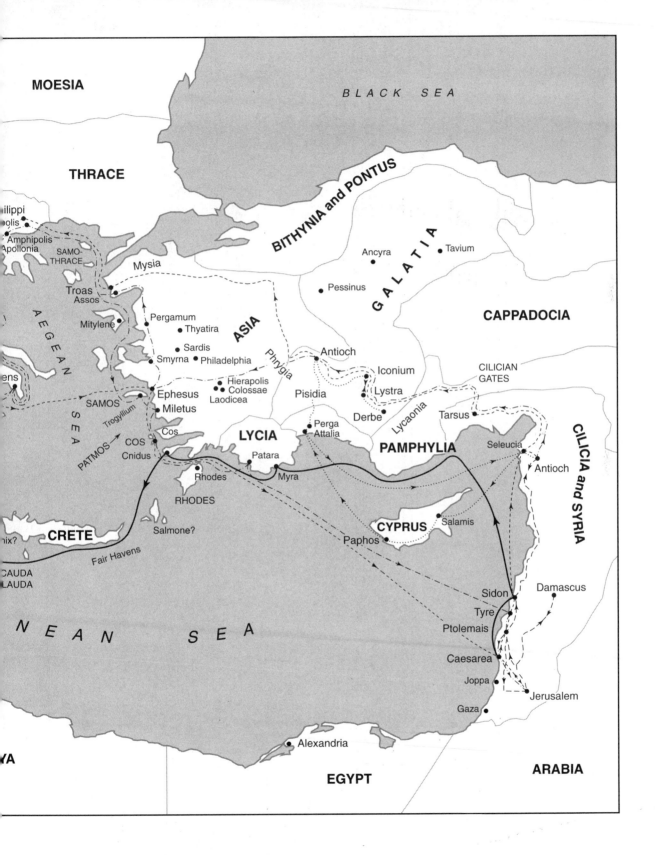